Unbeatable BMW

Eighty Years of Engineering and Motorsport Success

by Jeremy Walton

ROBERT BENTLEY
AUTOMOTIVE PUBLISHERS

Contents

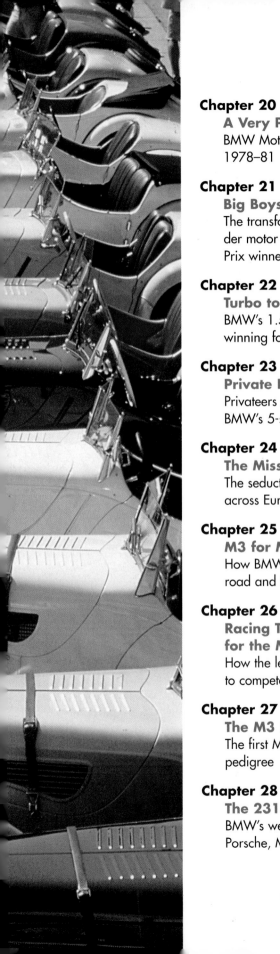

Information that makes
the difference.®

1734 Massachusetts Avenue
Cambridge, MA 02138 USA
800-423-4595 / 617-547-4170
http://www.rb.com
e-mail: sales@rb.com

Copies of this book may be purchased from selected booksellers, or
directly from the publisher by mail. Please write to Bentley Publishers at
the address listed on the top of this page.

Library of Congress Cataloging-in-Publication Data

Walton, Jeremy, 1946–
    Unbeatable BMW : eighty years of engineering and motorsport
success / by Jeremy Walton.
        p.   cm.
    Includes bibliographical references and index.
    ISBN 0–8376–0206–8 (alk. paper)
    1. BMW automobile—History. 2. Automobiles, Racing—History.
I. Title.
TL215.B57W35   1998
629.222'2—dc21   98–29667
                                                            CIP

Bentley Stock No. GBUB
01 00 99 98 10 9 8 7 6 5 4 3 2 1

The paper used in this publication is acid free and meets the requirements of the National Standard for Information Sciences-Permanence of
Paper for Printed Library Materials.
Unbeatable BMW: Eighty years of engineering and motorsport success,
by Jeremy Walton
© 1998 Jeremy Walton and Robert Bentley, Inc.

Manufactured in the United States of America

Cover photograph: The GTS3 class winner at the 1998 24 Hours of Daytona was this 4-door BMW M3, from Thomas Milner's PTG (Prototype
Technology Group) team. Photo courtesy of Klaus Schnitzer.

Front endpaper: Water drops glisten on the badge of a 507. Photo courtesy of Andrew Yeardon.

Rear endpaper: Detail of the inboard rear suspension on French Team
Oreca's BMW Z3 ice racer. Photo courtesy of Hugh Bishop.

This book is dedicated to
Marilyn Walton
and
Edmund the Bright Lurcher

Preface

The Faltz of Essen Group 5 320i at the 1977 Nürburgring 1000-kms. Driven by Hans Stuck and Harold Grohs, the car retired with a broken gearbox, but a similar BMW Junior Team car was 3rd—the only non-Porsche in the top ten.

See page 294

BMW cars are an under-written subject when compared with the horde of books available on other high-performance marques, such as Jaguar, Ferrari, MG, and Porsche. This absence of literature surprised me, especially as the story of how BMW came from the abyss of financial destruction or take-over by Mercedes was worthy of a book in itself. I wonder if any other motor company has traveled from the grave to such rippling prosperity in such short order?

The extent to which competition—particularly touring car competition—has helped BMW establish its present enviable image is central to this book.

BMW's sincere belief in production-based car racing (I use the term "production car" in its loosest sense, since the engineering behind some of these production cars is far more expensively complex than that in Grand Prix racing) has been the result of early necessity coupled with a growing sense of identification with its public.

When the Grand Prix BMW on the race track had a turbocharged 1.4-liter engine and weighed half as much as its cousin in the parking lot, most owners enjoyed seeing "their car" beating all comers. It also had the unique distinction of carrying a mildly-modified iron production cylinder block.

What I should have realized in the 1970s was that there was a very good reason for this shortage of BMW literature, especially on the sporting side, where BMW has such a fine record of achievement on two wheels or four. The reason was the lack of archives: there was little available to the researcher interested in competition results until May 1972.

That date marked the inauguration of BMW Motorsport GmbH in its original format. From that moment on, the records become as good as those of most rivals. You then have the problem of paying proper attention to what has been achieved by BMW in its intense overseas sports programs, especially in the USA and the nine countries that supported a 2.0-liter SuperTouring regime and national championships.

Faced with this shortage of material in the 1970s, I decided that the only way to trace the history I had not seen for myself was to talk to the people who were directly involved. A legendary BMW engineer insisted that part of my research for this book be conducted in a Munich graveyard, where acres of mute white head-stones were testimony to what the waves of American USAAF and British RAF bombers did in their effective 24-hour routines.

I also took a morning off from a Munich business trip to visit Dachau Camp. I am glad to see that these dark hours when the Nazi party was in power are now properly documented in English. When I wrote the first edition of *Unbeatable BMW,* such a perspective was not available.

Without two BMW engine engineers of legendary ability, I could not have known the struggles of the 1950s and 1960s, when half a dozen men founded the modern BMW image of supreme engine engineers. So I must say a public thank you to Alex Freiherr von Falkenhausen (who died in 1991) and Paul Rosche, who still puts the Power behind MPower on his own Munich-born-and-bred terms, for 1997 and beyond.

Today, working in a Britain where our largest indigenous mass manufacturer (Rover Cars) is owned by BMW and with the prospect of 1999 Rolls Royces powered by BMW motors (the two companies are already partners in an aero engine business), I am proud to have recorded those individual engineering efforts in a more nationalistic age.

A new edition of the book would not have been prepared without American enthusiasm and the private and professional support of Chris Willows, Public Affairs Manager at BMW (GB) Ltd.

It was also important to gain an appreciation of what BMW meant to a Bavarian, and that required extended German travel. Bob Constanduros, now a contributor to BBC's "Top Gear Motorsport," generously shared his VW camper van with me that I might gain these insights at the extremely low costs that have always attracted authors.

Herr Burkard Bovensiepen, the founder and owner of the Alpina concern, specialists in quality wines and legendarily effective BMWs, was an inspiration. His Schnauzer hound was not so pleased to see me (I still have the scars), but Burkard's undiminished enthusiasm helped buoy me through the task of making sense of some of the earlier touring car racing efforts. I also learned that this man would modify anything, when we spent a memorable evening driving his 350-bhp BMW 750 Limo with the sort of vigor reserved for smaller rally cars.

Contemporary comment on German and British attitudes toward racing sedan-car modification came from my Ford competition experience and the incisive insights of Dr. Fritz Indra. Fritz was then at Alpina, but later better known at Audi (Father of the Sport quattro 20-valve motor) and GM-Opel.

Former German Champion Josef Schnitzer was killed while I was assembling material for the original version of this book in 1978. Josef's quirky genius for making powerful engines and spectacular sedans was badly missed, but the legacy of his work at the factory lived on and inspired further BMW motor developments.

I was fortunate in that I had met and talked with Josef and his brothers (Herbert Schnitzer went on to become the workshop's driving force), before Josef died in that road accident. Charly Lamm was a youngster debating his future when I first met him at Schnitzer. Luckily for BMW and journalists around the world, the charming Charly decided Schnitzer was his destiny, rather than further academic studies in America.

Typically, Josef Schnitzer was the man behind the fabulous turbocharged CSL with which the late and equally great Ronnie Peterson menaced the all-conquering Porsches in 1976. I do not think there has ever been a more exciting combination than that of Peterson and the BMW touring cars.

I hope this book goes a little way toward reminding us of the efforts of three individuals who all died in 1978: Peterson, Josef Schnitzer, and the friendly, effervescent Gunnar Nilsson, who showed that he could drive a BMW touring car just as sympathetically as a Grand Prix Lotus—and attract more girls than Derek Bell in a memorable weekend bet.

Race for long enough, and an aura must attach to your products. Race successfully, as BMW has all over the world, and the message is crisply transmitted: "We are committed to motorsport, we intend to stay committed, and our cars are the better for it."

Jeremy Walton
England, 1979 and 1998

Forewords

Foreword by Nelson Piquet

I have always been interested in the technology of racing, so it was natural that BMW and myself should be partners in the turbocharging revolution that swept Grand Prix racing in the 1980s.

That I became the first driver to win the FIA Formula 1 World Championship in a turbocharged car in 1983 was due to the intelligence, courage and skills of many at BMW, Brabham and many suppliers.

But BMW has been winning races and powering aeroplanes before—and since—that turbo racing revolution. So I was glad to hear that this story of those other sporting BMWs tells the story of not just the machines and the results that they achieved, but also the men who motivated such success.

Today I race just for fun, but I still enjoy the partnership with BMW, whether it is at Le Mans in a McLaren BMW or a smaller event in a 3-series.

Nelson Piquet
World Champion,
1981/83/87
Sao Paulo, Brazil, 1997

Foreword by Karl-Heinz Kalbfell

I have known the author of this book for many years, so I have also known of his passion for the BMW marque and BMW Motorsport. In fact, one night when we launched the second generation M3 coupe in Majorca, Spain, he kept me up most of the night. We were arguing about the character of the new M3, compared with the older model and the classic coupes of the 1970s.

I enjoyed our discussions then, and at many other press gatherings held since. So long as BMW cars have strong sporting characters, in a world full of cars that are often so similar, we at BMW will attract the strong support that Jeremy Walton has written of in this book.

It is a story full of human heroes and mechanical achievements. This was true, whatever our activity: flying at record altitudes, setting two-wheeler speed records, or beating the best at the race track. Always we take part to win, but also we compete to improve our products and the strength of the human spirit needed to overcome the greatest challenges in sport.

Karl-Heinz Kalbfell
Head of Central Marketing of BMW AG
(responsible for Motorsports)
Munich, Germany, 1998

Foreword by
Jochen Neerpasch

I am pleased for myself and BMW Motorsport to write a few words about this book, for I think it was important that somebody should write such a story of BMW.

For me, it has been interesting to see the start of BMW's racing today by ideas developed from a little car with a rear-mounted motocycle engine! Today, we would not recognize such a motorcar as a racing machine, but it is good to see the progress we have made.

When Jeremy Walton came to me and asked if it was a good idea to make this book, I was surprised. Why had nobody done this before? I do not know the answer to this question, but I think the twenty years from 1959 to 1979 were the most important to the development of the main company and the Motorsport departments. So I welcome *Unbeatable BMW.*

For us, Motorsport is an enjoyable life as well as a business. When I read of the people who went before, I realize that this is the international sport. We visited many countries from the works and many more people overseas run BMWs in competition. I must also say a real thank you to all those teams and mechanics who gave us so much to be proud of in the years written of in this book.

There is so much that we have done all over the world that people ask me what is left? I think this is the fantastic thing about motor sport: challenge. There is always some other car or driver to beat, a way to make the car faster, always an improvement can be made.

Jochen Neerpasch
BMW Motorsport GmbH
Munich, January 1979

A dramatic moment at the 1997 24 Hours of Daytona. This M3 finished 9th overall, and 1st in the GTS3 class.

See page 511

QUICK FACTS

Period

1896–1944

Products

Roots back to kitchen utensil manufacture, and initial links with Porsche
design and Daimler manufacturing;
we unravel aeronautical units from
46-liter piston power to pioneering
jet propulsion units

Performance

BMW's acceleration from 0–560-mph
products took 27 years

Achievements

Set benchmark standards for altitude,
lifting a 1919 design 6.06 miles
above earth

People

From aviation engine engineering
pioneers Franz Popp and Max Friz
to World War I fighter-plane aces;
includes Manfred von Richthofen
and Ernst Udet

Chapter 1

Airborne Excellence

How the "Unbeatable" BMW's legendary performance began in the air

"I feel the need for speed," mouths the Hollywood hero before blitzing politically incorrect enemies of the Star Spangled Banner. For BMW, there is no need to act the hero. Speed pumps through the corporate life-blood as a right: the legacy of brave men crouched in cold cockpits, half-starved of oxygen as their BMW six-cylinders clawed over 3.5 miles above Munich almost 80 years ago.

We could equally honorably recall those leather-clad figures with their merry aerodynamic helmets tottering on the bounds of reality at more than 175 mph on two wheels, precariously perched over a frosty example of the 1930s autobahn. But it is BMW and cars that will fascinate most of you, whether that fascination stems from an eternal image of immaculate white 328s stamping the company legend over 2.0-liter opposition before World War II, or the more recent images of striped "02s" and swoopy "Batmobiles" carrying the legend into an era when BMW fights for overall world-class honors.

For it was BMW who seized the world's first championship recorded by a turbo-charged engine. It is BMW who delivered 6 liters of V12 energy to motivate McLaren in an equally epic confrontation with Porsche and Mercedes in global GT racing and win Le Mans on its debut.

A desire to go 10 meters higher, 10 km/h faster, created a company of supremely fit internal combustion engines for land, sea (not so prominently) and air. It's ironic that the BMW Roundel—conceived to illustrate the company's Aero heritage within a whirling propeller and its blue and white background—is now most famed in English-language countries for its firmly land-based motorcars and cycles.

We will pay homage to those pioneering aviation days, aware that since July 1990, BMW has partnered with old opponent Rolls Royce in the European aviation business of providing selected future jet engines. Yet the bulk of the book, beyond our opening chapters, concerns cars—an area in which I have worked for thirty years, which has taught me to respect BMW's abilities at a time when telling an English-language audience that BMW was "Unbeatable" was not a popular message.

My original *Unbeatable BMW* book drew on a British advertising campaign of the 1970s for its main title and was subtitled "A Racing Revival 1959–79." For this new edition, I have been able to focus on 70 years of sports success: 1928–1998. Instead of beginning with that bleak mid-winter shareholder's meeting of December 9, 1959, at which BMW was saved from becoming a division of Daimler Benz, I feel the true racing start-point of the "Unbeatable" four-wheeler legend came in the summer of 1936 with the winning debut of the 328 at the Nürburgring.

However, that sporting start date allows us only a glimpse of the truth, which is that Bayerische Motoren Werke AG (BMW to the everyday public) has always been involved in land, sea or (especially) airborne competition, not just autosports.

BMW's founding fathers

In 1916–17, BMW was still very much an embryo power-unit supplier: most of its business concerned servicing other makes of aero engines. BMW's forebears made 224 Austro Daimler 350 horsepower (hp) aero units under license, massive V12s that had been designed by one Ferdinand Porsche (yes, that Porsche!).

To grow, the fledgling BMW needed a more competitive aero engine and the patronage of the Prussian military. Therefore, the founding fathers, fittingly, were both engine engineers, although of varying abilities. Viennese-born Franz Josef Popp (1896–1954) came to Munich in 1914 to complete his post-graduate engineering studies of the embryo military engine business.

The chance of building the Austro Daimler motors at the Rapp works in Munich saw Popp embroiled as the Delivery Engineer of the Austro-Hungarian Navy, but it was obvious that the quality standards were appalling. Popp was acquainted with former Daimler (Mercedes) engineer Max Friz (1883–1966), and knew that the designer of the 1914 Grand Prix-winning Mercedes motor and subsequent successful Mercedes aero motors was available, following a petty dispute over pay with Daimler.

In January 1917, Friz reported to the Rapp premises (renamed to recognize BMW, that July, as above), to find that Popp had acquired

the magnificent Oberwiesenfeld green field site. This was to be home to BMW for their flying exploits, but it had an honorable role in the pioneering of German aviation previously (Gustav Otto, son of the inventor of the internal combustion engine, flew from Oberwiesenfeld from 1911 onward) and is better known today as the location of the Olympia Park, host to the tragic 1972 Olympic games.

To complete our present-day geography lesson, the Milbertshofen district, home to various BMW ancestors, lies in the same northeastern outskirts of Munich. That glorious testimony to modern BMW commercial muscle, the VierZylinder BMW Haus (four-cylinder BMW building) has overlooked the Olympia Park/old Oberweisenfeld sites since its 791-day construction between 1970-72 to coincide with the Olympic Games opening ceremonies.

BMW's first successful aero unit was a fundamental rethink by Max Friz of the 160-hp Mercedes D3, a six-cylinder. BMW's first branded engine was a sluggish (1,400 rpm) leviathan by modern standards and carried a bore x

stroke of 150 x 180 mm to yield 19.085 liters or 1,164.6 cubic inches (CI). It saw service only in the closing months of the 1914–18 war.

Although it fitted the same airframes as the widely used and proven Mercedes, BMW featured Friz design of many major components (cylinder head, lower-weight reciprocating parts, strengthened block) and a unique series of carburetor-intake modifications. These allowed mixtures to be corrected at altitude, retaining much of the ground-level horsepower via altitude-corrected air/fuel ratio mixtures.

Since altitude was essential to mastering the now-frantic airborne dog-fighting over the battlefields of France, the Popp-Friz alliance swiftly found their Prussian backing: the 3a went from a May 20, 1917 start via a wooden mock-up and September 1917 test-bed trials to flying its first missions in May 1918. It was quick enough to establish BMW an enviable reputation in the closing months of the war, but not quick enough to deliver more than a fraction of the 2,500 motors ordered by the Prussian military.

Today, many will tell you that the Red Baron of World War I Fokker Triplane fame was one of BMW's earliest and most successful customers. Manfred Freiherr von Richthofen (May 2, 1892 to April 21, 1918) was credited with 83 air combat victories, an unmatched total. In truth, von Richthofen never flew a pure BMW engine in a Fokker Triplane. It is possible that the Red Baron flew behind one of the service units that BMW or an affiliated company delivered in earlier times, but von Richthofen was killed in April 1918: the first thoroughbred BMW 3a deliveries to the battle front flew in May 1918.

Altogether, von Richthofen flew Fokker triples for only six weeks; it was enough to take a further 19 victories in the air. The Red Baron's killing skills were seen in other airplanes aside from the tri-decker: three types of Albatross, Halberstadt (once half-owned by Bristol Aircraft Co. in England—ironic, in view of post-war automotive history), and bi- and

tri-plane Fokkers, products of Dutch-born Anthony Fokker.

The Fokker Triplane was delivered with either Frankfurt-built Oberusel or Swedish-constructed Le Rhone 110-hp rotary power when von Richthofen deployed its deadly merits. The first BMW 3a motors, able to touch 200 hp and fly beyond 6,000 meters (19,685 ft/3.72 miles above earth), were delivered to the Richthofen fighter group a month after the Red Baron was controversially shot down over the bloody battlefields of Somme, France. The rotary motor from von Richthofen's last mission is preserved at the Imperial War Museum, London and is confirmed as an Oberusel, not a BMW.

However, demolishing such folklore does nothing to diminish the astonishing reputation BMW established in its early aeronautical years. The squadron for which von Richthofen finally flew—JG1, a group overseen by WWII Luftwaffe commander Herman Goering—was the elite of Germany's fighter resources. It was one of their number, Lieutenant Ernst Udet, who paid the BMW 3a engine a number of ultimate compliments.

Udet criticized the Mercedes 160-hp motors that had spurred BMW to produce its 3a in record time at Milbertshofen, a current BMW production site for 3-series. After reporting shortcomings in the Mercedes' performance versus the latest allied fighters at high (beyond 4,000 meters/13,123 ft) and low altitudes, the man who would become an architect of German military aviation in the second World War revealed, "During a summer leave in Munich, I heard about a fantastic new high-altitude engine which Bavarian Motor Works were said to have brought out.

"It was said that it produced 160 hp with the same weight as the 160-hp Mercedes engine, but did not lose power, even at high altitudes." This was because of the carburetor modifications that BMW had made.

Udet explained that the Richthofen Squadron received the first supplies at Bougneux aero-

The first man to articulately describe the benefits of BMW engine engineering—as a by-product of his main task of staying alive and destroying Allied aircraft—was this WWI ace, Ernst Udet (right: without a hat). You could say Udet was BMW's first works pilot. In fact, feedback from the Jagdstaffel 4-Jackdgeschwader Richthofen, the crack fighter group left behind after the legendary Manfred von Richthofen's death in April 1918, was equally favorable.

Picture: Chris Willows Library/BMW Archiv, released 1997

drome "during the push between Reims and Soissons." Udet added, "There were initially 22 of them, 11 destined for the squadron." This contradicts with aviation histories that put the initial number of BMW 3a-equipped Fokkers pressed into action at 13 in early May 1918.

Enough of the nit-picking. Udet's 1918 compliments summed up the key qualities that many have expressed of BMW products since, including the following: "The engine worked perfectly and had excellent throttle operation...I gave the BMW-equipped machine a first flight at the front, and noticed the enormous difference it had over the Mercedes Fokker.

"I needed to fly only at half-throttle if I was not to over-fly or overtake my squadron [who retained Mercedes power, initially—JW]. Its speed was considerably greater when pointing down, even at low levels, and rapidly increased over other planes at higher altitudes....Yet there was still a mass of power in

reserve, which could be very useful in emergency....Thanks to its superior power, I felt confident enough to attack the enemy from below, a tactic which I often used."

Udet concluded, "After 82 hours in service, I had the engine overhauled during leave. Wear on the bearings and other parts was minimal. There is no question that the BMW engine proved to be the high point of aero engines in the last stage of the War. Its only flaw was that it had arrived too late."

Udet's later life was just as relevant to BMW, for he went on to head up the German ministry that specified military aircraft, finally committing suicide in 1941. Ironically, Udet was threatened with concentration camp internment if he did not sign an order prohibiting the further development of high-altitude fighter equipment, especially engines.

Some official BMW historians believe that the first World War could have been won by

Germany, had supplies of that 3a BMW arrived earlier. Given the sheer weight of men and materials brought by the Americans from 1917 onward, to what had been a stalemate situation, this kind of emotional comment (along with criticism of German troops for surrendering) tells us more about the respect BMW gathered than the facts.

Ever-higher altitudes were the key to wartime supremacy and civilian respect. In 1903, the Wright Brothers flew just over 3 meters above that Ohio field in their Kittyhawk to record the first properly-observed powered flight. By the outbreak of war, 800 meters/2,826 ft were possible.

When BMW came to develop its high-altitude 3a, its answer was Type IV, a prophetic four-valve-per-cylinder design that retained an in-line six-cylinder configuration, countering the oxygen starvation and consequent power losses that fighter aircraft engines were experiencing beyond 4,000 meters/13,123 ft. That reflected wartime progress, but a year after Germany was defeated, Munich Oberwiesenfeld airfield was left over 6 miles (9,760 meters/32,021 ft) underneath the BMW IV-powered DFW airframe of Bavarian Lieutenant Zeno Diemer. It was just 16 years since the Wright brothers had made that first Giant Hop for Humankind.

Forging a corporate identity

What of the companies behind these astonishing aero-engine feats? How did they become BMW, and how did they fare in a Germany stripped of economic dignity and the right to field-powered military aircraft in the years after WWI?

We can establish BMW roots back over 100 years, to December 3, 1896. That date marked the formation of Wartburg works in

Eisenach, the BMW manufacturing center for all cars made from 1928 to 1940. From that site and Wartburg's numerous alliances before being sold to BMW in 1928 stretched activities as diverse as saucepan manufacture, powered mountain bikes, and the Knorr Bremsen (brake) company, the latter an outfit that today trades within sprinting distance of the BMW four-cylinder tower in Munich. The car-construction tale of the Eisenach arm is the subject of a subsequent chapter.

However, basics of the heartland Munich-based company of the 1990s arrived in 1916 when two airplane-engine manufacturing workshops (Gustav Rau GmbH and Rapp Motorenwerken GmbH) were subject to takeovers and closures that resulted in the March 7, 1916 registration of Bayerische Flugzeugwerke AG (BFW). Rapp had made over 200 of the 350-hp Daimler marine engines referred to earlier in the presence of Popp. When Karl Rapp departed the company that bore his name, that Munich company was renamed Bayerische Motoren Werke GmbH. Registered July 21, 1917, it was the first time

It could be Tazio Nuvolari, Dieter Quester or Nelson Piquet in that cockpit. The job's the same: operate in areas other mortals have neither the skill nor the courage to inhabit. Zeno Diemer is about to depart in the BMW IV-powered DFW biplane that netted them a world-record altitude after an 89-minute ascent. This technically amazing feat was probably one of the key reasons the Allies restricted German-powered flight so heavily before Hitler forced the issue in the 1930s.

Picture: BMW Archiv, released 1997

the basis of those now world-famous BMW initials was registered.

The most significant early move toward company identity came from Franz Josef Popp. He registered one of the world's most admired trademarks—the whirling propeller, complete with peripheral BMW initials—on October 5, 1917, at the Kaiserlichen Patentamt. Thus was BMW truly born of the aero engine business: motorcycles, marine engines and cars waited until the 1920s for their turns to carry the white and blue emblem.

Post-war, Franz Popp was faced with the task of enhancing BMW's reputation further while walking a tightrope—the company could be closed down at any time. While BMW-powered planes went on to set new altitude and endurance benchmarks—many unrecognized because Germany was not allowed to be a member of the relevant official bodies—the company required cash to survive the horrendous economic conditions of the 1920s.

Horrendous? Consider this: in July 1923, some 350,000 German marks would buy just one dollar! The mark had been devalued repeatedly by an ocean of near-worthless paper money issued by an increasingly desperate German Chancellor. In 1997, a dollar bought around 1.75 Deutschemarks.

An important breakthrough for BMW came when it became a publicly quoted company in 1918 with much augmented capital to produce the intended thousands of 3a aero engines, thus the AG suffix to the company name rather than the original GmbH.

However, that company restructuring happened just months before the close of WWI and the more relevant business was to first survive the Allied inspectorates—hiding items from connecting rods to templates—and then weather the money madness of the 1920s. The help of some very crafty entrepreneurs and the payments already received for the massive aero engine business helped BMW survive where others tumbled, but the key ingredient was BMW's reputation for fabulous flying engines.

Legendary engines

Aside from the company's own postwar altitude record, others used BMW sixes—or the IV and V six-cylinder progeny—and proved them superior for durability and serviceability in a number of extended journeys. These pushed the known limits of aircraft performance to headline-earning limits. Behind the scenes, BMW motors and personnel were involved in a number of sanctions-beating powered aircraft that performed well beyond the limits imposed by the WWI allies, especially within Germany's reciprocal military aviation agreement with Russia .

Perhaps the best story in this 1920s connection concerned an allied inspector who accepted a BMW employee's assurance that one prototype had exhausts appearing on either side for reasons of aerodynamic balance and streamlining. He neglected to tell the Versailles treaty enforcer that the exhaust belonged to a high-performance V12, a literally doubled-up version of the IV six. The 160 x 190-mm V12 displaced 45.8 liters/2,795 CI, performing way beyond BMW's apparent six-cylinder abilities, for the V12 unleashed 690 bhp at 1,650 rpm with 585 bhp at a continuous 1,530 revs reported in 1926.

Thus BMW's excellence in this field was established when powered flight was authorized with lesser technological restraints in 1926, but the company's philosophy was not immediately military.

At a time when water-cooled motors were seen as the solution for high-speed and high-altitude military use, Popp and BMW signed an agreement with Pratt & Whitney in Hartford, Connecticut to manufacture their air-cooled radial engines. These were nine-cylinder Hornet and Wasp designs, for supply to the burgeoning civil aircraft industry at 400 or 525 hp from 1929 onward.

The aero-engine trading link between American and German aero manufacturers could have gone further, but Washington stepped in.

Franz Popp correctly—but privately—anticipated that air-cooled motors would have military significance, but in the double row radial configuration. Pratt & Whitney were developing such an engine, but (fortunately for the UK and possibly the outcome of the air war) the US authorities forbade the American company from supplying the Germans with such a unit.

Franz Popp and BMW were told by the now rampant German air ministry to do the job themselves, but owing to personal clashes between the BMW bosses and those of Nazi officialdom, it was 1936 before BMW was authorized to go the air-cooled military route.

The most widely-used BMW aero unit of WWII was the 801, packing 14 cylinders in two rows and 41.8-liter displacement. The 801 was most famously used in the Focke Wulf FW190 fighter

plane of 1941 onward, but the long-nosed 152 variant was heaved through the heavens by the Daimler Benz liquid-cooled twelve.

Over 30,000 examples of the 801 were manufactured with ever-escalating power: the first A-series offered 1,600 hp, but subsequent use of water and nitrous oxide ("laughing gas") injection allowed almost 2,300 hp for takeoff and over 1,700 hp at 11,244 meters, or 7 miles above the earth. Depending on height (around 11,400 meters/37,400 ft was the operational ceiling of the later FW190s) and engine variant, the FW190 pilot could expect over 400 mph from this BMW-powered single-seater. If you settled for 298 mph cruising, the maximum range was over 640 miles.

Franz Popp, imprisoned by the American forces postwar, reflected that the potent BMW 801 could have been in production by 1934 instead of the early 1940s, following a "complete waste of effort" in further developing conventional large water-cooled motors for military use. He also told the Americans that Britain

Perhaps BMW's most famed—and feared—performance engine of all time: the 1940 radial 801 in C/D trim, complete with 14 cylinders in two rows. Displacing almost 42 liters, it was developed from 1,600 to 2,300 peak horsepower (55 bhp/liter maximum). It served single-engined fighters such as the Focke Wulf 190, a 400-mph weapon that could fly seven miles above earth and dueled for supremacy with Allied designs such as the North American P51 Mustang and Supermarine Spitfire.

Picture: BMW Archiv, released 1997

BMW was building twelves of enduring greatness back in August 1929. This was the world's largest flying boat and its twelve passengers plus four crew were lifted by 500 to continuous 750 peak horsepower BMW V1-U units.

Picture: Chris Willows Library/BMW Archiv, released 1997

would have taken the kind of bombing devastation that brought Germany to its knees, had his technical inclinations been followed. However, this was Popp's technical intellect speaking, not the voice of an intolerant warmonger.

Even in the 1930s, Popp was not well-liked by the Nazi authorities, having an English son-in-law (Dick Seaman, who died driving a Grand Prix Mercedes in 1939), regular Jewish contacts—defiantly including his doctor—and frequent cordial American business trips. It was not a surprise that he was demoted during the war, but given his working life in Munich, it was a surprise to find he died in Stuttgart during 1954.

Back in the 1930s, German authorities decided that both air- and water-cooled motors had potential. They divided responsibilities so that BMW and its 1939 forced acquisition—Bramo, of Spandau Berlin—worked primarily on the development of air-cooled radials (chiefly nine cylinders in a single row, or

14 doubled up), while Daimler Benz went with liquid-cooled 12-cylinders.

Such an expansion of military manufacturing capabilities distorted BMW's primary business so that one German-language account of BMW in the 1930s acidly reported, "BMW's car building nearly became a subsidiary operation." This non-factory source backed up its assertion with, "From 1933 onward, a quick production growth was once more provided by aero engines. In 1933, of BMW's 4,700 employees, only 2,400 worked in building cars."

The same source reported that 1936 saw part of the Eisenach site devoted to the manufacture of military apparatus: infantry and anti-tank guns, smoke canister throwers, and infantry carriers. You could also study the turnover and employment records and see how an income of 9 million ReichMarks (RM) from 1,000 employees in 1926 rocketed to 560 million RM and the best part of 50,000 workers. Another cross-check shows that employment

In the 1930s, the Focke Wulfe 200 Condor had a life as a civilian air/freight liner, setting long distance benchmarks (the crowd scene is at Floyd Bennett City of New York Airport in 1938), including Berlin to New York in 24 hours 57 minutes (averaging 158.6 mph outward bound). All this was achieved in a machine that lacked a pressurized cabin and could therefore fly no higher than 9,900 feet.

The same FW 200 Condor also covered 8,597.1 miles from Berlin to Tokyo in 42 hours 18 minutes (there were three brief stop-overs for a journey time of 46 hours), averaging 203.8 mph. The Condor became a war machine and was famously dubbed "Scourge of the Atlantic" by Winston Churchill for its U-boat liaison/Allied shipping attacks in the 1940s. It utilized a developed BMW 132 nine-cylinder radial in 1938 civil aviation mode; a quartet of BMW-Bramo Fanfir 332R nine-cylinders hauled wartime variants, with a peak of 1,200 horsepower each.

Picture: Deutsche Lufthansa and BMW Archiv/Courtesy Chris Willows, 1997

jumped tenfold in less than ten years (from 4,700 in 1933 to 47,300 in 1942) and it does not take a rocket scientist to know that a significant proportion of that workforce was not voluntary: BMW company histories now record the use of prisoners—slave labor or relevant prisoners of war (POWs) in manufacturing.

Perhaps the most familiar BMW-powered airplane of the 1930s and 1940s—certainly the least threatening with its Allied nickname of "Iron Annie"—was the tri-motor Junker JU52. Rather more affectionately known to German troops as Tante Ju (Auntie Ju), the Junker was the equivalent of the Ford tri-motor: square-rigged and almost indestructible.

The BMW nine-cylinder radials were of the 132 series and developed a best of 730 hp at 2,030 rpm for takeoff, allowing about 178 mph as the maximum speed by 4,500 ft (1,400 m). The BMW engines performed well in this unglamorous basic transport role, but a contemporary British report quipped, "Starting up the 725-hp BMW132A nine-cylinder radi-

als was rather like playing a Wurlitzer organ."

BMW aero engineers obviously listened to similar feedback from the Luftwaffe, because the better-known 14-cylinder radials of the 801 series had a mechanical version of today's engine-management systems. Called *Kommandgerat*, it effectively relieved the pilot of the job of controlling airscrew pitch, fuel/air mixtures, boost, and revs. This "Brainbox" contributed to the Allied accolade: "The FW190's magic as a fighter lay in its superb control harmony."

A senior British test pilot commented of a captured FW190A-3 with BMW motivation, "Despite the superlative job of cowling done by Focke Wulf designers, the big BMW 801D air-cooled radial engine was pretty obstrusive." However, Captain Eric Brown was forced to admit, "I was pleasantly surprised to find that, after clambering into the somewhat narrow cockpit, the forward view was still rather better than was offered by the BF109 [Messerschmitt], the Spitfire [Supermarine], or the Mustang [North American Aviation]."

Only two of the Messerschmitt 262 fighter bombers were equipped with BMW 003 turbo-jet power. This is the second such prototype: the more conservatively engineered Jumo unit was selected for service in the production 262.

Picture: BMW Archiv/Courtesy Chris Willows, 1997

The test report—concerning an FW190 that inadvertently landed at Pembrey, currently a very active race circuit in Wales—also included an engine commendation that many English-language car road-testers would later echo of BMW's more peaceable products: "We found that the BMW almost invariably fired the first time and emitted a smooth purr as it ran." BMW really had a very special brand of engineers, so to impress an enemy dedicated to its destruction!

Aside from the legendary 801s, BMW, or its 1939 acquisition, Bramo, equipped the fabled Focke Wulf 200C Condor with four 323R nine-cylinder radials that yielded up to 2,000 hp when boosted by water-methanol mixtures for short periods. Normally rated at 1,200 hp, these Fafnir motors pounded the fabled U-boat "eyes" across the Atlantic at up to 2,600 rpm and caused havoc among allied shipping lanes.

The FW200C was converted from the 1930s civilian airliner and had considerable combat weaknesses. These prevented it from adopting the four-engine bomber role that might have been expected to reply to the RAF Lancaster and the USAAF Flying Fortress carpet-bombing of Germany.

The Condor was an incredible technical achievement for the day, capable of flying over 2,700 miles at 158 mph in "economy" cruise mode or hitting 224 mph at 4,800 meters/15,750 ft.

BMW did produce a legendary unit in its 801, but was bombarded with German ministerial requests to get involved in every other kind of aviation propulsion in the hope that each would save the Fatherland from the

inevitable. This meant that BMW was a pioneer of the jet age, but "jet" is a very loose term: its most successful production result was the 003A to E-series axial-flow turbojets, of which more than a thousand had been made by the end of the war in Europe.

The 003 was most frequently found in the Heinkel HE162 Volksjager ("Peoples' Fighter") and was capable of hurling that tiny (under 30 ft long), tricky flying device to 562 mph at 20,000 ft.

An earlier BMW axial-compressor, turbo-fan jet design (P3302) was set to make the first flight with the twin-engine Messerschmitt ME262 (which went on to become the world's first operational jet fighter) on March 25, 1942, but suffered an ignominious failure of the vanes 50 meters off the ground and had to be brought back to earth on a standby propeller motor.

Unsurprisingly, the larger and better-proven Jumo 004 series became the chosen form of jet propulsion for the 262, and much the same applied to the high-altitude (13,000 meters/42,640 ft) abilities of the Arado 234B; but here, BMW's 003A-1 did rack up considerable test time in the four-motor 234C variant. BMW's initial advance in propellerless technology has largely been forgotten, but over 100 such engines had been delivered by August 1944, surviving 50-hour continuous test trials.

Time to put our feet back on the ground. How did BMW's accidental acquisition of a humble 15-horsepower Austin design in the late 1920s found the "Unbeatable" BMW legend of the 1930s? Read on....

The one that got away. This superbly elegant Arado 234 in test-flight guise with a quartet of BMW 003 turbo-jet motors flew first in February 1944, several years after the first "jets" became airborne in Germany and Britain. Capable of exceeding 42,000 feet in September 1944, its twin-engine cousins (also Arado 234s) frequently frustrated invading allied forces by flying beyond their technical abilities; but then power came from Junker Jumo units.

Picture: BMW Archiv, 1997

QUICK FACTS

Period

1922–45

Products

Boxer twins, R32 motorcycles to supercharged record-breakers

Performance

From 8.5 bhp and 60 mph to 90 bhp and 126 mph

Achievements

Setting 176.3 mph mark for motorcycles in 1937 and beating the previously all-powerful British motorcycle industry at home in their most prestigious event

People

The motorcycle heroes Ernst Henne and Georg "Schorsch" Meier, plus the creators of those world-beating designs, including Rudolph Schleicher

Chapter 2

Motorcycle Marvels

Breaking records on the ground and taking the sports battle to the British

BMW turned all kinds of activities, including shoe-making, to survive, but Popp and Friz were engineers, first and foremost, and there was no doubt that BMW would return to aero engine manufacture. Before that, motorcycles were seen as a necessary alternative to use their skills and those of a workforce that had turned from a WWI peak of 3,500 employees to less than 1,000. It was time to set new standards and create peacetime BMW's sporting reputation.

Sporting success on two wheels started almost immediately after making an all-BMW motorcycle. Previously, BMW was forced to make copies of prevalent English twin-cylinders (notably Douglas) to keep cash flow alive in the immediate postwar period.

In 1923, BMW produced its first complete motorcycle, which used the flat twin-cylinder (boxer) principles established in earlier Friz designs that were sold to other motorcycle manufacturing concerns. This time, the boxer unit—so-called because the crankshaft works the pistons in opposition, like the flailing arms of a pugilist—was disposed across the frame of the R32 design, instead of longitudinally. Some BMW motorcycles still carry the 1923 principles of boxer motors: shaft drive to the back wheel (most motorcycles use chain drive) and a double-loop steel frame.

Landmark motorcycle: the BMW R32 was conceived by engineeer Max Friz as Germany's aero industry went through the equivalent of Prohibition. The 8-horsepower R32 combined the "Holy Trinity" of BMW design hallmarks: shaft drive, a stiff frame, and the Boxer flat twin motor. It debuted at the 1923 Paris Show and its progeny are still manufactured in Berlin.

Picture: Courtesy BMW NA, 1996

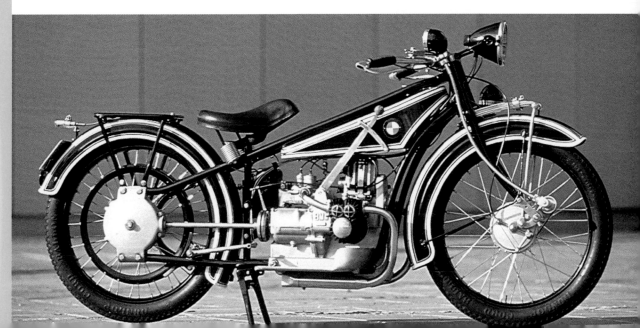

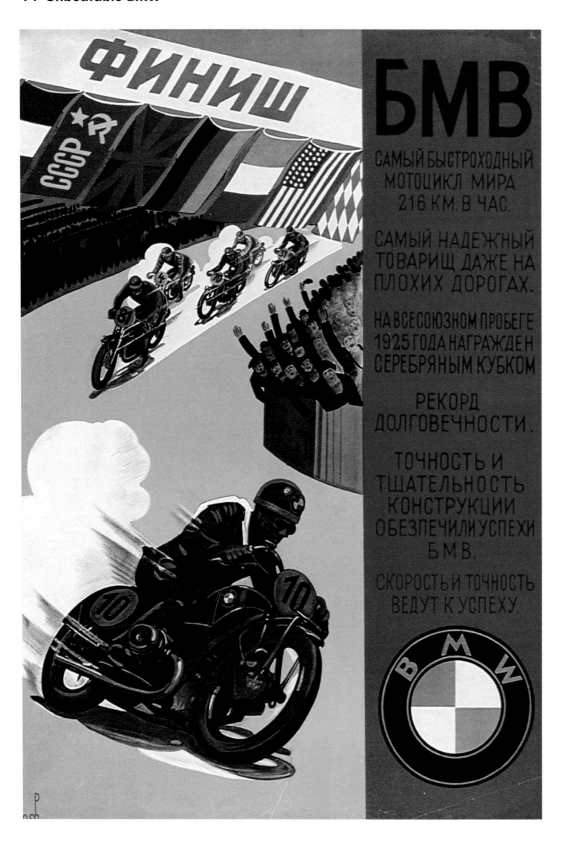

By 1925, BMW's commercial and competitive success with their motorcycles had spread as far as Russia. Rudolf Schliecher had uprated the R32 into an overhead-valve R37 that developed a double ratio of horsepower, totaling 16 bhp by 4,000 rpm, with the help of aluminum cylinder heads.

Picture: Courtesy BMW Archiv, 1997

Originally, the 500-cc unit yielded 8.5 hp and a maximum of 60 mph—not as fast as some, but as with today's BMW bikes, its durability, quality and reliability were appealing. The opposed-cylinder layout was still employed in 1997 Berlin-built BMW bikes, 74 years after its debut at a Parisian show. Now, BMW twins sit alongside a more sophisticated K-series four-cylinder, 16-valve engine line. Born 40 years after the twins, in 1983, it gave 90 bhp from 987 cc, enough to double the maximum of the 1923 original to 126 mph.

The 1920s boxer motors, designed by Max Friz with considerable input from newly graduated Rudolf Schleicher, were not immediate race winners. Indeed, they embarrassingly flopped on their Stuttgart track debut at Solitude. Decades of production and some heroic feats (just one of which I will recount shortly) have long since obliterated that sad memory. The Solitude wound cut deeper because it was enacted virtually on the doorstep of BMW's old sparring partners—and would-be owners—Mercedes.

The young graduate and ace rider Schleicher revolutionized the power of the BMW boxer motor with light-alloy, overhead-valve cylinder heads. These were drawn in October 1922 and manufactured to debut at the following Solitude event: May 19, 1923.

Now the "Unbeatable" legend could be replayed from ground level! A trio of BMW riders, including Schleicher, not only brought back victory from Solitude, but their specially tuned (20-hp) R37 racers founded a dynasty of German Champions that stretched from 1924–1932.

Unbeatable engineering

Throughout the 1920s and 1930s, BMW pushed its motorcycle engineering as ruthlessly as it continued to enhance its aero engines. The result was a disc-principle supercharger to boost the flat-twin motorcycle from 1932 onward. BMW raced supercharged twins with success, but were famed for a series of motorcycle land speed records set on closed sections of the then-new autobahn: they escalated from

The supercharged 500 underpinned some amazing "David and Goliath" feats from BMW. After some engineering experiments in the early 1930s, record-breaker Ernst Jakob Henne redeveloped a French Cozette supercharger to add valuable horsepower, utilizing both for record breaking and race-track performance. The bike shown wears the 1939 Tourist Trophy winning number with pride, BMW scoring a one-two result that confounded the motorcycle establishment. Other original BMW features for motorcycling included sliding front forks, enclosed valve gear, and independently-sprung rear suspension. The latter was the work of then-young recruit Alex von Falkenhausen.

Picture: Courtesy BMW NA, 1996

They raced the supercharged bike on ice, too! Ernst Henne needs a push to fire up the blown flat-twin, which hit 112 mph in Sweden, August 1931.

Picture: BMW Archiv/Chris Willows, 1997

244.4 kmh/151.5 mph in 1933 to a stream-liner 500's 279.5 kmh/173.3 mph in 1937.

Most speed records, including the long-lived 173.3 mph mark, were set by Ernst Henne. BMW agent Henne ran the supercharged BMW on an icy November morning, covering the same ground that was to kill Germany's contemporary Grand Prix star, Bernd Rosemeyer, just six months later. BMW's accumulating competition results and maximum-speed records could be compared fairly to the unrelenting Japanese overthrow of British and Italian motorcycle dominance in the 1960s, also via an escalating sports reputation.

It was the English, with their Midland-based Norton, Velocette, and Triumph sports designs that were the primary target and spur to BMW's sporting ambition. That leads to a hero's tale worthy of this competition-biased book, recalling how BMW served a warning of their increasing engineering prowess on the doorstep of Britain on the eve of World War II.

The "doorstep" was the Isle of Man (Manx): the occasion was the 1939 edition of the annu-

al Senior TT (Tourist Trophy) races, then the most prestigious motorcycle racing available. The word "race" is a bit of a misnomer for these hardy perennials (founded in 1907 and still held, but without the World-Championship status they once enjoyed), because the starts were staggered.

Thus, riders compete largely against themselves and the clock, combining tarmac rallying skills and reading largely unknown roads over the daunting 62-km/38.4-mile laps. I have covered the route in the comparative comfort of motor rallying and I can assure you it dwarfs the Nürburgring for its sheer scale and natural hazards, as the annual fatality list from TT week tragically emphasizes.

Georg "Schorsch" Meier took on the established might of the British bike factories, facing that two-wheeler challenge on his supercharged factory BMW 500, but the TT demanded the life of one BMW teammate in practice. The normally cheerful Meier was an acknowledged Auto Union Grand Prix ace, but

bikes came first for BMW and Germany's pride at Tourist Trophy time. Despite BMW's understandable bid to withdraw in the wake of that practice death, withdrawal was overruled at the behest of the accompanying Nazi party sports officials. So Meier—who had visited the island only once before—went into action on June 16, 1939, less than three months prior to the outbreak of World War II.

The Velocette and Norton opposition was white-hot, and Meier met personal abuse as a "German swine" from the traditional charm of a London cabby, so there was a lot more than just motorcycle commerce at stake. Those handicaps and the pre-race fatality made no difference to Meier, who recalled, "In practice, I had been fastest on practically every day, and the British did not think I could keep it up for seven laps, because I would have to ride flat out for three hours."

Wrong—the man who was nicknamed "Mad Meier," and whose other car was literally a Grand Prix Auto Union, had 50 seconds on

Two more historic moments from BMW's motorcycling roll of honor. "Schorsch" Meier pushes off at 11:00 am on June 16, 1939 for the traditional start of the Tourist Trophy's Blue Riband event, the 500 TT. In action with the 55-horsepower BMW, Meier scrapes one cylinder head over the pavement on the world's most unforgiving race track, one that claimed the life of a teammate in practice.

Meier recorded the first win for anyone but an Englishman, and the first on a foreign machine, hitting speeds up to 124 mph on the 37.5-mile, public-road layout. Today, the course is still used but the races no longer count toward the FIA International World Championship.

Picture: BMW Archiv, released 1997

the pursuing pack over the first tortuous lap! Then 29 years old, he later recalled building up his lead to some three minutes.

That was, and is, an eternity in racing victory margins, one that stands alongside the better-known Grand Prix drives of Nuvolari, Fangio, and Stewart at the Nürburgring. Yet that marvelous ride is comparatively unknown in the English-speaking world of the 1990s. The TT Trophy went back to Munich: the first time it had been won by a foreigner on a machine that was also distinctly not British! As a small compensation to wounded national pride, second overall had gone to Meier's British teammate Jock West, later well-known to British BMW bike buyers via AFN. Such a one-two result just underlined the unwelcome superiority of the German motorcycles on British soil.

Meier himself regarded it as "the greatest moment of my career," a pretty strong recommendation, as the former policeman and soldier was to enjoy one of the most varied working lives any adventurous male could imagine. These including a period working as head of security at BMW, an American appointment made during the immediate postwar invasion.

QUICK FACTS

Period

1928–41

Products

Dixi 3/15 and DA2; 303, 315 and 315/1; 319 and 319/1 to 328

Performance

15 bhp and 47 mph to 136 bhp and 143 mph

Achievements

From four-cylinder imitators to six-cylinder originators

People

Wartburg and the Austin of England connection

Chapter 3

From Austin to Awesome

The tortuous trail to the 328

In original 80-horse-power triple-carburetor trim, the hemi-head 328 set new standards for accessible power in the 1930s. But that was only the beginning of a six-cylinder tradition for ultimate, civilized power per liter that continues today in the M3 series.

Picture: Klaus Schnitzer

Sports success on four wheels came last among BMW conquests, but almost immediately followed the purchase of Wartburg's Dixi-manufacturing Eisenach car factory in 1928.

BMW's first major motor car sporting victory was celebrated in 1929, using a modified version of the Eisenach 15-hp sedan known as the Dixi 3/15. But there was a bit more to this story than BMW's first production car making good, or that first contact with one of the primary English companies (Austin) that went on to make up the Rover Group that BMW purchased in 1994.

The trail that would lead BMW to manufacturing one of the most respected sports designs of all time, and to becoming a true world citizen, traces back further than the aero engine business at Munich. It goes back a century to December 3, 1896, when Fahrezeugfabrick Eisenach AG was founded in the Thuringia region of Eastern Germany by arms-manufacturing millionaire Heinrich Ehrhardt. It tried to develop its own powered bikes, tricycles, and cars, but eventually settled for making a small French car, the Decauville.

Called the Wartburg after a local castle and hunting region, this 1897 coach-car design became the fifth car brand to be manufactured in Germany (beaten by Daimler, Benz, Durkopp, and now-GM-owned Opel at

Russelsheim). From 1897 to 1901, Wartburg offered either 3.5-hp air-cooled or 5-hp water-cooled motors of 500 or 750 cc, respectively, both utilizing chain drives.

The company that BMW bought in 1928 was in a vulnerable loss-making situation, but had proved a BMW-style winner even in its formative years, taking 22 gold medals before the turn of the century and proving a Wartburg to be a benchmark at 60 kmh/37.2 mph. Later, it participated in early Grand Prix racing.

By the time BMW of Munich took on Wartburg of Eisenach, the works were best known as makers of the Dixi range, a brand it had used since 1904. Dixi Eisenach Fahrezeugfabrik concentrated on small cars post-1926 and was trying to develop its own car. That, plus the German economic situation, brought it down even though it subsequently developed a successful product.

What had BMW bought?

Aside from 1,200 employees and a lot of debt at a time when economic disaster after the abandonment of the gold standard was looming, the Austin Seven was a state-of-the-art small car that had been proven since 1922—not just in Britain, but also licensed to Nissan-Datsun as its first product. The 748-cc four-cylinder yielded 15 brake horsepower (bhp) at 3,000 rpm and regularly returned nearly 50 miles to the gallon of expensive European gas.

The top speed of 47 mph was not going to frighten anyone, but BMW ensured the baby Austin transplant was stretched to its limits. Franz Popp took serious note of known Austin Seven defects—poor brakes (the back had only foot brakes, the front a hand brake!) and inferior front suspension—and decided that more interior space and grace would not be out of place.

The result was the DA2 (Deutsche Ausfuhrung) derivative of the Dixi, which was presented at the Berlin Zoo in July 1929, based on a body by Ambi Budd. Now without running boards to allow a broader body without interfering with the basic chassis, the DA2 also offered four-wheel cable brakes.

BMW knew what worth was attached to sports success and pushed its new acquisition to the limit, successfully answering all those in Germany who laughed at this reputable manufacturer getting involved in a foreign import of such cost-conscious appeal. It barely seems possible today, but the Eisenach-based team (Eisenach took responsibility for manufacturing, BMW kept design teams at Munich) got three of the little terrors home in the 1929 Alpenpokal, a 2,500-km forerunner of one of Europe's hardest motor rallies, passing over some of the highest Alpine mountain passes.

Piloted by a crew that included BMW directors Max Buchner, Albert Kandt, and Willi Wagner, it won BMW's most important and earliest major four-wheeler award: the team trophy and domination of three 500- to 800-cc categories.

The first international BMW Team Prize in four-wheel motorsports. Back at Eisenach in the summer of 1929, the trio of BMW 3/15s and the drivers who set 26-mph average speeds through the Alpenpokal Rallye on .75 of a liter were (left to right): BMW directors Max Buchner, Albert Kandt, and Willi Wagner.

A major asset was vehicle reliability and courage from the pilots of a machine notorious for its lack of brakes in normal street driving, nevermind Alpine competition. BMW engineers had, however, improved braking. That year, BMW announced the DA2 production model with uprated stopping ability—the first example of motorsports improving the BMW breed.

Picture: BMW Werkfoto, celebrating 50 years in 1978/ Courtesy Chris Willows, 1997

June 1927: a new car-building era for BMW begins with a convoy bringing 100 Austin Sevens for transformation into these 3/15 Dixis. They brought new life to the Eisenach works (part of which can be seen behind the trio of Anglo-German hybrids).

Since the destruction of the Iron Curtain, BMW has regained access to Eisenach, but only on a small component-manu-facturing scale. The big car plant in the area is now GM/Opel-owned.

Picture: BMW Archiv, reprinted 1997

Sports specials based on the 3/15 running gear pro-gressed rapidly in the early 1930s. Works cars similar to these time-trial machines also raced with success in the early days of the Nürburgring.

Picture: Courtesy Chris Willows, 1997

The baby Bimmers averaged speeds in excess of the required 42-kmh/26-mph minimum and convinced the German public that BMW engineering really had transformed the Seven/Dixi to the point where the laughing had to stop. In fact, *Deutsche Automobilzeitung* motoring news magazine was so full of praise that one suspects it had overdone the derision before the Eisenach-based BMWs took the start. Its comments enthused, "The Bavarian Motor Works took over the Dixi, and produced the improved Dixi as a BMW. Yet it must be considered a new make. It took part in the Alpine Rally and amazed the whole motoring world by giving a performance which left everyone flabbergasted."

Unbeatable? Not in overall terms, but that *Automobilzeitung* report added, "The BMW 748.5cc engines beat them all hollow!" So the rugged BMW reputation for enduring speed was up and running in the car world nearly 70 years ago.

This performance served as a warning that BMW was as serious about developing cars and winning with recognizable competition variants as they had been with aero engines and motorcycles, the latter having accumulated 100 major awards by 1925. BMW was quick to capitalize commercially on that sporting reputation, and sportier versions of the Dixi sprouted into the 1930s. They extracted another 3 hp and 500 rpm from the 748-cc and installed it in the BMW-Wartburg two-seater sports cars, of which only 150 were made.

Commercially, the DA2 was the success story of the BMW-Dixi generation, with over 12,000 made from 1929–31; but for competition, it was strictly limited to class wins. Something lighter and more powerful was required to satisfy BMW instincts, but as recent survivors of the financial horrors of the 1920s, BMW was never going to volunteer for the German state-backed Grand Prix programs of Mercedes and Auto Union status.

BMW needed a niche between poverty and prestige: an automobile that spoke of discriminating prosperity and sporting flair with aviation durability and performance as a pedigree bonus, something with six-cylinder potential rather than four-pot austerity....

The six-cylinders move in

The six-cylinders arrived in the brief (1933–34) but significant span of the 303, an upright sedan that debuted BMW's Lichtbau (lightweight) steel chassis, rack-and-pinion steering (just two turns of lock required), and the company's first use of the Nierformig (kidney-shaped) front grille.

That other familiar trademark of today, the cubic capacity preceded by a model number, came with the 1934 BMW 309, which simply meant 300 series and 0.9 of a liter, and developed more logically with the second best-seller, the 315 of 1.5 liters and 1934–37 production.

Today BMW sometimes eschews the 60-year-old tradition of model number and liters—both the UK and the USA have had 3- and 5-series cars with engine capacities different from their badges—but sales teams were happy to have the 328 legend back in 3-series format. Then BMW spoiled it by using the 2.5-liter alloy block in a 323i because of the previous pulling power of that badge! Generally, you can still tell exactly which BMW is in front of you, unless the owner has gone for the no-cost option of de-badging, which began in Germany and is now widespread.

The in-line six of the 1934 BMW 303 displaced 1,173 cc (56 x 80 mm) and developed double the original Austin Seven's horsepower. That meant a 5.6:1 compression, and a pair of Solex carburetors released 30 bhp at 4,000 rpm, enough to reach the magic 100 kmh maximum speed rating for the new autobahn that the unemployed recruits were digging.

Lest we forget, 1933 was a momentous year in German politics, and the implications of Adolf Hitler's rise to supremacy were particularly pronounced in the car business. Just 12 days after his accession to power, Hitler pronounced a four-point plan to get the national motorcar business moving. All five national company heads were present, along with Germany's motoring organizations, as Hitler pronounced that lower taxes and extensive road building would be implemented. BMW was definitely encouraged in its commercial and competitive aspirations, especially as the fourth point of the plan was "...the development of motorsports."

The 303's six—and much more that we shall hear of for 328—was the work of Rudolph Schleicher or the teams that he led. These included motorcycle engineer Alex von Falkenhausen, who figures prominently in our post-WWII account of BMW's return to rude health via motorsports.

Schleicher, who had redesigned BMW's bike cylinder heads in the 1920s, marked the beginning of a 1930s BMW partnership with Fritz Fiedler in which Fiedler was charged with overall vehicle design and Schleicher its development and testing. In modern parlance, Schleicher was the motor man and Fiedler's particular strengths came outside the engine bay, particularly in chassis engineering. They would plough through a mountain of models with their development work in the 1930s, setting resounding standards for BMW's automotive division to equal the achievements already accrued in aviation and motorcycling.

The pair had met at Horch, where Fiedler had designed a similar steel A-frame (narrower at the front than the rear) to show the benefits of 90-mm lightweight steel tubing and electric welding precision, and now the pair would produce the classic 328.

At first, the design partnership was a long-distance one, for Fiedler was in the Eisenach office, while Schleicher operated from Munich; but by 1937, Fiedler would join Schleicher at BMW's Munich headquarters.

The 1934 Alpenfahrt brought more glory to BMW, but now their six-cylinder 315/1 machines attracted international attention for their speed, supple suspension, and effective team management. The works 315/1s, seen here on the myriad twists that make up Stilfser Joch (Stelvio), were effective first steps along the highway to 328, also prompting major commercial inquiries for BMW import rights overseas.

Pictures: BMW Archiv/Chris Willows, 1997

The 303's key features spawned a line of mid-1930s BMWs that generally added to the firm's reputation for quality products. As a result, Mercedes declined to go on supplying the coachwork that had been a feature of so many earlier BMWs, which ended the long-running talks (since 1926) about BMW and Mercedes (or its Daimler Benz ancestors) becoming one southern German enterprise. It wouldn't be the last time Mercedes wanted to marry a Bavarian bride who proved too tough to convince!

There was, however, an English company that wanted to climb into BMW's bed. AFN Ltd. was the manufacturer of the Frazer Nash sports car in West London: hardy, lightweight designs that were traditional class winners in a variety of motorsports using an equal variety of power plants. Owned by the Aldington family, including keen and able competitor Harold (known as H. J. or Aldy) Aldington, AFN Ltd. contested the 1934 Alpine with a spontaneous "team" of three other Nash owners having a holiday that happened to involve one of Europe's toughest motoring trials.

After two previously successful outings in the Alpine, H.J. Aldington realized that opposition in the 1.5-liter class of 1934 was stronger than usual. Legendary *Motor Sport* reporter and Mille Miglia winner (with Stirling Moss driving) Denis Jenkinson reported, "The main opposition in the 1500-cc class came from a team of new 1.5-liter, six-cylinder BMW open two-seaters from the Munich factory. They were being run like a Grand Prix Team, to strict orders, strict discipline, and ruthless efficiency."

Aldington was not only aware of the efficient way the team was being run and the discipline of team members compared to his unruly lot, but also of the way in which the Type 315 BMW sports cars were performing. He knew his own ability as a driver and the potential of the TT replica Frazer Nash....Yet, here, an unknown driver/car combination was beating them.

"The BMWs were not only faster up the mountains, but also faster down the other side and were giving their crews a much smoother ride, for they had independent front suspension with supple springing and good hydraulic shock absorbers, while the cockpits were almost luxurious compared to a Frazer Nash," ended Jenks's telling comments.

Legend had it that the Aldingtons then went straight from a Sanremo finish to Munich to do the British BMW importation deal, but this was untrue. Local knowledge of the Aldington family through their later Porsche concession in postwar Britain reveals that they were a pretty cautious and canny lot, and Jenks unraveled their correspondence in his marvelous 1984/85 book, *From Chain Drive to Turbocharger*.

Documentation shows that the Alpine trial finished in Munich that year and that the Aldingtons wrote to the factory at the wrong address to arrange the first meeting! By November, AFN Ltd. and BMW had signed a formal contract that would lead to the importation of almost 800 BMWs—including 328s—to underline that competition actually sells the breed and improves its manners!

The BMW marque, available with right-hand-drive (RHD) for the first time (only the first Austin Sevens had RHD in Germany, and that was pre-BMW), were sold as Frazer Nash-BMWs. AFN was a significant force in the sports and commercial development of the marque in Britain and beyond, so well regarded that AFN drivers, including H. J. Aldington and A. F. P. Fane, were allowed to compete in one of the first three 328 racing prototypes (painted British Racing Green, on occasion).

The amazing 328

What were the 328's mechanical parents? Technically, production runs measured in hundreds of two-seaters (315/1 and 319/1) and

thousands of sedans on which they were based (315 and 319) contributed to the birth of the 328, and to BMW's "Unbeatable" sporting reputation.

Looking back at all the great BMWs, there is a tendency to think first of the power units and then of the chassis/body, for BMW did not set such absolute benchmark standards outside the engine bay as within. Indeed, some of its proudest aviation and motorsports achievements defer purely to power units. But the 328 was different.

BMW's most revered race and road car number would debut as a racing car. The most famous production-based racers from BMW, postwar, were all established road cars, made by the thousand, before a competition conversion (of increasing sophistication) took place.

The 328's first three prototypes initially ran without doors, no spare-wheel cavity, recessed headlamps, and a vestigial flat screen, unwiped. The latter screen replaced the two-

section vee-unit of production, which carried windscreen wipers for each half. Later, the original prototypes were partially updated to look more like production 328s and one of them competed regularly as a British AFN Frazer Nash competition entry. More of that, later.

As a racing machine, the 328 put a premium on track handling. It was always going to be competitively light—the sparse 90-mm steel tube construction of accurate electric welds saw to that—but it was also extremely strong, particularly at resisting torsional twisting forces. That gave it the foundation for the truly outstanding all-around performance that is the hallmark of a great sports design.

The first time you drive a 328—even in contemporary traffic—it is the balance of the chassis that wins you over. Modest grip, by today's standards, is accompanied by excellently-controlled breakaway characteristics and perfectly matched capabilities from steering and brakes that make you think you are the finest driver on earth—and my first experience of the 328 was in the early 1990s alongside a 1980s Z1. The 328 was not embarrassed in any department by the younger design, proving that the lack of BMW cash and the short development period were no handicap to providing a car that belongs with the gods of whichever Valhalla houses motorcars.

When I describe the simplicity that lay under Ambi Budd's coachwork, you may dismiss the above as fanciful flights from a BMW "nut behind the wheel." Here are some of the headlines from recent issues of the British classic car magazines, most of which approached the BMW 328 in cynical frame of mind....

Quote 1: "'Surely,' I thought, 'the BMW 328 can't be as good as everyone says?' Everything I had read suggested that it was the best pre-war sports car, years ahead of its time. Could this be true? It is! The 328 is a glorious car, both easy and immensely satisfying to drive." (Malcolm McKay, *Classic Cars*, May 1994.)

Still not convinced? Quote 2: "Way Ahead. BMW's great thirties sports car, the 328, set a standard the company was still struggling to match two decades later." (Mark Gillies, *Supercar Classics*, April 1988.)

You really are stubborn! Quote 3: "The 328 has the traditional characteristics of great German design: rational style and clean, undecorated surfaces, combined with purity of colour and detail....Rarely have I experienced such a sweet, willing, and easy car to drive." (Mick Walsh, *Classic & Sportscar*, October 1994.)

Such quotes underline the effectiveness with which BMW transplanted its simple ideals, born of 303 and descendants. A tube chassis, allied with the transverse leaf and wishbone independent front suspension and leaf sprung rears, was quoted at an enormous variety of weights: 550 kg as a simple chassis plus engine. (Apparently almost 60 were delivered without BMW bodywork. Not all were racers: wonderfully elegant lines were also concocted by Wendler, Drauz, and Ludwig Weinberger.)

Total weight was controversial too: eye witness accounts of the racing debut quote slightly over 800 kg for the door-less competitor, in line with a German translation I undertook which revealed 830 kg for a fully-equipped road car. However, an authoritative 1996 BMW Mobile Tradition publication records 780 kg in production, with 50 liters of fuel!

We can take it that the production cars, complete with their twin leather bonnet straps, averaged some 800 kg/1,760 lbs, working with a miserly low-cost overhead valve conversion of the American-style cast-iron cylinder block to provide a power-to-weight ratio of 101.3 bhp a ton. That is more than many small and allegedly sporty sedans can provide 60 years down the highway! It was also only a starting point for the competition cars, which reached 136 bhp prewar, and a lot more in a variety of postwar competitors.

Racing technology

To understand a competition 328, first you need to know that Schleicher had supervised the BMW in-line six's growth from 1,173 cc/30 bhp on the 303 through 1,475 cc (315 and 315/1) and 34 to 40 bhp. Then came 1,911 cc on the 319 (or 319/1) to peak at 55 bhp with triple sidedraft Solexes. Finally, the BMW became a 1,971-cc unit rated at least 50 bhp beyond that first 1.2-liter BMW six.

How was that road car's 80 bhp achieved? The big lift from the 319/1's advertised 55 bhp at 4000 revs came via a new cylinder head and its triple Solex 30JF downdraft carburetors tipping mixture down into hemispherical combustion chambers. Traditionally, running that classic pentroof combustion chamber would be allied with an overhead camshaft(s) valve gear operation, but BMW left the camshaft in the iron cylinder block to operate the inlet valves via long pushrods and rockers.

Exhaust valves were activated in a more cumbersome fashion, using a second pushrod to bridge the gap from inlet row to exhausts operated via a bell crank, rocker shaft, and shorter pushrod. BMW never claimed the idea was original, even in their 1936 patent application.

Team chief Schleicher candidly submitted, "A motor vehicle engine which can be converted through exchanging the cylinder head of an engine with sidevalves or parallel overhead valves into a high-performance engine with a valve arrangement having better combustion technology, characterized by the following well-known features," before describing the application in the technical detai already explored.

The cylinder head itself was constructed in cast alloy, the crankshaft and connecting rods in steel, pistons in Nural forged alloys, and the block using the cast-iron process Schleicher had debuted for BMW use in the 303. Power spurted from the cascade of mixture delivered via the triple Solex 30 JF carburetors, and the effi-

The 315/1 truly set BMW on the sporting trail; its works team exploits on the 1934 Alpine trial proved to be amazing international opposition for their 1.5 liter pace. A triple carburetor six foretold the way 328 would be developed.

Picture: BMW AG

cient combustion chamber design (spheroid) held a very high 1930s figure of 7.5:1 compression for the road, making it produce almost double the specific power: 40.9 bhp a liter in place of the parent 319/1's 28.8 bhp a liter.

That was far beyond anyone's natural expectation of a modest capacity growth from 1,911 to 1,957 cc, occasioned by a one-millimeter growth in bore and stroke of 66 x 96 mm to replace the 319's 65 x 96 mm.

So the six-cylinder motor—and much of the transmission around its sweet in-line cylinders—had roots in far less powerful BMWs, which was to prove a constant source of development aggravation as power increased.

The first 328 racer prototypes carried 86 to 88 bhp, rather than the road advertised minimum 80 bhp at 4,500 rpm. At that production rating, 135 kmh/84 mph was reckoned as the autobahn

cruising speed, 150 kmh/93 mph the maximum.

BMW's experimental department under Schleicher first progressed the competition 328, but from 1938–41, the company set up a formal competitions department that dealt with development as well as preparation and sales of parts. In the field, BMW's interests were represented by the managerial skills of Ernst Loof, the post-war founder of Veritas, who made eleven 328-based specials.

The unique valve gear dictated that little more than 5,000 rpm could initially be employed alongside a camshaft duration of 300 degrees. But development work, particularly postwar, saw the units rise to 6,000 rpm and beyond.

Originally, the four-bearing layout was supported in white metal for the mains, but this was displaced in 1938 by the overwhelming military need for that material, so an inferior

The most beautiful of the 328's relations, the 327 series in convertible (shown here) or coupe form, finally cemented its close technical links with the 328 by running the full triple-carburetor powertrain as the subsequent 327/28 coupe, capable of speeds nearing 90 mph.

Picture: Author (Car owned by Vasek Polak, USA)

"This is how it should be." BMW Mobile Tradition's Klaus Kutscher explains original OZ 80-stamped 328 motor magic.

Picture: Klaus Schnitzer, Munich, 1996

Even sixty years after the 328 was born, its engine was being redeveloped and raced. This example, said to be good for over 170 horsepower and fed by carburetors that came from a British Sunbeam Alpine, also offers radically-rethought tubular exhaust manifolding.

Picture: Author, Monterey, 1996

performance from lead bronze had to be accepted. In the late 1970s, Alex von Falkenhausen was still lamenting the bearing material change, knowing that durability and rpm were unfavorably compromised.

Other technical changes during the production run included a Hurth four-speed gearbox substituting for the original ZF and a slight lowering of axle ratio, but both road boxes offered synchromesh just in third and fourth gears.

In competition trim, transmissions were a problem, for the original back axle was conceived to withstand 40 bhp in the 319 era; the ZF gearbox did not like a sporting battering either, so these items were the most common reasons for 1936–37 retirements. Redevelopment of these Achilles heels saw the gearbox and axle from the 320 adopted in competition and for the last 180-odd production 328s. Competition actually did improve the breed!

Initially, the replacement Hurth four-speed proved to be the answer alongside the first of the 100-bhp-plus 328s of 1939; but when the factory extracted over 130 bhp for all its 1940 Mille Miglia entries, Hurth went to even heavier gear sets while the drivers had to baby the clutches if they were not to fail. ZahnradFabrik (ZF) did develop another generation of gearbox—and a limited-slip differential—just as you would expect from a company of their current reputation. These were not, however, widely available to the 328 prewar: today, a 328 employing an original ZF or Hurth box is a particularly precious specimen, especially equipped with the bracing bar that the factory used to keep for themselves and favored friends. This bar absorbs some of the flexing found in the 1930s casings.

Beyond adopting the heavier-duty 320 back axle, the competition department also offered an aluminium differential casing that housed Gleason (later known as Torsen-Gleason in the US) gear sets with 3.7:1 or 3.44:1 final drives. The road cars had used a 3.7:1 with the ZF box and 3.88:1 with the Hurth.

Post-war British transmission experience in motorsports led to many weekend competitor 328s receiving a Moss gearbox (a brand favored by Morgan and some 1950s and 1960s Jaguars). Or there was a Bristol copy of the heavy-duty Hurth used in the 1937–41 BMW 327 coupe. UK experience revealed that the donation of a Volvo Amazon box was practical and required no chassis alterations.

Over 50 bhp a liter was exceeded regularly by 1938 in Germany so that works cars or those for favored customers, such as the Nazi Motorsports Organization (NSKK), attained 110 bhp at slightly over 5,000 revs. The changes that brought the extra 30 bhp over a production example included oversize jetting for the triple Solexes, a replacement camshaft of higher lift, and carefully calibrated lobe profiles (they could not be too violent in this department with such a valve actuation train to support). Oversized combustion chamber valves were available—matched to enlarged intake ports—but these were not always reliable. Thus, a spread in achieved power could be expected. Improvements in production metals specified for the cylinder heads allowed compression ratios of 9.5:1 to be competition-specified on 80-octane fuel.

Alternatively, the Germans were masters of brewing special fuels, and BMW had two mixes—benzol and alcohol variants—that would allow a 10.5:1 compression and some 120 bhp, should the rest of the engine be prepared to withstand 5,500 rpm.

In fact, 6,000 revs were finally achieved with replacement chrome moly steel crankshafts used along with special fuel mixes. The ultra-high compression (nearly 11.5:1) version of the 2.0-liter Mille Miglia race motor, rated at 136 bhp, was the highest pre-war figure recorded for these now radically-reengineered units.

Aside from the restrictions of valve gear actuation—which also meant that the factory did not specify competition camshaft inlet durations beyond 300 degrees—the six-counterweight

production crankshaft was exhibiting worrying whip distortions over 4,500 rpm. The change to lead bronze bearings for 1938 production provoked markedly increased bearing clearances, and BMW encountered further lubrication problems that led to increasing the oil pump capacity.

These were only stop-gap measures, and the factory answer was a series of competition-only crankshafts—subcontracted to Alfing for manufacture—in chrome moly steels that also featured hardened bearing journals and a vibration damper. For competition, the crankshafts ultimately had Alfing's nine-counterweight crank of increased journal bore sizing (just about double the lead bronze shaft journal dimensions), and this was assembled with a number of lighter-weight components (mostly reciprocating) that saved them a third, dropping from 3,966 grams to 2,960 grams.

BMW achieved this valuable internal loss of just over a kilogram/2.2 lbs by measures such as a hollow camshaft, lightened valves, and connecting rods, plus an Elektron forged-piston design. Thus, the works BMW motors gained almost 1,000 rpm.

That pared-down weight put less load on the engine's antics between 4,500 and a finally-realized limit of 6,000 rpm. Incidentally, even in the ultimate 1940 trim, if a driver exceeded the chosen rpm limit, the damage was nearly always sufficient to require engine replacement, and this was the case with the winning Mille Miglia car less than 24 hours before the start.

Aside from the first BMW use of aerodynamic knowledge in competition cars—dealt with in our account that follows of the 328's competition career—there were always modifications to enhance the 328's low weight, fuel tank capacity, braking ability, and handling. Some of these were reserved for the works or favored customers, including replacement race seats that had either aluminium or (at Mille Miglia) Elektron magnesium alloy frames with deck-chair-style webbing.

Sports brakes sizes did not increase, but the Alfins drums of a stock 280 mm/11 inches were uprated with features such as ventilated steel back plates, riveted steel liners, balance weights, and, by Mille Miglia time, magnesium used in the ventilated brake-drum back plates.

The biggest handling tweak was to remount the rear springs and diminish the roll oversteer effects, but we can also be sure that spring and damper settings, front and rear, were thoroughly investigated and replaced as required for deployments as different as the Nürburgring, Mille Miglia, or the slippery tracts of early rallying.

How many modern sports cars could face such a varying work load? The 328 legend was based on a solid technical foundation and heroic driving: the subject of our next chapter.

QUICK FACTS

Period

1936–48

Products

Racing 328 and planned offspring

Achievements

Winning Nürburgring debut before production commenced; set the standard by which all other middleweight sports cars were judged; inspired a generation of more commercially successful British copycats

People

Ernst Henne debuts; British take up winning with A. F. P. Fane; Porsche's subsequent competition manager, Husche von Hanstein, wins wartime Mille Miglia for BMW

Chapter 4

The Legend Unfolds

The fabulous 328 sets the 2-liter benchmark

The start and finish apron of the old Nürburgring, 22.8 kilometers/14.1 miles of the most daunting and demanding racetrack ever devised by man, was a lonely place to be. It was lonely even when surrounded, as Ernst Henne was on the characteristically damp Eifel mountain day of June 14, 1936, by the din of 39 other competitors wishing to set new standards for 2-liter sports car motoring.

That huge concrete apron was a bleak place to wait for a race start, especially when the weather forecast is full of doom and gloom and Henne's previous four-wheeler experience—driving the ultimate supercharged Grand Prix Mercedes—was notable for poor fortune and broken bones. Ironically overlooked by an enormous Mercedes-Benz advertising banner, Henne looked apprehensive, his plain white overalls complemented by his equally pristine white BMW 328 prototype. Behind him was a career with many motorcycle world records—ahead, more reservations for the Henne name in the record books.

A look at the works-prepared BMW, brought right down to minimal weight (given as 810 kg/1,782 lbs) with no doors, and equipped with almost another 10 bhp over what would become the 80-bhp norm, should have reassured Henne. Still, the calculating ace had his doubts.

The 328 had survived many daunting sorties over the often-rough 270 miles of roads between Munich and Eisenach, but it had not appeared in public before. Now it had to conquer the Nürburgring on its debut, with an equally plain white Adler of greater front-drive traction for front-row company on the glistening tarmac. Both awaited the signal to start, two minutes behind bigger-class cars.

Henne need not have worried. He shrugged off any vestige of opposition in the opening stages of the first lap and went on to cover the 140 kms/86.8 miles at an average just over the magic 100 km/h mark, translating to 63.03 mph. On the way, the door-less BMW without a supercharger had blown away an example of the legendary Alfa Romeo 6C, finishing almost two and a half minutes ahead of the pack.

It was a fine start to a career that captivated a world-wide audience, before and after the war. Yet the initial problem was to keep the 328's motorsports momentum to placate what would inevitably be an elongated waiting list.

In fact, it was almost a year before series production of the 328 could begin, and even that is a relative term, for BMW sports variants of the 1930s were handmade by the hundred, rather than mass-made by the thousand.

BMW ensures that their Mille Miglia Italian racing tradition is unforgotten, vigorously taking part in the annual retrospective runs of the 1980s and 1990s.

Picture: BMW Mobile Tradition, 1996

A classic 328 in proper production form with opening doors and split screen—true, but look again at the registration and the RHD steering. Britain was the most popular export market for the 328, and many other BMWs, thanks to the sporting and commercial efforts of AFN Ltd. in West London.

Picture: Peter Osborne, Kent, England, 1993

For three years, beginning March 1937 and ending August 1939, BMW made more than 100 328s a year. Including prototypes, the final tally of 328s was just 464, but there would be many more half-brothers, cousins, and outright bastards based on the 328 inspiration, post-war.

Those who could afford the cost of a 328—and it was double the cost of the mass-produced 320 in Germany, or £695 for its UK debut at the London Motor Show—grimly awaited fulfillment of their dreams. Meantime, BMW got on with the job of beating the pants off of any class opposition. To put it bluntly, if

you didn't have a BMW in the late 1930s and you wanted 2-liter competition success, you were wasting your time with anything other than the white and blue roundel.

Across Europe, from Britain to Belgrade, via most current members of the European Common Market, the 328 racked up wins on everything from banked Brooklands to muddy fields and icy rally tracks: it was that versatile.

In total, there were 131 victories and 45 gold medals between 1936 and 1940, the latter wartime year devoted to events only in Italy (a pale echo of Mille Miglia) and Yugoslavia. Medals and an uncounted number of plaques

and trophies were usually won in endurance events that might be on a timed rally format or laps of a road-race circuit.

Because of the BMW-AFN trading links established after that 1934 Alpine Rally performance from the 315/1 BMWs, the British featured disproportionately well in the initial results scored by the 328, mostly in that original door-less format.

From June 1937 onward, AFN sold 45 of the original 461 production run—nearly all in right-hand drive (RHD) for UK—and additionally accounted for the use of a single works prototype (85.003, also RHD), which was officially delivered in October 1936 to be used as a demonstrator with competition use assigned to H. J. Aldington.

In fact, Aldington was allowed to take time off from a business visit to Munich in August 1936 to score a popular win in BMW's home-town Munich Triangle races with the very first (85.001) prototype. This lighthearted victory

tells us all we need to know of the mutual regard that existed between the Anglo-German trading partners, as it was the first event after Henne's historic win with the same 328 prototype.

Aldington repaid the BMW factory's faith in spades, for he scored the trio of wins that completed 1936 for BMW's triumphant debutante. He also organized the appearances of the cars in prestigious events such as the 1936 Ulster Tourist Trophy with a telling one-two-three result for the British-Racing-Green-sprayed 328 prototypes of A. F .P. Fane, Aldington and Prince Bira. That was an achievement to be ranked today alongside the US BMW importer winning a NASCAR round with the first three brand new sports machines off the line and the American boss driving, supported by world-class talent.

A week after his 1937 Shelsely-Walsh win, A. F. P Fane was fêted at the Nürburgring Eifelrennen. Beating the times of some supercharged machinery to win the 2-liter class, Fane was initially pursued by Ernst Henne (as here), but the German suffered an early accident, thought to have been prompted by a pit-lane mechanical mistake.

Picture: BMW AG, Historisches Archiv, reprinted 1997

(Top) A brace of views from the 1938 Tourist Trophy, which was held at the Donington Park Circuit in Britain after fatalities occurred in the earlier Ulster-based editions. In front of an enormous crowd—drawn by the prospect of seeing the all-conquering Mercedes and Auto Union GP cars—the mud-guarded sports racers await a handicap class departure. The works 328s are lined up on the left side of the second row.

(Bottom) Coming over the famous Donington brow—where the Grand Prix power-brokers flew—2-liter class winner Prince Bira flicks his works 328 past a more traditional Riley of the era.

Pictures: BMW Archiv/Courtesy Chris Willows, 1997

Fane's winning ways

Prince "B" Bira was a world-class single-seat driver of established reputation, but A. F. P. Fane has been severely underestimated by motoring historians, barring the original work of former Motor Sport colleague, Denis Jenkinson. Fane demonstrated winning ways in BMWs back to the 315/1: his performances in international class events, such as grasping third overall plus the 2- liter class in the 1936 Ulster TT on the fearsomely unforgiving Ards road circuit, showed he was much, much more than a rich man playing at sports car racing.

Fane was also a class winner in the 1937 edition of the Eifelrennen (in 85.002), qualifying quicker than Henne, who went off on the opening lap. By far the most successful 328 competitor, after the pioneering factory results of Ernst Henne, Fane was also a member of the BMW winning team's one-two-three class result in the 1938 Mille Miglia (finishing seventh, ninth, and tenth overall), which went to Alfa Romeo.

The factory responded to such obvious ability by fielding Fane at the international hillclimb on the Grossglockner that year, for another fine win with times faster than any other sports car, including the supercharged devices that were thought mandatory at this time to make a quick competition car. Fane finished off his fabulous 1938 season with a shared winning drive alongside Aldington at Brooklands.

There was more Brooklands success in 1939 for Fane, the India-born son of a mining engineer. Fane's name was originally Agabeg, but he was confusingly renamed Alfred Fane Peers Fane. He was a fanatically keen customer of AFN, and was famous for his exploits with the "Chain Gang" Frazer Nashes before and after the BMW deal.

Besides being a monstrously talented driver, Fane became a 20-percent shareholder in AFN to make the mass importation of BMWs viable in Britain. Ironically, he went on to become a very effective photo-reconnaissance WWII pilot for the RAF in an appropriately stripped-out Spitfire. This is doubly ironic, because he would occasionally fly over sections of Autobahnen and countryside that he knew better than many Germans. He is famous in Britain as the man who took pictures of the Tirpitz battleship, which led to its eventual destruction.

A. F. P. Fane died flying the Spitfire type that he loved on July 18, 1942, operating out of Benson, an RAF base now better-known for teaching Sarah "Fergie" Ferguson to fly.

Driving the legend

Back on the ground, there were other Britons who figured in 328s, but the best-known—Mercedes Grand Prix driver Dick Seaman—did not return the results expected of his prominence. It would be unfair to further overlook the achievements of the (mostly) German drivers who followed Henne's factory lead.

Best-known, post-war, were barons such as Alex von Falkenhausen and Fritz Huschke von Hanstein, the latter winning the 1940 Mille Miglia for BMW, while von Falkenhausen was second only to Aldington at the 1936 Munich Triangle races. Von Falkenhausen later showed rally pace enough to preview his post-war success. He became the father of BMW's engine engineering and competitive revival in the

1950s and 1960s, while von Hanstein was Porsche's archetypal competition manager in the 1960s and 1970s.

The bulk of the results came, however, from privateers who had ordered 328s early, such as Adolf Brudes, Paul Heinemann, Uli Richter (later a works substitute for Henne), Ralf Roese, Kurt Illman, and Paul Greifzu. But there were later works-backed drivers, such as Fritz Roth, who won the Finnish Grand Prix for sports cars, his Helsinki version of 85.002 now sporting doors.

Unhappily, politics entered every sphere of German life in this era, and we have to report differing kinds of works cars. Some were owned by the Nazi power sports organisation (NSKK)—who chose the drivers—but they operated through BMW under the managerial eye of the first traceable formal competition manager: Ernst Loof. Sometimes the privateers listed were allowed works cars and, occasionally, success came in a 328 actually owned by the German state post office!

Whoever owned the cars, BMW made sure it didn't spend too much on competition, for spending was simply not necessary: the 328 was truly unbeatable in the 2-liter class. Because supercharged cars were usually banned in German contests, there was only one logical choice, if you ignored the charms of the often successful Adler (Eagle), who was particularly adept at entering streamliners for high-speed events.

Le Mans in 1938 was just such an Adler event, but it led BMW to contest its first Spa 24 Hours. This event, on the Belgian border side of the brooding Ardennes mountains that also house the Nürburgring, was to become a BMW speciality when it hosted a touring car race in 1964.

Back in 1938, the 328 was good and strong enough to net the team prize for BMW in an arranged dead heat finish, the best Bimmer managing nearly 70 mph for the 24 hours, demoting the best Adler back to fourth in the class at an average almost five mph slower.

The first of many. Today BMW has racked up more than 20 wins in the Belgian 24-hour classic. A historic class victory and fifth overall went to the 328 of Prince zu Schaumberger-Lippe, who led a team of three Team Prize-winning 2-liter BMWs over terrain that included loose surfaces—thus the blasted center spotlight!

Postwar, the 24-hour Belgian classic switched to touring cars in the 1960s and BMW racked up their 20 outright wins—a feat unmatched by any manufacturer in endurance racing.

Picture: BMW Archiv, reprinted 1997

Aerodynamics come to competition BMWs

The challenge of developing streamlined bodies and enhancing the 328's overall pace was not long neglected. From September 1938 onward, the factory experimented with low-drag bodies through an official design department that built on their earlier work in 1938; the first efforts were far from stable but returned a maximum speed bonus that was attractive. BMW's technicians opted for an alternative to the Paul Jaray prototype approach—part of the Adler high-speed formula—and asked Professor Wunibald Kamm for input.

Time was running out to field a streamliner in the 1939 Le Mans, so the factory took a shortcut through Italy's Carozzeria Touring and made an appropriately reduced-scale competition Alfa Romeo body! Up against ultimate pacesetters such as the V12 Lagondas and aristocratic Alfas with Grand Prix power trains, Max zu Schaumberg Lippe and BMW engineering employee Fritz Weicher took the streamliner to fifth overall, leading two "normal" 328s home at over 82 mph. It was enough to forget about the Adlers, which had a very troubled event and posed no serious threat.

World War II broke out in September 1939, so British and French participation in the luxury of motorsports was terminated until after the war, but the Germans and the Italians did hold some events. Most significant was the 1940 Mille Miglia, which saw BMW debut not just new bodies for some entries, but also the ultimate motors discussed earlier, offering 130 to 136 bhp to haul their lowest-drag coachwork at more than 140 mph. Considering that the standard road car had trouble topping 93

Dubbed "The Ugly One" by some insiders, the Munich-built coupe using Kamm aerodynamic principles was also the fastest (143 mph) machine in the BMW factory-engineered Mille Miglia quintet. The aerodynamic drag factor was recorded as 0.25 Cd, a figure unequaled by any production car in 1998.

Picture: Courtesy Chris Willows, 1997

Not the same Mille Miglia roadster as our previous two pictures, but the uncreased lines of this Series 2 BMW 328-based Mille Miglia roadster have been thoroughly renovated and the machine is used regularly for publicity purposes.

Picture: BMW Mobile Tradition, 1996

mph, this was a fair indication of just how effective the four-year 328 competition development period had been.

The bodies used in 1940 were a pair of superb open two-seaters by Touring of Milan, the same company's low-line closed coupe, and the factory's own streamliner. The latter deployed inputs of Professor Kamm and Wilhem Meyerhuber, a BMW employee who established a separate design department in September 1938 at Munich.

Although our interest is primarily in the competition versions of the 328 they made possible, it is worth noting that BMW followed the American practice of having a separate styling studio during the 1930s. Meyerhuber was originally from the Opel branch of General

Motors, and so was his deputy (with appropriate experience at Fisher Body Co.). Also, the Ambi-Budd referred to earlier as BMW's increasing choice for coachwork was in fact the German division of Budd in the US.

Most of the competition bodywork used in 1940 was the result of mathematical calculations, previous experience, and practical trial and error on test autobahn runs. BMW planned a wind tunnel, but it was not operational prior to WWII, so outside facilities had to be used when required.

Despite these "suck it and see" methods and the obvious handicaps of military wartime requirements at BMW, the Mille Miglia results were spectacular. Kamm's drag measurements revealed that the aerodynamic drag factor (Cd)

of the standard 328, screen erect, was 0.54. The beautiful Mille Miglia open roadsters returned 0.37 Cd (competitive among open sports cars today: a Z3 2.8 recorded 0.42 Cd in 1997).

The Touring Coupe body did not allow much of a bonus on its open cousins, down at 0.35, but the company's combination with Kamm realised a sensational 0.25 Cd, still comfortably below that delivered by a any production coupe in 1998!

The practical benefits of such sleek aluminium paneling could be seen in a 6-mph top-speed bonus (143 versus 137 mph) when the two closed cars shared 136 bhp at 6000 rpm. The open roadsters were reckoned to be good for almost 125 mph on 6 bhp less, but had the advantages of improved vision, better handling, and driver comfort when the going got twisty.

BMW gained all the results that could be expected in a wartime version of Mille Miglia, titled Il Gran Premio Brescia delle Mille Miglia, set out over a triangular lap having its points

at Brescia (start and finish), Cremona, and Mantova. It was not quite a thousand miles around those laps, but Huschke von Hanstein and (for a final lap) Walter Baumer in the Touring-bodied Le Mans coupe remained on top throughout the 934 miles. They covered that distance in 8 hours 54 minutes, beating the second place 6C Alfa by more than a quarter of an hour!

The BMWs also took third, fifth, and sixth places with the open roadsters. The promising Kamm-inspired "Saloon" for Count Johnny Lurani failed during the last lap with an engine problem that pumped out most of its oil, after a run that had seen it hit a 134-mph maximum.

Perhaps the most lasting effect of this outing was that the elegant open bodies of the BMW-designed, Touring-built roadsters would inspire a postwar generation of production sports cars, obviously from Frazer Nash, but most famously the sensational 1948 Jaguar XK120.

BMW had already planned twin-cam successors to the 328, again using the style of the

Meyerhuber/Touring roadsters, which would have born the name 318 decades before a 3-series sedan wore that badge.

The war not only terminated that immediate 328 replacement activity, but the stored hardware was (mostly) seized as war reparations by Britain's Bristol Aircraft Company and AFN, along with the prototype 328 (thought to have been rebuilt from the original 85.032), which was described on the hasty 1945 import papers as one of the first three cars ever built—85.003, the original RHD British demonstrator/competitor!

This was the car that did become RHD in AFN's hands and was developed as a proto-

type Frazer Nash Bristol. After a spell in British club racing—the cruelest sport for hacking up any original motorcar—it luckily fell into the caring hands of the Bowler family. Michael Bowler sold it back to BMW in 1977, and it is regularly wheeled out on Mobile Tradition Assignments, now back in LHD Mille Miglia format. The fate of other original factory BMW 328s is more obscure, but a 1996 issue of Thoroughbred Classic Cars asserts that the Le Mans/Mille Miglia-winning Touring-bodied coupe is in the US and "has been on the market for several years." The BMW-designed-and-built "Saloon" used by Lurani had a brief postwar racing history (winning in the hands

Fresh from Touring Carrozeria in Milan, with period-dressed lady companion, this is the 1939 Le Mans 328 which won its class and finished fifth overall in the company's first 24-hour win of the year. BMW's factory machines also scored their first Spa 24-hours victory at Spa Francorchamps that season, lined up in perfect one-two-three class-winning order at the finish.

Picture: Courtesy Chris Willows, 1997

The legend lived on through a wartime victory celebrated in this 1940 poster.

Poster: Courtesy BMW Mobile Tradition, 1996

of Karl Kling at Hockenheim in 1947) but was cannibalized into one of the postwar Veritas sports cars. The trio of Mille Miglia roadsters are listed as living in Latvia, the US, and Munich (as above).

The postwar fate of the BMW 328 hardware, and future designs does not bear re-telling in a competition history, since BMW itself was not directly involved. Besides, a number of English authors have fully documented the Bristol developments of the materials that were claimed directly from BMW as war reparations, and their subsequent recycling as the basis for much-improved in-line sixes. These would yield over 170 bhp from the same basic layout.

That did not mean BMW did a bad job, just that those who redeployed BMW's example in the 1950s were able to do so in metals far superior to those available to BMW and with the knowledge of wartime techniques. Technology had inevitably passed into another dimension: aeronautically, with the transition from propellors to jets. So it was hardly surprising that Bristol, Frazer Nash and the rest found huge postwar gains....

For more about this postwar aspect of BMW history, of particular note are British authors,

especially the late Denis Jenkinson or Leonard Setright. Details of their work are given in our bibliography in Appendix 6.

There were no further factory entries of 328s after the war, and the record actually ends with the bizarre spectacle of sleek BMW factory cars, ex-Mille Miglia, travelling to Kronstadt, Romania for the Bucharest Grand Prix against the flow of refugees, who were lucky if they had horse-and-cart transport.

The Bucharest Grand Prix was canceled because battle was brought to this corner of Europe before battle could take place on the track. The NSKK did order BMW to have another trio of improved roadsters made at Touring during November 1940, but these 1940/41 streamliners were never actually raced, being brought back to Munich under their own power and stored for the duration.

BMW still has one such car (registered as M-MF328) and another is reportedly in the US. The fate of the final one remains a mystery, which means the fakers will soon fill that gap, just as they have for every other missing classic!

Unused beauty. A 328 Touring-bodied machine of the kind that would have been used in the 1941 edition of Mille Miglia: the race was not held that year, or any subsequent year until the end of WWII.

Picture: Courtesy Chris Willows, 1997

Huschke von Hanstein and the underrated Walter Baumer, victors of the unique 1940 Mille Miglia, flank leading BMW engineer Fritz Fiedler. Some subsequent picture manipulation has occurred: an SS crest from the Nazi party sports organization was removed from von Hanstein's chest, and a tactful pocket outline drawn in its place. Huschke was the only Mille Miglia driver to wear such insignia on his overalls.

Picture: BMW Archiv/Courtesy Chris Willows, 1997

Development of the 328 along increasingly radical aerodynamic lines was stopped by the war in 1940, but these two roadster designs (the Bugefalten "Pressed Crease" roadster by Touring in the center) inspired and influenced British postwar 2-seaters from Jaguar (XK120), MG(A) and Austin Healey (100/6 thru 3000). The hardtop coupe, aluminum-panelled by Touring, was a 1939 Le Mans class winner and the victor of 1940's unique edition of Mille Miglia. The coupe proved spectacularly efficient in promoting top speed, running close to 140 mph and averaging over 103 mph on closed public roads.

Picture: BMW Mobile Tradition, Munich, 1996

More variations on a 328 aero theme: this is how Bristol elegantly developed the BMW concept in postwar Britain, retaining the kidney grille but further developing both aerodynamics and motor, the latter assisted by the better-quality metals (especially engine bearings) that German engineers could not access immediately after the war.

Picture: Author, Goodwood, 1996

Another aerodynamic strand was this aluminum streamliner version of the 328, which runs a unique three-headlamp front end that lacks the famous kidney grille shape. Made by Wendlinger and designed by Reinhard Freiherr von Konig Fachsenfeld, just two survived the war. This one is part of a magnificent 20-plus BMW collection belonging to Dr. Knochlein at Nurnburg in Germany.

Picture: BMW Mobile Tradition, 1996

A trio of the leading BMWs pictured after their training runs in April 1940. This shows the three main types used (left to right): the only Series 1 roadster, the 137-mph Touring-bodied winner (the same BMW that won Le Mans in 1939), and the BMW Munich-built "Saloon" built to Kamm aero principles.

The winning 328 Touring coupe has lived in Canada and the United States since the war, and was listed as belonging to Robert Grier, a photographer in New York City: James Proffit acquired it after Grier's death.

Picture: BMW Archiv/Courtesy Chris Willows, 1997

Will it ever end? The 328 is still totally at home on the track, as seen at Monterey in 1996.

Picture: Klaus Schnitzer, USA, 1996

QUICK FACTS

Period

1945–65

Products

From factories turned to scrap to scrap aluminium recycling; the last German manufacturer back in car production; laying the foundations for the twin cylinder 700 coupe's motorsport success, via V8s and Isettas

Performance

From 40 bhp and 84 mph on less than a liter to 3.2 liters and 160 street bhp

Achievements

Survival! Husband and wife win international rally awards in a microcar

People

Alex von Falkenhausen bridges prewar to postwar, from the front line to the rebirth of 328 via AFM and 1950s sporting triumphs; Graf Albrecht Goertz, creator of the 503/7 sporting family; Quandt family rescue; enter a junior engineer by the name of Paul Rosche

Chapter 5

When we were small...

From American zone wreckage to reborn bikes and Germany's first aluminum V8s

BMW became a priority target during World War II and reaped a terrible reward for its famous aero engine and military prowess. By 1944, the "'round-the-clock" schedule of four-motor bomber fleets of the RAF (nights) and USAF dropped over 1,800 tons of bombs on Milbertshofen in Munich every 24 hours.

To put a human face on that devastating and apparently endless inferno, which destroyed about half of the buildings and interconnected units on that site, I traveled (ironically via VW Microbus) to summer in Munich during 1978. There, among many encounters, I met the man whose BMW engineering memories covered military, motors, and motorcycles, before he led the rebirth of BMW on four wheels and four cylinders for the 1960s.

To many, in Germany and outside, my contact was the man who created BMW's current sporting image. I consider it a privilege to have met him, for his efforts, whether in engineering or driving, are the stuff of which legends are made. However, this legend was very much a living one when I called in the middle of a July heatwave in 1978, his healthy vigor maintained almost until his death in 1991.

Alexander Freiherr von Falkenhausen's shock of pure white hair remained unruffled in the scorching heat rising from the pavement outside his home in a quiet suburb of Munich.

This had been his home for many years, but not always in its present pristine, white-walled form. As he explained, "It was all knocked flat in the war."

Von Falkenhausen smiled without rancor at his English companion on the peaceful street as we viewed the even quieter acres of an adjacent cemetery. Alex added, "You just cannot imagine it now. All the time the Americans and the British were bombing...yes, it was because of BMW...day and night they came."

As recorded in earlier chapters, BMW was one of the leading suppliers of piston engines and the newly-arrived jet turbines. Von Falkenhausen had spent much of his BMW time from 1934 onwards designing military vehicles, including a spell on the Tiger tank, which also involved another automotive designer of great repute, Dr. Ferdinand Porsche.

The war was not the most important point of our discussion, but it is of relevance to BMW's sporting record today. The Munich company proved more capable than most when it came to sorting out precision aero-engineering problems quickly and accurately, qualities as valid in competition as in war.

Alex von Falkenhausen rejoined BMW in 1954, forsaking his own small design business to do so. From 1948 to 1950, he had run his BMW 328-engined AFM (his initials with the

M-appellation for Munich) in any races he
could find outside Germany. As a German, he
could not drive outside Germany, so Hans-
Joachim Stuck Sr. qualified the car as an Austrian. "It usually had pole position, but the
bearings were no good. We could not get
Vandervell ones at this time," he commented
with a twinkle of a smile.

The AFM label was applied to seven original
328-motivated racing machines between 1947
and 1950, usually single-seaters that con-

formed to a Formula 2 category that was terminated in 1954, leaving von Falkenhausen with
no ready competition market. By then, he had
developed his racing concepts around alternative engines, including a sub-1-liter supercharged unit and the very special 2-liter
Kuchen V8, which came from Audi's present
hometown of Ingolstadt. It developed up to 200
bhp, and Stuck used it to beat Alberto Ascari's
166 Ferrari V12 in a Monza qualifying race!

Veritas and former 328 engineer Ernst Loof were an obvious postwar competitive and commercial alliance. Here, we have the badge and the Veritas Rennsport that surrounds it, as displayed at Pebble Beach, California. The superb Veritas RS is the work of the Feierabands, father-and-son restoration partners who were invited to bring their immaculate 328 and Veritas RS to American celebrations of the BMW marque in 1996.

Pictures: Author (badge) and Klaus Schnitzer (car), USA, 1996

This beautifully-detailed European Formula 3 car was powered by the BMW Boxer twin motorcycle motor and designed by Veritas creator and former BMW 328 engineer Ernst Loof. It lives in Missouri.

Pictures: Author (car) and Klaus Schnitzer (motor), USA, 1996

This extraordinary 1948 BMW Formula 3 streamliner was created by Ernst Loof at Veritas. It used Boxer motorcycle twin-cylinder power in front of its offset driver. The car was displayed by owner Robert Pass of St. Louis, Missouri, at Pebble Beach Concours in 1996.

Picture: Author

Veritas truly extended the 328 legend postwar, but achieved more racing than commercial success.

Picture: Author

June 1996: the streets of Munich reverberated to the beat of more than 100 BMW 328s that had gathered to celebrate the BMW benchmark's 60th birthday.

Picture: BMW Mobile Tradition

The 1954 Monte Carlo Rallye was graced by the BMW 501B of Ernst Loof and former factory 328 driver Hans Wencher. The six-cylinder 2-liters were overbodied and underpowered for Monte's hilly tests, but 501s did win a Team Prize at that season's Dutch Tulip Rallye. Hmmm...Holland is known for its flowers and flatness....

Picture: BMW Historisches Archiv, reprinted 1997

The Veritas

Of course, von Falkenhausen was just one of the many who redeveloped the 328 after the war. Most famous in Germany was the Veritas (Truth), a rebodied range of racers and road cars implemented by 1930s BMW competition chief Ernst Loof, the TT hero "Schorsch" Meier, and ex-BMW aero engineer Lorenz Dietrich.

Underfinanced Veritas moved from an outbuilding site to forest yards as it stayed one jump ahead of its debts. Veritas made 32 BMW Mille Miglia-inspired machines, from the 1947 open prototype to 1950 coupes carrying astral names such as Meteor Comet and Saturn.

In the early 1950s, Veritas rethought the basic themes of the 328—just as Bristol went way beyond the original format in technology and body design—using a Heinkel-manufactured (at Zuffenhausen, today's home to

Porsche) single overhead cam six, which was inspired by prewar BMW planning for the 318, successor to the 328. These motors—over 35 were made—released up to 150 bhp for racing and left the original 328 units for dead. Or they could be had at 110 bhp tuned for the road in a Veritas Nürburgring model.

Veritas did a good job with Germany's meager postwar resources, but the Truth title was a joke, for Loof had helped pack up the major 328 hardware and drawings that the Bristol aircraft company and British associates AFN claimed as war reparations. The owners of Veritas knew that BMW was in no position to make cars itself, so they went ahead and filled the obvious gap in the market. BMW acquired the destitute business in 1952 and shut it down, never having allowed it to use the BMW roundel anyway.

There wasn't much left of BMW immediately postwar, but the American occupation gradually breathed life back into its Munich manufacturing facilities with mundane tasks from refurbishing military transport to making cooking utensils! The initial attitude was that BMW would be razed to the ground and its talents scattered to the four winds, but that threat receded.

Back in business

BMW was back in the motorcycle business by 1947 (showing a revived R24) and mass manufacture by 1948. Now it could not be long before cars and competition came back into its life, for it would be the last German motor manufacturer to resume business. By contrast, Ford Cologne had managed to make cars within weeks of hostilities ceasing.

First, BMW became increasingly concerned with another 328 clone family, manufactured by the Russians at its old base in Eisenach. Even though 300 American tanks rumbled into the Thuringen city in March 1945, Eisenach was passed over to Russian control and disappeared behind the Iron Curtain until February 1990 (when BMW set up a small facility at its historic home in the wake of the fall of the Berlin Wall and German reunification).

Immediately postwar, the Russians pressed the old 321 design back into production at Eisenach, using much of the tooling gathered from the dismantled Ambi-Budd Berlin works. From 1945–55, a series of BMW-based designs were made in Eisenach, all sharing the 1,971 cc prewar six-cylinder at 45 or 55 bhp. They were branded Autovelo, BMW, or EMW, but BMW was strong enough in 1955 to legally prevent the use of its most potent image, the roundel trademark, in this application, too.

Just to round off the amazing production life of the 328 and its mutations, we should add that 1958 is reckoned as the date when Bristol

made its last recognizably BMW-inspired design, subsequently switching to Chrysler V8 power that sustains its minute production and stratospheric prices to date.

AFN fitted its last BMW engine to a Frazer Nash in 1957 and chopped all links with Munich in 1960, having taken on a parallel import license for Porsche (1953) while struggling to sell the 1950s BMW melange of motorcycles, Isettas, and V8 luxury cars.

The BMW range of the 1950s was oddball in its diversity, embracing both poverty and prestige, but none of the mid-range motorcars that the now-recovering middle classes could easily afford. This led BMW into immediate financial troubles, because the smaller designs made no money (and we mean small: the Isetta started life in 1955 as a quarter-liter, single-cylinder "Bubble car") while the big, baroque 501 sedans (debuted in 1951, manufactured 1952–58 with the Marshall Aid program buying new tooling) sold very slowly—"too like an English Austin and with the weak prewar six, too slow," said home-market critics.

Ironically posed carefully in front of the Mercedes publicity tower at Avus-Berlin, the factory 507 rests on the cobbled banking under the elbow of Hans Stuck Sr. Stuck's long career took him from prewar Grand Prix with the massive V16 Auto Union of the 1930s to becoming German Champion in the flat twin BMW 700 of the 1960s. He won over 400 awards, including a sensational sixth overall and GT class victory in the 1959 Gaisberg European Championship hillclimb.

Picture: BMW Archiv/Courtesy Chris Willows, 1997

The V8 packs in power

By 1954, BMW packed in Germany's first postwar automotive V8, an alloy 90-degree unit of 2.6 liters/90 bhp that had obvious power potential. BMW tripled sales with this big bomber—it weighed 1,440 kg, over 3,170 lbs—and decided to give the public more of the same.

This time, BMW went with a 3.2-liter/120-bhp version that hauled this even heavier automobile of Town Hall dimensions from 0–60 mph in 15 seconds and right on to 106 mph for as long as you could keep it in gas. Sometimes—it has to be said—the limiting factor was how long the earlier versions of the V8 would run before meltdown, but then we overlook the achievement of making such an advanced power unit with just a handful of engineers employed at that time.

Among that happy band was von Falkenhausen, who had two main tasks upon rejoining BMW, where he found Ernst Loof back on board as well, following the failure of Veritas. Loof was charged with creating a new line of BMW V8 sports cars that had the American market as a priority, but Loof's creation—unsurprisingly carrying Veritas and therefore 1940 Mille Miglia 328 styling cues—found no favor with the BMW board, and Graf Albrecht von Goertz got the job.

Von Goertz, long-time New York resident and still sprightly in evidence at the 1996 celebration of BMW sports success at Monterey, is best known for the Datsun Z-car (240Z). However, he also penned the 503 of 1955–60 and the curvaceous 507 of 1955–59, perhaps the most beautiful Corvette never to be made at a Chevrolet plant!

The trouble was that, although the coupes and cabriolets with V8 power of 140 or 150 bhp were quick (118 mph and 137 mph, respectively) and accelerated mightily by 1950s European standards (a 507 could nail 0–60 mph in 11.5 sec), they were slower to hand-manufacture over a base 502 and expensive to (equally slowly) sell.

Production figures from BMW in the 1980s update earlier reports, confirming that production of both types was in two distinct waves—the factory calls them 503/1 and 503/2 and uses the same system for 507/1 and 2—commencing in 1955 and 1957, respectively. A look at the figures explains why this was the case, for first-year manufacture was recorded at three units for the 503/1 and two units for the 507/1!

This was not viable, but BMW went on to make a recorded 407 of the 503 and 252 of the seductive 507, most of which seem to be in the USA today. BMW in Britain and Germany, naturally, have examples to show what these rare beasts were like. I've mentioned the Brits first, as it may interest readers to know that Hans Stuck Sr., Grand Prix god of the 1930s, did a lot of postwar BMW competition and promotion, one of the latter tasks being to go to Britain and frighten customers or the press with lurid demonstration rides in the AFN BMW V8s.

The V8 does not have a huge influence on our competition story—although that small engineering department included von Falkenhausen at the zenith of his motor engineering powers and Paul Rosche as very much the junior apprentice. Upon his return in 1954, Von Falkenhausen's first task was to manage the motorcycle racing activities, and the second task was to develop the 3.2-liter V8 for the 507.

Every one of the 252 V8s produced was personally checked by von Falkenhausen to ensure that the 150 bhp then claimed was actually provided, and that it was accompanied by a worthy body and chassis. Recollections of those personal tests still brought a smile to his tanned face and keen eyes decades later. Incidentally, BMW won every single world sidecar (three-wheeler) championship between 1955 and 1971.

Okay, V8 fans, this is your BMW corner! Germany's first post-war bent eight came in aluminum from the house of BMW and is shown in the multiple carburation 507 wearing wire mesh air filters, or with full production cold-air casings within a rare 3200CS. These examples and the "shark nose" of the 507 were all seen at the 1996 Californian Concours competition, but the superb V8 badge study comes from a specially-commissioned Munich museum series.

Pictures: Andrew Year-don (badge), 1992; Klaus Schnitzer (507s and 3200CS), USA, 1996

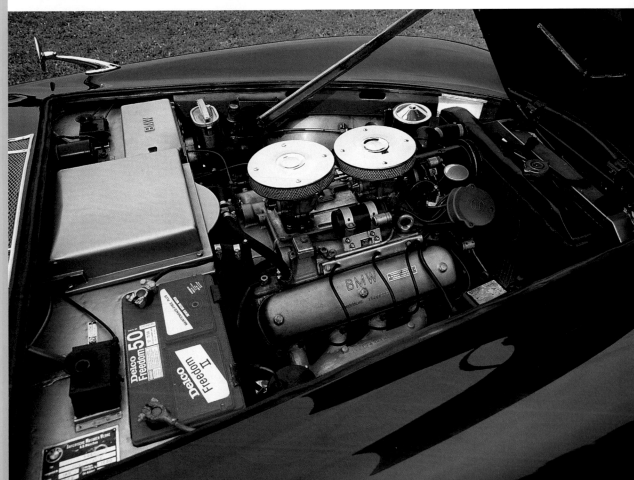

Von Falkenhausen would also take the V8s out to compete, debuting the 502 sedan in V8 format on the August 1955 Rallye du Soleil, Cannes. Run out of that Southern French seaside town, the Falkenhausens (Alex took his wife, Kitty) won the over-2.6-liter GT and sports group in an event that they had won outright in 1953.

Kitty and Alex von Falkenhausen were no strangers to international rallying success and would go on to blood the diminutive 600 in the tough Alpine rally (shades of the original Dixi giant-killing performances 30 years earlier). The aristocratic husband-and-wife pairing had scored classy European success with BMW-powered products, right back to the 328 with which they took third overall and class victory in the 1939 Rallye Paris.

On the first BMW V8, we should also note that the production motor was finally nudged to 160 bhp from its long-stroke 3,168 cc. It powered a Bertone 3200CS coupe, which gave us a genuine preview of the slim rooflines and uncluttered two-door chic that would evolve in a later generation of stimulating BMW four- and six-cylinder coupes.

Upon his appointment as chief engine development engineer with responsibility for BMW racing activity, von Falkenhausen's sporting concerns were the 700 sedan and coupe. Events outside his direct control gave the sporting potential of the new Michelotti-styled baby BMW a helping hand....

As the 1950s drew to an end, BMW prepared to meet the self-styled "swinging '60s" with a shudder of apprehension rather than with the joyful expectation of a bright future. Motorcycle production had resumed in 1948, and the six-cylinder 501 car made its appearance in 1951. But motorcycle sales slumped through the 1950s and BMW's car range offered no middle-range machinery.

The engineers and marketing people knew what they wanted—a good medium-range car worthy of the BMW name that could be afforded by the slightly wealthier-than-average citizen. But the company had exhausted its capital and its credit, the very finances that were necessary to make survival possible.

It was snowing when a Munich meeting of shareholders and company representatives was called on December 9, 1959, prompted by the

We know it is not a competition car, but it is a gorgeous performance BMW; and Hans Stuck Sr. used it to demonstrate the V8's abilities on both road and track. This BMW 507 was found within the BMW corral at the Italian Concours, Quail Valley, Carmel, in 1996. It's the best 507 the author has seen, including factory-owned examples, but there was plenty of equally attractive competition at Pebble Beach and Laguna Seca, 1996.

Picture: Author, 1996

The debut of the V8 BMW 502 in competition was, appropriately, a winning one. Driver/creator von Falkenhausen was navigated by his wife, Kitty, around the 1955 Rallye du Soleil in Cannes, France. Husband and wife took the GT class in the 2.6-liter limousine. Together, they won many rallying awards in a variety of unlikely BMWs, facing the toughest of events.

Picture: Courtesy Chris Willows, 1997

Deutsche Bank. Their objective was to announce a merger with one of Germany's bigger postwar automotive successes: Mercedes-Benz wanted BMW as a possible parts factory!

However, a band of the smaller shareholders fought, under the leadership of Frankfurt lawyer Friedrich Mathern, to keep the company independent. Fortunately, they succeeded, using an enormous loan from the Allach, the former aero engine satellite factory, to keep afloat.

In the interwoven history of these two magnificent German auto and aero engine manu-

facturers, this was the low point. BMW fans might regard 1992 as the high point, for that was the year 558,000 Bimmers streamed off the lines to exceed Mercedes car output for the first time....

The 1960s godfather to BMW was Dr. Herbert Quandt, along with his brother Harald, who acquired 15 percent of BMW. Herbert Quandt died in 1982, but his third wife, Johanna, and offspring still retain a controlling proportion (most accurately estimated at 60 percent) of BMW shares. In 1988, their value

was measured in billions of dollars as BMW announced the American adventure of manufacturing overseas for the 1990s.

Back at BMW's near-bankruptcy, as the 1950s turned to the 1960s, Herbert Quandt was so respected by the finance houses (despite increasing sight problems) that he was soon able to appoint a new management team. Given a steadier cashflow, BMW initiated vital new models into the showrooms, leading to the international company that it is today. BMW was also aware that sport was needed to promote the newcomers.

The key model for the future of BMW was the four-cylinder father of all the BMW single-overhead-camshaft engineering—the Neue Klasse 1500, an 80-bhp, four-door sedan.

The 1500 was remarkable because the under-financed engineers managed to include the sophistication of a chain-driven overhead camshaft (still a rare feature among cars intended for mass-production, even in 1961) and an independent rear suspension. Neither feature was unique, of course, but the 1500 was neatly detailed and capable of a lot more development: many of its four-cylinder principles and its chassis layout survived into the 3-series of the 1980s.

The 1500 swiftly grew into the 1600, 1800TI, 1800TI/SA, 2000, and 2000TI—the larger models worthy contestants in the European Touring Car Championship. Indeed, they won a title for the first time in 1966, the first of many for BMW, less than five years after the original 1500 was launched as a road car. It didn't take long for BMW to bounce back, once American-influenced niche marketing man Paul Hahnemann was appointed by the Quandts.

BMW's commercial and competitive future was partially indebted to these cheeky rear-engined chappies. This factory BMW 700 coupe, swinging around Monte Carlo Harbor in 1961, was driven by Prince von Metternich and Hans Wencher to finish tenth overall: teammate Karl Block managed fifth, a magnificent achievement.

Picture: BMW Archiv/Courtesy Chris Willows, 1997

Just because they were the smallest cars ever to carry a BMW badge (up to 1997, anyway) does not mean they did not have a 1950s competition history: the gallant Isetta-BMW, with its cloth sunroof open, tackles the Alpenfahrt's immense gradients.

Picture: BMW Archiv/Courtesy Chris Willows, 1997

Hahnemann's research among the German public showed that it took just seven years for BMW to originally establish its car-building reputation. The sporting BMWs of the 1930s—especially the 328—dominated how the German public perceived BMW in the early 1960s, so the sporting character was brought right back into BMW's accessible products at the design stage. That immediately established a different 1960s identity from that of Mercedes, which was seen as a company designing cars for older and stodgier clients.

Paul G. Hahnemann was a very public figure at BMW from 1961–71 and pulled off some notable sales coups, including the disposal of surplus 700s (unwanted by the public after the premature display of the 1500). But his flamboyant transatlantic style and former links through Auto Union back to potential BMW buyers Mercedes-Benz would never

allow popularity throughout BMW. He was disposed of as brutally and quickly as Henry Ford once dumped Lee Iaccoca.

Initially, it was the staggering total of 188,121 BMW 700s manufactured from 1959–65 that had to hold the financial fort in terms of cashflow and competition for BMW, since the 1500 was not shown until 1961 (Frankfurt) and was not truly ready for production until 1962.

Commercially and competitively, the sophisticated little 700 sedan and coupe, with their lightweight rear engines of BMW motorcycle parentage, were vital in redressing past mistakes. The two-door coupe, built by Baur, proved particularly useful for motorsports and was granted another 10 bhp even in showroom trim (1960–64), making it capable of 84 mph on just 40 bhp.

QUICK FACTS

Period
1960–65

Product
Racing and rallying 700s

Performance
From 30 street to 65 circuit bhp

Achievements
Hans Stuck Sr. and others take the 700 to German hillclimb and then to international circuit and test success

Chapter 6

Racing the 700 Coupe

The little car with the giant-killing reputation

When you have an engineering director this keen and this talented, the product tends to reflect such genius. Alex von Falkenhausen conducts some first-hand power-slide research at the Austrian Turrach-based hillclimb in the early 1960s. The climb was part of the May 1960 Austrian rally, and the Falkenhausens won their class.

BMW Archiv/Courtesy Chris Willows, 1997

In 1960, ADAC (Germany's premier sporting and touring club, with literally millions of members) organized its first Grosser Preis von Tourenwagen. This was a six-hour run for sedans around the 14.2-mile/22.7-km Nürburgring, an event that was able to draw over 100,000 spectators in its heyday.

Then, the unprotected grassy banks and curbs of the 'Ring made the ideal backdrop for the frequently spectacular sedans of the early 1960s, their suspensions groaning as they leapt over crests and plunged through violent camber changes around the world's longest artificial road-racing circuit. The braver, or less imaginative, began the flying antics that are still possible on today's Armco-protected and much-modified 'Ring, rather than the sanitized shorter circuit that serves as one home to the German Grand Prix in the 1990s.

In 1960, the newly announced 700's pushrod engine featured fan cooling, one carburetor, and a single-inlet manifold that had to split to feed both banks of the flat two-cylinder. It ran on a 7.5:1 compression ratio and obviously shared a great number of internal components (plus a bore and stroke of 78 x 73 mm—697 cc) with its motorcycle relations.

The coupe was just about 11.5 feet long (3,505 mm), rested on an 83-inch (2,108-mm) wheelbase, was fractionally under 50 inches

(1,250 mm) tall, and had a track of some 47.4 inches (1,265 mm). Even by European standards of the 1960s, we are talking small, though its chief racetrack rival (the Mini) was even stubbier at some 10 feet in length.

In sedan form, the 700's steel body was propelled by only 30 bhp, but von Falkenhausen and his team soon produced the sports version. This had twin Solex carburetors and individual short intake manifolds to allow 40 bhp at 5,900 rpm in production, 46 bhp with a little thoughtful assembly. It was followed by a blueprinted version for competition use, tuned by the factory around the same production components, but capable of producing 50 bhp. That was not a great deal of power even then, but it was certainly enough from 697 cc, equating to 71.7 bhp per liter and comparable to many current quad-valve-per-cylinder street motors.

A change in regulations allowed more motorcycle-sourced modifications to creep into the 700's BMW competition specification. It grew a pair of separate Amal carburetors and was eventually persuaded, by the appropriate head and camshaft changes suitable for these carburetors, to make 65 bhp. This was still from less than 700 cc (93.2 bhp/liter), so the "magic" 100 bhp level was being approached. My 1992 American encounter with Don Gibbs of Winston-Salem revealed that a Fort Worth,

Our 4-picture spread shows how one man in American preserved an important piece of BMW racing history. It is glossier and shinier than the originals, with a lot more paint (15 coats of lacquer!), chrome, and replacement American instrumentation in the stark dash, but it gives us the best possible idea of how the racing 700 looked and the extensive tuning measures used to lift the twin-cylinder motor toward 70 bhp. Don Gibbs of Winston-Salem, N.C. owned this 1960s 700 coupe for over ten years and the motor work was done by BMW Fort Worth, Texas.

Pictures: Author, Moroso Raceway, Florida, 1992

You could say the 700 inspired the revival of German motorsports! Over twenty road-registered 700s take the start at the Nürburgring of the early 1960s. Not only did the 700 mark the beginning of BMW's comeback to international racing, but it also provided the bulk of German entries in the Nürburgring 6-hours. Germany's effective contribution to the European Touring Car Championship was also founded in the wake of the enthusiasm generated by the Nürburgring, a great credit to one of the world's biggest auto clubs: Nürburgring organizers and promoters ADAC of Germany, and their Automobile Club Saar membership in Saarbrucken.

Picture: BMW Archiv, reprinted 1978

If you want to use the high-revving 700 on today's noise-regulated roads and tracks, these are necessary! Bernhard Knochlein uses this silver 1962 700S in 1990s vintage events. It's part of his father's astonishing BMW collection, which contains some examples of the marque that the factory does not possess.

Picture: Klaus Schnitzer, Nurnberg 1996

June 1960: the Munich factory 700 coupe for Hans Stuck Sr. and Josef Greger garners the laurels for its class-winning performance in the 12-hour race held at Hockenheim. That year, Stuck Sr. also won the German hillclimb championship in a series of giant-killing performances with BMW's twin-cylinder coupe. The alliance between von Falkenhausen and Stuck Sr. was echoed in a similar bond between Jochen Neerpasch and Hans Stuck Jr. in the 1970s.

Picture: BMW Archiv, reprinted 1978

Texas BMW outfit claimed 68 to 70 bhp from the engine of his competition 700 coupe, equivalent to 100.4 bhp a liter, if that production capacity was unaltered. I can only confirm that it was noisier than hell on Class A drugs and went as well as legend led me to expect....

John Bolster of Autosport added fuel to the British public interest in BMW for the early 1960s by testing the 700 coupe (then retailing at £728. 9s. 10d, almost $3,000 then) and commenting, "The performance of the BMW is really sensational, and one can understand its success in racing. When cruising at 80 mph (128 km/h), it is almost impossible to believe that only 700 cc of engine is propelling the little projectile." In 1964, the Brighton-based concessionaires (AFN was all Porsche now) advertised the coupe at the above price, but added that the specification included high compression, hemispherical heads, and a close-ratio gearbox.

Record of repute

Many Continental enthusiasts were able to cut their teeth on the 700, knowing that a good international performance in the 700 could bring greater things. As it did not offer massive straight-line performance, skillful cornering and minimal use of the brakes were highly developed attributes in the regular 700 competitor.

Notable BMW 700 drivers, aside from von Falkenhausen himself, included 1960 German Hillclimb champion Hans Stuck Sr. Exponents who grew with the 700 included BMW's future European Champion Hubert Hahne, Anton Fischhaber, Walter Schneider, and Jurgen Grasser. The latter two looked after the works representation in 1964 when it was busy with the bigger sedans. On occasion, Grasser had trouble with a young Belgian called Jacques "Jacky" Ickx.

This BMW publicity photograph was taken to commemorate its Monza 12-hour victory in 1960. The chief opposition in those days were the Abarth-modified Fiats. This win was taken by privateers Dore Leto di Priolo and Ottavio Prandoni.

Picture: BMW Archiv, 1978

At 60 years of age, Hans Stuck Sr. could not resist closing his career with a few more wins at the wheel of the 700. In 1960, the 700 took 34 wins—many courtesy of Stuck Sr., dubbed "The Mountain King," from the Alpine village of Grainau. The Stuck Sr./factory 700 combination won the 1960 German Championship, causing a minor problem for the Stuck household mantelpiece, as Hans Sr. won 403 events from 1924 to 1954: teenage Junior would soon be compounding the problem with an Alpina-BMW, beginning an equally rewarding career.

Picture: BMW AG, Historisches Archiv, reprinted 1997

The clean lines of BMW's 700 CS and the long rear deck required for the rear-mounted motor are clearly seen in this 1963 European Championship shot of a privateer car, complete with bumpers, in British action.

Picture: LAT, reprinted 1978

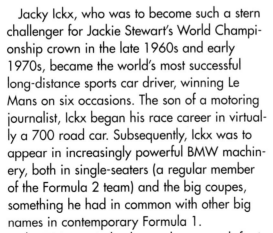

Jacky Ickx, who was to become such a stern challenger for Jackie Stewart's World Championship crown in the late 1960s and early 1970s, became the world's most successful long-distance sports car driver, winning Le Mans on six occasions. The son of a motoring journalist, Ickx began his race career in virtually a 700 road car. Subsequently, Ickx was to appear in increasingly powerful BMW machinery, both in single-seaters (a regular member of the Formula 2 team) and the big coupes, something he had in common with other big names in contemporary Formula 1.

The 700 was indeed a modern marvel, for it had 22 international class victories to its name between 1960 and 1965, though during the years after 1963 these were primarily in the

hands of privateers. Highlights embraced taking the German Hillclimb and national racing titles in successive 1960–61 seasons and regularly humiliating more fancied BMC/Rover Mini, Saab (2-stroke triples, as derived from rival DKW), and NSU opposition.

Sometimes it did appear, as English journalists were wont to grumble into their lukewarm beer when summarizing the class results of European Touring Car Championship rounds, that "the 700 class was made for BMW." However, as often as not, the car proved capable of taking on 1-liter or even 1.3-liter class cars, and still came away with the honors. The 700's marvelous handling and braking through its superb weight distribution (the motorcycle-based rear engine was very light) allowed some fine "giant-killing" sports performances.

The 700 appeared for its first race on March 5 and 6, 1960, in the white-and-blue color scheme carried in the company's whirling-propeller insignia. Von Falkenhausen was driving, but the car disgraced itself by swallowing a small o-ring from the induction tract. "They were never unreliable after that," commented the engineer-driver, the effrontery of the little car's behavior still sharp in his memory 17 years later!

In 1960, the 700 coupe, with its rear-engine location (dubbed "the working man's Porsche" in Germany), laid the foundations to what would be a very successful rallying career, returning with class victories in established international contests from Switzerland to the Tour de France. Here, its efficiency was rewarded with an Index of Performance award, similar to those doled out for many years at Le Mans, in the hope that a French entry would take the spoils.

On home ground, Germany's premier motor rally recorded not just the apparently inevitable class win, but also a fantastic seventh overall. The 700 under the direction of Klaus Block and Herbert Paul was good enough to beat machines of at least triple the engine capacity, disproving that old American cliché, "Ain't no substitute for cubic inches...."

The 700 also proved good enough to finish off Hans Stuck Sr.'s career on an honorable note, for he won the 1960 German National Hillclimb Championship for sedans with it at the age of 60! This was no mean achievement for, as von Falkenhausen recalled, "The car often had to beat Fiats modified by Abarth or even the Alfa Juniors." Since the latter were 1,300-cc cars, it can be imagined what an effective little machine the 700 was, an opinion endorsed by many Germans prominent in the successful post-1960s BMW sporting world.

Men such as Burkard Bovensiepen, boss of the internationally-known Alpina BMW conver-

The works car that scored the 1961 Monza 12-hour class victory. Driven by the legendary Auto Union pilot Hans Stuck Sr. and Sepp Greger, the little car had the usual factory attention to detail with tape not only covering the headlamps, but also securing the front luggage compartment lid. Note also the lack of bumpers and the use of standard steel wheels. Contrast this period in sedan racing with today's sophisticated composite fiber bodies covering full-race chassis and running gear.

Picture: BMW Archiv/Keystone, Italy, May 1963

Von Falkenhausen was behind this ultimate development of the 700 twin-cylinder theme. It was powered by a variety of the Apfelbeck-modified boxer engines with gear-and-shaft drive (as displayed in this Amal-carbureted engine) for the overhead camshaft on each cylinder bank. Known as either the 700RS or 800RS, the latter designation reflected the departure from the production engine size to 800 cc when power was up to 90 bhp. This made the light two-seater a very effective hill-climb car, especially when driven by von Falkenhausen as depicted in our picture. Note the early roll cage, screen cutaway, and sketchy front bumper.

Picture BMW Archiv, reprinted, Munich Olympics, 1972

sions and engineering concern, started his career hurtling around German sprints, hill-climbs, and races in the BMW 700. "It was the car that brought the company back some respect," Bovensiepen recalled in 1978. "The Isetta was not such a machine, but the 700! It was a fantastic little car to drive. So light in the steering and body, so it was good to drive as fast as possible, as often as possible."

In 1961, German motorcycle champion Walter Schneider tried his hand at sedan racing to such effect that the 700 won the national title, but the astonishing achievements were still in rallying. The 700 coupes went forth again, BMW having noted Klaus Block's driving merit, and he rewarded them with fifth place overall in the world's most prestigious rally: Monte Carlo. Of course, Klaus won the class again but, emphasizing the traction and agility of the

700, Prince von Metternich brought home another 700 coupe tenth overall.

Although the Monte Carlo Rallye had some strange classes and results in the 1960s, there is no doubt that BMW's comparatively shoe-string operation was bringing in results that major manufacturers would die for, and that reflected the true merit of this little jewel.

Klaus Block was put to work in the 700 on many other international rallies, slipping inside the top ten again on another subsequent World Championship round, battling home the 700 eighth overall in the Greek Acropolis event. In 1961, the 700 also recorded rally results of note in the Mille Miglia, a top fifteen placing in Holland's Tulip (a power event that a Jaguar E-type or XK120 could win) and a one-two-three class result in the Rally of the Midnight Sun, Sweden.

The best little rallyer

Those baby BMWs also managed a one-two-three class whitewash in the 1961 Tour de France, but their best overall international rally result came in August 1961, as Sobieslaw Zasada annexed not just the small capacity class, but also placed third overall in his home event, the Polish Rally. Zasada subsequently became a regular and successful Porsche 911 and 912 rallyist, but won the 1971 European title (not his first, it must be said) in a BMW 2002TI.

The 1961 racing season did not look so good on paper—BMW concentrating upon and winning its national title—but a one-off appearance for the 700 was to influence the English-speaking world. Appearing in a July supporting event to the British Empire Trophy at Silverstone, Herbert Linge took the startling twin-cylinder car to third overall at an average of almost 70 mph around the fast-perimeter track of the former airfield. September saw the 700s contest the Nürburgring 500-kms with class-winning results—first, second, and third for the sedan section, and a very creditable second and third among the 1-liter GTs. Linge led the Edgar Barth of (subsequently) Fiat Abarth fame.

In 1962, racing took center stage in BMW's factory plans, and the 700 roamed across Europe, taking in the odd hillclimb that would become part of the 1963 preview of the European Touring Car Championship. Anton Fischhaber became the blue-eyed 700 boy with class wins at Nürburgring's 500-km and 6-hour races, leading class clean sweeps for BMW on both occasions—shades of the 328 monopoly in the 1930s....

Walter Schneider was given a 700 coupe that could contend the GT categories and came away with three class results at Berlin-Avus, Hockenheim, and the GT supporting race to the German Grand Prix at Nürburgring. In that 1962 season, von Falkenhausen managed to win the Coup de Paris class battle and created quite a stir, just as the little car had done the year before when winning a similar class battle within a self-styled Brussels Grand Prix for sedans. A 700 coupe also won a special Ladies Cup at Britain's 6-hour Brands Hatch fixture in 1962, and the model scored five class wins in rounds of the European Rally Championship.

Also in 1962, von Falkenhausen drove the factory 700s to the Nürburgring for their annual summer outing in the 6-hours. The German aristocrat and his machinery received a rude shock, but one that was to yield BMW a works driver for many seasons to come. "Yes, I first met with Hubert Hahne at the Nürburgring. He is going faster than works cars, and always I remember this special sideways style." Hahne had demonstrated his potential with a second in class pursuit of Schneider's works 700S at the May 1962 Hockenheim meeting, which featured 17 BMW 700s in the fight for class honors!

For 1963, the ADAC at Saarbrucken wanted to stage a truly European Championship for racing sedans. Britain supported this aim, knowing that such a series could promote the charms of such diverse products as Jaguars and Minis, nevermind the Ford Cortina GT and Lotus hot shots that were now under development in the UK under Ford's global Total Performance initiative. Initially, Italy opposed the European series, but relented by the close of the year—Alfa was hard to beat, and so were the baby Fiat Abarths—and the series became officially FIA-blessed from 1964 onward. In fact, BMW very nearly won the outright titles, and predicted the unmatched record it would establish in this series—a true test of the worth of a sedan and its maker in the 1960s.

Hubert Hahne won the class for BMW at the Nürburgring 6-hours in 1963. Von Falkenhausen also tried him out in the European Touring Car Championship round at Mallory Park in July of that year. Hahne led the race,

The 700s went to Britain for the 1963 Motor-sponsored round of the European Championship and defeated both Saab and BMC (now Rover) opposition in the up-to-850-cc category. Mallory Park, Leicestershire was the venue, and Hubert Hahne dominated in the factory 700 grasp over the three-hour European qualifying round. Together with the privateer 700s, BMW came away with all first five positions, save second!

Picture: LAT, reprinted 1978

Motor Motor
LUCAS
NEWS WEDS 6P
EXIDE
Motor Cycle
THE DAILY
BOSCH
D
D

despite giving away 300 cc to the two-stroke Saab, finally settling for second just 1.2 seconds adrift and leading home all his BMW contemporaries.

The little BMWs scuttled away with the majority of class placings as well, causing Autosport to comment, "The remarkable performance of the Continental cars with top-line foreign drivers should make Mini enthusiasts stop and think, for it's quite obvious that Mini supremacy only exists in this country."

This aroused more interest in the 700 in Britain, not because of the rear engine—after all, sedans from Fiat, NSU, Renault, VW, and others had this configuration before front-wheel-drive became virtually mandatory for small cars—but because of its amazing performance. At that Mallory outing, the diminutive BMWs were first, third, fourth and fifth in the up-to-850-cc class, only one 850 Mini breaking up their runaway success at the close of three hours of racing.

Hubert Hahne challenged hard for that first title in 1963, scoring 90 percent of the BMW 700's perfect class-winning record. Hahne scored the same number of points (60) as the Jaguar-mounted winner of the first European Touring Car title in 1963, losing on a "class improvement" judgment. Despite finishing with the same points total as Peter Nocker (Jaguar 3.8), Hahne was relegated for sharing his Nürburgring win with partner Koch.

Incidentally, tenth in that exploratory season's points chart was Jochen Neerpasch, the future BMW competitions manager from Krefeld (a suburb of Cologne, now famous as 1994–95 World Champion Michael Schumacher's hometown), driving a Volvo 122S with distinction.

Another notable aside to the 1963 season: March's edition of a Sebring endurance event for small cars saw the first BMW international triumph recorded for the 700 in the USA. J. Stevens took a fabulous third overall in one of the rare American BMW imports. At that time,

BMW marketing policy was to concentrate on Germany first and the rest of Europe second, with the rest of the world to be given the big BMW sales message when they had their own back yard clear of the financial manure that had accrued in the 1950s.

Von Falkenhausen looked back on the those 700-mounted seasons with great affection; he drove a 700 on ten occasions and came away with ten class wins, including one on the Alpenfahrt Rallye. This was no sissy navigational event, as much of the route lay over proper, loose stages, and snow would frequently influence the results. In 1959, BMW's legendary competition manager actually won this Alpine event, in a BMW 600 (their four-wheel "bubble"), with his wife co-driving. 600s also won the team prize.

Highlights of excellence

The 700 proved capable of class-winning performances both inside and outside Germany through 1964 and up to 1965, but by then, the factory was well-enmeshed in developing larger-capacity four-cylinder variants that sprung from the 1500 sedan.

Full results for these seasons can be found in our Appendices, but there were a couple of highlights we cannot miss. These include Ickx scoring a class double for BMW and Ford, proving that a 700 coupe could get within 7.1 seconds of a Ford 1600 Lotus Cortina of more than double its capacity in a Namur hillclimb.

Also underlining 700's excellence was the performance of Jurgen Grässer at the Belgian Zolder European Championship round. Grässer rolled his works-backed Bimmer into a ball in practice. Undaunted, he whistled home, collected his 700 road car and won with that in the afternoon! Mind you, he had to struggle, for Jacky Ickx was coming on stream at that point and disputed the lead in an epic encounter with the flyweights of Europe.

Although the 700 coupe was raced at the production-engine size, von Falkenhausen and his engineering cohorts within the Munich department did produce a stretched version of the motor, using previous motorcycle technology. Measuring 800 cc and using a single overhead camshaft on each cylinder bank (chain-and-gear drive), the little engine could reach 8,500 rpm and produced between 85 and 90 bhp. The engine was mid-mounted within a very pretty tubular-frame, open racing car, and the ensemble was called a BMW 800RS, presumably acknowledging its links with the BMW 700RS motorcycles.

This pert 400-kg (882-lb) sports racer, constructed entirely on the engineer's initiative, was usually raced and hillclimbed within Germany or Austria by von Falkenhausen. This was not the only 700-based special, for there was also a rather crude, but aerodynamically effective, chop-roof fastback coupe that had an entirely smooth front and large side intakes before the rear wheels. This was the hand-built minimalist production work of Willi Martini, and was often the reason that 700 appeared in the GT class.

My lasting memories of Alex von Falkenhausen are of a courteous gentleman, smiling quietly as I struggled to absorb the breadth of what he and his employers had achieved, all on a budget that my previous multinational employers would have spent on press packs and hospitality. I met the Baron of engine engineering again in the 1980s, and he was the polite opposite of the temperamental genius described in German BMW histories. But then, I was not trying to argue engineering theory or impose marketing priorities on his amazing amalgam of intellect and pragmatic "real-world" talents.

Von Falkenhausen delivered a cool verdict on his Munich-based motorsport adventures over four decades: "My directors were only happy if things cost no money. Always I told them we went racing to make things strong...but always we go to race." He chuckled at the white lies that lay behind the reformation of this major motorsport force.

QUICK FACTS

Period

1957–64

Products

Creating the four-cylinder motors and
new class 1500, sportier 1800TI;
production design principles,
including slant motors, established

Performance

75 bhp and 92 mph to 145 bhp
and 125 mph

Achievements

First outright European
Championship race victory goes
to 1800TI; hillclimb success

People

Alex von Falkenhausen on motor
design; Burkard Bovensiepen on
the foundation of Alpina and the
full-time racers

Chapter 7

The New Pedigree

The new generation of 4-cylinder sedans

"I had five designers and one engineer for the test bed. The production people say I can go ahead on new engine work, but they say there must be no expense." Shrugging and suppressing outright laughter, Alex von Falkenhausen remembered the conditions under which his miniscule Munich department was allowed to develop a medium-range car, pulling the company closer to the success prompted by the agile 700.

In that department were youth and aged experience. While BMW's engineering Baron knew what he wanted, the vital combustion chamber shape—essential to promoting efficient power—was detailed by an unsung hero: Herr Rech. *Wirbelwanne*, or swirl bath, the principle of agitating the fuel/air mixture for the most complete combustion, was the handiwork of this gentleman's "...solid working methods and long experience," reported a former colleague who worked with Rech in the late 1960s.

Youth was represented in that department by Paul Rosche, who joined BMW in 1957. He recalls, "We were drawing all kinds of engines. We made designs of single-overhead-camshaft engines in sizes from 700, 900, 1,100 cc as well as the sizes we did come to make. All had four cylinders and water cooling." Born, bred and determinedly remaining in Munich, what-

ever company honors were heaped on him, Rosche was the spiritual, but more practical, less-intellectual heir to von Falkenhausen.

As the 1950s turned into the 1960s, von Falkenhausen was determined that the new middleweight BMW sedan's engine should be strong enough both to fulfill an effective role in modified form for competition and to take the inevitable increase in capacity and power needed for years of mass manufacture.

The department succeeded brilliantly, providing the basis of a four-cylinder that would last 24 production years (the 1964–88 1,573-cc unit) and contribute to BMW's 16 European Championship titles scored from 1966 to 1988. The BMW European Touring Car Championship tally between 1966 and 1988 is unmatched: 27 titles in all. In detail, 11 of those were makes titles, and 16 were prestige wins for drivers of BMW cars.

Those sound motor principles would expand through myriad permutations that included 2-liter displacement, turbocharging, and the cylinder-block base for competition engines of knee-trembling horsepower.

How did they do that? Alex von Falkenhausen commented, "Then, many cars had pushrods and three-bearing crankshafts, but I knew we must have something more. Alfa Romeo had already made many five-bearing

engines with two overhead camshafts, and so I fought for a BMW 1500 that could easily be a 1600, and that had the overhead camshaft and five bearings for the crankshaft. We made the block very, very stiff."

That was the aristocratic understatement of the century. During the 1980s, development of the 1.5 turbo Grand Prix motor, suitably treated (left outside to rust and season, then subtly reinforced) BMW iron blocks were literally taken off the 1,200-bhp dyno scale in the underground network of power test cells beneath Preussenstrasse, representing (albeit very briefly) some 800.5 bhp per liter!

A quality steel crankshaft with five (later, eight for 2 liters) counterbalance weights provided exceptional balance and operational smoothness. "We used quite a light penetration of the nitriding process for these 1500 engines. Today, they still use this steel crankshaft for the full racing Formula 2 engines...but the nitriding is a little heavier for this use at 9,000 rpm; we had designed the original for 6,000 rpm," von Falkenhausen revealed in the late 1970s.

In 1960s production, both the 1500 and 1600 engines shared the same 71-mm stroke, the smaller unit having an 82-mm bore and the larger an 84-mm bore, giving 1,499 and 1,573 cc respectively. Further production developments covered an 84 x 80-mm, 1,773-cc BMW 1800, which was uprated on the same dimensions for the sportier BMW 1800TI

with twin Solex carburetors and oil cooler, and the BMW 1800TI/SA competition cars detailed in the next chapter.

There was an important production change during the 1800's production life: the switch to an 89 x 71-mm bore x stroke. The capacity and power output figures of the base street car (90 bhp/106 lb-ft) remained as before, and the swap came too late to influence the 1964–66 span of the 1800s that we will discuss. The change is useful for parts knowledge though. It was put through at BMW because there were machine tooling advantages to the increasingly familiar 89-mm block bore, and the press thought the later 1800 ran sweeter still.

The BMW four-door 2000 sedans, two-door 2000 coupes, and the 2002 series all featured a 2-liter permutation of 89 mm x 80 mm to release 1,990 cc, which also proved to be a versatile sedan racing capacity. The BMW 1500-inspired family of four-cylinders with

their chain-driven overhead camshafts continued through the 1960s and into the 1970s, adopting a 30-degree slant angle in the engine bay after the original 1500, a feature that was shared by subsequent six-cylinders.

Some of the competition applications discussed here—2- and 3-liter-plus sixes—featured upright installations for ultimate power. On the street, however, BMW wanted the hood profile as low as possible. Thus they could not regularly employ the dry-sump oil lubrication systems that racers use for durability and to cut the depth of bulky sump pans.

The 1500 sedan

The 1500 was first revealed to the German public in 1961, but production did not get properly under way until the summer of 1962. Built on a 2,550-mm (100.4-in) wheelbase with a width of 1,710 mm (67.3 in) and a length of 4,495 mm (177 in), this rather tall (57 inches at the roofline) model was the medium-class savior that BMW had been waiting for. It was also the dimensional basis for the racers with 1.8- and 2-liter motors. It's worth noting that BMW played a road flyer with their

1800TI/SA homologation special, clipping street curb weight to an official 10 kg below that of the original 1500's 1,060-kg/2,310-lb debut statistic.

The MacPherson-strut front suspension and trailing-arm independent rear suspension had been tailored to suit the sporting driver from the start, but it's worth knowing that the trailing-arm system was originally developed for the baby 600. The showroom provision of front disc brakes and a good four-speed, all-synchromesh gearbox was appreciated, too, though sensitive rack-and-pinion steering, BMW's prewar heritage, was absent until 1975's 3-series cars.

Running on an 8.8:1 compression ratio, the 1500 unit produced 80 bhp at 5,700 rpm, but it was first shown with 75 bhp and an 8.2:1 compression. Power output was excellent for the period, but it did have a spacious five-seater sedan to pull along at the 92-mph (148-km/h) claimed maximum speed. The potential to run faster was obvious, and it prompted the start of perhaps the best-known name in high-performance BMWs: Alpina.

While the factory was pounding back down the road to prosperity—in 1963, it paid shareholders a dividend for the first time in twenty years—Burkard Bovensiepen was cautiously entering the competition arena. The young man had studied both engineering and economics in Munich, which gave him a good background for his position as the future founder and owner of Alpina. "I could not decide what to do. I already had a car business, yes, even while I was at high school [the equivalent of university]." Bovensiepen's ability to buy fine things (especially wine) seems only matched by his business acumen and philosophy, which have created a remarkable specialist business.

Despite a fair measure of pain and adversity to overcome in life—his distinctive limp is the result of a very bad road accident in his youth—Burkard Bovensiepen retains a rare ability to laugh at himself. Punctuated by frequent outbursts of joviality, the story of how this talented individual came to spend much of his working life connected with BMWs was told to me as follows: "I had a Fiat 1500 and I took this car to Nardi in Italy myself, to see how they would tune it to make it faster. On the

way home to Germany on the autobahn—I was only some twenty kilometers away from Nardi—I began to race with a Lancia...BANG! That was the end of my Nardi-Fiat!" The explosive Fiat showed him that the tuning business could still use some engineering expertise.

Bovensiepen recalled buying one of the early BMW 1500s: "This was a great car. The start of better things for BMW, I think. I liked this car very well, but always I am thinking how good it would be to go faster!" That was really the beginning of the Bovensiepen-BMW engineering link.

Working from part of his father's Alpina typewriter works at Kaufbeuren, some 12 or so miles from his present base at Buchloe and an hour west of Munich, Bovensiepen made up a twin-carburetor kit for the favorite 1500. "I made a kit for the two Weber twin-choke side-draught instruments. I was very pleased with this car, so we made a few copies, doing everything that was needed by the customer—manifold, linkages and so on—for 1,000 DM

Foundation of a competitive and commercial dynasty: a 1500 Neue Klasse brought together all the elements of a sporting four-cylinder BMW that would survive into the 3-series of the 1980s. Our drawing shows the front-engine, rear-drive layout with strut front and trailing-arm rear suspension. In one area, however, the 1500 was not the same as its successors, for it carried its engine upright, instead of at the traditional four- and six-cylinder slant.

Drawing: Courtesy BMW

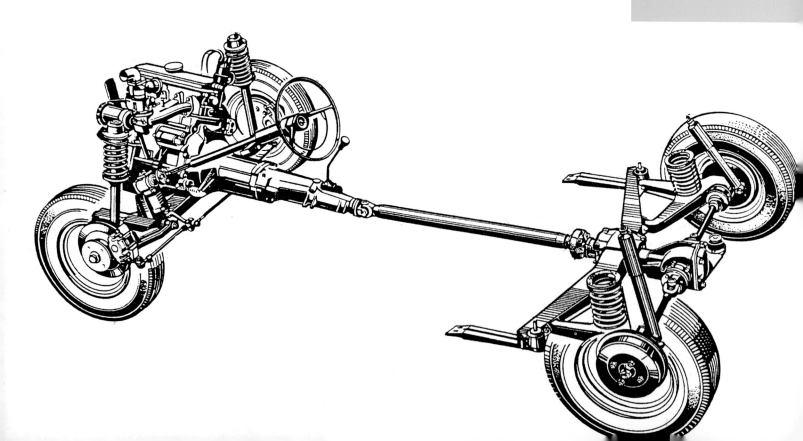

each." (At the time, the Deutschemark was less valuable than it is today.)

Bovensiepen continued, "One afternoon, because I was so pleased with the car, I went into the offices of *Auto Motor und Sport* magazine. There, I found a young journalist called Gerd Hack [still there, but now a very senior executive], and I told him about my wonderful car and he does not want to know about this. 'Always they are blowing up, these tuned cars,' says Hack. In the end I manage to show him the car parked outside and, after we do a lot of talking, he decides to test it for a couple of days."

The results were printed in that magazine's October 1963 issue, crediting the car with a top speed of five miles an hour faster than standard at 97 mph (157 km/h), and acceleration times that were a second or two quicker than the production model. A two-page spread was generously allocated to telling the full story of this new alliance, and the car was credited with 92 bhp at 6,000 rpm.

The magazine article stirred up some interest among potential conversion purchasers, and though most of the cars were used purely for ordinary, brisk transport, some must have found their way into competition as the first Alpina-BMWs. When the factory announced the 1800, with its single carburetor, it was an obvious candidate for the Bovensiepen treatment, while the 1800TI allowed Alpina to get a lot more ambitious. The cylinder head, camshaft, and pistons were replaced in an Alpina conversion. Bovensiepen also "threw away those Solex carburetors and changed many cars over to Weber."

Bovensiepen felt his customers wanted three things of Alpina: a factory standard of finish, fixed prices, and a valid guarantee. The accent was, and remained, on complete engineering work. Burkard cringed at the word "tuning," as Alpina made the transition towards manufacturing cars with their own engines, transmissions, suspensions and bodywork, using the BMW as a basis. By the early 1980s, Alpina

was an established manufacturer and utilized the services of engineers as fine as Dr. Fritz Indra—better-known for his 300-bhp Audi Sport Quattro 20-valve motor and GM-Opel Sport engine engineering today. Indra was particularly adept at harnessing turbocharging or oversize capacities to genuinely improve performance, while staying within prevailing emission legislation.

Alpina became the BMW tuners and frequently carried the factory flag in sedan racing. Later, they were joined by the Schnitzer brothers of Freilassing (just inside the southern German border with Austria), GS Tuning at Freiburg, Koepchen at Willich, and (in 1971) Hartge of Beckingen.

The Schnitzers, particularly eldest brother Josef, were to be deeply important to BMW, Josef even working in the Munich competition department on engine development. But at the pre-2002 era with which we are concerned, Josef Schnitzer was racing. "Sepp" was good: he was the 1964 runner-up in the German hillclimb championship and was the

1966 German circuit racing champion. Schnitzer drove and developed the four-cylinder BMWs, from 1800TI and TI/SA through to 2000TI, to attract customers to the Schnitzer business, established in 1966.

Today, Schnitzer is perhaps better-known than Alpina, being the favored race team of the factory since the 1980s. Note that the sale of public road performance parts was separated from racing operations in Europe during 1987, when a vast German BMW dealer (Kohl Automobile GmbH) signed a marketing deal to have public road products marketed by AC Schnitzer under license through more than 50 dealers. In the UK, both Alpina and Schnitzer products are channeled through the factory-owned importer, but two major dealerships—Frank Sytner in Nottingham and L&C Autos at Tunbridge Wells—are the public contact points for Alpina.

After Josef Schnitzer's death in 1978, Motorsport continued to be successfully handled by Herbert Schnitzer and Charly Lamm as part of Schnitzer GmbH. Lamm (brought up as part of the Schnitzer brood) has developed into such an outstanding manager that he has run the most successful BMW touring cars and was seconded to team manager on the McLaren-BMW GT racing program in 1997, returning to the German touring car scene for 1998.

Given the pace at which BMW turned around its fortunes, it was puzzling that the 1500 Neue Klasse did not immediately appear in competition. The factory actually had bigger problems in meeting demand and rectifying some worrying transmission and rear-suspension manufacturing defects, never mind the fact that the price was up 12 percent over the originally predicted 8,500 DM (then just over $2,100).

This beautifully-prepared 1600 with 2.1-liter M3 power was not just the most regular BMW winner in Britain through the mid-1990s, but twice won the premier overall championship. Owner/driver remained Simon Crompton of L&C BMW, one of two main outlets for Alpina products in the UK.

Picture: Mary Harvey, Pembrey, South Wales, UK, 1997

The 1800TI joins the race

Factory racing participation did not come until January 1964, when the 1800 sedan (displayed in September 1963 in Germany) had been joined by the 1800TI. The 1800TI was sold in the US by the controversial Hoffman Motors Corporation at some $3,500 in April 1965. It came painted in Germany's most emotive racing-associated color, forever linked to the Silberfeile Grand Prix Auto Unions and Mercedes...so it was "any color you like, so long as it's silver." The 1800TI marked BMW's comeback to full-size sports motoring, but with the twist that Alfa Romeo had popularized: family-car accommodation.

The 1800 single-carburetor sedan was capable of 100 mph (160 km/h) under good conditions, and this was in the era when "doing a ton" was traditional on Britain's pre-70-mph-limit highways and Germany's then-totally unrestricted autobahn. The 1800TI brought 110 bhp at 5,800 rpm through adoption of a pair of twin-choke Solex carburetors. *Car & Driver* proved the 1800TI capable of 107 mph (171 km/h) and 0–60 mph in 11.6 seconds, and under half a minute from 0–90 mph. The New York-domiciled 1800TI returned 16 to 23 mpg, including performance tests.

"It became important for us to have a competition version of our four-cylinder range," von Falkenhausen remembered, "but the 1500/1600 engines were not the way for us. In this class, there were the very fast Alfa Romeos and the Lotus-Cortinas. Yes, I think I knew these would be coming, too. So, for these reasons, we make a car that can win its class and that we can develop....The 1800TI and then the more specialized 1800TI/SA were those cars."

The mid-1960s saw BMW engineering take on a new recruit from Porsche: Otto Stulle (later to be found at Ford Cologne). It was this precision engineer, a stickler for correct procedure, who enlivened the 1800TI/Tisa engines for competition using the race-motor techniques of Porsche. The 1800TI's potential was "160 bhp with easy tuning changes," according to von Falkenhausen, "and we used to increase the compression ratio to 10.5:1." What von Falkenhausen left unsaid was the constant competition development work carried out by the small engineering team on the combustion chamber and the camshaft.

Working on the camshaft design, "because I was good at mathematics," he says nowadays with a grin, was Paul Rosche, who quickly acquired the nickname of "Camshaft Paul." He worked on the original profile for the 1500 and produced most of the sporting profiles thereafter, a subject he pursued through the 1980s.

In those days, the preparation of a racing sedan on the Continent tended to center far more around engine work, but with the influx of Mini-Coopers and Lotus-developed Ford Cortinas, this lasted only as long as BMW was running the 1800-bodied racers. Thereafter, wide wheels, the development of wheel-arch extensions, and sophisticated suspension systems proceeded apace.

Today, the 1800TI in racing form would look like a car taken off the street. Many people connected with BMW in those early sedan days confirm that impression. Paul Rosche remembers that the cars could be driven on the road to race meetings, and contemporary pictures show us they were road-registered, not the trailered formula-car hybrids of the 1980s and 1990s. The comparatively bulky BMW four-door, weighing in at 1,200 kg, also carried a weight penalty that would not be overcome in sedan racing until the advent of the two-door "02" series with its 2-liter punch.

Even when Dieter Quester started driving for BMW in 1966, the cars were very much tuned road cars. Narrow, steel wheels with Dunlop racing tires were the norm. The use of solid metal bearing rose-jointing (then called "the

As for the 328 and 700, the BMW 1800TI really caught the mood of German competitive driving ambition. Interrupted only by a lone Volvo P544, Hahne's factory car shares the front row at the Nürburgring, scene of the twin-carburetor 1800TI's first international outright win over six hours of the majestic circuit.

Picture: BMW Archiv, reprinted 1984

English way" in Germany) to replace the normal rubber bushings, and cut street-handling slop, had yet to materialize.

Integral roll cages, quick-steering layouts, and the possibility of replacing every fundamental part came as the big corporations like Ford started to pay the race specialists in Britain (Lotus, Cooper Car Company, Alan Mann Racing, Willment, et cetera) big bucks to turn mundane family cars into track warriors whose success could be commercially exploited.

Back then, homologation almost meant what the word stands for: the recognition of an existing production car for competition use. The art of adding "homologated options," which ranged from a thicker anti-roll bar to four-valve-per-cylinder engines and complete suspension, transmission, and bodywork transformations, is generally credited back to Stuart Turner's reign at BMC Abingdon, UK.

Jaguar sedans were fighting for top honors in Europe before that with a number of legalized options, and neither the Italians nor the French were slow to make the best of their products in competition. At the time, the German attitude to production-based rallying or racing seemed to owe a great deal to Mercedes-Benz, and that meant using as much as possible of the production vehicle. This attitude persisted until the end of the 1960s when Ford of Cologne produced an Anglo-German racing Capri. In turn, this revolutionized BMW's attitude to the sport, as we'll see in a later chapter.

Although Alex von Falkenhausen was still racing occasionally, Walter Schneider continued turning in good performances for the factory in the twin-carburetor 1800. At Zolder, in May 1964, Schneider practiced third fastest overall for the Belgian first round of the European Touring Car Championship. Ahead were Jack Sears (Willment-entered Ford Galaxie) and John Sparrow (Jaguar MkII-3.8), but behind, and most important, were former European Champion Eugen Bohringer and his factory 300SE Mercedes-Benz.

In the race, the positions were reversed, although, after a long battle, Schneider did have to concede his place to the Mercedes ace. But the 1800 had shown its worth in finishing fourth overall and winning the 2-liter class, just as von Falkenhausen had anticipated.

Touring-car racing was now popular enough to justify a two-day meeting at the Belgian circuit. Each of six classes were given their own race. In the 1,301–1,600-cc class, it was the Alan Mann Lotus-Cortinas that dominated the event. A comparison of practice lap times showed that von Falkenhausen was wise to avoid a direct confrontation at this stage, for the Cortinas were over five seconds a lap faster.

The 1800TI visited Britain for the first time on June 6. Then, Schneider and Hahne were not only leading their class but were also third overall before the clutch expired on Hahne. It was a popular outing with the British, for both drivers received sympathetic applause as they walked back to their pit.

A look at the qualifying times in Autosport's contemporary account shows that the BMWs were still in need of development. Around the Brands Hatch Grand Prix circuit, Sir John Whitmore flew the Alan Mann Cortina to pole position in 1 minute, 57 seconds. The lone BMW, Schneider's, was on row three with a practice lap of 2 minutes 1.4 seconds. Thus it was bracketed by Paddy Hopkirk's fantastic 2 minutes 1.0 seconds in the works Mini Cooper S and Handley's 2 minutes 2.0 seconds in a similar Mini!

However, the reporters (subsequent *Autoweek* expat Richard Feast and Michael "Mill Books" Kettlewell) noted that on the BMW, "all wheels were on the deck rounding South Bank, unlike the two cars that headed it!" This comment referred to the Lotus-Cortinas, which were inclined to corner on three, two, or even one wheel. The BMW was

The way we were. Thundering 7-liter Willment Ford Galaxie leads more agile Europeans from BMW (1800TI), BMC (Mini-Cooper S), and Ford (Cortina GT) around the British Brands Hatch circuit in 1964. The BMW was not as quick over each lap as the more radically-modified opposition at this stage, but its consistency put it into the top three, before mechanical mayhem intervened.

Picture: LAT, reprinted 1978

Spa Francorchamps in 1964 was this close! July 1964, and BMW is right back in the big league, battling with Mercedes-Benz for the lead of the Spa 24-hours in Belgium. After 18 hours, the BMW 1800TI of Hahne/Aaltonen (the original Flying Finn rally driver) had to stop for replacement wheel bearings.

The Mercedes 300 six-cylinder versus the BMW four-cylinder 1800 at this fast circuit (they averaged over 102 mph for 24 hours) was only going to end one way. After racing one afternoon and all Saturday night, through to 9:00 am on Sunday, the gap was just over 2 minutes. It was less than that at the finish, with Hubert Hahne/ Rauno Aaltonen coming in second overall.

Picture: LAT in Belgium, reprinted 1978

always set to finally oversteer to suit Hahne's sliding technique.

The first important win for the double-carburetor 1800TI came with a seventh overall and class victory in the Nürburgring 6-hours. The event was held on June 22, 1964, and was a dry, hard slog through Sunday afternoon.

In practice, characteristically damp and misty 'Ring conditions had kept Bohringer's winning 300SE down to 10 minutes 22.6 seconds (at that time, an unofficial sedan record). Hubert Hahne was paired with Anton Fischhaber (the Swiss who had also hillclimbed a Lotus 23-BMW successfully since 1963), and they overcame early "axle maladies" (in the words of Patrick MacNally's *Autosport* report) to record that placing.

The BMW was, however, not quick enough, being led by a German-crewed Volvo for much of the event, and was finally beaten by two Mini Coopers. By August, the BMW 1800TI was capable of winning the politically important supporting event to the German Grand Prix at Nürburgring, setting fastest lap on the way.

The 1964 debut season was unfolding as a good first year for the 1800 in competition. In the first week of July 1964, Hubert Hahne and Belgian driver Heinrich Eppelein won the Nürburgring 12-hours outright. They were favorites from the start, but when it came to the revived Spa-Francorchamps 24-hours later that month, there was really tough opposition lined up.

The Belgian 24-hour event had not been run since 1953, when it was for sports cars, set against the picturesque backdrop of the Ardennes forest on the high-speed Spa-Francorchamps track. The circuit is made by linking up public roads and closing them for racing. The Belgian revival attracted fantastic support from the European car industry. BMW entered two 1800TIs, with Walter/Eppelein in one and Rauno Aaltonen, taking a break from rallying to partner Hahne, in the other. To win, they had to overcome three works Mercedes, six Autodelta Alfa Romeos, the Alan Mann Lotus-Cortinas, and factory-backed cars from Lancia and Citroen.

Pole position in what was to be a dry race went to Sir John Whitmore on 4 minutes 46.1 seconds, averaging over 110 mph (177 km/h) around Europe's fastest road circuit. The swiftest Mercedes-Benz (Eugen Bohringer's 300SE) managed 4 minutes 48.4 seconds and the Hahne/Aaltonen BMW was fourth quickest at 4 minutes 54 seconds.

In the race itself, the BMWs showed their worth quickly, pulling up to third and seventh positions. As night fell over the dark pine forests of the surrounding Ardennes, the fastest Munich machine pushed into second place, and would even lead whenever the Mercedes stopped for fuel. After 12 hours of racing, the grimly determined Finn and the exuberant German were just 2 minutes behind Stuttgart's best. At 9 a.m., the gap was still only 2 minutes 13 seconds, so the BMW was fighting hard for supremacy rather than class honors.

Both cars ran into trouble—the BMW first. It had to stop for 15 minutes to have the front wheel bearings replaced—they took a terrible pounding on the outside of all of Spa's fast right-handers—and that cost BMW any chance of winning. In a late drama, the leading Mercedes was disqualified, and the sister 300 of Robert Crevits and Gustave Gosselin won instead. They covered 2,461.94 miles at an average of 102.45 mph (165 km/h). Hahne and Aaltonen averaged 102.18 mph for second place, and Aaltonen closed in on the Belgian-crewed Mercedes all the way to the finish, after having suffered that daylight pit stop.

BMW went from class winner to outright contender against Mercedes-Benz, and all in less than a year. Von Falkenhausen had reason to be delighted with his engineering colleagues, the tough car they had put together, and a good choice of drivers. In fact, he did not have time to be pleased, for still-better results lay in the coming months.

Just two weeks after Spa, Hahne was entered at Karlskoga for the European Touring

BMW and Alfa Romeo have always been rivals on the racetrack as well as in the showroom! The Milan-registered works cars attempt to subdue a Munich machine at Spa in 1964. Note the casual flag-marshal in sandals and shorts: if you crashed and burned at Spa of the 1960s and 1970s, assistance from marshals and medical teams was patchy. Fatalities were an all-too-regular feature of Belgium's premier 24-hour classic back then.

Picture: BMW Archiv, reprinted 1984

The Swedish public first saw the factory 1800 at Karlskoga when it amassed valuable class points, finishing sixth overall in Hahne's hands. Here, the factory BMW (M-VK 514-registered, again) pursues one of the surprisingly fast Saab 2-stroke triples (developed from a DKW base) around the tight, pinetree-lined track.

Picture: LAT, reprinted 1978

Car Championship round. After just over an hour's racing around the tight 1.86-mile Swedish track, the Fords had routed the opposition. There were Cortinas simply everywhere, the Alan Mann cars backed up by some rapid locals. However, Hahne was first of the non-Ford brigade, in sixth place, and the points did not go amiss in his class.

August had brought a fine first BMW outright win in the European Touring Car Championship series. The contenders had come to the fast Zandvoort track in Holland and the Hahne/BMW combination was in top form, as can be judged from the words of *Autosport* reporter David Pritchard, who noted, "...the astonishing brinkmanship of Hubert Hahne in his BMW 1800TI. This car looked as though it could never have got round the corner under attack except possibly upside-down, yet it lasted the whole twenty laps without an accident—as apparently it has done in the past."

Whitmore's fast but fragile Ford had led initially again, but the engine went on to three cylinders for a while. Jacky Ickx was obliged to stop harrying Hahne and drop behind his team leader, leaving the German (with his ral-

lying style) with a clear run to the finish, ahead of the two Fords.

Later, in September, came more good news—a second outright Touring Car round victory, no less. The scene was the cobblestones and city squares of the Hungarian Budapest 4-hours, allowing Hahne enough time to demonstrate the advantages of independent rear suspension and reliability over the Whitmore Lotus-Cortina. So the BMW had developed into a race winner; this trip behind the Iron Curtain allowed it to put both arch-rivals from Ford and Alfa Romeo firmly behind. The BMW 700 was already only a memory.

At the end of a year in which 18,000 employees had produced 61,300 vehicles for BMW, a very special employee—Hahne—had also captured the German national sedan championship title. So, 1964 turned out to be a very fine season for speedy BMWs.

Elsewhere, even the Munich police did their best for BMW in 1964. The International Police Rally was being contested by an 1800TI: it finished second overall. Internationally, the best BMW rally result was a sweep of the sub-2000-cc class on that year's Geneva Rally.

Period piece: BMW's works achievements encouraged overseas competitors to try their luck in the 1800s. Here, a more radically-developed Group 5 Bimmer takes on the contemporary Ford Anglia and Mini Cooper S opposition in the British Championship of the mid-1960s.

Picture: LAT, Silverstone, UK, 1966

BMW finished fourth overall, piloted by factory-backed Hans Joachim Walter.

Although BMW Rennsport supported the provision of a works 1800 to contest the Deutsche Bergmeisterschaft (German Mountain Hillclimb Championship) in the hands of 1962 title winner Heinrich Eppelein, not all went to plan. Opposition through the elevated turns included an increasingly rapid car-and-driver combination from Josef "Sepp" Schnitzer. The fiery Schnitzer beat Eppelein's factory runner

with increasing regularity and seized the runner-up spot in the overall title hunt that season.

Privateers had vehemently reestablished the Bimmer badge as a sporting recommendation, particularly in sports car racing. Anton Fischhaber took the Lotus 23-BMW four-cylinder to fifth overall in the competitive European Hillclimb Championship, skillfully exploiting its prophetic Anglo-German chassis and BMW power-unit alliance. But now we'll see how the four-cylinder racing sedans developed into winners in America as well as Europe.

In 1964, the factory also contested a number of rally and hillclimb events. This works 1800TI is out on the race courses that comprised the bulk of competition mileage on that year's 13th edition of the Tour de France.

Picture: Photo Junior, Nice, France, 1964

QUICK FACTS

Period
1965–67

Products
1800 and 2000 derivatives

Performance
158 to 190 bhp,
125 to 140 mph

Achievements
First 24-hour race wins and
trans-European titles

People
Dieter Quester on the longest of loyal
racing careers, and the ownership
roll of honor stretches to America's
first World Champion, Phil Hill

Chapter 8

Getting Serious: The 1800 "Tisa"

Predicting the pattern of sedan success

For the 1965 sedan season, the factory had a new weapon to show their increasing international commitment to touring-car racing. Called the 1800TI/SA (TI taken from Alfa Romeo's Touring Internationale designation, denoting a twin-carburetor high-performance variant; SA for *SonderAusfuhrung*, or Special Equipment), the newcomer was quickly nicknamed "Tisa," and goes down in BMW history as its first limited-production homologation special.

BMW should have made the 1800 TI/SAs in a run of 500 to compete in Group 2; research suggests that 200 were built between January and June 1965, sold primarily to competition-licensed drivers. Ex-factory "Sonder" goodies included a brace of twin-barrel Webers, an elevated 10.5:1 compression, and an official 130 bhp at 6,500 rpm. A five-speed gearbox was specified, along with an optional limited-slip differential that was needed to race competitively. Other Tisa tricks listed publicly included a slim rear anti-roll bar and plenty of bodywork drilling to support that 1,050-kg racing weight.

A factory racing Tisa boasted an uprated version of the 1800 SOHC engine; 158 bhp and a safe 6,500 rpm were quoted, but 160 bhp was possible. It also sported wider wheels than the street 5JK x 14 specification, although the rims were still seven inches or less, in steel.

However, the old twin-carburetor 1800TI was good enough for many sporting owners, as was revealed to the late Gregor Grant at the factory. The 1960s sports personalities who used them on the road included multiple World Champion Jack Brabham, America's Ferrari-mounted World Champion Phil Hill, Tony Maggs, Aston Martin sports car ace Roy Salvadori, and others.

One other personality who was important on the competition side, one of many men von Falkenhausen was to have running the team on a day-to-day basis, was Walter Schulte. He did not have an easy task in 1965: BMW Rennsport entered four or even five 1800s at some internationals that year.

The 1965 European Touring Car Championship program, comprising ten rounds with three main capacity classes, was tackled, but race results did not match that demon Tisa specification. There were teething troubles that cost Hahne dearly on occasion, but 1965 belonged to one man in European sedan racing, and that man was Sir John Whitmore. His red and gold Lotus-Cortina from Ford-subcontractor Alan Mann simply annihilated the competition, winning the Monza.

That Italian opener to the championship was typical of BMW's luck that year. Hahne's car, sporting drilled interior panel work and miss-

Dieter Glemser shows his and the BMW 1800 Tisa's approach to the fast corners found at the British Snetterton track in 1965. Wider wheels and stiffer suspension brought much-improved handling, though the drivers still used very large steering wheels by contemporary standards. Note the air intake ducts beneath the factory registration plate.

Picture: LAT, Norfolk, UK, 1965; reprinted

How it should be in the bay of an 1800 Tisa. This Clint deWitt Motorsport example was on display at the Monterey Historic event celebrating the BMW marque's sixty-year motor-sport history in 1996.

Picture: Author, Monterey, 1996

The Scuderia Bavaria engine bay on the 1990s update of the 1800 Tisa for European historic racing under international FIA rules. The camshaft was far more radical than could be managed in the 1960s and contributed to a 30-bhp boost in power.

Picture: Author, Paul Ricard, France, 1992

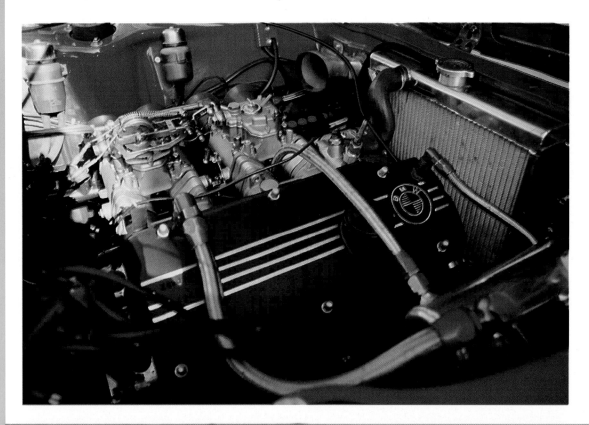

Arthur Porter's 1800 Tisa is a must for color spreads with its emotive tribute to another great sporting BMW—the thirties 328—created by artist Dennis Simon, the man who also did great poster work for the 20th Anniversary of Motorsport Oktoberfest gathering in 1992.

Picture: Klaus Schnitzer, Monterey, 1996

Multiple-BMW owner and Colorado Attorney Arthur Porter commissioned this fabulous 328-dominated artwork from Dennis Simon as a tribute to the BMW art cars on his shimmering 1800 Tisa. Bought as a rusty wreck in Pennsylvania, this Tisa (number 197 of the 200 run) was totally resurrected in time to be shown at the Monterey Historic meeting of 1996.

Picture: Author, Monterey, 1996

ing both hood and trunklid supports to lighten the load, ran third or fourth from a poor start. The gear-lever came adrift, and then the team had trouble with the new engine and clutch, so the BMW did not finish.

In June, only four out of the thirteen BMWs (not all factory cars) entered for the Nürburgring 6-hours actually finished the race. Hahne lost a wheel when lying second on the first lap. The rest did not do well against the Ford Lotus-Cortinas either, coming home fourth and fifth in front of the home crowd. Subsequent Ford and BMW competition manager Jochen Neerpasch was driving one of the two winning Fords that crossed the line in a humiliating (for BMW) "dead heat."

At first, it looked as if that year's edition of the Spa 24-hours could be even more of a disaster. Only one 1800 Tisa survived of the five gray cars entered from Munich. BMW sports manager Schulte was at a loss to understand the mechanical carnage among his five-car team.

BMW was not using highly-tuned engines, but all had overheated. There were also front suspension problems and a starter motor fail-

Hubert Hahne (left) and Alex von Falkenhausen pose beneath the light-weight, drilled hood of a factory 1800 Tisa at the British European Championship event in 1965.

Picture: BMW Archiv, reprinted 1978

Hubert Hahne at Spa's Eau Rouge in the 1965 24 Hours. It could have been a disastrous foray to Belgium for the works, for neither of the works 1800 Tisa models pictured finished, nor did four of the five cars BMW sent!

Picture: LAT, Belgium 1965; reprinted 1978

A superb study of the factory BMW 1800 Tisas at the Spa Francorchamps hairpin, Hubert Hahne leading one of four other entries. Just one car would finish the 24 Hours, but in the right place—on top!

Picture: LAT, Belgium 1965; reprinted 1978

ure, shared among a team that included Jacky Ickx/Dieter Glemser and Hubert Hahne/Willi Mariesse. Hahne had some compensation from a pole position time of 4 minutes 49 seconds in dampish conditions (he had managed 4 minutes 42.6 seconds in practice for May's Spa 500-km). He led for the first two and three-quarter hours, after which the Tisa needed some fuel.

However, one BMW Tisa was enough to provide a high point of the year, for BMW won its first of many 24-hour races at the demanding Belgian circuit. Jacky Ickx's brother, Pascal, shared the victorious drive with Gerald Langlois von Ophem, the Belgian pair putting 2,369 miles behind them at an average of 98.7 mph (159 km/h) in much tougher race conditions than had existed the previous year.

Spa 1965, and the mechanics fight to repair Hubert Hahne's starter motor on the car he shared with Belgian Willi Mariesse. Among the onlookers are a very youthful Jacky Ickx (left, in Dunlop overalls), von Falkenhausen (extreme right), and helmeted Hahne.

Picture: LAT, Belgium 1965; reprinted 1978

BMW's first victory in the Belgian 24-hour Classic on the Spa-Francorchamps circuit came in 1965. The surviving BMW 1800 Tisa was driven by Pascal Ickx and Gerald Langlois von Ophem; it was the Tisa's toughest international victory, applauded by the huge grandstand crowd. BMW's first outright win previewed a total 20 wins by 1997: an unparalleled hit rate for any manufacturer in 24-hour racing and a far more accurate guide to manufacturing quality standards than Le Mans, as the cars had such close production links for the majority of those victories.

Picture: LAT, Belgium 1965; reprinted 1978

A 3-liter limit was imposed at this 1966 edition of the Belgian classic, and Ford pulled all their toys out, as it was effectively a Mustang ban. There were no Cortinas, and Alfa was not strongly represented either, thus diminishing the glory in winning this edition. However, from a Munich engineering viewpoint, at least the right BMW survived with prophetic results: BMW sedans have won the Spa 24-hours, by far Europe's toughest touring-car test, more times than any rival manufacturers lumped together!

The 1965 domestic Bergmeisterschaft battles were tremendous, with Josef Schnitzer often beating works driver Eppelein to take a first uphill title for a business that had only been established the previous season. It would be almost 20 years before we realized just how mighty a competition force the first of the sporting Schnitzer brothers had established.

Tisa's American debut

BMW backed an 1800TI entry for factory driver Dieter Glemser at Sebring to open their 1965 American competition season. According to Hoffman Motors Corporation records, the 1800 Tisa entered American competition in April 1965. The first US victory was later that month at Chimney Rock, North Carolina, where the 1.8-liter streaked to third overall, the inevitable class win, and a new hill record.

The rest of the 1965 season was equally satisfying for the BMW 1800 special import, as it racked up racing wins across the country, beginning in Georgia. Also in May of 1965, the BMW racing message was received in West Palm Beach, Florida (an outright victory) and Santa Barbara, California, with an outright road racing win on Saturday followed by class and second overall honors on Sunday of a two-day meet.

(Top) Our fuzzy black and white picture shows a historic occasion in BMW and Quester lore: Quester takes his first start in an 1800 Tisa at Aspern, Vienna in 1966. Behind is Hubert Hahne, guesting in a British-prepared works Lotus Cortina.

(Bottom) Still crazy after all these years: Dieter Quester at the wheel of the 1993 Scuderia Bavaria rendition of the 1800 Tisa. Complete with all the trick bits, it was more like driving an E30 M3 than an old 1800, boasting 190 bhp in place of the original competition 158–160 bhp.

Pictures: BMW Archiv, Austria, 1966; Paul Ricard, France, 1993

June 1965 saw the Californian success continue for BMW with a class win, second overall, at Pomona (now better-known for its major-league drag racing events) and a good showing in a Hawaiian 24-hour race. The Tisa's debut American race season closed with an October event at Kent, Washington where the Bimmer—a baby by US standards of the mid-1960s—took another class best.

The 1966 season again offered a ten-round, three-class European Touring Car Championship. BMW results were magnificent, and there were some significant introductions on the factory and driver side that netted national and European titles. It was a year in which Alfa Romeos were showing a real turn of speed, with Andrea de Adamich taking particular advantage of the 1.6-liter/170-bhp GTA.

This new Alfa Romeo designation referred to the lightweight aluminum body panels and other competition modifications that made it hard even for 2-liter BMWs to keep up. In 1966, de Adamich alone scored four outright victories in the premier European series, and the Italians could occasionally summon the white-heat speed of Jochen Rindt in their tin tops, so Alfa was the hardest of acts to beat. However, BMW finished the 1966 season with a European 2-liter class title for Hubert Hahne, and Josef Schnitzer annexed the outright German racing title in a 2000TI, so it was a very successful season for the BMW name.

The 1800 Tisa continued initially, but from July onwards, the 2000TI—announced in January 1966—could be raced. As a street car in twin Solex 40 PH trim, it delivered 120 bhp, enough to release 112 mph maximum and 0–60 mph in 12 seconds. For racing, it delivered more bhp than the 1800 Tisa and a bonus in power-band spread with accessible torque. The 2000TI contributed toward Hahne's first driver's title in the European Touring Car Championship, and unruffled ascendancy in the poorly-contested 2-liter class of that series for BMW.

In March, the pretty 1600-2 (later designated 1602) coupe was announced at the Frankfurt Show. Though it subsequently gained a twin-carburetor layout allowing 105 bhp, it was not the basis for a competitive car until it evolved into the 2002 series, the subject of chapter 12.

From Vienna, Austria came a new BMW driver: inveterate practical joker Dieter Quester. Quester raced speedboats and motorcycles before a four-wheeler career that included a Porsche 356 before BMW. His merits were often overshadowed by the immense Grand Prix success of fellow countrymen Jochen Rindt (1970 posthumous World Champion) and triple World Champion Niki Lauda. Quester always had to make sure his voice was heard over the justified public praise for the depth of Austrian driving talent, Austria contributing a disproportionate number of race aces in relationship to its population.

Quester told me, "I bought an 1800 Tisa from Hahne for 5,000 DM [about $1,500 then] and used it to win the Austrian road racing championship and the BMW Cup. We prepared it ourselves, but there was a new 165-horsepower factory engine. This car was fantastic after the Minis and Abarths I had been driving."

Quester was to provide the mainstay driving force behind BMW's European efforts into the 1980s, winning the European title four times. Quester co-wrote a book about his exploits that was published in 1987 (see Bibliographical Notes) and was still driving both a BMW Formula 2 car and a 635 sedan thirty years after his first BMW contact, appearing at the 1996 Monterey historic races as an athletic testimony to the joys of a full life lived at 101 mph.

Back thirty years, in May 1966, Quester married Julianna von Falkenhausen, Alex von Falkenhausen's daughter. Quester had three outings for the works in 2000TI four-door sedans, as well as the success he enjoyed in the 1800 during 1966.

In 1966, BMW again won the Spa 24-hours in Belgium, but by this time they had homologated the 2-liter 2000TI. Winning crew were Jacky Ickx and Hubert Hahne; they averaged nearly 105 mph.

Pictures: Courtesy Autosport, July 1966; BMW Archiv/Courtesy Chris Willows, 1997

Driven by then-director of Altwood BMW Graham Parker, this 2000TI was competitive with Ford Cortina opposition in the British ICS historic series of 1994.

Picture: Author, Castle Combe, UK, 1994

Hubert Hahne surprised everyone by turning up at the second round of the 1966 championship (Aspern, on the outskirts of Vienna) in a Lotus-Cortina that BMW released him to drive, possibly to assess it further. Ironically, "Hubie" spent the race dicing with Quester, who appeared thereafter to get even more sideways than BMW's official number-one sedan driver. Hahne had secured the pole position for Ford, but when he had gearbox trouble, Quester assumed an untroubled third overall and an easy class win behind Whitmore and de Adamich.

July was the month for touring-car racing that year. There were three events: one in Germany, the next in Spa, and then a grand splash in Britain. Even the Nürburgring 6-hours produced victory for Italy and Alfa (as it did the following year), though two factory 1800 Tisas were second and third overall. Practice was notable for the fact that de Adamich recorded a touring-car lap of the 'Ring in under 10 minutes. The Alfa Romeo driver recorded 9 minutes 59 seconds, Sir John Whitmore (Lotus-Cortina) 10 minutes exactly, and Hahne's BMW was bested at 10 minutes 1 second.

Only two of the new 2000TI models were entered in the Spa 24-hour race, after the unhappy experience of running a large team the previous year. The result was the same, with another fine victory for Munich, despite the fact that there were no less than nine of the fleet Alfa Romeo GTAs entered, five of them Autodelta prepared. Hahne and Jacky Ickx secured pole position (4 minutes 45.6 seconds) by half a second from a local Ford Mustang. The BMW steamed away from the downhill start, leading away up the hill by a large margin in the strong sunshine.

The 2000TI did not lead all the way, but certainly had things under control for most of the race. They had to replace the radiator with less than four hours to go, but since the mechanics managed this in six minutes, that was not too much of a drama.

It was a popular and decisive win for Ickx and Hahne, with good conditions allowing a cracking 104.8 mph (169 km/h) average to be set, and they beat the second-placed Alfa by four laps. The second factory BMW of Dieter Glemser/Willi Mariesse was robbed of second place and a morale-boosting double finish when it started to overheat, subsequently retiring with suspected piston-ring failure.

The third outing of July, 1966 was Britain's Snetterton 500-km. Held in an absolute downpour, record-breaking crowds were not a feature of the breezy Norfolk circuit. However, the absentees from the spectator enclosures missed a competition full of intrigue. Alan Mann held out his ace driver Whitmore on dry tires, and the Baronet ended his race with dented bodywork as a result.

A pair of factory 2000TIs were present, facing up to a field that boasted high-quality drivers such as Jochen Rindt in his Alfa GTA. Whitmore put the Lotus-Cortina on pole position (1 minute 56 seconds), but the Munich machines were noticably faster than before. On the fast track, Hahne put in a 1 minute 58.2 seconds, good enough only for fifth place on the grid. But his performance demonstrated how the factory increase from a 145 bhp 1800TI to the 170 horsepower of the 2000TI had closed the gap on the highly-developed Cortinas.

In the race, Hahne and Glemser both showed real determination, Hahne seen jubi-

Dieter Quester has literally written a book about his memorable moments with BMW, and you need to read his comments about the 1800 to get the full flavor of racing in the 1960s. Here, he looks moody in the 2002 of 1968/69, complete with the roll cage and safety harness that were not featured in some contemporary factory cars!

Picture: LAT, Thruxton, Hampshire, UK, reprinted 1978

lantly grinning as he ran rings around the hapless Whitmore in the rain. Andrea de Adamich won for Italy again, but the BMWs were second and third, with part-time florist Glemser (later a factory Ford Capri pilot) a lap in arrears of Hahne.

Quester remembers those factory BMW sedans of the 1960s with wry amusement. Not because they were ineffective cars—far from it—but because things have changed so much. Looking back to his first works drives, Quester said, "Then it is so different. Nobody knows anything about suspension, so we drive the whole year on the same settings. Maybe we change tires—either we have Dunlop Green Spot or Dunlop White Spot. This is enough to take us through any conditions." He laughed, casting his mind back. "You know, we have to slide the car all the time with much oversteer. I was to do three races for the factory...but I never forgot the first....I go to Munich and pick up the car. Yes, my racing car for the Nürburgring. How will I get it there? By road, of course! I sit inside, all around me are wheels...anti-roll bars and funny things like this! I go with ten anti-roll bars, eight dampers,

and one mechanic [Klaus Miersch], and we drive to Nürburgring for a test session to try out different dampers and so on.

"It's my first visit, and I feel I should know the place like my rivals. I arrive at Brunnchen corner with 160 km/h [100 mph] for the left-hander. It is 50 km/h too fast! I fly off the road and crash the car 30 meters off the track, right under one of the old Nürburgring sections that had seen even the great Bernd Rosemeyer go off circuit in the past. I smashed the car completely. I tell you, it was a write-off! And my father-in-law rang to check our test progress, only to find I had done this. That was the end of my sedan car contract for that year...!"

In fact, he did great things for BMW in that private 1800 he had acquired earlier in the year, conquering Austria's national title with wins in Trento Bondone, Trieste, and Rossfeld mountain races. However, as we shall hear in a later chapter, Quester didn't always manage to keep even the most specialized of hillclimb BMW featherweights out of the scenery.

By 1967, BMW was engrossed in constructing pure racing engines, so touring-car racing took a back seat until the introduction of the 2002.

Way to go! Josef "Sepp" Schnitzer shows us how to power-slide any rear-drive BMW from the past thirty years. This is his 1966 German Championship-winning year on the circuits (this is probably a USAAF-zoned airbase track such as Wuntstorf) with a 2000TI, laying the foundation for a great privateer-factory partnership.

Picture: BMW Archiv, Munich, reprinted 1984

QUICK FACTS

Period
1963–67

Product
Forerunners to classic MPower motors prove explosive

Performance
From 250 bhp at 9,000 rpm to 330 bhp from 2 liters

Achievements
Initial standing-start world records; persistence in the face of tragic adversity; six European Championships won

People
Alex von Falkenhausen, Paul Rosche, Ludwig Apfelbeck, and a host of heroes, including Brian Redman

Chapter 9

Single-Seat Power

Developing four-cylinder power was an explosive business

Between 1973 and 1982, the BMW 2-liter four-cylinder development of the 1500 iron-block heart brought BMW the prestigious European Formula 2 Championship for drivers six times. Post-1973, after its initial works-only destiny had been fulfilled, the BMW Formula 2 (F2) unit was the first MPower motor to be made in Munich and sold by the hundred. It was always a competitive proposition, and it also served with distinction at the heart of those winged BMW 320 sedans.

Meeting the challenge of Renault (1976–77) and Honda V6s in the 1980s F2 racing seasons, until Formula 2 was replaced as Formula 1/Grand Prix racing's anteroom by Formula 3000 for 1985, BMW remained podium-placing competitive from 1970 to 1984. An unequaled record in the category, it must almost rank alongside Offenhauser's longevity in the old USAC days.

Much of this pace from the 16-valve, DOHC four was due to the fierce dedication of Paul Rosche, still designing more effective camshafts and remaining faithful to the BMW Motoren legend, even when Munich's directors forced him to run an illicit underground racing season! If engines have human fathers, then Paul Rosche was the parent for all the MPower generations.

The European roll of honor for the factory M12/7 BMW F2 power plant included pro-pelling the winning driver in 1973 (Jean-Pierre Jarier), 1974 (Patrick Depailler), and 1978 (Bruno Giacomelli). 1979 went to popular present-day BMW sporting ambassador Marc Surer, and BMW's final F2 victory—against all Ralt-Honda V6 odds—was scored in 1982 for Corrado Fabi.

International F2 rules changed in 1976 to admit racing engines that had no production link at all. Thus, motors like Renault's 24-valve V6 and Brian Hart's own 16-valve four-cylinder were admissible, along with the pedigree racing Honda V6s of the 1980s. Although the BMW unit was every centimeter a pure race motor, it still had the 2000/2002 iron-block production ancestry that all its rivals dispensed with in the creation of pedigree racing engines. So the BMW unit will always occupy a special place in race motor results.

Above, we listed only five of six BMW-badged titles, because they were all racked up by the M12/7 works engines in March single-seater race cars with alloy monocoques. The now-defunct UK race car constructors, March Engineering of Bicester, Oxfordshire, created chassis that were as logically labeled as BMW cars: a 732 was the 1973 F2 car while an 802 was the 1980 equivalent.

The sixth title went in 1975 to a non-works outfit with Jacques Laffite, a Grand Prix-grade driver (common practice in this era), in a Martini chassis powered by Schnitzer's fundamentally re-engineered S20/4 BMW 2-liter variant.

Competition four-cylinders

The four-cylinder competition engine was used with success in sports car racing and hillclimbing, sedan racing, and (to much less effect) in Formula 3. This basic four-cylinder design, dating back to von Falkenhausen's team in the late 1950s and early 1960s, has certainly served the company well. How did it begin to appear in formula racing cars?

The first such units were highly unofficial BMW SOHC engines in eight-valve form, proving themselves to privateers with a minimum of factory assistance. Best-known in the English-speaking world were the British Frank Nichols Elva sports racing cars. Yorkshireman Tony

Lanfranchi won the prestigious 1964 Autosport Championship for Elva-BMW. Elva coaxed a claimed 182 bhp at 7,200 rpm from the Bimmer motor, enough to race in the same second bracket as Jack Brabham. The Australian World Champion drove a BT8 equipped with a Grand Prix BRM 1.5-liter V8 and set faster lap times than Damon Hill's dad managed in a 1964 Ferrari GTO!

On the way to that title, a then-young Lanfranchi (who was still racing competitively at more than 60 years of age in the 1990s!) managed a magnificent third overall at Silverstone's heavyweight Martini Trophy meeting with the Elva Mk7-BMW. *Autosport* magazine ensured good publicity, and Lanfranchi's biography (see Bibliographical Notes) asserted, "Frank [Nichols of Elva] had some superb ideas. He was the first to bring BMWs into motorsport. Nobody even thought of getting BMW and doing something with it, but Frank did and did it well."

Frank Nichols then drew up and built five brand-new GT160-BMWs for 1964 of familiar

British chassis technique and German motor engineering have proved to be one of the most successful international motorsport combinations since the 1960s. The alliance of a Lotus chassis and a BMW engine actually preceded the better-known Elva sports racing and Lola-BMW; the Lotus 23-BMW tackled the mountainous continental hillclimbs in 1963.

Here we see a more basic Lotus-BMW single-seater combination: Willie Forbes winning the Jock McBain Memorial Trophy at Ingliston.

Picture: W.A. Henderson, Scotland, UK, September 1967

Here, the Ludwig Apfelbeck-patented 2-liter engine and cylinder head shows how the quad radial valve layout for each cylinder demanded an extraordinary head depth and complicated induction.

Pictures: Courtesy Chris Willows, 1997

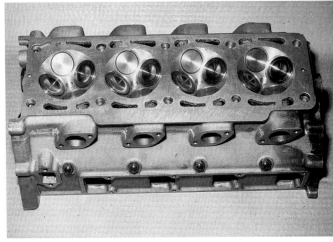

40-inch height (GT40), 1,200-lb weight, and claimed 160-mph capabilities. Unfortunately, Elva's commercial acumen did not match its competitive qualities, and the company did not see out the 1960s.

Actually, those damn foreigners were way ahead on utilizing BMW power in a sports racer, and they went for another English marque to do it: Lotus. Autosport reported in July 1963 that Anton Fischhaber had a new 1.8-liter motor enlarged to 2.0 liters and installed in the back of a mountain-climbing Lotus 23. Since the 1800 variant was not announced until September 1963, we can see that Willi Martini had excellent BMW factory contacts and had thought this British sports racer/BMW power combination through a season before Elva.

Martini and Fischhaber brought the Lotus 23-BMW to a fine fifth overall in the 1964 European Hillclimb Championship. This predicted an Anglo-German chassis/power plant alliance of the kind that would bring a lot more titles in the 1970s, 1980s and 1990s for March (F2), Brabham (F1/Grand Prix), and

McLaren (Global GT Racing), respectively.

Tony Lanfranchi's pioneering work with the 1964 Elva-BMW brought many more sports car racing clones and descendants. Usually these were 2-liter, two-valve Bimmers, popularized further when adopted as the basic power unit for Chevron's B8 international sports racing car. These units were the work of Chevron's Paul Owens and his team at the Bolton factory. They were capable of a reliable 180–190 bhp in 1968. BMW did lend Chevron a more powerful unit (slightly over 200 bhp), but that did not prove quite so reliable.

Driven by men like Chris Craft and Brian Redman, the Chevron B8-BMW proved capable of many class-winning performances on the international sports car endurance racing scene in the late 1960s, finishing as high as third overall in some full-blown multi-class internationals! In 1977, Osella, the Italian touring and sports car makers, won the 2-liter division of the World Championship series for Group 6 machines with BMW 2-liter, 16-valve power and Giorgio Franca driving.

So sports racing previewed MPower outside the sedan classes, but how did the company become involved with single-seaters? Paul Rosche recalled the first steps toward F2. "We had Ludwig Apfelbeck working in the BMW engineering department with us. He had much experience of four-valve-per-cylinder motorcycle speedway engines. He was always wanting to make a radial-valve engine for cars. First we make a one-cylinder of 500 cc; this gives 54 horsepower." Representing 108 bhp per liter, this was a very promising figure for the period, so BMW was encouraged to go further.

The Apfelbeck fours

During 1966, Munich made the first of the incredibly complex Apfelbeck four-cylinder engines at 2-liters, receiving approval from development director Klaus von Rucker. The cylinder block was the straight-forward BMW cast-iron one, and the complete race motor was coded M10 by the factory, "High and Heavy" by the laconic and shrewd Jack Brabham....

Eight carburetors had to be fitted, two per cylinder, and mounted at odd angles to fit in with the unique radially-opposed disposition of the valves. There were four valves per cylinder and, as well as the requirement for a carburetor on each side, there was also the need for

two exhausts per cylinder. The maze that was presented as each carburetor and exhaust dealt with one exhaust and inlet valve was horrific, especially to the pragmatic engineers of Munich who were used to simplicity in all but the original 328 motor layout.

Von Falkenhausen recalled that ex-KTM employee Apfelbeck was "a very good engineer...but he always had troubles to finish off his work." However, the engineering team did manage to complete the job. Later in 1966, Hahne and von Falkenhausen set off for Britain. Their mission was to buy a racing chassis in which to install the 2-liter wonder-motor and see how it worked away from the test bed.

In the test cell, an Apfelbeck behaved itself very well, and promised more power per liter than the Cosworth FVA, which was then being readied for the 1967 Formula 2 season (the Formula 2 category would go from 1 liter to 1.6 liters, top capacity). An obsolete Brabham 1965 Formula 1 chassis (which normally carried a Coventry Climax V8) was shipped to Germany. The Munich factory installed the engine, which was then producing 250–260 bhp at 9,000 rpm on gasoline.

In 1966 the Apfelbeck 2-liter engine was both tested and run in record-breaking trim at Hockenheim. Here, Hubert Hahne tries the Solex-carbureted Apfelbeck unit in the converted Brabham at the empty stadium. Lucas fuel injection was adopted for the racing 1600 version and subsequent hillclimb/sports car installations.

Picture: BMW Archiv, reprinted 1984

(Right) Puzzled and perplexed. Both Alex von Falkenhausen (with the silver hair) and Klaus Steinmetz (balding) trying to sort out the 2-liter Apfelbeck BMW unit installed within a Lola T110 for 1967/68 mountain-climbing duty.

(Left) Look at the onlookers in the background of the Steinmetz picture and you'll see one BMW fan with his hand to forehead in despair: he was not alone!

Pictures: BMW Archiv, reprinted 1978

Hahne took the new combination to a hillclimb near Innsbruck and won with it. Von Falkenhausen recalls, "Of course, we were very pleased...but it was only a small event, and to win a hillclimb you do not have to run the engine for long." Later in 1966, the converted Brabham felt the sharp twist of 330 bhp as BMW converted the 2-liter engine to run on nitromethane fuel for a number of world record attempts.

The first attempt was at Hockenheim, in September. Von Falkenhausen has good cause to remember the occasion, for he was driving: "I think this was perhaps the highest power output seen for a normal-aspiration 2-liter. I remember I was very worried because of this explosive fuel and the eight carburetors which kept spitting back. I was happy when it was all over, for I knew there was a good chance for an explosion with this banging from the carburetors."

Von Falkenhausen set an average speed of 128.581 km/h (80 mph) for the standing quarter-mile and Hubert Hahne took over to record 142.236 km (88 mph) for 500 meters. Later Hahne recorded 135.746 km/h for a kilometer. The kilometer figure was recorded after a trip to Monza had to be abandoned because of snow!

Serious 1.6-liter development through the winter saw the bored 1500 block equipped with the Apfelbeck head and Lucas fuel injection. The result was 225–228 bhp at 10,500 rpm, slightly more than Cosworth was declaring for its FVA, but there were severe development problems.

One basic setback was the fact that the 2-liter engine's 9,000 rpm had placed comparatively little stress on the valve gear. Running beyond 10,000 rpm brought a problem Paul Rosche described as "flexing in the double rockers." The valve gear was unreliable at higher crankshaft rpm and this weakness was to haunt the Apfelbeck design during its 1.6-liter competition life.

The Lola T100

For the 1967 season, von Falkenhausen, Hahne, and new team manager Klaus Steinmetz (later to have his own Opel-tuning business) ventured to England again to buy their chassis. They came away with plans to compete four Lola T100 monocoque chassis. A pair would be entered by Lola Racing—a John Surtees operation—for the English motorcycle and car World Champion to drive with people like Chris Irwin, Andrea de Adamich, and David Hobbs. The second pair would be driven

The 1967 hillclimb season featured Dieter Quester in the BMW 2000-labeled Lola T110 with Apfelbeck BMW power. His first outing ended in a crash, an experience repeated in Formula 2 and touring-car racing when first trying these categories in factory machines. This combination—seen in June that year—notched up a trio of third places in that year's European championship.

That hillcimb Lola-BMW slides under the power-oversteer exuberance that Quester applied to the Apfelbeck 8-trumpet motor, which we see in static detail as a shiny newcomer. With and without bodywork, the G767 BMW "Monti" Bergspyder flattered the 2-liter Apfelbeck engine, as we can see in these stunning side and top studies.

Pictures: Courtesy Auto-sport, June 1967; BMW Archiv, Courtesy Chris Willows, 1997

primarily by Jo Siffert and Hubert Hahne, entered by BMW themselves, and run from Germany.

In addition, a slightly modified (later comprehensively altered) Lola T100 sports car chassis was used to contest the European Hillclimb Championship and some sports car races in Germany and Austria. In 1967–68, European hillclimbing (Germans call it mountain climbing, which is more accurate) was the province of leading-edge-technology teams from Ferrari and Porsche.

While the factory was wrestling with the problems of the radially-disposed valve gear in 1,600-cc Formula 2 form, Quester attacked the 1967 European Hillclimb Championship series in the reworked BergSpyder BMW 2-liter. That Lola-BMW had a sharply defined "waist" behind the cockpit, hiding its parentage well. Quester vividly recalls doing 200 km/h (124 mph) through the woods in these skinny devices, all of which tried to emulate the flyweights of the works Porsches. Under the Group 7 prototype regulations, as Americans saw in Can Am, you could do almost anything.

Quester reported, "In 1967, Porsches had deadly rivals Gerhard Mitter and Rolf Stommelen, Ferrari fielded Ludovico Scarfiotti, Mario Casoni, and Gunther 'Bobby' Klass, but Bobby was killed in a practice accident, which shows you how dangerous it was."

The BMW works driver for this Europa Bergmeisterschaft effort was Quester, who recalled, "Later in 1966, I was allowed back as a works driver [following his 1800TI adventures at Nürburgring, as discussed in the previous chapter] with the monumental Apfelbeck 16-valve motor. It then produced about 260 bhp in a 522-kg [1,148-lb] total weight in one of the most elegant and best cars I have driven for BMW, but we started off with another catastrophe!

"In my first event with the car—it was in the Styria region of Austria—I crash. This time it's Klaus Steinmetz, the new BMW team manager, I have to tell! After this, all the races were

okay, and we finish fourth in the championship. But it's unbelievably dangerous, this sport. There are chips and stones all over the road...hard stone walls...and enormous drops to the ground below!"

Despite his feelings, Quester was one of the few to shine in anything but a Porsche or a Ferrari during 1967 mountain climbs. The young Austrian and his silver-finished "Monti" collected third overall results at Mont Ventoux in France, Ollon Villars in Switzerland, and the Austrian Gaisberg climb in 1966. Hahne took a third at one event as well, but none of it was enough to disturb the brilliant Gerhard Mitter in his flat-eight-cylinder Porsche hillclimb car, which won the title and seven of the eight rounds counting towards this 2-liter title!

The cars were very, very special. Quester remembered that the Porsches used every lightweight material known—titanium, magnesium, and beryllium brake discs were features in a rival Alfa Romeo. When the legendary Porsche family member and later Audi-VW engineer/director Dr. Ferdinand Piech arrived at an event, the Porsche entry was not light enough for his taste.

By 1968, the Porsche 909 hillclimb development of the 908 had a super-light spaceframe, just 15 liters (about 4 US gallons) of fuel for the 280 bhp flat eight and only 380 kg (836 lbs) curb weight. That is a power-to-weight ratio of 700 bhp a ton, Grand Prix talk for many years....At this stage, BMW still carried 430 kg-plus, was blessed with a large rear wing, and ran 253–260 bhp.

Quester managed to rack up four second places during 1968, and was second overall to Rolf Stommelen's super-Porsche 909 in the European Bergmeisterschaft with the rebodied and lightened (by 92 kg/202 lbs) BergSpyder.

Quester's second places came at Rossfeld in Germany, Cesana-Sestriere in Italy, Freiburg-Schauinsland in Germany, and at the Gaisberg climb on the outskirts of Salzburg. He did have a chance for the overall 1968 title, but had to

By 1968, the factory and Quester had produced this modified version of the Lola-Apfelbeck BMW. Quester raced it with considerable success in Austria and Germany, enjoying some encounters with the Porsche-mounted Jo Siffert.

Picture: BMW Archiv, reprinted 1978

miss the last hillclimb round in a successful effort to secure his first European Touring Car Championship with the 2002 in Spain.

Bumpy road ahead

The opening 1967 races in the new Formula 2 were in Britain, at Snetterton and Silverstone. In von Falkenhausen's words, BMW's Easter weekend debut was "a fiasco." Surtees tried both Cosworth and the BMW-engined T100s, and elected to drive the Cosworth version, leaving Irwin to tackle the BMW-powered car. Unfortunately, Irwin was involved in a startline crash in the second heat at Snetterton and severely damaged the top of the tall radial-valve motor, leading to retirement. Hahne finished well back, "looking a bit lost on the wide open spaces of Snetterton," according to one contemporary report.

Siffert came to drive the sole remaining car at Silverstone on Bank Holiday Monday. It didn't make any difference: the Swiss ace

could only manage twelfth overall in the first heat. The second heat was a low point, as *Motor Sport* reported: "The BMW people were not feeling in the same happy mood, their 16-valve engine not approaching the Cosworth engine, and they gave the second part of the race a miss and crept away."

Subsequent factory investigation showed that test cell horsepower was not matched by the second and third Apfelbeck 1.6s, which raced with just 205 and 206 bhp. What was the problem? According to von Falkenhausen, it was "...the dry-sump system working very well—too well! The oil is staying up in the cores and the engine is losing power as it tries for the highest engine revs through the oil." That was a specific installation setback, but they also had to tackle the problem of an excessively peaky power band. It was not until they had a 2-liter readied for the 1973 season that the importance of torque, rather than impressive bhp figures, was fully realized.

Von Falkenhausen subsequently confirmed that BMW's conventional parallel-valve (as per Cosworth) motors had won regularly with the

April 1967: the 1600 Apfelbeck engine with fuel injection makes its debut in Britain with a Lola T100 chassis. This is one of the works-entered cars. John Surtees also had two such Lola-BMWs that season, but it was a very troubled year for both the factory and the English effort, Surtees reverting to a Lola-Cosworth FVA. Note how tall and complicated the four-cylinder engine is, resembling a V8. It seems there was a small test-bed power advantage over its rivals, but when installed within a racing car and asked to perform at over 9,000 rpm, both the valve gear and lubrication systems were troublesome.

Also shown, a revealing contemporary shot of the treaded Dunlop racing tire that preceded the universal adoption of slicks (abandoned in favour of grooved tires for 1998 Grand Prix). The attractively-chromed but skinny Lola front suspension and gridded pedals were normal practice decades before inboard rocker-arm suspension became the norm in most single-seater formulae.

Pictures: Courtesy Autosport, 1967

Other scenes from that British Silverstone debut: the Apfelbeck 1.6-liter Formula 2 with Jo Siffert at the wheel, at speed through Copse corner; and Siffert in conversation with Hubert Hahne.

Pictures: Courtesy Chris Willows, 1997

same or less bhp than the opposition in the 1970s and 1980s, but with more available torque. This was a hard lesson to learn in a purpose-built race car and engine combination, but BMW learned it the hard way. Its full F2 specification M12/7 motors did have more accessible power—even more than Ford Cosworth motors in rally trim.

In April 1967, BMW's troubled team was at Nürburgring for a non-championship race around the shorter (4.76-mile/7.69-km) Sudschliefe, the southern loop to the main 14.2-mile circuit. "After practice, the directors were not happy," an insider recalled. "They telegrammed to withdraw the cars, but then the organizers said this could not be done. Finally, Surtees was second in the race results and Hahne was fourth." Siffert had been lying sixth, but he crashed in this event, which was dogged by persistent snow.

(Top Left) John Surtees tries diametral power in the Lola and does not look pleased. Today, his relationship with BMW is extremely cordial, Surtees having elegantly preserved examples of both a supercharged 1930s motorcycle and the fabulous 507 sports car.

(Bottom Left) meanwhile, with an umbrella and the prospect of a wet run around the Nürburgring, Hubert Hahne is shown in the Dornier-Diametral chassis.

(Right) we also have the atmospheric sight of Hubert Hahne out in the original Lola T100-Apfelbeck BMW at Nürburgring in April 1967, when collapsed suspension terminated play!

Pictures: LAT; BMW Archiv/Courtesy Chris Willows; Fast Man-Fast Car postcard series from Sebring Sportsspiegel

In May 1967, Lola Racing in England stated that it would not be running its BMW-engined cars—at least, not until late June, when the Reims Formula 2 championship round was to be held. Lola said an intensive development program would be pursued.

The Apfelbeck BMWs did appear at Reims, driven by Siffert and Hahne. However, they proved uncompetitive in practice, and the valve gear gave way. Only Hahne had an engine for the last day of practice! The Munich men went home before the race, but Chris Irwin did compete—only to retire after the engine was seen to be "...blowing a lot of its valves and parts out through exhaust pipes," in the words of *Motor Sport*.

Englishman David Hobbs captured BMW's second best result of 1967 in the Formula 2 division of the August German Grand Prix. He was third in the Surtees-run Lola-BMW, a promising omen for his subsequent services to BMW in the US as driver of the McLaren Turbo 320, among others. However, only four other class rivals finished.

How von Falkenhausen must have wished for the 2-liter limit to come to Formula 2, for in the German Grand Prix, Hahne participated a second time (in 1966, he drove a Tyrrell Matra-BRM 1-liter) and the 2-liter version of the engine went well to qualify thirteenth fastest, among the full Formula 1 cars. He was tenth slower than a troubled Graham Hill in the Lotus 49.

Hahne was up to ninth in the race, but the front suspension of the Lola collapsed after seven laps. It showed more promise than expected, but was overshadowed by Jacky Ickx's performance in the Tyrrell-Matra F2 1.6-liter Cosworth FVA. The Belgian was fourth overall among the F1s at one stage and set the third fastest practice time overall, which said a lot about Jacky Ickx, the power of the FVA and the agility of the Matra chassis. BMW took note, and Ickx was subsequently hired in both single-seaters and sedans.

At the end of 1967, BMW's first full-year in Formula 2, they could have been forgiven for quitting. There were no outright international wins. The company's official history from 1972 does show a victory for Surtees at Mallory Park early in the year, but this placing was scored in the Lola-FVA! The best placings were those non-championship results at the April Eifelrennen, when Surtees was second, and the Hobbs result in the German Grand Prix. The cars were brought out again, late season, but both Hahne and Siffert found it impossible to finish any better than the lower half of the top ten, even when the car did run reliably.

BMW was in good company. Ferrari had also hoped to contest the superiority of the Cosworth FVA, but the Ford-financed engine made mincemeat out of Maranello opposition as well as that from Munich.

QUICK FACTS

Period

1968–70

Products

Diametral valve layout to "Cosworth" quad-valver, Lola to Dornier chassis, big wings, and still the changes kept coming

Performance

Diametral layouts gave 220 bhp to 252 bhp at 10,700 rpm, all with the 1.6-liter

Achievements

Now a winner; less powerful (248 bhp) conventional valve layout boosts accessible power and race results/durability further

People

Hubert Hahne, Dieter Quester, and the usual suspects

Chapter 10

European Formula 2 Racing

Borrowed principles lead to success

Although the 1968 season did not bring anything concrete in the way of results in international Formula 2, both the engine's technicians and Lola produced new ideas to try to increase the effectiveness of the Munich company's challenge to the almost all-conquering Cosworth FVA.

Late in 1968, BMW reappeared with the Lola T102 monocoque—which had a tubular subframe at the rear—and a completely new cylinder-head layout for the 1,600-cc motor. The Apfelbeck radial valve layout was dropped, but the engine was still unusual. There were triple spark plugs and four valves per cylinder, but the valves were transposed so that, on each side of the combustion chamber, they had one inlet and one exhaust (the conventional method is to have the inlets on one side and exhausts on the other).

The BMW layout meant that a fuel injector was necessary on either side of each cylinder, as was an exhaust, sandwiching the heavily-divided vee of the twin overhead-camshaft rocker cover. Externally, it could be mistaken for a very narrow-angle V8. Another complication was that the three spark plugs per cylinder were placed transversely across the quad-valve chambers.

The engine made its debut at Hockenheim on October 13 and was known as the "Diametral," from the diametrically opposed disposition of the valves—inlet diagonally opposite inlet and exhaust diagonally opposite its counterpart on the opposite bank. Then, peak power was quoted as 220 bhp at 10,500 rpm, compared with Cosworth's 215 bhp at 9,200 rpm. Unfortunately, Quester still described the pulling power as inferior to a Ford-Cosworth, especially those supplied to his countryman, Jochen Rindt.

BMW also tried to assist its Lola's straight line speed at Hockenheim by the provision of side fairings, but these were only used in practice. With Siffert and Hahne driving the Lola T102-BMW, the new motor scored finishes for Hahne in both the Wurtemburg Preis at Hockenheim (seventh overall) and the Grand Prix di Roma (tenth). Siffert failed to finish.

Another new feature to arrive during 1968 was the wing. Wending its way down from Formula 1, the Formula 2 cars took to aerofoils in a pretty big way, many of the cars running in the bi-plane form that Jack Brabham popularized in the premier league. BMW incorporated the sophistication of electrical adjustment for the rear wing of the Lola. The wings only

(Top Right) 1969 was the year of bodywork experiments for BMW. Here is the monstrous tall rear wing on car 14 used at Jarama, Spain.

(Top Left) The result of such tall wings folding up in GP racing (notably at Barcelona) can be seen in the BMW version of post-wing aerodynamic bodywork as Siffert drives car 5.

(Bottom Left) The unumbered car at rest is the 1970 Dornier, which retained its full aluminum monocoque and started the season with the triple-plug-per-cylinder Diametral rated at 240 bhp from 1.6 liters (its ultra short stroke, 64.2 x 89-mm stroke and bore, allowing 150 bhp per liter), which ran to 10,000 rpm.

Pictures: LAT, Spain and Germany; BMW Archiv

Brave result.
Hubert Hahne slith-
ers through
Nürburgring's
Karussel concrete at
the 1968 German
Grand Prix.
Equipped with the
2-liter Apfelbeck
BMW motor, mount-
ed in the Lola chas-
sis, Hahne was
impressive. In dia-
bolical conditions,
he finished tenth in
a field composed
mainly of 3-liter
Grand Prix
machines with V8
power, beating four
of them. Talk of the
day was Jackie
Stewart's record-
breaking margin of
outright victory:
more than four
minutes!

*Picture: LAT, Germany,
August 1968; reprint-
ed 1978*

faded into sensible proportions after the Rindt-Hill near-tragedy at Barcelona in the Spanish Grand Prix of 1969, which resulted in wings being cut back severely for several seasons. There was also an incident within the BMW team when Siffert ended up with a particularly big rear wing around his ears!

In 1968, BMW ran the Apfelbeck motor again, with Hahne appearing in the 2-liter Lola once more at the German Grand Prix. It was a wet and foggy last outing for the racing version of the Apfelbeck unit in that August 4 classic. Jackie Stewart (Matra Ford Cosworth V8) dominated the race, finishing over ten minutes ahead of the BMW. Stewart was even four minutes ahead of second home man Graham Hill (Lotus-Ford V8), the biggest winning margin seen in modern Grand Prix. The Stewart drive was only recently paralleled by Michael Schumacher's 1996 Spanish Grand Prix mastery for Ferrari.

Though it was pouring with rain and Hahne's knowledge of the 'Ring was unparalleled, 2 liters was not enough against the now better-sorted 3-liter Formula 1 cars. In practice, the car was third from the back of the grid (10

minutes 42.9 seconds), but they could take some comfort from finishing tenth overall out of fourteen finishers. Hahne was the last driver to go the full distance ahead of four full 3-liter Grand Prix cars.

The 1969 season was to prove much better for BMW, although the engine was still not as reliable as the Cosworth. In fact, it could still be very unreliable. BMW engine changes became the toast of Formula 2 paddocks all over Europe until later the following year.

An early-season second overall for Hahne at Hockenheim disguised how much he disliked the Lola's handling. In this fraught second round of the 1969 European Formula 2 Championship, slipstreaming was so intense that timekeepers had to add up the results of two heats to find that Hahne had failed to beat Jean-Pierre Beltoise's Matra-FVA by just 0.61 seconds. Beltoise feigned engine failure on the last lap, braking in front of Hahne, so as to get the towing slipstream game right and lead across the line. The 80,000-strong crowd was not amused, but things looked better for BMW MPower.

In Bavaria, they do not just brew legendary beers. The now-elderly Lola chassis was to be

It looks as though he is enjoying himself, but Hubert Hahne actually elected to drive the Lola chassis in preference to the Dornier when the aircraft company's chassis was first produced for a race.

Picture: LAT, Hockenheim, Germany, 1969

replaced by a Len Terry-designed monocoque fabricated at the Dornier airplane factory, some twenty kilometers outside of Munich. Externally, the cars did not look too different, but the lines of the new monocoque were sharper and flatter, especially around the nose cone. The monocoque now extended to the rear, on both sides of the engine, and was carried up above the driver's legs in the cockpit. The suspension was made up of conventional double wishbones with parallel links at the rear. Oil and water radiators were mounted in what was the conventional nose position of the time.

For the third round of the series, one Dornier-built, BMW-powered monocoque appeared at Nürburgring. As it was so new, Gerhard Mitter drove this car, which also carried wings like that of its Lola brethren. Siffert qualified his Lola-BMW on its first pole position (9 minutes 3.8 seconds), Hahne's similar car managed 9 minutes 20.5 seconds, and Mitter's Dornier, complete with its huge lattice-work construction to support the grotesque rear wing, did 9 minutes 27.6 seconds. Both Lolas ran well in the race and finished second

(Siffert) and fourth (Hahne). The Dornier had to be retired when the steering failed.

The fourth round of the series saw only Hahne appearing. The curly-headed German tried the Dornier chassis in practice at the Jarama circuit, but found it too much of a clinging fit and opted for a steady drive to fifth place in the Lola.

The next race was a non-championship round, which was just as well, for all three BMW entries retired at Zolder in Belgium. They were not well-placed on the grid for this June race, but Dieter Quester made his now-traditional BMW team debut. Driving in Formula 2 for the first time, he rammed Hahne under braking.

This was also the first time Kugelfischer injection had been used on a Diametral engine, easily identifiable from a casual exterior glance, as the inlet trumpets were now in metal instead of fiberglass. Siffert used the Dornier on this occasion, but succumbed to the other big Dornier problem they still had to fully conquer: that of persistent overheating. At this stage, with over-140°C oil temperatures, retirements

Jo Siffert at Thruxton in 1969 with the adjustable wing and vestigial front wings on the Dornier BMW. His best result of the year was a second at the Nürburgring for BMW.

Picture: LAT, England, April 1969

were frequent, but the later aerodynamic changes made things even worse. Temperatures of up to 170°C were not unheard of before the inevitable retirements.

A pair of Dorniers were on hand for the next weekend's non-championship Formula 2 race at Hockenheim. Hahne disliked his so much that, after practice, he opted for the old Lola chassis to be brought back up for him from Munich. Despite his indiscretion, Quester was Hahne's teammate, destined for retirement when the clutch packed up. Hahne justified his selection of car by finishing second yet again at Hockenheim. Brian Hart, of subsequent engine-building fame, was the brainy winner.

Because of cancellations, the European championship provided only seven rounds that year. At the fifth round, in Austria, Hahne managed to pick up seventh place overall. He arrived at what was to be the penultimate round—on the Sicilian Enna circuit in late August—with a six-point lead in the ungraded driver's championship (graded Formula 1 drivers and the like not being eligible to score European title points).

At the fast Sicilian track (which is adjacent to a lake full of snakes!), the works BMWs appeared with fully streamlined bodywork for Hahne's Dornier chassis. BMW debuted its streamliner back in June for a non-championship event at Reims in France, which Siffert led at one stage. Hahne did not even make the start of the critical Sicilian race. In practice, the luckless Hahne hit a crash barrier pretty hard, breaking his foot.

Three Formula 2 machines were entered for the German Grand Prix on August 3, in which there was the traditional Formula 2 section. The drivers were Quester, Hahne, and Mitter. The cars went well in the first session, with Hahne recording the fastest time in the division (8 minutes 24.7 seconds), but in the second practice session, hillclimb hero Mitter crashed at more than 150 mph on the downhill sweep from Flugplatz, with fatal results.

Since there was a strong suspicion that a chassis component was responsible for an accident occuring at this point on the track (and as a mark of respect), the remaining BMWs were withdrawn. As von Falkenhausen later said to

"That's stuffed that...." Hubert Hahne's championship ambitions in the 1969 European F2 series were ended by this crash at Enna-Pergusa Circuit, Sicily. The young German broke a foot and finished runner-up in the Championship.

Picture: LAT/Mike Doodson, Italy; reprinted 1978

me, "It was not easy being the racing director for BMW." Apparently the team manager shared these views, for Klaus Steinmetz left BMW before the end of the season.

Hahne did recover to contest the final round of the European Formula 2 series at Vallelunga, Rome, on October 12. He lasted until the eleventh lap of the first of two heats when, in Motor Sport reporter Michael Doodson's words, "Hahne slewed sideways on one of the fastest of the bumpy circuit's corners...." The result was a comprehensive accident involving three other cars, including Quester's sister BMW.

Johnny Servoz Gavin (Matra MS7) won the race on aggregate, and the overall European title, leaving Hahne and BMW as runners-up. This was their reward for attending all the rounds, for Hahne's driving was inconsistent,

as was the reliability and preparation of the BMW task force in the 1969 F2 season.

Preparations for 1970 included pre-season testing of the Dornier chassis with designer Len Terry to sort out some of the handling deficiencies and to spot any structural weakness, as there had been three worrying crashes the previous season. After three years' effort, some progress had been made, but with the death of Mitter the previous season, some BMW directors (particularly sales wizard Paul Hahnemann) were unhappy about continuing in single-seater racing. Von Falkenhausen summed up his feelings after Mitter's death by saying, "It was not the car that was to blame, or the driver—it was the circuit. Nürburgring is not safe for this kind of racing—it's too long a distance for medical help to arrive quickly."

Victory at last

BMW drivers for the 1970 season would be drawn from Quester, Siffert, Jacky Ickx, and Hahne. Hahne was not felt to be in top form in 1970, and sedans were felt to be more suitable to his talents. 1970 was his last year of international racing for BMW, but Armin Hahne continued the family tradition in the 1980s and 1990s with rides for TWR Rover and BMW.

Hubert Hahne did not go out like a lamb. On June 14, 1970, he and the BMW team achieved the result they had been looking for since they started the single-seater project. That was the date on which Hahne beat Brian Hart by the same margin as the Englishman had defeated him by in 1969. Just 0.3 seconds separated Hahne and Hart, the BMW power unit winning its first outright international victo-

ry at an average of 115.63 mph (186 km/h) despite the presence of two chicanes inserted to slow down the cars on the Hockenheimring.

For the crowd and the team, it was a victory worth waiting for. The BMW factory had acquired a March Formula 2 chassis, and this helped Dornier with its 1970 chassis modifications. The modified chassis was simply dubbed a BMW (Hahne's was a 269, but the BMW 270 became the norm that season), and it represented an enormous amount of work and expenditure. Now that the three-plug engine was proving reliable, there was the chance for some results.

In late June, at Rouen in France, Jo Siffert's 270 won BMW its first European title points-scoring round. This win was an awe-inspiring, one-man war against the best in Formula 2 at the time. Siffert beat Ronnie Peterson and Jack Brabham by a tenth in his heat, then led by

The Kugelfischer mechanical injection system served BMW well in many applications. It is seen here in the winning Dornier 270 design of August 1970, feeding the third primary 1.6-liter engine created by BMW for European Formula 2: the basis for the subsequent 2-liter M12/7 series.

Picture: LAT, Salzburgring, Austria, August 1970; reprinted 1984

Peterson's March for five of the last six laps in the final. Peterson made a last-lap mistake that let Siffert win by a tenth over Clay Regazzoni's Tecno-FVA, subsequent IndyCar and World Champion Emerson Fittipaldi's Lotus-FVA, and Jacky Ickx, who ended up in fourth place. Ickx was just seven-tenths of a second behind the leader after 100 miles of heart-stopping racing.

With no touring-car racing to distract BMW Rennsport division—Alpina had been charged with the responsibility of defending the 1600 and 2002's sporting repute in 1970—development accelerated. Quester recalled, "It was so much easier for the factory to work with Dornier locally than it had been with Lola in England, especially for testing. Now problems could be examined and finished at the factory. The result was a better-handling car, a car much easier to drive fast than the touring cars, or the old design."

BMW Rennsport still suffered major engine failures on occasion. They managed to fit in a second/third overall for Siffert and Ickx—just outfumbled by Regazzoni in a slipstreaming contest at Enna—before unveiling what BMW engine technicians had been working for so long to perfect.

The date for the first Formula 2 race on the recently-opened Salzburgring in Austria was August 30, 1970. Bolted in the engine bay of the Ickx BMW 270 was the familiar BMW 1,600-cc block, but it was topped by a third and final cylinder-head configuration. BMW had bowed to convention: the 16-valve engine featured two inlet and two exhaust values per side of the combustion chamber, usually with one central spark plug. This motor was dubbed the *Parallel Ventiler Motoren* (Parallel Valve Motor) and was coded M12/2.

Cynics and some company insiders dubbed the parallel valver as "the Cosworth" layout, since the basics were the same. But Cosworth would not claim to have invented the classic 4-valve, DOHC, pent-roof combustion chamber

Jacky Ickx was a top Grand Prix driver, capable of beating the best in 1970. Here, he hustles the BMW 270 into oversteer through the Thruxton complex of slower corners. Ickx finished sixth, best of the four-car squad from BMW, after a tardy start to the final.

Picture: LAT, England, April 1970; reprinted 1978

For the simpler, and later, Formula 2, an alternative layout of conventional 16-valves was complicated by a triple-spark-plug-per-cylinder layout, plus an appropriate cam-driven distributor layout. It (and later twin-spark-plug variants of the M12) was abandoned for a single-spark-plug layout in 1973.

Picture: LAT, reprinted 1984

Historic for BMW fans and sad occasion for race fans everywhere: BMW's first F2 win and Jochen Rindt's last. Rindt died a week later at the Monza Grand Prix. August 31, 1970 was a winning debut for the third and final BMW four-cylinder F2 engine specification. Colloquially known as the parallel-valve motor, it reverted to the conventional layout of valves and required only one set of Kugelfischer injectors, placed opposite the four-into-one exhaust system.

Using the "Moby Dick" bodywork, Jacky Ickx is seen taking the BMW 270 chassis to victory at Salzburgring in Austria; second on aggregate was Quester in the 269 model. Second here is Jochen Rindt, the great Austrian Posthumous World Champion for Lotus, who won a heat in this home event with the works Lotus 69-FVA. Rindt is pursued by Lotus teammate Graham Hill, father to 1996 World Champion Damon Hill.

Picture: LAT, Austria, August 1970; reprinted 1978

layout. They did, however, refine four valves per cylinder to new levels of efficiency, becoming increasingly relevant to production engines requiring maximum power versus low fuel consumption and efficient emissions.

Externally, the new engine bore little resemblance to the old. The cast-alloy head casting still carried a deeply divided vee between the overhead camshafts, the whole engine being vertically installed rather than at the usual slant of the production cylinder block. The injection was mounted to the right and the exhaust to the left (looking from the back of the car forward).

Internally, the exhaust valves were left at the same diameter used on the Diametral, but the inlet diameter of the valve heads went down from 38 mm to 35.8 mm. The basic configuration, with gear-driven overhead camshafts, was to be a feature of both 1,600- and 2,000-cc versions of the BMW 16-valve, four-cylinder motors. When the Parallel Valve BMW cylinder head was introduced, the Diametral 16-valver

was producing 252 bhp at a screaming 10,700 rpm and 14 Kh/sq cm BMEP at 9,000 rpm. The conventional valve layout gave 248 bhp at 10,300 rpm and 14.65 Kh/sq cm BMEP at 8,500 rpm. Bore and stroke of the last BMW 1600 Formula 2 design was 89 mm x 64.2 mm.

Thus, the double ration of fuel injectors and exhaust pipes (and Diametral engine) was almost obsolete, for Ickx managed to win the two-part Festspiel-preis von Salzburg by 1.8 seconds over Vittorio Brambilla's Brabham-FVA, using the new Parallel Valve unit. Quester was third overall. Two weeks later, Ickx used the same engine cylinder-head layout to beat Jack Brabham and François Cevert (Tecno-FVA) at another Austrian event at Tulln-Langelebarn in late June. Brabham had led but suffered motor trouble.

Why did BMW adopt parallel valves when the Diametral was winning? Rosche explained some years later, "The test bed is not the same as racing. The Diametral engine had more power, but the parallel-head design we used and won races with at the end of 1970 had better response, ran more smoothly, and there was more torque—less power, it's true, but more torque. It had a better power curve than we had before. So, we discovered that the power curve is more important than a small difference in maximum power. We suspected the reason was that combustion was more complete and stable than was possible with the Diametral valve layout."

Now relying on BMW's own chassis expertise and the provision of its own aerodynamic bodywork for the faster tracks, the cars truly became BMWs. According to contemporary accounts, they were faster than the Cosworth opposition, and just as reliable as one could expect of a racing four-cylinder engine spending much of its life on the noisier side of 10,000 rpm.

The team was now managed largely by engineer/driver Dieter Basche in place of Steinmetz. It had every reason to look forward

to 1971, the closing year of 1,600-cc capacity Formula 2, with great confidence. The three-plug Diametral sounded its own death knell on September 27, 1970, when two of the engines had piston failures and Ickx had alternator trouble. Ickx, however, proved to be in top form—he was then winning races for Ferrari in Formula 1 as well—by snatching the fastest lap at the Italian Imola track. BMW had not been overawed by Hahne's driving during the season. His retirement from the BMW team and racing was announced in September.

On October 11, 1970, the factory sent two cars to contest the last round of the European Formula 2 series. Held at Hockenheim, the event naturally attracted all the top championship runners, though BMW preferred to send just the ungraded Dieter Quester with a parallel valve BMW 270, while Dieter Basche stepped into the driving seat of an older machine.

Quester qualified right up at the front and became involved in an almighty tussle with

The Dornier BMWs were retained by the factory and snoozed together in the 1990s Motorsport collection, alongside retired E30 Junior Team 3-ers, original race M3s, and E36's M3GTR of 1993: the machine that inspired the winning PTG North American program of 1995–97.

Picture: Klaus Schnitzer, Munich, 1996

Clay Regazzoni's Tecno-FVA. As a former sedan driver, Quester was absolutely determined to make the grade in single-seaters, and he was the only member of the team who had not, so far, won a race for BMW in that year.

The result was the physical clash of two wills and their attendant cars as they entered the giant Hockenheim stadium on the last lap. There was no way that Regazzoni was going to give way, while Quester could hear—yes, even through the protective clothing and the raucous engine noise—the crowd cheering him along. The two cars bounced off each other and the track!

Quester gathered his wits together and managed to persuade his car to move before Regazzoni's, limping through the infield, on the track, and over the line 1.7 seconds ahead of

"Regga." It was an astonishing and appropriate end to the 1.6-liter European Formula 2 series.

It was also to be the last time that a BMW Formula car in factory colors won, or appeared at, a European Championship round. So it was also appropriate that team manager Basche should have driven himself into seventh overall in the other car.

Clay Regazzoni won the Championship chase by forty-four points to the thirty-five of subsequent quintuple Le Mans winner Derek Bell. Emerson Fittipaldi was third with twenty-five points, and Quester tied with Ronnie Peterson in fourth place with fourteen points. The only other ungraded BMW driver—Ickx and Siffert were graded Grand Prix stars—was Hahne, and he finished down in fourteenth position.

QUICK FACTS

Period
1970–84

Products
M12/3 to M12/7 pure Formula 2 race engines

Performance
Final M12/7-1 reaches 321 bhp at 10,200 rpm from 2 liters (160.1 bhp a liter); late 1970s March BMW tests 0–62 mph in 3.5 seconds, 0–100 mph in 6.6 seconds

Achievements
Staying 17 years in the game until the End-Game! Last of six European Formula 2 titles taken in 1982

People
The underground fighters versus BMW establishment leads to a commercial business selling over racing motors and more than 200 single-seater thoroughbreds; Corrado Fabi of Italy is the last BMW-powered European Champion (1982); Philippe Streiff of France wins the last F2 event for BMW in September 1984

Chapter 11

The Winning Years: 1970-84

BMW becomes the dominant force in European Formula 2 racing

Experts predicted that the fastest combination for 1971 would be the March chassis and the BMW engine, and development along these lines was to be part of the factory's works schedule. Only nine days after Quester's 1970 Hockenheim win, the bombshell fell.

On Tuesday, October 20, 1970, the directors of Bayerische Motoren Werke AG, Munchen announced the company's withdrawal from motorsports. No reason was officially given, and it was also said that the four team cars and their twelve engines, plus associated spares, would not be available for privateers. The decision was to be implemented at the close of the 1970 season.

Recalling the shock, von Falkenhausen commented, "I think it was the death of Mitter that did this. Even though it was the year before, it makes bad publicity for BMW and, of course, the directors do not like this." Certainly, it seemed that the directors were worried, especially the influential Paul Hahnemann.

BMW itself was working all-out, starting to make full use of the Glas facility it had acquired at Dingolfing in 1966 and completely rebuilt through 1968. Production exceeded 160,000 cars in 1971, so the directors had

become blasé about motorsports' significance, particularly as the death of a national hero such as Gerhard Mitter had undone much of the good publicity acquired by BMW's competition resurgence.

On Sunday, October 25, 1970, the team traveled to one of the suburbs in Munich, to the Neubiberg airfield, for a ten-lap race to pay tribute to the company's achievements. A similar event had been held the year before, and Peter Westbury's private Brabham-FVA had just managed to beat Quester's BMW.

This time, no chances were taken, and the event's status was changed to allow BMW to run the 270 in prototype 2-liter form. That 400-cc gain was coded as M12/3, utilizing an 89.2 x 80-mm bore and briefly developing 270 bhp at this stage. That debutante expired in practice, but Quester was still on pole using Dieter Basche's 1600 crossflow, F2-engined 270. By the end of the 1,600-cc formula, the BMW engine was developing between 250 and 255 bhp regularly and reliably.

Quester won the race comfortably over Vittorio Brambilla and Westbury in their Brabhams, the BMW averaging 94.14 mph in its last European victory, an affair dubbed the "Straw Castle" races because of numerous intrusive chicanes. All the BMW mechanics wore black armbands, and a shroud—complete with company emblem—was laid over the victorious car afterwards! The BMW did race again, but in a rather exotic, non-championship event. The Macau Grand Prix was a rather grand title for the race run in that Portuguese colony, and Quester was an easy winner against local opposition.

The winners go underground

Did all competition stop because the directors had said it would? Myth says that the Germans obey orders without question—would the team who won seven events in 1970, plus one second-place and two third-place titles, be content to fade from the scene, just when things were going right?

Dieter Quester, Paul Rosche, and two mechanics (Walter Schmid and Fritz Gruber) went out and hired themselves a small garage in the northern suburbs of Munich. Quester had attracted sponsorship from Eifelland, the German caravan purveyors, and with their cash he purchased a new Formula 2 March 712 and a Mercedes transporter. For power, Quester had mysterious access to two of the twelve late-1970, parallel-valve, crossflow 1.6-liter engines with 255 bhp potential.

I did not inquire as to how these engines escaped out of the factory gates, but von Falkenhausen certainly risked his neck by continuing to sign off development costs as routine series-motor developments for the

Soaraway Surer success! Marc Surer celebrates his and BMW's 1979 European Formula 2 Championship victory with lift-off at the Nürburgring in his March 792-BMW, a car retained by BMW in Munich and still fast enough to frighten Formula 1 cars when Surer drives in historic events of the 1990s!

Picture: BMW Werkfoto, Germany, 1979

accounts department. He also remembered their racing nickname vividly: "We call it 'Underground Racing!'"

He chuckled at the memory and added, "It is only a small workshop [on nearby Knorr Strasse] and the mechanics come there only after working in the factory." Rosche would amble over to the workshops in the evening and add his own infectious enthusiasm to that of the other helpers, all determined to see the BMW legend live on.

For the first race, Rosche's private bank account would be raided in 5,000-DM batches, leaving his wife bewildered when she went in to make routine withdrawals! They all suffered a lack of cash during the year, but Eifelland at least made it all possible.

Quester improved on his standing in the European Championship, compared with 1970. Eifelland and March-BMW won one 1971 round outright (a slipstreaming contest aptly called "Monza Lottery"), finished second five times and third once, with all but one of those results achieved in European Championship rounds. That left Quester third overall in the European title hunt at the close of the year, beaten only by Carlos Reutemann and champion Ronnie Peterson. Incidentally, that Monza win was the fastest winning speed recorded that year—135.63 mph (216 km/h) average, which was rapid for 2-liter Europe.

Quester told me that the March-BMW 712 was very heavy to steer compared with the BMW chassis, "...so you had to be in good condition to drive it!" Looking back over several seasons with various forms of the BMW engine, in both hillclimbs and straightforward racing, Quester recalled, "The Diametral motors in 1968 and 1969 were better in pick-up than when I first try driving the hillclimb car in 1967, but still they do not pick up as well as the FVA at the bottom end. Against the FVA at low revs, the BMW engine was very bad, but it had good power at the top. Then it is always a problem to finish!"

"When we have the new Dornier chassis, everything is much better. The car is easier to handle and the new engine is much better at high and low revs; all the way to 9,000, it is good. For the driver, this later engine is completely different. No more jerkiness—now the engine is smooth, yes, very smooth and powerful!"

The 1972 season was bound to be a quiet year for BMW in F2. The engine was not homologated for competition in European Formula 2, so the inaugural year of 2-liter Formula 2 passed without any BMW competition at all. The season was notable for the number of tuners practicing their hand with the Belt Drive A-series (BDA) Cosworth-Ford, this being the only unit that was eligible under the new production cylinder-head rulings. For 1973, however, BMW did know that it had the chance of gaining admittance for its conventional 16-valve alloy cylinder head engine mounted on a 2-liter iron block, if it could satisfy the authorities that 100 such heads had been manufactured.

But the stubborn persistence of the "Underground Racing Team" was certainly not going to be thwarted by the change in Formula regulations. Somehow, Dieter Quester managed to put together a deal with a number of companies, including Denzel, to support him in an assault on the European Trophy for 2-liter sports cars. The car he used was a modified Chevron B21, weighing 20 kg less than standard in the chassis and carrying small rear upright fins.

Under the white fiberglass body, Paul Rosche and the rebel mechanics inserted the 2-liter version of their old 1600 Formula 2 unit, coded M12/6 and officially rated at 275 bhp by 8,500 rpm. Initially, M12/6 allowed some 276 bhp, but by the season's close, 285 bhp was being reported. The 2.0 BMW hit 9,000 rpm reliably to make some 15.5 kh/sq cm BMEP.

BMW engineers accrued a lot of racing experience with the new unit, for Quester

attacked most of the nine rounds in that series. He drove with flair and completed the second Underground Racing season with a first place (scored at Salzburgring, where the car completely dominated the proceedings) and a second place in the championship rounds, plus some rapid individual outings that deserve recall.

The highlight of the Chevron's year was the Austrian 1,000-km race. Quester was ill, so Rolf Stommelen and Toine Hezemans alternated in the small cockpit. This pairing of the shrewd Dutchman (later a major shareholder in the Lotus GT Racing Team) and the bespectacled German (who died at Riverside, California in 1983) was dynamite.

It was expected that Ferrari's 3-liter sports racing cars would finish first, second, and third, but in the fourth Ferrari, Arturo Merzario and rallyman Sandro Munari (best-known in Lancia's Stratos-Ferrari V6) were paired. Despite Oesterreichring's lap speeds and the

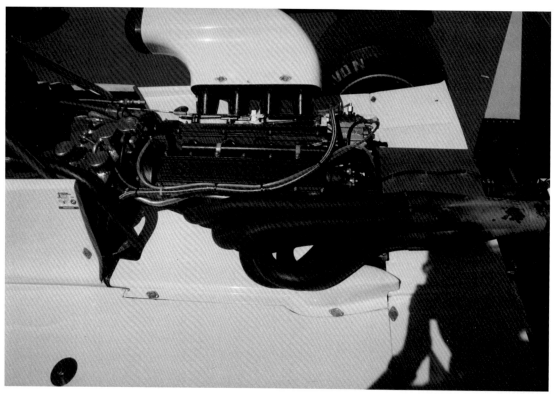

handicap of being minus a liter from the fabled Maranello machine ahead, Rolf and Toine attacked vigorously throughout the race.

The Ferrari was reportedly suffering with an unwell engine, but that could not detract from the enjoyment and respect generated among the onlookers for the pursuing BMW. The Chevron B21-BMW headed its Italian 3-liter rival before the water cap flipped. That forced the crew to ease off with low water, but a lot of steam, in the block. Even so, the Chevron-BMW finished only 37 seconds behind after five hours of racing, comfortably winning the class over the established Cosworth 1.8-liter FVC-powered opposition at an average of 120.59 mph (194 km/h).

Motorsport is born

Jochen Neerpasch arrived from Ford Motorsport in May 1972 to form the unique BMW Motorsport GmbH, a "company within a company." This at the invitation of today's Chrysler heavy-hitter, Bob Lutz, then an effective BMW director. More details about Motorsport GmbH are given in chapter 14.

By August 1972, it had been announced that March Engineering at Bicester, in England, had signed an exclusive agreement to supply customers and run works cars in Formula 2 and the 2-liter European Sports Car Trophy with the BMW 16-valve engine. Quester's countryman, Niki Lauda, was out in the March 2-liter sports car (later to become the March 73S-BMW), testing at Silverstone, that month.

Now that Neerpasch was in charge and competition was again an acceptable word around the boardroom at Munich, Rosche reworked his 2-liter motor, ready for the challenge of Ford and Cosworth in the 1973 season. Designated the M12/7, the unit depended on an 89.2-mm bore and 80-mm stroke for a cubic capacity of 1,999 cc. It developed a best of 290 bhp (145.1 bhp a liter), but would go on to break the 150 bhp/liter barrier by 1977.

The overhead camshafts ran in five main bearings and were driven by spur gears from the nose of the crankshaft. Valve diameters were 35.8 mm for inlet and 30.36 mm for exhaust. Instead of the original Apfelbeck 70-degree radial-valve displacement, the 1973 BMW Formula 2 engine ran an included valve angle of 40 degrees. Provision was made in the cylinder head for incorporating three plugs, and the factory did experiment with the layout that they had used for so many years in the Diametral engine.

However, it was found that the slight power advantage generated at the top end was not worthwhile in terms of reliability and complication. If the central plug did fail, then the prospects for the pistons were terminal. An 11.0:1 compression ratio was used and retained for most of the engine's racing life. Maximum power between 8,500 and 9,000 rpm was rather too close for comfort to the absolute limit of 9,100 rpm.

One unusual feature was the provision of titanium connecting rods. They were unreliable in the early stages, but these large connecting rods and forged Mahle pistons (with crowns in the piston heads to clear the valves) were proven, the pistons carrying two compression rings and one scraper ring apiece.

Through the winter of 1971/72, Josef Schnitzer had been working hard at the family business on a completely new 16-valve engine, taking a different approach to BMW. The brothers had considerable experience with the engine in sedan racing—they had a fuel-injected 2-liter giving a reputed 190 bhp in 1968—but this was with the two-valve production head.

Schnitzer went his own way, designing an alloy DOHC cylinder head that could easily be fitted to the production base, whereas the works head was installed through a total 180-degree rotation. For a start, the Schnitzer F2 race motor, coded S20/4, was laid over—

open the hood of a modern BMW to find the same slant principles—and the double overhead camshafts in this Schnitzer-designed alloy cylinder head were driven by chain rather than by the factory gear-drive system. Naturally, fuel injection and exhaust equipment were transposed, compared with the factory layout, and Schnitzer went to the trouble of designing a unique magnesium oil pump for the engine. It developed into an exceptional unit and also had ramifications for rally use in 2002.

For the 1973 season, March had prepared a pair of STP-red March 732-BMWs, to be driven by the Jean-Pierres (Jarier and Beltoise) from France. Hans-Joachim Stuck, Jr., having left Cologne for Munich with Neerpasch for the 1973 season, had his first Formula 2 race in April of that year at Hockenheim. He drove on many occasions that year and in subsequent years, becoming one of the mainstays of the March-BMW Formula 2 team. Also on the side of March-BMW, but as customers, were Colin Vandervell (son of Tony, the Vanwall Grand Prix car manufacturer), Jacques Coulon, and Mike Beuttler.

Vittorio Brambilla explored the potential of the Schnitzer S20/4 unit, which was first tried by Wilson Fittipaldi (works Brabham BT40) after it had been homologated for use in Formula 2 as of July 1, 1973. As the factory BMW unit was a success, the Schnitzer S20/4 engine (the only BMW-based unit for sale, outside of March) took off in sales and, subsequently, performance.

Ranged against BMW, Germans saw the opponent as Ford, but that multinational was represented by a large number of different engines and specialists. The Cosworth FVD was used with some success, but was declared illegal by the FIA during the season. Subsequently, a variety of Cosworth BDA/G motors in an equal variety of racing chassis were deployed.

The most consistent BMW opposition in 1973 came from Jochen Mass (Surtees-Hart

CASTROL CASTR

BDA) and Patrick Depailler (Elf-BDA). Initially, March-BMW was the underdog. Nobody gave the men of Munich pre-season respect, for it was not Ford that BMW was aiming to beat, but Cosworth at Northampton, who had created the Ford-badged DFV Formula 1 V8.

Many "experts" overlook the fact that BMW, through its own engineering resources and those of surrounding companies given sub-contract work, delivers the racing goods as a factory, rather than simply signing large checks for others to compete on its behalf. This was true until the winter of 1995/96, when BMW Motorsport decided to assign responsibility outside the engine bay for 1996–98 to McLaren for the SuperTouring 3-series (320) as well as their Global GT with BMW V12 motivation. For better or worse (and it is generally for better) BMW competes as a company, and employees do feel a sports involvement that is not present at Ford.

Beginning on March 11, 1973, at Mallory Park in the Midlands of England, two works-backed March-BMWs appeared. Beltoise sat on pole position (42.5 seconds), with Mike Hailwood and Jochen Mass looking threateningly quick in their Surtees-BDAs, and Jarier well in touch.

The opening laps were dramatic, Beltoise leading before his three-plug-per-cylinder engine almost literally exploded—the race control tower actually lost some glass as a result of its bombardment with BMW engine parts! It was the last time BMW used the three-plug layout for this engine.

The other single-plug-per-cylinder car was in no danger, and Jarier proceeded to win both heats at an average of 112.18 mph (179 km/h). For good measure, Jarier left the lap record at 41.8 seconds/116.26 mph (185 km/h).

Jarier was known to be temperamental, even in his subsequent Shadow and Lotus

Formula 1 career. Yet the combination of this former law student from Paris, a flyweight March, and the reliable power offered by the now-thoroughly proven BMW, was to prove the target for 1973. In 19 starts, "Jumper" won eight times and finished second twice to win the championship for March and BMW, defeating the Ford Cosworth BDA-propelled cars of Mass and Depailler into the bargain.

Speaking in November 1996 and celebrating 30 years of racing, Jarier nominated both the March-BMW and the 1973 season as his best, incidentally also nominating the Shadow-Dodge DN8 CanAm car of 1978 as the worst: "impossible to drive, dangerous, and fragile."

It was one of the healthiest years for international Formula 2, then the nursery for apprentice Grand Prix pilots. In 1973, the series visited Italy, France, Germany, Great Britain, Portugal, Sweden, and Austria. So BMW, March, and STP certainly had a wide audience for their rout of the Cosworth-Ford league. BMW's number of 1973 wins was 12; there were seven second places for the Munich

motor and eight third places. The closest the BDA brigade could get was six wins (an FVD-engine car won the remaining round), ten second places, and 11 third places.

Not all those BMW-powered podium placings could be attributed to Munich. The unique Schnitzer F2 engine's best result in 1973 was a third place, scored by Henri Pescarolo's Motul Rondel at Norisring, but it had shown the potential. A frenzied burst of activity saw Schnitzer produce sixty engines, plus associated spares, for the 1974 season to hit the jackpot. For 1974, the engine from Freilassing was mounted vertically. The previous slant motor was confined to the sedans.

A projected March-BMW assault on sports car racing was not so successful. In fact, the only race won by a BMW engine in that 1973 season was by Gerard Larrousse's Lola!

The 1974 factory M12/7 motors were sold to customers outside March and were generally more freely available, in an effort to help the competition department stay afloat in the very tricky financial aftermath of the fuel crisis.

Hans Stuck and Patrick Depailler were the 1974 March 742-BMW works drivers, and they headed the league table one-two at the end of the year, Depailler winning the coveted European Championship. Just how hard the BMW engine had hit Formula 2 and overthrown the traditional Cosworth-Ford dominance can be seen from the fact that not one of the championship rounds was won by anything but a BMW-block engine! In fact, over the year, the BMW monopoly was broken only twice in the first three home in each championship round—truly "Unbeatable BMW."

BMW domination continues

In 1974, the Schnitzer engine scored three of the 12 wins notched up by the BMW units, the remaining nine wins shared at four apiece by Depailler and Stuck, plus a guest works drive victory taken by Ronnie Peterson.

In 1975, the BMW domination continued, all but three finishing places in the top three in each race over the year being provided by BMW-based engines. Once more, no other marque of engine won a race!

However, it was not the traditional formula of March-Munich BMW engine that triumphed overall. Patrick Tambay and Michel Leclere tied for second place overall in their blue Elf-sponsored March-BMWs, but Jacques Laffite won the title, using the Schnitzer S20/4 in his French-built Martini. For most of the year, the motor was rated at 290 bhp, but the higher-lift valve gear used toward the close of the successful season took it to a claimed 300 bhp, representing 150 bhp per liter.

Laffite took six of the 16 wins notched up by BMW power units that year, driving former kart-builder Tico Martini's capable monocoque machine. By the end of the year, there were money problems in this team and the

Schnitzer engines started wilting and becoming unreliable, but the title was won. Josef Schnitzer was now off to BMW at Munich to do a little more development work, but first he uprated his Formula 2 engine to a claimed 305 bhp by the close of 1975 and left brother Herbert to run the shop.

In 1976, the focus for supremacy in Formula 2 racing power plants slipped from inter-marque struggles to the emergence of a newly-admitted Renault V6. This was a non-turbocharged development of their sports car engine: a DOHC, 24-valve design.

March-BMW's factory team was caught comparatively unprepared, for the ragged performances turned in by Maurizio Flammini and Alex Ribeiro were not enough to face the assault mounted by the French. To be fair, Gunnar Nilsson should have led the team, but his Lotus Formula 1 commitments were too heavy.

In the championship title race, Renault-powered Frenchmen (headed by Jean-Pierre Jabouille, who had given the Schnitzer-BMW its first victory) slammed home one-two-three. By using a number of drivers and chassis, the BMW unit was still a very common sight in the top results, and it only won two races less than the eight notched up by the Renault V6 units during the year.

The Renault took six second places to the five of BMW (significantly, a new Hart unit took a second place during the year), but Renault amassed eight third places to the four scored by BMW and the two by the new Hart.

The pressure was on for 1977. Rosche extracted 300/305 bhp and a 10,000-rpm limit from an engine still coded M12/7. Most progress came from continuous cylinder-head and camshaft development, but by the 1978 season, a new exhaust was also part of a very driveable package that had stabilized at 306 bhp (153.1 bhp/liter).

Despite the appearance of drivers like Jochen Mass in the factory March-BMW cars, it was the works-engined Ralt-BMW of

Jacques Laffite's Schnitzer-BMW-engined Martini took the European title in 1975. Here, the popular Frenchman is at Hockenheim and we can see the exhaust and injection systems are transposed on opposite sides, compared to the factory 2-liter race motor.

Picture: BMW Pressfoto, Germany, 1975

American Eddy Cheever that proved the most effective points opposition to Renault in 1977. Cheever finished second in the series, and Rene Arnoux's works Martini-Renault V6 won, with Didier Pironi finishing third in another Renault V6 machine.

The scoreline that year read: BMW six wins, six seconds and nine third places; Renault four wins, five seconds and two third overall positions; Brian Hart two wins and the same number of second and third places during the season, which actually comprised 13 rounds, a Ferrari V6 winning the other race. It was widely known that Renault would abandon Formula 2 at the close of the 1977 season, and the French kept their word. The Ferrari Dino V6 engine did take a win in just one 1977 Championship round—mounted in the back of a Chevron—but the handy four-cylinder Hart 420R looked like it was staying around for some time. Its main advantages over the BMW stemmed from the fact that it was designed as a racing unit around a light alloy cylinder block, and thus offered a distinct weight advantage as well as being a slightly more compact and tidy unit. You could say it combined the best of Cosworth

and BMW practice. Brian Hart later developed effective four-cylinder turbo fours for Grand Prix and became widely respected for delivering more durable power at less cost than many big-budget F1 concerns.

Back in 1977, BMW engines were available to a number of promising young drivers who had used them in various chassis. Though March did not figure in the overall top three in the championship, it did produce a very significant new chassis. The Formula Atlantic-based 772P scored three wins with the driver many picked as a star from his Formula 3 days, Bruno Giacomelli.

In 1978, the combination of Giacomelli—or "Jack O'Malley," as he was colloquially nicknamed by British-based mechanics—and March brought back the European Championship to Bicester and BMW. They seized six wins in the ten rounds held up until the end of July, sealing the title well before the end of the season.

At the close of the year, Giacomelli had won a remarkable eight races and factory March-BMWs had powered the first two in the series, Derek Daly's ICI Chevron-Hart finishing third.

Hans Stuck Jr. blasts past the stands at Hockenheim in his orange Jägermeister March 762 with BMW power logo on the airbox.

Picture: R.R. Kroschel, Germany, 1976

As a member of the BMW Polifac-sponsored Junior Team—the other two were Marc Surer and Manfred Winklehock—Giacomelli became the first Italian to win the title, following five years of French domination in the series. Surer—later a BMW roving ambassador and in-field team manager—was the runner-up to the 1978 title and won outright in the following 1979 season: total vindication for the Junior Team selection!

Talking of the BMW engine in 1978, its "father," Paul Rosche, commented, "Now I look for torque. It is easy to always get more power, but racing has a lot of braking and acceleration, therefore we must have torque for the best track performance. When you look on the test bed, it is the brake horsepower that people talk of. In racing on the track, I now look for good pulling power."

Rosche spent the winter returning to his old design love: camshafts. A new profile replaced the breathing arrangements that were yielding 306/308 bhp between 9,700 and 10,000

rpm. Even then, BMEP of 15.8 kh/sq cm BMEP from 7,500 to 8,000 rpm was too little for Rosche, even though it had shown a steady increase over the years. Peak torque was now up to 166.36 lb-ft.

Just what this meant on track can be judged from Manfred Winkelhock's 1978 Junior Team March 782-BMW M12/7. The 500-kg (1,100-lb) single-seater was tested at the close of the season by Germany's *sport auto* magazine and found to develop 307 bhp at 9,250 rpm. That allowed a massive 626.5 bhp a ton and figures such as 0–62 mph in 3.5 seconds, 0–100 mph in 6.6 seconds, and 0–124 mph a blink over 10 seconds.

That meant 2-liters could blow the doors off a 7-liter street machine, and the March-BMW from1978 did not compare badly against legends such as the Porsche 935 turbos of the Group 5 era, either. The Kremer turbo Porsche, at over 400 bhp, would hit 0–60 mph in 4.0 seconds and whoosh off 0–124 mph in 10.3 seconds.

The 1978 BMW brood of young European Formula 2 Championship challengers. Left to right around their state-of-the-art March 782-BMWs are: Ingo Hoffman, Eddie Cheever, Marc Surer, Manfred Winkelhock, and Bruno Giacomelli. Both Giacomelli (in 1978) and Surer (in 1979) were European Champions and both made it to regular Grand Prix rides. Racing prodigy Cheever is best known for US racing in the CART category during the 1990s.

Picture: BMW Werkfoto, 1978

In 1978, BMW F2 drivers included Eddie Cheever (seated in car 4) and Ingo Hoffman. The trio in and around the 1978 March-BMW are (left to right): Manfred Winkelhock, Marc Surer (in car), and that season's champion, Italy's Bruno Giacomelli. Both Winkelhock and Surer graduated from the 1977 Junior Team, which ran BMW 320i Group 5 cars in the German Championship.

Pictures: BMW Archiv, released 1984

Maximum speeds were not a priority—mighty braking and slick-shod grip were number-one items—so a turbo Porsche would exceed 180 mph, while the March F2 cars of this era would be geared for some 280 km/h (173 mph) at 9,500 rpm, with 7,000 to 9,500 rpm the normal working parameters.

Surer's March-mounted 1979 European Formula 2 title was the last the March-BMW alliance would take for two seasons. Then Corrado Fabi made a fantastic job of whirling the March 802 in ICI colors to five of 11 victories recorded by the BMW-engined March in 1982. Fabi not only contributed to an 11-3 scoreline for March-BMW versus Ralt Honda, but also narrowly defeated subsequent BMW touring car ace and ex-World Motorcycle Champion Johnny Cecotto in the March 802-Hart 420R.

I had the privilege of driving the Championship-winning ICI March-BMW at Silverstone in May 1982 with Fabi's guidance.

I can confirm that the M12/7 engine was truly flexible enough between 5,000 and 10,000 rpm to cope with a strange journalist on his first taste of a full ground-effect formula car. Learning new grip and braking levels at 100-mph lap averages was something else....

The 1983–84 closing F2 seasons were not glorious affairs, particularly the poorly-supported final year, which featured grids of 15 on average, rather than double that number in its earlier heyday.

The Ralt Hondas took the European title both years, but BMW was still not outclassed, winning two European Championship events in 1984 and supporting Christian Danner to third overall in the points. The honor of scoring the last BMW MPowered Formula 2 victory went to Philippe Streiff and his AGS JH19C-BMW at Brands Hatch on September 23, 1984.

In action at home: Bruno Giacomelli wields the 305-bhp March 782-BMW through the 160-mph pine forests of Hockenheim. The simple equation read: BMW Junior Team March 782 plus Bruno Giacomelli equals eight race wins and the 1978 European Championship.

Picture: BMW Werkfoto, Germany, 1978

Only the beginning

Looking back over its 17-year (1967–84) involvement in European Formula 2 as the most successful engine supplier, BMW could also reflect on some substantial cash inflow. More than 500 of the M12-coded motors were made, and the majority of those were sold profitably. The same went for March, for it had made more than 200 F2 cars, winning an extra title over BMW when March ran Ronnie Peterson to victory with Hart Cosworth BD power in 1971.

Recalling those racing seasons from motor carnage joke to championship class act, Paul Rosche observed, "By the end of Formula 2, our average maximum power had risen from 275 to 315 bhp [157.6 bhp/liter]. Then we saw it was 321 bhp [160.1 bhp/liter] and the normal maximum power was developed between 9,500 and 10,000 revs; our final evolution version [coded M12/7/1] gave best power on 10,200 rpm. The real point about F2

for BMW was that it gave us the basis for a lot of other projects, including the M3, the turbocharged touring cars of McLaren, Schnitzer, and ourselves.

"We had a start point for the M12/13 Formula 1 four-cylinder turbos between all these experiences, but I think Formula 2 was very important to us," Rosche paused. Then he winked and picked up another Warsteiner from the free bar at the 1995 annual Sport Pokal presentation evening. He quipped, "I had a lot of fun, as well as a lot of hard work with the people at March in England. It was a good time for all of us."

From despair to domination over the decades, BMW can certainly be said to have had its money's worth from a design that started off as a 1500 road-car engine of 75 bhp, "...with scope for further development."

The 1979 March-BMW European Formula 2 Champion and his 792 push through a race paddock. The youthful Surer is at the center of the rear wing, behind his helmet.

Picture: BMW Werkfoto, Germany, 1979

Future Champion: a superb study of 1982 European Champion Corrado Fabi (the late brother of CART competitor, Teo Fabi) at work in the March 812-BMW.

Picture: BMW Werkfoto, France, 1981

One of the hot runners in Formula 2 was the Ralt-BMW with Toleman-backed Stefan Bellof driving. Tragically, the German hope for Grand Prix acclaim—a decade before Schumacher—was killed driving a Porsche Group C car.

Picture: BMW Werkfoto, Thruxton, UK, April 1977

Another great German driver to die racing a Porsche was Manfred Winkelhock, elder brother of British and German touring car champion, Joachim Winkelhock. Here, Manfred wheels through the British Thruxton chicane in his March 802-BMW.

Picture: BMW Werkfoto, UK, 1980

The last hurrah! BMW's last European Formula 2 Championship came in 1982, courtesy of this works-backed March-BMW team. Left to right, we see the following drivers and their cars: Christian Danner, Champion Corrado Fabi, and runner-up Johnny Cecotto.

Picture: BMW Archiv, reissued 1984

Ground attack! This was the Pirelli-shod March 812-BMW ready for the 1981 season with full ground-effect side-pods.

Picture: BMW Werkfoto, UK, 1981

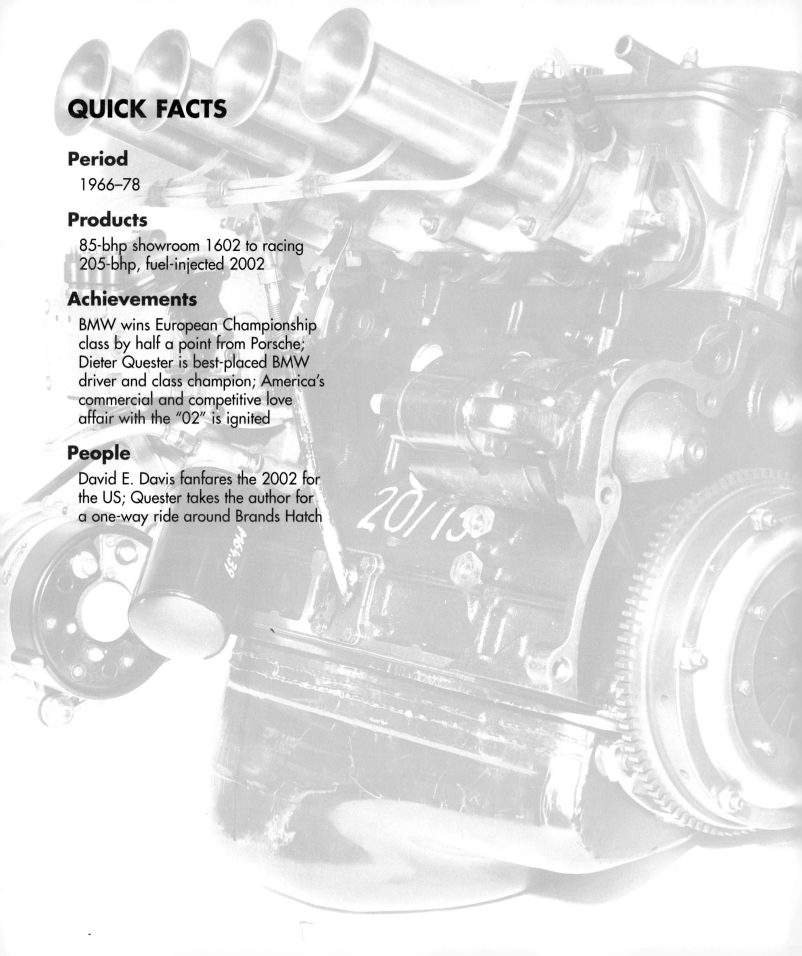

QUICK FACTS

Period

1966–78

Products

85-bhp showroom 1602 to racing 205-bhp, fuel-injected 2002

Achievements

BMW wins European Championship class by half a point from Porsche; Dieter Quester is best-placed BMW driver and class champion; America's commercial and competitive love affair with the "02" is ignited

People

David E. Davis fanfares the 2002 for the US; Quester takes the author for a one-way ride around Brands Hatch

Chapter 12

2002: "Born in the USA"

The versatile 2002 and turbocharged sons in road and race development

With a welcome like that which follows from such a major US motor magazine, you could say that the first BMW to be "born in the USA" was not the 1996 Z3 out of Spartanburg, but a Munich-made 2002 in February 1968. Accounting for almost 400,000 of a total 881,940 of the legendary "02" designs manufactured from March 1966 to July 1977, the 2002 represented a motor marriage proposed by the controversial Max Hoffman, BMW's New York-based official importer in the 1960s.

Hoffman was criticized for the way he represented BMW in the US, before the factory took over the import operation. But nobody quarreled with the performance logic of BMW's lightest, sleekest, and latest four-cylinder taking on the 100-horsepower clout of the 1,990-cc slant four. Replacing the 1966 original 1,573 cc at 85 bhp made sales and performance sense.

The result was a road and race driver's dream: one that handled a stock 100 European bhp to 170 turbo horsepower, or a regular 200 to a freakish 400 race horsepower. The 2002 did it all with a flair that flattered every driver into thinking these moments were the most exhilarating anyone had ever experienced in any form of auto, regardless of price.

Here's what David E. had to say in the *Car & Driver Yearbook*: "Unrestrained joy, unstinting praise. Turn your hymnals to 2002.

"David E. Davis, Jr. blows his mind on the latest from BMW. A super sedan for those who like to impress themselves and don't care very much about Kevin Acne and Marvin Sweatsock, and the guy down the block.

"Maybe the neatest part of the whole deal is the fact that the 2002 was originally proposed as a kind of second choice, American anti-smog version of the wailing 1600TI they were selling in Germany, but the second-choice version turns out to be better than the original....If the 1600 was the best $2,500 sedan C/D ever tested, the 2002 is most certainly the best $2,850 sedan in the whole cotton-picking world."

The BMW 2002 formed the bridge between the recovering BMW model range of yesterday and today's confident, competent, and million-selling 3-series designs. Judging by the number of 1990s keen competitors who still fly the 2002 flag in European and American historic races, driving schools, and autocross/sprint events, the 2002 was the definitive BMW stepping-stone to the automotive hall of fame.

America is truly home to the BMW 2002 cult and the further development of the machine the States dubbed "Pocket Rocket." This quartet of views from the Monterey Historic race meeting at Laguna Seca gives us a small idea of that enthusiasm, along with the superbly turned-out brace of "02s" at Lime Rock in a 1989 shoot for the *Roundel* magazine of the now 40,500-strong BMW CCA (Backdrop).

Pictures: Static shots, Author; Action shot, Klaus Schnitzer, California, 1996

The "Three" undeniably offered more creature comforts—even the fresh-air ventilation that seemed absent in the 2002's greenhouse—but many hardcore enthusiasts mourned the loss of the adaptable 2002.

Adaptable? Certainly: it was a basic road car with what had become BMW traits (slant four-cylinder engine up front, independent trailing-arm suspension out back), starting life in the showrooms of Germany in March 1966. It was badged 1600-2 with 1,573 cc (84 x 71-mm bore x stroke) and 85 bhp.

The 1600-2 (the "2" or "02" suffix designating two-doors) and 1600Ti of 105-bhp class competition potential occupied the market for nearly two years in Europe before the 2-liter derivative arrived. Then came 1,766 cc (89 x 71 mm) for the LHD (left-hand-drive)-only 1802 and the proven 1,990-cc (89 x 80 mm) 2002 made from January 1968 (a month later for US production).

This single-carburetor 2-liter was followed by the LHD-only twin carburetor 2002TI in Sep-tember 1968. A fuel-injected 2002Tii was sent to the US in two distinct production batches from August 1971 and September 1973. That meant a 1974 model year 2002tii (as the badge read) with squared rear lamps and an official admission of 125 SAE bhp rather than Europe's tougher DIN-rated 130 bhp.

The Tii debuted at Frankfurt in September 1969, after the competition cars had used Kugelfischer mechanical fuel injection (raced as 2002TI) for the best part of two years. The street 2002Tii utilized a carefully-devised, road-adapted version of the Kugelfischer system, with downstream injection and a single butterfly within a plenum chamber. The European Tii, with its 120-mph (193-km/h) top speed and capability of accelerating from 0–60 mph in under nine seconds, had a considerably uprated chassis to handle its 130 DIN bhp.

This was quite an advance over the basic 100 bhp DIN (98 SAE for the 1974–76 US model) offered for 2002 throughout that model's long Munich manufacturing life. From 1968 to 1976, over 382,740 fully-built "02" examples were created, plus 13,175 made in knockdown (CKD) format for overseas assembly.

Officially, the plain 2002 made 109.2 mph (176 km/h) and accelerated from 0–62 mph in just over ten seconds, but the US model was rated 105 mph and 12.3 sec for 0–60 mph.

The 2002 turbo

Toward the end of its series-production life, an ultimate 2002 turbo was made for the street, but its insensitive release in the middle of a European fuel crisis meant that only 1,672 were made between January 1974 and June 1974. By contrast, the 2002TI and Tii were made by the thousands. Some 7,449 of the US-spec Tiis were made from August 1971 to December 1974 alone.

The factory did not use the later street 2002 turbo in competition, despite the ill-timed bally-hoo at its September 1973 introduction which implied that this was BMW's greatest-ever competition weapon. The 2002 turbo was also falsely billed as, "the world's first turbocharged production ca," as stated in the authoritative *Guinness Book of Car Facts & Feats*. It was, however, Europe's first turbocharged production sedan, beating Porsche and Saab to the production line. America had the Chevrolet Corvair and the Oldsmobile Jetfire earlier.

The 2002 turbo was designed to add interest to a then-aging 2002 range, legitimately trading on a 1969 racing season that had seen BMW engineers debut turbocharging in this category. For production purposes, the familiar slant four was rated at 170 bhp on a 6.9:1 compression ratio, the KKK (Kuhnle, Kopp & Kausch) turbocharger blowing pressurized air into the injection system.

Chassis modifications were extensive and revealed the expertise BMW had learned from competition with the model. A bigger radiator,

ventilated ten-inch front discs with four-piston calipers (though drums at the rear were retained on road models), stronger half-shafts, and a ZF limited-slip differential (set at a slack 40 percent pre-load for this application) were included. Rim widths went back into the 1960s in competition terms, with steel rims of only a modest five and a half inches clad in 185/70 HR 13 radials.

Also changed were the gearbox internals, clutch, dampers, and road springs. The turbo boasted a very aggressive exterior, with spoilers and stripes, the optional front-spoiler signage causing howls of protest. It had scripted mirror-image lettering designed to intimidate those goggling into their rearview mirrors as the Bimmer blasted toward them on the autobahn. Since the future of gasoline-engined vehicles was at stake, thanks to the Arab-Israeli confrontation and consequent motoring bans imposed through Europe, BMW couldn't have picked a worse time to be described as "Bad Boys."

Racing the 2002

All 2002s had very clean lines for such capacious sedans, and this must have helped the fastest 2002 of them all gain a top speed of 131 mph (210 km/h), coupled with 0–60 mph acceleration quoted at 6.8 seconds.

Despite the commercial and competitive success accrued by this affordable legend, when the factory did compete the 2002, it had a brief official sports career that covered only 1968 and 1969. Since then, it has been beloved of non-factory competitors from Arkansas to Austria.

Von Falkenhausen succinctly outlined the 2002's factory racing advantages over the earlier Bimmer sedans for the 1968 season: "It was at least 180 kg lighter than the 2000TI we had been racing. It was also lower and was a better car for the aerodynamics—not so big

Racing for US glory: 1968-78

In America, the 2002 was fighting Alfa GTVs and BRE-prepared Nissan 510s to spread the BMW word. Gregory Racing, supported by US importer Max Hoffman, ran a two-car team of 2002s in the professional Trans Am ranks from 1968-72. These snorting double-carburetor cars still exist, thanks to the racing stewardship of Rug (not Reg, as my British printers used to insist!) Cunningham.

BMW dealer and racer Cunningham has a soft spot for the 2002 racers, born of a ten-race winning sequence in 1975's SCCA Southern Pacific region. Another Trans Am regular team driver was Carl Fredericks.

The team 2002s seem preserved in authentic 200-bhp, five-speed gearbox, 130-plus-mph trim—not so fast as some later turbo interpretations that ran in the same sessions at Monterey 1996, but absolutely great to watch. Since Monterey 1988, Cunningham has been plucking prizes for the preserved Trans Am period pieces, which won the BMW Cup for the company-backed Vintage Fall Festival, Lime Rock, 1990.

I was fortunate to see these 2002s in action at Monterey in 1996 and just wish we had preserved some of our top-line European racing sedans so authentically. They look like work-

Keeping the faith. American 2002s at work on the Corkscrew at Laguna Seca include the number 35 ex-Trans Am car as fielded by the Rug Cunningham team.

Pictures: Klaus Schnitzer, California, 1996

Nick Craw did a good job with the Miller & Norburn 2002 in American production-car racing during the mid-1970s, taking national titles against factory opposition from the big American Motors compacts, among others. Although he set winning records for driver achievement in the US, Craw (pictured in our inset) was subsequently better-known for his helmsmanship of the world's biggest competition auto club, SCCA.

Pictures: Author's archives, released 1978; Klaus Schnitzer; released 1996, US

ing racers, not pampered concours contestants. It was a rare pleasure to see them entertain the crowds alongside the bellowing Mustang-versus-Camaro wars—just as bitterly fought in 1996 as they were in the 1960s and 1970s.

One of the earliest successful privateer attacks came from subsequent SCCA President Nick Craw. Initially a single-seater professional—he drove for the rated Fred Opert Racing Team in the US, Mexico, Canada, and the UK—Craw found his place in BMW history for 1973. That season, he teamed up with Miller & Norburn and their 2002 production racer.

Big bumpers and all, Craw and the 02 proved too good for the opposition, winning his debut sedan season and the Goodrich Radial Challenge Driver's Championship. As a BMW

2002 driver, he won more races than any rival in the BF Goodrich series and was elected to both the Road Racing Drivers Club and All-American Racing Drivers Team.

Kermit R. Upton III was bred to speed-ski in his home state of Vermont, but switched to the automobile business in 1978, when he established Mountain Auto Sport. The aggressive skills he had displayed for the US ski team were transferred to racing, earning eight wins and three regional titles for his Mountain Auto Racing Team in his first 15 races!

Upton continued racing over the next decade, attracting Budweiser support for a Chevrolet Camaro before acquiring an M3 in 1989, which he raced on into the 1990s.

and square!" Remember, the 1800 series was a boxy four-door, while the 2002 was almost a two-door coupe, sold as such in some markets.

Klaus Steinmetz managed the factory race team and had eight mechanics for 1968, when the 2002 competed in the Group 5 category, which allowed the most radical modifications—a complete contrast to the early days of 1800 and 2000. The white 2002s began the season (belatedly, as they had to be legalized for competition first) with carbureted engines, yielding nearly 200 bhp at 7,500 rpm on an 11.0:1 compression ratio.

A Kugelfischer injection system was adopted and proved very satisfactory in providing a wide spread of usable power. The system mechanically injected fuel above the single throttle's slide. This injection system was retained for the rest of the 2002's factory-racing life and contributed to an average 205 bhp that would hurl the 2002 to 225 km/h (139.5 mph) through Brno's Czechoslovakian countryside in street-racing format.

Race drivers being ego-driven monsters, they complain about each other and their mounts, quotably. Quester's German-language biography is full of scathing commentary on "Kaiser" teammate Hahne and says that, aerodynamically, the 2002 was a silo in comparison to the rival Porsche 911. Yet the Porsche 2+(minimal)2 should never have been allowed in this sedan category anyway, as was shown by a subsequent international ruling.

The complete 2002s weighed 877 kg (1,929 lbs) and were flamboyant, carrying a peculiar set of wheel-arch spats that provided a streamlining downward U-bend before the wheel arch. The FIA banned these and a new-style front arch was introduced for the Nürburgring on July 7, 1968.

Suspension featured predominantly Dutch Koni damping and cast-alloy wheels carrying Dunlops. In this pre-slick-tire era, the road-registered cars carried substantial 4.75/10.00 by 13-inch diameter rubber. High-ratio steering and proper disc brakes were now also specified. Factory BMWs were soon trailered, not road-registered.

The biggest problem of that season and the following one was the Porsche 911 coupe, with

The 2-liter single-overhead-camshaft motor for the racing 2002 adopted Kugefischer injection before the double-overhead-camshaft single-seater Formula 2 motors. Despite those long induction trumpets and leading-edge power for the period, the units retained BMW's hallmark flexibility.

Picture: BMW Archiv, reissued 1984

its rear-mounted flat six. The Stuttgart factory did not bother to run a full factory team—but they did have some good, reliable, and wealthy privateers to represent them.

The Porsches were a little heavier than the factory BMWs, but they could resort to full twin-plug-per-cylinder Carrera racing versions of their flat-six engine, to wring 230 bhp from their four-cam 2-liters. Also on the scene were the Alfa GTAs (occasionally supercharged) and the Alan Mann Cortinas and Escorts, though these were 1,600s.

The fight was between BMW and the privateer Porsches, for the Alfas were not always present (and even when they were, their handling prevented all but the most competent drivers of the Italian marque from staying in touch with the Teutonic feud).

BMW Rennsport did not make the first March round of the championship that year (1968), but Bernd Henne and Dieter Basche did show the potential of 2002 by taking fifth place overall in the 1600 model at the Monza opener.

The second round on April 7 saw the victorious international and European Championship debut of the factory-prepared 2002 team. The venue was the Aspern airfield course, right on the doorstep of Viennese team driver Dieter Quester. In practice, Quester had to concede first place to Gardner's Ford time of 1 minute 9.3 seconds, but the BMW squirted and slid around the rough concrete course in 1 minute 10.6 seconds. Munich had closed the gap a great deal on lap times compared with the UK-based opposition. Now it was time to shift up a gear and start to take the initiative.

Quester beat one of the supercharged Alfas and two Porsche 911s at an average of 81.2 mph (130.6 km/h), and his fastest lap around the open track was 83.2 mph (133.8 km/h).

Round three of the European Touring Car Challenge (later a full championship) took the contestants to Snetterton in Norfolk, England, a former USAAF site for the Anglo-American bombing offensives of the 1940s.

BMW entered a trio of fuel-injected 2002s, although one was crashed in testing. Championship rules dictated that a certain number of starters should take the grid before full points would be awarded, so BMW ensured that a privateer brought his very unsuitable car along, and that Dieter Basche lent his road car to one Franz Pesch....

Both of the additional points-gathering 2002s were swiftly retired after the start, but the two factory cars for Quester and Basche practiced and raced competitively. Quester was third quickest in practice (1 minute 47.6 seconds) against Elford's pole-winning 1 minute 45.8 seconds (in the British-based AFN Porsche 911) and Basche's 1 minute 50.2 seconds.

The BMWs completed the opening laps in fifth and sixth positions. Then Basche's exhaust system loosened and Quester got away while battling with Gardner's Cortina, which was disposed of as the Ford overheated. After 25 laps, Quester was second and Basche had pulled back into fifth place.

After two hours and 20 minutes of racing, Basche lost positions by having a broken engine mounting replaced and Quester went out, as if in sympathy, with a rear transmission failure. Fitness fanatic Quester ran back to the pits and commandeered his teammate's machine. The BMW rejoined in fifth place and eventually made fourth overall, covering 111 laps, compared to the 115 laps of the winning 4.7-liter Ford Mustang in this 500-km event.

April 21 brought the 2002s a second European championship win, this time over Belgrade's streets, a four-hour grind around the former Yugoslavian track. Dieter Quester averaged 79.8 mph around the tight track, but more importantly, he beat Porsche entrant Erwin Kremer. There were two other Porsches behind, so BMW grins stretched to Munich and back.

Following a fifth-round cancellation, works BMWs did not appear again until it was time for the home fixture at Nürburgring on July 7. A gargantuan 93-car field actually started this

six-hour Grosser Preis von Tourenwagen edition. BMW entered three factory 2002s and employed Quester, Hahne, Basche, Kurt Ahrens, Ernst Furtmayer, and David Hobbs, the Englishman who would be so important to BMW in the US.

Hahne was BMW's quickest in practice behind two Porsches, completing a 9-minute, 45.9-second lap as compared with his 2000TI record of 9 minutes 58.9 seconds. That is progress, for a 10-minute lap was always a good formula car preserve in the "Good Old Days."

Ben Pon and Helmut Kelleners (Porsches) initially led Hahne, Lucien Bianchi's supercharged Alfa Romeo, and Quester. Bianchi's Alfa was one of a positive fleet prepared to try to hold Alfa's enviable record in the German event. Quester actually drove two of the factory BMWs, but it was Hahne who held the lead, fair and square, while both Porsches were fit.

Kelleners retired his 911, and Pon was later hindered by a slow co-driver and car trouble,

so BMW was able to lay on a magnificent and heartwarming display for its directors and customers. The Hahne/Quester car crossed the line just 0.2 seconds before the Ahrens/ Quester machine in line-ahead order. Five of the next six home were Porsches, so the victory went down doubly well. Incidentally, the third factory 2002 retired with differential failure on the penultimate lap, while in third.

The winning car averaged 84.2 mph (135 km/h) for the 36 laps/511.2 miles they covered, and the fastest lap went to a Porsche at slightly over 88 mph (141 km/h) at 9 minutes 36.6 seconds. To complete a good BMW day, Basche spent some time with Bernd Henne in the latter's private 1600TI. They won the class, following widespread mechanical malaise among the Alfas, and defeated an Alan Mann Ford driven by Frank Gardner and Dieter Glemser.

BMW missed the 1968 Belgian Francorchamps 24-hour annual, but a private Belgian 2002 driven by Raymond Mathay (subsequently killed in a dreadful, fiery accident

Eddie Regan's Mini gets that BMW blitz effect in Ireland as Alec Poole's imported road-legal 2002TI whips by on the last corner to win.

Picture: Autosport/ Elser Crawford, Ireland, May 1969

at Spa-Francorchamps in the 1970s) and Rob Derom did pick up sixth overall, fourth in its class behind the victorious Porsche of Kremer/Kelleners.

A new 8.5-mile street-circuit version of the Brno track in Czechoslovakia was attacked by a trio of factory 2002s for a four-hour event. By this stage, BMW felt the Porsche's extra straight-line speed (so clearly demonstrated on the faster circuits) was beginning to outweigh both the road-handling and driving advantage that Munich had so effectively employed thus far.

In practice, Porsches were first- and second-fastest: Kelleners/Jurgen Neuhaus zapped to 5 minutes 32.7 seconds against Quester's third quickest 5 minutes 35.6 seconds. On this occasion, Quester shared with Furtmayer, the second car was driven by Quester and Hahne, and the third by Hahne and Basche—you had to be a genius at musical chairs to run BMW race teams of the 1960s!

BMW suffered all kinds of race ills. A fuel-injection pipe came adrift on one car, Hahne had to drive a mile or so on a puncture, and Furtmayer made a comprehensive job of

demolishing the injection-troubled 2002 he shared with Quester. The excitement continued throughout the event, Kremer/Kelleners only winning after pulling back a 19-second lead enjoyed by Quester and passing the car the Austrian BMW driver shared with Hahne two laps from the end. Basche and Hahne were fourth—all in all, a good result.

The rest of the season covered three European championship events, but there were no more outright wins for BMW, despite its impressive reliability. At Zandvoort, Holland, Toine Hezemans took a popular local victory and another Porsche was second, the BMWs coming home in team formation to take third, fourth and fifth overall for Quester, Hahne, and Basche, respectively.

The Eigenthal hillclimb emphasized BMW's prowess at this branch of the sport: Basche finished second with one Porsche ahead and three behind. The 2002 was outclassed, puffing up hills on four cylinders against privately-owned flat sixes!

Things were tense going into the final round of the series on a then-new Jarama circuit near

Still developing. Metalbau Konig panelled some of this BMW Deutschland 02 Club member's machine (driven by Jurgen Schilling) in aluminium for the 1994 classic event that supported the Nürburgring 24-hours.

Picture: Chris Willows, Germany, 1994

Madrid, Spain. The Spanish decider on September 22 provided typically torrid heat in which to fight the final battle. BMW commanded that Quester miss the last round of a European hillclimb championship struggle against Porsche to seize this European racing title.

While Porsche and BMW battles dominated the headlines, Englishman John Handley's Mini Cooper was creeping away to a slight overall lead in the championship. Porsche and BMW totals were very close indeed in the over-1,600-cc Division 3.

The best Porsche was over a second quicker than BMW could manage with three team cars, driven by Quester, Hahne, and Basche. In the race, Helmut Kelleners proved too quick for the Munich trio, finishing nearly one and a half miles ahead after a three-hour struggle. The factory BMWs again managed to finish in order with Quester, Hahne, and Basche in third, fourth, and fifth places, respectively, and Jurgen Neuhaus grasping second for Porsche.

This reliable result still gave BMW Division 3 in the European Championship class, by just half a point's lead over Kelleners' Porsche after a season's racing. It also meant that Quester was runner-up overall to European Champion John Handley in the Mini Cooper, but BMW could claim the class.

In 11 rounds, Porsche won six, factory BMWs three, Gardner in the Ford Escort one, and a private Mustang one. BMW's finishing record and tally of places was marvelous. It was a great example of factory finesse—making the best of a four-cylinder sedan car that was not quite a match for the opposition, a reputable six-cylinder GT. Munich took three second places, two thirds, four fourths, and two fifths.

Looking back over that first 2002 season, Quester said: "This car was so much better than the big old 1800 and 2000. We had the wider wheels, and we could adjust the suspension a little, using the roll bars at the front and back. The car still oversteered, but it was much easier to control...and quite fast in a straight line with the fuel-injected engine."

The 2002Tii gets a press run

January 1969: while the factory was tackling the problem of turbocharging the 2002, von Falkenhausen, Quester, and Hahne visited England to give journalists a taste of life inside a 1968 Group 5 2002Tii. The venue was a cold and greasy Brands Hatch Club circuit and the "demonstration car" was white with red frontal panels to distinguish it from the other team cars (which had blue as one alternative).

I remember it well: I was 22, and "one of the invited."

The factory race 2002 stood over to one side of the start-and-finish line between runs, and I found it fascinating. The great squares of aluminum paneling riveted onto the main body extended out over the multi-spoke alloy wheels, which emphasized the low-set, wide body of this aggressive machine.

Today, it would look nude since the spoilers were absent, but then, we were all gawking at the amount of negative camber displayed. As the wheel and tire took the load on an independent suspension, it would be gradually forced to a vertical stance, planting the full tire-tread width on the ground and increasing adhesion.

My ride with Quester was notable for the many qualities of the road 2002 that were retained in the racing version. The ride over bumps was remarkable, and one sat in some comfort on the right of this fully trimmed LHD machine—fully trimmed, that is, until a famous journalist tore out the standard armrest as he tried to avoid landing in Quester's lap!

The compression ratio at that wintry Brands ride and drive was quoted at 10.5:1 for the injected engine, which retained much of the standard spread of power. Quester started by showing that there was clean power from 3,500 rpm.

Exiting slow corners such as Druids Hairpin (where it clambered over the curb), the amount of oversteer opposite lock that could be applied without the tail actually taking command of the alert Austrian driver's reflexes was memorable.

The car was not noisy, but as it rushed towards the paddock in the fourth of its five Getrag ratios, I do remember thinking that Quester's brain had fallen out. I was convinced that he was going to take me with him to that big BMW scrapyard in the sky. It was all routine to Quester and the competition 2002—the four-wheel disc brakes (the fronts inherited from the 2000TI) killed the speed without wheel lock on the slimy surface.

It was a memorable experience, an exhilarating step toward becoming the odd man out at British media centers—the Munich supporter in the days of British MiniMania.

QUICK FACTS

Period

1969–78

Product

The first 2002 turbos through Alpina privateer entries and onto the final "Schnitzer-Blitzers" that took 1.4-liter turbocharging to new heights; 2002 in rough road rallying with a Schnitzer formula car 16-valve motor

Performance

210 to 290 bhp in one 1969 turbo 2-liter step; then 400 bhp, 0–60 mph in 4.7 sec and 160 mph plus from 1.4 liters in 1977

Achievements

Winner, 1969 European Championship titles for class and driver with six wins in ten rounds for 2002 model; proved capable of winning a World and European Championship rally outright

People

Quester takes his first European title and Alex von Falkenhausen engineers a cunning plan; Josef Schnitzer repeats the recipe in the 1970s and predicts how a Grand Prix racing motor could be

Chapter 13

Competition 02s: Simply the Best?

The 2002's underfunded rallying career shows potential

BMW entered 1969 with renewed energy and a very significant second string to its bow: Alpina had decided to go racing properly in 1969 after those exploratory events of 1968. Alpina would enable a European championship success that is seldom acknowledged.

As Paul Rosche and Alex von Falkenhausen both recalled, just before Christmas 1968, the latter presented the engineers with the idea of turbocharging the 2-liter unit. As so often would be the case in later years with BMW's most successful touring car innovations, there was little time for theory or drawing up a fully-engineered installation for the KKK turbo.

Turbocharging was not well-known in Europe and had not been applied to a racing touring car before. The normal European practice was to supercharge, using systems that were pressurized by engine-driven compressors. The beauty of turbocharging was that a small engine did not have to devote energy to running the compressor, for it was driven—virtually free of mechanical losses—by the escaping exhaust gases. The gases hit vanes and turned a turbine wheel, which then pressurized air into the induction system to boost power.

Results were impressive. During 1968, the fuel-injection 2002s had gradually been developed

to give up to 210 bhp, peaking at 7,500 rpm, but capable of taking up to 7,800 rpm. A turbocharger boost between 1.0 and 1.2 atmospheres gave anything between 270 and 290 bhp, depending on the compression ratio utilized.

Von Falkenhausen commented, "So, in 1969, we had more power and certainly more flexibility from 2 liters than we can get from a full racing version of the Formula 2 engine. Always there is more flexibility with the turbo; this first one, it could pull from below 4,500 rpm to 7,500 rpm." Since the car could be raced down to as little as 860 kg, privateer Porsches now had a problem.

A turbo was not the whole answer, being unreliable and underdeveloped. Alpina's contribution proved critical to the year's points tally, and so did the now thoroughly-developed factory 2002Tii (the turbo was unofficially designated the 2002TiK, the K for *Kompressor*).

By 1969, Alpina had moved into its present Buchloe premises, and its reputation for BMW tuning was such that it played an important back-up role to the factory. Alpina even sold race cars to competitive drivers, including Jorge de Bagration.

For the European Championship, Alpina's number-one pairing in an orange and black

2002TI was Austrian Gunther Huber and German ex-Porsche driver Jurgen Neuhaus. The cars were a little heavier than the works cars and ran less-powerful, carbureted engines with less radical chassis modifications. They conformed to traditional Alpina ideals of aiming to finish above all. It was Alpina's first full season, but by the end, Alpina was the BMW preparation name outside the factory.

The 1969 season

The first round of the 1969 European Touring Car Challenge was the Monza 4-hours, where BMW fielded two normal 2002TI racers (as the 155-mph factory turbos were not prepared), supported by the Alpina car for Huber and Neuhaus. Opposition came, as it did for the whole year, from two very competent Dutchmen, Toine Hezemans and Gijs van Lennep, in two different 911 models (though they sometimes shared).

At its Monza debut, BMW was plagued with ignition troubles on both cars, with only Quester finishing, and in a lowly sixth place.

Huber and Neuhaus scored Alpina's first European win after the two Porsches retired, giving BMW a good start to the year—even if the points came from an unexpected source.

The next European Championship round was on April 13, but that day was not the debut of the 2002 turbo. The factory came to England to try its luck in the non-championship Group 5 sedan races over the Easter Bank Holiday, debuting the 2002TiK.

Quester practiced the turbo at Snetterton on Good Friday, but fuel supply to the engine was erratic, so the car did not start. Thus, it was on Easter Monday, April 7, 1969, that BMW fielded Europe's first turbocharged racing sedan in a race.

Quester made it an impressive debut, for the white 2002 brought a new whooshing sound-effect to the British scene, and BMW's abysmal F2 single-seater fortunes could be forgotten as the 2002TiK swished to a joint fastest practice time (1 minute 29.6 seconds) in a giant-killing performance versus one of two muscular 4.7-liter Ford Falcon V8s.

The brace of Falcons out-dragged Quester from the line, but he held down third place in the kind of short sprint-type racing for which

Without this "secret weapon," BMW could not have kept the 2002 in contention with the six-cylinder Porsche 911s then allowed in sedan events. The photograph shows us the turbo installation for the near-300-bhp 2-liter racing turbo of 1969 and the drawing takes us through the lower location of the also non-intercooled street cousin with over 110 bhp less.

In both cases, the 10,000-rpm turbocharging came from KKK, but mechanical fuel injection was credited to Kugelfischer and Schafer, respectively. The race motor regularly made up to 290 bhp, but suffered fairly severe detonation problems in its early life, as an intercooler was not part of the specification.

Picture & Drawing: BMW Archiv, 1969

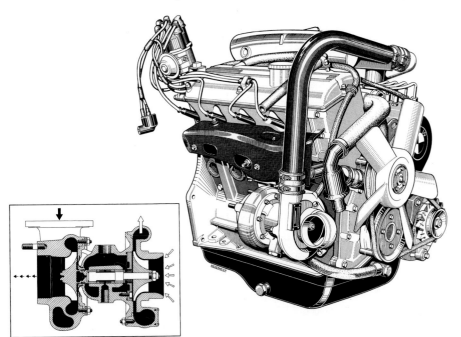

"Can I have one when I grow up?" 1970s works-backed Alpina with the squared arches is admired at the Nürburgring in 1971.

Picture: Autosport, 1978

the 2002 was never intended. Unfortunately, the fuel supply was again erratic. Quester spent some of the longest moments of his racing career up on two wheels when the engine cut out, retiring after 12 laps.

What were the problems with the turbocharged car? Paul Rosche explained some of them: "Herr von Falkenhausen told you that we only started this project very late. There was just no time to fit and modify parts correctly. Kugelfischer had two months to make the racing injection fuel pump, and it was often in trouble to maintain pressure—the gears inside would simply break. But these were not the only troubles.

"We had to reduce the detonation taking place in long races, and for this we would reduce the compression more and more, making the mixture richer....Often the fuel we had to use was not of such good quality as you can

get today...oh, and we did not have intercooling, so it was going to be trouble always....And with four cylinders and the turbo, the exhaust would split in early races. Even with the transmission, we had troubles when the turbocharged engine was fitted, for both the half-shafts and the gearbox had to take too much power."

That gloomy feeling was not reflected in the results, which were considerably better than expected in such endurance races. At the second round of the championship, Aspern in Austria, Quester's sole turbo expired. Basche's conventional works 2002TI did not score points either. Again Alpina struck gold, this time with a first (Huber) and second (Neuhaus) overall ahead of Dr. Helmut Marko's Chevrolet Camaro.

The third round was luckier. For two hours around the Belgrade track, Quester's sole turbo stayed together for a win ahead of Basche's TI and de Bagration's Alpina-BMW car, which Quester lapped. So, mark April 20, 1969 as the BMW's first turbo win: the first victory in an international event in the world by a turbocharged (as opposed to supercharged) sedan.

The fourth round at Budapest, Hungary, saw both works cars out of the top three. Alpina's workmanship and de Bagration's driving in the one-hour street race netted second place, splitting two Porsches.

The Czechoslovakian Brno circuit produced Quester's second win of the season, and BMW's second one-two-three, Basche holding that second place ahead of a locally-entered BMW 2002TI.

The sixth round of the series produced a last-minute cliffhanger finish and poor spectator attendance. Brands Hatch in Britain saw BMW produce a trio, led by Quester and Hahne (pole position, 1 minute 46.8 seconds). A sec-

ond turbo for Chris Craft/Basche (1 minute 48.7 seconds) was fourth quickest, and a normally aspirated 2002TI for Dr. Helmut Marko and Dieter Glemser (1 minute 49.8 seconds), demonstrated that the turbo had not completely overshadowed the injection 2002.

The turbo 2002s had been carefully detuned to improve their chances of lasting for six scheduled hours. Alpina had two backup BMWs in the bigger class and some 1600s to look after, but they lost one when Austrian Formula Vee ace Gerold Pankl suffered a driveshaft failure and hit the bank, breaking his leg. Another driver with a sore foot was Quester—Toine Hezemans ran over it in the pits!

Both the Craft/Basche and the Marko/Glemser factory BMWs retired with what was described as rocker-gear trouble (Craft's had actually seized its turbo). Quester and Hahne had to struggle with the electrical

The beautiful BBS cast-alloy, split-rim wheels first appeared on the 2002, providing up to a ten-inch rim width by thirteen inches in diameter for the Dunlop racing tires to rest on. These were pictured at Thruxton in April 1969 on Dieter Quester's 2002 turbo debut at the British Easter Monday Formula 2 meeting.

Picture: LAT, UK 1969; reprinted 1978

Britain, 1969: the two factory BMW turbos spring off the line for a 3-hour confrontation with Ford. It was close—very close—in this European Championship qualifier.

Picture: Autosport, released 1982

gremlins that left them with a flat battery after pit-stops and a slow, complete tire change.

Following the retirement of many of the front-runners—though it was by no means a tortoise, having practiced in 1 minute 50.4 seconds—the Broadspeed 1300-cc Escort GT was an unexpected leader. It was a very special Ford, but still 700 cc and a turbo light of the BMW, so it was in the psychologically-sound David position versus the German Goliath's turbo 2-liter.

Naturally, the British crowd was rooting for Fitzpatrick and former Grand Prix driver Trevor Taylor as they tried to retain the small Ford's lead. The turbo BMW, in Quester's hands, was flinging up the grass and kicking up the dirt as he slid in sideways pursuit of the regal purple Ford, catching up at three seconds a lap.

Just 28 minutes from the end, Quester made it, finally winning by just 7.6 seconds at an average of 84.36 mph (135.7 km/h). *Autosport* used the heading "Bayerische Brands" to describe the day's proceedings, for BMWs also won three other classes. Gunther Huber/Peter Peter (another Austrian Formula Vee man) were third overall, and took the 2-liter class. Yet another Alpina BMW was fifth and won the 1600 category for Paul Bergner/Walter Treser.

July brought Germany's 6-hour sedan Grand Prix; but, though BMW entered three cars (two turbocharged) and gained pole position (9 minutes 20.6 seconds), it was left to Alpina's Gunther Huber and Peter Peter to literally steam to the finish and take second place. Both the factory Bimmers led, Glemser crashing after seven laps, hitting a bridge in the TiK he shared with Basche (he was honest enough to admit he was looking in the mirror at Hezemans' pursuing Porsche). Hahne/Quester's 2002 suffered transmission failure after one-third distance.

Later in July, two factory cars were entered for the Spa 24-hours, Craft sharing again with Hahne in the turbo and Quester/Basche expecting better durability in a 2002TI. Chris Craft recalls that Hubert Hahne promised him a blind date that evening and that he had every intention of being there, even if their meeting was in Paris. Hahne knew that the TiK might be expiring sooner rather than later, and he was as good as his word—the turbo model blew a head gasket within one of the planned twenty-four hours!

In practice, the 2002TiK had proved a tenth slower (4 minutes 15.1 seconds) than Jacky Ickx in one of the big Mercedes (which did not take the start owing to tire and homologation incompatibility). The BMW's time was third quickest overall in this high-quality year. Also out was the Quester/Basche TI, making this one of the worst BMW Spa outings ever. The only compensation was a standard-looking and melodic Alpina 2800CS, which made the

magical coupe's first international race result with a ninth overall.

The ninth and tenth rounds of the 1969 series were at Zandvoort and Jarama, as there was no hillclimb in the schedule that year. Zandvoort again proved a Porsche circuit when the 911 driver was Hezemans. Quester squeezed around a tenth faster in practice (1 minute 40.2 seconds). Hezemans won by 22 seconds after an hour of racing, but it was Basche who took a tremendous second place, fighting off van Lennep's Porsche and Quester. The pace was such that fifth-placed Huber was lapped. Hahne, incidentally, was not driving either of two turbo 2002s because of an injury in the F2 BMW.

The final round at Jarama resulted in Quester's fourth win of the year, and the fourth for the turbo. The Austrian beat de Bagration's

It was never going to last! The works 2002 for Hubert Hahne explodes away from the start of the 1969 Spa 24-hours, and leaps up the hill from Eau Rouge. It left three Porsche 911s in its red-hot wake. Hahne and Chris Craft shared this 2002 turbo in the late-July classic. This is Hahne leading uphill from the start, though the car had recorded only its third-fastest practice time. Neither works 2002 finished that year.

Picture: Autosport, Special Stage section, 1/8/69

Picture: Autosport, released 1982

June 1969, and a dramatic finish to the Brands Hatch 6-hours saw Dieter Quester just haul the surviving 2002 turbo ahead of the fleet Ford Escort GT of John Fitzpatrick and Trevor Taylor. Quester and Hahne were just 7.6 seconds ahead after six hours' racing, following electrical troubles.

Porsche 911 and Alex Soler-Roig's Alpina-prepared 2002TI. That race was on September 28, 1969, and it was the last time the factory raced a 2002—a short but sweet career. During 1969, the BMW 2002 won six of the ten championship rounds, two of those wins scored by Alpina. There were seven second places and three thirds notched up by the BMW marque.

The 1969 season produced another Division 3 (biggest capacity class) European title for BMW—this time by a 5-point margin over the Porsches—but others had less opposition in their way, and two other marques scored more points in other classes. Quester took the driver's title in the division (over the consistent Huber), but was in the runner-up position, on overall points, to Fiat Abarth's "Pam."

In just two "02" seasons, BMW blitzed opposition from Porsche's pedigree GT and won races outright, quite a contrast to the class acts of the 700s and earlier 1800s. Ironically, BMW left the European Championship to Alpina in 1970, the season in which those fleet Porsches were banned from this category, as was turbocharging.

The 1970 season and beyond

Summing up the turbo, Quester told me, "For this time, the turbo has very good response to the throttle. For 1969 and the first season in turbo form, I think this was very good...the car had little of the slow take-up that is always talked about for turbocharged engines. The car was very comfortable to drive, mainly because it is so quiet." It was also a very quick car—capable, according to the factory, of 154 mph (248 km/h). That explains why a 2002 was able to turn in similar lap times to that of a 6.9-liter V8 Mercedes-Benz at Spa-Francorchamps.

I asked Chris Craft for his recollections of the 2002 turbo racer that he twice shared with Hahne. Craft was the up-and-coming international driver with a formula car and Broadspeed Escort pedigree. The British idea of good handling at that time was very different to that admired in Germany.

Craft frankly remembered the 2002TiK suspension as "...soft, dreadfully soft. It was like a family shopping car! Still, you soon got used to it: there were fair brakes and it did feel really quick in a straight line. I think it was probably the most comfortable racing car I have ever driven, with the quietest engine.

"I think turbos became part of Hahne and Quester's driving technique. For me, the turbo lag was noticeable—I would say something like one to one and a half seconds as you opened the throttle, before the full effect hit you. At the other end of any straight was the excitement though.

"I remember coming into Hawthorn's at Brands. I had shut off, but the engine was still going like a bandit! I just couldn't believe it. We survived, and I realized that it didn't supply the usual braking effect. The car always just seemed to be going faster and faster at the end of any straight, with me standing on the brakes like a cartoon character!"

Despite good omens, 1970 was not a good year for Alpina in the European race series. That was partly because it was struggling to develop the six-cylinder for the coupe, as well as continuing the now-conservatively powered (180–190 bhp) 2002TI, which remained on carburetors long after the factory had utilized fuel injection.

There was little chance of winning against a fierce, factory-sponsored Autodelta version of the Alfa Romeo GTA: the 205-bhp injection GTAm. Neither Alpina nor anyone else ever succeeded in winning a European Championship round with a BMW 2002 again, but Americans added further luster to the 2002's reputation, as revealed in the preceding chapter.

Alpina did win, twice, with the 2800CS, but otherwise it was Alfa all the way. Incredibly, a 2002 did not figure in the top three at the close of any championship round, Alpina's success coming either with the "six" or the class-winning 1600.

Developed to yield about 170 bhp, these 1.6-liter Alpina cars, in the hands of many drivers (notably Austria's Formula 1-grade driver, Dr. Helmut Marko), were enough to cope with Alfa Romeo. Marko won his class four times, and altogether the marque notched up seven class wins in the nine 1970 championship rounds.

For the first time, an overall champion was officially recognized, which did the BMW drivers no good (Toine Hezemans was Alfa's champion driver), but acknowledged that the Alpina-BMW 1600 had more points than any other manufacturer.

In 1971, engineer Dr. Fritz Indra came to Alpina. Though his arrival would make a lot of difference to the progress of the six-cylinder cars, the 2002s only developed in power by adopting the Kugelfischer injection system. The car still did not figure in the top three results of any European Championship event, for Alpina was now firmly preoccupied with the coupe and the domination of the Ford Capri in overall race results.

The 1600TI was a useful competitive introduction to the joys of 02 competition. This is another BMW baron at work: Ferfried von Hohenzollern in the leaning Alpina example. BMW left Alpina to represent their touring-car interests in 1970 and the Buchloe specialists conquered the smaller category with these 1600TI models. It was the spirited effort of Austrian Dr. Helmut Marko (later a Grand Prix driver before an eye injury tragically abbreviated his career) that brought Alpina that title in a year of no success for the 2002.

Picture: BMW Archiv/Postcard series, 1970

For 1972's European series, Alpina reverted to Teutonic logic and concentrated upon a single coupe. They did this instead of trying to run up to five cars per racing weekend, as they initially had in 1971 despite employing only four race mechanics at the time!

Thus, the 2002 faded away from top-level European results, although it was still as strong as ever in national events throughout the Continent and was a star player in the US in the mid-1970s (see chapter 30 for more on this). The 2002 was notably successful at events like Germany's own 24-hour annual sedan thrash around the Nürburgring, which Alpina has won on many occasions, using a cadre of drivers that includes women and even royalty.

The Alpina-BMW 2002 deserves special recall for introducing an 18-year-old Hans-Joachim Stuck Jr. to the taste of BMW success, when he finished second overall in a hillclimb held at St. Auerberg. His father is best remembered as a prewar Grand Prix star, but Stuck Sr. had also won a lot of postwar events for BMW, mastering the 700 to the 507 V8.

The Alpina-BMW 2002 also brought a woman home as co-victor in the tough 24-hours at Nürburgring. Miss Hannelore Werner became a winner in 1969 with Rudi Faltz, and she went on to become Dieter Quester's teammate in F2 for a single "Underground Racing" season.

Older and wilder

The 2002 assumed some wild European racing guises in private hands before it was finished. From 1973 onward, the 16-valve cylinder head was permitted internationally. Schnitzer's canted, production-style conversion initially proved just the right job for shorter events, starting off at 254 bhp (a 2-liter, 8-valve "02" usually delivered under 230 bhp).

The super Schnitzer 16-valver was even used briefly by Alpina when it thought it ought to be racing something in 1974. Koepchen fielded its own quick 16-valve 2002, as did Schnitzer and GS Tuning (run, engineered, and driven by

Still road-registered at nearby Kaufburen, a works Alpina BMW contests the 1969 Motor 6-hours at Brands Hatch in Britain. The smallest 02 was consistent but the lap times were a little faster than that of the pursuing 1.3-liter Mini.

Picture: Autosport, released 1978

Dieter Basche), in some European Touring Car Championship rounds in the 1973–74 seasons.

These hybrid 02s proved very quick indeed, but for the factory and overall victory, the 2002 was finished in European Championship racing. In England, the model was very successful in early Group 1 production racing, run by the official concessionaires, until Chevrolet Camaros and the Bimmer coupe were sorted for late 1972 and the remainder of the decade.

When the 2002 turbo road car was launched, it did look as though there might be

a serious effort to revive the fortunes of the model by the factory, but that idea collapsed in the wake of the 1973/74 winter fuel crisis.

Schnitzer never lost faith with the model—they were still front-running turbocharged versions in 1977 in the German Championship—but gradually, commercial sense prevailed. The 320 bodywork had to be adopted over the skeletal substructures that formed the base for any Group 5 car eligible for Germany's national series and the World Championship of Makes (1976 on).

Magnificent! As the 1960s turned into the 1970s, the 2002 appeal spread to racers at all levels. Here at Pflanzgarten, Nürburgring, the 02 of Kurt Fuchs strains every horsepower to stay ahead of the Alfa GT and the whirring Mini-Cooper S.

Picture: Motor-Presse Bild, H. P. Seuffert, Germany, 1970

Thanks to Schnitzer's later 1970s efforts, the 2002 raced in Germany with anything up to 400 bhp from its turbocharged 1.4-liter version of the plucky DOHC 2002 unit. Initially, the leading lights in keeping the 2002 competitive in Germany during the 1970s, where Porsche, BMW, and Ford wrestled for overall domination in successive seasons of increasingly radical re-engineering, were GS Tuning and Schnitzer, but the Freilassing brothers prevailed.

In 1974, the home series was still about Ford, with Dieter Glemser winning the title in a Zakspeed Escort. But class opposition came from GS Tuning's version of the 2002, which packed a normally-aspirated 282 bhp—enough to hit 0–62 mph in 5.3 seconds and 100 mph in 10.6 seconds in a stripped 2002 body that weighed under 900 kg (1,980 lbs).

For 1975, Schnitzer concentrated on a highly developed, 150,000 DM version of the big Bimmer coupe. GS Tuning redefined their 2-liter 02 and squeezed 285 bhp by 8,900 rpm from an 11.8:1 compression sprint version of 1,998 cc (142.6 bhp a liter). The series went

to a Zakspeed Ford Escort again, but Schnitzer won brownie points for its 485-bhp coupe, as driver Albrecht Krebs was the best-placed BMW driver in the 1975 series (third overall).

Unsurprisingly, this put Schnitzer back in the hunt for 1976. Utilizing the driving talents of Jorg Obermoser, they fought the factory-backed Zakspeed Ford Escorts. Meanwhile, Porsche (represented by diverse teams, giving it little chance for the Championship title) ran away with all the races in the early turbo monsters.

A 1976 Schnitzer 2002 remained normally aspirated, tipped the scales at just 854 kg/1,879 lbs, and spat 292 bhp from its big-bore, short-stroke 1,987 cc. That represented 147 bhp a liter, unmatched in my records for 2002 normally-aspirated power, and little less than the factory had from its 1969 race turbos, *sans* intercoolers! Such is true technical progress in the white-hot world of motorsports....

The provision of 347.6 bhp a ton allowed the Schnitzer 2002 of 20 years ago to rush from 0–62 mph in little over 5 seconds and embrace 0–124 mph in 17.5 seconds, all for a price tag of 70,000 DM.

For 1977, the 2002 had a very important role, previewing BMW's renewed interest in turbocharging and reminding us that Josef Schnitzer was now a technical pacesetter in the use of turbocharging for German national racing applications. Schnitzer had undertaken turbo research and development since 1974 (using a TOJ sports car as a neutral but swift test bed), and his links with BMW ensured that Paul Rosche was aware of Schnitzer's thinking. That turbo progress became relevant to BMW in both long-distance racing (an 800-bhp coupe monster), further turbo 320s (such as the McLaren 320T for the US), and the 1.5-liter Grand Prix turbo four.

Turbocharging was forced on German Championship contestants because the rules encouraged 1.4 liters, turbocharged, to beat conventional 2-liter category opposition. Even the early turbos—erratically and explosively at

first—belted out bonus bhp over their 600-cc-bigger, non-turbo opposition.

The 2002 turbo was very unreliable in its 1977 debut season, but extremely fast, with Albrecht Krebs setting Nürburgring's ultimate 2002 lap at 7 minutes 58 seconds, 171.98 km/h, and a 106.8 mph average. The 2002 turbo won two events for Kreb's colleague, Peter Hennige, and another for multiple Deutschemeister Klaus Ludwig, who was still racing (Mercedes "CLK" GTs) in 1997.

For 1977, Schnitzer had a 1,426-cc short-stroke version of BMW's famous four (80 x 71 mm) based on the 1.5/1.6-liter iron block. It had vertical mounting, gear-driven DOHC, and a single KKK turbo running 1.1 to 1.4 bar. The result was 400 bhp at 9,000 rpm, some 108 bhp more than 1976, with lower engine rpm and a figure of 280.7 bhp a liter.

A skeletal steel 2002 frame underneath wild, wide, and bold bodywork tipped official scales at around 800 kg /1,760 lbs, representing 555.5 bhp a ton. Impressive, with independent magazine time trials (as for all figures given here) returning 0–62 mph in 4.7 seconds, 0–96 mph in 10 seconds flat, and 0–124 mph in two seconds less than the normally aspirated 02s—just 15.5 seconds.

The last turbo 2002s could rip by at 160 mph on 1.4 liters. In a purely aerodynamic sense, the 02 was sleeker than its 3-series successors, but the 3-series of 1975 could not be ignored. BMW Motorsport (new 1.4 turbo motor, M12/12) and Schnitzer put together a 1978 alliance to secure the national title for the 3-series, the subject of chapter 21.

Neither BMW nor Schnitzer would devote front-line racing and engineering resources to the fabulous old 02 warrior after 1977—a season most German race fans remember for the BMW 320 Junior Team accidents!

Privateers continued to run the 2002 in turbocharged form right into 1978, and the car managed a best of fifth overall in the German series. However, there could never

Tiger by Schnitzer! Josef "Sepp" Schnitzer gives a works Ford Escort and the rest of the BMW babies a shock in a front-wheel-locking moment at the 1970 Nürburgring. The gifted engineer was a race and hillclimb winner with 1800, 2000, and 2002; but his legacy to BMW was leading-edge race-engine technology conceived on a practical "can-do" basis.

BMW Werkfoto, 1970; reprinted 1987

(Top) Private glory in Germany. Occasional works 02 driver Peter Koepchen developed his own breed of racing 2002 that was quick enough to hold its own with the very special Alfa GTAm, seen pursuing the Koepchen car around the Nürburgring in the early 1970s.

(Bottom) The GS Tuning 2002, seen up over the old serrated curbs on the infield loops of Hockenheim, was prepared and driven ably by one-time BMW Motorsport employee Dieter Basche.

Pictures: H. P. Seuffert; Author archives, 1970/71

How to corner your BMW 2002—for advanced students only! Avon Motor Tour of Britain 1975: some German competitors earn Spirit of 02 award.

Picture: Colin Taylor Productions

be the serious sponsorship cash behind an 02 as for a 3-series, when almost two years had passed since the last 02 (1502) left the production line.

The 2002 was a typical BMW—fast, practical, versatile, and reliable. From the factory racing viewpoint, 1969 was the racing end of the complete 2002, but Schnitzer's turbo engineering was significant in the 1970s.

The 2002 was and is the BMW that brought affordable and exciting motorsports to many, and it provided the factory with a chance to showcase engineering expertise and progress to the ranks of front-line international sedan racing.

(Top Left) Sometimes there is a substitute for cubic inches, and it comes from BMW! Starting life as a 1600, this Camaro-beating British 02 carries a 2,100-cc, M3-based motor. It was assembled by Roger Dowson at Silverstone and powered by a Lester Owen unit for BMW dealership (L&C Tunbridge Wells) manager Simon Crompton. This BMW has completed 33 races without failure as of mid-1997 and has won outright in the wet against 6-liter Camaros and Mustangs.

The L&C 1602-2.1 weighs 820 kg (1,804 lbs) and has 225 bhp by 8,000 rpm to regularly win its class (and appear in the top three overall) in the prestigious ICS Historic Racing Championship from 1994 to 1997. It is "prestigious" because the ICS Historics support the main British Touring Car Championship races. The gallant baby Bimmer also seized the overall ICS title in 1995 and 1996.

Picture: Mary Harvey, UK, 1997

(Bottom Left) The former Trans Am team 2002s at rest before their outings at the Monterey Historic meeting in August 1996. The equipe also had a rare Glas/BMW GT on display.

Picture: Author, USA, 1996

World rally career, 1969–73

The 2002 also jumped and slid spectacularly through a works-assisted rally career of six years. A single World Championship victory came in 1972 (Achim Warmbold won Portugal's TAP Rally), but the 2002 was never a regular winner at the World-Championship level. The 2002 was an excellent prospect over the tarmac twists of Ireland and was favored by many quick Irish rallyists before Porsches were imported by the ferry-load.

A sustained BMW rally program was impractical, and factory support fluttered so that racing had first call on often (very) limited funds prior to the Neerpasch era. BMW did allow Prodrive to rally the M3 in the 1980s, cooperating on the homologation necessities and becoming quite enthusiastic once more when a win at the World-Championship level was returned. The basic glossy marketing philosophy of BMW today always defeats any full-blooded World-Championship proposal, particularly as 4x4 is not a core value of BMW engineering.

In rally trim, the 2002s were campaigned from 1969 (debut at January's Monte Carlo Rally—neither

Archim Warmbold, later Mazda's rally team manager, and current Ferrari manager Jean Todt are shown in spectacular action on the 1973 Austrian Alpine Rally, an event they would have won in their works-registered 2002 on performance. They were disqualified after an organizational misunderstanding: teammates Bjorn Waldegard and Hans Thorszelius finished a fine third.

Picture: Author Archives, 1978

car finished) to 1974. The 2002 proved what a versatile machine it was by supporting the efforts of literally hundreds of privateers all over the world. Both BMW and Schnitzer derivatives of the four-cylinder unit have been used to good effect in rallying, too, but the factory stopped participating in this branch of motorsports in 1973.

Much of Toyota's success in 16-valve engine engineering traces back to Schnitzer and BMW. Schnitzer provided Ove Anderson's Cologne team with direct technical assistance in the 1970s that taught Toyota the basics behind the finest 16-valve engineering (and a brief racing liaison with a 1977–78 Celica Turbo that tried take on Porsche in the top classes).

The occasional works 2002s were potent in their later rally life. A 16-valve Schnitzer-engined works car appeared on the 1973 British RAC Rally and offered about 220 bhp, enough for Bjorn Waldegard to chase Makinen's leading Escort for the first half of the event, only to be badly delayed on the second leg when Bjorn parked it in some young trees. British rallyists Russell Brookes/John Brown oversaw a rescue, so the previously pristine white and Motorsport-striped 2002Tii ultimately finished seventh, run on a shoestring and the enthusiasm of a Munich hardcore.

Discussing BMW Motorsport's rally participation from 1973 onwards, when 16-valve heads were admitted, engineering executive Martin Braungart reported, "We started off with the Schnitzer engine, and Warmbold won the Austrian Alpine with that. Actually, we did quite a lot of development, and the car weighed about 1,000 kg and was strong and reliable. I think for rally events, the percentage of success owing to the car is not so high as in racing, but we had a good car with independent rear suspension and our engine.

"After the RAC Rally [1973], we ran out of money, but we did have a modified version of our own GmbH Formula 2 engine, giving about 240 horsepower, and we did do the 1,000 Lakes in Finland with that [it hardly starred, managing the lower half of the top twenty for an unhappy Warmbold/Jean Todt]," concluded Braungart, who is best-known these days for his continuing role in the famous wheel and accessory company he helped found: BBS.

The works rally team of 2002TIs made their debut in the 1969 Monte Carlo Rally. They were hindered by persistent braking problems and neither the car of Timo Makinen and Paul Easter (shown here at Monaco) nor the second team car made the finish. The factory rallied the 2002 with varying enthusiasm from 1969 to 1974 but was never able to apply the wholehearted support over a number of years that would have supplied the experience so necessary to succeed in this rugged branch of motorsports.

Picture: LAT, Monaco, 1969

Our 1977 shot is important for the period feel of the big Jaguar V12 coupe in gloriously unsuccessful motion (here driven by subsequent multiple British Champion Andy Roiuse), plus the fact that the 2002 was still seen campaigning in top-line internationals two years after its production demise. This one was run by the Lindner team, who subsequently won the European Touring Car title for BMW with the 1987 M3.

Picture: Werner Wilke, Germany, 1974

By 1974, Alpina had progressed to trying a rear-water radiator layout on a 16-valve, Schnitzer-engined 2002. Note squared-off wheel-arches as the car flies at Nürburgring. The venture was not a success and Alpina reverted to a policy of tackling events where their own race modifications inside the factory could be applied.

Picture: LAT, UK, 1977

QUICK FACTS

Period

1960–97

Products

All M-prefix road cars and their engine development

Performance

Motors of 60 to 600 normally-aspirated bhp; 400 to 1,200 turbocharged horsepower

Achievements

Limited-stock company established May 1972, offsetting 1970s competition budget initially, followed by generating millions of DM profit for the 1990s

People

Jochen Neerpasch brings BMW a commercial as well as a competitive edge; Dieter Stappert and Paul Rosche hit the Grand Prix trail; Karl Heinz Kalbfell guards the millennium M-spirit

Chapter 14

Motorsport, Inc.

BMW Motorsport GmbH: growth of a competition and commercial task force

BMW has always been interested in competition, but its massive 1996 turnover of 300 million DM ($189 million) in M-branded commercial exploitation of that interest is unique. From 1972 to 1993, Motorsport GmbH, a company-within-a-company, tackled BMW's involvement with increasing customer spin-offs to cover the M-prefix that originally signified Motorsport involvement.

Since then, we have had MPower (road and race motors), MTeam (usually works-backed race cars), MStyle (clothing), MTechnics (especially applied to uprated road-car suspension systems and usually called "MTech"), and the M1, M3, M5, M535i, and M635CSi/M6 cars.

The 1990s saw a logical continuation of this process, until BMW Motorsport GmbH split to breed a stand-alone concern (M GmbH, founded August 1, 1993), whose primary function is to deal with the public. That task is met by three M-divisions: BMW M Cars, BMW Individual, and BMW Driver Training.

The hardcore BMW Motorsport works racing business remained under the control of Paul Rosche at Preussenstrasse, within walking distance of the four-cylinder BMW Haus. Today, that traditional BMW Motorsport facility, with just over 100 staff and its entrenched under-

ground test cells, is primarily concerned with race-engine building.

A winter 1995/96 decision saw a nationalistically brave move to McLaren in Britain. That domestically unpopular decision covered all 3-series SuperTouring engineering, outside the engine bay, joining the same Anglo-German division of duties on the McLaren F1-BMW V12 GT program. This cooperation existed from the start of the 1995 GT race season to its contracted end in October 1997, when a new alliance was formed with Williams Grand Prix Engineering.

The German media was not amused when this British export decision was announced at a hastily gathered press conference, prior to the South American festive theme of the annual pre-Christmas Motorsport Awards evening. (But then, I don't remember the Brits hanging out the welcome banners when BMW bought Rover....)

BMW Motorsport (not separated formally until that 1995/96 winter) remained the insider source of engine expertise and works motorsport participation, the latter mostly in association with the Schnitzer and Bigazzi race teams, plus McLaren for all non-engine research and development. Paul Rosche remained at the helm, but other professional managers took the daily

Generation game:
Hans Stuck Sr. (left)
and teenage Junior
(center) in the early
1970s with the
guiding force behind
MPower throughout
the past three
decades: Paul
Rosche (right).

*Picture: Author
archives, circa 1971*

load of administration. Those who have recently contributed to the BMW fighting spirit at the circuits of the world include Klaus Mahrlein in the 1996–97 seasons on the organizational side and Marc Surer in driver management.

How did BMW develop such commercial and competitive muscle? Prewar, we have credited the personnel concerned, but there was only one lasting link between the prewar 1930s and the postwar 1950s and 1960s: Alex von Falkenhausen. He was certainly the inspiration behind the company's rebirth in the four-wheeled sporting world, prior to his retirement in 1975 and death at the age of 82.

Yet, many others tried to work at matching his stratospheric standards—men like Joachim Springer, a journalist who rallied himself with such enthusiasm, and Helmuth Bein, who ran the rallying department after having driven and co-driven with distinction in the company products. Then there was harassed Klaus Steinmetz, the engine-development engineer faced with Formula 2's biggest team and lead-

ing-edge aerodynamics. There were others, but these three (all of whom subsequently had some association with GM-Opel) soldiered through those days when being a BMW supporter was not a glamorous business.

The rallying side was entirely separate from von Falkenhausen's engineering/competition operation, though a five-man staff prepared rally cars at Preussenstrasse in the 1960s and early 1970s. The rally team operated on a small sales budget and was generally separate from the race-car technicians.

MPower is born

The pivotal change that brought MPower and M-everything-else came in May 1972. Jochen Neerpasch and Martin Braungart defected from Ford at Cologne after approaches from BMW personnel, including current Chrysler heavyweight Bob Lutz.

Klaus Mahrlein led the home-team effort in Germany's STW Cup of 1996 and 1997. In 1997, BMW drivers Johnny Cecotto and Joachim Winkelhock were the only effective opposition to Peugot of France winning the national title—painful!

Picture: BMW AG Presse, 1997

The aristocratic master: Alex von Falkenhausen in 1971, toward the end of a career that had linked prewar and postwar BMW sporting expertise.

Picture: BMW Archiv/ Courtesy Chris Willows, 1997

Neerpasch and Braungart settled in the sunnier south-Bavarian climate to construct a completely new company, responsible for competition and its commercial ramifications for the main BMW company. Since Neerpasch had been Ford's competition manager, running a team of then-invincible Ford Capri V6s in the European Touring Car Championship, he was a significant acquisition for BMW.

No less significance should be attached to the arrival of Martin Braungart, who came from Stuttgart and had been a regular co-driver in the Mercedes-Benz rally team while studying at university for engineering qualifications. After six months at Mercedes-Benz as an engineer, he joined Ford at Cologne soon after Neerpasch, who had been employed to establish Ford Motorsport in Germany as a counterpart to the earlier English Ford sports department. Both Braungart and Neerpasch had thus been through the grind of setting up a sporting department for a major manufacturer before coming to BMW.

Braungart's role was as deputy, taking technical responsibility for the cars outside the engine bay, a role in which he was supported by Rainer Bratenstein. Bratenstein worked for Auto-Union and for Porsche's racing and research departments before joining BMW Motorsport in 1973 as a competition-development engineer. That role stopped at the engine, for Paul Rosche and his engineers looked after power-plant development and maintenance as a separate responsibility, as true in 1997 as in 1972.

Neerpasch discovered some hidden advantages at BMW: the engine technology side was well advanced as a result of the Falkenhausen/ Rosche team's hard work, and Bob Lutz was there to push programs through at BMW board level. Like Neerpasch, Lutz was an outstanding individual. He was a former US pilot of German-speaking Swiss origin—one who had climbed to the top of the automobile industry in Germany and the US.

Bob Lutz headed Opel before moving to BMW as deputy to von Kuenheim. Lutz supported Neerpasch's sporting efforts to the hilt, especially in the marketing of the CSL lightweight coupes, which had to survive a hostile German-public attitude during the fuel crisis. When Lutz left to go on to Ford (and thence to Chrysler), Neerpasch had established himself as an achiever at BMW.

In 1972, Neerpasch arrived to find that a great deal needed to be done very quickly if he was to go out and beat the Fords in Europe the following year. Initially, there was an explosion in staff, as Neerpasch and Braungart hired extra expertise for BMW Motorsport, an enterprise with its own budget.

BMW had to start thinking in a new way. An increasing emphasis on pure competition engineering developed, rather than road and race versatility. When Neerpasch and Braungart were in Cologne, their Ford Capri deviant was designed to go racing; the early-1970s BMW coupes were little more than tuned-up road cars by comparison. While this technical chasm was closed rapidly, the structure and administration of BMW Motorsport was always a bit unwieldy, as it tried to knit diverse activities into one corporate pattern.

The first moves were to turn the sports department into a limited company within the BMW organization. This meant that it initially had to be seen as generating revenue of its own, which led to some bizarre money-raising activities over the years, including the early-1980s implantation of the BMW turbo diesel engines into the floppier American Fords.

"The money's okay, Mario?" BMW Motorsport GmbH founding fathers Martin Braungart (left), Jochen Neerpasch (center), and Italian-American hero Mario Andretti discuss the results of the first Procar race. Mario was then-reigning World Champion from his 1978 season with Lotus-Ford, but the 1979 season was not so rewarding.

Picture: BMW Werkfoto, 1979

More seriously, the "M" for Motorsport identity was established to sell anything from frivolity to serious speed.

Braungart recalled, "We sold anything we could, from rally jackets to complete 2-liter Formula 2 engines. We sold everything the department could make or market. It was a fantastic effort, and we stayed in competition, where we belonged, even through all the fuel crisis troubles."

Through the efforts of Braungart and Neerpasch, BMW Motorsport survived the 1974 season without sacking a single competi-tion employee. Recall that this was in an atmosphere of deep gloom and depression fol-lowing the fuel crisis, when literally thousands of car workers were laid off in Germany, so this was a fine achievement.

Something had to go to keep the 60-strong band at work, profitably, at Preussenstrasse during 1974. That something was the works racing team of CSLs in their smart midnight-blue paint (Neerpasch's favorite color), then packing over 430 bhp from their straight 24-valve, six-cylinder motors.

M-car development

M-branded car assembly began when the company gave its contracted race drivers something special to twirl between tracks. It is an irony of most M-badged BMWs that Motorsport was not their reason to exist, excepting E30 M3 and M1.

For the street, Hans Stuck drove a prototype V12 BMW coupe in 1973–74, but that came from BMW AG engineering, not Motorsport. From 1976 to his tragic death at Monza in 1978, Swedish F1 driver Ronnie Peterson spectacularly drove Motorsport-supplied E12 BMWs of the 3.3- to 3.5-liter 5-series that pre-dated any production 535, alternating with Saabs.

Back in 1974, Marks & Spencer's department-store-chain heir Jonathan Sieff (one of the main financial figures in BMW's importation and recognition in the UK through his key role at Cooper Car Company) was the recipient of an E12-bodied Motorsport 5-series. Truly the granddaddy of all M-branded automobiles, it carried 3-liter clout of more than 210 bhp and featured an uprated Bilstein-damped chassis. All this was at a time when a quick production 5-series came badged 525 and had but 150 bhp.

The first M-badged car to officially be sold was the mid-engined, 165-mph M1 of 1978–81. We tell that story in chapter 20, but for now, remember that only 450 were made, of which 49 were for racing requirements.

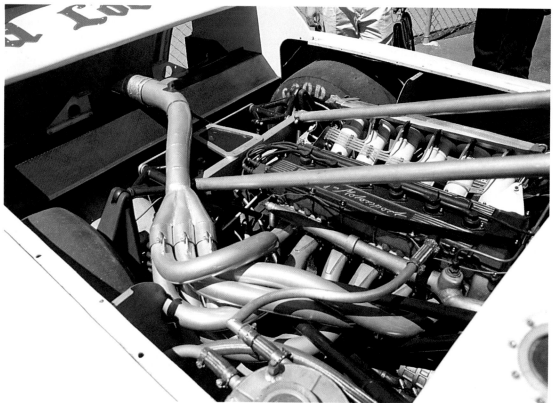

The big six-cylinders have done it all for M-generations, from 286 street horsepower at 3.5 liters to more than 750 turbocharged bhp from a 3.2-liter deviant. The race units we see in the States are Vasek Polak's CSL unit (Top Left) and the mid-motor M1 GTP installation for the Red Lobster team (Bottom Left). Then we have the blue unit, a production M5 motor (Bottom Right), which eventually ran up to 3.8 liters and 340 bhp with almost 300 lb-ft of torque.

(Top Right) And the red "M1"? This is where BMW NA never speaks to me again. Carefully posed alongside their corporate display is the All-American twist to a legend: whisper the truth...there's a big Chevy V8 packed in the back of that elongated rear deck!

Pictures: Author (3); BMW AG (M5 motor)

Marc Surer debuts the first M-product (M1) at the Nürburgring in 1979. Standing in the door is M-stalwart engineer Rainer Bratenstein, while his taller colleague in glasses is the BMW Motorsport manager who followed Jochen Neerpasch with distinction: Dieter Stappert.

Picture: BMW Werkfoto, Germany, 1979

That BMW ever adopted 3.5-liter sixes for larger mass-production purposes can also be credited to the fact that Motorsport made such oversize bore dimensions credible in competition. Descended from the M49-coded post-1974 racing CSLs, it was the in-line six cylinder DOHC engine from M1 (coded M88 for limited production) that formed the 24-valve basis for the M5 and the M635CSi, usually referred to in the US as the M6.

The long-term influence of those M49-coded 440-hp racing sixes of the 1970s was to provide the basis of arguably the finest in-line six ever supplied in production cars. M1, M5, M635CSi, and the ever-larger six-cylinder M5s all owed their mellow muscularity to that 1974 CSL racing unit.

BMW Motorsport listed all that was needed to make a 3.3-liter conversion to a basic 525 or 528 by 1978. That parts package included the ex-coupe/7-series 3.3-liter standard six-cylinder motor at 197 bhp, a close-ratio gearbox (dogleg first), a limited-slip differential (set at 25 percent preload), sports seats from Recaro or ASS Scheel, and a Motorsport steering wheel that accompanied chassis updates.

Such larger-engined 5-series proved especially effective and led directly to products such as the official 1980–81 BMW M535i in the E12 body (960 units in left-hand drive, and 450 in right-hand drive for UK). A second (E28) series of M535i, running from March 1985 to December 1987, featured the slightly facelifted original 5-series body and was criticized for wearing an M-badge while carrying very few M-features. It was a major commercial success, hitting almost 9,500 units in mainstream production.

Then came the ferocious 286-bhp M5 in the E28 outline, the pedigree and performance of which left nobody with any doubt of its M-

Big bomber. Officially referred to as the M635CSi but simply carrying an M-badge on its rump, the Americans had this superb Motorsport creation (manufactured at Dingolfing). They dubbed it simply the M6.

Picture: BMW Werkfoto, Munich, 1983

parentage. Some 2,145 were hand-made by Motorsport employees at Preussenstrasse and 1,370 were shipped to the US. That 24-valve M5 strand ran eleven years, from October 1984 to October 1995, and had three primary 5-series bodies (E28, E34, and E34 Touring).

While the M6/635CSi did not make it out of the 1980s—the 6-series replaced by the hopelessly excessive 850 V12 and V8 coupes in 1989—the M-band at Garching continued to develop and build the M5. Instead of the original 3,453-cc six (93.4 x 84 mm) rated at 286 bhp and 250 lb-ft of torque, Motorsport stretched the already-large six until you could hear the crankshaft creak. For 1988–93, it had 3,535 cc (same bore with an 86-mm stroke) for 315 bhp and 265 lb-ft of torque.

That was not the limit of Motorsport's street ambition. The six took another course of

steroids and became a champion weightlifter among straight sixes, hurling the spacious four-door across Europe on the 340-bhp thrust of 3,795 cc (94.6 x 90 mm).

You could have either sedan or Touring 5-series bodies, the latter having a curb weight of 3,740 lbs! Enlarged wheel-and-tire combinations had escalated to racing proportions, with the back of the Touring (and a Nürburgring sedan option) supported on 9J x 17 inch alloys and tire sizes up to 255/40.

Torque picked up to 290 lb-ft at the 4,750-rpm point, at which the motor went from mellow to bellow. This ultimate production BMW straight six—its DOHC 24-valve layout still owed to the CSL's 400-plus horsepower racing days of glory—needed a strong electronic limiter to stop it from launching the M5 down the autobahn at more than 170 mph. They settled

Sometimes they played the commercial M-product game for gain, not competition advantage. This British-registered "M" 535i was a production version of the big-engined 5-series theme that Motorsport had restricted in earlier 5-series to contracted personnel and VIPs. Thousands were made, amounting to a charming blend between the 3.6-liter six of the coupe/7-series and uprated running gear.

Picture: BMW (GB) Ltd., Bracknell, UK, 1984

for the 155-mph maximum that has existed for political reasons for many of Munich's finest since the 1980s. M5 acceleration from 0–62 mph occupied 5.9 seconds, which highlights the M5's inexorable progress, because the original (and lighter) upright M5 was also a 150-mph car with outstanding acceleration.

To give you an idea of how the M-cars mushroomed, consider that the M1 trickled through four manufacturing years to hit 450 units. That M1 production total was not unlike the equally-exotic V8 sports Bimmers of the 1950s: the 507 appears in factory records at 252 for 1957–59, plus one rogue parts-built during 1957 to give us 253 total. The earlier 503 made 407 series examples and five parts-built units in its 412 total.

More on M-manufacture: the E28-coded M5 was hand-made from October 1984 to December 1987 by the competition staff (and other sub-contractors) at Preussenstrasse to

commercialize on the original big-engine 5-series format of the 1970s. Altogether, 2,143 emerged from Preussenstrasse in almost exactly four years. Over ten times more would be made from 1988–95, some 12,249 made at M GmbH's headquarters in Garching.

The first M3 (based on E30) went straight to the production halls of Milbertshofen—designed and created by Motorsport staff led by Thomas Ammerschlager—and some 17,184 of these two-doors were made in a similar four-year span! And that figure ignores the M3-badged Cabriolet, again more of an individual Garching job at a sky-high European price, which covered just 786 power tops. Thus, total M3 output from 1987–91 was a fraction under 18,000 copies

The later E36-based M3 dwarfs even those commercial achievements. Over 36,000 coupes and sedans were made from 1992 to the end of 1996, and the grand total (includ-

These were the conditions when I first drove the M1, but it was still by far the best-natured supercar I've driven in 30 years of privileged motoring.

Picture: BMW Werkfoto, Garmisch, Germany, 1980

ing E36-based sedans and cabriolets) to the close of 1996 exceeded 39,200. The US was the biggest export market for both the boxy original and its sleeker successor, but the later M3—even with its horsepower deficit to the European motor—virtually doubled US M3 sales in little more than a full season!

One model that did not make it down the limited-production lines was a natural successor to the M-prefixed 6-series, of which 5,855 were made between 1984 and December 1988. Motorsport did rework the 850 successor in the hope of providing BMW with another supercar. The spring 1991 M8 prototype

featured over 500 bhp from a 6-liter, quad-cam, 48-valve version of the V12.

Tackling criticism of the 850's standard bulk (over 4,100 lbs), Motorsport expensively reduced weight using Kevlar, carbon fibers, and advanced plastics alongside the crudity of sliding clear-plastic windows. Wolfgang Reitzle, BMW's then-director of research and development, who had presented the original 300-bhp 850 to the press in 1989 as a flawless jewel in the Munich crown, would have none of the 188-mph M8.

Reitzle told reporters when the M8 was unveiled alongside other stillborn BMW babies (including an E30 M3 3.5-liter six

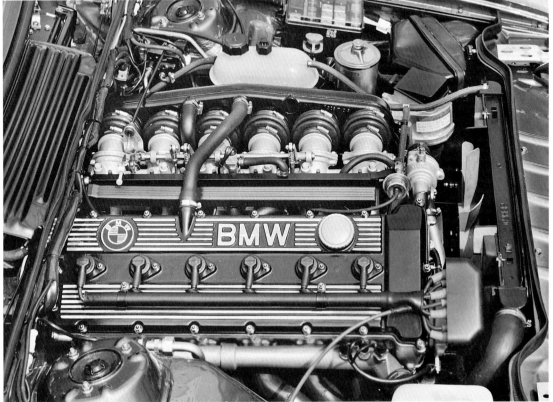

Same straight six 24-valver, different applications and badges. The 286-bhp unit carried the MPower logo for the 1985-built M5 and simply said BMW twice on the 1983-built M635CSi.

Pictures: BMW Werkfoto, Germany, 1983 and 1985

Smaller brother: the four-cylinder M3 (E30) motor was originally developed from an abbreviated six-cylinder, so they share the classic quad-valve, central-spark-plug combustion chamber layout. Inititally rated at 195 catalytic converter bhp or 200 with converter in 2.3-liter trim, the motor was persuaded to give 220 bhp in Evolution street form and over 350 racing bhp with a boost to 2.5 liters.

Picture: Klaus Schnitzer, US

and an M5 convertible), "We're just not interested in putting our name to cars like these anymore."

Instead, Motorsport reworked the 5-liter, 24-valve to 5.6 liters in single-cam-per-bank format to yield 372 bhp and over 400 lb-ft of torque. Complete with a further suspension drop (down 10 mm), a 17-inch alloy wheel diameter, the Getrag six-speed gearbox (an 850 feature), and a unique spoiler set, the 850 CS actually represented the closest thing to an M8 that the public would get. It shifted its 4,200 lbs from 0–60 mph in 5.7 seconds, but was electronically limited to 155 mph. At the wheel, it was a much better car than the original, but not enough to foster the halo effect needed to save the faltering fortunes of the V12 850 line.

M GmbH then and now

As of this writing, M GmbH does not supply customer 3-series racers—1996 was the first year when it simply sold off the dozen works 320i sedans—but you can get most of the parts to build such a Supertourer.

For sheer profit, M GmbH's past record of selling competition hardware is unparalleled in European motorsport.s. Ford probably outdoes the sheer volume when rally demand peaks, but for continuous specialist sales, BMW's commercial Motorsport Division is an enviable profit source. Our Appendices reveal that over 250 such Supertourers have been supplied, and past records include over 500 of the pure racing M12/7 Formula 2/320-Group 5 power units and significant supplies of the 320 itself.

In 1977, the sports division built 27 replicas of their 320 Group 5 series. Just how popular the four-cylinder M12/7 F2/Group 5 motor was can be emphasized by the fact that, when Formula 2 ended in 1984, BMW Motorsport GmbH had built over 500 such motors, priced at over £8,400 ($14,112 today). Over 350 were completed by 1978.

In 1977, BMW Motorsport made approximately 200 of those special 3.3-liter 533i road cars per annum as well. These alloy-wheeled machines pioneered the M-badged road cars that would follow the M1 and subsequent 5-series.

The redevelopment of Preussenstrasse was scheduled over an eight-month period in 1978–79, and was calculated to produce the world's biggest competition department for a mass-production manufacturer at that time. Within the new £1.32-million redevelopment of the old Preussenstrasse site, there was a showroom front protecting separate factory and customer competition workshops, engine dynamometers by Schenk, an engine assembly area, drawing offices for chassis and engine developers, and accommodations for all offices necessary to administrate the activities of 160 staff. For 1997, around 100 are left on competition-engine development for factory ends.

By 1978, Paul Rosche could call on the services of 40 engineers and 14 staff in the main BMW factory. Among that band were six design engineers and four test engineers for the four dynamometers then being used.

Back in 1978, BMW Motorsport thought internationally, having raced from the factory or with factory assistance in South Africa, North America, and Sweden. It pursued two major European programs in Formula 2 and Group 5, using teams and drivers from Germany, Italy, Belgium, France, and England.

In 1977, the two star drivers were Ronnie Peterson and Hans Stuck (another to move from Ford to BMW for 1973), but there were many, many more. Some—too many for comfort—are now dead, and some are famous for their work with other marques, such as Tom Walkinshaw of TWR.

In 1997, BMW Motorsport retained four star drivers who rotated among the championships and categories Motorsport dictated. They were all 36 years old, or more, at press time. They comprised Joachim Winkelhock from the home team, Italy's Roberto Ravaglia, Venezuela's Johnny Cecotto, and Britain's Steve Soper. Their biographies can be found in chapter 27.

Today, BMW Motorsport operates globally. During the 1990s, it has fielded factory-backed race teams, usually featuring 2-liter SuperTourers, sub-contracted to Schnitzer if it

Machining 16-valve cylinder heads at BMW Motorsport in the early 1970s. The resources beneath Preussenstrasse were simply astonishing for the period, especially with respect to the engine test cells.

Picture: BMW Archiv, released 1984

wanted a winning guarantee, and appearing in the major national championships of Japan, Germany, Italy, and Britain.

Furthermore, there have been serious efforts and varying levels of Munich cooperation in France (Oreca was the ace on this territory and was a pioneer with the Z3 as an ice racer during the 1996/97 winter!), Australia (with due past credit to former Ford sedan Champion Frank Gardner's administration and John Player's cash), Belgium, South Africa, and New Zealand. For 1998, BMW Supertouring efforts emphasized the German series, where the factory was represented by Schnitzer as a new 3-series was developed.

BMW Motorsport has also cooperated with BMW North America on a number of programs that were sparked by their appearance from 1975 onward with the CSL. BMW Motorsport also supplied technical liaison and homologation facilities to Prodrive in England to compete with the M3 as a winning rally car in the late 1980s. It also worked with both Brabham and McLaren in England to supply power units of World Championshi,p Grand Prix, and sports-car racing classes. As this is written, Motorsport is developing a Grand Prix power unit, of V10 layout, scheduled for its first runs in 1999 with Williams, who also cooperated on an unsuccessful 1998 Le Mans V12 sports-racing prototype.

This is truly a transformation since BMW was unloved and nearly bankrupt in 1959–60, revered only inside the boundaries of Bavaria.

The major players

Who were the men at BMW Motorsport who had the most influence in this transformation? Pole position goes to Jochen Neerpasch, whom we profile in an accompanying panel, but there were plenty more.

Austrian Dieter Stappert was the former editor of *Powerslide*, a Swiss-based, German-language weekly bible to continental enthusiasts. The knowledgeable Stappert arrived at BMW Motorsport in 1977 as Neerpasch's personal assistant and succeeded him in February 1980. Neerpasch had upset the main BMW board considerably with his "take it or leave it" negotiating style. That applied to the cost of ProCar (reputedly more than a Grand Prix budget) and his attitude toward the BMW Grand Prix motor that Paul Rosche and company were developing beneath Preussenstrasse. Basically, Neerpasch had told the board what he intended to do with the motor, rather than asking for permission before making his moves.

Motorsport under Stappert was a frenetically successful organization, but the commercial side began to gravitate away naturally, as Stappert was 120 percent committed to bringing BMW its racing ambitions, not making another 500 DM on sales.

Having succeeded on the Formula 1 front beyond the reasonable expectations of all but BMW, Stappert left BMW Motorsport in 1985 for a varied subsequent career. He tackled the HB cigarettes motorsports programs (extensive, including motorcycles) and he has more recently returned to journalism and TV commentary.

Stappert's committed "Racer's Edge" leadership was replaced by Wolfgang Peter Flohr. Berlin-born Flohr ensured that the commercial development of BMW Motorsport and the M-badges expanded. Best-known in the 1990s for his stewardship of the German-based ITC race series, managing the winning GM-Opel racing Calibra coupes (450-hp V6s that beat Mercedes in 1996), Flohr was not a confident competitions manager at BMW.

However, Wolfgang's 1985–88 managership saw the commercial side into profitable overdrive (turnover reached 70 million DM). Flohr established the Garching site that has become the public face of M-branded goods and services.

Jochen Neerpasch

Whereas Munich-born-and-bred Paul Rosche and amiable Martin Braungart were very approachable figures on the 1970s motorsports scene, Jochen Neerpasch was a more remote figure. Born in the Cologne suburb of Krefeld and the son of a major Ford dealer, Jochen rarely smiled, apparently ice-cool and calculating. These qualities were subsequently used on behalf of Mark McCormick's massively influential IMG sports management organization and the international motorsport controlling body in Paris (FIA).

Neerpasch also founded a Junior Team at BMW, subsequently taking the idea to Mercedes, and thus gave 1994–95 World Champion Michael Schumacher and 1997 Williams Grand Prix driver Heinz Harald Frentzen their breaks in international motorsports. Shrewd and far-sighted seemed apt adjectives for the man who put German drivers into the kind of worldwide prominence enjoyed by compatriots Boris Becker and Steffi Graf in world-class tennis.

Although Neerpasch is outwardly reserved, he does have a ready and dry sense of humor, which emerges whenever there is the chance to do more than exchange basic race-day civilities.

Neerpasch had been a top-rank driver. Paired with Vic Elford, he won a number of international events (including Daytona 24-hours) for Porsche. Ironically, his last outing for Porsche was at Le Mans, and his was the only car with a good chance of beating the victorious Ford GT40. Neerpasch had the managerial Ford contract in his pocket, but raced as hard as ever for Porsche.

Instead of creating a converted road car, Neerpasch guided Ford in Germany to borrow the British competition Ford Escort approach. That created a new race-oriented Capri derivative, the Capri RS2600. This is relevant to BMW, because the RS2600 had an alloy-head, fuel-injected engine specification—Ford's first in Europe—specifically created to act as a base for racing in two differing Capri variants. These Fords inspired the BMW CSL.

One Ford was sold, in a limited way, to the public; the other was a super-lightweight version to provide a basic lightweight framework for competition. When Neerpasch arrived in Munich, two years after the Capri had dramatically proved a consistent winner (it won all but one European Championship round in 1972), he and Braungart knew what was needed.

In four years at Ford, Neerpasch had absorbed things that most competition-drivers-turned-team-managers never learn: how to put together a winning team and forget one's own personal achievements behind the wheel. The nearest parallels I

Jochen Neerpasch had it all figured out until it came to Grand Prix power units....

Picture: H. P. Seuffert, Le Mans, France, 1973

have met are Roger Penske in America (Penske is much more of a businessman than Neerpasch) and Gerard Larrousse, who subsequently managed Renault's international sports program. It is significant that all were sports-car drivers of international standing, a category where persistence and intelligence are crucial for success in addition to the obvious need for sustained speed.

Neerpasch's motorsporting vision was wider than his contemporaries, and this was reflected in the variety of events and activities that BMW followed under his leadership. As a true European with German as his mother tongue and an excellent command of English and French, he took an international view, making his contemporaries—especially in Britain—seem petty and parochial.

From 1972–79, Jochen Neerpasch transformed BMW's competition philosophy from a part-time pastime to a massive motorsports machine. But Formula 1 would not be denied, and when Grand Prix came to BMW, it led to the downfall of Neerpasch and his departure from BMW.

More M-people, this time from the 1980s. Triple World Champion and former BMW Alpina CSL driver Niki Lauda (with Parmalat cap) stands alongside then-BMW Motorsport Chairman Wolfgang Peter Flohr. Lauda was a consultant to BMW Motorsport for several seasons before fulfilling the same role at Ferrari's Grand Prix team into the 1990s.

Picture: BMW Werkfoto, Germany, 1986

The talkative Flohr faced the acrimonious BMW years of fighting Ford worldwide, as well as the Mercedes home-championship challenge, but his heart apparently lay in a major Formula 1 return. When that was repeatedly denied by the BMW board, Flohr was replaced by another loyal company man, this time drawn from the marketing department. Karl-Heinz Kalbfell became Managing Director of BMW Motorsport on October 1, 1988.

Garching became home for the M5 in the later (E34) bodies. Manufacture started in September 1988 and in its heyday, settled at around 2,000 units a year, with a comfortable waiting list of half a year or more. Over 12,200 were made in six different bodies before its demise in July 1995.

Following Flohr's departure in 1988, Kalbfell—who had joined BMW in 1977 and had been the mainstream sales whiz who made both the M1 and the first M5 happen commercially—gradually assumed greater M-department responsibilities. Kalbfell enthusiastically occupied his new post of Managing Director at BMW Motorsport (Paul Rosche

tended to do all the hardcore sport stuff) into the mid-1990s.

By the conclusion of 1996, Kalbfell's brief had expanded to keeping the BMW board informed of all M-branded activities, obtaining the necessary motorsports budgets, and being the most senior public face between Motorsport and the mainstream AG. In fact, if you asked about the latest McLaren-BMW V12 racer or the driving thrills of BMW's emotive Mobile Tradition classic collection, Kalbfell would have the answer.

Today, BMW Motorsport GmbH at Preussenstrasse develops all works engine programs, but also provides technical information that used to support worldwide privateer teams.

M GmbH at Garching is really the public face of BMW in motorsports—the retailer, if you like. It also has responsibilities for the successful Driver Training programs (up to 30 near-stock 3-series based at Nürburgring).

In 1997, it was astounding to think how BMW's M-branded activities started as a minor offset to the costs of competition. In 1996–97,

Two decades old and still as strong as ever: this is the MPower M12/7 motor that powered Brian Redman's winning Chevron B19 spider at Monterey in 1996. Redman beat a bevy of bigger-engined opposition, but when he went past a Mirage-Ford V8 Cosworth on the run down from the Laguna Seca corkscrew, we all knew that neither he nor BMW's legendary 4-cylinder had lost any of their motivation since the 1970s!

Picture: Author, Monterey, August 1996

the M-branded division turnover exceeded 300 million DM ($189 million) annually and employed approximately 450—as it has for much of the 1990s—but it no longer builds the M-branded machinery.

At this writing, the M3 continued to occupy the manufacturing halls of Milbertshofen. The six-cylinder M5, after a total 1984–95 run of 13,373, was in abeyance, awaiting development of a V8-propelled M5 to straddle the much-acclaimed new 5-series line. A Z3-based M-sports car with M3 power was also awaited, with a definite promise that America would receive a unique version, subsequent to the February 1997 European press debut.

Other M GmbH responsibilities included the fantastically successful BMW Driver Training and BMW Individual programs. Under the direction of Peter Locker, Individual has flourished from a provider of fancy paint and interior colors to meeting every individual whim (at a price) on every twentieth BMW!

In 1996, BMW made more than 640,000 cars, and more than 30,000 went through some aspect of the M GmbH services. Usually, the paint or interior work is done at the individual production plants of Dingolfing or Regensberg, "on-line," but meeting requests "...such as fax machine in the back, whatever..." will mean that the vehicle visits Garching.

The Driver Training schedules—more than 500 of them in 1996, coaching more than 8,000 people a year "...who want to do more than just hold a driver's license..."—are directed by Josef Bucherl from Garching. They now extend to Finland, Canada, and a variety of mainland European haunts, including the fabled Nürburgring. Leading drivers who get involved on the more specialist courses (you can select anything from a half-day in a compact to a week in snow and ice) still include former Monte Carlo rally winner Rauno Aaltonen and 1979 European Formula 2 Champion Marc Surer.

QUICK FACTS

Period

1970–79

Products

Showroom coupes (2000C to 3.0 CSi) and their specialized racing cousins

Performance

100 bhp and 107 mph to 360 bhp and 170 mph

Achievements

Evolving a six-cylinder race sedan out of an elegant four-cylinder base; Schnitzer wins (twice) before the CSL appears

People

Alpina takes on Dr. Fritz Indra; BMW tries British technology; Schnitzer brothers hit the heavy-horsepower trail

Chapter 15

Toward Batmobile

Elegant Karmann coupe develops Batwing muscle

A competition car is often obsolete by the time it is winning. The designer is already firmly launched into drawing up its successor. Such statements apply, most of all, to Grand Prix cars, but even the humblest production-based categories reach their sell-by dates in four or five seasons. This chapter reviews the technical progress of the big Bimmers, from road cars to racers. Key racing memories from this era are related in the next chapter, covering nine amazing years.

BMW coupes (which trace their shape back to 1965 2-liter coupes by Karmann) raced and won internationally over a decade (1969–79). The elegant coupe became the "Bat-winged Terminator" and won six European Touring Car Championships, never mind its achievements in the US (IMSA) and the annual conquest of the Belgian Spa 24-hour classic.

To put it another way, from its 1973 factory-first European title to the 1979 close, the BMW Batmobile version of the big coupe was beaten only once for European honors (a Ford Escort nipped between battling BMW and Ford coupes to secure class and 1974 title). Since that winning record covers seasons which the aged six spent fighting a 5.4-liter factory-funded Jaguar XJC, this BMW's strike rate was immensely impressive.

In 1965, the coupe—styled by Wilhelm Hofmeister—was sold either with a 100-bhp, 2-liter engine or with the twin-carburetor, 2000TI unit (CS designated "coupe sport"). By October 1968, BMW had announced its return to the six-cylinder luxury-car market for the first time since the 1950s.

The big sedans, the 2500 and 2800, attracted the most attention, but German coupe taste was fed by a carbureted, 170-bhp 2800CS. This six-cylinder BMW took the established BMW principles and expanded on them. Trailing-arm rear suspension, MacPherson-strut front, and a chain-driven single overhead camshaft engine (a six-cylinder version of the existing four), all made the car a tempting proposition for competition life.

The 2800CS lost the distinctive one-piece headlight glass covering of the 2-liter model and carried a strong family resemblance to the new six-cylinder sedans, carrying quadruple headlights. In fact, it was mainly four-cylinder engineering underfloor, dating back to the early 1960s, so the chassis needed a fair bit of sorting for the showroom—a process not really tackled until the transition from 2800 to 3.0 CS. BMW succeeded in contemporary coupe terms: *Road & Track*

The 1965 face by Wilhelm Hofmeister launched a coupe legend as the comparatively rare 2000C/CS series. The four-cylinder engine and older technology under that center-pillarless roofline did not deter BMW and their specialist partners from reworking this theme into a six-cylinder machine that ruled European Championship racing through two decades.

Picture: Author, Monterey, 1996

When the 2800CS six-cylinder coupes arrived in 1968, they sowed the 170-bhp seeds of an enthusiasm that has yet to burn out in America. Now there is even a magazine devoted solely to the coupe faction: *The BMW CS Register*, currently published through the efforts of CS owners Amy and Wayne Lester. The contact address is in the Appendices; meanwhile, just drool over part of the 104-strong BMW CCA coupe corral at Monterey in 1996.

Picture: Author, Monterey, August 1996

described the 2800CS as "close to irresistible." The staff put their money where their mouth was, with then-engineering editor Ron Wakefield purchasing a six-cylinder coupe.

The coupe adopted a 3-liter engine in spring 1971 and became a much better drive, with four-wheel disc brakes and 195 tires to replace the original 175s. The extra 200 cc (approximately) came from the use of an 89-mm bore in place of 86 mm, the stroke remaining at 80 mm, for 2,985 cc. European power was quoted at 180 bhp, but in autumn 1971 came Bosch electronic fuel injection (and a CSi badge) to replace the 3.0's twin downdraft Solexes. Now 2,985 cc made 200 bhp, enough to realize 132 mph and 0–60 mph in 8 seconds. America got 170 bhp and the original 2800's 125-mph pace, with acceleration at 0–60 in 10 seconds.

Lighter is better

The company could not fulfill its sporting ambitions without preparing a lighter, high-performance CSL (the "L" suffix signifying "lightweight"), vital to sports success. The CSL was homologated and then sold with a full set of

"wings" to create aerodynamic downforce and cut uplift. Nicknamed "Batmobile," this car, with its addition of eight-part aerodynamic aids, so infuriated the German transport authorities that BMW had to resort to packing the aero wings away in the trunk when the car went on sale in its definitive 1973 format.

In September 1972, BMW produced the first of its CSL lightweight derivatives, which offered an aluminum hood, trunk lid, and doors in left-hand drive, with little in the way of luxury equipment. To qualify the car for racing in the over-3-liter division (reboring was limited to a fixed percentage in Group 2), the capacity was quoted as 3,003 cc and 89.25 mm x 80 mm, a strange bore figure that was retained in conjunction with an 84-mm stroke to provide 3,153 cc when the 1973 winged version was launched. In road form, this allowed 206 bhp at 5,600 rpm, which provides a pointed comparison with the original 100 bhp back in 1965.

The rebored six-cylinder was the most powerful engine offered to coupe road customers in a production run from 1968 to 1976. The CSL label needed only 1,000 cars to pass as far as the factory was concerned for homologation purposes. BMW made a total of 1,096 complete cars, and extra, super-light bodies for motorsports use only.

In the aftermath of the 1973–74 fuel crisis, when the last CSLs were made, they were hard to sell, as people panicked about fuel economy. Today, the CSL can rightly be regarded as a limited-edition classic, but it was almost impossible to define the car unless it had the full wing regalia and the (nominal) 3.2-liter engine, because there were three badged CSL derivatives, all running Bilstein dampers and 7J x 14 alloys (originally of Alpina inspiration).

Scouring factory production statistics reveals numbers for genuine CSLs with start and finish dates. The CSL trio began with the September 1972 3.0 CSL; some 539 were made inside two years, finishing in June 1973.

The second production spurt was of RHD UK-bound CSL models in a batch of 500, to a unique (and heavier) specification, between September 1972 and January 1973. UK information is that the last of these were sold in August 1974, and experts such as Tim Hignett of L&C BMW in Kent, who has the definitive

UK-based Batmobile, report that specification was "variable."

Officially, a UK CSL—some of which I have seen in Florida concours—came in RHD only, cost £5,828, and retained the chrome wheel-arch lips, external striping, and alloy body panels. They did not pack the wing kit and opted for electric winding glass to replace the lightweight's winders. Also returned for city-bound Brits were heavyweight bumpers with rubber facings and tinted side-glass, as opposed to the original CSL dietary demand for Plexiglass. (I have seen UK examples with winding front glass and electrically-operated rear three-quarter panes!)

Scheel bucket seats stayed in the UK spec, but thicker carpets were specified, and Brits could take a power steering option, by which time the CSL's weight savings over an equivalent 3-liter CSi was halved!

Finally, there were just 57 CSLs made between June 1974 and November 1975 to a

July 1969: the 2800CS ventures into long-distance racing with minimal modifications. Nicholas Koob and Helmut Kelleners, of Luxembourg and Germany, respectively, took the 2800CS to its first international competition result. The Alpina-prepared coupe (only the engine was much-altered) finished ninth in that edition of the Spa 24-hours.

Picture: Autosport, released 1978

specification referred to as 3.0 CSiL. My suspicion—and prevalent information from post-factory privateer teams—is that 50 more body-in-white shells were made at Karmann purely for Motorsport purposes. I am tempted to describe the cars above as fulfilling that purpose, except that factory records indicate manufacture of complete cars at Werke 1, Milbertshofen. Although Karmann did build bodies for the CS series, assembly was at Milbertshofen.

The original CSL of 1972 used Solex carburetors for its 180-bhp, 3-liter engine. The first CSL offered an important race homologation-orientated curb-weight savings of 286 lbs, tipping the scales at a minimum 1,270 kg versus 1,400 kg for the 3.0 CS. Under weight-saving percentage allowance from the FIA in Paris, the CSL raced at a little over 1,000 kg/2,200 lbs, rather than a typical CSi roadgoing weight of 3,080 lbs, hiking power-to-weight ratio radically.

This road-car weight was achieved with aluminum for hood, trunk lid, and door skins, although the door frames remained in steel. There were no front bumpers, and the rear was a polyester contraption weighing a little over five pounds. Lightweight seats and trim (including carpets and black headlining) plus manual front windows and Plexiglass fixed rear three-quarter panes all helped.

In August 1972, the 3,003-cc capacity was offered for 200 bhp with Bosch fuel injection. The concessionaires in Britain went on to offer their own 500 versions of this CSL with fuel injection only, and with a lot more luxury equipment than was offered in Germany. The 3,003-cc capacity was really a maximum rebore size—a motor-racing-capacity class trick.

The Batmobile

The third version of the CSL was the definitive winged "Batmobile" of 1973. It was always called the 3.0 CSL, but race teams would use the 3.2 CSL badge in a later Group 2 guise. In road terms, German sources took most of the accurate performance figures. You could expect the 1972 example to cut half a second or so off showroom 0–60 mph times (in the 7-second bracket) and to modestly exceed 130 mph on its 180 bhp.

The last 206-bhp, 3,153-cc units allowed close to 140 mph and 7-second acceleration, down to 6.9 seconds for 0–60 mph if the CSL was built to full German lightweight specification. That meant fixed side glass (not the earlier Plexi sheets), but a reclining mechanism was by then incorporated in Scheel front seats, and the trunk lid came in steel to counteract the bending forces imposed by the rear wing at autobahn speeds.

Sixties starter

The BMW factory was engaged in racing the 2002 in 1968–69 and concentrated heavily on Formula 2 in 1970. So there was not enough manpower available to race-develop the six-cylinders. Besides, its big drawback was always its weight for the size of its engine in pre-CSL days.

Private enterprise was called for and came from Alpina in the weeks leading up to the July Spa-Francorchamps 24-hour race of 1969. Then the big BMW made its debut in racing. Comparatively unmodified, it did not set the competition world on its ear, nor even the parochial sedan-racing scene. Who knew then that one day the floorpan would glow with the heat of an engine capable of generating over 750 turbocharged horsepower from 3.5 liters? Or that it would go on winning for years after production of the CSL had ceased, and even after the factory had replaced the 3.0 CS range by a 633CSi flagship for 1976?

When Burkard Bovensiepen and his Alpina staff recall the six-cylinder coupe's rugged competition debut in a 24-hour race, they smile a little. The car was so standard that it used the normal 6 x 14-inch diameter wheels, power steering, relied on barely-modified suspension with production brakes, and so on. Alpina had taken the engine apart, blue-printed it, and substituted triple twin-choke Weber carburetors as they reassembled it, claiming 250 bhp for a fenderless coupe.

In spite of consuming some 40 Dunlop racing tires in the 24-hours, the Alpina-BMW 2800CS completed the closed public road course with its pine-tree-lined, 120-mph bends and unique climatic blend of rain, fog, and humidity. Technically speaking, Alpina was now far too busy racing the 1602 and 2002 to progress much further with the six-cylinder car during the 1969 racing season.

In 1970, coupe competition interest escalated sharply. BMW asked Alpina to represent its interests in sedan racing while the factory pursued its hefty Formula 2 schedule. Alpina's work during the intervening winter saw the coupe biased toward racing sedan rather than converted road car.

Plastic wheelarch extensions covered wider alloy racing wheels, but still the brakes and suspension remained virtually unmodified. The engine progressed, and one great aid to reliability with the wet-sump lubrication then used (and subsequently required for the 1977 Group 2 season versus Jaguar) was Bovensiepen's patented piston displacement pump. This long auxiliary cylinder contained a piston and an emergency supply of oil to compensate for oil surge under heaving braking and cornering in the comparatively elongated wet-pan oil system.

When international Group 2 touring car regulations were altered to demand wet-sump lubrication again in the 1976–77 season (dry-sump lubrication had been used in the intervening period), the displacement compensator oil supplier became valid again. When Broadspeed took the Jaguar XJ5.3C V12 coupes racing in the European Touring Car

Alpina again prepared a 2800CS for the 1970 Spa 24-hours. Kelleners drove again, but this time he was partnered by Austria's Gunther Huber. They were rewarded with outright victory, a feat the model was to repeat for many years at the Belgian circuit, where its clean lines and high-speed handling were especially useful. To the right is the tenth-placed Alpina 1600TI of Nicolas Koob and Rene Herzog.

Picture: Deutsche Presse Agentur GmbH/Alpina Archiv, released 1978

Championship, Bovensiepen very generously supplied a pair of his auxiliary piston displacement pumps to try to solve the British car's enormous wet-sump lubrication problems. It helped, but the problem was a lot bigger on the Jaguar, and Broadspeed ran with a Cosworth-based dry-sump system for many of its ill-starred outings.

Some of the transmission problems apparent in 1969 were solved not long afterwards. The differential had been overheating, and Alpina developed its own ingenious external pump to defeat it. The gearbox also gave trouble, and a five-speed ZF was adopted virtually "from the start." However, in Dr. Fritz Indra's words, "We still had standard clutches, and the drivers were not allowed to use full power for the starts!"

CS success

Based on race results, the 1970 season was the beginning of the CS success story, for Alpina had outright wins in two international events counting toward the European title. This, in turn, created interest in making the 2800CS really competitive, both at the factory, where Gerhard Haerle was in charge of making sure the drivers were paid by BMW, and among other tuners. Enter the Austro-German border raiders from Schnitzer....

Down at Freilassing, Josef Schnitzer and his brothers had started work on the sixes. Charley Lamm told me in the 1970s, "We competed in a few small sprints and national races, where we got a few small wins." As always, Schnitzer produced a pretty powerful engine for the car, and progress was so encouraging that it entered its smart CS for its first European Championship race at the nearby Salzburgring, just over the border in Austria, in the spring of 1971.

In March 1971, Dr. Fritz Indra arrived at Alpina's Buchloe base. Born in Vienna, a grad-

uate of technical high school in Germany, "Fritzi" was a fair, curly-haired youngster tackling his first full-time job in automotive engineering. However, he had an honorable background both in competition and emission control work—both subjects that needed attention at Alpina. The speed-equipment industry in Germany has grown up with the requirement that its products should not produce high noise or exhaust emission levels, and that its equipment should pass rigorous tests. Indra's knowledge and his irreverent sense of humor were vital so that Alpina could legally sell more sophisticated performance equipment.

Bovensiepen joked that all his drivers were Austrian, and with the arrival of Indra, the Austrian atmosphere grew even stronger. To intensify this, Indra had been involved with Niki Lauda (subsequently a triple World Champion for Ferrari and McLaren) and Jochen Rindt in Formula Vee during a spell at Karmann.

Racing most weekends as a practical scientist had obviously taught Indra a lot about car behavior, but it left him rather unprepared for touring-car racing. "When I come to Alpina, these cars are terrible—just like normal production cars, only the instruments and seats seem to be changed!" More fearless laughter as he spluttered, "The 2800CS had won at Spa, of course, but it has the same disc brakes fitted, power steering. Everything is production compared with the Capris. It later had 13-inch diameter wheels [because you could get better rubber from Dunlop, and to lower the center of gravity] and the engine has 280 horsepower with the three Webers, but the car is so heavy, you just cannot imagine.

"Braungart and Neerpasch at Ford Cologne, they make a proper racing car. It was so completely new for us in Germany; the Capri had these big wheels, light homologation weight, racing suspension. They were so much faster than our cars then, maybe 10 to 15 seconds each lap at the Nürburgring. I remember a week or two after I arrived, we had to go to

Monza for the first 1971 round of the European championship, with three coupes and four 2002s!"

Though it was obviously going to be tough to get results with such a large team and only four mechanics, they set to work on the big coupes as their priority. Adhesion was enhanced via 8-inch-wide alloy racing wheels, and new competition shock absorbers were installed.

In the longer term, Indra knew they had an engine problem: "You could go 7,000 rpm, okay. Then go 7,100 rpm and the crankshaft is broken!" To overcome the torsional vibration that was inflicting such havoc, Indra decided to turn to the expert services of Freudenberg, specialist German consultants, on questions of torsional stress. They tested the crankshaft and recommended a successful solution: machining away a significant amount of weight.

At BMW, von Falkenhausen remembered encountering the same crankshaft problem, but tackling it by different methods to achieve a reliable 7,500 rpm when using the two-valve, six-cylinder motor. They installed both a lightweight flywheel and clutch, plus specially-developed crankshaft counterweights. There were the same number as on the production engine (twelve, in total), but they were smaller and lighter. The crankshaft was also nitrided.

The factory's role was more of a watching brief through the 1971 season, though it drew little comfort from watching the blue-and-white V6 Capris lapping up race after race. During 1971, the competition limelight on the BMW coupes was carried entirely by the tuners. Just how seriously BMW took the situation is emphasized by the fact that it commissioned a British racing-sedan preparation specialist to

More of a racing CS: the 1971 Alpina CS for Gunther Huber at Spa lacked any aerodynamic package, but the extended wheelarches and side exhaust were leading-edge moves toward more radical six-cylinder speed in the 1970s.

Picture: BMW Archiv, released 1984

complete a design study on the coupe at the close of the season. It also made sure that the 3-liter coupe (3.0 CSi) was homologated internationally in July 1971.

Back at Alpina in 1971, they felt BMW's attitude to homologation was: "You don't need any, the car is perfect." In other words, policy at the time was very similar to Bovensiepen's own inclination and Neerpasch's consistently-held views on Group 1: the less modification and consequent easier homologation, the better. In 1971, Bovensiepen still felt that big brakes and other radical modifications were not a good thing—he felt that the car should just be reliable and finish with honor—but others (Indra among them) wanted to hit the radical engineering button and win against the accursed Fords.

Pumping up the power

More power was needed. The lightweight CSL was still a future plan, a dream that the tuners kept asking for, but one that the factory refused to homologate until Neerpasch arrived. Thus, work began on fuel injection at Alpina. The big six-cylinder was sold to the public with a fine Bosch electronic system later in 1971, but for racing, the mechanical Kugelfischer layout was required.

Kugelfischer injection had been used by the factory for many seasons on the four-cylinder, but for the six-cylinder, Alpina enlisted the help of Quast, making use of the special lightweight pump that it had made reliable after experience with the four-cylinder factory engines.

At first, fuel injection did not yield the test-bed results Alpina had expected. Dr. Indra was amazed: "At first, there was no power, or no more than for the carburetors. We look on the test bed, and think this is impossible. Then we make new injection-trumpet lengths and modify

the combustion chambers to suit the injection. Then we get more power." These remarks applied almost equally to the four- and six-cylinder Alpina cars then being raced.

Using 3-liter engines on carburetors, Alpina found that power outputs were always below 300 bhp (Schnitzer claimed 295). Once those internal and external injection engine changes had been made, Alpina realized 330 bhp. Indra, and Dieter Quester for that matter, well-remember the debut of the six-cylinder injection system on an Alpina coupe.

It was at the Nürburgring 6-hours of 1971, and the original layout featured an enormous "guillotine" slide to admit or close off the air supply to the six chokes, which had no bearings to ease the slide operation. Naturally, this meant the throttle operation was very heavy and the linkage was subject to great stress.

The unfortunate Alpina boss, Bovensiepen, was struggling to solder the linkage together for Quester up until ten minutes before the start. They did finally weld it together, but the linkage fell apart in "...about half a lap," said Indra.

The advent of more power for the car produced other problems. Tires, brakes, and suspension were all found to be inadequate, though by this time the disc brakes had been slightly thickened for competition to absorb a little more heat; standard calipers were retained!

This braking handicap was an enormous disadvantage compared with the rivals at Ford. So were curb weights, which were roughly 970 kg for the Capri (then offering about 300 bhp) and a whopping 1,270 kg for the lightest pre-CSL BMW.

During the dour struggle of the 1971 racing season, when, in Indra's words, "We worked all night, every night, trying to beat the Capris," Alpina tackled a critical area of sedan-handling on track. It inserted harder bushings for the suspension, front and rear. Such a substitution, in which the softer rubber that allows a quieter ride is sacrificed for stiffer bushing location of all the suspension compo-

nents in the interest of greater driver control and "feel," was vital.

In Germany, such harder bushings were initially held in some suspicion, as it was thought (unjustly) that the stiff bushings would break. Back then, BMW coupe rim sizes averaged 8 by 13-inch front and 9 by 13-inch rear, and servo-assisted power braking was still retained. Power steering was deleted, and the big BMWs were showing a turn of speed in a straight line that emphasized how competitive they would be, if a lightweight could be swiftly sorted.

A 3.0 CS by Schnitzer had the honor of showing the Capris home for the first time in 1971.

Appropriately, it was driven by Dieter Quester, who did the damage to the Capri's invincible reputation at the fast Zandvoort circuit in Holland. Nose spoilers were now beginning to appear on BMWs; the Fords had deployed such spoilers under their long snouts since 1970.

At the close of the 1971 season, Alpina was not too pleased with itself. Obviously, the 3.0 CSi would become the spearhead of a new BMW assault on Ford's monotonous success, but it was not obvious how BMW was to proceed. For the time being, it seemed content to rely on the tuners to turn its prestige model into a winner; but which tuner would get factory blessing?

(Left) Growing up: the CS started to develop bulging muscles and ever-wider wheels as it prepared to flatten Ford's previously all-conquering European Championship Capri V6s. The first time the BMW six-cylinder coupes defeated the works Capris was long before the titanic 1973 confrontation and the CSL. Here is Dieter Quester en route to that 1971 first win in the Schnitzer machine at Zandvoort, ahead of two factory Fords and the very rapid Alfa GTAm. Later on, fellow Austrian Marko (who was driving a Capri) was to lap with the nose of his Ford resting on the BMW's trunk!

Picture: Bilstein/via Hugo Emde, 1971

Fuel injection was a great boost to the slant six in competition. This is the 1972 Broadspeed prototype unit supplied by BMW in pre-GmbH days with Kugelfischer mechanical injection.

Picture: London Art Tech, released 1984

BMW was undecided. As the racing season closed with the one Schnitzer victory, it decided to see what could be done by an independent consultant. Accordingly, Southam in Warwickshire became the Mecca for representatives of BMW Concessionaires (GB) planning a new image for the Cooper Car Company, which it had acquired.

The Broadspeed coupe

Southam was home to Broadspeed, headed by Ralph Broad, a bespectacled auto engineer who talks a little faster than a Thompson sub-machine gun. Broad murdered opposition across Europe with his versions of the Cosworth BDA-propelled Escort (previously Broadspeed prepared British championship-

winning Anglias and Minis), and he sought something capable of winning outright. So, as it happens, did BMW....

The result was the provision of two BMW-Karmann prototype lightweight bodies. These were made using the lighter-gauge steel and aluminum hood, trunk lid, and doors that were to become the CSL specification later on. There were no wings then, but Broad did fabricate his own alloy front spoiler, and the car carried massive (for the time) wheelarch extensions in fiberglass to cover 11-inch-wide front wheels and 13-inch-wide rears. Because Dunlop was able to supply the first of its ultra-low-profile touring-car tires for the 1972 season, Broadspeed opted (along with Ford and Schnitzer) to run 15-inch-diameter wheels. This allowed bigger brakes to be installed and took advantage of better rubber.

Some Alpina and Schnitzer know-how was used in the Broadspeed coupe, including a pris-

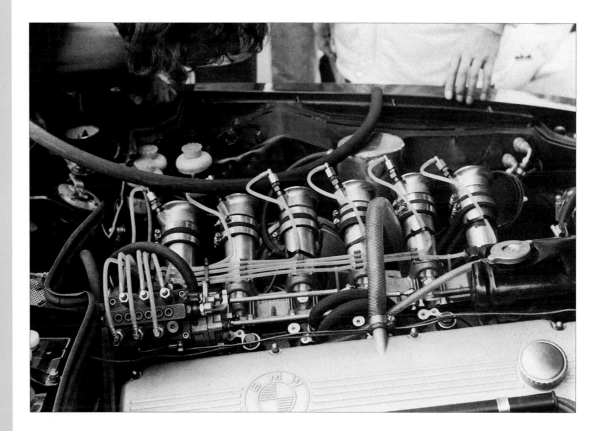

tine Kugelfischer-injected engine that had passed through the hands of Paul Rosche at BMW. This motor was claimed to give 332 bhp at 7,500 rpm with a limit of 8,200 rpm. With the assorted cooling pumps Broadspeed built for the ZF gearbox and limited-slip differential, it finished third and was reliable through a hard two-hour thrash in the snow of Salzburgring in April 1972, but the car did not race again.

Though the Broadspeed BMW finished third in the hands of John Fitzpatrick, it had been too advanced in specification. Scrutineers made Broad and the mechanics take off the aluminum body panels—which were not homologated prior to the race—and there was a great deal of general suspicion about the car's eligibility to race under Group 2 rules. The truth was that it anticipated by nearly a

year how things would be when the CSL was built, but it needed the arrival of Neerpasch and Braungart at Munich to pull together all the tuners and their own efforts.

The Broadspeed car had technical significance. I was privileged to drive the car one afternoon around the Silverstone short circuit when Niki Lauda also tried it for a few laps. I thought it handled and stopped superbly, with a melodious motor that sounded Italian in its passionate appeal.

The Broadspeed coupe needed a professional like Lauda to really get the best out of the car. Lauda had been driving the Alpina car occasionally in the 1972 season, and confirmed that Broad's variable-rate Bilstein suspension was a lot less twitchy than that found on the Alpina coupe. Lauda had experience

Zandvoort, 1972: the BMW effort is stepped up through the specialists. Here, Niki Lauda's Alpina CS power-slides in front of Rolf Stommelen (Schnitzer 3.0 CS), the two Grand Prix Germans just as keen to beat each other as Ford! Even with such fine drivers, the BMW coupes were too heavy to be truly competitive. About to be gobbled up is Englishman Dave Brodie's Ford Escort RS1600.

Picture: Werner Schruf/Alpina Archiv, 1978

A rare photograph. John Fitzpatrick races the Broadspeed BMW at Salzburgring in Austria, Easter 1972. It was the radical coupe's only race appearance, but many of its features—like the blade front spoiler and brake cooling ducts—were incorporated in later racing BMWs.

Picture: London Art Tech, 1978

with rougher race tracks, and knew that an absorbent ride quality was of some importance in European endurance events.

Lauda's other 1972 ride was a factory March 722, and he said of Broadspeed's coupe, with typical dry humor, "It's almost as good as my Formula 2 car!" As part of his development program after Salzburgring, Ralph Broad altered the rear center of gravity quite radically by lifting the BMW rear floor-pan three inches, lowering the car appropriately, and allowing the rear wheels far less camber change under varying throttle and cornering conditions.

This BMW also used solid metal jointed suspension instead of rubber bushings, hollow tube aluminum anti-roll bars with 10.9-inch diameter Lockheed discs, and servo-assisted front brakes carrying four-piston calipers. All these items were useful to BMW for evaluation when the cars and ancillaries were returned to Munich at the conclusion of the Broadspeed-BMW consultancy. With the benefit of hindsight, it might have saved Ralph Broad heartache—and his business—had the BMW link turned to a racing deal. Jaguar's XJ5.3C of 1976–77 stressed him beyond belief, and when his daughter died in a road accident, Ralph lost heart in Broadspeed, which did not survive the 1970s.

The 1972 season

Alpina trod its own lonely path. For 1972, it ran regularly with 310/320 bhp, and these cars were what Indra described as "Alpina's first racing cars." Having only one coupe to concentrate upon, it tried some fairly advanced ideas.

The disc brakes (with unventilated rotors) were mounted inboard and could be considerably larger than before, matching the units with the 14-inch-diameter wheels that had replaced its 13-inch-diameter units. A titanium flange to replace the production universal joint was mounted between the propeller shaft and the differential, and solid rubber blocks were installed to mount the differential to the rear subframe. Alpina also shifted the driver back nearly four inches and the engine rearward by almost two inches. Yet its biggest problems were wheel/tire combinations that simply did not put enough rubber on the road.

Again, the only BMW victory of the year came from Schnitzer, with that super silver-and-red coupe taking the pounding handed out by the home track at Nürburgring in its stride, and winning the 6-hours. Since this was shortly after Neerpasch joined BMW, it seemed a little bit as if it had been pre-ordained. The Schnitzer-BMW was tremendously fast (some 360 bhp was claimed, and rivals almost believed Schnitzer), running on the proper rubber and brakes.

It was also driven by the experienced and rapid trio of Rolf Stommelen, John Fitzpatrick, and Hans Heyer at the 'Ring. For Alpina and Schnitzer, winning races was all-important, as BMW had offered a substantial 10,000 DM to the winner of a European Championship round in a Munich machine, and 100,000 DM if either could win the title! That was to prove impossible against the Capris, and Ford won the European title for the first time since 1965.

Schnitzer über alles!
Left to right: Hans
Heyer, John
Fitzpatrick, the late
Josef Schnitzer and
Rolf Stommelen are
flanked by Herbert
Schnitzer and mem-
bers of the Schnitzer
team after they had
beaten Ford in the
1972 Nürburgring
6-hours. Since
Neerpasch and
Braungart had only
just left Ford for
BMW, this could be
seen as something
of a good omen!

Picture: H. P.
Seuffert,
Germany, July
1972

QUICK FACTS

Period

1972–79

Product

Lightweight CSL coupe technology

Performance

350 bhp from 3.3 liters, 12-valve, SOHC, to a maximum 480 bhp from 3.5 liters, 24-valve, DOHC, all normally-aspirated; turbocharged 3.2-liter delivered up to 1,000 bhp, or 750 sustained

Achievements

Flow of European titles from 1973–79 only interrupted once; adapted successfully to world silhouette-car and American IMSA regulations with individual race wins in these series; thrashed Ford in 1973, Jaguar in 1976–77

People

Martin Braungart creates the Batmobile, Paul Rosche powers it, and nothing—even its death on the production line in 1975—seems able to stop its international racing success

Chapter 16

Frightening Ford

BMW's answer to winning European sedan competitions

The days of winning easily were coming to an end for Ford. Alpina, Schnitzer, GS Tuning, Koepchen, Broadspeed, and BMW itself all agreed on the need for a lightweight coupe. The prototypes were already running around outside the Karmann works at Osnabruck. Neerpasch and Braungart were installed and operational from Munich in May 1972, Braungart having left Ford on just a month's notice. The ex-Ford duo had a year to produce a winning BMW in the European Touring Car Championship.

Swiftly, they went ahead with the lightweight project, which was already well under way from a road-going viewpoint. Indeed, Neerpasch had a lemon-yellow CSL, complete with its distinctive alloy "spats," at Salzburgring in April 1972. As Jochen had just announced his decision to leave Ford, following a working breakfast with Bob Lutz at the Munich Sheraton, it was little surprise to see that Ford Motorsport mechanics stuck a neat "Powered by Ford" sticker under the BMW chrome nomenclature of the new lightweight!

Neither Braungart nor Neerpasch had much time for smiling about such pranks. As Braungart quietly told me some years later, "There were the rally people doing their own thing in one corner at Preusenstrasse, and there was almost no development time. There was an engineer to do some drawing and me. We knew Paul Rosche would look after the engines.

"In four months, we had drawn everything and ordered it to be made—new front suspension, steel hubs, new castings for the MacPherson struts, center locking for the wheels [just one large nut and hub pegs secure the racing wheel, making changes faster and location better], completely new steel trailing arms to accommodate much bigger wheels, and a complete power train [a Getrag five-speed gearbox was homologated and replaced the ZF] from one end of the car to the other.

"We even had a new driveshaft made, and some other axle ratios, magnesium castings for the bell-housing and the gearbox, and several cooling systems. We had the belt-driven oil pump from the flange of the driveshaft for the differential, with the pulley built into the inner driveshaft flange. The brakes were also new, after cooperation with Ate," recalled Martin.

Rosche labored over the M52.2-coded race six. A dry-sump, 92 x 80-mm, 3.3-liter version was devised and homologated for use with the rest of the competition CSL on January 1, 1973. BMW Motorsport's M52 engine still retained the 30-degree production slant, which

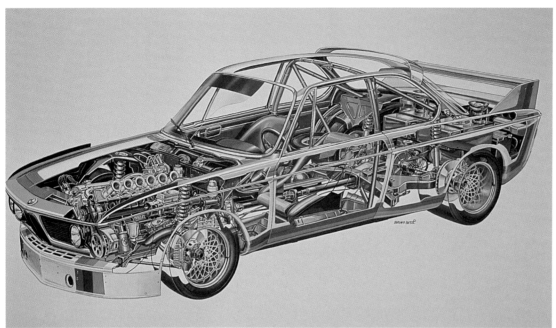

The racing CSL in its summer 1973 debut factory racing form, with full wing kit fitted and the 3.5-liter/370-bhp tune for the 12-valve slant six. Note how thin the roll cage tubing is by contemporary standards.

Picture: Courtesy BMW

Winter 1972/73 testing for the factory BMW CSL: the full wing set came later. Dutchman Toine Hezemans (second from left) confers with Martin Braungart as BMW prepares to beat the hitherto-invincible Ford Capris with science generated at sessions like this one at Paul Ricard, France.

Picture: BMW Archiv, 1978

(Left) Development force: Dieter Quester in his winning way in the 1971 Schnitzer CS at Zandvoort Holland, 1971. This car still exists in Britain.

Picture: Actions Pictures Holland/ Autosport ,1978

caused the oil to run up the bores in pre-dry-sump days, producing some 350 bhp fed by the usual Kugelfischer injection.

Then, manufacturers could only bore out their engines for Group 2, crankshaft stroke to remain as homologated. One of the reasons Schnitzer always seemed to have an edge over the others was risky over-boring. Rivals inside and outside the BMW ranks pointed the finger of suspicion at Schnitzer on this count, but no irregularity was ever established.

Oddly enough, when Alpina came to run at the first race of 1973, it had not gotten the homologated parts to make an "over-3-liter"

engine. Neerpasch chose this meeting to investigate. It was a surprise for the factory to find that the victorious Alpina car was undersize!

Ironically, Martin Braungart could not give the race CSL its first test runs at Ismaning—then a recently opened BMW proving ground outside Munich—the authorities said it would be "too noisy!" Braungart was able to drive the car up and down a runway at Dornier's local airfield. That was before Christmas 1972, and Hezemans was able to drive the car at Hockenheim soon afterwards. Through that 1972/73 winter, they kept plugging away at the testing, with help also coming from Hans

Stuck, then another Ford refugee.

The white cars, with their red-and-blue BMW Motorsport corporate livery from new chief designer Paul Bracq, carried full-width front spoilers, which had cold-air ducting for the large four-piston, alloy-caliper disc brakes fitted inside those large-diameter BBS split-rim wheels. Rim widths were fixed at 11.5 inches at the front and 13 inches for the rear, using at that time the Dunlop rubber they were to stay with until 1976. The replacement trailing arms had been necessary to accommodate a large inset on rim width and for wide wheels to fit beneath wing extensions.

Now it was time to see if this leading-edge technology worked in Italian race conditions....

The CSL's proving ground

The factory racing coupes covered 12 hours of pre-event testing at Monza, scene of the first round of the European Touring Car Championship. BMW's sports division arrived feeling in good shape. The cars had run excellent pre-practice times, and the only real

problem they had experienced in testing was some cracking of the new steel hubs. There was apparently no danger of losing the wheel altogether, but a change in material specification was completed.

Braungart smiled wryly at the memory of what happened in Italy that Sunday, when both cars were eliminated by dissimilar engine-related retirements . "It's always the same: after years in sport, you know the truth....Competition is completely different to testing."

The BMW factory mechanics had a tough time with ignition and injection problems, finally installing the last engine at 2:00 a.m. Toine Hezemans then checked it out at 2:30 a.m. with a full 7,800-rpm run through the wonderful parkland that surrounds the Monza circuit. Only in Italy could this happen—the equivalent of taking a run through Central Park in New York, assuming that amenity also hosted Daytona raceway!

The compensation at the Monza debut was that Alpina-BMW won—saving the factory's bacon, as it was to do so many times in 1973—and the works Fords shattered two motors as well. These stranded Capris included the V6 entrusted to the very-expensively retained World Champion Jackie Stewart.

More testing in the full body kit and stripes that began the 1973 season for the factory BMW CSLs. This time we are at Hockenheim in Germany with 1973 European Champion Toine Hezemans. Hockenheim was the subsequent regular venue for the German Grand Prix after the Nürburgring ran into safety trouble due to Niki Lauda's fiery Ferrari accident of 1976.

Picture: BMW Archiv, released 1984

Rare beast! The competition homologation base car: a 3.0 CSL in its third and final form with oversize engine and wing system properly displayed, front and rear. The 138-mph final evolution of the CSL was not actually allowed to be sold in West Germany in this form, but in Britain and some other European countries, the CSL arrived with the wing system erect instead of packed away in the trunk as it had to be on delivery in Germany! BMW confirmed a 0–60 mph capability of 6.8 seconds in street form.

Owners like Derek Bell in the UK confirmed that the wing system did give extraordinary stability, a fact echoed by the competition car's consistent lap times. As with many of BMW's brightest competition ideas, it was developed in a remarkably short time.

Picture: BMW Werkfoto

BMW made no major changes to the engine specification at that stage, though the six-cylinder did feature special sealing rings around the combustion chambers. These fit into grooving on the top face of the cylinder block, in an effort to counteract the head gasket failure at Monza. All build tolerances were tightened still further.

BMW Motorsport suffered engine trouble in the second European round at Salzburgring, too. Even though it was pure bad luck, Rosche was just beginning to get edgy enough to guarantee that he would personally inspect every component that went into the works engines in the future.

Then a lift came with the first factory win in the German Championship, Toine Hezemans beating a useful Porsche Carrera 911 combination around the 14-mile Nürburgring by 5.2 seconds, seizing pole position with an 8-minute, 33.5-second lap.

"We were racing to win in Europe, but any win is always good for morale," Braungart asserted. Technically speaking, there was still in-team skepticism about the engines, so Neerpasch and Braungart directed the team into the longest and most public test they could find: Le Mans 24-hours.

As Braungart said afterwards, "It was a big break to finish and beat the Fords to take the touring car classification award." Mechanically speaking, the engines were fine, but the first of many gearbox problems on the car driven by Stuck reared its head. Even five years afterward, Braungart admitted, "In theory, the gearbox was perfect, but we had persistent problems on the Stuck car. It had wider gears, bigger bearings, and a different lubrication system. Do you know, in 12 months, we made 30 gearbox modifications?"

The team went back to an aluminum casing for the gearbox. Despite work with Ate, the German braking specialists, to solve a very visible problem in night racing, the brakes were glowing red through the wheels and the pads needed changing every four or five hours—a difficult job with the heat generated. Ate attached cooling fins to the calipers, and the design of the four-piston caliper lived on in the 320 Group 5 sedans.

There was only one really competitive BMW without Ate brakes that occasionally appeared in Europe. This was Brian Muir's Alpina CSL, which used Lockheed components and was intended for the last 1973 season of Group 2

racing to be held in Britain. Otherwise, the Muir UK-based CSL was a twin to the one Alpina was campaigning in Europe.

Neerpasch and Braungart intensified their Munich crusade to beat their old teammates at Ford-Koln in the north. They had spotted an amendment in the International FIA regulations that permitted evolutionary changes to be added to existing models. They decided this meant they could offer the CSL for sale with a full aerodynamic wing set.

Braungart relived the decision as follows: "We just had no time to do anything. The next homologation date we could meet [after which they could use the optional equipment without fear of retaliation from Ford] was July 1. We had to get the papers into the FIA in Paris six weeks before that.

"There was no time for a normal development program. We took a racing CSL to the wind tunnel at Stuttgart, and we really just tried the effect of sticking on all sorts of wings, spoilers, and so on. The styling department had helped us with some ideas, but it was all such a fast job that we just tried to see what we could find that was best. Our problem was to cut lift in exchange for downforce on the back of the car; we had about two days to find the answer with the wind tunnel."

Braungart continued, "The standard car had rear-end lift of about 60 kg at 200 km/h (124 mph), and we worked until we had converted this lift into 30 kg extra downforce upon the back. I remember Hans Stuck showed how little downforce we had on the rear—he went off at the Nürburgring 1,000-km, when he blistered the rear tires by sliding so much. He ended up in the Armco!"

Braungart looked suitably amused, but the first test with the wings was to provide even more dramatic proof of their effectiveness. The team had competed in six events with varied

(Top Left & Right) What went on underneath? A Group 2 CSL, then belonging to prominent American BMW specialist Ricard Conway, recalls the fuel-injected slant six in 12-valve format, plus the safety fuel tank dominated trunk.

(Bottom Right) Then we have the example of a BMW NA-owned CSL's drilled replacement racing trailing arms, disc brake, and low-mounted anti-roll bar: all served racing BMW coupes for generations.

Pictures: Author, Florida 1992 and California, 1996

The combination of CSL and Alpina was not only effective on the track. An American customer displays a superb street car in the local BMW Chapter's corner of the Italian Concours at Carmel.

Picture: Author, California, 1996

success and was testing at the Nürburgring 22.7-km/14.2-mile Nordschleife a week before that circuit's 6-hour European Championship qualifier was due to be held.

A 3.3-liter six was installed (by this time producing over 360 bhp), and they were lapping in the 8-minute 30-second bracket. Earlier in the year, Jochen Mass had managed an 8-minute 25-second lap in the 2.9-liter Capri. Because time was short, the Motorsport mechanics were asked just to fit the slightly larger front spoiler and the tail wing. The BMW "Batmobile" in Stuck's hands immediately recorded 8 minutes 15.4 seconds—shaving nearly 15 seconds a lap! Incidentally, a similar Nürburgring experiment by Ford showed an 8-second reduction, but it could not move as rapidly to formalize the spoilers because of English managerial inertia.

It was a team manager's dream come true, and Ford could not homologate an answer that season. "Forget the splitters on the front wings and the hoop over the rear window," Braungart told me. "They show a small percentage improvement in the wind tunnel, but you cannot see this in the lap times."

But the effect of the wings was not just one of boosting lap speeds. A number of chassis problems could then be solved. Apart from the tire problems recounted in Stuck's case—which disappeared, since the cars were no longer excessively tail-happy—the winged BMW could generally run softer springs than the Capris. The faster the track, the better the Bat CSL worked, for it was literally pressed harder to the road because of efficient aerodynamics.

Rosche also added his own brand of engine magic to the BMW cause, producing a 3.5-liter version of the faithful SOHC, alloy, 12-valve-head, iron-block six. Rosche grinned widely when recalling the details, for at the time, they were a little worried about going to anything more than 90 mm on the bores, as there was not sufficient space left between the cylinders to allow water passage.

"Now we have it on the road cars," he chuckled happily in the 1980s. That forcibly reminded me of how much BMW benefits from the personal competition experience of its personnel. Subsequently, both the M1 road and race cars and M5 showroom models benefited from this CSL race development.

The finished result was coded M52.3 and measured 3,498 cc from a bore and stroke of 94 x 84 mm. Using the normal competition compression ratio of 11.0:1, this allowed "a lot more torque" and 370 bhp at 8,000 rpm.

The torque was important, for the CSL was still considerably heavier than the Capri. It raced at around 1,062 kg, whereas the Fords had dipped below 950 kg at Monza. Set against that, the BMW engines gave approximately another 50 bhp, for the Weslake-headed Ford V6 was really at the end of its life and was safest at 320/325 bhp from nearly 3.0 liters.

In theory, and on the track, the 3.5-liter engines and wing system were enough to slaughter the Ford opposition with an unbroken string of wins. It would be wrong to think they were all BMW wins, though, for the role of Alpina and Schnitzer was often the leading one, if the factory struck trouble.

Alpina said it could have won the 1973 championship, and beaten Ford on points, without the factory points, for they won quite a few rounds (notably the first and an epic struggle at Silverstone) and finished every race (except the Spa 24-hours, where the tragedy of Hans-Peter Joisten's death resulted in retirement of all Alpina-BMWs.)

Technically, Alpina went for a simpler car than BMW Motorsport. Alpina abandoned the magnesium transmission castings, retaining the 15-inch-diameter wheels and Dunlop tires when BMW and Ford had started working with the new 16-inch-diameter wheels. (Schnitzer used large-diameter wheels with Firestone tires.)

Alpina installed production-type struts and uprated them appropriately, rather than using the full-race and purpose-built factory struts.

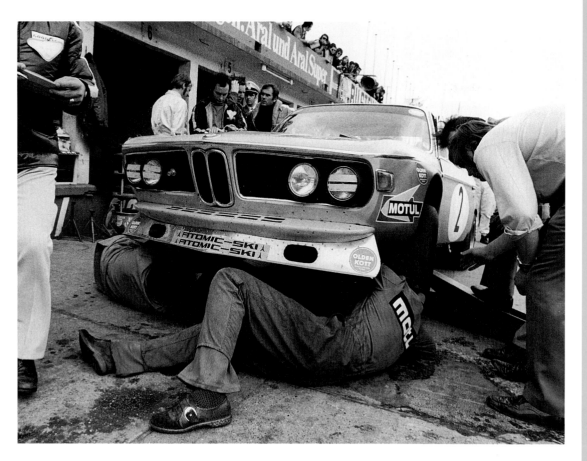

The path to the very top of the BMW preparation and tuning tree was turbulent for Schnitzer. Their coupes in the early 1970s were blindingly fast for the first hour of the 3–6 hour European routine qualifiers, but back in the pits all too soon for further investigation of leading-edge technology. This is the CSi that won their historic Nürburgring victory of 1972; Jochen Neerpasch stands beside the car at the pit stop with one of the Italian racing-driver Brambilla brothers looking puzzled (they are split by the official in the peaked cap). A Dunlop technician from Britain kept busy wondering if the team was still using its contracted rubber....

Picture: H. P. Seuffert, Germany, July 1972

The latter move was to try to make the steering lighter and more manageable in some of the longer-distance events. Alpina also reverted the rear disc arrangement to a conventional outboard mounting point from the previous year's inboard experiments.

The engine specification was also conservative. For Monza, it had to run the smaller engine (3 liters), and even when it had the full 3.5 liters, it reckoned to run up to 20 bhp less than Schnitzer in the interests of making the maximum number of race finishes, an objective it achieved.

According to Alpina, it had about 360 bhp at best, using narrower rims than most with 10 inches in front, 11 at the rear. Alpina's experience in 24-hour racing was excellent, with three Nürburgring night-and-day races to its credit; part of this was due to having relieved the engine of a little compression pressure,

knocking back the ratio from 11.0:1 to 10.5:1. The emphasis was deliberately placed on torque, and it had 275 lb-ft or more at 5,000 rpm, the engine pulling well from 5,000 to the bhp peak of 7,400 rpm.

Alpina tried to move as much weight as possible to the rear. One unsuccessful move was to rear-mount the water radiator, but it was both too big and too vulnerable to assaults from both the ground and the rear, which are not unknown in racing. Weight distribution was modestly improved by a flat fuel tank. A dry sump oil tank was placed within the trunk from July 1972 onwards.

Technically, 1974 was immediately notable as the era of the four-valve-per-cylinder racing sixes from Ford and BMW, but Alpina dropped right out of the picture and Schnitzer was not represented in this new era, which began officially on January 1, 1974.

1975 IMSA:
How the American racing CSL developed

When the CSL was prepared for its American challenge, it was time to take stock of all those components that were now non-stock:

1. The 24-valve motor shared only its x-rayed (to insure that enlarged bores were safe) iron block and the water pump with production items. Cylinder bore was 94 x stock 84 mm for 3,496 cc. Inlet- and exhaust-valve sizes were 1.41 and 1.19, respectively, with compression at the usual Motorsport 11.2:1.

2. Similar in principle to the four-cylinder M12/7 Formula 2 motor, the M49 racing six had a single chain to drive its twin overhead camshafts, not the gear drive of F2.

3. All suspension components were replaced/uprated, as for European racing practice. After 1975, the track at Sebring was boosted 2.5 inches a side, so appropriately wider fenders were installed. This reduced lap times by one second in trials.

4. The limited-slip differential was usually replaced by a locked differential action from mid-1975 onward.

5. Rack-and-pinion steering replaced production worm-and-roller.

6. Anti-lock (ABS) braking was used widely on the US-specification CSLs. It came from the Teledix cooperative, not the later Robert Bosch production system for BMW.

7. The final drive originally used many standard components, including casing, gears, and shafts. However, one driveshaft was used to drive a pair of oil-pump/cooler systems: one for the gearbox and the other for the differential.

8. Borg and Beck supplied a triple-plate clutch to mate with the heavy-duty Getrag 5-speed.

On the American racing front, Peter Gregg's CSL earned BMW North America two outright victories in the 1976 IMSA series.

Picture: BMW Archiv, 1978

Schnitzer's race results drooped as it began to feel the shortage of money among the big boys in 1973. Besides, it was busy with work for customer engines at Freilassing, and it was getting interested in formula car racing. Schnitzer returned to CSL work with a monster coupe for the 1975 German Championship.

Alpina was out because Bovensiepen had always tried to race what he could sell to customers. Four-valve-per-cylinder, six-cylinder racing engines were not on that list. It was a sad ending to Alpina's efforts after its pioneering role, but it was to be back with a vengeance, conquering the 1977 European championship against Broadspeed Jaguar.

Just as the six-cylinder road engine was a close cousin to the four-cylinder, so the racing six-cylinder with four valves per combustion chamber was a very close relative of the four-cylinder, four-valve engine first raced in Formula 2 in 1970 and then successfully developed into the dominating force in 1973 Formula 2.

There was chain drive for DOHC, but the six was otherwise similar to a racing four with the same hemispherical combustion chambers, titanium connecting rods (first born in the 1.6-liter Formula 2 days), and the cast-alloy Mahle pistons. Of course, the nitrided steel crankshaft was different, and it did have to be made in a more-resilient steel than that used for the two-valve sixes.

Coded M49, this engine first raced and won at Salzburg in March 1974, when it developed around 435 bhp at between 8,000 and 8,800 rpm. As von Falkenhausen points out, theoretically, the heads, with the same valve angles and the same dimensions as the Formula 2, should have provided more than 9,000 rpm as well, but the length and natural whippiness of the six-cylinder crankshaft restrained revs.

The single-slide fuel injection and lightweight pump from Kugelfischer were retained. The M49 engine remained the basis for all the factory efforts with the CSL, but Josef Schnitzer

subsequently (in the winter of 1975/76) increased its effectiveness in a number of interesting ways when he arrived for his spell at the factory. First, he sorted out the exhaust system and had the engine mounted vertically in the car, instead of at a production slant.

This helped in several ways, for the inlet system could be straightened out, the head design modified so as to take advantage of the bigger exhaust pipes provided, and the engine could become a 460-bhp unit—not far off Formula 1 standards, and very impressive for a production-block unit 20 years ago. Then the head's water circulation and temperatures were improved for its higher power ratings in the new Group 5 with an external water line going out of the head between the spark plugs.

For the 1974 European season and the 1975 American season, when the CSL embarked on an IMSA racing program, the pace of development slowed. The wings remained, but for 1974, a slinky dark-blue basic body color was adopted. The car proved shattering in speed, but rarely appeared in the 1974 European season ("not interesting for us anymore," I was told several times, but money and fuel-crisis politics played the major role). However, the mildly-redeveloped CSLs gave a remarkably good account of themselves when sent to America in 1975–76. Altogether, the CSL won seven IMSA races outright, Hans Stuck taking four such wins in 1975.

Meanwhile, back in Europe, 1976 saw some major regulation changes for racing sedans. Group 2 changed over to a more-restrictive formula, aimed at employing fixed wheel-rim widths, small body-wing extensions, comparatively unsophisticated suspension systems, and wet-sump-lubricated engines, without the option of using four-valve-per-cylinder heads unless they were mass-produced as original equipment.

BMW was not directly interested in contesting this category, but Belgian preparation specialist Luigi Racing was keen enough to assemble hardware and drivers that took the 1976

European title once more for the big Bimmers. Luigi had been a force to reckon with in 1975's Coupe L'Avenir, a hybrid series necessary because of the poor support for the European Touring Car Championship after the Ford versus BMW war had fizzled out in 1974.

Based at Comblain-au-Point, near Liege in southern Belgium, Luigi Racing had developed out of the enthusiasm and practical skill of Luigi Cimarosti. A most unlikely team proprietor and garage owner, Cimarosti exhibited all the fire of his Italian ancestry, yet endeared himself to everyone by working all the hours under the sun on his cars, surrounded by a team of part-time timekeepers and team managers.

The Luigi BMW team achieved international recognition in 1974 when it won the modified Group 1 Spa-Francorchamps 24-hours, a feat it followed up the next year. By 1976, its activities had achieved some factory support (mainly for parts, especially lightweight body shells, the very last of which it fielded from 1977–78), and both Gunnar Nilsson and Hans Stuck were occasionally drafted into its cars to meet the very rare challenges offered by Group 2.

Using mainly Belgian drivers, the 370-bhp CSLs turned the clock back almost to the beginning of BMW development with their four-speed gearboxes and modest bodywork, though the wing system was still there. The 1976 European season was spent mostly waiting for the Leyland Jaguar to appear, which it did belatedly in September at the Silverstone Tourist Trophy. Luigi still won and secured the title, as Lotus Grand Prix star Gunnar Nilsson (who subsequently died of cancer) forced a CSL to match the pace of the 2.2-liter larger Big Cat for Derek Bell, negated his own chances in the process, and allowed Luigi a most important victory.

Neerpasch was right to choose Group 5 for his main effort. While the factory-supported BMWs from Luigi simply mopped up the 1976 Group 2 title, Munich was not expecting much in the way of results in the new Group 5. Porsche had been developing its turbocharged

911 into the 935 racing car, and it was too formidable an opponent for pessimistic Germans to predict any hope of modified sedans such as the CSL having any success. In fact, BMW did very well, winning three rounds outright and turning the "silhouette" championship into a more-interesting contest than we had any right to expect.

BMW took the decision to contest Group 5 in December 1975, but none of the cars were built before February 1976. A brief test program at Ricard established new lightweight and more aerodynamic bodywork. The plastic front wheelarches and spoiler were similar to what had gone before, but the spoiler extended in real cow-catcher style. At the rear, the wing extended out further, with revised side-plates, and the wheelarches were enormous. They now accommodated Goodyear rubber—BMW had flirted with the idea during its American program the previous year—and were of 16-inch diameter, 12 inches wide at the front and 14 at the back.

Somehow, BMW managed to build four of these 1,030-kg machines in time for the first round of the Championship on the tight Italian Mugello circuit in March. It had one 1,370-meter/1,500-yard straight where drivers reported maximum rpm in fifth gear, corresponding to 161 mph (260 km/h). An elongated straight would see them tip 170 mph. The four BMWs were for Alpina-Faltz, Schnitzer, and a British-based Hermetite team run by Carl "Tivvi" Shenton (a US resident for many years by the 1990s), and a car retained by the works to push ahead with development.

The idea was that the three customer cars would be reliable and pick up points, while the works developed its legendary turbocharged version of the 24-valve six-cylinder motor. That is exactly what happened.

The Group 5 CSLs proved remarkably consistent. Horsepower, between 470 and 480 bhp at 8,700 rpm, was provided by the Munich factory, and the cars apparently all started off weighing within five kilograms of each other, a remarkable and rapid achievement. Though the green Schnitzer CSL and the other two customer CSLs were spectacular in the hands of drivers like Brian Redman, Dieter Quester, John Fitzpatrick, Tom Walkinshaw, Harald Grohs, Sam Posey, and Albrecht Krebs, everyone was waiting for the turbo CSL to appear.

That the debut was as exciting as it was owed a great deal to the car, which the normally-serious men of Munich saw as virtually a "motorized joke." Braungart described every fault lovingly as if describing some mischievous woman who entranced everyone. And that's virtually what the big white CSL, with its huge stripes, did when Ronnie Peterson climbed behind the wheel for its three race outings in 1976.

Braungart recalled with astonishment, "Even the floor glowed red with the heat from the engine—it was colossal! We knew the car could not last for long—in fact, we were surprised when it lasted close to an hour at Dijon—there was no way the transmission could take this engine. Did you know it could produce twice as much power as our Group 2 engines? But we did not turn the boost up this high...For sure, these engines will make 1,000 horsepower one day...."

Braungart blinked thoughtfully behind his brown-tinted glasses as he detailed the chassis alterations made to try to help the car's 56 percent front, 44 percent rear weight distribution of its 1,080 kg. Despite moving the water radiator to the rear and the use of 19-inch-diameter rear wheels, the irrepressible Peterson could set the tires smoking in third gear as he headed for a fifth-gear maximum reported as 178 mph (286 km/h) on Silverstone's Hangar straight. Reports from a subsequent Le Mans foray put the beast's ultimate maximum at 212 mph....

The engine that made this possible actually measured out at 3.2 liters and had two KKK turbochargers set at 1.3 bar boost. That allowed 750 bhp at 9,000 rpm, compared with the best

1977 European Champions: the immaculate green Alpina 3.2-litre CSL is driven by Dieter Quester. Here in the opening race of the series at Monza, Quester is chased by Martino Finotto's ex-1976-Luigi CSL, which is driven by Italian veteran Carlo Facetti. In 1977, Alpina not only made sure that the two-car attack by the Jaguar V12 coupes went without a race win, but they also defeated the other BMW opposition.

Picture: BMW Archiv

Opening shots. In March 1977 at Monza, the big European news was the arrival of a two-car team of Jaguar V12 coupes from Broadspeed/ Leyland. The 5.4-liter Jags were powerful in short bursts, but BMW's Gosser Bier Alpina partners—and gross unreliability from the Jaguar—ensured that the Leyland-financed Jaguar never won a Group 2 race in its 1976–77 life.

Picture: Nigel Snowdon with LAT, 1977

of 480 bhp that was seen for the Group 5 unit of 3.5 liters with Kugelfischer injection.

The installation was neat enough, but the extra weight was nearly all added in the nose. Although the factory regarded this as appalling, Alpina had raced with far worse distribution figures, going up as high as 58.6 percent front/41.4 percent rear in 1974.

The turbocharging work was very much Josef Schnitzer's baby, and he left behind a legacy of practical experience that allowed a better installation for the later M1 coupes. Compared with Porsche, the engine always had one advantage: a four-valve head.

Those quad valves allowed BMW to use comparatively low boost for a high output, which has been reported all the way to 1,000 bhp. The 750 quoted above was the most accurate the factory could supply for a volatile

unit. Supplying power was never a problem with this CSL: harnessing it for more than an hour without transforming the transmission into plasticine was insurmountable.

That was the glorious swansong of the factory BMW Motorsport-prepared CSLs. There were cars at the closing rounds of the Group 5 championship in North America (which went to Porsche in the end), but at Silverstone and Dijon, the late and great Ronnie Peterson proved he and the "Munich Monster" could run with Porsche and create some excitement. Redman drove the CSL turbo at Le Mans, where it held third overall, but retired with gearbox troubles.

In November 1975, production of the BMW CSL was completed on the last 59-off batch, and the CS itself died with it. The last consignment of production CSi types for the US was

Brands Hatch, 1978: Carlo Facetti hurls the ex-Alpina CSL onto two wheels around the British circuit. The car was purchased and co-driven by wealthy Italian industrialist Martino Finotto and could have won both this Championship round and the title, but internal disagreements and a lack of preparation were handicaps too strong to overcome. Finotto and Facetti finished second at Brands.

Picture: Colin Taylor Productions, 1978

In 1977, BMW was well-represented in the European fight for title honors. Luigi Cimarosti (left, in the open door of striped car number 6, alongside subsequent European multiple champion Umberto Grano) ran these gaily-painted CSLs. Here, the cars are awaiting practice at the Nürburgring with Jean Xhenceval in the front car and Eddy Joosen in the second team car.

Picture: Strahle, Germany, 1977

completed almost exactly a year earlier, in December 1974. Some 44,327 of the grand coupes (2000CS to 3.2 CSL) were made in the decade, from September 1965 onward.

All the six-cylinder coupes contributed handsomely to putting a sparkle back in BMW's image, as well as into the company coffers—none more so than the CSL. Now it was time to leave the CSL to a twilight run of success that actually saw the spotlights relit as Alpina-BMW racing spirit was reborn to meet the challenge of Broadspeed Jaguar in 1976–77 Europe.

The CSL proved as successful as ever in European Group 2 championship racing. In fact, no other marque or type won an individual European qualifying round between July 1974—when a Zakspeed Escort pulled off a surprise win in the Nürburgring 6-hours—and the CSL's championship appearance in October 1978. This was despite some highly professional opposition, including the Jaguar assault from late 1976 (one race only) throughout most of 1977, when then-Leyland-owned Jaguar financed a costly team of Broadspeed XJ5.3C V12s.

To meet that Brit invasion of its territory, the 1977 season saw Alpina produce its pride and joy, which amounted to a brand new CSL, built

up from one of the CSL shells supplied originally by Motorsport GmbH for Group 2. Alpina expressed every talent it possessed, with gleaming green paint and glittering mechanical components speaking louder than any publicist's voice of the enormous care and enthusiasm that had gone into building perhaps the best-presented touring car seen in Europe to that date. The works cars were always highly professional and eye-catching, but this beauty was ready to concours before every competition. Back 20 seasons ago, Alpina's greatest CSL was not just a pretty face, though. On-board air jacks, 16-inch-diameter center-lock wheels, and a rear alternator driven from Alpina's unique driveshaft-belt arrangement (similar in principle to the oil-pump differential cooler) were employed.

Everything Alpina had learned about BMW coupes was within this remarkable racer. The engine began the year in wet-sump form with some 325 bhp produced from 3.2 liters (standard 84-mm stroke and 89.8-mm bore), but when Leyland's political pressure made the CSI change the Group 2 regulations to allow dry-sump lubrication late in the season, Alpina did install such a well-proven system. It was chiefly this freedom from wet-pan oil drag that allowed a yield of 340 bhp at the close of the year, with 8,000 rpm the recommended maximum on the production steel crankshaft.

The 1,075-kg Alpina CSL had to use a four-speed Getrag gearbox under the new regulations, and this was equipped with the following ratios: 2.33:1, first; 1.47:1, second; 1.17:1, third; and direct 1.00:1, top.

It was the European Championship-winning car that year, and it scored five victories. Most featured Dieter Quester, who won his third of four BMW-mounted titles. Quester recalled all the technical tricks Dr. Indra incorporated in his winning machine (sometimes shared with Tom Walkinshaw, who would restore Jaguar racing glory in the 1980s and win the European title personally), commenting, "We raced with a sixth of the Jaguar budget."

I agreed with Quester as he simply said of the Gosser Bier-sponsored Alpina CSL, "It was the best car I ever had. Fantastic handling, brakes, everything was good enough to win." He was not so enamored of the constantly changing overseas co-drivers that he had to endure to boost Bovensiepen's export trade. Alpina-BMW simply outpaced the rest, however many liters the Jaguar had (German-language sources credit it with 6.2 liters, rather than the homologated 5.3/5.4 tolerances!).

The gorgeous Gosser Bier CSL lives on. Ironically, the Big Cat-Eater resides with BMW specialists Munich Legends, honored in England in the 1990s—although I last saw it at Monterey in 1996.

Luigi was also strong on the scene with two of its own CSLs and an ex-Luigi CSL developed by Carlo Facetti, driven by himself and

And here is the car that won that March 1978 British European Championship round...just! Tom Walkinshaw is seen here in the Luigi-prepared CSL that took the penultimate title for that honorable BMW warrior of the European scene, the champion being Italian leather-goods tycoon Umberto Grano (seen driving the same car in 1979).

Picture: Courtesy of Enny, 1979

The Alpina mechanics crane the 3.2-litre straight six with its five-speed Getrag gearbox into position at the opening Monza Championship round, 1977. The wet-sump engine provided over 340 bhp—more when dry-sumping was allowed.

Picture: Alpina Archiv, 1978

Martino Finotto. This one was often very fast and occasionally used Goodyear tires, while the others stuck to Dunlop.

Alpina withdrew after winning the title and humiliating Leyland-owned Jaguar, saying there was nobody to beat. It sold the car to Carlo Facetti and Martino Finotto. Once away from Germany and Buchloe, it simply lost its polish and preparation in 1978.

It was left to one of the persistent Luigi BMW CSLs, driven by wealthy Italian leather-goods specialist Umberto Grano, to take the model's fifth European Championship in 1978, and 1979 saw its last European title. The Italians got their act together: middle-aged Carlo

Facetti, the former Alfa Romeo star, paired with wealthy industrialist Martino Finotto, secured the CSL's sixth, and last, European Touring Car Championship. The Bimmer that brought winged science to touring-car racing in Europe boomed to the final flag, winning all the way.

QUICK FACTS

Period

1969–75

Products

Racing CSi to CSL in Europe

Performance

330-bhp, 12-valve and on to
400-bhp, 24-valve layouts

Achievements

Six European championship titles;
Group 5 World Championship
race winner

People

The best battle it out in sedans;
New Zealander Chris Amon tells
how he adapted from Grand Prix
to CSL technique

Chapter 17

Old Glory

CSL's world-wide racing feats that made BMW an international name

In this chapter, we highlight some of the action memories of the charismatic CSL coupes. We also take a round-by-round look at the factory's 1973–74 seasons, up to the point where Neerpasch had to announce that BMW would no longer contest rounds of 1974's European Touring Car Championship. Ford and BMW continued to do battle at German Championship rounds after 1974, but Porsche did more outright winning. By 1976, only Porsche turbos won outright, so the home championship battlefield shifted to weapons such as the BMW 3-series and Ford Escort, rather than the CSL versus Capri.

That 1974 season was traumatic for both BMW and Ford competitions departments, as finances dried up after the fuel crisis. Keeping BMW Motorsport alive, nevermind expanding it to today's multi-million-dollar operation, was a major management success (as covered in chapter 14).

Before Neerpasch, the turning points in the big BMW's career were the result of the tuners' efforts. In July 1969, the German Helmut Kelleners shared credit with Luxembourg's Nic Koob for the Alpina 2800CS that made the car's international racing debut at the Spa 24-hour race. Between the consumption of 40 racing tires,

it showed bursts of speed that spoke of its potential, finishing ninth.

In July 1971, Alpina and Kelleners were back in 24-hour business. Using Gunther Huber as co-driver in a more professionally-prepared car, they scored a prestigious first major international win for the six-cylinder BMW coupe, which was backed by the German national airline Lufthansa.

That year, Alpina also scored a victory in the Austrian round of the European Touring Car Championship with the Spaniard Alex Soler Roig. Yet, these wins were not a true indication of the car's speed, for the Alfa Romeo GTAm 2-liter driven by Toine Hezemans was the dominant force that season. Incidentally, Porsche 911s were excluded from European Group 2 Championship racing from 1970 onward—too little rear-seat headroom to qualify as sedans— but 911s would still be the major headache in national German and American events.

In 1971, Schnitzer was developing his version of the 2800CS, and in August of that year, Dieter Quester showed its pace. Previously, 1971 had been the year of the lightweight Capris, and they had won literally every European qualifying round prior to the Dutch race.

Quester and the Schnitzer coupe administered Ford's first defeat on this fast course, where the BMW weight penalty was not such a handicap. Quester qualified second fastest to one of the works Ford V6s and took the lead early in the race. Having pitted for fuel and tires, the Austrian had six seconds to make up on fellow countryman Dr. Helmut Marko's factory Ford. He just managed to make up the deficit as they came to cross the line at the end.

A further morale-boosting win in the face of Ford Capri unreliability went to John Fitzpatrick/Rolf Stommelen/Hans Heyer—again in a Schnitzer coupe—at the Nürburgring on July 9, 1972. There were still no lightweight CSLs homologated to race (though road prototypes existed), and wins against the specially-developed Ford had looked impossible.

The 1973 Season

Through the 1972/73 winter, BMW labored at Munich, preparing what basically would be a two-car team of works cars for the eight-round European Touring Car Championship series. In Freilassing, the Schnitzers worked on their own silver CSL (destined to have a bigger engine than most, earlier than most, most of the time), backed by Atomic Skis.

East of Munich, the small agricultural community of Buchloe resounded to the bustle and scurry at Alpina's headquarters as it prepared another of its famous orange cars, sponsored by Jägermeister. The whole of Bavaria must have been caught up in the mood as the local marque prepared to take on those big, bad American-financed Fords from the north.

Driver preparations were not neglected either. As Fritz Indra of Alpina said, "It was like a Grand Prix grid out there." During the year, Grand Prix drivers Niki Lauda, Chris Amon, James Hunt, and Jacky Ickx, plus Henri

Pescarolo, all appeared in BMWs. Ford hired even bigger names (Jackie Stewart and subsequent IndyCar Champ Emerson Fittipaldi), but to less racing effect.

Round 1 was at Monza, in northern Italy, in March. There were 25 cars on the grid; 14 were Fords and nine were BMWs. Only eight cars mattered; three works 3-liter Capris were barraged on one side, with pole position to their credit (by just 0.2 second), facing two factory BMWs, two Schnitzer cars, and a single Alpina.

In the background, Alpina had the spare CSL normally used by Brian Muir in England as back-up, and Harald Menzel had a third development works car. Menzel was contesting the German Championship that year and finished fourth in that 1973 national series with three victories.

In Capris were Dieter Glemser/Jackie Stewart (pole: 1 minute 38.2 seconds), Jochen Mass/Jody Scheckter (1 minute 38.8 seconds), and Gerry Birrell/John Fitzpatrick 1l minute 39.6 seconds). The Schnitzer CSL of Vittorio Bram-billa/Bob Wollek did 1 minute 38.4 seconds as the fastest BMW, pursued by the two works cars of Stuck/Chris Amon (1 minute 39.4 seconds) and Hezemans/Quester (1 minute 39.9 seconds). Alpina's Niki Lauda/Brian Muir came in at 1 minute 40.4 seconds and Ernesto Brambilla/Walter Brun in the other Schnitzer coupe returned 1 minute 42.9 seconds.

The war was bitterly brief. Vittorio Brambilla lost the lead after five laps with the Schnitzer CSL's gear lever in his hand. Mass, Stewart, Stuck, Birrell, and Hezemans were left to fight it out, some way ahead of Lauda. Lauda mastered the Alpina car with its lower-stage-of-tune engine, a significant 40 bhp light at 3.0 rather than 3.3 liters.

The factory BMWs were out after 14 laps (head gasket) and 31 laps ("major engine failure," reported Braungart years later), but Lauda and Muir outlasted the Fords. The Austro-Australian pairing in the German CSL covered 142 laps/507.35 miles at an average of 126.06 mph (over 200 km/h) for the four hours. Then, it was the fastest sedan-race average recorded in Europe, boosted by a special dispensation to run without the Formula 1 chicanes, a freedom subsequently rescinded. The joint-fastest-lap record time was shared by Ford and BMW—the 1973 World Champion (Jackie Stewart) and Vittorio Brambilla. They put in 1-minute, 38.3-second (130.69 mph or 210 km/h) hot laps. So it was Round 1 to BMW, albeit Alpina-BMW.

Following a cancellation, Austria's Salzburgring became the next round, only two hours on the autobahn from Munich. It was snowed out from its original date—Lauda served notice of his intentions by posting

fastest lap before the organizers quit. BMW then went to the April 29, 1973 German Championship round at Nürburgring for the morale reasons mentioned earlier. Toine Hezemans won, but it was a rough race that wrote off Brian Muir's Alpina CSL and sidelined Menzel's CSL after war in the Ford ranks.

Ford and BMW met again in the non-championship Spa 1,000-kms and the supporting Coupé des Spa. It was all BMW in the 1,000-km race, but in the Coupé des Spa, war was resumed. Jochen Mass (factory Ford) fought Niki Lauda (Alpina-BMW) in a superb high-speed display that left some of the Porsche contestants breathless and brought new respect to sedan racing.

What it was all about: BMW versus Ford. Even at the close of the season, the fight was going on. Here, the protagonists are Muir's Alpina CSL versus Broadspeed protégés John Fitzpatrick (works Capri) and Andy Rouse (Broadspeed Capri) at the British Championship round in September 1973. Ford won the wheel-waving contest.

Picture: London Art Tech, reprinted 1978

Mass led the opening lap, but as they scrambled around the eight miles of classic curves on the old Belgian road circuit, the lead would change, apparently on each corner. Capable of slightly more than the Capri's 161 mph, the CSL was still bothered by the Ford at every slower-speed turn; fortunately, there were not that many of those at Spa.

Eventually, this glorious battle came to an end, with the blue-and-white Ford limping to the side of the road and exiting at the slowest corner on the course—the first-gear La Source hairpin—as it was shedding a rear wheel! That Spa outing had been good to Lauda and Alpina-BMW. Lauda left the 1,000-km race having shared victory with Stuck in the Group 2 category within the World Championship of Makes (seventh overall). Lauda also shared the second car home in that race (with Muir), won the Coupé des Spa, and recorded a fabulous new outright sedan record of 3 minutes 52.8 seconds (135.5 mph or 218 km/h). This was only to stand until July's European Championship edition of the Spa 24-hour race, by which time Grand Prix commitments and an accident to his wrist prevented Lauda from sharing the fated Alpina entry.

Salzburgring was held belatedly in May as European Round 2. The entry was reduced by the hectic schedule for Ford and BMW: Munich sent only one white CSL down for Stuck and Quester. It recorded pole position, but retired after 41 laps with a bent valve caused by sucking in stray debris.

There was Alpina back-up from Muir/ Hezemans, but Hezemans had a spin avoiding a backmarker and was not able to secure more than second place. The Schnitzer CSL's ZF gearbox (as opposed to the works Getrag) expired after the car showed competitive speed against the Capri.

Only one works Ford was running in this event, as Birrell had a massive shunt following a tire failure at 150 mph (241 km/h) in practice. A true Scot, he was burrowing in the

headlining for his small change and watch when the rest of the Ford crew and I found his inverted Capri! The world was a sadder place when the cheerful Birrell was killed later that season, driving a single-seater.

Salzburgring brought the score to one-all for Ford versus BMW, as Glemser and Fitzpatrick won an anti-climactic Austrian race.

Round 3 was at the Mantorp Park track in Sweden, in the first week of June. With Le Mans scheduled the following weekend and both Ford and BMW entered in the French classic, the entry was depleted again. No works BMWs attended, and only one works Ford took part, facing Muir/Hezemans in the UK Alpina CSL and Brambilla/Wollek in the Schnitzer CSL.

Mass/Glemser's Ford took pole exactly a second quicker than the Schnitzer duo could manage, with the Alpina coupe a further 0.3 second slower. The race was not much of a contest; the Ford won with 124 laps to the 122 of Hezemans/Muir, and the Schnitzer car retired on five cylinders. The European Championship score-line now read Ford 55 points, BMW 50. Muir led the driver's championship with 51 points to the 41 of Glemser.

A public defeat for Ford at BMW's hands in Le Mans boosted BMW morale, though its full impact was minimized by the fact that the touring cars supported the main sports-car act at Sarthe. Motorsport entered a brace of CSLs for Amon/Stuck and Quester/Hezemans, to face a trio of factory Fords.

As ever, the Amon/Stuck car suffered gearbox trouble, stuck in fifth or literally hammered through the linkage to release third and fifth only. Mechanics and management conspired, and five gears were restored for Stuck. Neerpasch quipped that BMW's first six-speed gearbox could have been created if the race had been 30 hours long, so skilled was BMW Motorsport in deflecting officials from its persistent transmission troubles while miraculously rebuilding to full health!

Unfortunately, the mechanics could not drive the BMW as well, because Stuck stuck it into a Ferrari—and the sand—during the night. So the perpetually unlucky Amon and Stuck were out. The Quester/Hezemans CSL survived where all the Ford Capris failed (valve-gear troubles, lapsing onto five cylinders—a persistent trait as they tried to keep the Bimmers in sight that summer). The BMW made eleventh overall, conquering the sedan classes.

The wings have it

European Round 4 was to prove the conclusive halfway point in the series. Held on July 8, 1973, with practice for two days preceding the event, Germany's contribution to the European title series was the 6-hours of Nürburgring. It was the single most important race to the pro-

tagonists in the fight. Victory around these hallowed 14.2 miles was worth almost as much as the whole series.

Both the crowd—over 100,000—and the entries (over seventy cars started the race) were at an all-time high. TV, national press, radio, and specialist press from all over Europe attended. Jochen Neerpasch had more demands for pre-event interviews than Marlene Dietrich.

The weekend was a technical knock-down of Ford in practice, followed by an absolute rout of the Ford forces in the race. In a dramatic event, two of the Capris rolled over into retirement, a very rare occurrence with the wide-track configuration of these racing sedans.

The tussle for pole position was all BMW, with Lauda determined to show Stuck the Nürburgring fast track. Stuck and Mass were always the sedan stars on the Nordschliefe, but Lauda—then driving for British BRM in Formula

Brian Muir at Thruxton early in 1973 with the Alpina CSL. It had to face Frank Gardner's 7-liter Chevrolet Camaro throughout the British season, but did score a win and was always driven in entertaining style at the front of the field. It was maintained in Britain by specialist Ted Grace, the man who was also responsible for the gleaming preparation of an ex-Penske ,Sunoco-blue Camaro for Muir.

Picture: Colin Taylor Productions, released 1982

1—proved living legends can die, smashing the orange Jägermeister-sponsored Alpina CSL in 8 minutes 17.3 seconds. Stuck settled for an airborne, tail-thrashing 8 minutes 20.4 seconds.

The wings had arrived, and Ford was demoralized, for it was not even allowed tail spoilers. At maximum speed, the Ford would actually lose speed as the rear wheels started to rise from the tarmac! Mass put in a brilliant 8 minutes 23.0 seconds to be, easily, the fastest of the three factory Fords entered; but even the presence of Jackie Stewart and Emerson Fittipaldi in one Capri could not prevent their impending defeat.

Despite the omen of changing from the new 3.5-liter engines (which Stuck had debuted at Mainz the previous weekend, retiring with a broken crankshaft) to the 3.3-liter sixes for the race, the works winged-wonders finished first

(Stuck/Amon) and second (Hezemans/Quester/Menzel). Lauda and Hans-Peter Joisten were in third place, four laps behind the leaders, after spending time in the pits, completing a fabulous one-two-three BMW whitewash.

Later, when BMW engineers read the race statistics, they could see the real significance of the wings in providing consistent speed and handling. The winning car had led 22 of the 42 laps; Lauda had led on 17 laps and Stuck/Amon's winning average of 158.5 km/h (just short of 100 mph) was 3.9 km/h faster than the quickest record-breaking lap put in by Mass in the 1972 race with the Capri!

Lauda's fastest lap of 8 minutes 21.3 seconds (164 km/h or 101.84 mph) was no fluke. The Austrian ace had repeated a time of 8 minutes 23.8 seconds exactly for three consecutive laps. Lauda's skills were a factor, but the pre-

Winged flyer! This was the debut of the "Batmobile" wing kit, then-newly homologated in July 1973. Stuck demonstrates exactly what the wings were meant to prevent!

The Nürburgring 6-hours saw the winning debut for the demonic wing system of BMW, which slashed lap times by over 14 seconds on the 14-plus miles of the 'Ring, effectively smashing the Ford European title challenge. BMW won the remaining four rounds of the European Championship. "Hanschen" shared his victorious 3.3-liter CSL at the 'Ring with Ferrari Grand Prix star Chris Amon.

Picture: BMW Archiv/Postcard, released 1984

dictable handling element of the car's new winged stability, along with the ease with which these times could be repeated over 14 miles, in race traffic, was decisive. Ford was effectively finished.

No Fords completed that Nürburgring Round 4, so the result of what Clive Richardson of *Motoring News* in London called this "homologation Tomfoolery" was that, at the halfway point in the Championship, BMW had 70 points to the 65 of Ford and 60 recorded by Alfa Romeo.

On a score of wins at two-all in the European series, Belgium's Spa 24-hour race comprised Round 5. BMW entered its usual two works CSLs, backed by an Alpina car for Joisten/Muir and another Alpina car whose crew included the very swift Spa specialist Alain Peltier.

Practice at the super-fast Spa-Francorchamps circuit preceded the two-day race of July 21–22, the start taking place at 3:00 p.m. on Saturday. Though the factory was not keen to extend its 3.3-liter, 360-bhp units (Alpina ran that capacity, too), Stuck could not be restrained. "Hanschen" romped around the course, taking the Masta Kink S-bend flat out at over 160 mph in the process and shattering the time Lauda set in the spring (without wings). Stuck left the pole position to the factory at 3 minutes 49.9 seconds, the first sub-3-minute, 50-second lap of Spa by a sedan. Co-pilot Amon exhibited his legendary lack of luck, punting an Alfa off at huge speed, but the CSL was repairable to race.

The Joisten/Muir Alpina sat in the middle of the all-BMW front row, while the second works car of Hezemans and Quester recorded

Spa 24-hours, 1973: New Zealander Chris Amon eases the works CSL off the pole position on the left of the front row. In practice, partner Hans Stuck averaged nearly 138 mph around the closed public road course! This works car retired in the early hours of the morning, but the second Munich machine for Hezemans and Quester won easily over a sick Ford. The ill-fated Muir and Joisten Alpina-BMW coupe is on the right of the front row and the author's Ford (destined to finish a lucky 13th) is being battered by Alfa Romeos at the back of the grid.

Picture: Courtesy Colin Taylor Productions, Kent, UK, 1973

The Alpina-BMW at Spa 1973 displays the full factory wing kit in dramatic three-wheeling action at one of the World's most challenging corners, the downhill Eau Rouge. This picture is of Hans-Peter Joisten driving the Malcolm Gartlan Racing-loaned coupe he shared with Brian Muir. Tragically, a matter of hours later, Joisten, one of Germany's most promising young drivers, had died—one of three competitors to die in a particularly bloody edition of the Belgian classic.

Picture: Colin Taylor Productions, released 1982

3 minutes 52.5 seconds. The fastest works Ford was 7.3 seconds per lap slower, even with Jochen Mass doing his best in one of two such factory Capris.

The race was a long-winded tragedy that eventually cost the lives of three drivers during the night. The works BMWs established their early supremacy, running first and second at 1:00 a.m. In those early hours, Hans-Peter Joisten, the 30-year-old Essen garage proprietor in his first full season of professional motor racing, died in a multiple pile-up. The rapid Joisten—whom Lauda preferred as a co-driver—was one of two drivers killed on one of the fastest sections of the track, exiting from Malmedy. Competing cars (mine among them) threaded through the garishly illuminated wreckage and continued the race, but Alpina naturally withdrew. Later during the night, Alfa Romeo's Autodelta team also retired all their cars upon hearing the extent of what later proved to be fatal injuries to one of its drivers in a separate incident.

At Spa, BMW Motorsport lost the Stuck/Amon car at 3:30 a.m. after it irreparably dropped a valve. The other works Bimmer handsomely thrashed the only Capri to finish: the Fitzpatrick/Mass Ford, running only on five cylinders and very sick.

In 24 hours, Quester/Hezemans covered 2,746.67 miles to lead the Ford by over 20 laps at the finish. Stuck had also put in an official new record that was to stand as the circuit evolved. Stuck's "flyer" was 3 minutes 49.4 seconds, which represents a staggering 137.69 mph (221.5 km/h), an astonishing average speed for a sedan on a closed public road in variable conditions and race traffic.

Going into Round 6, BMW led Ford by ten points in the ETC. Ford's hopes were raised by practice and race performance at Zandvoort, Holland. The wing system of the BMWs did not seem to matter. Moreover, the heavier BMWs were wearing through tires faster; the team had to cut holes in the spoilers to relieve the temperatures on the near-side-front (NSF) rubber.

BMW entered its usual pair of Batmobiles, equipped with full 3.5-liter engines. In a weekend when Jean-Pierre Jarier also made sure of the European Formula 2 title, the factory touring car team had all sorts of problems, including a practice crash from Hezemans that caused them to worry that the hub fatigue problem was not solved. Subsequently, tire failure was found.

Motorsport was backed up by a 3.5-liter Schnitzer car for Henri Pescarolo/Harald Ertl. Alpina's scoop was hiring fast-rising Formula 1 star James Hunt (now deceased) to share the UK Alpina CSL with Muir. Just what a troubled weekend Alpina had can be judged from the engine capacities installed before the race: 3.3, 3.5 and the original 3.3-liter unit for the event itself....

The grid featured two front-row BMWs: Stuck/Amon (1 minute 35.2 seconds) and Hezemans/Quester (1 minute 35.7 seconds). Gallant former sailor Jochen Mass had put the Ford he was sharing with Glemser into third place on the grid, just 0.2 second slower.

Former Monte Carlo rally winner Gerard Larrousse paired up with Fitzpatrick, their Ford a further 1.1 seconds adrift.

The seaside race through the sand dunes was a full four hours of drama, starting off with Hezemans and Stuck being attacked by Mass in the Ford, with Fitzpatrick drafting along behind. The four cars sped around the abrasive Dutch course with a fair-sized crowd baying against the wind for compatriot Hezemans to come good, mindless of the BMW and Ford fight.

Then Fitzpatrick's Ford lapsed onto its fashionable five cylinders. There was a fabulous confrontation between the two fastest sedan regulars for the rival teams, Stuck versus Mass. Both had Formula 1 careers at stake, not to mention the honor of being Germany's fastest driver since the 1960s days of Wolfgang "Taffy" von Trips (Ferrari).

In Holland, Stuck was eventually outmaneuvered going into the large Tarzan loop at the finish of the giant straight. Flat-spotting his tires, he shuffled off to the pits, while Mass charged around with the suspicion of a grin on his face. Not for long, though.

The factory Ford suffered a halfshaft failure, and it was left to Chris Amon to show that he had acclimated to sedans by belting the big works coupe around a second a lap faster than the leading Schnitzer car, then in Ertl's hands. The gearbox gave way on the works car of Amon (again) and Pescarolo suffered a flat tire on the Schnitzer coupe.

Round 6 went to the BMW of Hezemans/Quester, who managed 143 laps at an average 93.72 mph (150 km/h), a lap ahead of Hunt/Muir, who were in turn a lap ahead of the surviving Ford, that of Fitzpatrick and Larrousse. Fastest lap of the race was shared between BMW and Ford at 1 minute 36.3 seconds (98.10 mph, or 157 km/h) for Hezemans and Fitzpatrick.

Ford had fought hard despite an obvious technical handicap, but the winged BMW

Batmobile was on course for European title glory. Surely Ford could not stop it with only two rounds left! The points stood at 110 for BMW and 90 for Ford....

Trouncing Ford, European style

Round 7 involved trekking down to the boring but well-rewarded Paul Ricard circuit in the south of France during September. Earlier in the month, it was announced that Lauda, his wrist recovering fast from a single-seater shunt, had signed with Ford to drive Cologne Capris in 1974. He was not to be the only BMW defector for 1974.

At Paul Ricard, BMW just stamped Ford out of existence in the dusty heat, despite all the star names Ford employed. Stuck took pole in

one of the two usual 3.5-liter factory coupes and headed an all-BMW front row with a time five seconds less than Mass had set the previous year in a factory Ford. Altogether, there were seven CSL BMWs on the grid versus two factory Fords and a privateer in Capris.

The result was the first predictable no-contest of the season, and BMW smashed home first, second, and third again. Hezemans and Quester grasped their third straight victory and secured the driver's title for the Dutchman, as well as BMW's claim to the 1973 European Touring Car Championship.

Stuck's winning average over the six hours was 95.70 mph (154 km/h), and he covered just over 574 miles. On the same lap were James Hunt and Jacky Ickx in a new Alpina CSL, and less than 30 kilometers behind them were Amon and Stuck, recording their first finish in four races. Inevitably, the gearbox was losing gears again, but they had stuck at it in fifth and still managed to keep within ten seconds a lap of their normal times!

BMW's unbeatable score from this penultimate round was 130, with 100 each for Ford and Alfa Romeo. The final European qualifier looked to be all cut and dried later that month at Silverstone, but Round 8 served up raw excitement for the English crowd.

Stuck seized pole position again (1 minute 32.7 seconds), but this time he had no Amon to share (Amon drove the third Elf Tyrrell at Watkins Glen), and the company on the front row was made in Detroit, rather than financed there! Frank Gardner's 427-ci/7-liter Chevrolet Camaro wanted a change from its normal UK diet of gobbling up Muir's Alpina CSL. Gardner, subsequently a successful BMW team manager in his native Australia, found the German-based teams in endurance racing a very different proposition from the opposition in British 20-lappers.

The Chevrolet was just 0.02 second slower than Stuck but ahead of Hezemans/Quester (works 3.5-liter CSL), three works Fords (one

driver per car, in a pair of two-hour heats to be aggregated), and the unusual Broadspeed Capri of Andy Rouse, which had a radically different suspension set-up from the works cars and experimental underfloor spoilers.

The first heat was only exciting in the initial stages. Just as Stuck applied the pressure to Gardner's opening lap lead, the tires went off. Munich had been trying out some 16-inch-diameter wheels, and Stuck did not like the handling, but he retired with a broken clutch. "Striedzel" was a little deflated, having set a superb record lap of 1 minute 32.4 seconds (114.04 mph, or 183 km/h) in pursuit. The Camaro lasted only 15 laps, but cost Burkard Bovensiepen 1,000 DM as he had bet it would not manage more than 10 laps....Stuck's speedy Batmobile time must be judged against Gardner's 1972 record in a 5-liter Camaro, which was 2.2 seconds slower than Stuck's 3.5-liter "Batmobile."

Ford could not alter the overall result of heat 1, which was: Ertl (3.5 Alpina CSL) first, followed by two works Fords (the Broadspeed car was sidelined in an accident) and Hezemans in fourth (the only factory BMW to finish). Stuck's retirement was too early on to allow a restart.

The second race had the crowd on their feet and is still recalled as a classic. Second time around, Gardner lost an early lead when the Chevy's tires went off, but this time Mass was really making the superhuman effort in the Ford. Wings or no wings, he forced his evil-handling machine up on two wheels almost permanently to equal Stuck's record-breaking lap of the earlier heat, a record that was never broken because of circuit changes. It looked as though the Ford could not stand the strain in the same way as the muscular Mass, though, and it was in for over half a minute for extra water to cool the overheating V6.

Mass rejoined the race on lap 15 and found himself alongside the leading BMW of Dieter Quester. This was convenient, for he could attack for all he was worth, knowing that

Mighty Munich: a classic study of the works cars in united action, showing Hans Stuck leading Toine Hezemans at Silverstone, 1973. This was actually one of their most chaotic outings, but the factory's debut season was a championship triumph, for they also secured the European Formula 2 title.

Picture: London Art Tech, reprinted 1978

Fitzpatrick in the other Capri might be able to make ground and that—as at lap 20—Fitzpatrick's Ford had taken on enough fuel to run the remainder of the race, while Quester still had to stop. Maybe the Ford could still win while the BMW was refueling!

The result was about the closest racing, without today's bent panels, that has been seen in Britain. The constant attack from Mass meant Quester was using more fuel, more emotion, and more personal energy. The crowd was quite exhausted with "oohing" and "aahing" as Mass and Quester dived around each corner, often changing positions on entry and exit of virtually every one.

Fitzpatrick did eventually get up to second place when the Alpina car (now being driven by Derek Bell) pitted for a new tire, but that was all. The Ford reverted to its favorite five-cylinder form.

The question then was, which BMW would win? Quester was hauling in Bell very quickly

after the 13-second fuel stop for the works CSL, intent on scoring a fourth straight win. To this day, in Munich, nobody says anything about it. The fact is that Quester ran out of fuel with two laps to go while fast catching the Bell/Ertl Alpina coupe. When it happened—just two laps from the end, with Quester still well-tweaked-up for a win—he was beside himself with rage. Few have the nerve to shout at Neerpasch, but Quester did on that day.

The result in that heat was a one-two-three for BMW, but Jochen Mass secured second place on aggregate to make the overall result: first, Bell/Ertl (Alpina-BMW), 150 laps at an average 108.78 mph (172 km/h); second, Mass (Ford), 147 laps; third, Muir (UK Alpina-BMW), 142 laps. Toine Hezemans was confirmed as European Touring Car Champion driver, with BMW the leading marque.

Harald Ertl, the 1978 German Champion, is shown here two-wheeling at Beckets corner; he drove with five-time Le Mans winner Derek Bell. This Anglo-Austrian combination won the September final British round of the 1973 European Touring Car Championship for BMW, the CSL and Alpina. Silverstone was a dramatic race—as ever—bringing out the best in touring-car spectacle.

Picture: H. P. Seuffert/ Alpina Archiv, 1978

Designing for 1974

So the main 1973 European conflict was over, but both sides were arming themselves for even faster competition in 1974. BMW made an appearance at the Kyalami 9-hours in November 1973 with its new chassis (20 kg lighter) ready for the 24-valve engine it had homologated back in July, but that would not be fully ready to race until 1974.

At Kyalami, the car attracted more attention than any other, setting the first-ever 100-mph-plus sedan lap. Driven by Ickx and Stuck, it also proved quicker than many of the pure sports racing cars on the grid. In the race, brake-pad trouble demoted them well down the results list, but the CSL was seventh.

Meanwhile, world events were moving around both Ford and BMW's competition thinking. The Arabs applied the oil squeeze, and Germany was one of the countries to react most violently.

The rival designers got on with their tasks. For BMW, Herren Zinnecker (drawings) and Rosche added the M49 24-valve engine to a proven chassis. Ford made a new RS3100 Capri with a rear spoiler on the trunk lid, and Cosworth in Northampton finished its Mike Hall-designed stock cylinder-block V6, which also had 24 valves and was born into a Britain of fuel-emergency-prompted 50 mph limits.

The battle rages on

In 1974, both BMW and Ford would have over 400 bhp to call on, but would the economic situation allow them to be used?

The answer to that question was, "No." The big CSLs met the Fords only twice, noseto nose, Batwing to tail spoiler. Tantalizingly, each won a race. However, it was the humble 2-liter Zakspeed Escort that did the trick for Ford, tilting the balance with class wins to secure the 1974 title.

The opening Monza round of 1974 was won by the ex-Hezemans/Quester 1973 works car of Jean-Louis Lafosse/Alain Peltier, with no factory cars from either side sent along. The factory also sold a car to Martino Finotto, who shared with Manfred Mohr and had some

Grand Prix CSL technique

Courtesy of Nigel Roebuck (*Autosport* magazine), I was allowed access to the talented Chris Amon's recollection of that epic 1973 season. One of the youngest men ever to participate in Grand Prix and the widely-experienced successor to compatriot Bruce McLaren, Amon revealed, "Compared to a single-seater, it felt harder-sprung, yet rolled more. You could brake late, like an F1, but cornering called for a totally different technique.

"You entered the corner later and drove a wider arc around it. Getting sideways in this saloon, with so little surplus power over weight, meant scrubbing totally sideways until you came to a gentle halt! The CSL was a nice car to drive, but about 300 lbs heavier than the Capri, which meant we got blown away on acceleration. Once we got the wings on the car, Stuck and I usually had the legs on the rest."

Hans Stuck generously (and characteristically) remembered Amon as "...the best driver I ever shared with. I learned a lot from him."

(Right) Testing at Salzburgring in 1974 for the first race outing of the 24-valve CSL. The midnight-blue factory machine topped 170 mph. Economic constraints following the fuel crisis of the previous winter prevented BMW from contesting more than two European Championship rounds that season. BMW entered only one works CSL at Austria's Salzburgring against two works Fords. In a thrilling battle, Jacky Ickx and Hans Stuck defeated both Capris which, by then, had Cosworth 24-valve V6 motors.

Picture: London Art Tech, reprinted 1978

(Left) The 1974 colors for the works CSLs were a midnight-blue allied to the BMW Motorsport striping. The cars appeared only twice in European Championship rounds in the aftermath of the fuel crisis. Here, Hans Stuck shows his usual three-wheeling flair at a German Championship round of that year.

Picture: H. U. P. Nicot

good results during the year, including finishing inside the top ten at Le Mans, improving on the factory's 1973 result.

At the Salzburgring second round, the normal order of things was reversed with two works Fords (one driven by Hezemans, who was another BMW defector) against a single, now midnight-blue (officially violet), factory CSL of Stuck/Ickx. However, there were nine private CSLs entered.

Stuck secured pole (1 minute 17.14 seconds) after the clutch had been changed, a persistent misfire gradually rectified, and a worrying black-smoke haze eradicated. We could see it was going to be a good race though, for Hezemans/Glemser's Ford recorded 1 minute 17.44 seconds and close behind was Gardner's 7-liter Chevrolet Camaro (the engine size shows how effective factory engineers and four-valve-per-cylinder layouts were). Lauda, with Mass, in the second Ford, was fourth on the grid.

The three works cars set off in a battle of their own, blasting around the Austrian speed-bowl at such a speed that within 39 laps—with all three sedans still fighting for supremacy below the spectator-packed hillsides—they had

lapped Gardner's Camaro! After their first pit stop, Mass managed to pull out 15 seconds over Ickx.

Former BMW employee Braungart remembers two conversations that day. As he watched the three cars scream around, nose to tail, Mike Hall of Cosworth asked Martin, "Will that car of yours go for four hours?"

"No problem with my bit," answered Braungart, hoping Rosche wouldn't hear of it!

The second conversation featured Hezemans and Braungart. "What are you doing here?" the BMW engineer jovially asked the new Ford recruit, after his Capri had retired.

"I have two engines in my Capri," said Hezemans laconically, referring to a severed cylinder block!

Both Fords had to be retired in the last 90 minutes of the race, leaving to an anxious Neerpasch the duty of trying to slow down Stuck on the way to a ten-lap victory over the next-placed, private BMW!

Both BMW and Ford gave the third round of the championship a miss. Although that Vallelunga, Rome event was won by a private BMW, the 2-liter Escort won its class again and finished third overall, bringing Ford and

BMW dead level on Championship points for the fourth round in Europe.

At the Nürburgring 6-hours in July of 1974, BMW really had a first-class driver team. In the first of two works CSLs, it offered the huge home crowd the debut of "SuperSwede" Ronnie Peterson. He was paired with Stuck, and the car recorded a staggering 8 minutes 11.7 seconds for pole position.

The equally formidable duo of Lauda and Mass were second on the grid in 8 minutes 14.8 seconds with the Ford Cosworth Capri; the second factory Ford did 8 minutes 29.5 seconds and Ickx and Bell in the other Munich-prepared BMW managed 8 minutes 29.7 seconds.

BMW probed another aspect of Formula 1 expertise: that of Goodyear. They went back to Dunlop for the race, but the factory did contract with the American company in 1976. Stuck's car also publicly debuted an early vari-

ant of ABS, the anti-lock Teldix-Ate braking system. By 1978, BMW offered the production Bosch system for sale in the normal production 7-series, but it did not return to racing until the German Championship runners of the late 1980s. (However, ABS was used in the 1975 American season, again by Teldix.)

Nürburgring in 1974 offered more in the way of changing conditions (mist eliminating many of the starters that year in spectacular crashes) than in outright racing. Stuck cleared off at incredible speed in the fastest BMW, slashing around the jumps and fabled profusion of corners and gradients to put in a lap of 8 minutes 10.9 seconds (104 mph, or 167 km/h) on his standing-start lap.

Stuck hurtled past for the first time with a 14-second lead over Hezemans, who had about the same advantage over Ickx. Mass pitted the Ford with low fuel pressure. After nine laps,

German home crowds saw more of the 24-valve 1974 works CSLs than did the European Championship, as the 1973/74 winter fuel crisis hit motorsports hard. This is Hans Stuck at Norisring in one of two domestic outings that season, both of which he won. The 430-bhp Munich machine hit 60 mph in less than 5 seconds, 0–100 mph zapped by in less than 9 seconds, and it covered only 5 miles on each gallon of gas!

Picture: BMW Archiv, released 1982

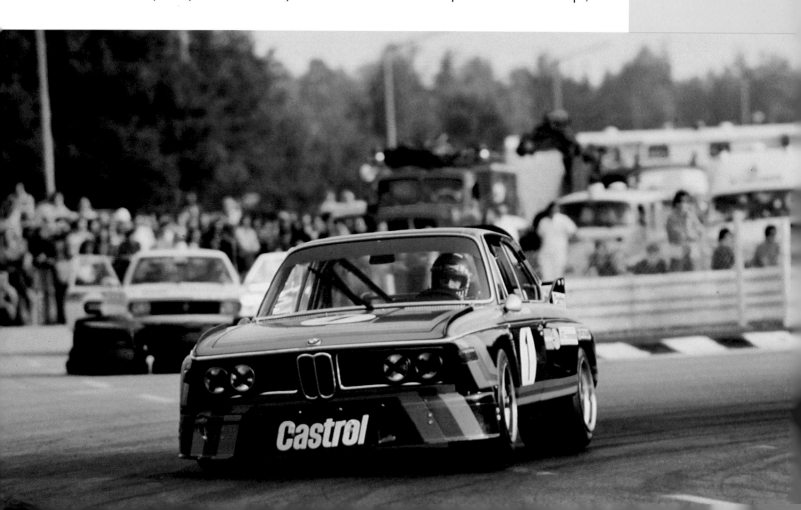

The spirit of night racing and the enduring toughness of the CSL: here is the British-based car of Brian Muir (right) up on stands along-side the winning Hans-Peter Joisten and Niki Lauda orange Jägermeister coupe in the 1973 edition of the Nürburgring 24-hours.

Picture: H.P. Seuffert/Alpina Archiv, 1978

the factory BMWs reigned supreme over Ford in first and second places, but this time luck was on Ford's side.

Stuck hit a backmarker and was badly delayed returning to the pits with the nearside front suspension collapsed. Mass also crashed the Ford, which left Glemser in charge of the situation while the remaining healthy BMW changed tires. Peterson was installed and was a minute behind Glemser in the Ford. On the next lap the gap was 32 seconds! However, conditions changed fast, and the BMW had to come in again for tires.

Stuck retired when the bell-housing on the gearbox split, just ten minutes after half-distance, in the last factory CSL. Some six laps and nearly an hour later, Glemser's Ford was in for 25 minutes to have its final drive rebuilt. That was enough to see a 2-liter Zakspeed Escort win the prestigious Nürburgring Grosser Preis von Tourenwagen. Ford went on to win that year's title with the little Escort, but CSLs won it (in private hands) in every subsequent season until 1979.

That July of 1974, Nürburgring was the last European Championship confrontation with Ford of Germany, whose sports boss, Michael Kranefuss, has become a familiar figure on the US motorsport scene.

In 1975, a factory-prepared CSL appeared rarely, but privateers won four of nine German qualifying races with the CSL. Encounters with the growing Porsche army and the now news-paper-backed Fords resulted in a ray of final domestic glory with third in the final points. That was for the Schnitzer-run CSL of Albrecht Krebs, which scored three outright wins and should have taken the title, but for an engine failure in the final Hockenheim round. The 1975 Schnitzer CSL was a formidable 1,090-kg/2,398-lb machine capable of 0–62 mph in 5 seconds and stomping up 0–100 mph in 9.1 seconds. This Schnitzer CSL cost 150,000 DM ($92,700 today). The Schnitzer blaster set pole position at 183.59 km/h (114.1 mph) to lap faster than any Porsche that day in September 1975.

QUICK FACTS

Period

1974–79

Products

Racing CSLs for American IMSA, World Group 5, and European Group 2 Championship success

Performance

480-bhp 24-valves of 3.5 liters to 1,000-bhp sixes of 3.2 liters, normally aspirated and turbocharged, with 175–200-mph maximums

Achievements

Continuing European titles (1975–79); six IMSA and three Group 5 World Sports Car Championship wins

People

American wins, pole positions, and jokes by Hans Stuck; sandy stunts from Dieter Quester; more wins from Brian Redman and Sam Posey; perfectly-prepared wins for Peter Gregg

Chapter 18

Exporting Excellence

The CSL racing beat goes on in the US

Those 1974 European factory cars were sold off, and one of the pioneer importers was John Buffum, better known for his motor-rallying exploits. Buffum and Libra Racing imported the 1973 Le Mans class -winner and reportedly the "first Motorsport-built CSL." Those cars emerged in Trans Am trim for 1974, beating the factory to American participation. (Buffum was also something of a pioneer when it came to the M5, winning the 1992 *Car & Driver* One Lap of America event.

For 1975, BMW Motorsport contested both the IMSA series in the US (1975) and the World Championship of Makes Group 5 in 1976 with the big CSLs, but it was hard to find a level playing field. In America and Europe, the problem was always the same— you spell it Porsche, and add the word turbo.

However, that did not prevent the big BMWs from putting on a fabulous show. In America, BMWs did not secure the IMSA title, but Stuck displayed the astonishing wheel-lifting speed that Europeans had enjoyed watching in previous years. Stuck managed the fastest time in American qualifying on five occasions, winning four races in 1975.

Even in the Group 5 World Championship of 1976, the three cars built for outside

teams and the CSL in BMW Motorsport colors made Porsche sweat for its honors. The prediction that BMW's 3.5-liters, at 1,020 kg, had no chance versus Porsche's 600 bhp, with less bulk, mercifully proved inaccurate.

The opening round at Mugello in Italy provided the expected Porsche win, but when the series came to Silverstone in May for that circuit's 6-hour race, BMW really gave Porsche a shock. First, it brought along the CSL turbo with its monstrous power output and the swiftest of Swedes, Ronnie Peterson and Gunnar Nilsson, to drive it.

Ickx and Mass took pole position in their Martini Porsche 935 turbo, but the CSL turbo in Peterson's determined care whooshed around the now-revised Silverstone circuit, complete with chicane, in a time little over a second outside that of the Porsche, representing an average speed of over 120 mph. Braungart remembered, "It was ridiculous, this car—the floor glowing with heat, no way to transmit power, and the wing on full downforce position to keep the back on the ground. It was mad, but fun...."

At the standing start, Peterson gave the big Bimmer a huge "go" message, browbeating Ickx to the first corner. Rear tires wreathed in

Caution, test team at work! BMW gets the measure of Daytona prior to their 1975 debut as a works team in America. Competitively and commercially, it was a great success, ensuring that the public knew the factory had taken over its US import and distribution operation.

Picture: BMW Archiv, released 1988

blue smoke, the CSL shook itself into motion and Ickx simply blew it—the clutch, that is. The Martini Porsche lurched back to the pit, but could no longer win.

Peterson's machine soon lost its lead (stopping for new Goodyears after just 14 laps, or 40 turbocharged miles!), with the transmission in meltdown. However, the fuel-injected CSLs, especially the slowest one in practice—that of John Fitzpatrick/Tom

Walkinshaw—was out in the lead, Fitzpatrick driving like a demon.

Behind "Fitz" and closing rapidly was Bob Wollek in the Kremer Porsche turbo. A crowd of 13,000 jumped up and down in non-traditional British manner, willing the CSL to finish ahead of the Porsche, Fitzpatrick already having driven a straight three hours because Walkinshaw had flown off to win another race in a Ford.

Le Mans loan: qualified fastest among the Group 2 cars, this was actually a spare IMSA-program machine that was painted by Alexander Calder (American inventor of the mobile), managed by BMW's Jochen Neerpasch, and driven at the 1975 edition of the French 24-hour classic by Sam Posey and then-owner Herve Poulain.

It lay first in class, a fine fifth overall, when the engine let go at 8:00 p.m. on Saturday. It was a shame, for it would have been BMW's best result until the McLaren-BMW won in 1995. The car is retained by the Munich factory and was exhibited at Monterey in 1996.

Picture: BMW Archiv, 1988

The beast! Ronnie Peterson eases the CSL turbo away from the start of its first race ahead of Jacky Ickx and his Porsche. The car did not finish here (Silverstone, England) or at Le Mans (three laps, but Redman was third overall, up among the proto-type sports cars when forced out). Its final appearance was at Dijon, France, where Peterson headed the works Porsche again. The car last-ed for an hour, but in the end it expired, leaving behind the memory of the most power-ful sedan seen in Europe, controlled by one of the fastest drivers of all time.

Picture: LAT Library, 1978

Fitzpatrick had about four and a half seconds in hand on the last lap. He flashed into view for the last corner with the Porsche right behind him—a mere 1.19 seconds separated them after six hours racing!

This gave the Group 5 series new hope that it could be the beginning of a proper contest. Although BMW CSLs won three rounds of the series outright and were well placed in the ten rounds that were held (many were canceled), it was not enough to win the Group 5 World Championship of Makes in its inaugural year.

Last European outings

For the record, the last time a factory-prepared-and-entered CSL raced in Europe was September 4, 1976. It was then that Ronnie Peterson put on another maestro's display in the CSL turbo on the tight track in Dijon, France. He managed to head the factory

Porsche for three-quarters of an hour before bowing to the inevitable transmission maladies.

That car was as spectacular-looking as Peterson's driving, with its Frank Stella paint in graph-paper-style fine lines on a basic white background. As an appropriate farewell (though he did not have any time for sentiment), Peterson climbed straight into the Schnitzer CSL that had been used by Dieter Quester/Albrecht Krebs. He finished the Dijon race in sixth place overall, the first non-Porsche turbo home. This shows how hard it was for BMW to take results in the Group 5 championship.

The last international victory and appearance for a factory Group 2 BMW CSL came on November 6, 1976. Although they suffered various transmission troubles (including a gearbox problem), Jody Scheckter, Harald Grohs, and Gunnar Nilsson won the Wynns 1,000 km at Kyalami, South Africa, by four laps over a Zakspeed Escort. A second works CSL for Peterson and Fitzpatrick was forced to retire at half-distance by a split fuel tank.

"The world's fastest painting," was how BMW described the graph-paper-style finish applied by American artist Frank Stella to the 1976 factory CSL turbo. The car appeared in this form at Le Mans and Dijon in France and was officially credited with 780 bhp at that time.

Our pictures show Stella (Bottom) with the car at rest in front of one giant BMW articulated transporter (note the artistic cigar prop!), and Ronnie Peterson (Top) in even finer form than usual at the Dijon round of the Group 5 World Championship of Makes. They failed to finish either event; and like many other "Art Cars," BMW retains it for publicity purposes in the 1990s.

Pictures: BMW Archiv and Werkfoto, 1976

(Top) The 1976 Group 2 season belonged to the Luigi BMW CSL team from Belgium. Their 3.2-liter coupes won seven of the nine ETC rounds outright to take the title. The side view shows the CSL of the Belgian pair who were acclaimed joint Champions: freelance journalist and driver Pierre Dieudonné, Luigi's brother-in-law, and hardworking all-rounder Jean Xhenceval. The CSL is seen at the British Silverstone race, which it won with current BMW Belgium executive Hughes de Fierlant also driving.

(Bottom) Our head-on shot has Xhenceval hard at work in the now-obsolete machine, albeit one that could still rule the touring-car roost in the new era of 6-series.

Pictures: Colin Taylor Productions; BMW Werkfoto

Up she goes! The Luigi team ran in these UFO Jeans colors for 1977 and came within a backfire of winning the European Championship again. Here is the official number 1 car of what was usually a two-car team driven by Jean Xhenceval and Pierre Dieudonné most of that season. This spectacular shot is on the way to victory at Mugello; there were no other wins that season for this pairing, but they did have five second places and two thirds to emphasize their reliable challenge for the title.

Picture: R. R. Kroschel

Belgian faith

Belgians persisted with the CSL when others had lost interest in European titles. Over nine years after that first Alpina outing at Spa, a Belgian crew—Antwerp jeweler Eddy Joosen and Raijmond van Hove, the son of a wealthy haulage contractor—won the last round of the 1978 European Touring Car Championship, held on the Belgian Zolder circuit. It had won its last 1978 race with honor. The CSL led by a lap and averaged 123.5 mph (196 km/h) for 4 hours, 14 minutes, and 3 seconds of racing.

Somehow, the old warrior was reprieved, and four years after production ceased, the CSL went back into privateer battle. Italian veterans Carlo Facetti—best know at Alfa Romeo—and wealthy chemical industrialist Martino Finotto won the 1979 title to complete BMW's run of six European Championships in seven years, a record that is unlikely to ever be matched internationally.

The American scene

Over 20 years of factory ownership produced some spectacular US competitors, well before Spartanburg was a gleam in North America's eye. Legend has it that Jochen Neerpasch could not afford to ignore the US challenge when one American asked him if BMW stood for "British Motor Works." More seriously, the factory thought it needed to reestablish its American presence, following a long legal battle with Max Hoffman's import organization and subsequent factory takeover of the import and dealership process for 1975.

BMW products had been seen competing in the US long before the CSLs arrived in the mid-1970s as official representatives. A 700 had won at Sebring back in the early 1960s and the 1800TI/SA had Hoffman's backing, importing these ultra-rarities and selling specialist parts. The 328 earns as much respect in North America as it does in Europe, and

The trunk of the 1975 CSL displays European technology with twin-filler-bag fuel tank; central belt, one driven from a driveshaft flange pulley for the alternator; the early racing anti-lock braking system hardware (right); fire extinguisher reservoir for the automatic system; and dry-sump oil tank (Left). All of this was meant to balance out a front-mounted, iron-block, six-cylinder engine, the priority of BMW's engineers for 1970s competition.

Picture: BMW Pressefoto, 1975

Americans have more of the exotic 328 derivatives in competition or one-off trim—especially strong on the Veritas and single-seater survivors of postwar chaos.

Competition's commercial importance was thoroughly understood at BMW by 1975, and it immediately instigated an IMSA Camel GT program for the CSL. This program would support the transition from Hoffman to BMW of import rights and declare that the factory was serious about a long-term future in the US. We did not know they were serious about Spartanburg back then, but any race-goer could see that this was an ambitious manufacturer of quality speed...

Thus, in 1975, four CSLs were shipped to America, one returning for use in the distinctive Stella-painted Le Mans project of 1976.

For American racing, they could get a little closer to 1,000 kg, because both trim and some of the side-glass could be removed (even the dashboard could be taken out). Also, there was greater freedom over the wheelarch extensions, so larger extensions were fitted.

BMW, like Porsche and Ford, had been expecting the International Group 5 Championship of makes regulations, based on a car's silhouette, to come into force for 1975. Marketing requirements of the States appealed a lot more than grinding the non-existent opposition into the dust in the European series as a factory.

So, the old Group 2 24-valve cars were sold off in Europe (Alpina bought one), and BMW based itself on the premises of stock-car driver Bobby Allison at Hueytown, Alabama, in the heart of the South.

The wild CSLs—an example of which is retained in thundering order by BMW North America to this day—carried enormous screen-top banners proclaiming Bavarian Motor Works as their origins. I do not think race-goers would need such education in the 1990s.

The substantial CSLs were capable of close to 180 mph, having 470–480 bhp under their lighweight hoods. They were driven by a team that included Hans Stuck, Sam Posey, Brian Redman, and Ronnie Peterson.

The American experience was extended to 1976. Peter Gregg, better-known for his activities as a Porsche privateer, represented the Bavarian factory that season. The car continued to be quite competitive, though the sheer speed of the American V8 home-grown machinery—and Porsche's reliable speed—prevented Gregg from enjoying the kind of success Braungart certainly felt the American deserved as a driver.

"I remember, at Daytona in '76, it took Gregg only a few laps to settle down to Redman's time in the same car. That's why we wanted him for 1976," the BMW executive told me. Gregg won two races for BMW in 1976 and returned to running his own Porsche in subsequent seasons, prior to his death.

The funniest story from those American CSL seasons is one that Quester told in his biography, but which deserves an English-language audience. Back in 1975, Dieter was testing ABS systems—as debuted in Germany the previous season and redeveloped—on the big Bimmer at Riverside, the now-defunct layout in the California desert that was a cresty blast to drive.

Dieter laughed as he translated that near 20-year-old memory for me at the Florida 20-Year Oktoberfest Anniversary bash for BMW Motorsport: "I suppose I was doing maybe 250 km/h [155 mph] when I hit the braking area for a 180-degree curve. When I hit the brakes, I spot my teammate, Hans Stuck, standing in the dunes with his girlfriend of that time. She was a very well-built woman—like the US TV show, Twin Peaks! Anyway, Hanschen decides to let me see how beautiful she was: lifted up her T-shirt and gave me a show!

Ready to run: the factory CSL is shown ready to ship in 1975. Under the caption "BMW Sporting Muscle for the USA," the size of those muscles was listed as 430 DIN PS for the 3.5-liter six in a 1,062-kg/ 2,347-lb "Fighting Weight." Technically, the car was interesting for the move to a full side-radiator installation, with much weight shifted rearward to balance the bulky straight six, including oil cooler for both engine and transmission around the rear-axle line.

Picture: BMW Pressefoto, 1975

The American debut season. By 1975, BMW abandoned the European touring-car scene as a factory effort and sent modified 3.5-liter CSLs to America, contesting rounds of the IMSA Camel GT series. Here Hans Stuck tackles the challenging up-and-down sections of California's Laguna Seca track. Note the three uprights supporting the rear wing, back wheel-arch air inlets, and Dunlop tire supply sticker. Goodyear was the contracted tire company to the factory from 1976 onward.

Pictures: BMW Archiv

Inside the cockpit of the 1975 IMSA racing CSL: note the inverted VDO 10,000-rpm tachometer for best readout. Other driver aids included a substantial footbrace to the left of the clutch and the placement of ignition and starter switches to the center console surrounding the five-speed Getrag gear lever. Compared with European racing, the IMSA CSL could be modified quite substantially and was appreciably lighter, but note that the door-panel trim was retained.

Picture: BMW Pressefoto, 1975

Pit-stop action from BMW in the 1975 US season. Here is the factory CSL for Ronnie Peterson (in car) and Brian Redman (waiting) at the team's Daytona debut. Peterson practiced the car second quickest overall (in a field that included a 600-bhp, 7-liter Corvette) and held second place in the race until a rare engine failure (camshaft drive chain, reportedly) sidelined "Superswede" and Redman. A second team car, driven by Sam Posey and Hans Stuck, moved into second place, only to suffer another engine failure, this time prompted by a connecting rod seeking fresh air.

Picture: BMW Pressefoto, 1975

BMW was always conscious of the role color plays in emphasizing speed. Herve Poulain's coupe has been retained by the factory, as have some of the other BMW Art Cars seen here, including the Frank Stella-inspired 320i by Roy Lichtenstein for 1977 Le Mans and an M1 by Andy Warhol. Exhibited in the reception area at Spartanburg, Warhol's crudely-daubed M1 caused one onlooker to quip, "They should have saved the money and left it out on a street near the New York subway—the graffiti's in a better class around there!"

Picture: Author, USA, 1996

Pristine! The factory-prepared engine compartment for the 1975 CSL is shown with its fiberglass airbox and cramped exhaust system. The restricted exhaust manifolding was one of the reasons for later mounting the 24-valve engine vertically, on the advice of Josef Schnitzer.

Power was publicly quoted as 430 DIN PS at 8,500 rpm and 292.9 lb-ft torque. Not bad for a 3.5-liter straight six more than twenty years ago.

Pictures: BMW Pressefoto, 1975

Brian Redman is shown in the 1976-modified factory CSL he shared with Peter Gregg for the opening World Championship race in America. Gregg impressed the Munich management from the outset and proved capable of competitive lap times immediately. The pairing won this shortened 24-hour race, seen beaming with pleasure as they hold up their silverware. In this event, which ran for only 20.5 hours, Gregg and Redman averaged 104 mph to win, assisted by current Silverstone BRDC boss John Fitzpatrick.

Pictures: BMW Archiv, 1978

Laguna Seca, California, 1975, and the works CSL, one of three originally sent to the States, plunges through the famous downhill section. Drivers during the year included Sam Posey, Brian Redman, Hans Stuck, and Ronnie Peterson. They took away an IMSA class title for their pains (Gregg's Porsche won the GT title that season) and nobody ever called BMW "British Motor Works" again!

The best result of the season was a one-two on the Riverside long track, Hans Stuck and Dieter Quester completing over 600 miles at 103 mph. Stuck—second overall in the 1974 European F2 championship and under pressure to perform on the March Grand Prix team—finally finished fourth in the 1975 IMSA Camel GT standings.

Picture: Author archive, 1975

"Jeezus! Now I was going into a complete U-turn corner and no chance to make it around...into the sand I went with Hanschen laughing like anything. Was not so funny when they found the motor completely kaput through eating up all the sand. Big bill for that, but luckily we make a one-two win the following day," said the experienced Austrian, who has more strange stories to tell than "The X-Files."

Away from the laughter, the CSL in its debut American IMSA season in the Camel GT category won at Sebring 12-hours (Redman, Stuck, Posey, and the Australian Alan Moffat) and took solo driver wins for Stuck at Laguna Seca and Daytona Paul Revere 250. It also netted

Quester and Stuck a victory after the T-shirt comedy at Riverside. CSLs also posted five second-place results and six pole positions.

Stuck was the hero, but it took a toll on his European single-seater performances. Hans Stuck Jr. always found it hard to get the respect he deserved in Formula 1 or 2, where the combination of a famous father (not always recommended: ask Damon Hill) and his wild sense of humor clashed with the increasingly money-oriented business of Grand Prix racing.

Now, BMW's problem was how to follow the CSL's class act. Something smaller was required—something 3-series-sized....

NASCAR stock-car winner Benny Parsons (left) was assigned as partner to David Hobbs for the 1976 Daytona 24-hour endurance race. They finished tenth after suffering the same fuel-feed problems as the other two works CSLs, for there was water in the race fuel supply that year.

Picture: BMW AG Presse, 1979

Generation gap: The 1992 Spa-Francorchamps winner (BMW's 15th such Belgian victory!) for Jean-Michel Martin, Steve Soper, and Christian Danner is retained by BMW in Munich, while the 1976 CSL behind won that year's Daytona (over 20.5 hours rather than the planned 24) for Brian Redman and Peter Gregg. It is retained by BMW NA and was sign-written for Redman and Sam Posey at the 20th Anniversary of BMW Motorsport/Oktoberfest event in 1992 .

Picture: Author, Sebring, Florida

Fitting farewell: here are Peter Gregg and the BMW CSL as they would like to be remembered, powering ahead. Note the riveted rear wheelarch extensions with matching extractor slots on this 1976 car, the widest of factory-backed CSLs.

Picture: BMW Archiv, 1978

The most common view of the Alpina BMW in 1977: Gunnar Nilsson co-drove with Quester at the Nürburgring 6-hours that year, and they won the home round in front of an enormous crowd. It was an unusually close race, though, for the Jaguar team scored their highest placing of the year, a second. Note the Group 2 plastic wheelarches, complying with regulations that also included a requirement for wet-sump lubrication at the start of the season. By the end, Leyland had persuaded the authorities to allow dry-sump lubrication, which was readily fitted to this Alpina coupe, but not to the Luigi CSLs in 1977.

The Alpina-BMW CSL scored five victories in twelve championship rounds, the remainder all won by either Luigi or ex-Luigi CSLs.

Picture: Unknown/ Author archive, 1978

QUICK FACTS

Period

1977–79

Product

Normally-aspirated and turbocharged racing 320

Performance

125-bhp street 320 to 654-bhp
BMW North American 320t

Achievements

Class champion in Germany and the
World Championship series trains a
new generation of chargers; eight
times a winner in the US

People

Sweden's Grand Prix ace, Ronnie
Peterson; Britain's expat American
ace, David Hobbs; additional commentary from Brian Redman

Chapter 19

Junior Makes Good

Enter the 3-series, from international trainer to turbo blitzer and Grand Prix prophet

When, with a final turbocharged flourish, the 2002 series expired in 1975, BMW faced contemporary image problems. New 3-series sedans, factory-coded E21, were launched with substantially the same four-cylinder running gear, trailing-arm rear suspension, and MacPherson-strut chassis. Their engines were giving slightly less performance in the plusher, larger 3-series bodies.

BMW engineers, including Rosche, were working on a premium new range of 2.0- and 2.3-liter straight sixes which would power the 320 and 323i models from early 1977 onward. These small sixes, with belt-driven SOHC and the familiar slant installations, allowed a performance progression over the 2002 icon—and reinvented BMW's prewar reputation for lower-capacity in-line sixes of powerful quality.

These six-cylinder models countered initial public criticism that the 3-series lacked sporting character. Many felt that the four-cylinder range—even a 320i injected with 125 bhp—was a let-down after the heritage of the 2002. Comparing the 2002Tii, with 130 bhp and a lighter body, with the 320i often saw the more recent Bimmer severely criticized in Europe. Initially, soft 320 suspension settings

were also a godsend to aftermarket companies like Alpina.

By 1977, the chassis and braking modifications offered with the six-cylinder engines overcame some prejudices. At 143 bhp in European showroom trim, the 323i lacked little, returning 126 mph and 0–60 mph in 8.3 seconds during independent tests, causing some to wonder why the six-cylinder was ignored for competition.

Rosche, who had been seconded to develop the BMW small sixes for two years and who demonstrated to me (on our way to the Hockenheim Grand Prix) that the road version could happily sustain over 7,000 rpm, without modification, definitely seemed the right person to ask.

He said decisively, "For Formula 2, I think the four-cylinder is better. It is lighter, uses less fuel, and can make more revs." From an installation viewpoint, the four was also more compact, though the small BMW straight sixes were not then as bulky as today's 24-valve units.

So, BMW raced a four-cylinder car while the six-cylinder carried all the road-going prestige. That status was preserved into the 1990s with four-cylinder 318/320s defending worldwide company honor in SuperTouring, while the cur-

Back at Le Mans for 1977, this was the Roy Lichtenstein 320i Art Car at work on a Porsche 911 pace. Driven by art enthusiast Herve Poulain and Michele Mignot, it finished a fine ninth, a place behind the 3.2-liter Luigi CSL for Jean Xhenceval and Pierre Dieudonné.

Picture: Colin Taylor Productions, 1977

rent E36 M3 is the street performer. As the M3GTR, it won the ADAC German national championship of 1993 and was America's IMSA GTS2 champ of 1996. It has also shown well at Nürburgring 24-hour events, but the four-cylinder still bears the brunt of BMW sedan warfare.

Besides BMW Motorsport preparations for improving the 3-series' sporting image in the 1970s, some bold privateers developed production-based versions of the 3-series. The 1976 season was the first for a more restrictive Group 2 that barred many homologated extras, such as four-valve engines and durable five-speed gearboxes.

A German-speaking Swiss outfit called Eggenberger (later winners in Europe for Volvo and Ford) produced a very neat 320i. At its first appearance in Britain (also the debut of that big Jag) this neat white machine impressed everyone at the September 1976 Tourist Trophy at Silverstone. It ran reliably, finishing sixth overall and winning its class while the Luigi team racked up another notch on the CSL's outright winning record.

The Eggenberger 320 weighed around 1,570 lbs and featured a fuel-injected four-cylinder engine that owed a lot to Alpina parts and practice. It was purported to give 220 bhp in two-valve-per-cylinder form.

Group 2 went through a temporary renaissance in 1977. While the big Jaguars fought unsuccessfully to finish and beat the BMW CSLs, Eggenberger ran a (mainly) two-car 320i team built around Swiss Walter Brun, a former European Champion in a CSL shared with Siggi Mueller. Opposition in the 2-liter class was not fantastic, and Eggenberger accrued enough points to win that division for BMW as well.

Eggenberger did not have a particularly lucky year. Transmission troubles were constant, either through the four-speed gearbox or the single-plate clutch. Honest horsepower was less than the Cosworth BDA-engined Escorts, but they were unreliable without a trick gearbox. Eggenberger also suffered the complete loss of one 320 when the Group 2 circus went down to Enna and Brun rolled the 320 into a ball.

Another interesting non-factory effort was from Georges Benoit's team in France. It prepared a 323i for the 1978 Spa 24-hours, the car having made its debut in a supporting event to the French Grand Prix earlier in July. The car was very mildly modified, indeed, having little over 150 bhp, but it did prove reliable and finished the race, though not within the top ten.

The Motorsport-backed 3-series

BMW Motorsport moved quickly once the BMW board approval for a proper racing 3-series was received. Motorsport took two development paths: a surprise contract with McLaren's operation in Detroit and, for Germany, a three-car BMW Junior Team mounted in Munich-made 320i Group 5 sedans.

Both moves were officially announced at the annual competition conference in December 1976. Though the Formula 2-engined (M12/7) 320i would be basically the same for both operations—McLaren taking over its unit from the works after Daytona 1977—there could not have been a bigger contrast in drivers.

The Junior Team had an average age of early twenties, while the experienced and communicative David Hobbs from Britain was assigned the majority of American events. The

This beautiful orange 320i Group 5 machine, entered by Rudiger Faltz of Essen and sponsored by well-known German beverage concern Jägermeister was a regular sight in German and World Championship events of 1977. The superb side shot of the 320 was taken at the May Silverstone 6-hours, where Ronnie Peterson and Helmut Kelleners finished fourth overall. The classic jumping shot of Harald Grohs at the Nürburgring was irresistible, as are the many scale-model versions of this attractive BMW, which was also driven by Hans Stuck. The Quartzo metal model of this car sat on the author's computer throughout the writing of this book.

Pictures: Colin Taylor Productions (Silverstone); Author archive

Bodywork for the 320i was developed with cooperation from the Pininfarina wind tunnel in Turin during the 1976/77 winter. It was only altered in detail for subsequent seasons in normally aspirated trim.

Picture: BMW Werkfoto, 1977

Junior Team members were Eddy Cheever (then only 18 years old), Manfred Winkelhock (elder brother to 1993 British Champion, Joachim Winkelhock), and Marc Surer. Competition was white-hot, as the winner would have the best possible chance of moving up the single-seat ladder with BMW.

All three were entered to contest rounds of the German national championship, but on one occasion, when they were exceptionally unruly, they were smacked by Neerpasch and sent to their rooms, suspended for one round! Hans Stuck and Ronnie Peterson took the naughty babies' places and tried to set a standard, but the 320 was so easy to drive that even experienced warriors got caught by the rasher dashers.

During 1977 and the following winter, BMW Motorsport GmbH pumped out many more of these popular Formula 2-engined 320s, and they appeared all over the world in a supporting role at the World Championship of Makes, which was run on much the same Group 5, highly-modified touring-car rules as the German national championship. So popular and reliable were the 320i racers in Group 5 form that Neerpasch reported sales of twenty-seven cars at slightly over £30,000 apiece (just over $50,000 today) halfway through the 1978 season. It should be remembered that the engine alone represented £8,200 ($13,694).

What made this "production run" so remarkable was the complexity of the race 320. It

Naked! Without its fiberglass suit of clothes, the main structure of the 320i Group 5 car can be clearly seen. Note the side-mounted oil radiators in the rear-wheel cavern; also note that the water radiator is moved to the rear. Curb weight was quoted at 765 kg/1,683 lbs, almost halving the bulk of a standard 320i four cylinder at 1,080 kg/2,376 lbs.

Picture: BMW Press Pack, 1977

featured inner production framework in steel—floor pan, roof bulkheads, and so on—clothed by aerodynamic fiberglass bodywork developed in a wind tunnel at Pininfarina in Turin, Italy. The doors, hood, front end, large wheel-arch extensions (front and rear), and separate front air foil were all fiberglass, as was the rear cover and wing support, though the wing blade itself could be made in aluminum.

Because so many different teams ran the Group 5 320, all looking for some small advantage over the others, aerodynamic alterations were often made. Primary changes were to the wing, to the enclosures of the open air feed to the front of the rear wing extension (where the side radiators were located), or to the tail sections.

Where the factory was involved in the turbocharged 2-liter program (from the World

Championship of Makes in late 1977 until the end of the US IMSA series in 1979), it further developed the body, removing weight and extending the rear air foil. Both works and privateers left the "running boards" (from front wing to rear, below the doors) intact. A small hoop was fitted above the rear window as for CSL, but the CSL's front wing splitters were absent.

Rainer Bratenstein was the quiet and precise young man assigned with developing the race 320. As a development engineer at BMW Motorsport, Bratenstein had traveled throughout Europe and America, where his excellent English and sense of humor helped him contribute greatly to BMW North America's CSL and 3-series racing programs.

Recalling the development of the 320 into a racing car, Bratenstein said, "In the three months we had to do the job, it would have

Neat and functional: this is the driver's view of the 320i compartment, showing the handsome LHD leather-rim steering wheel, VDO instruments, and center console mounting for all controls. Note that the driver must reach the controls from a position considerably further back than in a normal street car.

Picture: BMW Press Pack, 1977

The heart of the 320i in Group 5 trim was the fabulous M12/7 2-liter Formula 2 engine. It mounted lower and farther back than in the production car, partly for handling and partly because the vertical engine is taller than the slant production unit. Power output was maintained at over 300 bhp, despite the heavier body, restrive exhaust and longer races that were successfully tackled.

Picture: BMW Press Pack, 1977

been quite simply impossible to develop this car in the conventional way on the drawing board. Even if we had 50 designers, it wouldn't have been possible."

The E21 pressed-steel bodyshell was the starting point, together with the knowledge that it had to be mated to a conventional front-mounted, north-south installation of the M12/7 Formula 2 four-cylinder racing engine. In a successful effort to find some basic balance within the design, Motorsport's engineers and mechanics moved the engine 120 mm (4.7 inches) back toward the front bulkhead. Simultaneously, the engine was lowered in the chassis by 60 mm (2.4 inches).

Such radical re-engineering slashed a lot of sheet metal to make way for the bulk of the engine moving toward the passenger area,

plus widening and refabricating the central transmission tunnel as the new Getrag 245/6 five-speed was installed in a rearward position. The turbo version had to accommodate the heavier duty, ex-CSL Getrag 265.3.5. A twin-plate Borg and Beck clutch sufficed for the Formula 2-engined version (more about the turbo later).

To complement the lower and rearward disposition of the high-revving formula engine, BMW also moved the driver's seat to the rear. Subsequently, that meant moving back the foot controls, brakes, accelerator, clutch, and remounting the steering column with its replacement steering wheel to suit the new driving position. Because of the time element, a large number of components came from the CSLs, including the gear-change linkage and

Rear disc brakes were radially ventilated with coaxial Bilstein and a coil-spring unit above. Note the threaded tube of the shock absorber, allowing rapid ride-height adjustment. The abbreviated and lightened (see the tell-tale holes?) trailing-arm rear suspension mounts to a rigid ball joint on the left. Again, much of the principle comes from that established by the bigger CSLs.

Picture: BMW Press Pack, 1977

More than 20 years after its debut, the 320 turbo motor still appears in America on high-profile occasions. Only in the US did the 2-liter ever deliver anything like its winning potential, more than doubling the power offered in the normally-aspirated version, with a total 650-bhp best.

Picture: Author, Monterey, 1996

Simple and effective: the front MacPherson strut for the 320i carried an aluminum-tubed Bilstein shock absorber. Comprehensively-ventilated Ate disc brakes featured massive 4-piston calipers. The layout works along principles established with the factory CSL coupes. Note how little steel bodywork remained!

Picture: BMW Press Pack, 1977

the basic shape of the roof spoiler. Many of the suspension components were adapted to a 320 application.

Unusual features included employment of titanium coil springs with linear spring rates and the lack of a conventional limited-slip differential on the works cars (there have subsequently been other rear-axle layouts). Other features included a straightforward locked ("locker") differential action mated with a new differential casing and quick-change access for the final-drive ratio.

Contributing towards the final balance of the chassis and the rapturous driver comments that the Group 5 320 always attracted throughout its normally aspirated career, the battery, alternator (driven from the inner driveshaft flange à la CSL), fire extinguisher, and dry-sump oil tank were all mounted within the trunk. Other detailing included Plexiglass for all but the front laminated windshield and the intelligent use of Teflon-insulated electrical wiring harnesses for both safety and neat installation. Bosch supplied the electrical equipment, which

Look for the missing grille on Manfred Winkelhock's Junior Team 320 and you get an idea of just how close the contact was between the ambitious Juniors in 1977.

Picture: Author archive, obtained 1988

included an 0–8 hp starter motor, a condenser ignition with an electronic rpm-limiter, and surface gap spark plugs.

The floorpan of the 320 not only had to be altered with respect to admitting the new and relocated engine and transmission parts, but also to accommodate the completely-revised rear suspension arms. These were curved and capable of accommodating rear rim-widths up to 14 inches.

Alloy-tube Bilstein MacPherson racing front struts were used with magnesium uprights, aluminum hubs, and "floating" Ate calipers. "Atmo" 320 racers used Ate ventilated discs, front and rear, of very generous dimensions. At the rear, a shortened CSL trailing-arm competition suspension was designed, mated to Bilstein aluminum-cased dampers and titanium coil springs.

At the front, fabrication was needed to provide rack-and-pinion solid race mounts, and fresh brackets were required to locate the competition anti-roll bars and the extra provision of longitudinal front-strut location arms.

The car was tested extensively, despite the original lack of time allowed to the engineering department. Drivers included Ronnie Peterson, Gunnar Nilsson, sometime US-based Brian Redman, and the three 1977 Junior Team drivers. Redman—still a winner at the 1996 Monterey Historic races—particularly remembered the 320, commenting, "I liked the car very much indeed. It was a fine little machine with a lot more balance than the big CSLs we had been driving up to then.

"I did my test miles at Zeltweg, around the Oesterreichring. Now that is a fast track, but if I remember rightly, we were only a second or so off the pace of the 3.5-liter cars with this 2-liter. I think it was Ronnie who got round the smaller track at Paul Ricard faster in the 320 than he had in the CSL."

Juniors (Surer on the
left) gang up on an
unfortunate priva-
teer at the
Nürburgring. Often,
it ended in tears....

*Picture: BMW
Werkfoto, 1977*

3-series performance

Everyone was pleased with the car. Toward the end of the 1977 season, Tom Walkinshaw had reason to share a 320 with Manfred Winkelhock at Brands Hatch, and he just couldn't get over the brakes. "They just stop the thing dead, miles before you think it's possible," he exclaimed. Since Walkinshaw's experience then included outings in all types of formula cars, this was high praise, indeed.

However, there was a snag to such good track manners. Although Ronnie Peterson also commented in conversation that the normal 320i racers used by the Junior Team were "the

best handling saloon cars ever," he also admitted that this created some driver problems.

Even the redoubtable Swede felt a touch anxious when Cheever virtually destroyed Peterson's car in one epic Nürburgring confrontation. As Peterson asserted, "These cars have so much chassis that almost anybody can drive them fast." This was obviously the case, and it was the primary reason for Cheever, Surer, and Winkelhock indulging in so much spectacular pushing and shoving in 1977. At times, this just got out of control (Surer having his racing license suspended at one stage), but it certainly made for fantastic entertainment.

How much performance did these baby Bimmers pack? In normally-aspirated and fuel-injected form, the 320i Group 5 racer weighed

1,683 lb/765 kg and boasted almost 400 bhp (actually 397.3) a ton. Hauled by a 2-liter M12/7 creating 305 bhp and limited to 9,250 rpm, independent tests established 0–62 mph in 4.4 seconds and 0–100 mph in only 7.7 seconds. Some 3-series!

How did the 320 fare in initial European action? I reported a July 1977 support race to the German Grand Prix at Hockenheim, Germany, when the Junior Team was at a fever pitch. There were rival Ford Escorts to defeat—even Porsche was there with its 1.4-liter "Baby" 935.

The crowd and the press concentrated on one race—the Junior category. The white cars with their Motorsport striping and consecutive numbers 11-12-13 (no fear at all!) jinked round the drab Motodrom's curves, hopped over curbs, crawled along in a three-car continuous train, or simply barged off each other

under braking at any opportunity! Ickx beat the BMWs into two-three-four placing, but the Bimmer train also demoted the best Escort (Armin Hahne) to fifth.

It truly was a breathtaking spectacle: how BMW Juniors ever accrued enough points to win the 2-liter division of the German Championship that season, I will never know. The overall title went to Porsche that year, but BMW's best Junior, Manfred Winkelhock, was third overall in a series won by Rolf Stommelen's Porsche 935, just besting Ford's Hans Heyer and teammates Eddie Cheever (USA) and Switzerland's most successful export to BMW, Marc Surer.

By 1978, the BMW Junior Team was transferred to single seater Formula 2 racing (see chapter 11). For that 1978 season in Germany, BMW and Schnitzer had developed a baby turbo Bimmer "320" of 1.4 liters that

Lesson learned? Because of the rough tactics seen among the 1977 Junior Team, Neerpasch turned out 320s for a "BMW Gentlemen Team." The old wisemen included Hans Stuck and Ronnie Peterson.

Picture: BMW Archiv, 1978

could collect the championship for Harald Ertl. Because of its importance to Grand Prix racing, that story is told in our chapter devoted to the development of that world-title winner.

Less spectacular, but a lot more predictable, was BMW's win in the 2-liter division of the world championship in 1977. There was no real opposition to the factory-replica 2-liters, which showed their inherent reliability by finishing 4- and 6-hour races comfortably, quite often with a place in the top five as a bonus.

Official BMW factory participation at most Group 5 World Championship rounds in 1977 was a no-show. BMW Motorsport could not campaign the old CSL coupe because it was obsolete, and the turbo 320t was not ready to come to Europe until late September.

Motorsport aces like Peterson and Stuck joined many other worthies in racking up championship points. Among them were

Walkinshaw, Kelleners, Stommelen, and Manfred Winkelhock, with the cars in a number of varying color schemes, including Jägermeister and Faltz of Essen.

In 1978, the BMW domination in the 2-liter division of the World Group 5 Championship was complete, the 320i certainly winning the class without interruption. Nominally, these 320s were divided up into countries. Belgium's car was mainly driven by Patrick Neve and Harald Grohs, Italy's by Eddie Cheever and Giorgio Franca (this car had a special short-stroke Osella motor and Pirelli tires), Sweden's by Bo Emanuelsson and Anders Olofsson, Heidegger's Swiss example by Freddy Kottulinsky and Marc Surer, and one shared by Scotland and Austria in Gösser Bier green going to Dieter Quester to share with Tom Walkinshaw.

Surer tests the 1978 specification 320i at Hockenheim. It was one of five such cars intended to contest the 2-liter category of the Group 5 series, each one generally entered under the country of the drivers, though this could be stretched on occasion. There were cars representing Sweden, Switzerland (shown here), Belgium, Italy and a kind of Anglo-Austrian machine for Quester and Walkinshaw. Between them all, they made sure of the 2-liter section of this world title series.

Picture: BMW Archiv, 1978

Turbo technology

The turbocharged 320i developed by BMW, from later in the 1977 season, was called 320t, and its turbo motor was coded M12/9. It was plumper, transporting 26.4 gallons of fuel instead of 22.0 gallons, plus it had all the ancillary weight created by the turbocharger at the front. A 320t weighed 1,936 lbs/880 kg in World Championship guise, considerably less for the US. The best power ever recorded was from the American version—slightly over 650 bhp—so the power-to-weight ratio was better than 800 bhp a ton in the US, under 700 bhp a ton elsewhere.

In contrast with the Garrett AiResearch tur-bocharged 2-liter developed in America, we should also note that peak torque was 166.4 lb-ft for the Formula 2 motor, against a tur-bocharged 353.7 lb-ft on higher-octane American fuel: McLaren at Livonia, Michigan.

BMW Motorsport succeeded in making it an American race winner with a Garrett AiResearch installation puffing at 1.3 bar.

Unfortunately, the turbo motor's World Championship life was limited by piston fail-ures in face of the lower-octane fuels of Europe. Despite lowering the compression from 8.0:1 to 7.0:1, it was never a long-distance competitor for the Porsches.

McLaren personnel under the supervision of Tyler Alexander at Brands Hatch in 1977 told me that the turbo unit initially differed from its Formula 2 brother only in the insertion of some American parts. For example, the connecting rods were made by Carello, pistons by TRW, and the turbocharger was also American, rather than the traditional German KKK unit. Reprofiled camshafts were obviously needed for the turbo application and so, too, were heat-resistant materials for the Formula 2-sized valves.

The "softer" camshaft timing and inherent docility of the turbocharged unit was emphasized by a power range 1,000 rpm wider than the normally-aspirated version (6,000–9,500 rpm for the turbo, 7,000 the start point without).

At his Brands outing in 1977, Ronnie Peterson noted how easy it was to lose time if there was any race traffic about. By Grand Prix standards, a 320 had a comparatively heavy body and a small motor to overcome any inherent turbo "lag." The offset was stunning handling and braking for such a conventional layout of the main mechanical components. Peterson maximized such characteristics

to show how talent combined with a manageable car could overcome cubic inches.

Running gear of both types of factory Group 5 320i owed a great deal to the hefty CSL. Although this meant the components were strong, some privateers looking for an edge in shorter German national races used lighter components.

For the turbo model, extra clearance had to be obtained on the abbreviated trailing arms to accommodate 14-inch-wide rear wheels of 19-inch diameter. The "normal" racing 320i specification used BBS composite wheels with their beautifully polished spun-aluminum rims,

While "Hanschen" Stuck looks thoughtful (right), Martin Braungart probes the engine department of the 320i turbo at its European debut. Note the deeper front spoiler fitted to the factory turbo model as compared with the Junior Team 320s of the previous year. The BMW 320i turbo made its European debut late in the 1977 season. While Stuck looks on, the mechanics prepare this international hybrid. It used American turbocharging expertise, the German rolling chassis, and engine rebuilds, in Europe, by John Nicholson in Britain.

Picture: Colin Taylor Productions, 1977

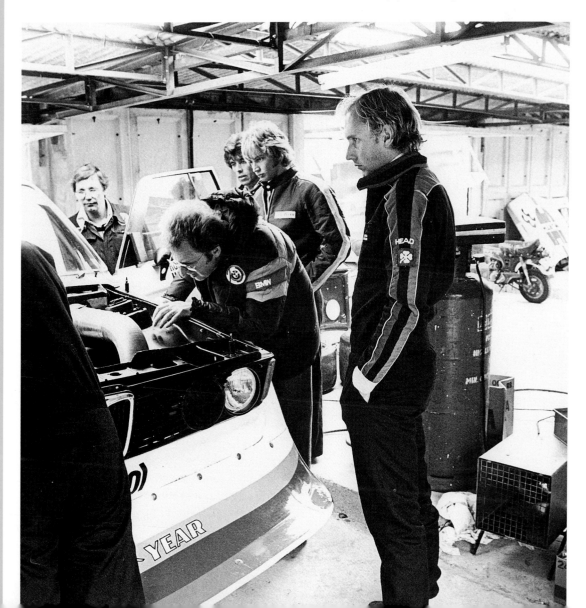

Only in America. The BMW NA truck and Monterey hills are the backdrop for the preserved 320 turbo that punished Porsches in the late 1970s and is regularly reunited with ex-pat British driver, David Hobbs.

Picture: Author

Brewed in Germany, reworked in the US

BMW North American sources report importation of a trio of 320 racers to get the US racing job done. Chassis 001 was the normally-aspirated, 300-bhp ex-Junior Team car referred to in the main text and raced just once in its original format (at Daytona in February 1977).

It was then reworked by McLaren NA around the turbo motor. Body moves included the "cow-catcher" front spoiler, a custom rear item (stretched a lot further rearward with expanded side sills/rear wheelarch extension to house 19 x 14-inch-wide rear wheels in place of the usual 16 x 12.5 inches), plus additional radiators and intercooling.

"001" was crashed at Sebring early in 1978 and rebuilt as a convenient further extension to the European turbo work then proceeding to establish the validity of a 1.5-liter Grand Prix motor. This was the unsponsored, plain-white 320t run at Mid Ohio in 1978 by Tom Klausler and David Hobbs, while the regular car wore Citicorp identification. That it finished in such terrible heat—pun-

ishing the drivers severely—was an important boost to the ongoing F1 turbo program back in Munich.

The 002 chassis was always a turbo 320 and debuted at Mosport in August 1977. Unfortunately, IMSA rules changed rapidly, and that led to the construction of the lightweight 320t mentioned below, conforming to the more radical GTX category.

The final (003) chassis shipped for BMW North America's most successful road-racing program prior to the 1990s was the lightweight car mentioned in our test. It had a one-piece nose, radiator remounted behind the back tires, NACA extraction slots in the rear fenders, and an even boxier profile!

Dubbed the "Flying Bricks," that trio of BMW North American McLaren 320t-types recorded eight outright victories. They also annexed the same number of pole positions, established six fastest laps, and set ten lap records in three seasons. They are often remembered as the "Fire and Wind" Bimmers and were most successfully driven by David Hobbs, who in 1992 recalled them as "...quick as hell, easy to set up in corners in a four-wheel drift."

BMW North American 3-series gang, plus cheeky Ford/Grand Prix/Porsche chappy, Jochen Mass (right). The M-people are (left to right) Sam Posey, David Hobbs, and Ronnie Peterson. Both Posey and Hobbs remain well-known because of their TV commentaries, but David Hobbs also played the key role in driving and progressing the American-based 320T program.

Picture: Author archive, obtained 1978

but it specified 16-inch-diameter and 12.5-inch-wide rims at the rear. At the front, the BBS wheels were of 16-inch diameter on both cars, and 11 inches wide. Goodyears to then-Formula 2 specification were fitted.

The transmission was rather clumsy, according to factory engineers, but proven. That was important for dealing with customers and the demands of a turbo version, as soon as possible. The works fitted the Halibrand drop-gear final drive with driveshafts adapted from the big coupe's last days in Group 5. The Halibrand final drive weighed 35 kg, so some of the privateers in the German championship saved nearly 19 lbs/9 kg by using lightweight differentials with aluminum casings.

The five-speed Getrag gearbox was specified, but it could be either a production casing with five gears installed within or what the engineers quietly called "the big Getrag"—nearly bomb-proof, like the Halibrand rear end. Again, the fight was between lighter weight and ultra-reliability. But for the turbo 2-liter, they used the bigger unit in Europe. In the turbocharged version, a triple-plate clutch

was necessary, supplied by Borg and Beck.

Whereas factory racing 320s sported side radiators, revealed by those side openings at the front of the rear fiberglass wheel extensions, the 1978 320t specification placed water radiators behind the rear wheels. The repositioned water radiators not only offered weight distribution advantages, but also contributed to an average 20-degree lowering in engine temperatures.

Running in shorter events, the American McLaren 320t was lightened considerably in 1978 (90 kg/198 lb has been quoted) by the use of a new body and associated plastics, a front subframe assembly, and the substitution of many lighter components in place of those developed for endurance events.

That meant it should have had 1,738 lbs/790 kg, boosting power-to-weight from around 700 bhp a ton to 849 bhp a ton, the best for a race 3-series, but not enough to regularly cope with the US-based Porsches encountered in the 1977–79 BMW NA program. (See the side panel for individual details of racing 320 turbos in the US.)

Turbo: The world-wide picture

The exciting BMW turbo four-cylinder made its debut at Brands Hatch, Britain, in the penultimate round of the 1977 Group 5 World Championship. It was to be driven brilliantly by Ronnie Peterson in practice, but crashed early on by Hans Stuck in the wet race. It was a poor omen, and the car's racing career in turbo form within the World Championship proved unreliable. However, in the US, McLaren's BMW North American 320t and David Hobbs won eight races (four in 1977) during some spectacular 1977–79 motoring.

The biggest racing problem was getting away from the start line competitively with what Hobbs once candidly described as the "zero torque" engine. This remark was untrue in engineering terms, but very apt when launching a 2-liter BMW to war against 3-liter Porsches equipped with rear-engine traction and double turbocharger units. Such advanced customer 935s produced nearly 800 bhp, and that, in a chassis honed over the years, was tough to beat.

This handicap was emphasized throughout the 1978 season when the McLaren BMW 320t won only two races. By the close of that season, with some help from an improved water-cooling layout, Hobbs reckoned McLaren had squeezed 610–620 bhp from 2 liters. "I just don't see how we can wind much more horsepower out of it. Even if we do, we still don't have the torque, and that sheer pulling power away from slow corners," Hobbs revealed in August 1978. Subsequently, the highest horsepower claim was reported at 654 bhp in America.

In 1977, without the turbo for one race, the American BMW team scooped its national 2-liter class. BMW sent over one conventional 320i, which McLaren then reworked, adding the 2-liter AiResearch turbo engine early in the season. The second turbo—the one that appeared at Brands Hatch—was built up by BMW in Munich. McLaren in the US built a second turbo for 1978 with the biased rear-radiator location and modifications listed in our side panel.

By the end of 1978, the 320t's best-ever European performance had been at Silverstone, England, in April. Contesting the 6-hour international, Hans Stuck/Ronnie Peterson managed four very competitive hours and were second overall at one stage, right in among the Porsches (but were not competitive with Porsche's factory 3.2-liter twin-turbo). Then the differential failed, robbing BMW of some superb driving from Peterson and Stuck in the flame-belching 320 turbo.

In America, the winning started a season earlier. By July 1977, the McLaren-run machine in CitiCorp suit won its first IMSA race outright by nine seconds at Road Atlanta.

The 320t first raced in turbo trim in the US on April 17 that year, driven by David Hobbs, and great things were expected in Europe. Practice around the ups and downs of the twisting Kentish Grand Prix circuit in the spring of 1977 produced a sensational time of 1 minute 26.37 seconds—sensational because a factory 2.9-liter Porsche turbo for Jacky Ickx managed a time only 0.12 second faster than Ronnie Peterson.

On the day before official practice, Peterson was giving people rides around the circuit. Even as dusk closed in, the amiable Swede was charging around, lighting up the twilight and the other occupant's frightened features with long flashes of flame from the side exhaust.

Unfortunately, Stuck crashed in the Brands race after just four laps, following the wet start. That was that—it was the end of the best chance BMW ever had to beat the Porsche turbos outright in Europe since that inaugural Group 5 season of 1976.

In its European debut at Brands Hatch in Britain, the factory 320i in Ronnie Peterson's hands gave Jacky Ickx a real battle for pole position in the Martini Porsche turbo. Hans Stuck did the race start and crashed within a few laps in the conditions you see here; he was bravely trying to keep the BMW ahead of Ickx in the Porsche!

Picture: Colin Taylor Productions, 1977

Lime Rock, 1977: the Garrett turbocharged 320 for David Hobbs is paddock-prepared for battle. In action later that day, we can see that the 320 needed a turbo twist to keep up with the V8 domestic opposition and the ever-present Porsches.

Picture: Klaus Schnitzer, US

Road Atlanta, April 1977: the third round of the American IMSA series. This was the world racing debut of the 320i turbo. After a misfire in qualifying and an electrical short in the first heat race, Hobbs started from the back for the main feature event and finished fourth on the same lap as the leaders. This excellent shot also reveals the rear window stays used in American events and the normal driver's door safety "net." Rear wheels were 19 inches in diameter as opposed to the normal 320i Group 5 car's 16 inches.

Picture: Via Teddy Mayer, McLaren UK/US, 1978

Transatlantic trauma

Translating turbo technology on both sides of the Atlantic led to some basic errors, but the biggest problem was always Porsche! In 1978, there were two separate concerns putting together turbo 2-liters: Nicholson-McLaren Engines at Hounslow on the outskirts of London and the American end of McLaren Engines in Michigan. Though the material they worked with and the way they operated and assembled the motors had much in common, the results were totally different—the Americans achieved better results than the Europeans.

Toward the end of a season curtailed by engine failure for the works turbo in Europe, a very disappointed John Nicholson told me what he thought the big transatlantic problems had been. "First, we had no time to bench test and get acquainted with the engines. It took us over a year to get to grips with the Ford Cosworth DFV eight cylinders when we started on that, and the BMW demands even more care. We just didn't know the engine at the start of the year, and we have only recently understood the real problems."

There was (and still is) an astonishing difference in octane between premium fuels (particularly Sunoco) available in the US and the best race gas then in Europe. Sunoco was happy brewing well above 100-octane, a rarity then in Europe and now unknown as pump fuel (unleaded 95- and 98-octane are most common, and 97-octane leaded is on the wane).

The 1977 result was a disastrous spate of piston failures when BMW Motorsport contested World Championship Group 5 rounds in Italy and in pre-season turbo testing at Paul Ricard. Eventually, research and subsequent specification of the motor revealed the transatlantic octane difference.

For Europe, the compression ratio was cut back to 7.0:1, when it had been 7.5:1 and even 8.0:1 in the States. Boost was around 1.25/1.3 atmospheres in either case, with two intercoolers placed at the front where the radiator would normally be. With the boost well up for qualifying, 600-plus bhp at 9,000 rpm was released in Europe—nearly double that of the already-effective Formula 2. More realistic figures for racing in 1977 were 550 bhp in American trim and 500 in Europe.

Teddy Mayer, who ran the Bruce McLaren Grand Prix and USAC team effort in Britain, recalled how McLaren and BMW got together for the 1977 season. He reported, "I knew of Neerpasch for some time before this business came up. It was obvious BMW wanted to continue racing in America, and we had the right facilities, especially the engine shop. BMW were looking for the right people, and it just seemed kinda logical we'd get together."

McLaren created its premises in December 1969 in a Detroit suburban area, to have a base for both its Indianapolis and Can-Am operations. There have been several business managers over the years, but it is MacLaren's long-term engine man who provided the link: Gary Knudsen. Gary gathered a lot of American turbocharged racing-engine experience through MacLaren's single-seater USAC formula racing cars.

A separate McLaren North America Corp. to look after BMW's racing interests was established from 1977 onwards. By 1978, it had nine employees and was headed by Englishman Roger Bailey as the racing team manager. He was known as a F1 mechanic with Tyrrell before directing the Indy Lights race series.

Mayer felt, "The 320 seemed just ripe for turbocharging. That Formula 2 engine base was just a super engine, and you've got to hand it to Paul Rosche for one of the best little racing engines around. Our job was strictly about IMSA, but we did some World Championship rounds on the North American continent too—Sebring, Daytona, Mosport, that kinda thing.

"We were able to stiffen the car up a little by making the roll cage do some more of the work, and we stitched the front end together a little. That first season, we found the Porsches weren't quite ready, and you have to say we were unlucky not to win more than the four races we did get.

"In 1978, it was a different game. It's asking a lot for a 2-liter sedan to take on a twin-turbo with 3 liters and more. On the fast tracks, the aerodynamics are not comparable to a Porsche, and it's been uphill all the way. We could have done a little more to the car, but it really would get very expensive. All we or BMW can do is regard 1979 as the interim year while we wait for the M1 coupe to come...."

Stand by for heartache as the most beautiful Bimmer of the 1970s breaks cover!

Coming and going. Seen at Lime Rock in 1978, the BMW North America 320T reveals its lightweight accessibility (note the one piece "hood"), adjustable rear aerofoil blade, hidden radiators, and an uncanny ability to multiply beyond the original singleton 1977 entry.

Pictures: Klaus Schnitzer, US

Wide, wide body. The McLaren BMW was just like your regular 600-horsepower showroom 320, but more so....

Picture: Klaus Schnitzer, US

The 320T attacks Laguna Seca's Corkscrew corner almost twenty years after its debut. This example, still driven by David Hobbs, is kept by BMW North America and still turns heads at historic events, like this Monterey meeting in August 1996.

Picture: Klaus Schnitzer, US

QUICK FACTS

Period

1972–81

Products

M1 street and race, plus sports racing descendants (450 built, including 49 ProCar)

Performance

Street-rated 277 bhp and 162 mph with 0–62 mph in 5.6 seconds; ProCar, 470 bhp and 192 mph with 0–62 mph in 4.5 seconds

Achievements

Looking gorgeous, driving like the dream, raising BMW profile, retaining value

People

Rosche's first MPower for the street; Bernie Ecclestone and Max Mosley do The Business; David Cowart and Kenper Miller make BMW North America and Red Lobsters everywhere very happy

Chapter 20

A Very Professional Car

BMW Motorsport's original M1 supercar, 1978–81

The two-seater, mid-engine M1 was unlike any BMW made to date or any other member of the supercar breed. The principles of ultimate performance through the mid-motor configuration sound like those for the McLaren BMW V12, but that project was initiated and marketed by McLaren. BMW's McLaren interest escalated only as it became possible to win GT races in the 1990s, so the 1970s M1 was the first time—and, to date, the last time—that BMW was responsible for its own mid-engine supercar for public sale.

The basic specification was not to build the fastest car in the world—six cylinders and 277 bhp were not going to achieve that task, even in 1978. Rather, it was to create a memorable machine: one that could and would mark Motorsport's entry into car manufacturing ranks. The M1 would also serve as a base for the homologated Group 4 competition variant and subsequently more-radical race-car engineering.

As it hit the street, the M1 weighed 2,860 lbs, most of that attributable to the sturdy mixed-steel chassis construction and good-quality fiberglass panels which were styled by Italy's Giugiaro.

The in-line six ran at the big bore 3,453 cc (93.4 x 84 mm) and amounted to a Paul

Rosche rationalization of the CSL coupe race motors from the 24-valve series—coded M49/5 in test trim, M88 for production. For M1, Kugelfisher mechanical injection was employed; but later variants on the same theme rated 286 bhp, were electronically managed by Bosch, and were injected to provide ultimate street manners that served most M5 generations as well as the M6. So the M1 motor's race and production life could fairly be said to have extended two decades, from the 1970s into the early 1990s.

The M1 came to the public with superb mid-motor manners, a handling rarity in itself. A 162-mph machine, the M1 was capable of 0–62 mph in 5.6 seconds on 225 bhp a ton and sported excellent Pirelli P7 traction. The Group 4 variant added a tiny sliver on the bore (the full 94 mm) for 3,500 cc that yielded an honest 470 bhp at 9,000 rpm. The factory quoted 282 lb-ft of torque at 7,000 rpm.

According to BMW, these specifications gave the 2,240-lb/1,020-kg Group 4 machine a performance of 0–62 mph in 4.5 seconds and a maximum speed of 192 mph (309 km/h) on the right axle ratio. Those were the bare facts, but the charismatic M1—worth around five times its original sell-

The showroom M1 was an excellent road car with the balance and manners to cope with the snowy conditions shown here. Official performance figures reported 163 mph and 0–62 mph in 5.6 seconds, but what mattered was the charismatic charm of driving such a well-developed example of the often-disappointing supercar breed.

Picture: BMW Werkfoto, 1980

Start points: first, we have the front and back of the BMW turbo show car (Top Left, Bottom Right), which clearly donated its front and rear treatment, but not the four-cylinder powertrain or gullwing doors.

In the production M1 for the street, there was Italian ancestry throughout, especially in the tube frame extensions that hold Motorsport's first production engine, mid-mounted ahead of the 5-speed transaxle in an upright stance learned on the race tracks.

The engine and its installation in the road car were the responsibility of Paul Rosche's engineers in Munich. The engine retained the four-valve-per-cylinder layout of the racing engines and dry-sump lubrication, but had modified fuel injection with butterfly control instead of a slide, and chain-driven overhead camshafts. Power was almost 200 bhp less than the 9,000-rpm competition motors.

Pictures: BMW Werkfoto, 1978

ing price in the mid-1990s—deserves a bit more background than that....

In 1975–76, Jochen Neerpasch knew he could either go into Formula 1 with a BMW engine or he could make the mid-engined M1 coupe. He could not do both. Influenced by the BMW board of directors, BMW stayed with a form of racing that had some link with its everyday production. Like Porsche, BMW was convinced that Group 5 racing for the World Championship title was the way to go.

However, when BMW had been through the trauma of trying to produce the M1 at Lamborghini in Italy, and had finally brought the work back to Germany, it was too late to fight Porsche. So Neerpasch hit upon the M1 ProCar series for 1979, concocted in collaboration with current FIA President Max Moseley.

Neerpasch described his objectives as follows: "We wanted to make the production type of car racing more popular with a bigger audience. Formula 1 is so big that nobody is interested to come to Group 5 races, so we must take the racing to them...."

Establishing BMW Motorsport as a separate entity led to the logical thought: Why not manufacture its own car? Sell it, service it, supply parts, and race it? Much of 1978 was spent preparing to do exactly that with the logically-named M1 supercar. The results were 401 wonderfully manageable mid-engine road cars, 49 racers, and some stunning sports expenditure on a scale that made the subsequent Formula 1 engine program look reasonable.

There was a good, sporting, primary reason for M1. German manufacturers supported replacement of the World Championship for Makes (Group 6) sports cars by the adoption of a formula for touring cars. The argument, chiefly propagated by Porsche and BMW, with muted approving noises from Ford, was that Group 6 sports cars were no longer relevant.

As pure sports car racing became weaker through the 1970s, the Anglo-German group pressed for what became popularly known as

the "Silhouette Formula," or Group 5. This meant that the cars would retain their visual identity in outline from the side, but any other body or mechanical modification would be allowed, so long as the engine was of the same basic type and located in the same position as on a production model.

For example, a Ford Capri could not have a mid-mounted V8, even if it were out of a Ford Mustang. The euphoria faded once the others realized how long and how thoroughly Porsche had been preparing for Group 5. A start to silhouette racing was postponed to 1976, and then a thoroughbred sports racing Group 6 series was retained as well.

Inevitably, Group 5 began on a weak note, for there was simply nothing that could touch the rear-engine Porsche turbos. Lancia did field a semi-works Stratos turbo, but that car was burnt out twice and showed little more than flashes (!) of promise. Ford shuffled off to World Championship rallying (again), and nobody wanted to take on Porsche.

All this left BMW with a big image problem. It had said it would support this new Group 5 series, but BMW did not have a suitable car to fight Porsche. The stop-gap answer was to field three BMW CSLs in normally-aspirated trim and to try to develop a works CSL turbo of its own that would deflect the Stuttgart championship steamroller. That temporary answer was rather more effective than anybody expected, but a victory dependent on a rival's failure was not for BMW.

BMW Motorsport had an engine for Group 5. That CSL twin turbo developed with Josef Schnitzer's assistance had shown a potential that was undeniable. Now they needed a car to transmit its gargantuan power to the road, reliably and effectively.

There was a safety-inspired BMW show car (BMW Turbo) doing the rounds in October 1972, not long after Neerpasch arrived at the factory. A Bracq in-house design, the gullwing two-seater coupe (two were made) featured a turbo version of the 2-liter, four-cylinder motor and attracted a lot of attention when it was debuted at the 1972 Paris Show. It implanted the idea that BMW could produce a flagship supercar, too, and Neerpasch traded on this idea to sell a similarly advanced concept to top management.

In 1976, BMW Motorsport management placed an order with the exotic and erratic Italian Lamborghini group to detail and produce a fiberglass body for a two-seat, mid-engine coupe. It had to be aerodynamically sound in basic shape, and it had to look good enough to draw the customers, 400 of them at

Inside the M88, chain rather than racing gear drives operated the double overhead camshafts and quad-valve-per-cylinder layout. Then rated at 277 bhp from 3.5 liters, this M88 development of M49-bred CSL racing sixes sired a production series of 24-valve sixes that stretched to 3.8 liters in the early 1990s M5.

Official drawing released by BMW Presse, 1980

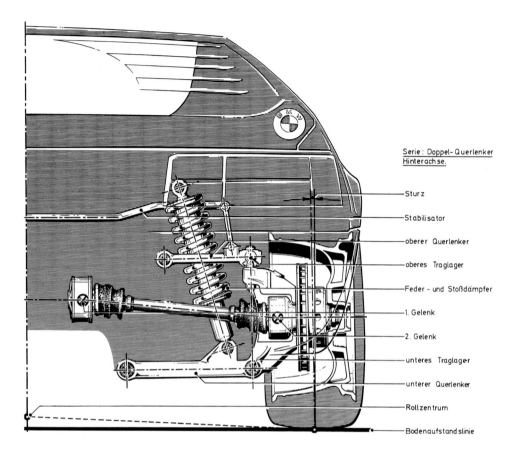

Serie : Doppel- Querlenker
Hinterachse.

- Sturz
- Stabilisator
- oberer Querlenker
- oberes Traglager
- Feder - und Stoßdämpfer
- 1. Gelenk
- 2. Gelenk
- unteres Traglager
- unterer Querlenker
- Rollzentrum
- Bodenaufstandslinie

(Left) Cross-sectional view of rear suspension shows that there was nothing haphazard about the way BMW prepared the double-wishbone rear axle with its coaxial spring/damper layout and generously-proportioned vented disc brakes for the showroom M1....But there's always a better way on the race track, and the side view of the rear suspension was the intended 5-link rear end for Group 5 competition use.

(Right) Finally, up at the front, BMW engineers used another version of the double-wishbone theme with a drop-link anti-roll bar to the lower, wide-based, lower arms.

Official drawing released by BMW Presse, 1980

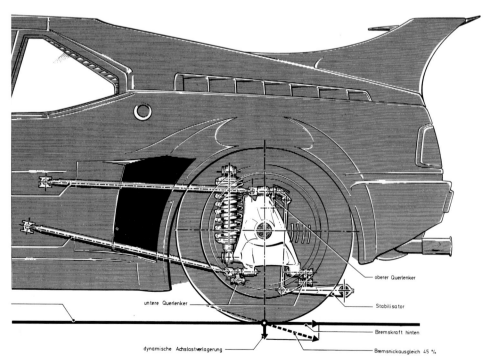

- oberer Querlenker
- untere Querlenker
- Stabilisator
- Bremskraft hinten
- dynamische Achslastverlagerung
- Bremsnickausgleich 45 %

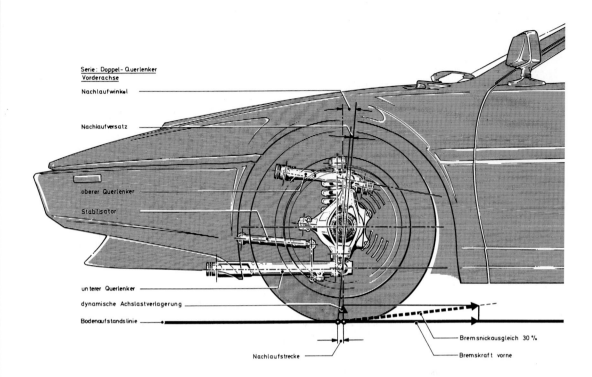

least, who were needed to satisfy homologation requirements before the car could be raced internationally.

The order was placed with Lamborghini at St. Agata Bolognese, near the heart of the Italian super-car industry in Modena, to marry the Marchesi-made tubular steel chassis with Ital fiberglass bodies and to assemble the whole car around the mechanical parts provided by BMW or its sub-contractors.

The body design was produced by Giugiaro's Ital Design, and the M1's outstanding chassis balance and amiable characteristics were the reponsibility of Ing Dallara, better-known for his motor racing work and the Lamborghini Countach.

However, Lamborghini was becoming more and more financially distressed. When the time came to assemble the components at its factory, the Italian concern could not even afford to buy sub-assemblies....

Moving the M1 forward

Early in 1978, things had reached a crisis point for the M1 coupe. At the Turin Motor Show in March, BMW executives were meeting under the main exhibition hall, looking for a solution to their dilemma. Neerpasch had been told that the M1 coupe project was okay, but only for as long as it did not interfere with other BMW production.

Now BMW was faced with an insolvent Lamborghini, a company incapable of turning its prototype cars (already very late, for it had hoped to race them toward the end of 1977) into production motor cars. No production motor cars meant there would be no prestigious international racing, either. There were many who began to wonder whether it was all worth it.

BMW's superb-looking M1. Here, the striped version equating to FIA Group 4 is posed in its Munich debut. Such a car was tested throughout 1978 in readiness for the 1979 ProCar series (as seen in our vigorous action picture). I make no apology for also showing the definitive road car, as it must rank as one of the all-time classic BMWs and was the first officially M-branded complete car.

Pictures: BMW Archiv

Group 5 as a championship was faltering badly. Only Le Mans, which allowed virtually everything with wheels into the competitors' paddock, was prospering. Was it worth millions of Deutschmarks to try to beat Porsche in front of sparse European audiences? Porsche bitterly attacked BMW for failing to support the series.

In 1977, BMW Motorsport attended rounds of the series only sporadically with its troubled 320t, and Porsche gained little joy from beating its own customers. BMW attempted to keep faith—and provide the North American effort with further marketing muscle—through the BMW 320 turbo project. Neerpasch remained persistent in the face of all this carping, for the M1 project survived both internal and external criticism.

By July 1978, Neerpasch was happily able to talk of producing 800 M1 coupes (nearly double the number actually made) and of a new super-series to support the World Grand Prix Championship races: Die ProCar Rennserie 79. Ironically, the manufacturing answer had been found in Stuttgart, home to both Mercedes and Porsche!

Baur, specialists in coachbuilding prototypes for the German motor industry as well as earlier BMW cabriolets, agreed to take on the assembly job from Lamborghini. The complete body would be shipped from Ital Design to Baur, and some of the suspension fabrication would also be sourced in Italy.

The whole thing would be assembled at Baur, but Motorsport in Munich would complete all quality control and would officially be known as the producers of the car. Some 400 left-hand-drive cars would be made in time to meet the target homologation date of July 1,

1979, with more cars made after that, according to demand.

BMW factory records show that what actually occurred was the manufacturing output recorded in the following table:

Year	Output
1978	29
1979	115
1980	251
1981	55

That meant a round total of 450 complete M1s, but no more than 401 were pure street cars because factory records reveal 49 listed as having ProCar race specifications. The original plan called for three basic types of M1 coupe: the 277-bhp road version, the Group 4 racing model with 470 bhp, and the very limited-edition, pure-factory racer with a turbocharged version of the six-cylinder motor, giving anything from 850 bhp upward. (The latter was sporadically developed to race nationally by Schnitzer.)

M1 for the road

Where Neerpasch astounded both his colleagues and the rest of the sporting world was in his answer to the question, "What do I do with all these cars before they are homologated?" Some hard talking and a mound of cash encouraged Max Moseley and Bernie Ecclestone (both then based at the Brabham headquarters in Chessington, Surrey, England) to produce the answer. They would promote the world's most magnificent one-marque racing series.

The scale and cost was far beyond what had been previously contemplated. Some manufacturers had managed to obtain the right to run one-marque races on or before the day of a Grand Prix. None had thought of running a series of one-marque events, supporting Grand

Prix in eight of the countries visited during a season. Ironically, the Porsche Supercup has filled this role in Europe during the 1990s and is now well-established.

So BMW produced the M1 coupe to Group 4 racing specification alongside the early road cars, long before it was ever homologated. It was a fiendishly costly and clever idea.

BMW would get promotion at a Grand Prix weekend for a car that would automatically have the cachet of being driven by some of the world's leading drivers. Originally, the fastest five Grand Prix drivers in practice would feature on a 24-car grid of M1s, but tire and manufacturer contracts put a stop to Ferrari participation.

Still, there would be 15 privateer cars on the grid—each one priced at £38,500 in 1978—and some good names to race against. BMW's generous prize scheme and other money injected into the Formula 1 world would lubricate that supremely successful circus, enough to allow BMW to join in as a supporting act, playing after Formula 1 practice had concluded.

The series regulations, using the traditional American dollar as the prize-fund currency, included $5,000 for a win in each round and a free M1 coupe for the overall champion after eight such races. That was not the extent of BMW support, though. Encouraging the hopefuls to beat the Formula 1 drivers, BMW held out the offer of $50 a lap for each lap that a non-Formula 1 driver led a Grand Prix star. There were obviously other private incentives to ensure that the highly-paid Grand Prix drivers were willing to go out and risk their reputations and necks in these 186-mph-plus (300-km/h) machines.

Although the basic mechanical layout sounded very similar between the road and racing M1, there were large differences between the two. These involved the Motorsport engineering staff in a terrific amount of work, especially for the engine team under Rosche.

The racing Group 4 engine was not a problem. It was installed north-south and mounted

vertically in the same way as the racing CSL,
giving a very similar power output. The ZF five-
speed gearbox—the unit used in de Tomaso
Ford V8-powered mid-engine cars—sat behind
with a hydraulic twin-plate clutch operation.

The development of the road engine involved
the design of a new (84 x 93.4-mm stroke)
version of the 3.5-liter six. Gone was the train
of gears used in the Formula 2 four-cylinders.
The new engine was designated M88 and had
chain-driven double overhead camshafts, com-
paratively-heavy pistons, new camshaft profiles
to go with the small-valve head, and a new
injection system.

Instead of the traditional Kugelfischer one-
slide "guillotine" and lightweight racing pump,
a new timed-injection system with six individual butterflies to admit air in each choke was

developed. This virtually solved the emission
control problems with continuous-injection road
systems. With these changes, the engine provided good low-speed response and a flat
power peak of between 6,000 and 6,700
rpm. Maximum rpm were initially set at 6,900
rpm, allowing gear speeds of 48, 71, 101 and
136 mph in the first four longish ratios.

From a competition point of view, the work
done in the big CSL coupe was to prove the
engine ready for installation in the mid-engine
machine. BMW knew that the mid-engine layout would pose cylinder-head overheating
problems, and that was one of the reasons
Schnitzer and the team provided the revised
cooling arrangements with external water pip-
ing and mounted the engine vertically, where it
could not only be relieved of the extra heat from

It looks good wherever you stand! This was the sight that greeted BMW visitors at the 1978 German Grand Prix announcement of the M1-based ProCar series in Hockenheim.

Picture: London Art Tech, 1978

the exhaust system (which lay below on the previous 30-degree slant) but could also have less cramped exhaust, allowing better power.

The dry-sump arrangement was vital for the mid-engine machine, in competition or road form, if the length and height of a straight six-cylinder engine was to be neatly accommodated. Using the dry-sump, the engine could be mounted as low as possible, and in turn the handling would benefit from a lower center of gravity. A small clutch and flywheel diameter were also required, but the use of the twin-plate unit was designed to get over such snags.

The 1978 test program emphasized the correlation between road and race versions of the M1. Driven by many of the BMW-contracted drivers (including Markus Höttinger, the young Austrian whom BMW saw as a future international star), the cars were covering over 930 miles a day in reliability testing. Some 43,470 miles were completed in the few months that prototypes had been avail-

able prior to July 1978. Most of the testing miles were at Nürburgring, Zeltweg-Oesterreichring in Austria, and Salzburgring. All the testing was aimed at getting some distance on the design to evaluate its durability rather than to fine-tune it for racing.

Another person to drive the car in its prototype form was Alex von Falkenhausen, the former engineering chief. Despite a heavy rainstorm, he pushed on at speeds approaching the car's 160-mph (258-km/h) maximum in road-going form. He arrived back in Munich very pleased with the car's stability in poor conditions and the way in which it had been developed into a civilized road car.

Dallara's work for Lamborghini to mate the front-suspension geometry to Pirelli's P7 road tire had been worthwhile, and development was completed with BMW assistance. Tire sizings for the street were 205/55 VR 16 fronts and 225/50 VR 16s rears, mounted on 7- and 8-inch rims, respectively.

The original racing test bed for the equivalent of the 470-bhp Group 4 specification was this striped M1, shown with Hans Stuck's name at the German Grand Prix of July 1978.

Picture: BMW Werkfoto, 1978

Street racers! Here is the M1 let loose on the 1979 streets of Monaco. It was a spectacular sight, especially with talented drivers such as Patrick Depailler (middle M1), who had won the main event for Tyrrell-Ford the previous year. Leading this group is double World and 1989 IndyCar Champion Emerson Fittipaldi.

Picture: David Winter/BMW Archiv, released 1988

The Group 4 specification outside the engine included racing-style double-wishbone suspension at either end, magnesium wheel uprights, and the usual BBS center-lock lightweight racing wheels (11 inches wide by 16 inches diameter front, 12.5 inches wide by the same diameter rear). The road car looked slightly less like a homogenous entity on its five-slot, cast-aluminum wheels. There were also twin master cylinders with adjustable brake balance for the four-wheel Ate ventilated disc brakes, which had alloy calipers. All this was needed to stop an imperial ton from regular excursions beyond 160 mph....

Other chassis detailing covered anti-roll bars front and rear with a number of quickly replaceable alternatives, aluminum wheel hubs, and the inevitable higher-geared rack-and-pinion steering. Inside the stark Group 4 version, a black, functional roll cage, steering wheel, seat, and skimpy dashboard full of vital instrumentation were all that the driver had for company.

The body naturally varied between the two versions. The road car had a separate add-on plastic front spoiler that was a good deal shallower than the racing version. However, the aerodynamic shape was promising for no add-on rear wing was fitted to the Group 4 model prior to 1978. Large rear wings were tested early in 1979 and were retained for race use.

Both models also shared pop-up headlights and small rectangular auxiliaries set into the front grille, which hid the water radiator and the engine oil cooler. Both the ZF differential and the gearbox unit had an oil cooler installed on the racing model, too. The racing model was developed with wing extensions and a deeper spoiler as an integral part of the body.

Racing the M1

In race action, the M1 was no European threat to Porsche, but it did a marvelous job of elevating the BMW image, especially as the 24 race cars—with Grand Prix stars aboard most of the front-runners—went thundering through high-rent venues such as the Monte Carlo harborside. Those huge Bimmer tail pipes boomed out across the packed decks of million-dollar yachts, conveying their 180-mph ability to every TV camera on circuit.

Then-Brabham Formula 1 teammates Niki Lauda (1979) and Brazil's Nelson Piquet (1980) took the ProCar titles in successive years. There were links to McLaren's future owner (Ron Dennis) in the preparation of these winning M1s at Project 4, and the series established the links that would see Nelson Piquet exploit the BMW four-cylinder turbo in Grand Prix.

Those Piquet-BMW links are far from severed today. Following Piquet's huge IndyCar accident in the early 1990s, BMW deployed his talents at Nürburgring 24-hours and other 1993 events. Nelson drove at Le Mans in 1996–97 and renewed his acquaintance with a factory M1 at Monterey in 1996, driving immaculately. The former triple World Champion continued to win South American sports/GT races in a McLaren-BMW V12 during the 1996/97 winter, and has proven to be a quietly-spoken but effective ambassador for BMW over the years.

Back in April 1979 in Europe, the BMW M1 made its first international appearance outside the ProCar series on April 8, with Marc Surer at the wheel, for an unhomologated development run at the Nürburgring Eifelrennen.

A flotilla of Porsche 935s monopolized the top five places. Ford stole a little of BMW's thunder by sending a turbo Capri (later a Mustang for US appearances through the Roush organization) into the bigger classes and using the services of BMW's 1973 European Champion, Toine Hezemans, to finish ahead of Surer and his M1 debutante.

Two seasons of ProCar Championship success went to Brabham Grand Prix teammates Niki Lauda and Nelson Piquet. Shown here in 1979 (Right) and in his Championship-winning year of 1980 (Left), the last ever ProCar series, is subsequent triple World Champion Piquet. Note the grilled and masked radiator on the 1980 car, which also features as much downforce setting as possible on the "fenced" rear wing.

Pictures: BMW Presse, obtained 1988

The factory had a patchy policy toward its home series in Germany, and the M1 appeared more popular with privateers than with its creators. In the large class, it was usually spanked by 700-bhp turbo Porsches from the house of Kremer or Loos. The late Manfred Winkelhock won a race on the road (300-kms Nürburgring, March 1980), thrashing the Porsches by over half a minute, but was not allowed to score points.

The highest German Championship round points position for an M1 was Helmut Kelleners securing third overall at the same March 1980 meeting during which Winkelhock beat Stommelen. Otherwise, Manfred Schurti equalled that third place at the April 1980 Eifelrennen.

Lanky Christian Danner (a BMW-contracted single-seater regular) managed a fifth with a works M1 at the Hockenheim close of the 1980 Deutschrennmeisterschaft, but the main BMW works effort had long been directed at getting at Hans Stuck the overall German title with a charge in a 320 turbo. The Schnitzer belter netted a quartet of small division wins versus the hottest competition from Lancia, Ford, and rival 320 turbos, but Stuck finished second under ten points from the overall title.

American success

For sheer results, the American-domiciled Red Lobster restaurant-backed M1 was the king, delivering winning results in all but four of 16 IMSA Camel GTO events contested. This 1979 M1 remains superbly fit and was a welcome sight at Monterey in 1996.

During 1981, the Red Lobster M1 so dominated its IMSA GTO category that drivers David Cowart and Kenper Miller finished one-two in their division—the first time this had been achieved in the US. Their fabulous M1 racked up 12 wins that season alone, contributing to Miller's BMW record of 13 IMSA wins and adding to Cowart's national championship tally, as he had won the 1978 IMSA/GTO national title.

For 1982, Cowart/Miller Racing opted for the combination of March ground-effect chassis engineering and the M1 race motor. The BMW March 82G was again backed by Red Lobster restaurants, but the ferocious formula car approach brought only two podium finishes (a second and a third) in a year that saw Cowart and Miller finish tenth in the competitive IMSA GTP pure sports-racing category. The Red Lobster race organization ran cars until 1985, while in 1986, Kenper Miller

Things don't always happen according to plan. The 1981 race program of the Red Lobster M1 driven by Kenper Miller and David Cowart was rewarded with the most consistent winning record ever recorded by an M1. Here, our photographer at Lime Rock shows that even lobsters can suffer punctures!

Pictures: Klaus Schnitzer, US

scored his most significant international result with a third overall at Le Mans 24-hours.

The most serious BMW North America competition program prior to 1996 was the IMSA GTP challenge to Porsche, Nissan, and (Bob Tullius, not TWR) Jaguar V12s. This high profile 1985–86 program, managed by the US branch of McLaren and based on BMW four-cylinder turbo power in a March 85 or 86G chassis, was racked by unreliability and aerodynamic problems.

Driven by Formula 1 old guards David Hobbs and John Watson (both now excellent motorsports TV commentators), with junior hot-shoes John Andretti (Mario's amiable nephew) and Davy Jones (later the US hotshot for TWR-Jaguar), the BMW-March GTP turbos harnessed up to 850 qualifying bhp from 2.0 liters and made a magnificent sight circulating Daytona beyond 200 mph, on their way to pole on their debut. Official statistics for their motors: 2-liter BMW Motorsport turbos, coded M12/14. They gave an average 800 bhp at

Seen shortly before their withdrawal at the conclusion of a BMW NA 1985–86 assault on the IMSA GTP category, these 2.1-liter hybrids with a March 85 or 86G chassis found their form too late to attract the necessary budget for 1987. The number 18 racer is for John Andretti and Davy Jones, while the number 19 GTP was piloted by British elder statesmen David Hobbs and John Watson.

Pictures: Courtesy BMW NA, 1986

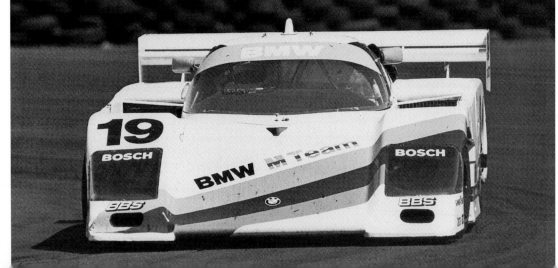

(Left & Bottom) Two views of the radical March 81G-BMW. Even this radical ground-effect chassis (look at the depth of the rear exit tunnels!) did not offer a solution to making the M1 motor a regular sports-car winner. Descendants of this March chassis were, however, used for subsequent US competitors.

Picture: BMW GB, 1981

9,000 rpm by October 1986, enough to allow 210 mph as their speed-gun pace at Daytona.

However, BMW-GTP race results were rarer than rocking-horse manure. David Hobbs revealed how much work had gone into overcoming the protracted problems when he commented, prior to Daytona on October 12, 1986, "Changes have been made to these cars from the car I drove onto the front row at this race in 1985. It is the same basic car and package, but we've fine-tuned and developed it to a level of not only competitiveness [they had won the preceding IMSA GTP round when David was interviewed—JW], but also reliability.

"We have also simplified the fuel system and made the cooling much

Farewell, oldtimers. Part of the BMW NA collection at rest at Lime Rock. Over the enormous side radiator and air snorkels of the IMSA GTP, we see its predecessors (left to right): the David Hobbs 320T fielded by McLaren and BMW in North America, the M1 to Group 4 specification, and the IMSA-specification CSL of BMW NA that won Daytona in 1976.

Picture: Klaus Schnitzer, US

more efficient. Most obvious are the changes we made to the body: it is much lighter, stronger and features a much smoother, aerodynamic line," concluded BMW North America's most loyal and articulate driver.

Right at the end of the program, which had literally been proven in the fire of battle, Jones and Andretti plastered the Porsche 962s and brought home the team's first and—because they were unexpectedly withdrawn for 1987—last win. That win was at Watkins Glen, September 21, 1986, and owed a lot to then-22-year-old Jones, who set pole position, a new lap record for the picturesque and twisty 3.77 miles, and secured an historic win.

The BMW GTPs raced only twice more, qualifying well but failing to establish the consistent winning record that this expensive program needed. The sports-racing BMW flag, this time carried in Camel Lights by the Gebhardt JC853-BMW, was carried across Europe prior to its arrival in the US.

Alf Gebhardt and Greg Hobbs (David's son) then drove it in the 1987 Daytona 24-hours, but the motor failed after 10 hours—a shame, as it had been leading the class. Another Floridian venue, Miami, saw the Gebhardt take a fine third in the 1987 IMSA Grand Prix for Stanley Dickens/Garry Robinson. Otherwise, it failed to finish a number of events, save sixth at San Antonio, Texas, and was financially starved into permanent absence from IMSA during 1988.

Master blaster! Despite the ferocious horsepower reputation of the Group 5 Schnitzer M1 and the wet-weather skills of driver Hans Stuck around the Nürburgring, the combination never achieved the Porsche-busting pace that BMW had originally foreseen for a turbo M1.

Picture: BMW Werkfoto, obtained 1988

April 1979: the 180-mph BMW M1 makes its racing debut at the third German Championship round, Nürburgring. Although the car looked terrific and ran reliably to the finish, it was no match for the ruling turbo Porsches and the Zakspeed Ford Capri turbo (later, the base for Jack Roush-run Mustangs in the US). It did not make the top five, was not eligible for points, and was never run by the factory as a German Championship contender.

Picture: BMW Werkfoto, 1979

BMW's automotive version of paradise came to earth at Monterey in 1996. On the next two pages, check out our single shot of the important IMSA GTP.

(Right) In this shot, you can play Spot-the-Bimmer. I count 16 important competition or performance BMWs in this elevated (I hung off the bridge!) picture. You can also see the 320 turbo and sports-racing company in another corner, outside the tent BMW used to show off the amazing variety of machinery assembled to honor the marque at Monterey in 1996.

Pictures: Author, Monterey, 1996; Klaus Schnitzler (IMSA GTP)

Outside Germany, the 1979 season saw BMW gather its World Championship Makes points via the 320, but a private entry at Le Mans with some BMW factory support saw Winkelhock lead French co-drivers Herve Poulain and Marcel Mignot to sixth overall.

Across Europe in 1980, Nelson Piquet shared an M1 to ProCar-plus specification with Hans Stuck. They hurtled around 621 miles/1,000 kms of Nürburgring in all its old glory and returned in May 1980 with a fine third overall—noted as the M1's best World Sports Car Championship result, and therefore its best international outing.

Other 1980 international results for the M1 included a more comprehensive effort at Le Mans, fielding two cars. Considering that Grand Prix ace Didier Pironi was retained in one M1 with Dieter Quester and Hans Stuck on call alongside locals, fourteenth and fifteenth overall were poor rewards.

Elsewhere, Quester and Pironi had managed a sixth overall in Mugello, laps behind the leading Lancia prototype turbo. The enormously successful Red Lobster team in the US squeezed in 1980 Watkins Glen International and could be proud of placing tenth overall for David Cowart and Kenper Miller. More about that later.

The author drove a trio of road M1s in Britain and Germany, on road and racetrack. They all packed excitement and startling practicality into one immortal package that would delight any serious BMW collector.

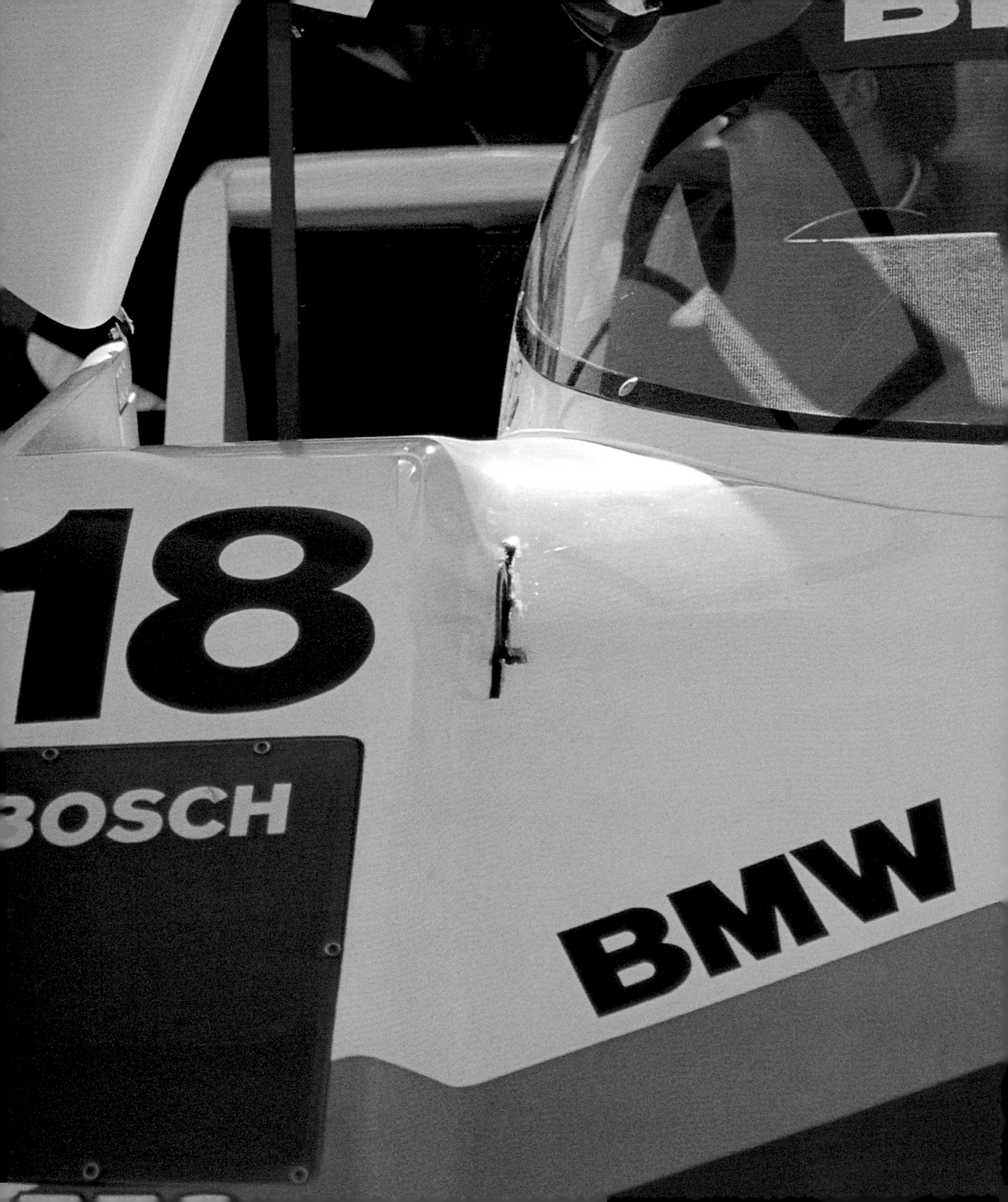
18
BOSCH
BMW

QUICK FACTS

Period

1978–88

Products

BMW 1.5-liter turbocharged four-cylinder Grand Prix race motor; aborted flat-eight and V12 motors; the first production BMW twelves

Performance

557 bhp in 1980; "over" 1,200 bhp in 1986; in 1987, Benetton B186 rated approximately 900 bhp and, driven by Teo Fabi, returned 0–100 mph in 4.8 seconds in trials for *Road & Track* (this combination would have recorded a 0–100–0-mph acceleration/brake test in 7.5 seconds)

Achievements

1983 FIA World Champion Driver Nelson Piquet wins first World Championship for a turbocharged car; Brabham-BMW comes in third in FIA World Championship Constructor's series

People

Brabham (1980–87) and Benetton (1986) in Britain received Munich works motors; BMW also supplied various degrees of support for Arrows (1984–86, then Megatron BMW in 1987–88), ATS (1983–84), and Ligier (1987)

Chapter 21

Big Boys, Power Ploys

The transformation of the BMW four-cylinder motor into a 1,200-horsepower Grand Prix qualifier

To understand BMW's recent absence from Grand Prix (Formula 1) World Championship racing, know that a strong faction among BMW board members will always vote against its inherent (and near obscene) expense. Even among the pro-motorsports senior management—typified by Karl Heinz Kalbfell, current board member for sales and BMW Motorsport—Grand Prix is no shoe-in for automatic participation. Thus, it took from 1988 to 1997 before BMW would welcome a comeback to Formula 1.

The first priority was always generous European funding to support BMW's ambitions in the touring-car classes. Many customers expect BMW to win in these categories, as it has since the 1960s. That touring car task becomes tougher every year, as opposition multiplies and the regulations tighten.

GT Racing with McLaren has been a recent, welcome diversion that paid an unexpected bonus with a 1995 Le Mans victory, hence the increased BMW funding behind McLaren (who ironically runs with Mercedes in Grand Prix, through a separate organization) in both GT and touring cars for 1995–97.

Debating Formula 1 with BMW senior personnel over a decade since the last BMW-pow-

ered Grand Prix victory (Mexico, 1986), I understood that the technical side of producing a competitive power package was not the major issue. BMW Motorsport produced and tested at least two V12s before settling on a V10 design. Politics over the true commercial worth of single-seater racing was the major obstacle to a BMW comeback.

American readers may wonder why BMW bothers, since Grand Prix has had little recent US impact. In the rest of the world, Formula 1 attracts TV audiences measured by the billion, even if it fails to put butts on every paying seat, NASCAR-style.

BMW 3-liter V-type motors will probably be powering a new generation of Grand Prix racers, as the Millennium parties decimate the world's champagne stocks. However, such plans were hidden from public view at this writing, confined to the underground test cells beneath Motorsport's Preussenstrasse engine-engineering headquarters.

An unexpected flashlight on the serious way BMW has studied Grand Prix engine engineering over many years came from Alex von Falkenhausen in 1978. "At the end of 1975, I drew up the plans for a Formula 1 BMW engine. This was after my official

Underground magic: here is the BMW Motorsport engine shop underneath Preussenstrasse, suppliers of winning Grand Prix power to both Brabham and Benetton teams.

Picture: BMW Pressephoto, 1985

retirement, but I sat down to make a serious suggestion.

"The engine was a flat eight-cylinder, a layout which I am choosing because it is short and low with the advantage over the Cosworth V8 of a lower center of gravity and can allow air to the rear wing. Why not twelve cylinders? Because the friction and fuel consumption of the twelve-cylinder make it so you have no advantage except power over the eight-cylinder, and you need the power to overcome the extra fuel load and other extra weight you carry with twelve cylinders. Besides, the eight is cheaper and faster to make than twelve.

"My engine would have a little shorter stroke than the Cosworth—76-mm bore x 55-mm stroke—and by revving to 12,000 rpm should have had the same power as Cosworth can make. The power would be less than for twelve cylinders and I could see problems with the exhaust system—but Ferrari got over that—and with the system of firing order in the cylinders. With the crankshaft of my flat eight, firing would take place at the same time on either side. At low revs, this would mean the engine would be much rougher than a vee of eight cylinders, and it would be impossible for road use."

The mainstream company engineering department also had a great deal of experience with V12 engines, and these gave rise to the rumor that BMW would enter Formula 1 after it had conquered Formula 2 in 1973. In fact, the engines were purely for contemporary road use, and very different from each other.

In 1973, BMW built two of the big 2500-series slant sixes into a V12 of 5 liters. That was installed in a contemporary large sedan and happily used on the road, for it gave 310 flexible bhp. In 1975, BMW engineering constructed another V12 from the new small-capacity, six-cylinder engines designed and developed by a team headed by Paul Rosche. This engine had a capacity of 4.5 liters and

would not fit a contemporary BMW, though it obviously could have been further developed for the later 7-series.

During this period, BMW management, right to the highest executive, repeatedly denied that BMW would manufacture a V12 motor for road use, but this happened with the 1989 announcement of the world's first catalytic-converter twelve. Created in aluminium within a 60-degree vee, the 4,998-cc (84-mm bore x 75-mm stroke], single overhead camshaft (chain drive) Bimmer delivered 300 bhp and 332 lb-ft of torque. It was marketed for initial use in the factory flagship 750i/750iL (longer wheelbase) sedans; by September 1989, it was also offered in the 850i coupe.

These twelve-cylinder units are important as the basis for a BMW Motorsport-created 5.6-liter that enlivened later 8-series (381 bhp and 405 lb-ft) and for a radical S70/2-coded redevelopment at the heart of McLaren F1 GT road and race cars of 6.1 liters, 627 bhp, and 479 lb-ft torque (see chapter 28).

Thus, pure race V8/10 and V12 motors were extensively studied by BMW Motorsport in Munich for Grand Prix. As of this writing, there is a separate eight-cylinder development of BMW's alloy 3.0- to 4.4-liter V8 road-engine family, progressing to meet BMW North America racing requirements.

Touring twists

Back in the 1980s, how did BMW become the first to seize the FIA World Championship with a turbocharged four-cylinder? It was a long and winding trail, hard to trace through turbocharged touring cars, but worth following through all its twists.

In the aftermath of the M1's chaotic creation in the late 1970s, the author debated the Formula 1 question with Jochen

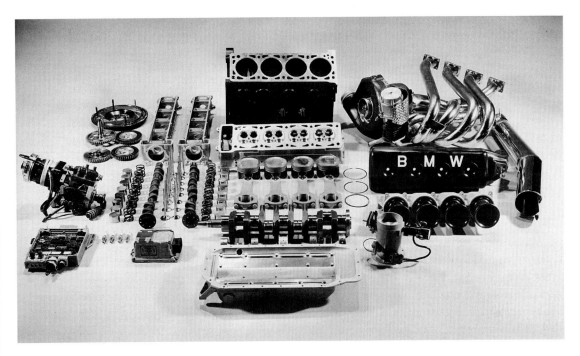

Master the art of assembling these 700 components correctly and you, like BMW in 1983, could be rewarded with 600 horsepower from 1.5 liters. It also helps to have a truck-sized KKK turbocharger operating at 1.9 bar/27 psi and the finest electronic ignition and fueling managment from Robert Bosch.

Picture: BMW Werkfoto, 1983

Neerpasch: "Is BMW content to play the supporting role in Motorsport forever? Will it continue with its production-based competition activities, ignoring the glittering world of Formula 1 to which the M1 has introduced it, first-hand?"

Neerpasch replied, "I wanted us at BMW to do it, but look at the Renault turbo effort. It is not good to be more than a first year without results. You must be like Lotus in 1978. And maybe you can do it and beat all the teams if you spend a lot, lot, of money. Then you spoil Formula 1 if you succeed, because you spend all this money and there is no way to beat you.

"For a manufacturer like Porsche or BMW, production racing is best—we cannot race without success. The company must have success in racing. And this you cannot be assured of in Formula 1."

BMW and Formula 1 politics

As ever, the politics were more convoluted than the technicalities: it would be a protracted birth for Germany's first Grand Prix motor since the 1.5-liter Porsches of the early 1960s. At the time, Jochen Neerpasch was still in charge, but his ambitious Austrian deputy, former motoring journalist Dieter Stappert, was in direct conflict over a suitable destination for the BMW Grand Prix engine.

Neerpasch, always an ardent Francophile, promised the Talbot Sport organization in France that it should be recipients of the BMW Formula 1 motor. Stappert and many of the Bavarian sports staff, especially the powerful Paul Rosche, violently disagreed. There was plenty of lobbying in the corridors of power bisecting BMW's dramatic four-cylinder building—a brisk walk over a couple of blocks from Motorsport's power base at Preussenstrasse.

Stappert and the loyalists, including the directors of sales, engineering and public relations, prevailed. By November 1979,

Neerpasch had elected to leave, still working on the Talbot project. In February 1980, Stappert confirmed that "...serious development [had] begun." Dieter became the new BMW Motorsport manager, a position for which Neerpasch had groomed and recommended the bespectacled former media man.

Spring 1980 saw BMW management destroy the Talbot Formula 1 engine supply agreement. From March 8, 1980, BMW opted to supply Brabham on an exclusive basis with their Grand Prix motor.

Why Brabham? There were three key factors in favor of the Chessington team founded by triple World Champion Jack Brabham:

1. An existing working relationship with contracted BMW Motorsport drivers Niki Lauda and Nelson Piquet;

2. The demonstrable power of Bernie Ecclestone at FOCA, who continues to rule Formula 1's money machine today (Ecclestone

owned Brabham and had been an essential part of BMW's progress into the M1 ProCar series); and

3. The sheer talent of designer Gordon Murray and the excellent direct working relationship he had established with Paul Rosche, another facet of Anglo-German relations that continued in 1995–97 with the BMW-McLaren alliances.

Technically, BMW reverted to its origins as motor engineers, leaving Britons, Americans, and South Africans to provide motorcar and running-gear surroundings to their powerful products. By 1983, the combination of Nelson Piquet, Brabham BT52, and a turbocharged BMW 1.5-liter realized the world's first Formula champion to rely on turbocharged power—achieved in 630 development days.

The trio that created the world's first Grand Prix Championship-winning turbo car and driver: Paul Rosche, then fifty years of age, is flanked by Nelson Piquet (wearing cap) and Gordon Murray (right), then the Brabham designer.

Picture: BMW Werkfoto, 1982/ Courtesy Chris Willows, 1997

Technical development

Paul Rosche commented in the late 1980s, "The four-cylinder was further developed in turbocharged form, first for saloon car racing and then, as the M12/13 series, for Grand Prix racing. So M12/ 7 Formula 2 experience in the single-seaters with over 300 bhp was important to us, as were the developments we made with McLaren and Schnitzer in the turbocharged racing saloons."

Keen to enhance public perception of 3-series virtues, after the sporting 2002 series died, the BMW sports department transformed it into an international racing project with factory support in America as well as Europe. We have discussed the factory 320s in Europe and the US in chapter 19, but there was another 3-series program in German national racing that would be vitally important to the future of any Formula 1 four-cylinder.

Schnitzer set the initial tiny turbo technical pace, through an idea it originally developed in 1975 for sports-car racing. The Schnitzers left the 1.4 to one side through most of 1975 and 1976, as it was outlawed in the sports car for which it was originally intended (a Toj), and there seemed no hope that it would be admitted in the pre-Porsche era of the German championship either.

Schnitzer developed a 2.1-liter turbo BMW motor, which was very rapid and reputed to produce 560 bhp for the Toj, in which it appeared in 1975. It was also the basis for a late 1970s Toyota Celica turbo of 2,090 cc that also developed 560 bhp for German championship races of the period.

It was a 1.4-liter (bore x stroke, 89 x 57.5 mm) version of the BMW engine that first caught BMW Motorsport's attention. That ultra-short stroke turned into a more amenable 1,425 cc (80 x 71 mm). Turbocharged via KKK and running a 6.9:1 compression, this realized 400 bhp at 9,000 rpm by 1977, or 280.7 bhp per liter. That represented an obvious bonus over the 280–305 bhp offered by the normally-aspirated 2-liter-class opposition, because of the FIA international turbo cubic-capacity equivalency formula, and one that could not be ignored. The 2002s in which this 1,425 cc was bundled weighed but 800 kg/1,760 lbs. They could hit 0–60 mph in 4.7 sec, 0–100 mph in ten seconds, and 0–124 mph in a little over 15 seconds.

In 1977, Schnitzer appeared with a pair of 2002-based Group 5 cars for the German series in turbo trim. Drivers were Peter Hennige and Albrecht Krebs; Klaus Ludwig also drove on occasion.

It was a troubled year, which seemed filled with head-gasket problems whenever the engines went beyond 9,000 rpm. Another recurrent trouble was that of the lighter Getrag gearbox. As far as the transmission was concerned, Schnitzer had to revert to the bigger Getrag as used in the old CSLs. On the second 320 Schnitzer constructed for the 1978 season, the team adopted an oil cooler for the gearbox and employed another for the differential.

After demonstrating the potential of the turbo unit in 1977 in 2002, Schnitzer received direct support from the factory to press ahead with its development in 1978, including a complete 3-series, so that the factory could run two 320i racers and one driver: Harald Ertl. This bearded sometime-journalist/Grand Prix racer (subsequently killed in an airplane accident) brought along Sachs as sponsors and shock-absorber suppliers. Thus Schnitzer became the only builder in a series sponsored by Bilstein to run anything other than that massively popular gas-filled damper, and Schnitzer was also the only team in the small division on Dunlop tires.

Based on the competition 320i, the Schnitzer baby Bimmer had to race for 1978 at 1,426 cc to fall within the 2-liter class

when turbocharged. The M12/12-coded engine drew on KKK turbocharging and developed 410 bhp (287.5 bhp per liter) at 9,400 rpm.

The 1978 results were encouraging, with Ertl proving more than capable of winning. Unfortunately, halfway through the season, two clouds appeared on the horizon. Having given succor to the perennial head-gasket problem, a quadruple-side-radiator installation was tried. This gave rather poor water circulation, so a triple-side-radiator layout was also tried. However, a bigger problem was the emergence of a Ford-backed Zakspeed Capri 1.4-turbo. Turbo Porsche was the only way to go in the bigger-capacity division of outright winners.

Also in 1978, BMW ran the 1.4-liter motor in a BMW North America 320t of the Citicorp generation—but in plain white—at Mid Ohio for Tom Klausler. It turned into a hot-weather endurance session, but allowed valuable data to be collected, particularly when David Hobbs climbed in to finish second overall!

Speaking at the Preussenstrasse headquarters that Motorsport engineers still use in the 1990s, Paul Rosche recalled, "The Schnitzer car of '78 was interesting, so we got behind the 1979 GS Tuning 320 for Markus Höttinger."

This Jaegermeister orange 320t won its sixth event, the September 2, 1979 Hockenheim penultimate round of that year's German Championship. What's more, it was one of four BMW 320 turbos in the top five home, and its extraordinary receptiveness to further power boosts made BMW engineers and executives think a Formula 1 race program really could be "on."

Grand Prix potential

When BMW Motorsport applied more serious boost (1.5 bar) and modified the breathing of that 1.4-liter M12/12, they realized a maximum of 610 bhp (a fantastic 427.8 bhp per

A powerful and adaptable family: from left to right, BMW shows the iron-blockers that took them from a carburated 80-bhp 1500 (this is actually a 90-bhp, 1.8-liter cousin on show), through Formula 2's M12/7 at more than 300 bhp, to the complexities of the turbocharged four on the right, which could be made to (briefly) give some 1,200 bhp in qualifying trim.

Picture: BMW Werkfoto, 1981

liter)—more than enough to be competitive in contemporary Formula 1.

Rosche and the Preussenstrasse team then made a 1,499-cc (production-based 89.2-mm bore and ultra-short 60-mm stroke) version of the Formula 2 M12 series (M12/13) to withstand the specialized demands of single-seater installation in turbocharged form. The closest production link ever in modern Grand Prix hardware came from the 1500 block of the BMW Grand Prix motor, which became a 1.5-liter turbocharged showcase for technology such as Bosch Motronic engine management in the 1980s.

The BMW iron blocks were carefully aged—simulating 100,000 km/62,500 road miles—and lightened 5–7 kg by machining casting projections not required in a race application. The cylinder head dated back to the successful 1970 Formula 2 parallel-valve program, gear drive for its DOHC and 16-valve layout, but with three significant changes for turbocharging:

1. Lowered compression, from the F2 ideal of 11.2:1 to less than 7.0:1 (see piston details below);

2. Hardened valve seats and replacement valves of 35.8 mm inlet and 30.2 mm exhaust (the same as early F2 on the inlet, just 0.1 mm smaller on exhaust); and

3. Rosche's own turbo cam profiles, inlet and exhaust.

Engine builders among the readership may think the author has forgotten to mention a replacement head gasket or the insertion of cylinder sealing rings. Both features remained as for the normally-aspirated Formula 2 unit, which shows the enormous margins Munich provided in those 300-bhp units.

Other vital hardware included forged Mahle pistons running 6.7:1 low compression in association with a 1983 race ceiling of 1.9 bar/27 psi boost beyond atmospheric pressure. These abbreviated, ultra-short-skirt pistons were a proven item and weighed just 365 g/12.8 oz apiece.

The steel crankshaft was taken over from the M12/7 Formula 2 motor, but put through an additional gas-nitriding process and incorporating extra oilways for the turbo application. The 153.6-mm connecting rods were the most exotic part of the specification, being milled and turned from forged-titanium shot-blasted blanks.

Lubrication was by the ubiquitous racing practice of a magnesium dry-sump (pan) layout, 10 liters/2.1 UK gallons were circulated by a single discharge pump and scavenged by four more pumps. Two of those pumps concentrated on turbo and cylinder-head scavenging duties.

Fuel capacity was limited to 220 liters/48.4 UK gallons, meaning that consumption could not be less than 4.13 Imperial mpg when the engine was rated around 640 race horsepower. It should also be noted that BMW used some very special fuel blends—especially in qualifying practices—now banned in Grand Prix.

Paul Rosche recalled that the technical parameters for the Grand Prix unit were rapidly established—it was making it all work within the aerodynamically-demanding confines of a Formula 1 car that was the biggest challenge. "We always knew we would use the four-cylinder, and when we saw that the Höttinger's 320 engine would stand over 600 bhp, our job was developing what we already had through years of Formula 2 and saloon cars."

A Director of McLaren Cars and BMW Motorsport in the UK during 1997 ("only the third proper job I have ever had"), the original-minded Gordon Murray was employed as Chief Designer at Brabham through most of the 1980s. Brabham was then run by Formula 1 supremo Bernie Ecclestone.

"Bernie let me have my technical head, so long as it didn't cost too much," Murray recalled. That prompted a number of ingenious ways in which they slashed costs for wind-tunnel and carbon-fiber monocoque construction, using a little lateral thinking.

In a series of deft sketches on lunchtime napkins and the author's notebook, Murray explained how the installation problems posed by the BMW four-cylinder upright engine were surmounted. "We couldn't stress the engine as part of the car, as has always been the Cosworth tradition, so we made up a four-bolt solid aluminium shear plate, a second rear plate, and a light steel tubular frame—which stretched back toward the gearbox—to divert and spread the loads, the engine sandwiched between the plates.

"There was not a weight penalty compared to the opposition, because the BMW motor, even with its iron block, was quite light, being only four cylinders versus the V6 turbo opposition or the normally-aspirated V8s. That installation was satisfactory, but we still had the aerodynamic problems of sticking

Four cylinders and half the cubic capacity was the transformation Brabham undertook to test the BMW motor as a replacement for the familiar 3-liter Ford Cosworth V8. It was not an easy transformation to make, and would never have worked reliably, but for the electronic managment and test telemetry systems mounted to the right of the upright four. To the left, the long sweeps of the exhaust manifold are seen running down to the heat-shielded zone around the KKK turbo and wastegate. Closest to the camera and hidden underneath the final section of the exhaust are the inboard coaxial spring/damper units and pull-rods to activate the suspension systems that pull obstructive springs and dampers out of a single-seater's airstreams.

Picture: BMW Werkfoto, 1981

Installation for test purposes only in the BT50 Brabham-BMW, far from the shiny show unit seen in the next picture....

Picture: Author archives, 1997

The first Formula 1 car to be crash-tested was the Brabham BT49-BMW. Such experience of a major manufacturer's resources was incorporated in the design of the Championship-winning BT52-BMW that debuted March 3, 1983.

Picture: BMW Werkfoto, 1983

the four-cylinder airbox out in the wind, finding a home for the turbocharger [and its sprawling exhaust]...plus the sheer power of the thing!

"I don't think there has ever been a time when power has escalated so rapidly [from an official 557 in 1980, almost doubled in six years—JW]. We had just a simple rear-drive of no weight at all [588 kg/1,320 lbs initially] to take a power-to-weight ratio that I don't think has been matched in motor racing," said Murray modestly.

That BMW motor raced much of its life at over 850 bhp (a phenomenal 567 bhp per liter or 1,603.8 bhp per ton!). Furthermore, BMW prepared "grenade" qualifying motors that could hit more than 1,200 horsepower. That meant at least 2,264 bhp/ton, a figure more familiar to 8-liter dragsters, which have only a quarter-mile straight to navigate. No wonder Gordon Murray commented, "Nelson used to say that qualifying

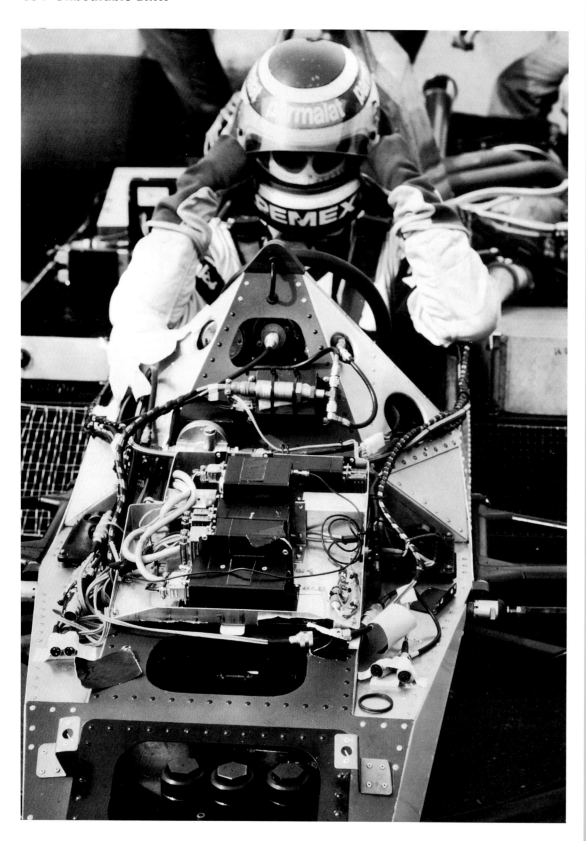

One of the rare Grand Prix talents who put as much energy and intelligence into testing as he gave to racing, even Nelson Piquet (helmeted head in gloved hands) must have wondered if the turbo motor would ever run reliably at the stunning power outputs per liter it generated. Note the black boxes above the driver's knees, revealed in this test day shot. They are all part of the pioneering telemetry systems used by BMW and Bosch to monitor motor behavior.

Picture: BMW Werkfoto, 1981

was just a question of aiming the car down the middle of the road and constant prayer!"

Paul Rosche added, "We kept the production 89.2-mm bore. At Motorsport, we took the 56-mm stroke crankshaft of the Höttinger project out to 60 mm with titanium parts for the connecting rods, all to give 1,499 cc. The compression began at 6.7:1 and boost was around 1.8 bar for 570 bhp, but of course these things varied between test, qualifying, and race sessions." Those figures were the official BMW ones for a motor that was coded M12/13.

Rosche compressed some character-building test and race seasons between 1980 and 1987, occasionally having to firmly assert BMW's rights in the harsh world of F1. On the technical front, he recalled, "At the beginning, we had Bosch-Kugelfischer mechanical fuel injection and the twin-intake KKK single turbocharger; but in these areas, things changed a lot over the racing seasons. Sometimes, for more power, but also for durability.

"In later seasons, there were boost restrictions that made a four-cylinder a bad choice

against the V6 twin turbos. They could rev higher to get better power under controlled boost—and their exhaust pulses to the turbo on each cylinder bank were more frequent.

"We started at 7,500 to 10,500 revs power band and increased to 11,200, but that put us very near the point at which the engine would explode! One missed gearchange and that would be it, whereas the V6s were happy at 12,000 and more rpms." According to year, regulations, and race/practice specification, peak power could truly be quoted between the initial 550 or so to "...more than 1,200 in qualifying form," grinned Rosche. "Our dynos cannot read any higher!" In the World Championship-winning 1983 season, an enlarged KKK turbocharger was supplied from the Dutch Grand Prix onwards; this allowed a regular 640 bhp at 11,000 rpm.

For 1984, BMW Motorsport proved an increased compression (7.5:1) in alliance with a phenomenal 3.9 bar boost (absolute) that would release a racing 950 bhp. There were a lot of failures attributed to fuel composition at the time. An insider commented, "BMW got fuels from BASF Chemicals, and it is thought that some of the mixes were based on old wartime piston engine practice during the time when Germany had to make gasoline substitutes. I don't think these mixes—impressive though they looked, with a heavy haze, like a big diesel on boost, hanging over the cars—make more than a couple of percentage points on the horsepower. A crap engine was still crap, whatever the fuel!" said our experienced observer acidly.

There was an allegation, never proved, that BMW exceeded the 102-octane ruling and transgressed the regulation chemical compositions laid down during this period, but the company could point to both internal BASF and BMW test procedures specifically created to eliminate the possibility of besmirching their reputation.

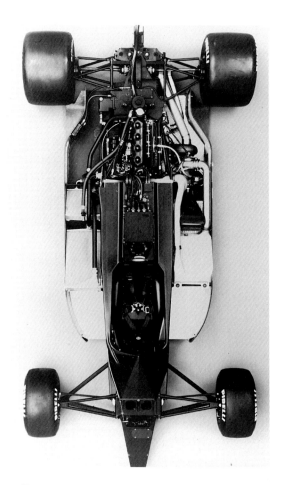

The power game

Official 1984 power quotes for BMW were almost 100 bhp less than previously. Such outputs became closer to the truth in fuel-economy-conscious 1985 when "900 to 910 bhp was usual," said Rosche. The factory BMW rpm-peak power quote was extended to a marginal 11,200 in the unsuccessful "lay flat" 1986 engine era for Brabham. Some 1,050 to 1,100 bhp was the expected qualifying power for a "maximum of two laps, when the engine would be completely destroyed," according to one insider.

Why did the "lay-down" unit and seating for the Brabham BT52-BMW concept not work in 1986? In March 1997, Gordon Murray admitted, "I think there were three peripheral

Laid over, but not laid back. The clever idea of getting the BMW motor to hide out of the airstream and increase traction through shifted mass for the BT55 design was counter-balanced by a lack of testing, insufficient scavenging effect for the lubrication system, and little of the gains in traction that were anticipated. Gordon Murray commented that the principle was later applied to his McLaren MP4/4 Grand Prix car, which proved virtually invincible, so there was nothing wrong with the theory.

Picture: BMW Werkfoto, 1986

things that I did not take into sufficient account. First, I really have to take all the blame on my shoulders, but the fact is that—although I hate to work more than a year ahead to produce each new design—I should have put the car out for testing a year before it appeared. Second, the motor could not scavenge sufficiently because of the slant angle, particularly pronounced in the corners. Third, traction was poorer than anticipated, partially because of the low center of gravity and weight distribution. When I did get the chance to execute the concept at McLaren, it won 15 of 16 races as the MP4/4, so the theory was sound," he asserted.

In its closing 1987 season as the official BMW M12/13 motor (Arrows with Megatron BMW power continued into the final 1988 restricted 2.5-bar-boost era), BMW's four-cylinder continued to be rated around 900 bhp at 11,200 rpm. BMW engineers were less happy about their competitive state as maximum boost controls allowed no more than a sustained 4 bar.

With the benefit of 1988 hindsight, Paul Rosche noted, "I would say the development of Bosch Motronic engine management systems was a most important part of our success." BMW had three distinct stages in electronic management from Bosch. Another significant technical move echoed the original McLaren 320T, for BMW Motorsport switched to Garrett turbocharging. That was in 1985 at the French Grand Prix, which Piquet won in extreme temperatures that suited previously-recalcitrant Pirelli tires.

Gordon Murray forthrightly commented of that switch from KKK to Garrett, "The original KKKs cost us the 1984 Championship. We actually deserved to win the title more in 1984 than 1983: the car was better, Nelson drove to nine pole positions, and we led time

It goes in there and comes out over there! Intercooler, turbocharger, and wastegate plumbing on the 1985 Garrett-turbocharged BMW unit. Despite maximum boost regulations, BMW could now cheerfully admit to 800 bhp from the original 1.5 liters at 10,400 rpm. The maximum torque rating was "only" 540 Nm/398 lb-ft torque at a frenzied 8,500 rpm, so the driver had around 1,900 rpm of operational rpm band.

Picture: John Townsend for BMW Presse, 1985

Testing prior to their Championship year, Riccardo Patrese in the Brabham BT52-BMW shows the car's clean front end as a contrast to the need for extensive radiators and inter-coolers in front of the rear wheels. Moving mass rear-ward was crucial, as Gordon Murray anticipated the enor-mous power gains being made at BMW.

Picture: BMW Werkfoto, 1983

and time again, only to have a turbo failure. There was not a single cause, but differing problems, such as bad welding, imbalances, incorrect construction. That kind of thing resulted in the turbo expiring and we were out. The move to Garrett came too late, in my view."

The M12/13's cubic capacity and major components remained throughout BMW factory involvement with Formula 1, but a canted installation was needed to supply

Brabham in 1986 for the unsuccessful "lay-down" BT56.

From 1980 to 1982, BMW factory engines were supplied only to Brabham, whose con-tracted drivers were 1981/83/87 World Champion Nelson Piquet of Brazil and Riccardo Patrese, the Italian who had con-tested more Grand Prix races than any rival in 1989.

By 1983, the German-owned ATS team had gained BMW engine supplies for their D6

To finish first, first, you must finish: more test miles at Paul Ricard in France for Nelson Piquet in the 1984-season BT53-BMW. But for the unrelia-bility of supplier components, BMW and Brabham should have scooped a second World title.

Picture: BMW Werkfoto, 1984

driver and BMW-contracted Manfred Winkelhock. Gordon Murray pointed out that ATS designer Gustav Brunner deserved a place in the Grand Prix record books. "All but two or three books tell you that Hercules, John Barnard, and McLaren invented the carbon fiber tubs that everyone uses today, and which have so transformed driver safety.

"To the best of my knowledge, Brunner at ATS produced the first full carbon tub, years before McLaren. We had used some carbon constructions at Brabham back to 1978, but had a bit of a hiccup when two low-speed accidents at Monaco with the BT49s saw the carbon shatter and turn to dust.

"I put the all-carbon construction program on hold—and when we came to do the BMW program, Brabham did the first-ever Formula 1 crash test with BMW facilities, using the high-speed cameras and all the road-car facilities.

"By then, we had included resins and Kevlar to the carbon mix to improve the resilience—I was very keen to see how it would perform, and the results were incorporated in the BT52 world championship design of March 1983. For the record, I would estimate that the BT52-BMW had some 60 percent carbon construction in 1983 and we were up to 100 percent for the tubs at Brabham when I left at the close of 1986. At McLaren, I found they were on 75 percent carbon fiber construction," reported Murray.

Did the Grand Prix BMW perform? Did it ever! But, as shown in the next chapter, it could have collected even more world titles.

Now on show at Spartanburg South Carolina's Z3 factory is the back end of a Brabham-BMW, which demonstrates just how big those intercoolers and water radiators had to be to make such power from the smallest of small iron-block BMW fours.

Picture: Klaus Schnitzer, US, 1997

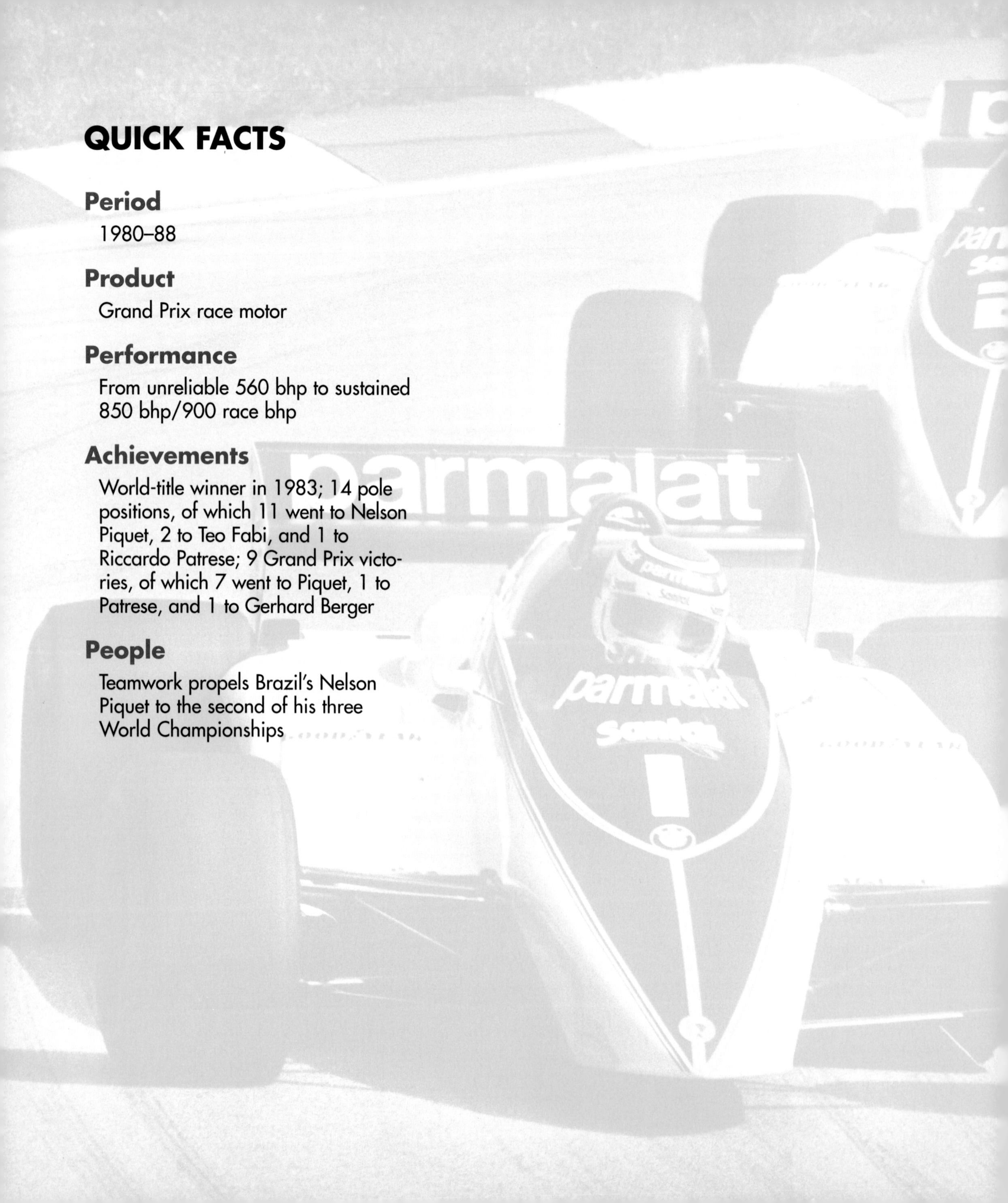

QUICK FACTS

Period

1980–88

Product

Grand Prix race motor

Performance

From unreliable 560 bhp to sustained 850 bhp/900 race bhp

Achievements

World-title winner in 1983; 14 pole positions, of which 11 went to Nelson Piquet, 2 to Teo Fabi, and 1 to Riccardo Patrese; 9 Grand Prix victories, of which 7 went to Piquet, 1 to Patrese, and 1 to Gerhard Berger

People

Teamwork propels Brazil's Nelson Piquet to the second of his three World Championships

Chapter 22

Turbo to the Top

BMW's 1.5-liter turbo in Grand Prix-winning form

Dynamic Duo: the BT50-BMWs fly in formation for Nelson Piquet and Riccardo Patrese during the racing debut season of 1982. Piquet took the car from Detroit non-qualifier to Montreal winner in seven days after the motor's flexibility was transformed. During the season, it set one pole position time, won its first Grand Prix, and set three fastest race laps.

Picture: BMW Werkfoto, 1982

In successive seasons, until their withdrawal as a factory engine supplier at the close of 1987, BMW continued to supply Brabham. Benetton (1986) and Ligier (1987) also received BMW or Megatron-branded turbo power units for Grand Prix, as did ATS and Arrows at Milton Keynes.

During the early 1980s, Gordon Murray and the Brabham team pioneered a number of technological moves, setting the pace to such an extent that a 29-year-old Nelson Piquet won his first of three World Championships in a Brabham-Ford Cosworth V8 in 1981. Pit stops and tire warmers were Brabham moves that are still current; but for BMW, Gordon Murray also had to guess how much weight would need to be moved rearward in the wake of banned ground-effect aerodynamics, harnessing the ever-sharper thrust of the Bimmer turbo 1.5 liter.

The first track test runs (October 13, 1980 at Silverstone onward) saw a modified Brabham BT49T at an initial 557 bhp by 9,500 rpm. The Brabham BT49/50 hybrid appeared publicly for the July 18, 1981 British Grand Prix at Silverstone and practiced as fourth fastest on July 16 and 17. These early Brabham-BMWs were more cut-and-shut monocoques,

conversions from V8 Brabham designs, rather than purpose-built BMW racers.

As on so many subsequent occasions, the BMW unit was not raced at Silverstone in 1981, even though it proved capable of cracking 190 mph on the fastest sections. After weeks of testing in southern France and an explosive winter of destroyed BMW motors, BMW's engine was out racing in 1982, although BMW identification was modest (on the orders of an apprehensive BMW management).

When it came to racing the BMW M12/13 unit, intended pilot Lauda had retired (for the first time). Lead driver Nelson Piquet set the second fastest practice time in the first race outing. In South Africa on the weekend of January 23, 1982, Riccardo Patrese qualified fourth. South Africa was not a successful debut for the BT50 Brabham BMWs, nor for Piquet, who got involved in off-track politics and found that Ecclestone had effectively barred him from participating in the first practice session!

Piquet bogged the start and did just four race laps before sliding off the circuit, while Patrese ran as high as fourth before the oil pressure zeroed. The BMW-Brabham relationship sank to its depths, and the Munich motor

Out of the car, you can see the near-vertical motor in its previous upright position, alongside the near-horizontal version of the motor coded M12/13/1 for the 1986 season. Motorsport worked on the concept through early summer 1985, and turned the upright motor through 72 degrees inclination to the left, saving a reported 9 inches/ 23 cms on installation height. Engineers had to design and create a new crankcase, oil and water systems. It should have worked well, especially as BMW now quoted 900 race bhp and 1,050 practice horsepower as routine from the 374-lb/170-kg package.

Picture: BMW Werkfoto, 1986

was not fielded in the next three Grand Prix. Some of the reasoning was political rather than technical, as the British-based runners fought to preserve ultra-low race weights in association with the proven Cosworth V8 and water-cooling reservoirs for the brakes.

For a tense and agonizingly-prolonged period, Brabham preferred to race the Ford-Cosworth V8s. When BMW issued a statement threatening the end of any further cooperation (April 28, 1982), Brabham recognized the inevitable. The Surrey constructors turned their talents for innovative design, concours presentation, and sheer hard work toward a formidable alliance with BMW.

The initial driver faith in a project that had looked very wobbly in its early stages came from Piquet. Subsequently abused for his lacklustre Camel Lotus Grand Prix performances, Piquet always sought the "Racer's Edge" over the opposition from his British Formula 3 championship days onward. The BMW turbo engine fit the Piquet philosophy perfectly, and he used every bit of his triple World Championship-winning talent during prolonged BMW test, development, and racing days. Of 9 BMW Grand Prix wins, Nelson Piquet scored 7; and 11 of 14 pole positions (fastest practice times) recorded by BMW engines were Piquet's intelligently rapid handiwork.

Missing three Grand Prix, and just seven days after the BMW public threat to terminate cooperation, the Brabham BT50-BMWs reemerged for the Belgian Grand Prix of May 1982. In Belgium, Piquet made it to the finish at the humpy Zolder circuit, albeit sixth. Piquet was laps behind the winner, and Patrese retired when running fourth, but at least one BMW proved it could go the distance....

They won the World title together, but it could have been even better....Nelson Piquet and the turbocharged Brabham BMW did thousands of miles before the 1983 World driver's title was netted, but their pace was equally quick in 1984 (the BT53-BMW turbo from that year is shown here), only to suffer constant turbocharger-related failures. They set eight pole position times that season, but the car only lasted long enough to score wins in Detroit and Canada. A change of turbocharger suppliers came too late to save their chances for a second successive title.

Picture: BMW Werkfoto, 1984

Grand Prix power came from BMW for Nelson Piquet's leading Brabham BT52 and the yellow ATS carbon fiber monocoque pioneer behind him.

Picture: BMW Archiv, reprinted 1996

Aside from dubious reliability in the early days, the BMW unit offered sharp on/off power characteristics until the 1982 Canadian Grand Prix. Thus, a thirteenth position on the grid qualification at Monaco was unsurprising on this tight street circuit, Piquet retiring after 50 laps with a transmission failure—not a rarity at this stage. To rub salt in BMW's wounded pride, Brabham took a Cosworth-Ford BT49 and Patrese won. Very tactful!

There were some desperate moments when neither competitive nor reliable performances came from the Munich four-cylinders, severely stressing the Anglo-German alliance. The amiably intelligent Dieter Stappert performed an underrated feat of diplomacy, keeping BMW management and the rugged Brabham racers from tearing each other apart. The respect of Paul Rosche for Murray's genius was another factor that saw this alliance eventually reap its just rewards.

Illustrating just how temperamental the turbo task was, the first victory came on a cool Canadian evening (June 13, 1982), just a week after Nelson and Brabham BMW had failed to qualify for the previous weekend's Detroit Grand Prix! Running a Grand Prix at twilight had become a necessity, as a fatality had occurred on the first start, so Piquet deserves extra respect for controlling his emotions. Applause also for the BMW technicians who found that a relatively simple mixture alteration turned the turbo four from misfiring street beast to cohesively flexible Cosworth crusher.

There were no more wins that 1982 season, and a lot of retirements, but the Brabham-BMWs did secure the top three practice positions on five occasions. Nelson Piquet secured second in the Dutch Grand Prix, so the alliance still looked to be a competitive proposition.

Grand Prix success in 1983

For 1983, Gordon Murray took the brave pills, creating the beautifully-effective "Arrow" concept Brabham BT52-BMW in Munich on March 3, 1983. The principle was to get rid of the side pods: like the now-flat floor, they were no longer allowed to generate significant ground effects. Brabham shifted all the heaviest cooling components to the rear for better traction from the 7-percent increase in rear-end weight.

The intercooler and the water and oil radiators trekked aft as part of a bold gamble that saw "56 to 57 percent of the car's sub-600 kg on the back, which I designed to allow separate engine removal via four bolts, plus the clutch, brake, and accelerator cables," recalled Murray. But that was not the total extent of his gamble: "It was the most non-adjustable car I have ever drawn," he noted in 1997.

"We had locked ourselves into this concept: there was no rear anti-roll bar to adjust, simply a fence around the rear wing. The only adjustable factors were the front wings, ride height, that kind of thing. It would be absolute death if I had misunderstood the changes prompted by the ban on ground effects, the loss of 60 percent downforces generated with the assistance of side skirts, and the consequent need to accommodate a center of air pressure that had moved forward, along with the center of gravity.

"Even at 60 mph, such aerodynamic losses are obvious. Emphasized by our rapidly-developing turbo horsepower, I had to bet that traction would become a vastly higher priority," Murray remembered. His courage included continuing with the principle of planned mid-race pit stops: "Luckily, the others were initially slow to imitate that," he said, still puzzled, before concluding, "We had just three months after tearing up the planned ground-effect car. I lived on chemicals, and none of us had any

Now that's what you call a rear wing! BMW power was harnessed in many other chassis besides Brabham. From 1983 onward, the German ATS (funded by the sports road-wheel manufacturer of that name) showed advanced engineering in carbon fibers and intermittent promise for BMW's favored drivers. Here, Manfred Winkelhock gets in some test miles with the 1984 ATS-BMW D6 at Rio de Janeiro, Brazil.

Picture: BMW Werkfoto, 1984

sleep. Only the wheels and pedals were carry-over items."

Just ten days after its Munich media bow, the Brabham BT52-BMW faced its adversaries for the torrid 197-mile Brazilian Grand Prix. Although they qualified comparatively quietly (fourth and seventh) around the 5-km/3.1-mile Rio de Janeiro track, the Brabham-BMW BT52 gamble paid off with a 20.6-second victory over the conventional Williams-Ford Cosworth V8. The bonus was a fastest lap beyond 112 mph for Nelson Piquet in his home run.

North America would not be so kind. At Long Beach, California, the bumpy streets left the Brabham-BMWs struggling, way off their normal pace. They were not the only major team to suffer: McLaren went from the back of the grid to a one-two win, but the BT52s both failed to finish. Piquet was uncompetitive and quit when in the midfield, while Patrese managed third before his motor electronics died.

The French Paul Ricard track, on which Brabham-BMW completed so much of its winter testing, saw Piquet back in the frame with a fine second place, about half a minute down on Alain Prost's revitalized Renault V6 turbo. Now that the other teams had caught on to the

pit-stop strategy—of special benefit to turbos in allowing higher fuel consumption/higher boost tactics to be employed—the Brabham-BMW-versus-Renault-turbo pattern of the season became apparent.

The Italian independent state of San Marino and its punishing Imola circuit handed no finishing points out to the BMW effort, but Patrese took quickest lap (119.38 mph). So, what was the trouble? The nuts behind the wheel! Piquet qualified second, but bogged his start, staged a magnificent recovery to fifth place, then had a valve disintegrate. Patrese led, but stuck it into the wall for no fathomable reason.

The tight street circuit of Monaco was a technical challenge to the turbos in their early days, but Piquet came home with second-place points and fastest lap (just under 85 mph) in the summer of 1983. Patrese was sidelined by the motor electronics, plus his brief encounter with a guard rail.

The 7-km/4.3-mile Spa track in Belgium used some public tarmac to wind through the "Battle of the Bulge" Ardennes forest and featured the fast track that turbos adore. The front four carried turbocharged motors, headed by

Prost's Renault. Piquet managed to get up to second place before the Brabham-Hewland gearbox gave selection trouble, but he still soothed it home fourth.

The transmission had been a perpetual problem and was not truly fixed until Murray renewed an old trading link with America's Pete Weissmann. Gordon Murray paid him this tribute, upon Weissmann's death in 1996: "He was a truly practical, 'can-do' engineer, and our direct working relationship ranked alongside that with Paul Rosche. There is no higher praise in my vocabulary."

Back to the States and another street fight: Detroit. Piquet exhibited his command of colloquial Anglo-Saxon when he recalled this race, because he qualified on the front row and led most of it, only to suffer a nailed rear tire. He recovered to fourth, but once again Patrese was sidelined, so the points-gathering was slowing down. Some consolation came from an encouraging ninth to ATS-BMW with BMW-contracted Manfred Winkelhock aboard.

The French-speaking public in Canada got a one-two Renault result to celebrate, while the Brabham BMWs collected zero points, with Piquet suffering a snapped throttle cable. The British Grand Prix at Silverstone was the fastest of the year and the Championship challengers went at it, head-to-head. Fastest lap (142.2 mph) and the win went to Prost and Renault, but Piquet was second and looking forward to the fast tracks in Germany, Austria, and Holland.

Germany (Hockenheim) was kindest to Patrese, who came in third, while Piquet shared BMW's home crowd embarrassment with a big blaze in the motor department that forced him out of his meritorious third position. Piquet was third at Zeltweg, then the second-quickest European track. He finished only by soft-pedalling the turbo, after it had started to wilt under the pressure of near-140-mph averages and a maximum speed of more than 195 mph on 1.5 liters.

Zandvoort in Holland saw Piquet hit pole position with aid of an intercooler water spray and British specialist Brian Hart's boost-control valve. From the start lights, Piquet lead by a huge margin, but he was uncharacteristically barged out of the way by Prost at the slowest hairpin.

(Right) What should have been: Piquet and the 1984 Brabham-BMW shoot away in the lead on one of the fastest tracks ever on the Grand Prix schedule: Oesterreichring. Snaking through the Austrian country-side, the brilliant Brazilian leads Alain Prost (McLaren Tag), Elio de Angelis (Lotus-Renault), Niki Lauda's Porsche-powered McLaren (Lauda was destined to win a third title that year), Patrick Tambay and Derek Warwick in their turbo Renaults, and Teo Fabi in the second factory-backed Brabham-BMW. Piquet and Fabi were fourth in one of the team's better 1984 outings but, as for the season, Piquet should have won.

Picture: BMW

(Left) One of Grand Prix's longest runs without a Grand win has been the fate of Arrows, who was a loyal BMW and Megatron customer in the 1980s. Here, Gerhard Berger hurtles past the Hockenhein Grandstands in the Arrows A8-BMW.

Picture: BMW Werkfoto, 1985

Prost didn't benefit directly, since the Renault went off as a result of sustaining running-gear damage, but he still led the championship decisively. Now there were just three events left: the fabulous Monza Park circuit in Milan, Britain's Brands Hatch, and the South African finale at the high-altitude Kyalami circuit.

Piquet and Brabham-BMW simply went into overdrive with wins in Italy (at 135 mph for the 187 miles) and Britain (123 mph and 199 miles), plus a fastest lap (137.4 mph) in Monza. Now there were two points between Prost's Renault and Piquet's BT52-BMW, but the Brazilian BMW pilot was on a roll....

A cunning Brabham-BMW pit-stop strategy allowed an initially commanding lead in South

Africa, held until it was obvious that Piquet could be absolutely sure of the Championship because Prost's Renault retired. Brabham teammate Riccardo Patrese was handed a South African victory at the end of the season, as Piquet made sure of the 1983 title.

"A very special moment," recalled Murray, "winning the Championship with one driver and the race with the other....And that BMW beat Renault to the title, the first for a turbo car, for just a fraction of what the French were spending, that just made our Kyalami satisfaction complete, especially as I was on home turf."

The only win of 1985 for Brabham-BMW came at Paul Ricard in France. Here, Nelson Piquet sees the checkered flag after his Pirelli-shod Brabham coped with conditions better than any rival. This was the first time the BMW motor raced with Garrett instead of Kuhnle, Kopp & Kausch (KKK) turbocharging.

Picture: John Townsend for BMW, 1985

Monaco 1985: Piquet takes to the streets of the southern France principality with BMW MPower. The gleaming Brabham-BMW failed to finish, its concours presentation tarnished in an accident.

Picture: John Townsend for BMW, 1985

For 1986, Benetton had a British-based team that grew out of the Toleman operation and fielded the B186-BMW. It was only a one-season deal, and BMW still had both Arrows and Brabham to supply. Still, the Benetton relationship produced a Grand Prix win (Mexico) as well as sixth (Makes) and seventh (Driver's) places in the World standings: better results than either Brabham or Arrows harvested with MPower.

Picture: Author archive, 1986

The BT53 gets mixed reviews

In 1984, the 1983-uprated BT52B became a BT53-BMW and faced races without planned fuel stops (which were temporarily banned) on 220 liters/48.4 Imperial gallons of gas. The Brabham-BMWs should have won the title again, but their turbo and motor-related retirement rate was awesome.

Piquet picked up eight pole positions but only two victories (Canada and Detroit) in a chain of explosive outings with new teammates Teo Fabi and his younger brother Corrado. Piquet slipped to fifth in the driver rankings and Brabham-BMW was fourth in the constructor's leagues.

The latter constructor's result was equalled in 1985, when the four-cylinder combination grew less technically competitive for reasons that Paul Rosche outlined earlier. Piquet slumped to eighth in the driver's world title trail in 1985, having won at Paul Ricard and set only one pole position during the fuel-conscious season.

Gerhard Berger and Anglo-Italian Benetton-BMW were the heroes for BMW in 1986, winning one race (Mexico), taking third in San Marino but suffering nine retirements! Benetton managed sixth in the constructor's series, and

Berger was seventh—BMW's best-placed driver. Benetton went for Ford in 1987, so the last BMW-powered Grand Prix win of all went to BMW protégé Gerhard Berger and his Benetton B186 in the Mexican Grand Prix on October 12, 1986.

BMW officially withdrew from Formula 1 engine supply at the close of 1987, but its techniques lived on in the upright four-cylinder form of the Megatron engine (serviced by Heini Mader in Switzerland). Megatron powerfully served the 1987–88 Arrows equipe at Milton Keynes, achieving a best placing of sixth in 1987 (America's Eddie Cheever at Detroit) and beating Brabham in both the world driver's and constructor's league tables of that season. In 1987, Cheever was eighth, ahead of Patrese, and Arrows Megatron led Brabham-BMW to seize sixth in the Constructor's Cup: the official works team was eighth and Ligier-Megatron was eleventh.

BMW's final Grand Prix score totalled nine Grand Prix victories, all but one scored with the official Brabham-BMW alliance. Piquet won seven Grand Prix races for Brabham-BMW in the 1982–85 seasons, Patrese won one (1983), and Berger (Benetton-BMW) took the final 1986 accolade. Brabham-BMW netted not just the 1983 driver's title for Piquet, but also took third in the 1983 World Championship for Constructors, the partnership's best result. BMW motors scored 14 official practice pole positions.

British sources were correct to anticipate that BMW will return to Grand Prix racing as the powerhouse behind the all-conquering Williams Grand Prix team in 1999/2000, but Paul Rosche indicated that a Grand Prix unit (a V10, if current trends are followed) would take at least two seasons to reach a competitive level. The BMW board is adamant that it sanctioned such expenditure just a week before the September 9, 1997 official announcement that the company would return to Formula 1 with a BMW-Williams design.

At this writing, Williams has the assurance of winning Renault V10s until the close of 1998, so BMW's most likely comeback season would be 1999 test-running with Williams, followed by the year 2000 race season with Britain's most recent Grand Prix benchmark team.

In fact, the hottest tale at press time was that BMW would pay Williams to partly-fund an interim Renault V10, badged and built by Renault supplier Mecachrome, while BMW's motor was readied. Stranger things have happened in the moneyed world of Grand Prix!

(Left) The livery changed during the race season, but green bought BMW and Benetton better fortune than white. Here are Teo Fabi and Gerhard Berger on their way to World Championship points for fifth and sixth in April 1986's Spanish Grand Prix.

(Right) Our second shot was taken ten years afterward, with Steve Soper taking a cautious Californian outing (the tub was visibly cracked!) in the B186-BMW that the factory retains through Mobile Tradition.

Pictures: BMW Werkfoto, 1986; Klaus Schnitzer, 1996

CHRYSLER CORPORATION presents
REY HISTORIC AUTOMOB
Chopard
GENEVE
MONTEREY HISTO
AUTOMOBILE R
benetton
DUCKHAMS
10
benetton
RIELLO
20

QUICK FACTS

Period

1972–83

Products

E28 5-series in European Group A, for production runs over 5,000 annually; British, Belgian and South African "Fast Fives"

Performance

528i 2.8-liter in-line six at 184 bhp/130 mph with 0–60 mph in 8.9 seconds for showroom format; 240 bhp/145 mph with 0–60 mph in 8.0 seconds for racing format

Achievements

Privateer's choice wins the July 1977 Spa 24-hour race in E12 530i (US) homologated trim; 1982 European Champion's car

People

Scotland's Tom Walkinshaw uses the E12 5-series to make a name for TWR; Germany's Helmut Kelleners and Italy's Umberto Grano choose the E28 to take the 1982 European Championship

Chapter 23

Private Prancers

Privateers show winning speed with BMW's 5-series

The missing link in the racing history of BMW is the story of the four-door 5-series sedans and the two-door 6-series coupes, which were often raced by privateer and semi-works teams. The factory supported the 5-series, ensuring that it was properly homologated for the new Group A regulations of 1982 and earlier national races for Group 1 production sedans.

As for the later racing career of the 6-series coupe, BMW never raced the engine that could have beaten the best and may have prevented Jaguar from winning the 1984 European title and Volvo the 1985 title. But for the last three years of the European series—abandoned after 1988 in exasperation by the FIA in Paris after so many disqualifications and allegations of cheating between the participants—BMW were winners once more with the original M3.

The mass-production years of the 5-series were from April 1981 to December 1987, for E28 528i only (80,775 from April 1981 to December 1987). This compares with 11,310 of the US-spec 533i made from September 1982 to September 1984.

Despite the handicap of never homologating the 286-bhp 24-valve six that honestly pow-ered the M5 and M6/635 derivatives, these BMWs still came away with European titles in 1982, 1983, and 1986. These challengers used 12-valve sixes and legendary durability to intermittently beat V12s, V8s and a very special turbo car from Volvo.

Why did BMW never homologate the 24-valver? In a word: numbers. The German sports authorities at ONS would not allow a national manufacturer to cheat production numbers, unlike rival nations who actively supported the competitive ambitions of their national manufacturers. BMW could not prove sufficient annual output of the 24-valve-engined 5- or 6-series to make the cut. They got awfully close to genuine qualification and honestly made more M6s annually than Jaguar made of the V12 XJS in some production years, but it wasn't enough.

The Jaguar had qualified on a cunning transfer from the earlier Group 1 category. BMW missed the implications of that smart move, which was ironically implemented by former BMW-contracted driver Tom Walkinshaw. Thereafter, BMW found that the racing seasons of the 1980s, pre-M3, took place on a playing field that tilted more than a battered pinball machine.

First, we'll tell the tale of the racing 5-series, which traces back to Britain and the fortunes of former Alpina-BMW CSL and Group 5 320 driver Tom Walkinshaw. Tom Walkinshaw Racing (TWR) then of Kidlington, Oxfordshire, in England, was a former BMW competition subsidiary of the later 1970s.

TWR remains in Oxfordshire, but has since spread its wings far beyond BMW, having prepared racing Mazda rotaries, Jaguars, Rovers, Audis, and Volvo sedans at the international level. All except Audi (even with Stirling Moss and Martin Brundle aboard) have been winners. Jaguar was TWR's most successful international marque, with a European title for the XJS—gained at BMW's expense—and both Le Mans and Daytona 24-hour race wins, along with the World Sports Car title.

Today, TWR employs over 1,000 people and has production car/racing connections with General Motors/Holden in Australia and Volvo

in Sweden. TWR is famed for partnerships that resulted in the creation of the Jaguar XJ220 and Aston Martin DB7.

Walkinshaw's TWR of the late 1970s consisted of a number of private companies, handling everything from complete car conversions to accessory sales. The pedigree of that TWR outlet went back to an operation mounted within BMW Concessionaires (GB) Ltd. and inaugurated in 1972 to contest British national championship races.

Although BMW Concessionaires was not then a factory subsidiary, it was able to wield a fair influence with the parent company, as Britain was such a good market for the higher-priced models, lagging only behind the Arab states and the United States as an export customer. Britain took a particularly large (500-off) allocation of the lightweight CSL coupes.

In 1972, BMW Concessionaires appointed club racer/sales wizard John Markey to be

Silverstone, 1978: battered but unbowed. Tom Walkinshaw breathed life into BMW GB's enthusiasm for racing again. The Scottish pro enjoyed good results at home and abroad in 1977 with his 530i, but the 1978 season started very badly. By the end of the year, Walkinshaw had got the car back into the winning circle again, but its comfortable four-door weight was always a handicap in the short (under half an hour) UK events.

Picture: London Art Tech, 1978

its UK competition manager. At first, the 2002 Tii was campaigned with great success by journalist Roger Bell, and then a 3-liter CSi was acquired, which was also prepared by Mathwall Engineering. That car made the Concessionaires' first and last sortie to the Belgian Spa 24-hour race of that inaugural year, where it won its class, just beating a factory-backed production racing opponent, and finished seventh overall. The author was honored to share that Belgian foray with Peter Hanson.

The UK Concessionaires also had a great deal to do with the Cooper Car Company/Broadspeed coupe sent to Salzburgring earlier in the year, a full Group 2 machine that only raced in public once (detailed in an earlier chapter). Toward the end of the 1972 season, the results were not so bright, and a great deal of money had been spent.

Then, in 1973, a series of British races was contested using the 3-liter Si sedan for Bell and veteran Tony Lanfranchi, and at least one of these cars now lives in the US. Brian Muir's Alpina CSL also contested the premier British series (in its last season of Group 2 regulations), so that season was expensive. In 1974, the fuel crisis hit BMW in the UK hard, and recently-recruited competitions manager Lanfranchi was one of the casualties, though the Si sedans continued to appear in their usual wallowing, tire-spinning style. One even contested the 1976 Silverstone 6-hours and survived in a sea of turbo Porsches.

That 1974 season looked like the end of competition for BMW in any organized form in Britain. Not so. Early in 1976, Tom Walkinshaw became involved in Group 5, driving the Hermetite-sponsored, factory-prepared CSL with John Fitzpatrick. This brought the shrewd young Scot into contact with the Neerpasch "method" and reminded him that his other employers at Ford were not very interested in sedan racing on a big scale any more.

In late 1976, Walkinshaw approached the BMW factory with a scheme to investigate the potential of the E12 original 5-series in competition, taking away a 528i from the British Concessionaires in September for evaluation. However, the factory already knew about building faster E12s, for Neerpasch had encouraged the production of converted 5-series cars with anything up to 3.5-liter engines, special suspension, braking, and other equipment appealing to the enthusiast or BMW contracted drivers for road use.

So the Munich department had a fair idea of what was required in a track 5-series, but it did not have the manpower or inclination to become involved in racing at a national level. This attitude multiplied, leaving BMW France, BMW Italia, and BMW Belgium to administer competition programs that suited their conditions. In Britain, France, and Belgium, it was the so-called Group 1 1/2 BMW 530i for any national racing task.

In Britain, Walkinshaw ran the 528i through its paces in late 1976. His racing mechanics stripped the car apart to measure every relevant component and to assess the geometry, corner weights, and likely performance in competition trim in a modified Group 1 form suitable for racing across Britain, Belgium, and France.

The result was confusing: BMW managed to homologate a special 530i (US), and also to register the concept of the 5-series with a 3-liter engine as an evolution of the 528 for racing! In America, there was such a car (listed from 1975 with 176 SAE-measured ponies), and BMW made 27,073 examples between October 1974 and August 1978. In Europe, it was only possible to have a 530i by having one specially converted at the factory or by other specialists.

It was this gray homologation aspect of production racing that put BMW off earlier forms of Group 1 or 1 1/2 racing, especially as there was later a Swiss CSI delegate

Not a common sight, but it just shows most BMWs have a sporting spirit. The British regularly raced the largest contemporary Bimmer in its fuel-injected form in production touring car events. An American collector (Arthur Porter) has just such a car. This Manitou Forklift Trucks example was driven by David Taylor at Brands Hatch in 1977.

The privately-owned BMW Concessionaires also backed a team of 3.0Si limousines in the hotly-fought 1973–74 production categories, where they proved they could powerslide like rally cars for the photographers and were a short-circuit match for less-ambitiously-funded Chevrolet Camaros.

Picture: Colin Taylor Productions, 1977

investigation into the weights and equipment that Group 1 cars were using for competition. This resulted in the homologation for the 530i (US) being dropped as a valid international recognition for the car, and it was then raced only as an evolution of the 528 for the 1978 season, having competed at many 1977 events in US trim.

Tom Walkinshaw enjoyed quite a promising first season with the 5-series in 1977, holding a couple of British lap records and finishing within the top three on occasion. However, the elusive outright win did not come the small team's way. For 1978, Walkinshaw received a lot more backing and was able to set up in premises of his own that could handle not only a two- or even three-car 530i team, but also Formula 2 (South Africa's Rad Dougal) and the many other activities that would make him and TWR an international name.

Walkinshaw found that the 530 produced in Britain was faster than those raced in France, which he attributed to the fact that they did not use the same suspension top mounts, tires, or engines as the British. Suitably encouraged, he tackled both the Spa 24-hours and the Nürburgring 4-hours with

the 530i (its first appearance in European Group 2 at the 'Ring), with mixed results. At Spa, neither car finished, but at the 'Ring, the car was tenth overall and won the 3-liter class, which was a good result for what amounted to a British sprint racer with a deep spoiler tacked on the front.

The 1978 British season offered high hopes with Pentax and Tolemans Deliveries as sponsors, and with drivers like Andy Rouse, Dieter Quester, and Rad Dougal booked to appear. True, the cars were heavy at 1,230 kg/2,706 lbs, and engine specialists Racing Services had struggled to reach 245–248 bhp after the loss of the US specification, which permitted a compression ratio of well over 10.0:1 (now they were limited to 9.5:1).

Just how hard TWR worked to even get back on terms with the 2,200-lb, 225-bhp Ford Capris can be judged from the fact that, although the cars started the year on Goodyear tires, by the end of the season, Dunlops were being used for dry conditions—and Michelins for wet!

What went into a Group 1 1/2 BMW 530i? In the 1970s, I asked Walkinshaw that question, and found that most of the points he covered

Tom Walkinshaw raced the BMW 530i against stern Ford Capri opposition in the British Championship through 1977–78, occasionally appearing in Europe. Here, Walkinshaw races the 3-liter Funfer at Brands Hatch in October 1977. The combination controversially won races and laid the foundation for a TWR empire that spanned three continents and employed over 1,000 people in the 1990s.

Picture: Colin Taylor Productions, 1977

were held in common with other similar cars prepared throughout Europe. To squeeze an extra 45–50 bhp from the 2,985-cc six (89 x 80 mm) takes a great deal of work and patience. The 3-liter motor normally developed a European-rated 195 bhp on a 9.0:1 compression ratio, while the racing unit was persuaded to give almost 250 bhp only by designing and profiling a camshaft to conform to the tolerances listed on the homologation form. Walkinshaw's team also increased the valve lift.

Otherwise, engine work had to be confined to pulling each engine apart and building it to the often advantageous tolerances listed on the homologation form. Port sizes, governing the amount of fuel mixture that could be dragged in and quickly exhausted, could be enlarged if the manufacturer's casting provided smaller orifices

than those listed on the homologation form. The whole engine could be set up to operate with the least possible friction from bearing or other heat-generating surfaces.

The chassis work is where much of the "1/2" in Group 1 1/2 comes from, for there were marked differences from the Group 1 "showroom" intention of the international regulations. To start with, all the rubber bushes were replaced by steel rose joints. Bilstein gas-filled dampers were used front and rear for the classic BMW MacPherson-strut/trailing-arm all-independent suspension. Complete with threaded alloy casings, the dampers could be quickly adjusted with respect to ride height, and the suspension geometry was swiftly altered with respect to camber angle, castor, and toe in/out. Camber and castor were both subject

to change through the drilled alloy top-mounting plates for the MacPherson struts. All the suspension parts, including the variable front and rear roll bars, had to pick up on the production mounting points.

The car was allowed to race on seven-inch-wide alloy wheels. The Continental European teams used Michelin tires only, but some fitted Dunlop for dry-weather use. The brakes, cooled by a cold-air feed, were ventilated disc units front and rear, which Walkinshaw described in glowing terms: "Without doubt, the best feature of the car. You can make up three car lengths on a Capri going into a corner. They are slightly bigger than those of the 528, and we use no servo booster. With this set-up, the driver can modulate the pedal just like one of those Maxaret aircraft braking systems, right on the point of lock-up. If you have the booster fitted, you tend to lock up wheels and flat-spot tires."

Walkinshaw was also driving the car himself again after vowing at the beginning of the season that he would not drive a car his works had

prepared. It would be the mid 1980s, with a European title under his (Jag) belt, before he gave up driving the race cars TWR prepared.

Walkinshaw drove in seven 1978 races, scoring four pole positions and winning two late-season events, including the TransEurope Trophy round held at Silverstone—this after an RAC tribunal that vindicated TWR's stripping off trim in accordance with the somewhat-confused regulations. Now you can see why the factory was not keen on Group 1. The BMW-TWR link did not blossom, and Walkinshaw went his increasingly-successful way, but only after TWR had also prepared the 323i for a one-season, one-marque racing role.

The 5-series was also campaigned by Luigi Racing (Belgium) in international races toward the end of the 1977 season. Luigi Racing was a former European title-winner with the CSL. Luigi continued to race the four-door E12 in 1978, though it actually won the European title with the CSL before going with Chevrolet for 1979.

BMW indirectly supported the preparation of 5-series Group 1 1/2 racers in France through

Georges Benoit at Villefranche in the south of France. From the same region, former hillclimb champion Pierre Maublanc was its driver. Such BMWs were highly-popular racing mounts in France during these seasons, and some fine drivers participated, including Jean-Pierre Beltoise, who won the French championship with his Benoit 530 in 1977.

The French rarely ventured outside their own territory, and the Belgians scarcely needed to as they had one of the world's classic races on their Ardennes doorstep—the 24-hour annual at Spa-Francorchamps. In 1977, Belgian BMW competition manager Hughes de Fierlant, former long-distance racer of many seasons' standing, administered the efforts of several rival tuning establishments well enough to scoop the BMW 530i's most impressive international win, averaging over 100 mph (160 km/h) while covering 2,536.06 miles/4,081 km from Saturday, July 23 to Sunday, July 24, 1977. French rally ace Jean-Claud Andruet and Eddy Joosen won outright in their Juma-modified BMW. Similar cars were fifth and seventh, while Alain Cudini/Guy Frequelin in their Benoit car were credited with the fastest

lap: 4 minutes 25.9 seconds, at 118.71 mph (191 km/h).

De Fierlant masterminded the appearance of two teams with a pair of 530i models apiece in the 1978 race, prepared by Juma and Serge Speed, respectively. The Belgian competition manager had massive support, for there were 12 other 530s entered among the 60-car field, including those of Luigi (who had won the 600-km international earlier in the season) and Benoit. Even though Derek Bell shared one of de Fierlant's machines with Joosen, and Jean-Claude Andruet was again on the team, the Capris proved to be just too fast in 1978.

The fastest 530 was tenth after practice. Even though Gordon Spice suffered a few dramas, making it one of the most exciting finishes ever between the British-based Capri team and the Belgian BMWs, the 530i for Joosen/Raijmond van Hove (Bell had crashed the car he shared originally with Joosen) finished second, having covered just four and a half kilometers less than the winning Ford. Other 530s finished third and fifth to reinforce the reliability image, but de Fierlant

Under Salora-Castrol colors, automotive entrepreneur Eddie Keizan scored around 40 South African victories from 1976 to 1978. BMW South Africa constructed the original production batch required to race. That meant 100 cars were built to homologate the main points for racing (about 100 kg lighter, with 3-liter injection sixes and five-speed gearboxes). These lightweight four-doors were the nearest thing to works 5-series BMWs that existed prior to the factory supporting Group A development in 1981–82 Europe, France's wild M5 Supertourisme of the mid-1980s, and the 1990s BMW North America-supported M5s for John Buffum and David Donohue.

Picture: Courtesy John Dunbar/Zoom Photographic, 1979

immediately set off for the German Grand Prix and embarked upon a series of discussions with BMW to find some way of gaining the extra speed they needed! It never really happened in Europe, but before telling what BMW did allow for the 5-series in the 1980s, we need to visit a very resourceful motor-racing nation indeed, somewhere a bit off the beaten track....

The most exciting BMW 530s did not come from Europe at all. The story of the incredibly successful South African BMW team is inspiring, showing everyone what could be done with this upright sedan.

The remarkable Eddie Keizan, then a director of several automotive businesses including the Tiger Wheels manufacturing and retailing concern, was the man behind these South African BMWs. Keizan had twice won the country's modified sedan championship before he was approached by BMW South Africa to run a new racing team on its behalf.

South African rules were a law unto themselves. Although most countries have their little idiosyncrasies, the South Africans provided very fast specials of some kind or another in the 1960s and 1970s. Decades ago, it was Ford Capris with V8 engines. Then came a cross between international modified (Group 2) and production (Group 1) competition, to provide BMW with a chance to win.

To comply, 100 examples of the type of car to be raced had to be built. Although this was quite an undertaking, it was modest compared with international requirements that now reach up to 25,000 units a year for SuperTouring 2-liters. The regulations allowed racing wheels and tires, 2-inch/50-mm wing extensions (as for Group 2), and engines modified by the substitution of pistons, camshaft, exhaust system, and carburetors.

The 100 road BMW specials were built in time for Keizan's team to start racing in 1976, each of them as road cars equipped with a 3-liter engine and five-speed gearbox. Even

The South African 5-series cars were also permitted tail spoilers and wheelarch extensions, far more radical powertrain changes than were permitted in contemporary Europe.

Picture: Courtesy Keizan/Dunbar, 1979

these machines were some 100 kg lighter than the usual production 528.

The late Josef Schnitzer completed the original engine development while he was at Munich. Further detail changes in South Africa allowed the straight six 280 bhp to propel 1,170 kg. Under those wheel arches, they could fit 10-inch-wide front BBS alloy wheels and 12-inch rears, carrying Goodyear tires.

At the close of 1978, the South African BMWs, driven to success by either Keizan himself or former single-seater pilot Paddy Driver, were set for a second championship title. The original car was ready to race in June 1976 and had a remarkable race record up to 1978. It did not finish its first race, but it did finish over 40 subsequent events. In all but one of those finishes, it was a winner. Initially, another 530 was raced by Alain Lavoipierre, but at the beginning of 1978, that was absorbed into a two-car works team with backing from Castrol and Salora Racing, Driver taking over the second seat.

Obviously, the 1976–78 seasons have been most successful for the dynamic Keizan, who was "...responsible for technical and management supervision and promotion, aside from driving." There was opposition from Wankel-engined Mazdas, which certainly had the straight-line speed but lacked endurance. However, the 530 was hampered by the standard inlet manifold rule, and the sheer speed of the Japanese cars was becoming an embarrassment in 1978. Keizan felt that "...the 530s had made up in their handling what they lost in straight-line speed, this in spite of their rather heavy weight."

A totally new South African championship for the 1978–79 season allowed a great deal more freedom. The provincial-based Modified Saloon Car Championship continued, while the new series allowed only South African manufactured bodies, engines from the same factory, and only broad restrictions in respect of weight and engine capacity. For this formula, something of an ultimate 5-series sedan hybrid was constructed, mating the 5-series body with

These are the official homologation pictures for the 1982 season Group A 5-series (E28 body) for recognition by the FIA sporting authority in Paris, France. BMW Motorsport sold a complete body and all that was needed to make a racer into a rolling chassis. Motors could come from Heini Mader, Hartge, and others. The racer was strong, but not very fast, having "only" 240 bhp to heave its four doors along at some 145 mph.

Picture: BMW Werkfoto

a 3.5-liter, 24-valve motor like that used in the CSLs, plus the Group 5 suspension developed by the factory for the 320. It was quite a mongrel, and one that was first seen at the end of 1978 when the annual Kyalami race (formerly the 6-hours) loomed up. It proved fast enough to lead, but was robbed of a win by misfortune in a dramatic race.

For a car that was certainly not intended to race, the 5-series has had quite a career. Like all modern BMWs, except the M1 coupe, it has been required to cope with a number of engine and trim options. One could not have dubbed the old 518 or 520 (even in its later 520, six-cylinder form) as competition-biased cars. However, when it came to the bigger six-cylinder engines, the 2500 and 2800, it could be seen that the car had potential.

Installing a bigger six- or eight-cylinder, the 5-series became fun, a fact recognized back in the 1970s by the factory and its supply of the 177-bhp 528i to Europeans, or the special 200-bhp-plus 3.0-, 3.3- or even 3.5-liter Motorsport GmbH machines to accredited customers. That was as far as Munich was prepared to go, though, and the nearest the

5-series cars have come to being factory racers has been outside Germany.

European title-winner

The most successful format for the racing 5-series proved to be the 1982 introduction of Group A. This formula allowed radical chassis changes, such as replacement brakes, hubs, and suspension components, yet tightly controlled engine power, demanding standard head castings, and inlet and exhaust manifolding.

BMW accepted the challenge of these new regulations, accepting that the minimum production run of the basic vehicle used would have to be 5,000 annually. Unfortunately, this would bar the forthcoming mid-1980s BMW 5- and 6-series variants with 3.5-liter, 24-valve, DOHC sixes, and the 3-liter motor variations of the hefty 5-series that Walkinshaw had deployed in the 1970s.

From February 1, 1982, BMW Motorsport received recognition for a racing variant of the

Eggenberger preparation, Pirelli tires, and the talents of Umberto Grano and Helmut Kelleners were enough to overcome more obvious and powerful opposition in the 1982 European Championship.

Picture: BMW Werkfoto, 1982

528i. Duly homologated on that form were full
racing suspension with center lock wheels,
shorter-ratio steering box for ball-and-nut layout, 5-speed racing gearbox (dogleg first
Getrag), and a big (up to 35 mm/1.4 inches
thick x 332-mm/13-inch diameter fronts) and
ventilated disc brake system, complete with
dual master cylinders and cockpit adjustment.
Traction was assisted via a limited-slip differential, pre-loaded at 75 percent.

BMW Motorsport supplied 528i race bodies,
painted but without soundproofing. Those bodies came with all that was needed to build a
racer, usually in left-hand-drive, including all
electrics, radiators, crossmembers, differential
and trim (such as the roof lining and door
panels), but supply of the race items listed in
the preceding paragraph was confined to outside specialists "due to capacity reasons" quoted in their customer letter of July 22, 1982 to
the author.

Eggenberger in Guemlingen, Switzerland
was given the nod as engine and hardware/
complete car suppliers. Hartge was also a recommended motor supplier, and Heini Mader

did the design and development program on
the 528 race 6-series through 1982.

The Group A 528 was only front-line equipment for BMW privateers for one 1982 season, but that was enough to give Germany's
Helmut Kelleners his third successive BMW-
mounted European Touring Car title in the
Eggenberger four-door. Kelleners shared with
Italy's Umberto Grano, who was also a previous European champion for BMW (1978 and
1981, CSL and 320 respectively).

By one of those strokes of fate that motor
racing specializes in delivering, I actually saw
one of these one-season Eggenberger Group A
528s close up—very close up—at some 135
mph. I had a grandstand view down
Silverstone's Grand Prix circuit main straight of
the 528's excellent braking and chassis capabilities. I probably had another 30 bhp from
the engine of my Ford 3-liter V6 as I pursued
the Eggenberger car during practice for the
1982 edition of Britain's oldest motor race, the
Tourist Trophy.

The Ford was fully 15 mph faster in a
straight line than the 240-bhp BMW, but

lacked durability, decent brakes, or the rugged chassis that BMW had supplied, so the lap times were not that different in practice. The difference was that a BMW would usually go on turning those times for two, six, or 24 hours. That was the essential difference in racing a private Ford, but a properly sorted Capri V6 was always a more affordable proposition in Britain (because of the plummeting £-versus-DM rate of the 1980s) than the 100,000-DM race 528.

It takes a very good car to succeed without direct factory preparation. That the BMW 5-series made such a fine international career says a lot about the engineering that BMW has put in over the years. Some of the components may have been proved elsewhere, but that is no bad thing when a non-works team is involved. Engineering integrity was certainly a significant factor in the square-rigged BMW 5-series success against the odds in competition.

QUICK FACTS

Period

1980–86

Products

BMW 635CSi coupe, road and race
models

Performance

SOHC, in-line six of 12-valves: showroom at 3,430 cc, 218 bhp, 1,430
kg (3,146 lbs), 138 mph, 0–60 mph
in 7.5 seconds; race at 3,473 cc,
285 bhp, 1,185 kg (2,607 lbs), 155
mph, 0–60 mph in 6.7 seconds

Achievements

A 3.4-liter winner of the 1983
European Championship against
5.3-liter Jaguar V12s, Rover-Buick
V8s, and the turbos; also won
European title in 1981 and 1986
under differing regulations and Spa
24-hour races of 1985 and 1986

People talk

Dieter Quester's last European title
scored in 1986; Stefan Bellof and
Gerhard Berger show F1 speed
in coupes

Chapter 24

The Missing Link

The seductive 6-series races with honor across Europe and into American hearts

After years of winning with the CSL through the 1970s, BMW's many supporters in the European Touring Car Championship had to find a new weapon for the 1980s. A 320 won the 1980 laurels, but 1981 saw the first of three titles for the most radically-modified of those European Champions. Prepared to Group 2 specification by Eggenberger in Switzerland, this was the machine that did the winning in the hands of Helmut Kelleners and Umberto Grano. The same Italian-German-Swiss alliance took the title again in 1982, using a 528i.

Picture: BMW Werkfoto, 1981

BMW's biggest coupe found it as tough to replace the CS/CSL series in the hearts of "der BimmerHeads" as had the original E21 3-series when asked to substitute for the legendary 2002. On the street, BMW could dictate the pace of change: if you wanted a new BMW coupe after 1976, it had to be from the 6-series. On the racetrack, it was not so simple: the old "Batmobile" CSLs continued to race long after any factory sell-by date.

Right through 1979, with barely a trace of factory backing and with their homologated right to race expiring at the close of the season, the three-years-obsolete CSLs continued to race and win. In 1979, the CSL won 12 of 13 European Championship rounds to score title gold in six of seven possible European championship years. In fact, the only missing season since BMW's big-coupe home run in 1973 began was 1974. Then a Zakspeed Ford Escort nipped between battling BMW and the Ford Capris to interrupt the succession of BMW driver titles that even a change in regulations could not stem.

Just as for the 3-series versus the 2002, the 6-series was designed for a more-demanding public, not the racetrack. They carried more weight, had a larger cross-section to cut

through the air, and the 6-series powertrains—at least until the 3.4-liter 24-valve motors came on stream in the mid-1980s—were not a significant advance over their lighter predecessors. Production years for the mass-produced 635CSi were June 1978 to April 1989 (45,213 were made, including all markets).

By 1980, it was obvious even to the keenest of CSL supporters that the old warrior had earned retirement, particularly as BMW would not support those who raced it. The first stumbling steps for racing the 6-series were taken under the FIA European Group 2 formula (from 1980–81), followed by the 1983 homologation in then-current Group A of the 635CSi. It was the latter model that grabbed most international success, but the following will outline how those pioneers performed before getting into the more production-linked Group A racers.

The first racing 635CS for the European title hunt came from Racing Corporation Vienna and was prepared to the tightened Group 2 regulations that had banned many of the trick items—four-valve-per-cylinder heads, non-production gearboxes—in the later 1970s.

This early race 635 weighed in at 2,618 lbs/1,190 kg, quite a bit heavier than the last

That would have been nice...twice! The 1983 BMW-powered World Champion driver, Brazil's Nelson Piquet, straddles the bonnet of a 24-valve "M6" coupe: a combination that would have netted BMW even more success for the car they dubbed "The Gentleman's Racer." In fact, Piquet did take delivery on at least two special M635CSi coupes. The machine acquired at Hockenheim Grand Prix in August 1984 was an all-black Motorsport 3.7-liter stretch of the original 3.5. It developed 330 street horsepower in place of the production-line 286. Maximum speed, then unfettered by electronics, was quoted at 170 mph. The all-black machine would now be the ultimate collector's piece.

Picture: BMW Werkfoto, 1983

of the 24-valve CSLs. It also had another 100 bhp over the 367 bhp that the 12-valve six offered 1980 lead driver Umberto Grano. The Italian's teammates were Austrians Herbie Werginz and Harald Neger, and this trio won the opening two rounds of the 1980 European Championship, those of Monza and Vallelunga (Italy). The race 6-series then had to concede best to the title-winning Eggenberger BMW 320i of that year, winning only one more race, albeit the prestigious British Tourist Trophy round at Silverstone. From September 1980, BMW Italia became more seriously involved in the European Championship and backed a second 635CSi, whose drivers included Belgian Spa 24-hour winner (in a US-spec 530i) Eddy Joosen.

During 1981, the 635 again appeared in Group 2 for Europe, this time with more overt BMW support and Enny leather goods sponsorship. Drivers were Grano and German veteran Helmut Kelleners, who wrapped up a series that became more competitive with the advent of the new Group A regulations for 1982.

BMW met the European challenge of a Jaguar V12 XJS prepared by TWR and backed by Motul. From 1983 onward, Volvo 240 turbos and TWR Rover SD1 V8s (running the alloy eight descended from a 1960s Buick) wanted to come and beat the TWR Jags, which had become official works entries, resplendent in British Racing Green for 1983 onward.

The European race pace heated up, but BMW was not well-prepared for the rule-bending that inevitably followed. BMW was forced to field the less-powerful 528 for 1982, while the 635 CSi was not homologated for Group A until March 1, 1983 and the 24-valve M5/6 motor never made it to Group A recognition at all (for manufacturing/ONS inspection reasons noted in the preceding chapter).

Having homologated and modestly supported the 2.8-liter 5-series, BMW knew it needed more cubic capacity to meet the challenges of the 5.3-liter Jaguar and turbocharged models from Volvo (a 240 variant) and Mitsubishi (Starion). The 635CSi was the only variant with BMW's largest power plant produced in sufficient numbers to qualify for 5,000 per annum Group A, so this dictated the decision, rather than any sentiment for echoing the great feats of the charismatic CSL coupes.

There were to be no dramatic homologation moves from BMW on the 635CSi, and it turned out to be the (glamorous) workhorse of European championship racing. It was good enough to secure Dieter Quester another European title (1983), and strong enough to dominate the first six places in the last Nürburgring 6-hours to be held (also 1983).

Underlining the 635's fortitude in all-weather racing, current Formula 1 ace Gerhard Berger shared a winning 635 in the 1985 Spa 24-hours, and the second car home that year was a 635, too. In 1986, the 635 proved the 24-hour point comprehensively, the big Bimmers monopolizing the front four places, and BMW also came in fifth with a gallant 325i. BMW has really "been there, done that" and earned our respect.

One of many distinctive paint schemes applied to BMW factory competition cars was the Original Parts livery for the Schnitzer Group A 635CSi coupe, seen from 1983 onward. The reliable 285-bhp racing version of the single-cam engine was strong enough to win at classic European events around the Nürburgring and Spa-Francorchamps. The tanned Dieter Quester on the 635's handsome bonnet is an optional extra, available to those who allow him to "drive for food."

Picture: Author

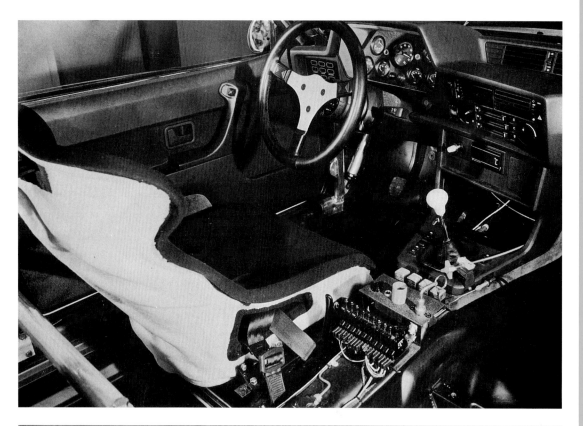

Enduring speed, with some of the world's best drivers thrashing it literally day and night, was the 635's racing strength, not track performance. The official race homologation (into FIA Group A) and press launch of the 635CSi reminds us that this BMW, like the Group A 528i in our previous chapter, was closer to its production roots than could have been expected after years of ever-wilder turbo machines in the German Championship.

In the cockpit, much of the door trim/ dash had to be retained and the later 3.4-liter six was modestly boosted to 285 bhp rather than a showroom 218. Weight was slashed by 539 lbs and the Group A car recorded 155-mph maximums alongside 0–60 mph in 6.7 seconds.

BMW Werkfoto, 1983; printed 1984, obtained 1988

The racing 635CSi

What went into a racing 635CSi? A lot of detail work, and some factory production changes that assisted in lowering race curb weight (1,161 kg/2,554 lbs) to the point that it had to be ballasted up to reach the class minimum of 1,185 kg/2,607 lbs. In June 1981, the production 6-series had gone through substantial alterations, including adoption of the 7-series double-link front suspension, the 5-series-based rear trailing arms (13 degrees), and a decrease in curb weight of 60 kg /132 lbs.

There were no lightweight panel tricks. BMW had anticipated the worst in crash test regulations during the 6-series' production gestation. Once in production, BMW found that it could provide at least the same crash-test performance without the designed bulk in steel grade or body construction. Weight was shaved back, but still the fundamental changes continued.

The summer of 1982 saw the 635CSi become an unbadged 634, as the single overhead-cam six dropped from 3,453 cc and a 93.4-mm bore (originally a Motorsport-only move) to 3,430 cc on a safer 92-mm bore (as found in 3,210-cc BMW six-cylinders). Allied to a familiar stroke of 86 mm, this 3.4-liter replaced the 3.5 for duty in 635CSi and 735 derivatives.

For the street, a 635 continued to be rated at 218 bhp at 5,200 rpm and 224 lb-ft of torque at 4,000 rpm. Compression escalated from 9.3:1 to 10.0:1 in the changeover to 3,430 cc and reflected more sophisticated Bosch Digital Motor Electronics (DME).

In race terms, the most radical engine engineering was applied to the camshaft timing and lift, plus a rise in compression to a minimum 11.0:1. I had the privilege of driving an Alpina-engined 1983 example, normally raced by Hans Stuck in the UK. A works-supported car, the extraction of an extra 67 bhp for the Alpina under Group A rules had Alpina boss

The keys to so many BMW Motorsport successes since the 1970s (left to right): BMW dealer/driver Roberto Ravaglia of Venice, Italy; Rudi Gmeiner, BMW Motorsport technical liason from Munich; Charley Lamm of Schnitzer at Freillassing; and Johnny Cecotto, Venezuelan former motorcycle champ who lives in Italy.

Picture: BMW Werkfoto, 1986/Archiv, 1997

Burkard Bovensiepen sighing, "Much of the work is in the electronics from Bosch, and this is so expensive for the private tuner or owner. Bosch doesn't want people re-programming their electronics, and the prices are too high for customers."

Alpina succeeded on that occasion, although the Stuck BMW never managed to beat the Rover on the racetracks of Britain that season, despite some epic encounters with the TWR machine for Steve Soper.

This electronic programming era and racing sedans that became progressively more race and less sedan did not suit the Alpina policy of supplying parts to privateers. Alpina's race star began to lose its twinkle during the mid-1980s, and Schnitzer—who would farm its public performance conversions and parts supplies out under a licensing agreement—became ever stronger.

The 635 represented that Schnitzer turning point, for Charly Lamm's team management was unmatched for European endurance racing strategy. Add that intellect (Charly was top-grade US university material, diverted by the Schnitzer family racing business) to BMW durability with speed, and you can see how BMW became the most successful long-distance sedan racers.

The 1983 Stuck car was pretty typical of how the 635 stayed in touring-car trim for 1983–86, for the restrictive Group A regulations strangled normally-aspirated motors. German officialdom and its reluctance to falsify production figures meant the 635CSi stayed right around 285 bhp on 6,000 rpm and 254 lb-ft of torque on 5,500 revs. That gave a power-to-weight ratio of 243.6 bhp per ton—better than the 528 but no match for a V12 Jaguar or a turbocharged Volvo.

BMW 635 race compensations were the 6.9- to 8.0-mpg fuel consumption (incurring fewer fuel stops than their rivals), dependability, and BMW Motorsport's hiring of some extraordinary driving talent. The 1997

Benetton and former Ferrari pilot Berger was the most obvious example, but Motorsport also hired Stefan Bellof to pedal a 635. They reckoned the young hot-shoe (like Manfred Winkelhock, subsequently killed in a racing Porsche 962) was worth "over a second a lap, saving us hundreds of thousands of development Deutschemarks," spluttered a happy Dieter Stappert of this budget-conscious bolt-in speed.

The rest of a racing 635 was pretty conventional. The suspension had to act on the same principles as those found in production, but quite a few bits were carried over from the Group 2/IMSA CSL via 528 to 635. These including some of the big brake/wheel-bearing options and fabricated suspension components.

BMW Motorsport offered replacement lower arms for the MacPherson struts, replacement rear trailing arms (significantly stronger), center-lock wheel nuts, and a selection of three spring damper (Bilstein) choices that multiplied as the seasons rolled by. In 1983, wheels and tires were BBS multi-piece 11 x 16-inch alloys, shod by Dunlop in the UK. Pirelli was, however, the favored supplier for the most successful Schnitzer BMW 635s of 1985–86.

I drove the ex-works Group A 635 on 1,200-lb/in front springs and 750-lb/in rears, but the British demands were at odds with Europe for increasing spring stiffness and stiffer anti-roll bars. That Donington circuit test car had 32-mm front and 20-mm rear bars. The steering remained on the ball-and-nut steering box system, but the standard 14.5:1 or a quicker 13.6:1 ratio were options.

Similarly, there were three choices of final-drive ratios—a ZF limited-slip differential set at 75 percent pre-load when I drove. The gearbox definitely had CSL heritage and the Getrag provided the same good-natured command of four ratios in an H-pattern, first isolated on a dogleg, closest to the left-hand driver. Gear ratios were radically different, with a

2.33 first gear as compared to a 3.822 on the wide-ratio stock gearbox and appropriately close ratios thereafter. This allowed a suitably "tall" first for racing getaways—most of which were rolling-start affairs in Europe. In Britain, they stuck with standing starts for their national race series, and the standard single-disc plate would wilt under that strain.

6-series for the record

What results did the 6-series achieve in Group A trim? In hindsight, the best year was the first, when the turbo cars were not quite so feisty and the big-capacity Jags and Rovers were not always durable enough for the long slogs around Europe. BMW won the first encounter—held at Monza in March—against Jaguar. BMW filled eight of the top ten spots after 500 km/310.5 miles of the legendary Italian track!

The final European round, on September 25, 1983, was at the badly-organized venue of Zolder in Belgium. The season could not have been closer, since both BMW and Jaguar had won five European Championship rounds apiece, the only other qualifier going to Rover. The front runners—16 of them—practiced within 2.5 seconds of each other, and there were 46 runners and riders to watch.

Stefan Bellof hit the front for BMW and led much of the opening 35 laps, but nothing could take that much abuse and last an hour, never mind a slog from sunshine into twilight. The other BMWs did last the pace and supported Dieter Quester as his Schnitzer coupe scooped up another championship. It was BMW's 13th title in the 17 years since it had contested the European Championship when Hubert Hahne won its first European driver's title back in 1966.

This was Quester's fourth and last European title, but BMW won again with the 635 in 1986, and took two more titles with the original M3 before the European series folded in 1988. Today, BMW continues to contest events that were part of that European series, its record in the annual Spa 24-hours apparently strengthening by the year. Nobody offers BMW serious opposition at home on the old Nürburgring, but today the international accent is on national 2-liter SuperTourers, a category that is no automatic BMW domain in the late 1990s.

In 1984, TWR returned with a trio of the V12-powered Jaguar XJS coupes in factory livery. The BMW wins became scattered, with only Helmut Kelleners and Gianfranco Brancatelli offering consistent opposition. That said, a Belgian BMW team entry for France's Danny Snobeck/Alain Cudini did win an early

event, despite a freak accident that involved another BMW mounting their coupe!

The only other 1984 compensation was that Volvo had enough pace to win, so it was not all Jaguar all the time—it just seemed like it. At home in Germany, the press gave BMW a roasting. Then national German media turned to the preparation of the winning Jaguars. German magazine-market leader *auto motor und sport* asserted British illegality, illustrating its complaints, particularly with regard to fuel carried and engine size: both were alleged oversized.

Nothing was proven, and the combination of Tom Walkinshaw and the Jaguars that his company prepared took the 1984 European title. In contrast, TWR's unstoppable run of wins in the 1983 British series was successfully protested by BMW dealer/driver Frank Sytner. TWR Rovers contesting the British title only were retrospectively disqualified halfway into 1984,

Racing across Europe: Hans Stuck in the "Original Teile/Genuine Parts" 635CSi from Schnitzer opens a slight gap on Eggenberger's 1981–82 European Champion, Helmut Kelleners.

Picture: BMW Werkfoto, 1984

The Wurth company, long-time supporters of leading German Championship race teams, backed this Schnitzer-prepared-and-entered 635CSi in the European Championship of 1984. Despite the presence of drivers like multiple touring-car Champion Roberto Ravaglia (seen here), BMW lost the title Dieter Quester had won in 1983 to the cars of former BMW driver Tom Walkinshaw's TWR. This time, TWR won with Jaguar V12 coupes, but BMW failed to win the European title only twice in the 1980s [1984 and 1985], before the series was axed in 1988.

Picture: BMW Werkfoto, 1984

Although BMW Motorsport/Schnitzer lost the European title to Eggenberger Volvo turbos in 1985, the 635 still pounded around the Belgian Ardennes to bring back another Spa 24-hour win. Here is that Schnitzer multinational winner, driven by Roberto Ravaglia of Italy, Grand Prix winner Gerhard Berger of Austria, and Marc Surer of Switzerland.

Picture: BMW Werkfoto, 1985

This was exactly the racing opposition BMW faced in the mid-1980s. At the 1986 Spa 24-hours, a factory Rover V8 races for the first corner with the winning BMW 635CSi of Roberto Ravaglia, Gerhard Berger, and Emanuele Pirro. Behind is one of the very quick turbo Volvos (dubbed the "Flying Bricks"!) and one of two works Ford XR4Ti turbos. At Spa, as ever, BMW ruled the roost and finished up with a one-two winning result.

Picture: BMW Archiv, released 1997

with fines totaling £100,000 imposed by the national sporting authority.

BMW finished 1984 with just three European wins, failing to secure that season's Spa 24-hours, while a lone Jaguar won its first day-and-night victory of the 1980s.

For 1985, Volvo did get its turbocharged act together, and the 350-bhp Swedish box-cars became regular winners, securing the European title for Brancatelli. The high spot of the BMW racing year was the victory of Gerhard Berger/Marc Surer and Roberto "Bob Ravioli" Ravaglia over its sister Schnitzer coupe at Spa 24-hours, but BMW struggled for qualifying pace.

A brace of Eggenberger Volvo turbos surprised most to manage third and fourth on much reduced boost. So even at Spa, the 1985 Volvo race-winning threat was as real as it became during 1996–97 in England and Australia. Those 1990s race 850/S40 Volvos were created by TWR, while other divisions of Walkinshaw's empire raced Nissans at Le Mans, Yamaha motors in Grand Prix, and Holdens for Australian 5-liter V8 rules.

Berger set fastest lap at over 96 mph over Spa's now purpose-built Ardennes curves in 1985. There were six BMWs in the top ten finishers, versus a brace of Volvos and Alfa GTV6s. The rest of 1985 was pretty unhappy

Winning 6-series warriors battle the spray and each other (look at the headlamps on the lead car) to win not only another Spa 24-hours but also the return of the European Championship in 1986.

Picture: BMW Archiv, 1997

for von BimmerHeads, and the best Championship points tally at the end went to Ravaglia, ninth in the over-2,500-cc class behind a horde of Volvos and Rovers.

It was the worst result I can recall in my research for BMW in the European sedan series. Schnitzer did not contest all the championship rounds, while Berger put in some fabulous work at the wheel of the outclassed 635 on their combined appearances. His new-found Formula 1 confidence allowed not only speed, but that sedan rarity, pace without curb crawling and underbody damage.

In fact, 1986 was the season BMW won the overall driver's title again—Ravaglia and his Schnitzer-entered works 635CSi won out by just one point to Briton Win Percy (Rover V8) on an official recount. The contest went right down to the final wire. Some compensation came from a BMW 325i winning its division

and completing the top three, overall. More about that in the M3 development chapter.

Back on the 635CSi front in 1986, Roberto Ravaglia starred in four first-place finishes for the Schnitzer equipe, but (unusually) the Spa 24-hours was not one of that winning quartet. What happened to Ravaglia and the leading 635CSi he shared with Berger and Pirro at the annual Spa 24-hours? As you would expect, it was a leading runner. Unlike the BMW 635 that would win for Dieter Quester/Altfrid Heger and the injured Thierry Tassin, it avoided the sand traps and any subsequent need for an illicit tow!

Ravaglia and company were leading until 2 hours 15 minutes prior to the 5:00 p.m. finish. Then an alternator bracket fractured and its Schnitzer-BMW teammate (both in the famous black-and-white BMW Parts/Original BMW Teile livery) thundered through to win. The result was the BMW 635 haul of the first four finishing positions, with the fifth taken by BMW as well, for the Vogt 325i defeated a French-prepared Mercedes 190.

As expected, "Bob Ravioli" was always on the top-three podium pace throughout the 1986 season, and he took the fight to the last Portuguese round at the Estoril Grand Prix track. Others did the physical stuff: Dieter Quester even rammed an Australian Holden V8 (GM product) in an effort to improve Ravaglia's finishing position versus the Rover of Win Percy!

Disproving the dictum—often credited to Roger Penske—"Show me a good loser and I'll show you a loser," Roberto Ravaglia was finally declared the official champion by the FIA at the close of 1986 play. It was this sort of reversal of on-track race results that weakened the credibility of the European series to the point where it was dropped at the end of 1988.

Ravaglia progressed to become not just BMW's most successful driver, but also the holder of most European-centered championships: the Venetian BMW dealer gathered up European, Italian, German, and world titles for BMW. The only title I have seen Ravaglia conspicuously fail to secure was Great Britain in the 1996 McLaren-BMW Motorsport assault.

In the 1986/87 winter, BMW Motorsport was intensively developing the M3. There was the possibility that the 3.5-liter 635CSi might prove quicker than its 2.3-liter junior—so much so that the possiblility of running the 635CSi on into the opening three races of 1987 was published.

Back-to back trials were conclusive: the M3 was up to two seconds a lap quicker, even when it was far from its predicted 300 bhp. At last, the coupe that BMW never intended to race could be pensioned off, complete with a pedigree that many purpose-built competition cars cannot equal.

Ten years on, and one of the "Original Parts" 635s is still taking a racetrack airing for Dieter Quester in the heat of a Sunday afternoon. This time, the venue is California, and the 6 is just one of many competition BMW treats laid out by BMW Mobile Tradition and the North American operation to celebrate the BMW marque. Most of the exhibits were still driven flat out!

Picture: Klaus Schnitzer, US, 1996

QUICK FACTS

Period

1983–92

Product

The first production M3 and its Evolutions

Performance

Original 2.3 (200 bhp) allowed 0–60 mph in 7.0 seconds and 145 mph maximum; Sport Evo 2.5 of 238 bhp gave 0–60 mph in 6.2 seconds and 154 mph maximum; Showroom Stock engine/motor layout was 195 or 200 bhp in 1986 and 238 bhp in 1990 at 2.5 liters; in-line 16-valve DOHC four of 2.3 liters (1986–89) had enlarged bores, with same configuration for 2.5-liter

Achievements

Commercial as well as competitive success; raced in European Group A, N, and more-radical German National Championship trim; also rallied at World Championship level, Group A

People

BMW's Rosche on engine butchery; Thomas Ammerschlager on design briefs; Prodrive's David Richards on rally lore; author on road and track action

Chapter 25

M3 for Muscle

How BMW Motorsport created E30s for road and track performance

Outside Germany, the creation of "Homologation Specials" (cars manufactured to serve a motorsport purpose) was usually regarded as a necessary chore to be completed at minimal cost in the shortest possible time to gain a competitive advantage. This resulted in a number of British, French, and Italian street machines that were hastily slung together. They often had to be properly assembled by their owners after being dumped at dealers or open-air-stored at their respective factories.

Germany played to different street rules. Government rules demanded that the cars meet road regulations and were fully (TUV) inspected, while the customers demanded far more civilization and durability than the British and Italians expected in the 1970s and 1980s.

All of that meant that you could buy (whisper it) a 1981–90 Quattro turbo knowing that it had been through the same proving process as its Audi classmates and was fully equipped. The mid-1980s gestation of M3 followed the same pattern of total street-development of the kind that, for instance, Ford abbreviated violently for their turbocharged Cosworth Sierras of the same period.

BMW Motorsport GmbH was assigned responsibility for the ultimate E30, which had to be made at the rate of at least 5,000 units a year to qualify for International Group A and N competition recognition (homologation). Just how seriously BMW Motorsport took the M3 project can be judged from the fact that it allowed Paul Rosche on the engine program and transferred former Ford Cologne and Audi development engineer Thomas Ammerschlager to take charge of the road-car project. The race car was subject to parallel evolution, but was the work of a separate team, as detailed in the next chapter.

Every major aspect of the M3 that boosted its motorsport potential was examined, but not all such features had to be built for the street. Braking and handling were improved, but not to serious competition standards, for that was not a requirement of the homologation process.

The heart of the M3

As for any BMW, the heart was its engine. A massively-overbored four-cylinder was constructed using traditional BMW twin overhead-camshaft, 16-valve competition-engine principles. It had immense strength, both in durability

Lights, music, action! Enter the M3, a four-cylinder automotive barrel of fun that made even 2002 diehards think, "Well...maybe, just maybe, there is another way to have more fun from A to B...."

Picture: BMW Werkfoto, 1985

and potential horsepower, but was a little bulkier than strictly necessary for a racing four-cylinder, owing to its six-cylinder heritage.

Basic engine research started in the summer of 1981. The first principle to establish was the worth of a light and simple 16-valve four-cylinder over BMW's proud in-line six-cylinder traditions. The marketing men were worried, too, for the 3-series performance options for the public from June 1976 onward were promoted first around the carburated 320 and then the 1977 fuel-injected 323i.

Of course, the M3's E36 successor did have an in-line six, but (although originally planned) that model did not enjoy an international Motorsport career with the factory.

So why did BMW Motorsport not pick the six for the original M3 back in the 1980s? Paul Rosche recalled, "The most important reason was our experience with four-valve-per-cylinder Formula 2, but the six-cylinder M1 and M635 were also important. We had proved the large cylinder bore (93.4 mm) for motor racing and production. The cylinder head design of the M635 looked so good for us that

we did the first development work in two weeks by cutting up the head for a six-cylinder and fitting it to a 2-liter four!

Rosche gusted with laughter, "We cut off the end from an M635 of 24 valves; two cylinders were removed and the water passages closed off. Yes, now we have a cylinder head to put on the iron-block four. That's what we needed to show us the M3 could work!"

Braveheart! Originally cut down from the M5/6 24-valve six, the S14-coded unit contained the classic central spark plug, quad-valve technology to make 195 bhp at 6,750 rpm with a catalyst or another 5 horsepower without "Der Kat." Torque dropped 7 lb-ft from 177 at 4,750 rpm when the catalytic converter was fitted, but BMW soon learned to run all M3 derivatives, Evos included, with catalyzator exhaust.

Picture: BMW Werkfoto, 1986

Thus all the vital dimensions—bore and stroke, valves—were set to be those of the pedigree six-cylinder M1 motor. Rosche added, "It worked well, straight away. Remember, a six-cylinder motor would just have been too heavy for the best race handling of a front-engine car, and the crankshaft for a six is longer than we would like for racing rpms. It is a more compact engine, the four, and we knew the four very well for motorsports," summarized Munich's motor legend.

An enlargement to the production 2,302-cc for maximum effect in the 2.5-liter racing class was possible via a steel crankshaft and an 84-mm bore to cooperate with the 93.4-mm block. The bore and stroke remained true to the M1 for all but 600 examples of the final 2.5 liter Sport Evolution, which had an even bigger bore (95 mm) and 87-mm stroke to support 2,467 cc.

The M3 had to go through all the usual BMW factory durability tests, but in a far shorter span than normal to meet homologation and consequent production schedules. Development tales told me that the M3 spent its time in all the usual durability tests for hot and cold climates. The M3 was fully crash-tested and also had to go through a pretty severe emissions control panic, occasioned by a late decision to make a politically correct catalytic-converter version available at launch.

As for most BMWs, there were numerous proving sessions at Nürburgring. The M3 racked up at least 6,200 miles at this historic venue, relying on the famous old track sections to prove the suspension under duress from October 1984 onward. The most spectacular high-speed tests were three flat-out sessions held on the southern toe of Italy. The Nardo speed bowl saw the M3 hurtle round at more than 140 mph for a minimum of 31,000 miles.

That four-valve-per-cylinder head layout, as used in earlier M635/M5, was descended directly from the mid-engine M1 of 1978–81. The resulting engine was internally coded S14, stamped on the block as 234 for all 2.3 liters, a point worth remembering when analyzing motor and chassis codes.

M3 motors were built in a Munich factory corner, alongside the V12s, by the highest-paid hourly workers in BMW AG; even "bathroom breaks" were streamlined with women bringing these aristocrats of the engine-building craft their beverages. It wasted too much expensive labor time if they downed tools. Politically incorrect, but this practice predicted how Spartanburg and American production costs would become vital to BMW in the 1990s.

The M3's European debut

In February 1983, BMW Motorsport's M3 project took on more impetus as the factory racing replacement for the 528i/635i sedans and coupes, which were less competitive propositions. The surprise was how many M3s the public would buy. Such homologation specials traditionally cost the factory money; instead, BMW's experience with the M3 was selling close to 20,000 at profitable price margins.

The chunky M3 made a static debut at the September 1985 Frankfurt Show. Reactions were predictably warm, some effusive in the German-language press. BMW Motorsport needed this kind of support since there was a hidden agenda: a 3-series/3.5-liter motor marriage was mooted, one that specialists such as Alpina were to profit from when the factory (thankfully) decided to steer a more maneuverable M3 course.

Another internal hurdle that was overcome was to convince high-level management of M3's public road abilities. This was done in a direct-comparison test, back-to-back, with the 325i and the Mercedes 2.3-liter 16-valve Cosworth sedan. The latter had beaten BMW to the high-performance two-door production line. Yet Mercedes was frequently sneered at in Germany for having a rough, British-made, Cosworth-headed, 16-valve engine.

After the toughest tests, BMW management was convinced and the Type Approval reference machines could be built, following managerial sign-off. The project received further practical street engineering expertise in 1985 when Thomas Ammerschlager entered BMW Motorsport.

Ammerschlager assumed overall responsibility for developing a product to be mass-produced by the mainstream BMW AG in Munich. He coordinated the overall conception and production of the M3 until he left in the middle of 1989 for a senior-management position in the chassis-engineering development department of the parent BMW AG concern, based at the Fiz facility.

Another internal obstacle that had to be overcome was that of producing a car on normal production lines with so many plastics. Steel was used for the extended wheelarches, which were designed to accommodate racing wheel rim widths of up to 10 inches. Otherwise, the Motorsport engineers were able to use more plastics than had been seen in a production 3-series. The fact that steel would be used for the main body meant that development time for the body was minimal, owing to the need to get the body-in-steel tooling prepared.

Radical body changes were finally allowed by the parent company, including raking the enlarged rear window to provide better airflow to the 40-mm/1.6-inch rear trunk-lid/spoiler assembly (in SMC-plastic). Hard plastics also completed the side and front spoiler "body kit," but the square fenders, as for the Audi quattro coupes of the 1980s, remained of steel.

Aerodynamics were also critical for BMW competition aspirations. These were not just confined to the obvious spoilers, for the rear trunk-

The rear end of the E30-based 3-series was most radically modified in M-guise, the trunk-lid height raised and the back screen raked to suit aerodynamic demands, cutting the rear-end lift that affects all mass-production cars.

Picture: BMW Werkfoto, 1986

lid height was elevated and back window raked. Cutting aerodynamic axle lift by harnessing modest downforce energy would be priorities throughout the M3's career. Specifically, such aerodynamics contributed to 160-mph racing stability and road car aerodynamics of 0.33 Cd, not bad for such a boxy outline.

Fit, finish, and paint standards were as would be expected of BMW. I have now seen 55,000–100,000-mile examples that have creditably resisted the ravages of British and North American weather.

For used-car buyers, I would recommend ensuring that your potential choice is not a faked M3 of cheap body-kit parentage. Also, make sure that genuine BMW standard panels have been used in any crash repairs: some of the aftermarket stuff is rubbish, or is very poorly installed.

Engineering the street M3

New engineering influences were most pronounced in the modified-strut front suspension, the geometry featuring "triple" the castor of the 3-series and a "quicker" power-assisted rack with a 19.6:1 ratio. Both moves increased feel and high-speed stability: in fact, the M3's outstanding handling characteristics were unmatched by any contemporary sedan.

Other relevant chassis changes covered new front and rear roll bars of sturdy girth, which were associated with new pivot points, and twin-tube Boge gas dampers were installed. However, the basic layout of the rear axle, with 15-degree raked semi-trailing arms was retained, albeit with stiffer springs and bushings. BMW never put the effective M3 chassis work at the disposal of lesser 3-series.

Why not? A BMW engineer, who declined to be named, revealed in 1990, "All the M3 suspension parts can be fitted to less expensive 3-series. Indeed, the basic mounting points are the same, but it was very expensive to make this change. The parts were more expensive to produce than the standard ones. I think this was another good reason why they were not adopted for any other 3-series in production."

On record, the engineering contact would do no more than nod at the suggestion that BMW mainstream managers were unconvinced that clientele buying the 325i were sufficiently appreciative of vehicle handling to justify the expense of changing to a system created by Motorsport, rather than mainstream, BMW engineers. There was a strong feeling of NIH (Not Invented Here) about the rejection of M3 agility for lesser E30s of mainstream parentage.

Engineering sufficient braking capability involved some expedient raids of the contemporary 5-series (E28) for a set of wheel bearings and vented front discs in 284-mm/11.2-inch

diameters. Rear M3 brakes were 250-mm/9.8-inch solid units. The quartet of discs was beautifully balanced and monitored by ABS from Bosch on all production M3s.

Standard equipment within the German price included a ZF multi-plate limited-slip differential torqued to a soft 25 percent pre-loading, a bigger 70-liter/15.4-gallon fuel tank, tinted glass, electric twin mirrors, and a Getrag five speeder with Borg Warner synchronizers. First gear was isolated closest to the left-hand-drive pilot in contemporary competition style.

The cabin was completed with the BMW-built sports seats that were optional on lesser 3-series, and a tactile three-spoke Motorsport steering wheel added to the solid air of the gray-toned environment. The seats were adjustable via three levers and knobs to cater for height, thigh support, backrest rake, legroom, and tilt.

Original options included a simplified onboard computer (I managed 26.9 mpg in 93 public-road miles at the launch). Also offered were air conditioning, power windows, central locking, leather trim, and the usual plethora of stereo sounds.

The usual BMW "command post" driving position emphasized switches and red-needle instrumentation as an object lesson in comprehensible clarity. The original had a 260-km/h (161-mph) speedometer. That was matched by an 8,000-rpm tachometer with a 7,300-rpm redline. The rev-counter carried an oil temperature gauge instead of the usual 3-series econometer. It could be punished to a constant 140 autobahn mph on a summer day (say, 30° C ambient) and the oil temperature needle stayed steadier than BMW's bank balance sheets in the 1980s.

First of the Evolution M3s with improved aerodynamics for racing purposes came in 1988 in Europe. Power was also increased to 220 bhp, all with catalytic convertor exhausts. All known BMW Evolution and production M3 variants are listed in a chart within this chapter.

Picture: BMW AG/GB, 1988

The front and back of it. Aerodynamics were constantly featured in the "Evo" process. This 1989 UK model displays a fenced lower addition to the rear wing and the jutting front spoiler first seen in 1988. This one was plated as a Roberto Ravaglia limited edition and the "blacked-out" alloys were standard, along with 215 bhp. Continental Europeans (France, Germany and Italy) had a similar machine with a plaque signed by Johnny Cecotto. Both had production runs of around 500.

Pictures: Author, UK, 1989

The Evolutionary M3 developments

The further Evolutions of the M3, which began to trickle through in its 1987 international racing debut season, were the cream topping on already-fine chocolate cake. For BMW Motorsport and its marketers, Evolutionary M3s were an opportunity to wring the most out of the same basic format for competition or commerce.

It was not until the final 600-off 2.5 Sport Evos that engine capacity altered, so there were some pretty tricky aerodynamic and engine enhancements to follow. BMW Motorsport reported the development of the following M3 variants and supplied their build dates.

The European derivatives were listed as follows:

Type	Bhp	Production dates	Production limit (units)
2.3 M3	200	9/86 to 7/89	Unlimited
2.3 M3 Kat	195	9/86 to 5/89	Unlimited
2.3 M3 Evo 1	200	2/87 to 5/87	505
2.3 M3 Evo II	220	3/88 to 5/88	501
2.3 M3 KAT, Europameister'88	195	10/88 to 11/88	150
2.3 M3 Ravaglia/ Cecotto	215	4/89 to 7/89	508*
2.3 M3 Kat	215	9/89 to 12/90	Unlimited
2.5 M3 Evo III	238	1/90 to 3/90	600

*The author's official UK test car was number 73 of 508, according to the plaque on its body.

The above data gives the basics of what was done in the Evolution or limited-edition M3 market, but for competition purposes, the most important derivatives were the Evo I, II, and III of 1987–88 and 1990.

All Evos marked BMW's allowable annual attempts to incorporate updated competitiveness in the homologation procedure for international racing only. This could only be done once a season, and the homologation procedure through the "Evo" process was not permitted to alter the specification on Group A or N rallying format.

What was the effect of those vital dimensions on M3 ownership, dynamics, and performance? The benchmark performance figures for an original European M3 were impressive. Some 6,750 rpm and 200 bhp were 1986 specifications for the M3, sold only in left-hand-drive to the public (or 195 bhp in catalytic-converter trim), enough to claim up to 146 mph and 0–62 mph comfortably under 7 seconds, with or without a cleansed exhaust. Independent tests in Britain showed that the M3 in any trim was substantially the fastest of the E30-bodied 3-series.

The UK weekly *Autocar* ran a trio of 2.3 M3s, including a brace of 200-bhp examples (one convertible, one sedan) and reckoned they were good for up to 146 mph with 0–60 mph in the 6- to 7-second bracket, and 0–100 mph in less than 20 seconds.

Externally, the 1987 Evo I was identified by extended front and rear spoilers and used a lightweight trunk lid. This model gave no practical road benefits, save a slight increase in stability at higher speeds.

Autocar's most consistent results came from the 1988 Evolution II with 220 bhp on the original 6,750-rpm peak. The motor generated that 220 bhp using replacement camshafts, pistons, lightened flywheel, air intake trunk, and Bosch Motronic chip. It was mated to a slightly taller final drive (3.15:1), and BMW claimed a substantial increase in performance.

Usual factory M3 figures were 146 mph and 0–62 mph in 6.7 seconds. For the Evolution II, BMW recorded 152 mph and 0–60 mph in the usual 6.7 seconds, and *Autocar* certainly found an improvement over its 200-bhp M3 test experience.

Instead of recording 7.1 seconds for 0–60 mph and 19 seconds for the 0–100 mph drag, *Autocar* returned 6.6 and 17.8 seconds respectively. They timed 148 mph around the banked Millbrook speed bowl, equating to 150 mph on a flat road; their best M3 fuel consumption was 26 mpg.

The 220-bhp level was the best road M3, smoother than the later 2.5 and practically as fast, so long as you kept the revs in the 5,000–7,000 rpm band. The chassis, running Pirelli P700s of 225/45 section on 7.5 x 16-inch BBS alloys, never seemed to run out of dry-road grip, understeering wide of an apex if overdriven. In the wet, this M3 would still slide if the full 7,300-rpm redline was employed in second or third, as would the later 2.5 M3.

Evolutionary clues

For the secondhand buyer, here are a few general M3 variant identification tips. The first Evolution model (200 bhp) had an "E" punched onto the cast eye of the cylinder head, which is underneath the fourth cylinder throttle housing—it can only be seen by using a mirror!

Evolution II (220 bhp) carried an air collector and valve cover in white, also painted with Motorsport stripes. Evolution II also sported additional spoilers, these carrying front brake ducts and the extra lip on the rear wing, resting on a lightweight trunk lid that was supported by further weight saving in material thickness for the rear wing, bumper supports, back screen, and rear side windows. Altogether, the factory expected to save 10 kg/22 lbs to lower the racing weight.

Identification clues on the Ravaglia/Cecotto machines included the Evolution II spoilers and the use of body color for the air collector and rocker cover, which meant either Misano Red or Nogaro Silver. The test car I had bore a

plaque inside that announced it was "M3 73/508 1989 BMW Motorsport GmbH." Cars from these series should be signed either by Roberto Ravaglia (UK only) or Johnny Cecotto.

Mix-and-match M3 Evos

The factory also supplied some exceptionally helpful notes on updating engine power between models, meaning that you can update a 200-bhp M3 into full Evolutionary specs, but only among 2.3-liters.

BMW Motorsport tells me that the standard 200 bhp (non-catalyst car) can be uprated some 20 bhp to the level of Evolution II via its parts sales department (Rennteilevertrieb) and a reprogrammed Bosch Digital Motor Electronics (DME) microprocessor. The latter is identified as the usual Bosch 0261.200.090, but has a modification to the labeling that cannot be revealed for security reasons. This indicates that Motorsport has reprogrammed the standard unit.

Bosch I.D. codes for all M3s run the prefixes 0261.200, followed by 071 for the 200/195-bhp machines and the 1988–89 Cabrios, 090 for Evolution II, and 091 for all 215-bhp M3s and the last (1990–91) Cabrios. These were the Ravaglia/Cecotto specials, plus the M3 KAT sedan (only the 1989–90 production span). The 092 suffix is reserved for the 238-bhp 2.5-liters.

The same kind of hardware and reprogrammed software approach will increase output of the catalyst M3 from a showroom 195 horsepower to 210 bhp. The Bosch DME programming I.D. is 0261.200.091. Hardware replacement includes new inlet manifolding and heavy-duty valve springs. Motorsport also gave us some handy hints for identifying specific M3 types. Aside from the chassis data, other useful statistics include motor identification codes which are based on 23 4E A to cover initial production from the M3 sedan to Evolution I, uprated beyond this point to I.D.-specific rarities.

Again because of security, genuine customers must withdraw such valuable details from their BMW network. A genuine 2.5-liter does follow logic in using 25 as the initial engine number numeral, but leaves the rest of the code for BMW to reveal upon application.

M3 convertibles

BMW Motorsport hand-made convertible M3s from May 1988 to July 1991, constructing that strictly-controlled number at substantial prices. You could say this was the beginning of BMW Individual programs, but a purist would argue that BMW Motorsport had always been open to hand-tailoring cars for their initially-rarefied commercial clients. To expand such trade (and other assembly projects), Motorsport was subdivided and expanded in 1986 to embrace the factory at Garching, as detailed in chapter 14.

BMW Motorsport employed over 400 people at the two factory sites in Munich and Garching suburbs in the late 1980s and early 1990s. Some created the original M3, but it was built (save for the subsequent 1988–91 convertible) on the main Munich production lines. The soft-top rarity (less than 800 made) was crafted at Motorsport's Garching plant.

The M3 convertible almost did not make it into production for 1988 as a four-cylinder at all. The first show car had a 4x4 drivetrain hitched to the usual BMW 325i power plant. This became a one-off when the realists persuaded management to opt for the four-cylinder M3 unit and rear drive. The original M3 convertible has never sold in large numbers (the total was 786) , but it was never intended for huge sales. Yearly production figures, as well as those the for M3 sedans, are appended at the close of this chapter.

The ultimate production E30 M3

A 2.5-liter final competition-prompted twist to the original M3 theme was briefly produced (four months and 600 examples) in the gap between E30 lines closing down and E36 output commencing. Detailed specifications for the M3 Sport Evo, drawn alongside the later 215-bhp M3 of 2.3 liters for instant comparison purposes, is found in in the statistical data at the end of this chapter.

The big changes began with a capacity increase from 2,302 cc to 2,467 cc, via an elongated crankshaft throw and bigger

The final Evolution. The 1990 ultimate twist to the E30 outline was a 2.5-liter of almost 240 bhp that had a three-way adjustable wing set. This lasted the racers until the summer of 1992, when they received yet further extensions, front and rear, to put them back on the German Championship pace in their final season.

Picture: BMW Werkfoto, 1989

bores. Power escalated by 18 bhp and torque by 10 Nm. Then BMW radically rethought M3 aerodynamics. Both front and rear spoilers could be adjusted, there was a small degree of ground effect, the front wheelarches were enlarged, front suspension was lowered, and the interior was made over. Sport Evo featured a distinctive Motorsport look, along with a suede look to the leather steering-wheel rim, gear knob, and hand-brake grip.

The story behind the M3 Sport Evo was far from the "bigger is better" manufacturer development trail. The 2.5-liter had been conceived as the basis of a more-effective weapon against Mercedes in the German Touring Car Championship.

It was announced against the festive backdrop of the 1989 BMW Motorsport Christmas conference celebrations, for the company had won the national title in 1989 (against the Mercedes odds) and intended to win again. Even though Mercedes had been equipped with full-production 2.5-liters (plus subsequent short-stroke Evolutions), and BMW had won, BMW Motorsport felt it wanted to offer an equivalent big four-cylinder to compete right up to the class capacity limit.

German TV audiences watched as the menacing black 2.5 M3 Sport Evolution was unwrapped with due fuss and fanfares. Truth to tell, there was not much to see externally—just the bolt-adjustable wing set and the hint of serious intent given by the lowered front end and enlarged wheel arches. These would hold the accurately forecast move to the 18-inch diameter wheels in 1990 Group A.

BMW engine engineer Franz Zinnecker commented, "For the 2.5-liter M3, I had rejoined BMW Motorsport whilst Paul Rosche was moved onto another project that I cannot discuss [McLaren V12 of 48 valves—JW]. Our priorities were to keep on increasing the competition potential of the 2.3-liters: I think that M3 race unit went from 295 bhp to a best of

317 bhp before we added another 5 bhp with another 500 rpm.

"That took us up to 9,800 competition rpm, but we did not think we could gain more under the regulations, without an increase in capacity, so we make the 2.5 liter. Now I think we may have to come back to an 8,800-rpm limit, but we have more power and new crankshaft balance weights to increase in the future," concluded the frank Zinnecker before the 1990 season.

By the 1990 racing season, the 2.5-liter Sport Evolution III was regularly credited with 330 bhp at 9,500 rpm, but it had started the year at 9,200 rpm. More of that in our competition chapter, but we can see that the 2.5-liter did the job that was intended and, courtesy of Franz Zinnecker, we can also pick up on a previously-forbidden BMW engine engineering topic.

"Originally, von Falkenhausen would not let us have Siamese bores. This rule was broken with the bigger six-cylinders and, therefore, we have this feature on all M3 motors as well," Zinnecker said. The 95-mm bore of the 2.5 Evo III is the biggest the author knows of for a sports four-cylinder outside the obsolete Porsche 3-liter (104 mm). Building on a reputation for constructing engines that give the ultimate in bhp per liter in normally-aspirated, catalytic-converter-equipped vehicles, BMW Motorsport went close to the street-elusive 100 bhp per liter.

Such road-car power was released in the M3 2.5-liter by installing oversize inlet valves (38.5 mm/1.52 in) instead of the usual M3 sizing of 38 mm (1.5 in). Camshaft timings went from a duration of 264 degrees to 282. Compression ratio was dropped from 10.5:1 for the series M3 to 10.2:1. Internal engine modifications included sodium-cooled exhaust valves (the head diameters as before) and oil injection jets to spray beneath the pistons.

Externally, red leads for the spark plug caps and a polished exhaust pipe were the only frivo-

Together with a racing companion (bottom of picture), 66 of the planned 600-off production run in 2.5-liter Sport Evos are readied for homologation inspection and approval as of March 1, 1990.

Picture: BMW AG Presse, 1990

lities allowed the sales force. The company claimed a 154-mph maximum and 0–62 mph in 6.5 seconds. There was reduction of 0-to-1-km time to 26.7 seconds, rather than the 2.3-liter model's 27.3 seconds. The Evolution's final drive did few favors to fifth-gear acceleration (slower than a 2.3), but fourth gear let the engine rev a little and returned a reasonable 7.6 seconds for 50 to 75 mph. The factory quoted 22.6 urban mpg and that was so close to the truth, it should have won an integrity award!

The 2.5-liter chassis was refined in detail. From a racing viewpoint, the most significant alteration was a new front and rear wing set that could be adjusted (albeit slowly and carefully for the showroom car) via soft-metal bolts to provide three basic positions fore and aft, or nine permutations.

The aerodynamic progression was from fully retracted (front spoiler in, rear laid almost flat)

to a full extension of the front "lip" and a distinctly Grand Prix look to the back blade. The effect was to maintain the usual 0.33 Cd in the retracted position, cutting front-end lift and allowing "slight lift forces" on the back. Fully extended, BMW claimed "virtually zero lift" in the front and "slight downforces at the rear." A Venturi was integrated forward, artificially accelerating the flow of air beneath the car by means of a "V-shaped wind deflection profile. As a result, the air flowing beneath the car accelerates to a higher speed and creates an under-pressure, the car being literally sucked onto the road," the BMW press department airily explained.

The front spoiler also deleted the usual auxiliary lamps in favor of extra brake ducting. Friction materials (but not front discs or calipers) were replaced with uprated, heat-resistant pads.

Other front-end changes included lowered suspension ride height (by 10 mm/0.4 in), a further flare to the wheel arches (to accommodate ever-larger diameter racing slicks, racing 18 inches now homologated through production 16-inch diameters) and yet more attention to close up the lattices of the front "kidney" grille.

All those front-end openings were additionally streamlined (headlight mountings, front grille attachment areas, and surrounds to the hood), usually using rubber fillings, which were first raced in 1988.

Curb weight remained quoted as before—1,200 kg—but that had meant quite a lot of additional lightening to offset the extra engine capacity effects and generous standard equipment. Specifically, the company attacked the fuel-tank capacity, substituting the 320i/325i unit of 62 liters/13.64 UK gallons instead of the usual M3 reservoir of 70 liters/15.4 UK gallons.

Other dietary requirements were to carve out more of the front and rear bumpers and rear trunk lid, reducing the thickness of the rear and side glass, just as for the first Evolution M3. Similarly, deletion of the roof grab handles and map reading lights helped trim those bulges.

Lower and ever wider, Michelin MXX tires of 225/45 ZR 16 dimensions were accompanied by 7.5J x 16 cross-spoke alloys with "Nogaro Silver" hub and spoke finish. Grip, on all but the slipperiest of surfaces, was prodigious.

Showroom trim changes allowed only "Jet Black" or the snappy "Brilliant Red" body color, each contrasted by red or black bumper insets. A green band was prominently tinted into the windshield. The interior was freshened, deploying suede leather for steering rim, gear lever, and hand-brake handle, plus red seat belts (shades of modern MGs). Door trim panels were also unique, and an M3 logo was placed on the instep.

Motorsport seats were then new to BMW and extremely effective, but no Recaro option was offered on this model. Thus, seat heating

was also not available. The seats were normally finished in anthracite cloth and wore Motorsport striping.

Black leather was an expensive option, as was air conditioning. On one demonstrator I tried, the engine did not run cleanly through 90-degree days when the air conditioning cut in. Otherwise, the M3 2.5-liter seemed to have been engineered with surprising effectiveness, given the short development period, a pressing motorsport need, and the impending end of the E30 line.

BMW was beginning to dismantle E30 lines as these last M3 Evo Sports were pushed through at the usual Munich M3 manufacturing site. New E36s were being built by the thousands from July 1990, so the Motorsport engineers did an outstanding job to get this final tweak to the M3 E30 theme out on time....

Memories of performers

There is not much point in discussing the road-going M3s unless we recall their enduring driver appeal. For this was a classic sports BMW of prowess sufficient to wean even diehard 2002 fans away from their religion.

At M3 introduction time, I was lucky enough to attend the epic Italian media launch, on and around the Mugello race track. I had driven over 2,000 miles to attend for one British monthly magazine (*Performance Car*) in a similarly powerful (204-bhp) Ford Sierra Cosworth for a back-to-back test. I also reported the event for the weekly *Motoring News*.

All that meant lots of track and road time, with a unique timing session held in front of the start-and-finish line that saw the normally-aspirated BMW of 2.3 liters right on the Ford-Cosworth 2-liter turbo pace. Remarkable.

I reported for *Motoring News*, "The BMW engine idles with Teutonic-Motronic precision, has plenty of torque from 2,500, and marches through the close ratios with resonances galore around 4,500 (particularly annoying, and ultimately tiring, in motorway use), but it is a real joy from 5,000 to 7,000. Then it struts into real power production, comfortably outpacing the Mercedes Cosworth alliance by 15 bhp.

"The gear-change is naturally super for the track, but less attractive when you are shifting between first and second, across the gate. After three full-throttle departures, this knack was acquired once more. A good example of the normally-obstructive competition shift layout. This Getrag also has the advantage of being perfect for use out of town, within the second to fifth H-pattern.

"The 5/6-series-derived brakes (and wheel bearings) were superb, on circuit or road. On track, the ABS acted only when provoked from 125-mph fifth into a U-shaped 65–70-mph curve that required third. As anticipated, the chassis proved memorable. It will cope with four-wheel circuit drifts, usually preferring to understeer when pushed too hard, but capable of holding a third-gear tail slide over a particularly greasy section.

"On the road, it's even better and would have saved BMW a lot of past criticism over the oversteer of past 3-series, or the rather soft production specification of current 325i [referring to the 1986 E30]. The ride is outstanding by sports saloon standards, the steering informative, and the whole plot works better than we have any right to expect of a conventional saloon. 10/10."

This was my conclusion upon the international debut of the M3 for *Motoring News* in May 1986: "The 2.3-liter M3 amounts to a 146-mph package of old and new BMW goodies that sets new standards of pace and chassis grace amongst rear-drive saloons."

The Evo Sport 2.5-liter M3 was mine for several weeks. Aside from using it in Britain alongside a Mercedes 2.5 Evo II for a newspaper comparison, I also took in six countries in seven days for a 1990 *Motor Sport* magazine extended trial with then-BMW executive Scott Brownlee as the brave navigator.

That was the outing that netted a cross-checked 22.68 mpg: the worst a modest 21.09 mpg and the best almost 26 mpg for an event that included keeping track of veteran competition cars (drivers included Stirling Moss: it was not an economy run!) and a maximum speed run in Germany at over 7,000 rpm and 158 mph in fifth.

I came back from that trans-European run convinced that the Sport Evo was the ultimate incarnation of the M3 in terms of cross-country speed, but still sticking by the comment that the evolutionary 2.3-liters were marginally smoother. Neither Evo M3 was as refined as the equivalent Mercedes Cosworths, but neither was the Mercedes as much raw fun as the Bimmer. You pays your money and you takes your choice....

The M3, whether as an original or the final Sport Evolution 2.5, was a magnificent reminder of the simple pleasure of effectively developed rear-drive motoring. It had rough, gruff habits as the big four worked through its broad rpm range, but I cannot recall more driving pleasure from the production sedan ranks. Even so, the track versions wrung yet more magic from the MPower formula!

Specifications for the 1986 BMW M3

Engine

Inline DOHC four with 16 valves and Bosch ML Motronic injection/ignition

Bore x stroke

93.4 mm x 84 mm (2,302 cc)

Compression

10.5:1

Power

200 bhp @ 6,750 rpm and 176 lb-ft torque @ 4,750 rpm. Bhp per liter: 86.8. Option: 195 bhp with catalyst at 6,750 rpm, 170 lb-ft (catalyst) at 4,750 rpm

Transmission

5-speed with Borg Warner synchronisation, 3.25 final drive, rear drive and limited slip. Ratios: first, 3.72; second, 2.40; third, 1.77; fourth, 1.26; fifth, 1.0. Final drive: 3.25:1

Body

Basic unitary steel 3-series augmented by SMC plastic trunk lid/spoiler and body kit; front and rear bonded glass. Fiberglass-reinforced resin 3-piece bumper/spoiler with foam filling; also used polyurethane skins. Rear bumper, same construction and side sills. Aerodynamic drag coefficient: 0.33 Cd

Dimensions

Wheelbase, 2,562 mm/100.9 in (2,564 mm with 225/45 VR 16 option). Overall length: 4,360 mm/171.7 in. Width: 1,675 mm/65.9 in. Height: 1,365 mm/53.7 in

Weight

Full tank of fuel (70 liters), no extras: 1,200 kg/2,640 lbs

Brakes

Based on current 5-series (vented fronts) discs + ABS. Sizes: Vented fronts had 284-mm diameters; solid rears, 250 mm. Single-piston calipers

Wheels and tires

Alloy BBS 7J x 15; Uniroyal or Pirelli P700, both 205/55 VR

Suspension

Uprated strut/trailing arms, uprated 15-degree trail angle for trailing arms. Boge twin-tube gas-pressurized shock absorbers and inserts, unique coil springs. Anti-roll bar has twice standard leverage, pivot point outside spring/strut axis. Replacement stub axles encase 5-series wheel bearings. Steering: rack-and-pinion, 19.6:1 ratio, servo-assisted

Performance

BMW quotes 146 mph, 0–62 mph at 6.7 seconds, 50–75 mph in fifth at 7.1 seconds. With catalyst, maximum speed is 143 mph, 0–62 mph at 6.7 seconds, and 50–75 mph at 7.5 seconds

Fuel consumption

Urban, 24.3 mpg. At 56 mph, 48.6 mpg. At 75 mph, 37.6 mpg

1986 price

DM 58,000 without options

M3: the vital statistics

According to factory sources, the E30 M3 sedan was actually rendered in one 1985 pre-production example. It went into full manufacture in July 1986, but a batch of 20–30 very accurate production prototypes were finished to meet the press at Mugello in May 1986.

Some 2,396 M3s were built in 1986, and it was recognized for competition in Group A and N (5,000 examples built in one year) by March 1, 1987. You can see how production then fared from the accompanying tables, reaching its peak in 1987. America accounted for over 33 percent of all sales, but the subsequent E36 M3 smashed all export records for M3 in the 1990s.

The number of M3s made totaled 17,184 on the main Munich 3-series lines, including 600 of the Sport Evo III 2.5 made between December 1989 and March 1990. A further 786 M3s were hand-made from 1988 to 1991 as Cabrios at BMW Motorsport, Garching.

M3 sedan production

(excluding Motorsport prototypes, all from Munich 1.1 plant)

Year	Production All M3	Sales of M3 in US
1985	1	---
1986	2,396	---
1987	6,396	2,524
1988	3,426	1,103
1989	2,541	987
1990	2,424	686
TOTAL	17,184	5,280

M3 Cabriolet (convertible) production

(all from BMW Motorsport, Garching)

Year	Production
1988	130
1989	180
1990	176
1991	300
TOTAL	786

M3 Convertibles: Power levels & numbers

Model	BHP	Span	Number Made/Year
2.3 M3 Cabrio (no Kat)	200	5/88–7/89	42/1988 94/1989
2.3 M3 Cabrio (Kat)	195	1988–89	88/1988 86/1989
2.3 M3 Cabrio (Kat)	215	1990–6/91	176/1990 300/1991

Comparative specifications for the 1986 2.3 M3 KAT versus the 1990 2.5 M3 (Sport Evo III)

	M3 KAT	Sport Evo III
Engine	In-line 4-cylinder	In-line 4-cylinder
Layout	DOHC, 16-valve, alloy head, iron block	DOHC, 16-valve, alloy head, iron block

CAPACITY		
	2,302 cc	2,467 cc
Bore x stroke	93.4 x 84 mm	95 x 87 mm
Compression	10.5:1	10.2:1
Peak power	195 bhp @ 6,750 rpm	238 bhp @ 7,000 rpm
Max torque	230 Nm/169 lb-ft @ 4,600 rpm	240 Nm/176 lb-ft @ 4,750 rpm
Bhp/liter	93.4	96.5
Fuel	Unleaded, 95 octane	Unleaded, 95 octane
Tank	70 liters/14.7 gallons	62 liters/13.64 gallons

TRANSMISSION		
Final drive	3.25:1	3.15:1
5-speed ratios:		
First	3.72	Same
Second	2.40	" "
Third	1.77	" "
Fourth	1.26	" "
Fifth	1.00	" "
Std. tires	205/55 ZR 15	225/45 ZR 16
Std. wheel (alloy)	7J x 15	7.5J x 16

BMW FACTORY PERFORMANCE FIGURES		
0–62 mph	6.7 seconds	6.2 seconds
50–75 mph (5th)	7.8 seconds	10.7 seconds
Top speed	227.2 km/h (142 mph)	248 km/h (154 mph)
Urban fuel consumption	22.8 mpg	22.6 mpg
@ 56 mph	45.6 mpg	45.6 mpg
@ 75 mph	36.2 mpg	36.2 mpg
BODY	2-door	2-door
Length	4,345 mm/171.1 in	The same
Width	1,680 mm/66.1 in	The same
Height	1,370 mm/53.9 in	The same

	M3 KAT	Sport Evo III
Front track	1,412 mm/55.6 in	1,416 mm/55.8 in
Rear track	1,424 mm/56.1 in	1,430 mm/56.3 in
Aerodynamic drag coefficient	0.33 Cd	0.33 Cd
Curb weight	1,200 kg	1,200 kg
Steering	Rack-and-pinion, power-assisted, 19.6:1 ratio	The same
Suspension	MacPherson strut, anti-roll bar	Same as M3 KAT, further lowered by 10 mm/0.39 in
Rear	Trailing arms (15-degree trail)	The same
Brakes	4-wheel disc, as original M3 (from 5-series) with electronic ABS	Same as M3 KAT, plus air ducts from front spoiler and change in front pads

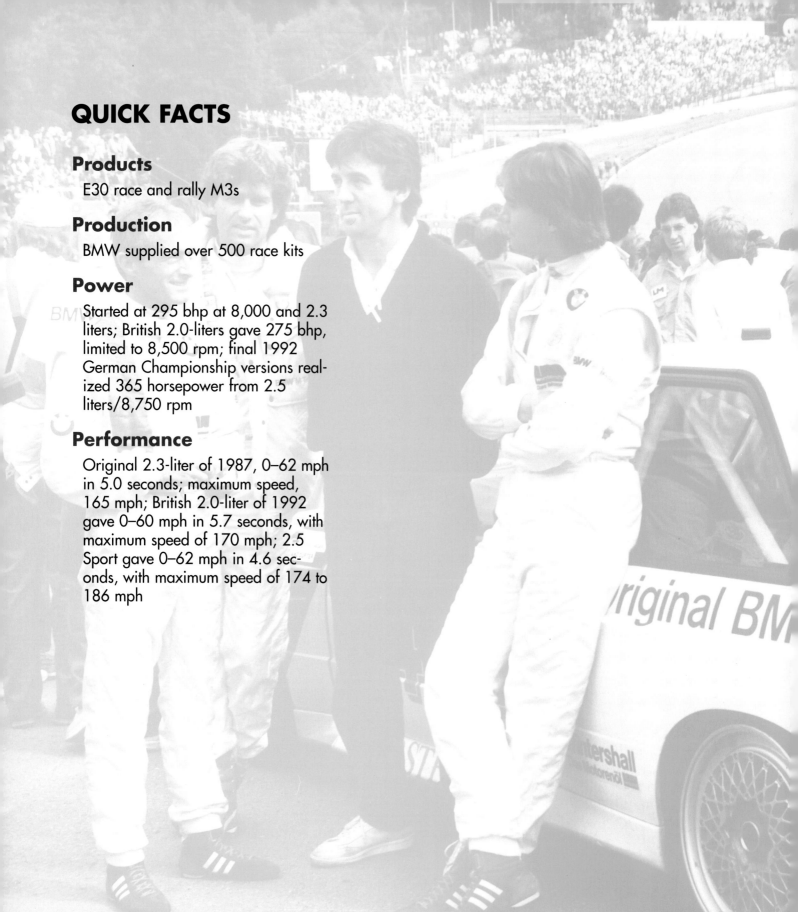

QUICK FACTS

Products

E30 race and rally M3s

Production

BMW supplied over 500 race kits

Power

Started at 295 bhp at 8,000 and 2.3 liters; British 2.0-liters gave 275 bhp, limited to 8,500 rpm; final 1992 German Championship versions realized 365 horsepower from 2.5 liters/8,750 rpm

Performance

Original 2.3-liter of 1987, 0–62 mph in 5.0 seconds; maximum speed, 165 mph; British 2.0-liter of 1992 gave 0–60 mph in 5.7 seconds, with maximum speed of 170 mph; 2.5 Sport gave 0–62 mph in 4.6 seconds, with maximum speed of 174 to 186 mph

Chapter 26

Racing Technology for the M3

How the legend amassed horsepower to compete successfully against the opposition

Winni Vogt (left) is seen here, before the start of 1987's Spa 24-hours, talking with Christian Danner, BMW's favored F1 pilot in the 1980s. In "civvies" is Ludwig Linder, who prepared Vogt's winning E30s—and many other excellent race BMWs—with Altfrid Heger (to Linder's right), a subsequent Spa winner for BMW.

The factory retains an M3 from this era and it was shown in the US during the 1996 Monterey Historic meeting.

Picture: Hugo Emde/Bilstein, 1987

Before launching into the considerable racing saga of the M3, it is worth remembering that 3-series without the M-prefix also competed with European honor in the 1980s seasons prior to the M3's launch. In the 1,601- to 2,500-cc category of 1985, the promising Winni Vogt and the 323i BMW were flattened by five Alfas on their way to the overall manufacturer's title for Milan. Better days would, however, come for BMW and Vogt in 1986.

Winni Vogt (in an E30 325i) snatched third overall in the driver's contest, beating off Mercedes to hold that 2.5-liter class. Vogt intelligently took ten class wins and finished in the top six overall on five occasions, a remarkable achievement for the 2.5-liter 3-series. Vogt would secure a European title of his own in the 1987 M3, but the quiet German died away from the race track, long before his natural span was done.

As the press was trying the first M3 road cars around the delights of the Italian Mugello circuit in May 1986 (see previous chapter), BMW Motorsport had covered thousands of kilometers with its racing counterpart. At this stage, the machine was prepared to pure Group A international rules (production of 5,000 per annum). By the early 1990s, the versatile M3 would be progressively adapted to more radical German Championship rules to yield another 70 bhp, or reduced to 2 liters and given a sixth gear for British SuperTouring. In both cases, the M3 continued to show championship-winning class.

Back in 1986, the M3 was struggling for serious horsepower and was certainly not up to the 300-bhp levels attributed by the publicists to the debutante 2.3-liter. Yet it was obvious that the Pirelli-shod BMW chassis was not going to be merely a middle-class car. It would challenge for outright victories in the world, European and national title races, despite the World Championship opposition from viciously quick (360 to 480 bhp) turbocharged Ford Sierra Cosworths and the rumbling presence of 5.8-liter Holden (GM) V8s.

BMW Motorsport and its parent company fell asleep on the job when it came to getting the M3 to race market, so Mercedes was an established force. However, BMW's development, both of competition kits and road M3s, so excelled that privateers always had a good chance of winning with BMW. Plus, showroom customers were prepared to pay for the extra verve of the M3 over a 190E 2.3/16 Mercedes.

This super cutaway by Bruno Bell shows the M3 in 2.3-liter racing guise for its initital 1987 season. The car was an immediate competitive success and managed to defeat the turbocharged opposition for the 1987 first—and, so far, last—World Touring Car title.

Cutaway: Bruno Bell/BMW Presse, 1987/88, Courtesy Chris   Willows, 1997

Winni Vogt made the transition to Group A before the M3 was available and scooped up some good results with this 323i E30. Vogt went on to win the European title with an M3 in 1987.

Picture: BMW Werkfoto, 1984

Commercial back-up

The M3 formula was undoubtedly the racing sedan success story of the late 1980s, but BMW had more in mind than simply winning races (and, almost by accident, rallies). The company, and particularly its Motorsport off-shoot, was ready to commercially exploit the M3 as well.

The Garching premises supplied equally thorough competition packages to provide everything required to assemble a competitive M3 (Group A or N and subsequent equivalents). It was left to the buyer to choose the engine specialist. One British-based Prodrive professional said to me, "If you have a single nut or bolt left over, it's your fault....Motorsport never makes basic mistakes!"

Demonstrating the sheer value of competition M3 business done by BMW Motorsport, press officer Friedbert Holz confirmed in June 1991, "Around 300 M3 racing cars/kits were supplied" up to that date. As of November 1991, a further breakdown was supplied by BMW Racing Team Manager Karsten Engel, revealing that Motorsport GmbH had supplied so many M3s that 250 originals "...raced regularly, all over the world."

Further inquiries revealed the number of Group A kits supplied by BMW at 270, with a further 60 supplied in Group N trim to make a total of 330 BMW M3 racing packages supplied from Munich. Our appendices reveal further customer sales figures beyond 1991.

The 1987 competition M3

The showroom M3 of 1986 was a very fine car, but it was only the start-point for a world-class competitor. This chapter recalls how it was developed for international Motorsport, while the following chapter fleshes out the results and the personalities at the wheel.

Racing cars change specification from hour to hour, track to track, but BMW did follow some patterns that translate for a mythical average racing M3 during 1987.

Placed alongside a production M3, the obvious body changes were the lack of interior trim and an extensive computer-calculated roll cage which had been tested in scale model trim and manufactured by Matter in Switzerland (reinforcing torsional strength as well as crash stress). As testimony to the extraordinary abilities of the 28 meters of lightweight steels welded within the M3, a BMW engineering source told the author that they provided "three times" the torsional and bending rigidity of a standard 3-series.

We can quantify some of these dimensional changes by saying that the Group A Bimmer competed at 960 kg rather than the production 1,200 kg, a sharply effective diet that slashed 25 percent from curb weight and immediately boosted power-to-weight ratio.

The next body trick was to let the car ride as low as was feasible, dropping the center of gravity as far as possible, postponing body lean and two-wheeling cornering antics. Replacement wheels carried racing tires and the radically-lower ride height.

In the case of the M3, the roof line touched 1,370 mm in production, and 1,330 mm for Group A racing. That 40-mm/1.57-inch savings also helped the car slice through the air cleanly with less air drag.

Naturally, more fuel was required by the competition M3, so a larger safety tank made from Kevlar and nylon-reinforced synthetic rubbers (with foam lining to protect the "bag tank" fuel reservoir) was adopted. When compared to a road-going M3, another 40 liters was allowed, taking the racer to a total 110 liters/24.2 UK gallons.

The wheelbase was altered by the adoption of racing hardware, climbing from the usual 2,562 mm to 2,565.5 mm, an insignificant

Roll-cage development continued to beef up the overall cabin and car structure to extraordinary levels of stiffness. Here, we see the winning Spa 24-hours M3 of 1992 in its red Bastos livery (Right) and an old warrior in white with Wintershall livery that the factory has preserved (Left).

Pictures: Author, US, 1992 and 1996

3.5-mm matter next to the extra millimeters generated by BBS replacement wheels and Pirelli or Yokohama racing rubber. The standard set up was 205/55 VR on a 7J x 15-inch wheel. For competition, the rim and overall diameters were permitted a maximum increase of 2 inches, so BMW generally adopted a 9 x 17-inch 3-piece alloy with a magnesium center and 245/610 rubber. Some teams were equipped with 16-inch rollers, which meant the tire sections shrank to 235/590-16. Others used both 16- and 17-inch diameters, the smaller size at the front to promote turn-in on sharper corners.

Other front-end moves included Bilstein aluminum-tube front struts. These encased low-pressure gas damping and were encircled by markedly increased coil-spring rates. The lower suspension arms for the struts were also in forged aluminum and were cross- braced. New hubs and cast-magnesium uprights lay behind the center-lock wheel attachment.

Huge hubs carried enlarged 13-inch by 1.25-inch (332-mm diameter x 32-mm thick) vented disc brakes, big bearings, and single-nut location to speed pit-stop wheel changes. Those discs were served by four piston calipers and were originally supplied largely by Brembo in Italy. More teams changed to AP Racing in Britain during 1988, and their later six-piston calipers made them a regular components supplier to the fastest M3 equipes by 1991, and on factory-backed E36 racers by 1995.

A faster steering-rack ratio of 17.0:1 was recognized in place of the production M3 19.6:1 ratio, and the showroom power steering was deleted. Rose joints and adjustable anti-roll bars completed the competition picture at the front.

For the back end, semi-trailing arms had to be retained, but the arms themselves were extensively reinforced with pivot-bearing mounting points and provision for immediate (albeit via wrench) camber and castor adjustment to tune the car to each track. As at the front, adjustable spring plates were also employed to vary vehicle ride height, again in search of ultimate circuit suitability. Once more, there was a jointed and adjustable anti-roll bar and central wheel-nut hubs to carry

Before the 2-liter regime in Britain, Prodrive and BMW GB campaigned the only effective class opposition to GM-Vauxhall's Astra assault. Here is the 1989 machine, complete with carbon composite induction manifold and the bigger front and equally fearsome rear cross-drilled AP race brakes that were typical of the period.

Pictures: Author, Silverstone, 1989

bigger brakes—vented units of 280 x 20.7 mm that were also served by four-piston calipers.

Pirellis were the initial tire selection for factory-backed BMWs, but Japanese Yokohamas became the quickest lap-time choice during the 1987 world championship season. "Yokos" were the preference of the works-backed Schnitzer and Bigazzi teams into the early 1990s, but Michelins were adopted on the 1992 works M3 of Johnny Cecotto, and today's factory-backed E36s also sport Michelins.

Motor magic

The slant four-cylinder built on its DOHC, 16-valve layout to create a substantial power bonus, but the layout of production exhaust manifolding and the restrictions of Group A regulations (standard size valves, standard inlet manifolds) kept power beneath the old Formula 2 levels. A competition M3 was usually slightly overbored (from 93.4 mm to 94 mm) to reach 2,331.8 cc rather than the showroom 2,302 cc.

Running a Motronic engine-management system that had been expensively redeveloped by a BMW-Bosch alliance, BMW Motorsport was able to operate at a 12.0:1 compression ratio to replace the usual 10.5:1. Power was always quoted by the Munich press department as increased by 50 percent over standard. This meant 300 bhp at 8,000 rpm, some 128.6 bhp per liter. Don't read too much into the far-higher bhp-per-liter levels of German championship 2.5-liter M3 motors, though. The domestic championship regulations were a lot more liberal, particularly on induction system and all manifolding, than the original Group A, so power was built disproportionately for the later 2.3 and 2.5 liters in Germany, reaching 146 bhp per liter.

Experienced engine rebuilders reported that the pre-Evolutionary engines (roughly March

1987 to July 1988) actually had "285 to 290 bhp at 8,000 rpm," with a first season rpm-limit of 8,500 revs. The real 300 bhp was only available courtesy of a new (Evo 1) exhaust manifold for the bulk of the 1988 season.

Maximum torque was far from fabulous in that it was delivered only at a sky-high 7,000 rpm. Yet the Group A M3 boasted some 20 percent bonus over standard, at 270 Nm (198.5 lb-ft) rather than 230 Nm.

The factory gearbox choice was a five-speed Getrag with close ratios stacked from 2.337 to a direct (1:1) fifth, and choice of final drives that encompassed 3.15 to 5.28:1. The factory picked a 4.41 to demonstrate a 0–62 mph time of 4.6 seconds (the standard figure was nearly 7 seconds) and reported speeds up to 280 km/h (173.9 mph) that first season, although those maximums were recorded on the taller 3.25:1 final drive.

For racing, the bigger Getrag used in the 6-series coupe was initially employed, 6-speeds prompted as part of the M3's narrow rev-band 2-liter armory. The factory settled on the sequential-shift Australian Hollinger box, as pioneered in 1991–92 by the Vic Lee team in Britain, and it is still in use today for 2-liter factory-backed BMW-McLaren 320s.

There were other 6-speed choices, however, including an H-pattern shift Getrag for the beefier 2.5-liter German championship racers and a Prodrive-engineered unit with Xtrac gears for the UK-based Prodrive 2-liters. To be all square on gearbox knowledge, BMW street 3-series did not get 6-speeds (pioneered on the unloved 850 of 1989) until the Evo M3 six-cylinder 3.2-liter of 1995.

Who is Prodrive?

Based in Britain's motorsports Midlands belt at Bicester, Prodrive is a group of professionals with a reputation founded in World Championship rallying, winning the title for Subaru in 1996–97.

The 1981 World Rally Champion's co-driver, David Richards, established Prodrive in the mid-1980s at Banbury in Britain. Initially, it ran Rothmans-backed Porsche 911s and Rover mid-engined Metro supercars in rallying, but when BMW wanted to get more involved in 2-liter SuperTouring, Prodrive went from the self-proclaimed " biggest sales outlet, anywhere in the world, for BMW Motorsport cars and parts" to valued BMW partners.

The relationship only soured in the early 1990s, when Prodrive itself was outmaneuvred by another British racing organization (Vic Lee Motorsport) in the vital liaison with factory personnel. Prodrive achievements included the creation of its own BMW 6-speed, non-synchromesh gearbox (H-pattern shifts, not the universally-adopted sequential shift of today) in six months by former Williams and Benetton transmission consultant John Piper.

Prodrive boss David Richards left even the most determined 1980s Yuppies deflated. He had the balls to sit with 1981 World Champion Ari Vatanen from his British debut onward, but when Richards retired from world-class rally co-driving, he achieved even more! Richards won his own championship titles solo, hovering his helicopter through airborne aerobics.

Prodrive expanded rapidly when it "pushed" BMW into allowing it to run the 3-series in rallying and racing. The UK company was forced to move from Silverstone to Banbury in January 1988. It moved in 32 additional personnel and now has over 100 staff.

The acceptance of BMW's 4x4 325iX for international competition depended on a Prodrive initiative, but that was nothing compared to the idea of taking the M3 into international rallying.

Richards recalled, "We really forced them into it, step by step. BMW were not keen at first, but we have always had fantastic support from the national sales companies, particularly BMW France. They were the best export market for the 1980s M3."

They really were BMW fanatics in France: The Oreca race organization that now runs Chrysler Vipers in World GT Championship events grinned when recalling the large M1 running along their tiny tarmac trails of French national rallying....In 1997, Oreca ran Z3s for ice racing! Their expression is "Tete en Feu," meaning "heads on fire"—and they call the English mad!

So, it was appropriate that the French island of Corsica saw Prodrive

For 1989, in the days before the British series went over to an all-2-liter format, BMW and Prodrive fielded this class-winning combination. Here is previous champion and major UK BMW dealer Frank Sytner beside professional British ex-pat James Weaver, a man as well-known for his IMSA exploits in the US as in front of his home crowd. Sytner had taken 11 class wins from 12 outings in 1988, but this 1989 combination could be explosive on some televised occasions!

Picture: BMW GB, Snetterton, 1989

British-based Prodrive and immaculately-presented BMW M3s were inseparable for both racing and rallying. Its BMWs wore very simple production bodywork for its 1991 season, when Prodrive was beaten to the UK title a second time, mainly because of a Pirelli tire choice in an era when Yokohamas were measurably quicker and more race-consistent. This is young hopeful Tim Sugden, who managed a race win from the recalcitrant UK combination.

Picture: John Colley Photography, 1992

engineer BMW's first and last World Championship Rally win. Such success had its own commercial rewards. "We built 28 of the 120 competition M3 kits released by Motorsport," asserted Richards in 1988. "Besides building the front-running M3s for championship honors in France, Belgium, Italy, and the competitive European series that Patrick Snijers led, Prodrive had built M3s or materially assisted in the national motorsport programs of BMW, in Holland, Spain, Switzerland, Greece, and Norway."

Prodrive's rally record, 1987–90

BMW's success at World Championship rallying culminated in that 1987 Tour de Corsica World Rally Championship qualifying-round victory. Prodrive contested national rally titles with success, particularly in France, where the Prodrive M3 won the 1989–90 titles and was a runner-up in 1987–88. In 1988, Prodrive also won the Belgian rally title (repeated in 1989) and also finished second in the national rally series of France and Italy.

The British-based Prodrive M3s also secured the 1988 British Touring Car Championship for BMW GB and Frank Sytner. In 1989, the success continued, with class success for James Weaver and national championship titles accrued from Finland to France.

The Tour de Corsica victorious M3 won against the cream of World Championship rallying machinery from Fiat-Lancia and Ford. The drivers for this rough tarmac road race

amidst bandits and rock faces were Bernard Beguin and J. J. Lenne.

The 1989 BMW season was notable for a unique rallying double: the M3 won both the French and Belgian titles. Naturally, Prodrive was behind this prestigious coup, but to prove it was no fluke, the rally championships of Holland (John Bosch), Spain, and Yugoslavia also fell to M3 drivers.

Francois Chatriot and Michel Perin were triumphant in France. Marc Duez and Alain Lopes took their similar 2.3 M3 into the Belgian limelight. Incidentally, Prodrive efforts had put BMW as high as third in the World Rally series during the 1989 season, but this was only when the tarmac surfaces were the majority of competitive mileage.

French ace Chatriot was aided by a near repeat of the earlier M3 World Championship Rally victory. He flicked the M3 into second place on the spec-

The M3 preparing to meet the rigors of rallying: this was the first body to receive the Matter/Prodrive treatment in the 1986/87 winter season. Note the transverse stays from the front bulkhead to the transmission tunnel.

Picture: Courtesy Chris Willows, 1986

tacular Mediterranean island, giving best only to Didier Auriol in a works Lancia Delta integrale, then the master of World Championship rallying.

Furthermore, the 1989 Corsican event also saw Prodrive BMWs for Beguin and Duez snatch fifth and sixth positions. It was at that stage (round 5 of the World Rally series) that the M3 had elevated BMW to third overall in the World Rally Championship! Belgian Duez had also scored an encouraging eighth overall in that year's Monte Carlo Rally.

Prodrive continued to prove the worth of the M3 in rallying with a national double in 1990. It added the French national title to its bag with the efforts of Francois Chatriot and Michel Perin.

The Prodrive M3s were effective rear-drive contenders in the age of turbocharged four-wheel-drive on many other World Championship events, although muddy forests were not an M3 strength. BMW had no wish to see the car out in those less-glamorous locations. It was amazing that Prodrive managed to persuade BMW management that its glossy image should take in a "bit of rough" on the road to becoming a motorsports legend.

For 1991, BMW GB and Prodrive were very serious about the British 2-liter BTCC title and hired former Tyrrell GP driver Jonathan Palmer (left) to compete alongside Steve Soper. The season was not a success, but the VLM team did win for BMW.

Picture: BMW GB, 1991

Techniques for M3 racing development

How did the M3 progress over the 1987 race specification? Between 1987 and 1989, the 2,332-cc engine capacity was deployed: the only real progress possible on those basic racing fronts of aerodynamics, tires, power, and gearing. The four-piston brakes remained as did the 18-inch wheels, but the M3 Evolutions had a vital effect and also brought with them extended spoilers (1988). An increasing number of lightweight panels, which had seen the factory M3s outlawed at Monza in 1987, were recognized.

According to factory records, there were the logical three Evolution models (1987, 1988, 1990), and their basics are described in chapter 25.

The biggest change in race-engineering principles of the 1988–89 seasons was the occasional adoption of the Prodrive 6-speed gearbox, but German touring-car runners just as frequently reverted to the 5-speed, and an alternative Getrag 6-speed was more widely used. For 1991, other 6-speed options had emerged. Steve Soper premiered the ratio sextet of Australia's Hollinger in German use, as introduced by Vic Lee Motorsport (VLM) in their British Championship cars. The continually developed M3 motor was winding toward a 10,000-rpm rev limit and an increasingly narrow power band.

In 1989, the World and European Touring Car Championships were dead, but the white heat of the German international touring-car title hunt meant that BMW worked harder to find a winning edge from a machine that was looking positively brick-like in the age of aerodynamic ordinary sedans.

Maintaining a 12.0:1 compression ratio, BMW Motorsport changed most key motor parameters under the engine direction of Franz Zinnecker. German regulations allowed the use of slide-throttle air admission (as opposed to the Group A use of standard intakes), and this allowed a small power bonus, but the real search in 1989 was for higher rpm and, therefore, extra horsepower. BMW Motorsport engineers overhauled their racing M3 motor. A stronger crankcase, lightened camshafts and pistons, and a BMW—as opposed to Bosch Motronic—Electronic Control Unit (ECU) were allied to double injectors to boost rpm and mixture flow.

The process was effective. At the beginning of 1989, the drivers were allowed 8,800 rpm. Early summer brought 9,200 rpm, and the year ended with 9,800 rpm at their disposal. Despite this elevation, official power peak was 8,500 rpm and 320 bhp, plus fractional augmented (5 Nm) pulling power, rated at 275 Nm/202 lb-ft of torque on the usual 7,000 rpm.

German regulations up to 1992 allowed weight alterations at the whim of the organizers and the success of the drivers. The 1989 M3 was forced to race at 1,040 kg/2,288 lbs, approximately 100 kg/220 lbs heavier than the engineers could now provide as a racing weight.

A wide choice of final-drive differential ratios remained, but 0–62 mph was still quoted as "around" 4.6 seconds with top speed elevated to 300 km/h (186.3 mph).

The cost of such M3 speed? In his valuable annual Tourenwagen Story 1989, author Thomas Voigt quoted typical M3 "on the line" cost at DM 220,000. At the time, that was equivalent to some $116,000.

ABS race braking

Anti-lock braking (ABS) was not initially used by the factory Group A racers. It was co-developed during the winter of 1990/91 by BMW Motorsport and Alfred Teves GmbH to contest the German Championship.

Steve Soper, Roberto Ravaglia, and Johnny Cecotto were the development drivers at a crucial Salzburgring progress test. It took some spirited discussion before the system was adopted. Even then, some T-car back-up M3s for factory-associated teams lacked this item.

BMW had been a pioneer in the use of ABS braking for competition, right back to the 1970s CSLs, in Germany and America. Such 1970s experiments were not a total success, with wheel lock and delay a constant complaint. By contrast, the 1991 German Championship season proved ABS to be a success.

A BMW-Teves system seemed particularly adept at overcoming the wheel-locking moments that the rival Mercedes-Bosch ABS deliberately did not totally prevent (they allowed the driver to overcome ABS at preset pressures). Today, the 3.2 Evo M3 sports a unique BMW-Teves anti-lock braking system.

BMW also included the feature of absenting ABS during high-speed rear-ward travel (i.e., a spin) so the driver could stamp on the pedal and lock the wheels when homing in backwards on those unfriendly barriers!

BMW drivers could switch out the ABS from the cockpit if they thought it was hindering progress. Lap-speed gains in the wet for ABS brake operation were measured in seconds, according to Steve Soper and other top-liners.

Track action with the 2.3-liter M3 E30

Here is the author's account of driving the 1988 Evo M3 as prepared for racing in Britain, as published by *Performance Car*:

"Most familiar to BBC TV viewers through the two-car team it runs under Mobil 1/BMW Finance colors for Frank Sytner, Prodrive has also contested some European races this season. The July 1, 1988 homologated 6-speed gearbox successfully survived the 23 hours of the Spa 24-hour race that the engine failed to complete!

"Our test cars were two of the three Prodrive Evolution M3s contesting the UK series: the much-repaired Mike Smith machine and the series-leading M3 of BMW and Alpina UK retailer Frank Sytner.

"The differences between the first M3 and the Evolution model were not so radical as to force new cars upon Prodrive. They share the new front and rear spoilers, lightweight [trunk] lid, and rear glass, but it is worth noting that neither power nor weight are notably changed in Group A racing guise.

"Prodrive's Senior Race Technician Peter Holley explained, 'The road-car changes do not effect the racing systems that we use, so power remains around 300 bhp for a really cracking example, with 285 to 295 the norm.' Race Engineer David Potter added, 'The quality of the panels used and the slight glass thickness reduction do not drop weight appreciably below 1,000 kg, which is still above the M3's class minimum of 940 kg.'

"In Group A racing, M3 power is augmented little over 35 percent in the best examples, less than turbo teams would expect, which leads to inevitable discontent. For example, the Sierra RS500 gushes from 224 road horsepower to a widely available 440–480 competition bhp.

"Such disparity has led the Germans to thrice restricting the Ford's power output in their national series by constricting air restrictors this season, and allowing the BMWs up to 330 bhp from the use of single-slide fuel injection. The British series remains unfettered, save in the less prestigious production (Uniroyal/Monroe) series.

"M3 torque is promoted on the rallying engines down as low as 5,500 rpm via camshaft replacements. For racing, 270 Nm will not report until 7,000 rpm, thus the need for the closest and biggest gear ratios for ultimate track speed.

"Compared to a conventional synchromesh, Getrag synchromesh 5-speed gearbox, the 'Prodrive Six,' offers the following ratios (Getrag in brackets): First, 2.449 (2.337); Second, 1.913 (1.681); Third, 1.579 (1.358); Fourth, 1.332 (1.1.50); Fifth, 1.148 (1.00); Sixth, 1.00 (–). That means a more appropriate ratio for most racetrack cornering quandaries.

"Peak power is at 8,200 rpm, but the Bosch Motronic chip in the digital engine management system of Frank Sytner's car allows a maximum 8,800 rpm. On Britain's short tracks, that will allow Mr. Sytner to brush 150 mph, but the wide choice of axle ratios are claimed to yield up to 175 mph on longer circuits. German magazines have electronically timed the M3 over 0–60 mph in some 4.5 seconds. There is no reason to think the Prodrive examples would be slower.

"The cabin is functional in the business tradition, but far from stark. The door panels are trimmed and the predominantly white color scheme extends to the steel scaffolding Matter sells as a roll cage.

"As you would hope in a cabin that is going to be subjected to considerable G-forces from 9-inch-wide Pirelli slicks, the driving position bolts you into the car as an integral component, one located by six-point Sabelts and the clinging embrace of an ultra-light Sparco racing seat and braced by a massive aluminum footrest. There is little chance that your feet will slip off a foot pedal or the floor, anti-slip grids literally applied.

"Instrumentation is extensive via six dials and functions such as ignition, lighting, and fuel pumps are supported by nine fused push buttons over the transmission tunnel. The Stack rev-counter is a memorable device, for it recalls the maximum rpm utilized on two recall commands and can be plugged into a microprocessor analysis to spew forth rpm readings at regular circuit intervals.

The 2,332-cc quartet (slightly over-bored from standard at 94 mm x the usual 84 mm) literally starts on the push of a button. It pays not to touch the throttle pedal as the engine management automatically accelerates the engine beyond the 1,150-rpm tickover to produce perfect starts on the power of a Pulsar transplanted helicopter battery.

"You study the gear shift pattern...apprehensively, but such fears are quickly cleared by the instant selection of first. There is the inevitable 'clonk' of a generously-dimensioned dog-gear box without synchromesh, and the 4–5 downshift takes some finding. Yet the deft speed at which each shift is made thereafter will be familiar only to motorcyclists and formula-car drivers.

"Naturally, the engine does not like full throttle in racing trim below 4,000 rpm. You are better waiting to 5,000 for a rude response. In practice, 7,000 to 8,800 is the natural habitat of this tough 2.3-liter 16-valve.

"For our test, the British championship silencing was fitted. Below 5,000 rpm, the noise emitted really wasn't much more than a sporting road car. Above 5,000, there is a definite increase in interest, and from 7,000 onward, the whole unit seems to pull its short-stroke act together, soaring for the highest rpms. 'You hardly ever hang on to a gear for more than a couple of seconds,' says

Sytner with enthusiasm. You share his glee when the tachometer blinks barely 400–500 rpm on each marvellous change and the engine resumes its Supercar thrust.

"As noted, the M3, even in Evolution guise, does not have much power by the standards of the 'boosty boys' who utilize turbocharging in Sierra and Nissan, but it transmits every drop to the pavement and preserves every 0.1 mph of cornering speed.

"The sheer grip available is hard to comprehend in something that bears such a close relationship to a road car, but the steering is not monumentally heavy on the move, even without the standard power steering.

"Basically, you point the M3 at a corner under full throttle, and it either screams through...or not. Ask Frank Sytner to list the virtues of his white Evolution steed, and he will list, in comparison to the original car, 'The Evo M3 feels better, it has more aerodynamic bite, and it just turns in terribly well.'

"I later learned that part of the reason for this lies in the use of BBS 16-inch-diameter front wheels and 17-inch rears. Stir in a thoroughly-sorted suspension based on freshly-fabricated parts for the MacPherson front struts and vastly-stronger rear trailing arms. A layout that deploys 1,000-lb/in front springs (about eight times stiffer than those of a sports hatch!) and 675-lb/in rears. Additionally, the suspension is swiftly adjustable in most respects, and has a number of alternative leverage points for the 27-mm front anti-roll bar and 20-mm rear, to transform roll stiffness.

"Of the M3 in general, [Sytner] feels its winning qualities are: '1) Robustness—it never feels that you should drive it anything but absolutely flat out; there are no worries about boost levels, or any of that nonsense. It will run to nearly 9,000 rpm for 24 racing hours. 2) The handling gives it the capability of qualifying in amongst Sierras with nearly twice the power. They brake like hell where we might dab and go flat-out. You have to work really hard in this car for a lap time, but it's supremely satisfying when you succeed. 3) The brakes are excellent. At 300 bhp, you try not give speed away, but when you do need brakes, they are brilliant. Not as good as they have been, because the authorities made us lose an inch of rubber width this season, but still fine,' concluded the 1988 British national sedan Champion."

Here is the M3 in full German Championship trim, and the first thing you notice is the extended spoilers. The cars ran at 2.5 liters in this, their closing international works race season (1992), and had 365 bhp. Even with the post-Nürburgring further growth in wing area seen here, it was not enough to hold the similar-capacity Evo II Mercedes 190 2.5/16.

Pictures: Author, Germany, 1992

M3 Sport Evolution, 1990–92

The 2.5-liter stretch of the M3 engine was logical for racing purposes, given the 2.5-liter Mercedes opposition. The 1989 BMW Sport Trophy dinner in Munich on Saturday night prior to Christmas was used to unveil a new M3 competition and road car for 1990.

Called M3 Sport Evolution (see details in the preceding chapter), it featured a 2.5-liter stretch of the 2.3 and advanced aerodynamics, including front-end Venturi for limited ground effects plus adjustable front and rear spoilers.

Due for homologation on March 1, 1990 (production of the necessary 500 began December 1990), the M3 Sport Evolution defended BMW's unexpected 1989 German victory over the 2.5-liter Mercedes.

Ford quit the German series in a huff over further turbocharger air restrictions. GM-Opel went for an unsuccessful 24-valve 3-liter Omega/Carlton and Audi had over 400 bhp in its weighty V8 sedan, so power was at a premium for BMW.

The racing M3 Evo started aerodynamic development in July 1989. Power came from 2,467 cc developed by the Preussenstrasse BMW Motorsport engine department, managed by Franz Zinnecker. He predicted,

"Compared with last year, we will start with another 10 bhp, probably 330 bhp at 8,500 rpm, and there will be more torque." Racing weight was 1,040 kg/2,280 lbs for Germany, 160 kg/352 lbs less than a road M3.

The 1990 Evolution featured the manually-adjustable front and rear spoiler extensions of the road car to vary downforce, as well as the use of ground-effect Venturi at the front end. Further lightweight panels were evident, and detail aerodynamic updates extended to reprofiling the traditional front radiator grille and sealing off front-end openings.

M3 personnel

Bigger engines, stronger BMW-supported teams, and much more serious recognition of Group N production racing were the primary messages from BMW at that annual Munich dinner. Established BMW sedan stars, including multiple champion Roberto Ravaglia, stayed on the German championship strength in company with Johnny Cecotto and then-Monaco-based Steve Soper.

One new recruit was former TWR Rover and Ford contractee Armin Hahne. The younger brother of 1960s BMW Champion Hubert

The Evolution 2.5 Sport racing version of the M3 prolonged the sporting life of the E30 original to six full seasons. Here is Armin Hahne continuing the Hahne family BMW tradition with the 1991 Evo, his second season at Bigazzi with Steve Soper. By 1992, this high-tech German Championship series was fought between BMW and Mercedes only, Audi having withdrawn the V8 saloons that won both 1990–91 titles. The series continued from 1993 to 1996, without BMW; but in its latter years, it went international and finally proved too expensive to survive.

Picture: Author archive/BMW, released 1992

Hahne, Armin was still on crutches following race and mountain bike (!) leg fractures.

Also driving the latest M3 in 1990 International Group A events were Dane Kris Nissen (fully recovered from his Japanese Porsche crash), Fabien Giroix, and veteran BMW contractee Dieter Quester, who was postponing retirement yet again. Double Spa 24-hour winner Altfrid Heger rang in to publicly proclaim on TV that he would stay at BMW.

BMW kept its word on production and homologation dates for the 2.5 M3 Sport Evolution. In detail, the 2.5-liter stretch meant the racers could use a 95.5-mm bore (production was 95 mm dead) with the standard 2.5 liter 87-mm stroke to achieve 2493 cc in place of 2467 cc. Utilizing the traditional 12.0:1 compression and reworked BMW electronic management allowed another 10 bhp (a total of 330 at 8,500 rpm in 1990) and a 15-Nm boost in torque to a seasonal average of 290 Nm/213 lb-ft. This gave some 500 rpm up on the older 2.3-liter, peaking at 7,500 rpm.

The engineers were worried at the beginning of the year that this ultimate four-cylinder stretch would leave them down 1,000 rpm on the 1989 "screamer," and they set an initial target of 9,200 rpm. This target was not

observed by all the teams, although 9,500 rpm was safe by the end of the season—a fine achievement for this large-bore four.

The extra horsepower for the 2.5-liter M3 was vital, as the Mercedes Evolution 190E 2.5/16 had even more-radical aerodynamics than the BMW and 333 bhp to propel the same organizational race-weight minimum of 1,040 kg. Still, Motorsport engineers were confident that the car could be raced at 940 kg/2,068 lbs, but that was never allowed on home turf because Mercedes could not get down below the 1,040-kg/2280-lb minimum. Despite the modest horsepower and torque bonus, however, no performance advances (initially, 0–62 mph in 4.6 sec, 186 mph maximum) were reported over 2.3 liters.

Revised aerodynamic and power were apparent to the drivers in the extra muscle between 50 and 150 mph. Roberto Ravaglia, the most successful of all M3 drivers with four international driver's titles to his credit by 1990, commented, "The old motor had its power at 8,000 rpm; the new [2.5-liter] is beautiful at 7,000 rpm. It is the best M3 I have driven." The statistics from the Nürburgring Grand Prix circuit backed up that judgment emphatically: the 1987 M3 best lap upon

debut was eight seconds slower than the hottest 1990 best lap!

Contributing to that dramatic rise in lap speed was the replacement aerodynamics (particularly the Venturi under the engine bay) and the use of 18-inch wheel diameters as routine for the Yokohamas, which gradually proved vital if one was to get the best from an M3. By 1991, some teams in Italy (CibiEmme) were certainly using 9 x 19-inch-diameter rear wheels regularly, usually in association with 18-inch-diameter fronts and Pirelli tires.

Detail chassis changes were headed by the availability of six-piston brakes, and BMW Motorsport specified an increase in vented-disc diameters to 350-mm/13.8-in fronts and 11.8-in rears. Yet the major technical advance for 1991 was the adoption of an anti-lock (ABS) braking system, the cooperative result of work by BMW and Alfred Teves GmbH engineers (see sidebar).

Steven Soper reported, "I knew the potential of such systems from a track test I did in Britain for *Cars & Car Conversions* magazine in the late 1980s. The championship-winning Group N Sierra of Robb Gravett had the ABS disconnected, so I tried hitching it up. I then went faster than Robb with the car; that made me think positively about ABS in racing."

Other leading drivers did not share that view, but BMW Motorsport knew that its rivals would be assessing the system, so it decided to develop a system of its own. During the 1990/91 winter testing at Salzburgring, it showed that Soper could lap over 3 seconds faster than without ABS. That was enough to convince his fellow front-running drivers, Ravaglia and Cecotto, that ABS might be a very good idea indeed!

No dry-lap time saving was quoted to the author, but the merits of the system were obvious in heavy German Championship race traffic, allowing the M3's basic agility to be exploited even in emergency situations. If the driver suffered a spin, on-board sensors allowed the system to "lock-out" and the driver to lock the brakes—very handy if the driver was pirouetting backwards into a barrier and wanted to lessen the consequent impact. In the BMW system, ABS was then automatically reset, so the driver could carry on immediately. If, however, the driver decided to dispense with ABS, the system could be locked out with a cockpit button—a set-up similar to that of generations of Audi quattro road cars.

Incidentally, Mercedes got together with Bosch and created a rather different ABS action for its winged 190E, allowing the wheels to lock beyond preset (heavy) pedal pressures. The BMW drivers felt that the Teves layout was better. This layout, plus the high-rpm ability of the stretched BMW 2.5-liter, often gave the M3 driver a technical edge over Mercedes opposition.

BMW did not win the 1990–92 German titles, but the M3 scored some superb results in sprint and long-distance races. The 2.5-liter

featured enough technical progress to ensure that the arch-rival Mercedes was frequently defeated in the home series. However, as we'll note in the following chapter, another 0.2 liters was not enough to put BMW back in the championship-winning game.

Against a 4-liter Audi V8 and the increasingly technically-sophisticated Mercedes, the M3 was a simple, often effective, but quite backward device. This 1990–92 period saw the German home-based manufacturers spending Formula 1 money (say, $25 to $40 million annually) on their national series, but BMW did not have its heart and soul in it, as their 2-liter programs went so well and the association with McLaren through the 48-valve V12 was progressing with expensive promise.

My favorite blobby color scheme came from Valier for Engster to drive at the 1992 Nürburgring German Championship round. Nearing the end of its competition life, the M3 was allowed extra front and rear wing area to make it more competitive and end its German Championship career.

Picture: Author, Germany, 1992

Trackspeed 2.5 action

In November 1991, the author had the privilege of driving a 2.5-liter Evolution M3 racer. A spare Bigazzi M3 for Altfrid Heger, this M3 lurked at a short track outside Perugia, Italy, and I enjoyed about half an hour in its 9,000-rpm company.

The major attractions were whip-sharp handling, steering that was sensitive to every track nuance, and brakes superior to any race sedan I have driven in thirty years.

The motor was tired after a long, hard afternoon doing double duty (an Italian "race instructor" demolished the intended ABS-equipped demonstrator!) and rumbled in the mid-range. Compensation came from the guttural motor hitting the spot: its lust for 9,000 rpm from 5,000 remained, well, lusty! Even I could plant my foot down and enjoy the small-track action in a car that made me feel like the Ace of all Aces.

The highlight of the day was a subsequent run as Steve Soper's passenger in the same 340-bhp package. Using some curbs that apparently had been dragged in from local Autostrada reconstruction work, Soper clambered aboard and monstered this abused M3 into a performance it knew was possible. Steve lapped us 2.79 seconds faster than I had lapped, solo.

The M3 was the finest four-cylinder racing sedan constructed: zestful, adhesive, strong, and fit to fight any rival in bouts from 10 laps to 24 hours. It was a BMW in the finest competition tradition, and one that I am proud to have seen at work, inside and out.

QUICK FACTS

Period

1987–92

Products

M3 in race, rally, and hillclimbing trim

Achievements

Winner of the World Championship in 1987 and the European title in 1988; two-time winner of the Australian and German Championships; three-time British Championship winner; three-time Italian Championship winner; won two race titles and one rally title in France, one race and one rally title in Holland, two rally titles in Belgium, and two race titles in Portugal; winner of the Scandinavian Cup, Finland, and numerous lesser national hillclimb and rally championships; won Belgian Spa 24-hours at every works-backed attempt from 1987–93

People

Biographies of BMW's "Big Four" drivers: Steve Soper, Joachim Winkelhock, Roberto Ravaglia, and Johnny Cecotto

Chapter 27

The M3 race record

The first M3 establishes a winning pedigree

In the 1980s and early 1990s, as a racing spectacle, the M3 was a totally different experience from that of the 1971–86 BMW CSL/CSi era. European spectators and drivers had become accustomed to the big six-cylinder coupes and their sonorous straight sixes as the BMW trademark in long-distance sedan events. The bark of four BMW cylinders belonged to formula-car racing or to the jinking silhouette 320 racers that appeared alongside sports cars in World Championship events.

The M3 was the first of the European sedans to take structural stiffness into the formula car league. It was not the full American space frame-plus-body-panels-as-cladding layout. Yet the M3 was a superb amalgam of hidden roll-cage strength (tripling body torsional resistance values) and bullet-proof running gear—sound foundations that ensured its late-braking, apex-clipping, zippy-motor response values. It was an inspiring sight at all the cornering zones, entertaining spectators and drivers alike.

Pitched against the straight-line speed of GM-Holden V8s and the turbocharged Ford Cosworths, the boxy Bimmers had such cornering capabilities that their hottest lap times were little inferior. A top team such as Schnitzer could run its M3s closer to their ultimate pace, for longer—simultaneously consuming less fuel, brake friction materials, or tire rubber than the Ford and GM dragsters.

Thus the 1987 contests between BMW's 300-ish horsepower David and Goliath's 360 to 450 bhp was a closer call than anticipated. Only when Ford fitted a truck-size (T04) Garrett turbo to the "Cossie" did the Black Texaco-backed biplanes pound the Motorsport-striped Best-of-the-Bimmers into the tarmac through 1988. There wasn't too much publicity profit in that for BMW, but since both world and European title hunts were cancelled by the close of 1988, Munich could honorably scatter its zippier M3s into the national contests of Germany and Britain.

The results were very different M3s. In Germany, they went for more radical engineering, and the original 2.3 sprouted 2.5 liters and extended wing sets. Over 350 bhp became the norm, along with 180-mph capabilities. These were the DeutscheRenn-Meisterschaft (DTM) machines that took on a similar normally-aspirated formula from Mercedes, a straight-six 3-liter GM-Omega Opel, air-restricted turbo Fords, and 4.2-liter V8 Audis.

Ready to go! The original version of the 2.3-liter M3 was pushed to make an honest 300 bhp, but could defeat rivals with 200 horsepower extra, thanks to a superb chassis, outstanding drivers, and the best-organized teams in the business.

Picture: BMW Werkfoto, 1987

Two-class society: James Weaver heads for another class win with the 1989 Prodrive BMW at Silverstone Grand Prix track, while keeping a wary eye on the 500 bhp turbo Ford behind!

Picture: Courtesy Avenue Communications, UK, 1990

Eric van der Poele was the talented winner of the M3's first German national title in 1987 with former Ford allies, Zakspeed.

Picture: Author archives, 1992

These colorful corporate battles were brilliant to watch, especially at the packed Hockenheim stadium. There the massed ranks bayed for their chosen marques with more ferocity than football supporters, while the 30-car fields sprayed concrete stadiums with more disjointed decibels than a heavy-metal concert.

The UK spec became 2-liters in the 1988–90 formulae that led to the rev-limited (8,500 rpm) 2-liter becoming the only game in town from 1991 onward. There were severely restricted aerodynamics, as well as minimum curb weights and wheel widths, all in the interests of close racing. There was also a minimum length that ruled out specialist hot hatchbacks. Thus was the net spread to catch the major manufacturers, who all had mundane front-drive 4-doors in the showroom to sell against equally dull opposition. A British sedan-racing boom began, propelled by escalating manufacturers' numbers (eight or nine) and bulging budgets.

BMW was always a big-time spender and professional about any class of sedan racing it contested, and it mopped up the first three 2-liter titles in the UK with the original M3 (1991–92) and the E36 318iS coupe (1993). The opposition got smart and expensive, hiring in the formula-car set: Williams for Renault, TWR for Volvo, Reynard at Ford, TOMs Toyota, and so on.

Annual British race and hospitality budgets went beyond $7.5 million for the biggest players and currently stand around $10.4 million for Renault Williams. BMW Motorsport stayed in touch through 1993, but thereafter the British scene needed an individual approach. This led to closer links with McLaren on the touring-car side, maintained from 1995 to October 1997, alongside the GT racing deal of that period.

An astonishing first season

Even BMW was to be astonished at the initial and continued success of its 1987 newcomer, the M3 motorsport baby. At the conclusion of the first season, Motorsport manager Wolfgang Peter Flohr said, "We knew we could win class victories and hoped there would be success overall as well. But we had just won the European Championship with the 635 Coupe from Schnitzer. Herbert Schnitzer and Charly Lamm told us there was no way that our little twerp of a car would be as fast as the 635. Even in the opening development months of the M3, it was immediately 2 seconds a lap faster than the 1986 coupe 635...."

The M3 was justly hailed as "...the most successful racing car from Munich in its first season. No other BMW has achieved so many victories so quickly and reliably." The record behind those words was equally impressive, and the newcomer had not been content to stick purely to racing.

By the close of 1987, the M3 had won the driver's section of the first and last World Touring Car Championship, a series so wracked by bitter regulation controversies that it was dropped by the international authorities immediately! Ford won the parallel series for manufacturers.

Yet the achievement of Italian Roberto Ravaglia in taking four outright wins with the Schnitzer-prepared M3 was one of the giant-killing feats of modern motorsports. It was a triumph for Schnitzer teamwork and the shining abilities of compatriot codriver Emanuele Pirro, who accompanied Ravaglia on all his winning runs.

Additional spoils in that first M3 season included the European Championship, which went to German Winfried "Winni" Vogt in the Team Linder M3. Honors were equally shared among the top preparation specialists in the BMW fold, for Belgian Eric van de Poele initi-

ated the Zakspeed move from Ford to BMW with the greatest success a German preparation company can wish for: the German Touring Car Championship title.

That was far from the close of 1987 M3 achievements. The simple fuel-injected 2.3 brought BMW the FIA Group A Trophy for makes in the European Hillclimb Championship, plus national titles in Australia, France, Finland, Holland, and Portugal. This was a stunning win list for a newcomer, but double merit points should go to the Australian equipe behind veteran Jim Richards. Sedan racing is a premier-league motorsport in Australia, and preparation standards can outshine the best in European teams.

World-wide success

Once Ford was armed with the Sierra Cosworth and BMW had the M3 for 1987, the first and last World Championship was a struggle between two contestants of totally-opposed ideologies. Fittingly, both won a 1987 world title, but BMW repeated its driver success in 1988 before the European series was abolished.

It was a chaotic first 1987 World Championship round in Italy, where all the leading Fords were outlawed before the race (illegal engine-management systems). All the M3s were disqualified from the top six places (plus eighth) for lighter-than-lightweight body plastics!

The M3's lack of turbocharged power was offset by chassis agility and the sheer weight of BMW M3 numbers—all telling factors versus the embryo Eggenberger Sierra team.

Ford then beat BMW outright by a touch of the Evolution homologation game that had seen BMW defeat Ford in the 1970s. It took the arrival of the evolution Sierra, coded RS500 and reworked with a larger turbocharger and extra Batwing sets, to complete the 1987 World Championship job.

The 1991 British Champion in a Vic Lee Motorsport 2-liter on Yokohama tires was Will Hoy. Looks easy, doesn't it? Look again and you'll see our three-car shot is a typical action sequence from the pre-aero-package era of BTCC, with more passing than an Italian city center! Closest to the camera is David Leslie's private M3, sandwiching GM-Vauxhall's John Cleland, with Hoy attempting something terribly brave on the outside of this Silverstone circuit lunge for the final corner.

Pictures: BMW GB/John Colley Photography, 1991

Now the 2-liter turbo Ford could be developed to exceed 500 bhp, while BMW and its normally-aspirated 2.3-liter could do no more than detail the 2.3 liters, exceeding 300 bhp only under favorable circumstances or German national regulations.

Why no turbo for BMW, too? I asked this question when I took the Ford down to meet the M3 for the road-car confrontation detailed in our previous chapter. I received no convincing answer, aside from the fact that BMW had its eye on the similarly-specified Mercedes opposition and did not feel turbo cars fit with their sales plans. Look back, and you'll only find two turbocars listed by BMW: 2002 and 745i. Neither were a great sales or warranty success.

The 1988 Evolution M3 had 220 bhp for just over 500 road customers, but it was for lighter body panels and extended aerodynamic spoilers that competitors valued the car. Although the RS500 Ford was an outright winner (outside Germany) from its mid-1987 season introduction, the M3 continued to garner racing and rallying victories across Europe.

The second (1988) season for BMW and its factory-supported teams headlined the successful Schnitzer campaign to secure the European Touring Car Championship for drivers. This was the last time that the title was offered, and it was fitting that an M3 won the last European edition: BMW drivers had won the title, or the class contested, 16 times since 1965!

M3 took both 1987–88 European honors via Winni Vogt (Linder) and Schnitzer's Roberto Ravaglia. Outside Germany, the M3 enjoyed a successful 1988 season, scooping up British (Frank Sytner), French (Jean Pierre Malcher), Dutch (Arthur van Dedem), FIA Asian-Pacific Championship (Trevor Crowe), and Swedish (Lennart Bohlin) titles.

Even the Portuguese Touring Car racing title went to an M3, but it was Prodrive who really outdid itself on BMW's behalf. It not only stood behind that Frank Sytner UK title victory, but also snatched the Belgian Rally Championship.

The same Prodrive crew—Patrick Snijers and Danny Colebunders—also finished as the runners-up in the European Rally Championship itself. So BMW almost collected a unique sedan double in European racing and rallying titles.

The German national story

In Germany, the M3 remained competitive over six astonishing seasons. Here, organizers handicapped winners on a weight and power basis for close racing. The 1988 German home international series was not the happy hunting ground for the M3 that it had been in 1987, but the M3 still acquitted itself well versus Champions Eggenberger Ford, whose RS500 was strangled back on turbocharger air supply for 1989 in the cause of ferocious track action that clipped the Ford's winning ways.

In the 1989 season, BMW bounced back on the home front. Its fabulous M3 beat the best from Mercedes—even though the 190E now bore 2.5 liters—to add the 1989 title to its 1987 home championship victory.

Eggenberger Ford and its air-restricted RS500s were strangled to 360 bhp in 1989 and withdrew from this enormously wealthy and well-attended series from 1990 onward.

Ford was little missed, as Audi joined the fray with its V8 4-door for 1990–92. The biggest quattro came home with the title in its debut season. Ingolstadt also mugged the home opposition again in 1991, wrenching a second title from unimpressed opposition. BMW got its revenge in 1992, and it was Audi's turn to leave in a mid-season huff, after BMW spotted a flat-plane crankshaft that did not comply with regulations.

The big Audi V8 sedan also wore a rear wing for 1991 and was credited with over 500 bhp by the leading BMW and Mercedes drivers. Audi claimed 462 bhp and definitely enjoyed a power-to-weight advantage, never mind the benefits of 4x4 on comparatively narrow tires with (again comparatively) heavy bodywork.

The result of this 1990–91 Audi double was to redouble pressure for new regulations, the car company engineers unhappy at the German racing-by-weight-handicap system. Yet the public and the media seemed to be delighted at the resulting close competition.

BMW Motorsport fared better than Mercedes under German regulations in the 1980s, but BMW could not agree with the framing of the 1993 regulations for their home series. Munich withdrew its planned E36 six-cylinder M3 entries, which would have faced Mercedes, Alfa Romeo, and (later) GM-Opel in the German/ITC (International Touring Car) Championship that was on television from 1993–96.

Then the ITC three-way battle between Mercedes Alfa and Opel was smashed asunder by Alfa's decision to quit a now-obscenely expensive exercise. The prime attraction in Germany in 1997 was a 2-liter SuperTouring series that looked more competitive than that of originators in Britain, but there are many television race fans around the world who miss the colorful old excesses of high-tech German/ITC Championship racers.

Audi took the German national title in 1990 with Hans Stuck and its V8 limousine, but the BMW fleet put Johnny Cecotto in second (Schnitzer) and placed six M3 drivers in the top ten of the most fiercely contested sedan series in Europe. Briton Steve Soper was fourth in the 1990 title hunt, and continued to race right on the pace, thanks to the 2.5-liter variant.

Soper's Bigazzi MTeam teammate Joachim Winkelhock was sixth and fellow Bigazzi driver Jacques Laffite was also in the top ten in a fine year for the Italian M3 team. It had given Schnitzer a hard run for the 1989 Italian title, and provided much of the inspiration behind the original Vic Lee British M3 that scooped UK titles and out-maneuvered Prodrive so dramatically.

For 1990, Zakspeed was assigned 51-year-old Dieter Quester and the only woman to be regularly seen in this championship: Annette Meeuvissen. She was valuable for publicity, but was no more likely to win races than Quester was in 1990. Zakspeed was confined to the use of Pirelli tires, while BMW favorite son Schnitzer clung to the Yokohamas that had brought it so much success since 1987. Unsurprisingly, Zakspeed departed BMW for Mercedes money in 1991.

The M3 record in the 1990s

The BMW M3 continued to be a versatile winner for the early 1990s. It utilized three very different engine specifications: original 2.3-liter guise for some branches of the sport (such as rallying), 2.0-liters for the British Touring Car Championship and equivalent overseas 2-liter categories, and 2.5-liter Evolution motors for German and similar Group A contests.

In 1990, Johnny Cecotto, Fabien Giroix, and Markus Oesterreich headed a BMW M3 record result culminating in a one-two finish at the Spa 24-hours, the toughest event on the sedan calendar. It was an event won six times by BMW M3s, but on this occasion, the "sprint" car distinguished itself by spending only 7 minutes 30 seconds of the 24-hours in the pits, much of that time required for mandatory driver changes!

Other notable M3 achievements in 1990 were the acquisition of the Italian, Dutch, Finnish, Swiss, and Belgian national championships, with a fine one-two result in Italy for MTeam Schnitzer drivers Ravaglia and Pirro. There were runner-up positions scored in the national title hunts of Britain and Germany. European titles did not mean much by this stage, but BMW had Frenchman Francis Dosieres down for the European hillclimb trophy, Group A.

Winning at the Spa 24-hours for the lucky 13th straight time is the Fina-backed car operated by Schnitzer in 1990. BMW M3 pace and durability netted three 24-hours race wins that season: Belgium, Germany (Nürburgring), and Snetterton (Norfolk, UK).

Picture: BMW Pressefoto, Germany, 1990

Johnny Cecotto fought valiantly for the Schnitzer team and BMW Motorsport in 1990 and was a German Championship contender, but Audi's 4.2-liter V8 4x4 was too much for 2.5-liters on tight tracks such this layout at Norisring.

Picture: BMW Pressefoto, 1990

Norisring, June 1991: the four-marque fight for the Deutsche Tourenwagen-Meisterschaft (DTM) was between BMW (leading), Audi (two quattros in hot pursuit), and a field full of Mercedes and GM-Opels. Audi aside, it was one of the most competitive years in DTM, and this sort of entertainment could have kept the series alive today.

Picture: ITR, 1991

The 1991 season

In 1991, in the wake of former Ford specialist Zakspeed's departure for Mercedes Benz, the BMW factory line-up included Johnny Cecotto, Kris Nissen, and Joachim Winkelhock for Schnitzer. Bigazzi retained Steve Soper and Armin Hahne. A freshly-created MM-Diebels Team was awarded former BMW-backed Grand Prix aspirant Christian Danner. Linder was served by the fast but unlucky former F3000 driver Altfrid Heger.

After 14 races, the M3 was once again embattled in the thick of German champi-onship wars, but no title resulted. Steve Soper (Bigazzi) and Johnny Cecotto (Schnitzer) fought Frank Biela's Audi V8 quattro. Klaus Ludwig, in the best of the factory-backed AMG Mercedes, also showed some late-season form.

So the series resolved into a five-way fight. Former BMW 320T factory pilot Hans Stuck, the 1990 champion for Audi, was also in contention for the 1991 title in a Schmidt Motorsport Audi V8, but teammate Frank Biela finally prevailed over his taller and older rivals, leaving Mercedes and BMW without the coveted championship.

War! BMW M3 holds off Mercedes and straight six-powered GM-Opel Omega. At this stage of the 1991 German Championship, two of BMW's drivers—Cecotto and Soper—had a chance for the title versus two Audi V8 conductors and Mercedes "King" Klaus Ludwig. The V8 numbers won!

Picture: ITR, 1991

The 1992 season

1992 turned out to be the last season for BMW in the 2.5-liter German Championship, and a turning point for the German national series. The 1992 season also marked massive progress made by the 2-liter SuperTouring formula, then spreading from Britain to the rest of the globe.

The year was dominated by AMG Mercedes and ultra-trick suppliers who supported another successful title bid for Klaus Ludwig. Using Bridgestone tires, a British X-trac 6-speed gearbox, and a steel connecting-rod specification that allowed a sustained 375 bhp and 10,200 rpm without trick fuels (a feature of 1991 German races), the 190E was a winner.

Its computer-controlled tricks implemented variable cooling slats (closed for longer straights), variable anti-roll bar settings corner-by-corner, and the anti-lock braking systems now banned in Grand Prix. The 1992

Mercedes Evo II was always going to be too much for BMW to fight with what had become an obsolete machine.

Save for a sentimental final round and a brief summer run of victories for the now-aged M3, it was a hard job to get the M3 onto the first three podium positions. BMW was assisted by a rear-wing extension from the mid-summer Nürburgring date onward, allowed by the organizers to improve competitiveness in much the same way as NASCAR alters aerodynamics mid-season to boost inter-marque competition.

The most effective 2.5-liter BMW runner was a very special Michelin-shod runner for Johnny Cecotto, which was Fina-backed and domiciled at BMW-owned premises adjacent to the Nürburgring track. This was, effectively, the factory car, used for leading-edge development with considerable technical input on chassis stiffness from Simtek's Nick Wirth in Britain.

Among more familiar BMW Motorsport-liveried warriors were Schnitzer (Roberto Ravaglia

and Joachim Winkelhock) plus Bigazzi (Steve Soper and Emanuele Pirro). Linder ran some interesting M3 drivers, including Armin Hahne and World Championship motorcyclist Wayne Gardner. Gardner remained a very effective touring-car driver in the late 1990s, driving in his native Australia in the big banger V8 wars between Ford and GM.

Most wins went to Cecotto, but even the viciously-quick Venezuelan could hold no higher final championship position than fourth overall, a fair reflection of the qualifying and race pace of the BMWs battling along in the wake of the quickest Mercs in 1992.

Cecotto represented the only BMW among six Mercs by the close of play. Ravaglia took seventh overall in the series and the last two wins of the 1992 season: a double header at Hockenheim that saw the M3 out in a blaze of one-two-three-four-five glory.

It was a grand finish for a fabulous fighting machine in the finest sporting traditions of BMW, but there was to be no equally impressive E36 M3 successor. BMW announced its withdrawal from the 1993 German series for 2.5-liters just six weeks after it had committed to fielding at least four factory M3s with 400-bhp straight sixes.

The reasoning? BMW and Paul Rosche swore it was because the authorities would only let them have one year with the in-line six moved radically rearward, so it would be too expensive to make such cars for just a season.

Outsiders swore that BMW knew it was going to get a beating because all the rest—Mercedes, GM-Opel, and Alfa Romeo—had, or were preparing, high-rpm V6s. Rosche swore to the author—and at the opposition—that the BMW straight sixes would sing beyond 10,000 rpm, happily. All we, the public, saw was a few test pictures of the most exciting BMW 3-series racer yet, a 190-mph machine destined to remain on the test-only factory list. America would be the scene of the six-cylinder successor's greatest international status perfor-

mances, while BMW Motorsport backed a low key ADAC National GT and Nürburgring endurance race program for less-radically-modified M3s.

The factory Bimmer M3 never raced, because BMW went for the 2-liter format, before all its national rivals, and earned titles all over the world. But that's another tale, told in a later chapter.

British-based BMWs were peculiar 2-liter conversions for the UK series, but they remained rev-limited (8,500 rpm) winners. Prodrive was still winning UK races in 1992, having provided the 1990 class champion, Frank Sytner.

Now there was stronger opposition from VLM (Vic Lee Motorsport), who had provided

In Britain, the M3s were raced to the 2-liter SuperTouring formula and won the first two titles outright. This is the 1991 Champion, Will Hoy, in the Vic Lee Motorsport machine with Yokohama rubber and 275 bhp by the mandatory 8,500-rpm limit.

Picture: John Colley Photography, 1991

Still capable of winning in the heat of summer, 1992. Steve Soper hustles the Bigazzi M3 Sport Evo to victory at Nurnberg's Norisring track. Joachim Winkelhock won the second DTM event of that weekend, making it a bright spot in an often-unrewarding final DTN season for the E30 M3.

Picture: Bilstein Werkbild, 1992

the British champion's car in 1991 (Will Hoy) and scrapped for every tenth of a second or sliver of a budget Deutschmark with Prodrive. Or at least they did until the VLM proprietor was sentenced to 12 years at Her Majesty's Pleasure, following the discovery of millions of pounds worth of forbidden white powder in a capacious gas cylinder.

The unique UK Prodrive 2-liter M3 formula featured 93.4 mm x 72.6 mm for 1,989 cc and 274 bhp by 8,000 rpm of the mandatory 8,500-rpm UK limit. Such M3s were handled on rotation by Steve Soper, Christian Danner, Dr. Jonathan Palmer, and Tim Sugden (the latter Prodrive-contracted over several years after a maiden 1991 win at Brands Hatch in a Prodrive M3).

Although Prodrivers Soper and Sugden won events, the VLM M3 for former World Sports Car Championship charger Tim Harvey

secured the 1992 British series. It was a fine achievement against the front-drive Vauxhall of John Cleland and the Andy Rouse Toyotas, which were allowed to race at 100 kg less, especially as the team had to be reorganized for the losing rounds of the series after proprietor Lee's imprisonment.

A 2-liter formula was good news for the company in Britain, for the 3-series won the UK title outright in 1991–92 with the E30 M3. Then, following the change in German championship plan, BMW abandoned six-cylinders at home for the 1993 UK Championship with an E36 coupe (officially an 318iS). Driven by Joachim Winkelhock and operated by Schnitzer with another M3-derived powerplant, its story is in Chapter 29.

How it could have been: this is the German Championship prototype of the E36 that was intended to race from 1993 onward. It had straight six-cylinder power (tested beyond 400 bhp) but BMW could not get the long-term concessions they wanted on rearward engine location, so the racing six was never developed to this ultimate specification.

PTG worked through 1995–1997 to make the most powerful sixes endure and win under US conditions. This Munich prototype was handed over to Sandro Chia for one of BMW's bold Art Car paint schemes.

Picture: BMW AG PR/Postcard, 1993

In five successive years, Italian Roberto Ravaglia won titles for MTeam Schnitzer BMW, four of those with the M3. Here, Ravaglia adds the 1990 Italian title to the World, German, and two European Championships.

Picture: BMW Pressefoto, Italy, 1990

Peter Kox of Holland did much to sort out the McLaren revisions for racing the E36 in 1996. He was also a winner in the 1996–97 McLaren F1-V12 as a reward. Christian Menzel (Far Right) came from a racing family background and promised much in the summer of 1997.

Pictures: BMW AG Presse, 1996

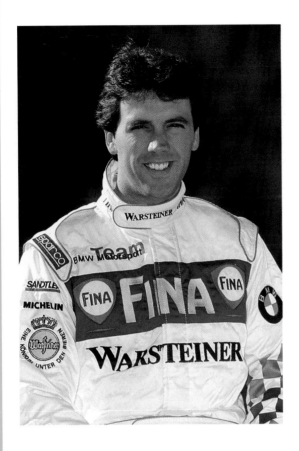

Leading BMW M3 M-Team drivers

Steve Soper, Joachim Winkelhock, Roberto Ravaglia, and Johnny Cecotto are the "Big Four," BMW Motorsport-contracted aces who have competed all over the world to extend the winning reputation that Bayerische Motoren Werke has earned in 80 years of sports success. All are superb drivers who handled the M3 with distinction to complement the engineering skills of the Motorsport division. We only had space to print biographies for this quartet, but all were 36 years old, or more, at this writing, so we can expect the next generation—drivers like Peter Kox from Holland and second-generation German racer Christian Menzel—to fill more motorsport headlines after the millenium.

It would be nice to think that David Donohue, who did so much for the E36 profile and performance in the States, would be among those year-2000 BMW racing headliners. However, when this was written, he was (reluctantly) outside the Bimmer fold earning a living on the Chrysler-Reynard 2-liter Stratus program. I also want to pay my respects here to those who have won for BMW overseas, particularly 1997 Australian champion Paul Morris, 1996 Australian champion Geoff Brabham with the 320i, and 2-liter M3 E30 British champions Will Hoy (1991) and Tim Harvey (1992).

Steve Soper

The first Briton to impact German Championship racing since John Fitzpatrick, Steve Soper is a natural winner whose trademark is sartorial and circuit neatness.

Soper has known racing life on a shoestring as well as the sharp-suited trappings of success. He is the only driver to make the German grade from the ranks of the British one-make race series for the underpowered Mini, Metro, and Ford Fiesta, winning titles in all three national categories.

Soper felt that it was this early success in low-powered, front-drive machines that taught him to squeeze a racing advantage from nothing. Certainly, it is his racecraft that allowed him such a prominent role in the tightly contested German Championship. Soper secured a single pole position at the close of 1991, yet he always figured among the German lists of most successful race winners at the close of a season.

Soper's mechanics always comment that he has a very light touch on the car, particularly the steering, but it was his sheer precision that dumbfounded the author when Soper gave him rides around the Silverstone Grand Prix circuit in one of the infamous TWR Rover V8 winners and the E30 M3 of 1992.

That Rover V8 would have netted Soper the UK title outright in 1983, had not a preparation scandal erupted. He continued to drive for TWR Rover until 1985 and built a reputation as a hard man.

From Rover, Soper graduated to the turbo power of the Eggenberger Ford Sierras. In 1986, these were US-homologated Sierra XR4Ti models, and he was a winner in that inaugural year. He stayed with Eggenberger for the 500-bhp Cosworth era and looked likely to secure outright titles on several occasions, but took individual victories: three in 1987 and a fantastic seven outright wins as the Ford RS500 outpaced all comers in 1988.

BMW's British driving force, Steve Soper, graduated to the "Big Mac" McLaren in 1997.

Picture: BMW AG Presse, 1993

Soper first appeared in the German Championship to take a brace of second places at Wunstorf in 1988, a season when he also appeared in Britain driving the black-and-red Eggenberger Sierras to engage in some fantastic dices with Andy Rouse. The switch to the official BMW MTeam came in 1989, following the close of the European Championship, and Soper immediately proved ultra-competitive.

In 1991, he was serving a second season for the Bigazzi equipe and led the German series at the halfway stage, finally finishing fifth after four more outright wins and three fastest laps. Brits may remember him best in 1991 for a fighting second place to Frank Biela (1996 British Champion) in the monster Audi V8 quattro at Donington.

By 1997, Soper had won the Japanese Championship outright—a tough fight against the might of the national Japanese teams in 1995—and should have won the 1996 German title, only to have a teammate trip him up!

Soper had fought his way to the top of the BMW Big Four pecking order with much the same determined grind as Nigel Mansell exhibited in single-seaters. BMW Motorsport gave him a 1997 drive in the McLaren-BMW factory team for the FIA team, earned on the merits of his "rookie" pole position at Silverstone in 1996.

At press time, Soper had shared his 604-bhp long-tail Schnitzer McLaren-BMW V12 with J. J. Lehto to achieve four wins and tied with Lehto to finish second in the 1997 World FIA GT series. Not bad for a West London boy (born September 27, 1953) who first attracted BMW managerial attention in a 100-bhp Mini-Metro racer!

Soper is married to Lulu, has a young son and daughter, and holds a helicopter license which he attained from scratch in the late 1980s. He has been a Monaco resident, rather than using a tax-exile address, but drove an M5 to races rather than flying in the early 1990s. Today, his home is almost the racetracks of the world, but he is a familiar sight in Britain, usually laughing as he tells sharply-observed race tales between global engagements.

Joachim Winkelhock

He is a counterpart to Soper, but Joachim "Jockel" Winkelhock is the youngest of the BMW quartet (born October 24, 1960). Like Soper, his former teammate in the UK, Winkelhock was a national hero born into motorsports—one who evolved from modest one-make racing into an international title winner.

If the Winkelhock name is familiar, that is because elder brother Manfred also made it all the way to Grand Prix with BMW power. The elder Winkelhock died racing a Porsche Group C sports car. That was back in 1985, and Joachim now puts family values above all else in his life. Home security is in Waiblingen, Germany, where he lives with wife Sabine and their two daughters, Sina and Nina.

Winkelhock borrowed 10,000 DM from his elder brother for his 1979 race debut with the hot hatchback Renault 5, but took his first title in 1985: the hard-fought Porsche 944 Turbo Cup. In 1987–88, he reverted to single-seaters (having experienced Formula Ford in 1982) and managed a second overall in the German Formula 3 series, followed by a significant win in that German Championship of 1988—a Reynard-VW victory that propelled him into 1989 Formula 1 the next year, but with the uncompetitive AGS-Ford V8 equipe.

By 1990, Winkelhock reported for duty to the BMW touring-car squad and began to win once more. There were three national victories plus the tortuous Nürburgring 24-hours won by Winkelhock by the end of 1992, all with the old M3. A switch to the E36 318iS coupe brought Winkelhock British honors in 1993—beating teammate Steve Soper to the title—and he also used the two-door for an Asia-Pacific title before switching to the current four-door 320i layout for his first Spa 24-hour win (1994).

At press time, Winkelhock had served seven years with BMW and harvested three successive championships: British (1993), Asia-Pacific (1994), and German 2-liter SuperTouring (1995), all in E36 3-series. In Britain, he was as popular as in Germany, nicknamed "Smokin' Jo" after his perpetual cigarette habit and fabulous standing-start abilities.

Joachim Winkelhock has been both British and German Champion in the E36 era.

Picture: BMW AG Presse, 1993

Roberto Ravaglia

The most successful of the BMW M3 squad in terms of garnering titles—and some very prestigious individual race victories—Roberto Ravaglia was originally set on a conventional single-seater career. Born May 26, 1957 in Mestre, outside Venice, Ravaglia won the Italian National Kart Championship twice...before he left school!

Ravaglia graduated to single-seater Formula 3, finishing fifth in the European title hunt of 1983. It was 1985 before Ravaglia and BMW began their international winning connection. Ravaglia and the 160-mph 635CSi coupes gelled immediately. He was part of the winning equipe at the Spa 24-hours of 1985.

The man with more titles than the monarchy: Italy's Roberto Ravaglia.

Picture: BMW AG Presse, 1993

Ravaglia's long-distance talents were confirmed with further wins at Spa in 1986, 1988, and 1994, in various 3-series. The rapid Venetian has also secured wins in the 1989 and 1994 Nürburgring 24-hour bashes. The latter do not have the opposition that Spa brings, yet the legendary old long circuit is at its most formidable with rain, sleet, and fog, which is the norm to beset drivers facing a series of 90- to 150-mph crests and twists.

However successful "R. R." has been in terms of individual records, they pale beside his aptitude for securing sedan championships. In eight successive years, he brought back as many titles: European (1986 and 1988), German (1989 and 1992), Italian (1990, 1991, and 1993) and World (1987).

Since 1993, Ravaglia's championship pace has slackened. He had a tough time stamping his previous authority on the German series of 1995, while his entry in Britain's rough-and-tumble 1996 season (with a 3-series that hated UK circuit bumps) brought only a sixth overall.

For 1997, Ravaglia was drafted into the FIA GT Championship, still with Schnitzer, but driving the awesome McLaren BMW V12. Facing the challenge from Mercedes-Illmor V12 opposition, Ravaglia and Peter Kox won the second round of the 1997 FIA series and finished eighth overall in the year-end rankings.

An amiable and approachable man off the track, Ravaglia retired at the end of 1997 to run very successful BMW dealerships. He is a family man of great loyalty to his chosen race team and to his wife Franca. They have two daughters, Stefania and Francesca.

Speaking in the winter of 1988 of the Schnitzer team that helped create his winning ways, Ravaglia said, "The M3 is a staggering racing car, but I would never have made it without Team Schnitzer and Charly Lamm's fantastic mechanics. They're real professionals and take care of your car at the pits faster than any other team in touring-car racing." Whatever the car, the remark is equally true today.

Johnny Cecotto

Rated by his rivals as the fastest man on a single-lap basis, Johnny Cecotto was a world-class winner long before he appeared in a BMW. Cecotto was a born racer, who began competition life on a motor bike in 1972 when he was sixteen.

A year later, he was a national champion of South America and was soon seen on the world circuits, where he scraped knees with the best in biking. Cecotto was the 1975 world champion at 350 cc, securing the world 750 class in 1978.

"Johnny be Good," as he has been dubbed in European paddocks,

A World Champion on two wheels, former Grand Prix driver, and a winner for BMW in E30 and E36: Johnny Cecotto.

Picture: BMW AG Presse, 1993

switched to single-seater cars in 1981. He was immediately quick and proved to be one of the stars in European Formula 2, a category in which BMW was always a major player. Inevitably, he ended up in a March-BMW (1982), and, equally inevitably, Cecotto proved an able companion to that year's March 882-BMW European Champion, Corrado Fabi, finishing runner-up in the series.

Cecotto's single-seater career was extremely promising, but a severe accident at the wheel of a Toleman (the forerunner of Benetton Grand Prix) put an end to those ambitions. Cecotto then turned to touring cars for his motorized living.

In 1985, Cecotto was recruited for Schnitzer and the BMW 635 program, but he has not been at BMW all throughout his sedan-racing career. Cecotto drove turbocharged Volvos in 1986 (for two European Championship wins) and Mercedes in 1988.

In 1987, the Italian CibiEmme MTeam benefited from his talents: co-driving with Gianfranco Brancatelli, Cecotto seized four tough European victories including Dijon, Estoril, and Zeltweg.

For 1989, he was back from Mercedes with Schnitzer BMW. Ever since, Cecotto has proved to be a wiry and athletic performer, winning the 1989 Italian Touring Car Championship and just missing out on the 1990 German title at the last round.

In 1991, Cecotto was similarly competitive and finished fourth in the DTM, scoring three outright victories with a brace of pole positions and two fastest laps to his credit. In both 1991 and 1992, Cecotto was runner-up to the overall German title—series then blitzed by Audi 4x4 V8s—and left the tough series with ten wins.

In 1993, BMW switched emphasis and played the Cecotto hand in the "less important" ADAC German Cup. Despite insider misgivings about the series, a new M3 GTR 3-series was created and won the title straight out of the box. The following year saw Cecotto remain in ADAC-organized competition, but this time he was armed with 2-liter E36 SuperTourers.

In fact, the German ADAC series was never enough racing for Cecotto. He competed in Italy occasionally at first (seventh overall in 1994), then more seriously, finishing as runner-up to a new generation of 4-cylinder Audi quattros (A4) in 1996. For 1997, he was assigned to Bigazzi, alongside Jo Winkelhock, facing the very tough task of beating Audi, Peugeot and many more in the 33-car strong German ADAC SuperTouring Cup. Initial signs were encouraging with podium finishes for the pair, but the 320-bhp Pug was a little stronger down the straights than BMW's 320i. Both Cecotto and Winkelhock were beaten by France's Laurent Aiello in the factory Peugot 406.

Born January 25, 1956 in Venezuela of Italian parents, Cecotto has now found a natural home in Italy with a German wife and a son who may follow a different career: his name is Johnny Amadeus.

QUICK FACTS

Period
1988–98

Product
McLaren-BMW V12 F1 and GTR/LM derivatives

Performance
From 627 road horsepower to 640-bhp racing format (with air restrictors); normal 1995–96 max rpm at 7,500–7,800; official 1997 max at 8,000 rpm (telemetry reveals "quite regular use of 9,000 rpm," reports an insider, "and the most we have seen without a blow-up on a missed shift was 13,000 rpm!"); aerodynamic downforce rules slow street maximum of 231 mph to 205 racing mph; street F1-BMW at 0–60 mph in 3.2 seconds, better for GTR/ LM replica

Achievements
Won Le Mans at first 1995 attempt; winner of BPR Global Cup in 1995 and 1996; winner of Japanese GT Championship in 1996; fourth at Le Mans 1998

People
Gordon Murray on converting the world's fastest road car into an immediately-successful GT race winner; J. J. Lehto on winning Le Mans 1995

Chapter 28

The 231-mph GT

BMW's weapon for WSC racing against Porsche, Mercedes and the best of the rest

Created after a conversation in 1988 between McLaren directors who had lost their first—and, as it turned out, only—Grand Prix of that season, the McLaren-BMW F1 set unmatched benchmarks for production-car street performance. The F1 incorporated carbon-fiber flyweight chassis/body-panel construction alongside 103-bhp-per-liter parameters of track performance from its magnificent Munich-built V12.

The last McLaren F1-BMW for public road consumption was built in the fall of 1997. A $957,770 baby that blew everyday assumptions about supercar performance and price to new highs, the F1 failed commercially to reach more than a third of its targeted 350-unit production run or return a profit for McLaren.

Equipped with a tired development BMW Motorsport twelve coded S70, its 369 cubic inches struggling against 40° C ambient air at the Italian speed bowl of Nardo (ironically owned by Fiat, Ferrari's parents), this McLaren F1 prototype rewrote the rule book. Even with a Bimmer V12 reckoned to be 50 bhp down on the 627 bhp sold to the public from March 1994 to June 1997, the "Big Mac" was logged on its computer telemetry at 231 mph.

That was 18 mph faster than contemporaries such as Ferrari's F40, Lamborghini's Diablo, or

Bugatti's bulging quad-turbo EB110. Some 237 mph was the expectation for a fully-freshened McLaren-BMW in street guise, but this McLaren was about much more than sheer track speed.

Designer Gordon Murray, who designed the Brabham chassis that wrapped around BMW's Grand Prix championship-winning turbo motor, had "wanted to design a sports car since I was a kid. I got side-tracked by racing, but right back to 15 years of age, I had produced sketches of a mid-engine sports car with three seats and a central driving position. That is basically the whole concept of the F1 we built for the road, and which we currently [summer of 1997] continue to support in FIA GT Championship Sports Car racing with BMW Motorsport backing."

The price tag and the comparatively low cost of Ferrari F40/F50 opposition (never thought I'd write that without laughing) kept demand for showroom McLaren-BMWs down to 86. An additional 14 GTRs were for motor racing only—an official 100-strong run at the close of F1 public-sale production (official, because the first two McLaren road car prototypes had the proven Ultima chassis alongside BMW running gear, and they may have been included in the grand total.)

Open wide! The production McLaren F1-BMW V12 road car rewrote the supercar rule book. The 230-mph performance shattered previous benchmarks, but it also accomodated luggage in side compartments (like a coach!) and three people across its central-driving-position cockpit. In 1997, it remained the only GT racer that had genuinely been conceived as a road car rather than as a pure racer.

Picture: Courtesy McLaren Cars, UK, 1995

Gordon Murray insisted on ultimate driving pleasure, plus the functional best. He eschewed popular palliatives like ABS and power steering. Murray did allow a purpose-built Kenwood CD system (his second passion is rock music) and the air conditioning that is vital in such a generously-glazed street design.

The deal to utilize a specially-designed BMW Motorsport 48-valve version of the V12 was announced in February 1991, but had been negotiated since November 15, 1990. McLaren had been winning with Honda when the car was conceived, but the Japanese were not interested in the 500-bhp street numbers and cubic capacity that Murray wanted to meet and beat with the emerging supercar crop of the 1990s.

Ferrari was a possibility among seven alternatives, but it was the working relationship with Paul Rosche at BMW Motorsport that clinched a necessarily rapid development pro-

Gordon Murray "...wanted to design a sports car, since I was a kid." He achieved his lifelong ambition, but along the way the South African also designed winning Grand Prix cars for Brabham and McLaren (the latter were almost invincible in the late 1980s).

Picture: BMW AG Presse, 1997

gram—one to match Murray's insistence on at least 100-bhp-per-liter output.

Beginning in March 1991, Motorsport drew up what amounted to a total revamp of the company's 60-degree V12. Murray had set the parameters tight for the longitudinally mounted engine (the gearbox is transversely mounted) with 550-bhp minimum, cylinder-block length of 0.6 m/23.6 in, and a 250-kg target for the twelve, including all ancillaries. The Munich motor measured out at 6,064 cc, equivalent to 6.1 liters and 396 cubic inches, to produce 103 bhp per liter from its aluminum block, heads, and magnesium cam carriers. The final S70/2 production unit was also was the correct length, weighed 266 kg /585 lbs and yielded a 14 percent power bonus, some 627 bhp at 7,400 of an available 7,500 rpm.

During the 1996/97 winter redevelopment for racing, Motorsport hit 237 kg/521 lb as the dressed weight for a slightly smaller (5,995-cc) version of the V12. This utilized hugely-expensive carbon fiber for the coils and valve housings. The latter were originally in magnesium. Motorsport made more-traditional moves, such as a lighter flywheel, exhaust manifold, heat exchanger, and wiring harness to clip off 29 kg when compared to the original.

Back in pre-production, the real BMW point was a massive torque curve, one recorded at more than 479 lb-ft from 4,000 to 7,000 rpm. Such gentle-giant pulling power was always among the major impressions of those who have driven the street car. It has not been neglected in competition, either.

The 4,288 x 1,820 x 1,140-mm (168.8 x 71.7 x 44.9-in) package dimensions of the McLaren-BMW were uncompromisingly small when compared with conventional supercar opposition. The McLaren result was a 230-mph motor car packaged some 100 mm/4 inches shorter than a BMW 3-series sedan. A curvaceous 3-seater with central driving position and transverse 6-speed gearbox, it also

weighed less (at 1,140 kg/2,508 lbs) than BMW's then-smallest sedan.

When it came to racing in 1995, McLaren was able to remove the obvious clutter like the CD player and enormous catalytic-converter exhausts, part of the rear crash structure on the road car. When McLaren studied the discarded 100 kg of road equipment, they found they had to put back in 60–70 kg in the form of a steel roll cage, fire-extinguisher system, and sundry other mandatory safety measures. There were also race-weight gains involved in beefier transmission and suspension components.

So the astonishing McLaren F1 street power-to-weight ratio of 560 bhp per ton was little bettered by the earlier racers, which hit the circuits at 582 bhp per ton. The 1997 derivative runs around 645.2 bhp per ton, thanks to a new minimum weight from its reduced engine size.

What prompted McLaren to change its mind about a racing version of the F1 in 1994–95?

West Germany's former private bank owner Thomas Bscher was a major force in persuading McLaren to take the F1 from road to race trim. He owned and drove both road and race versions of McLaren's million-dollar baby.

Picture: Author Archive via West Racing, 1995/96

The most effective requests from McLaren customers came from former private bank owner Thomas Bscher (he had street and race McLarens to beat Big Mac withdrawal symptoms), who used to control Oppenheimer. Former sports car champion Ray Bellm of Britain added his voice, and between them, they convinced McLaren that the emerging BPR Karcher Global GT Championship could be a happy hunting ground for the F1-BMW, as well as a valuable source of extra business.

The author is convinced that McLaren and Murray did not set out with the idea of creating a competition car in the F1, but slower sales than anticipated, plus the prospect of raising McLaren's profile worldwide at the non-championship Le Mans 24-hours, tipped the balance.

Murray recalled, "All of us involved in the original 1988 discussion to created the F1 had agreed that the goal was the ultimate sports car for the road. McLaren's Ron Dennis and Creighton Brown, plus TAG's Mansour Ojjeh and I all agreed on that—if we even started thinking race car, we would not make a good road car." However, Bscher and Bellm were good customers and, Murray added, "We had the design group standing idle at the time they asked....It was worth investigating."

That was 1994, and the response was a converted road car (tagged GTR) for 1995, one that nevertheless won Le Mans and the Global GT Championship for drivers. That prompted a more serious racing program for 1996, when Porsche drove into town with a "911" based on pure racing technology.

McLaren-BMW had to react rather more fiercely if it was to stay in the 1997 game, for Mercedes was preparing an even more-radical

Father and brawny son. Here is Paul Rosche, BMW Motorsport Ltd. manager, with Motorsport V12 in 604-bhp/6-liter race trim for 1997: those exhausts cost a little more than a 328 coupe!

Picture: BMW AG Presse, 1997

racer: a "CLK" coupe outline with oversize Grand Prix engine from Illmor. McLaren announced a full-blooded "long tail" McLaren F1-BMW GTR for 1997, when BMW funding became much heavier and the Schnitzer team was switched into GT racing alongside McLaren and its customers.

Aside from the weight losses recorded earlier, on the BMW front, the V12 engine continued to run its primary hardware—block and most major reciprocating items from the crankshaft upward—in stock form. Paul Rosche credibly claimed that the V12 could serve "...a full season, including Le Mans..." without major replacements. Since each engine accounted for at least $57,750 and was as advanced as possible in its street format, this should not be a major surprise. Seriously expensive factory work was done to offset the effect of the 39-mm air restrictors imposed by the international authorities for 1995.

It was estimated that more than 100 bhp would be lost from the 1995 street engines if the air restrictors were simply bolted into place, so how did they obtain a modest (13 bhp) gain in 1995? Murray and Rosche initiat-

ed an extensive re-mapping program with McLaren's business partners and electronic aces, TAG. Rosche's role was to ensure that the cylinder head could breath under this revised regime and to provide alternative settings for the showroom variable valve timing system (VANOS). The modest boost in horsepower was accompanied by even more torque.

From 4,000 rpm upward, they reported a bonus 15 percent in torque (542 lb-ft compared to 479 lb-ft for street) and one extremely tractable racer. Alternative non-factory figures suggested over 580 lb-ft of torque was on tap.

Recalling these early moves in 1997, Murray pointed out that many of the expensive changes made to the V12 were to reduce weight (a total of 25 kg/55 lb in the engine bay), but "if that had not been a factor, the street specification engine was perfectly capable of standing up to racing demands...with few obvious exceptions." That meant that the standard dry-sump lubrication layout was modified, as was the fuel-system pump and scavenge layout, to pick up the last 100 cc and lengthen the period between pit stops.

For a race car that was intended to change direction, rapidly, on slick racing tires, more fundamental suspension and engine mounting changes were required. Drivers of the highest standard found the initial tail-happiness through sharp directional changes disconcerting.

If the driver realized that the world's most expensive car could be drifted through this unhappy transition, then astonishing feats could be realized, even in 1995: for example, J. J. Lehto's astounding laps of Le Mans, seconds faster than the opposition and his teammates. These were skills that made the original race GTR 001 a winner when more established McLaren customer cars were waylaid.

Another 1995 Le Mans feature that worked beyond its obvious enhancement of (stopping) performance was the substitution of £40,000 Carbone Industrie disc-brake systems for the showroom steel fitment. Of course, the slowing

distances were shaved, although wet weather and lower temperatures could upset their carbon consistency. Yet the real Le Mans point was that pad changes could be cut to just one in a marathon, rather than several.

In 1995, there had been minimal money, and time, to revise the aerodynamics. McLaren spent just a day in the MIRA (Motor Industry Research Association) facility at Hinckley, Leicestershire, UK. It managed a record 60 separate set-ups in that day, but were not allowed to use the fan-assisted systems of the road F1. Still, the fans remain to ventilate engine bay and driver.

The most obvious changes for 1995 were a fixed rear wing, minimal counterbalance from a revised front bumper, and extra cooling slots. The rules dictated a flat under-floor until the rear axle, robbing ground-effect downforce that Formula 1 designers like Murray were used to harnessing. A diffuser and tail-end ground-effect tunnels were allowed in back of the rear axle to a maximum depth of six inches.

As J. J. Lehto commented at Le Mans, this meant that the McLaren-BMW was light to drive in comparison with the heavily downforce-loaded Grand Prix car. The McLaren-BMW needed considerable set-up skills to balance its flexible and massive power against limited aerodynamic and mechanical grip.

In 1995, McLaren utilized modified production uprights that took bigger wheel bearings, and was rated 2.2 G rather than the 1.1 G expected from showroom specification.

Developing the McLaren-BMW further

McLaren itself listed its work step-by step, so that the 1995–96 changes could be seen in detail. The overall themes were living with the tightened

The most exclusive of all

To celebrate its 1995 Le Mans victory, McLaren executed a limited edition (just five were constructed at $1.2 million apiece) of the already-exclusive F1. Called McLaren F1 LM, previewed in a screaming orange that recalled the immortal "Bruce and Denny Show" M8D Can Am racers, this was the closest the company could get to offering the public a replica of the Le Mans racing experience...on the street.

Mechanical alterations made this the fastest of the fastest, including an unrestricted version of the 6.1-liter/396-cubic inch 12. Instead of 1995's 39-mm restrictors, BMW Motorsport was commissioned to build much of the Le Mans knowledge into a unit that drew through unfettered 85-mm orifices. Yet another camshaft profile, more TAG programming of the management electronics, and the original 10.5:1 compression were featured.

The massive result was 668 bhp at 7,800 rpm, plus 520 lb-ft of torque at 4,500 rpm, representing 110 bhp per liter. There were nearly 630 bhp per ton, for curb weight was recorded at 1,062 kg/2,336 lbs.

Using race-car aerodynamics, the LM was not going to crack the original car's 230-mph maximum. Some 220 mph was the quoted maximum, but the stripped-out advertisement for the merits of carbon fiber (now including the rear wing) dropped

0–60 mph into unknown road-car territory (below 3.0 seconds).

McLaren set new handling and adhesion benchmarks, using the solid mounting system for the first time on the road, rather than the rubber-insulated suspension-mounting points of the first F1. A further grip bonus was conferred via OZ race specification 18-inch diameter magnesium wheels (10.5 and 13 inches wide). These were clothed in Michelin tires of up to 345/35 section, rather than the original 315/45 maximum Goodyear 17-inch F1-coded tires.

The most exclusive of all McLaren F1-BMWs, and certainly the most powerful to hit the road, was this 668-bhp F1 LM variant. Prompted by the Le Mans win in 1995 and wearing the traditional McLaren colors for their years of Can Am dominance (with aluminium V8 Chevrolet power!), just five LMs were made and pre-sold at some $1.2 million each.

Picture: Courtesy of McLaren Cars, UK, 1995

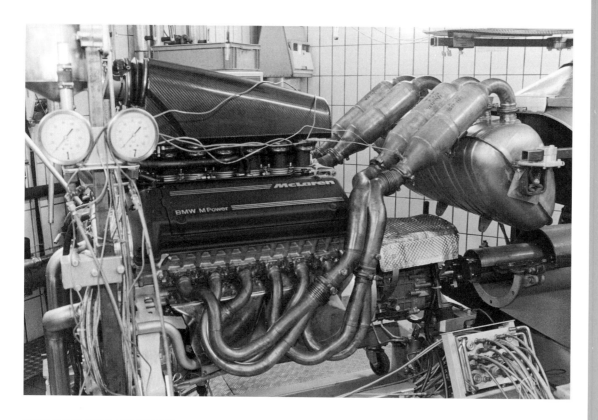

In or out of the McLaren F1, the BMW V12 is an impressive sight. Here, we see a 1996 Munich test cell and the racing implant in a 1996 Bigazzi-Fina machine, when it was rated around 600 bhp at 7,300 rpm, owing to tighter air restrictors.

Pictures: Klaus Schnitzer (cell), Germany, 1996; Author (racecar), US, 1996

air restrictors on the engine—which cost around 35 bhp in 1996—by lowering curb weights, substantially overhauling the suspension, and a thorough aerodynamic overhaul.

For 1996, the most fundamental change was lowering the motor 15 mm/0.60 inch in the chassis. A replacement magnesium-alloy casting to the upright was employed, because the predictions of 2.1 G cornering capability (double that of the outstanding road cars) proved accurate.

Also uprated in the chassis for 1996 was the usual unassisted steering rack, which was shortened to lessen steering turns (from a street 2.7 turns lock-to-lock to a flick-wrist 2 turns) and stiffened. Critical circuit shocks, fed in through the front mounts, were handled a little more gracefully. There were double spherical bearings placed at either end of the rocker-arm layout, part of the 1996 extensive suspension redesign work that saw McLaren insert solid bushings and beefier race components to complement the revised motor location.

That second (1996) season was much more challenging technically. The opposition, headed by Porsche, became more radically-engineered and used the turbocharging systems that are so hard to equate with normally-aspirated engine engineering. And our heroes suffered additional air-induction restrictions (another 3-mm constriction) from the FIA administrative authorities, which limited horsepower considerably.

BMW Motorsport responded with a hike in compression from 11.0:1 to 12.0:1 in 1996, reprogrammed TAG electronics, another cam profiling set from Paul Rosche, and revised induction tracts in the cold air and filter feeds. Most radical was a reduction on pumping rates for oil and water systems, bidding to improve mechanical operating efficiency.

As expected, 1996 peak power (600 bhp at 7,300 rpm) and torque (511 lb-ft at 4,000 rpm) dropped from 1995 levels. However, McLaren knew it could compensate in other areas. Among the smaller changes were the provision of a 100-liter/22-gallon (UK) fuel tank, in place of the original 90-liter unit, plus two race-specification radiators installed in the nose, a feature Murray had used in Grand Prix Brabhams.

Those GTR carbon-fiber brakes were 14 x 1.42 inches thick versus the 13 x 1.26 inches of the steel street items. For track use, the Le Mans specification brakes measured the same, front and rear, whereas street cars had the 14-inch units up front, 12-inch rears, and a full road-legal handbrake—dispensed with on the race car, of course.

For 1996, McLaren moved back to the Activa wind tunnel that Murray had created as a cost-saving exercise in his Grand Prix days with Brabham. It took an array of alternative rear wing profiles, which had to perform without 1995's multi-plane elements, but it was allowed to retain the ubiquitous Gurney flap.

McLaren also attacked the front with a notable front splitter to work alongside a realigned front panel, both cutting production lift that had given a high-speed understeer in the 1995 racer.

"The whole package was a lot more aerodynamically adjustable in 1996 than it had been in 1995, when I felt rather sorry for our customers. All they could then do was crank on more rear wing when searching for extra downforce. Then they would run into understeer and excessive front tire wear as the limiting factors.

"For 1996, we got a lot more aerodynamic adjustment into the F1, including high or low downforce rear wings, so it was a lot better to aerodynamically adjust to differing circumstances in 1996 than 1995," concluded Murray, regarding the aerodynamic answers that could now be explored.

1997 race specification

External changes were pronounced this season, with the long-tail body (20 in/500 mm longer; 8.7 in/220 mm wider) designed to dramatically increase downforce in the era of purpose-built racing challenges from Porsche and Mercedes. The 1997 McLaren body had much increased area to generate downforce (approximately 2,000 lbs at 150 mph) at the lower race weight. Murray estimated that the lowest downforce position of 1997 equaled the maximum available the previous season.

BMW Motorsport had hit the total commitment button in GT racing, while it devolved touring-car responsibilities (outside the engine bay, which remains sacred) to Bigazzi in Germany, subbing Schnitzer to global FIA GT duties.

Technically, the 1997 McLaren F1 GTR was most radically-changed in a clever S70/3-coded Motorsport move from 6.1 liters to less than 6.0 liters and 6,064 cc down to 5,990

cc. That meant a virtually square bore x stroke ratio (given as the usual 86-mm by either 86-mm or 85.95-mm crankshaft stroke, depending on source).

Maximum torque dropped to 506 lb-ft, some 1,000 revs further up the scale (5,000 rpm), and horsepower was hard to maintain at 604 bhp. The point was that the now FIA-promoted GT Championship allowed a weight drop at the new engine capacity. A racing weight up to 75 kg/165 lbs lighter (1997 total: 950 kg/2,090 lbs) would significantly improve power-to-weight ratios over 1996.

The gearbox was new, too. Instead of the H-pattern transverse unit with McLaren casing and straight-cut replacement racing gears used in Le Mans 1995 and 1996, the 1997 GTR sported a sequential shift (in-line, as for a 2-liter SuperTourer or a motorcycle) racing box from X-trac in Britain.

To stop the plot from 205 mph at Le Mans, McLaren went up again on carbon brake disc sizes, this time settling for 15-inch units, but clamped by Brembo eight-piston units rather than the previous four-piston practice. These hid behind the usual 18-inch diameter OZs of 10.85-inch front width and 13-inch rear breadth. Cornering forces were now reckoned to be up in the 2.5 G league, close to the routine, rather than ultimate, levels of Grand Prix racers.

A revised carbon-fiber chassis was necessary to underpin those further weight reductions, and TAG electronics data acquisition and instrumentation were added to the 1997 specification for the eight race chassis scheduled.

Looking back over three seasons of race development (1995–97), Murray commented, "If I had set out to design a racing McLaren-BMW, I would never have devoted the time to getting a dedicated sound system with a clearly defined weight target, installed air conditioning, or put the suspension system on sound insulating rubbers. In fact, the F1 would not have looked the way it looks, nor have the unique luggage accommodation—

For 1997, BMW Motorsport appointed Schnitzer race-track strategy supremo Charly Lamm as racing director of the BMW-McLaren GT program. The immediate results were sensational, with four wins in the six opening races of the year, but nobody expected the road-converted McLaren to hang on for the first FIA World GT Championship in the face of race-bred pedigree Porsches and Mercedes.

Picture: BMW AG Presse, 1997

In all its glory, the
aerodynamically-
revised and length-
ened McLaren F1-
BMW V12 for 1997
proved harder to
beat for the later
Porsche and
Mercedes designs
than anticipated.

*Picture: BMW AG
Presse, 1997*

more than for some family hatchbacks!
Instead of making more than 25 cars a year,
we'd have sold six in total!"

Turning to those individual season modifications, Murray recalled, "The 1995 racer
really was a converted road car with 30 percent modifications. The 1996 was a halfway
stage to being a racer. The engine work was
quite extensive at BMW Motorsport, including slowing down the oil and water pumps.
The gearbox was a bit lighter—we did more
race-orientated fabrication, and there were
some different castings and a lot more lightweight materials.

"For 1997, we'd probably reversed those
original percentages. Now we had a 70 percent race car in GTR spec, 30 percent left from

the road....But, it's important to remember that
all our fundamental principles—central driving
position, the mid-mounted BMW V12, suspension systems—all remained," said Murray with
justified pride.

One development peculiarity was that
McLaren completed a massive ABS anti-lock
braking program for the GTR in 1997, in association with Germany's ITT Teves. This was
required because the authorities at Le Mans
looked like they were going to permit this feature, even though it was not permitted in the
BPR or FIA Global/World GT series...and the
F1 does not feature ABS for the showroom.

This GT racing/road-car link at McLaren-
BMW was definitely not the case with either the
Porsche "911," Nissan's 390 with TWR at Le

Mans 1997, or the Mercedes CLK. All were conceived purely to race, and the road car variant was not on sale when they first competed.

Jeff Hazell, McLaren/BMW Motorsport Chief on the GT Racing and Touring Car programs, reminded me of another unique aspect of the GT racing operation. The customer service is amazing and has been an built-in part of the way McLaren-BMW races, with technicians, a $3.3 million truckload of spares, and technical support inherent in supporting those—like Bscher and Bellm—who prompted such a customer-based program. By monitoring telemetry and radio messages, the McLaren customer-support technicians have occasionally managed to have a component/assembly waiting for the inevitable pit stop before teams were aware they had a problem!

Unlike normal race practice, there were few trick or development pieces that were not freely customer-available until McLaren had to support the BMW-funded 1996 Le Mans assault from Bigazzi, which included a preliminary Silverstone warm-up race. Thereafter, the pace of development quickened.

Full customer service remained, along with availability of the 1997 long-tail GTR at some $1.98 million. A Schnitzer-McLaren alliance for Le Mans 1997 and FIA GT championship racing meant that there would be a factory-funded development stream of parts, with the priority to ensure these GTRs set the pace: customers continued with proven parts.

Race record: 1995–97

The highlight of all highlights was the 1995 Le Mans win, but the "Big Mac" managed much more than that. Tested over 5,000 kilometers from January 1995 and destined to endure 6,000 successful kilometers at Le Mans, the first GTR (001) looked to be a durable winner. In fact, the GTR was a breed of winning machines, from its 4-hour February 1995 debut in Jerez, Spain, through Le Mans (the first time a manufacturer has achieved a debut winning run in the 24-hour classic), to Zhuhai in China, the final 3-hour encounter. Considering that the opposition included Porsche's customers cars (twin-turbo GT2 911) and Ferrari followers (twin-turbo F40), McLaren and BMW could be proud of that season. They knew they owed particular thanks to the pioneer customer teams of GTC and West.

Right from the Jerez opening round, the BPR Global series developed into a duel between the Ray Bellm-owned GTC McLaren-BMWs (managed by former Williams F1 manager Michael Cane) and the David Price-run, West cigarettes-sponsored McLarens, inspired by Thomas Bscher and exceptionally co-driven by John Nielsen.

All three McLaren-BMWs proved at least two seconds a lap faster than the quickest GT2 Porsche in that season opener, but the final flag fell fittingly on Ray Bellm's car (shared by Maurizio Sala) just 16 seconds ahead of the best Porsche after 4 hours racing. Close call....

There were four McLarens out for the second round at Paul Ricard in France, and they finished the event first, third, fourth, and seventh. Reliability of the major mechanical components was already above expectations. Gordon Murray would quote just three retirements through mechanical causes from 51 starts for McLaren BMWs in their debut season—an unparalleled achievement for any race car, never mind a winning V12.

Despite fiercer opposition from Ferrari on home ground at Monza (Swedish former touring-car ace Anders Olofsson planted the Ferrari Club Italia F40 on pole) and a Porsche leading at three-quarter distance, McLaren won again in Italy in 1995. This time it was the West pairing of former Le Mans winner Neilsen and owner Bscher, who took a narrow three-in-a-row-result for McLaren-BMW.

Big Mac to go with Gulf dressing. Despite winning half of the McLaren victories recorded, the Michael Caine-run Gulf McLaren-BMWs had to settle for third in the 1995 Global series. They made up for it in 1996....

Picture: Courtesy Gulf Oil Corporation, 1996

There were six McLaren-BMWs entered for Jarama's four-hour Spanish encounter: one Big Mac got rolled pre-event (the safety equipment did its job). Pacesetters Bellm/Sala and Nielsen/Bscher returned a one-two McLaren finish, just 17 seconds ahead of that pesky Larbre Porsche.

This was the drift of the debut year. McLarens with BMW power won all but two of the twelve BPR Karcher Global GT Championship rounds for 1995, plus an imposing one-three-four-five-thirteen finish for the BMW Motorsport-engined Big Macs at Le Mans. In a further testimony to the sound engineering behind the McLaren F1 GTR, five of seven McLarens finished at Le Mans. The two non-finishers both had accidents, not mechanical failures, that sidelined them.

That Le Mans victory was in doubt up to the last two hours of the day-and-night marathon. The odds were 2:1 that McLaren-BMW would come away with the goods, as there were two McLarens in the Sunday morning top three. Odd man out was then 55-year-old Mario Andretti, sharing a Courage Porsche and looking to equal the Graham Hill record of winning motor racing's equivalent of the Holy Grail: Indianapolis 500, World Championship, and Le Mans.

If Derek Bell had won in the Harrods-backed McLaren F1 he shared with son Justin, that would have equaled the record number of LM victories posted by one driver: Bell has won five times; Belgium's Jacky Ickx scored six.

It did not happen that way. J. J. Lehto's sheer speed won through alongside triple-winner Yannick Dalmas of France and Masanori Sekiya, the first Japanese to share a Le Mans outright victory. They shared the daddy of all GTRs, the prototype GTR 001 development car rented out to Kokusai Kaihatso and managed by Paul Lanzante in the sinister stealth-bomber carbon black livery. Only one primary advertising legend broke the black theme of car 53, that of Ueno Clinic, which specializes in...umm...let's try a hint: the car was dubbed "Free Willy," a reference to its sponsor's specialization in male circumcision and associated services.

GTR 001 hit the front first at 9:00 am with Lehto decimating Justin Bell's lead, but it relinquished the lead to the Harrods McLaren during stints by Bell Sr. and former winner Andy Wallace. The Ueno-backed F1 finally hit the front for good when its rival F1 suffered the apparently inevitable gearchange/clutch dragging problems that afflicted many of the front-running McLarens.

Lehto's mastery of the midnight hours is recorded on video tape (see bibliography) and allows us all along for the winning debut ride. It was a privilege to watch a scandalously underrated former Grand Prix driver show his superiority at the wheel of the booming BMW.

The use of some magic lightweight camera technology lets you virtually press the clutch for the winning drivers. You can work through the long-throw 6-speeds to 200 mph, extend that rocker-arm double-wishbone front suspension and the long strut/coaxial twin-wishbones rear, deliver this ultimate rear-drive through the wet track zones, and watch the others slither off. The McLaren continues to supply astonishing, treacherous track traction, acceleration that Lehto gleefully taps with old fashioned rear drive and power slide.

Lehto—dropped by Grand Prix team Benetton after returning to the fray too quickly for a full recovery from a heavy testing crash—supplied a heroic Le Mans drive in 1995, backed by the solid speed of Dalmas, whose recent record for Le Mans wins stood at three from four entered by the close of play. Lehto's legendary performance saw the McLaren putting 10–15 seconds per lap on the opposition at some splashy stages. The calm Finn said with a grin afterwards, "We pushed very hard during the night. The gearbox got a bit stiff around two in the morning, but other than that, we were okay." His team manager seemed to suffer more stress, trying to contain the exuberant Lehto.

Ray Bellm, multiple millionaire and talented gentleman driver, at the wheel of the 1995 McLaren he shared with Maurizio Sala. The Gulf team, run by GTC Motorsport in the UK, was the most successful in terms of outright wins that season, but West was more consistent. Either way, Porsche got a regular beating: one that made Stuttgart thirst for 1996 revenge with the GT1, rewriting the rule book...again!

Picture: Courtesy Gulf Oil Corporation, 1995

Lined up for Le Mans 1996 were two works-backed McLaren-BMWs. Run by touring-car aces Bigazzi, this one was driven by Steve Soper, Jacques Laffite of France, and Belgian Marc Duez. Like its teammate, it was a force to be reckoned with until the twilight zone inflicted a 90-minute delay to replace one of many failing gearboxes and transmissions that would haunt McLaren at Le Mans 1996.

Picture: BMW AG, 1996

Other 1995 seasonal pots to be collected with McLaren-BMW's formula for success included the BPR Championship for drivers (Thomas Bscher/John Nielsen). That went to the consistent West/Price Racing entry, while rivals GTC/Gulf won half (five) of all McLaren-BMW wins that debut season, but still had to be content with a third place in the driver's series.

During the ten-month 1995 season, McLaren created GTRs 01 to 08, but there were actually seven complete GTRs that year, as number four was based on the intended GTR 08 to be rebuilt after its Spanish roll-over accident. For 1996, the test and development GTR was number 10, with GTR 14 under construction in April 1997, GTR 15 servingand as the spare to fill any unexpected (usually accidental) further orders.

Porsche was obviously not going to take McLaren-BMW's invasion of its traditional endurance GT racing territory forever, and 1996 marked the return of a full factory team. Porsche fielded a mid-engine, rather than rear-motor, 911. Aside from the carbon-fiber tub, it had much of the race-car ancestry of its dominant 1980s Group C World Sports Cars evident. This "911" was eligible for an official class win (second and third overall) only at Le Mans, contesting—and winning—selected BPR rounds for no points rewards.

This led to a nonsense situation in 1996 where the Porsche won BPR races at prestigious venues such as Spa in Belgium and Brands Hatch in Britain, but the points tables remember only McLaren-BMW. Gulf/GTC Motorsport was rewarded for its F1 loyalty by taking the BPR global driver's title (owner/driver Bellm paired with popular Anglo-American sports car winner James Weaver) with five wins. In fact, these only record the number of times Gulf/GTC Motorsport collected maximum points, for the Porsche was pretty well unbeatable in 1996.

Porsche-powered vehicles finished one-two-three, but the Stuttgart factory was not ecstatic. The winning machine was an open sports-racing design by TWR (intended for Jaguar at Daytona and Sebring) and run by Joest in Porsche flat-six turbo trim. The Joest-Porsche hybrid left the two factory "911s" with the minor placings on the podium. One of the winning drivers was former BMW GTP pilot Davy Jones.

The best that BMW-engined McLarens did at Le Mans 1996 was a fourth overall for the

In 1996, Bellm paired up with James Weaver in the revised McLaren F1-BMW. They came away with the BPR Global title and five wins accorded to the two-car team that season. Le Mans was not on the winning menu for the McLarens in either 1996 or 1997.

Picture: Courtesy Gulf Oil Corporation, 1996

West/DPR machine of John Nielsen/Peter Kox and Thomas Bscher. Prodded by the need to maintain a faster pace than anyone could have anticipated in the hot conditions, the other McLarens had their worst reliability run.

Gearboxes begun to succumb, but a more bizarre delay hit the Planet Hollywood/BMW North America entry driven by Danny Sullivan/Johnny Cecotto/Nelson Piquet. It dropped from sixth to tenth when an air jack failed to lift it, finally fighting back to hurl its Stars n' Stripes livery across the 24-hour line in eighth overall.

1997 and beyond...

The 1997 season for the BPR's successor—the FIA World Endurance GT Racing Championship —was only three races old when it became clear that BMW Motorsport's appointment of

Schnitzer to work with a redeveloped McLaren GTR was paying terrific dividends.

The team's drivers had won all three opening rounds of the series, despite the formidable opposition of newer Porsche and Mercedes designs. The Steve Soper/J. J. Lehto combination was equally effective, taking two of those famous wins.

For the 1997 Le Mans, BMW Motorsport (Munich, McLaren and Schnitzer personnel to total 60 staff) supported two aerodynamically-altered GTRs and six factory drivers: 1995 winner J. J. Lehto, his regular 1997 winning partner Steve Soper, Roberto Ravaglia, 1997 BMW test driver Eric Helary, 1996 test driver Peter Kox, and 1982 World Champion Nelson Piquet.

There were a lot more McLaren-BMW GTRs in the entry (six total), but the back-up team (David Price of DPR having absconded to Panoz-Ford for 1997 dollars) was Gulf Team Davidoff/GTC Motorsport. They fielded their 1997 GTR brace for another half-

Aerodynamically-redeveloped around a long-tail formula and able to run a lighter weight with a downsized 6-liter version of the Motorsport V12, the McLaren/BMW Motorsport/Schnitzer alliance proved to be astonishingly successful in 1997. "Big Mac," with its original central seating position, led the 1997 FIA GT Championship title race at the halfway stage. Driving stars were J. J. Lehto of Finland—the most underrated driver outside Grand Prix in 1996–97—and Steve Soper. McLaren-BMW had won four of six qualifying rounds as we went to press, but Mercedes blitzed the remaining two....

Picture: BMW AG Presse, 1997

Winning combination for BMW Motorsport's McLaren-BMW team were (left) Britain's Steve Soper and (right) Finland's J. J. Lehto. Soper memorably described the sophisticated V12 McLaren as "a proper racing car. It's got a bit more grunt than grip...."

Picture: BMW AG Presse, 1997

dozen, including the 1995 (Thomas Bscher/John Neilsen) and 1996 (Ray Bellm) BPR champions.

Gordon Murray worked on the aerodynamics for Le Mans over five weeks, commenting, "We looked for maximum speed balanced by good fuel consumption. The enormous speeds generated by the long straights make Le Mans a Mecca for aerodynamicists." The most visible modifications were the 70-mm/2.75-in-taller rear wing, but most work went into the hidden underbelly to further reduce drag. Murray also studied optimization of higher-speed wind flow over the upper body, including the "schnorkel" roof-top air intake.

Mechanically, little was altered—the 5,995-cc V12 running the usual 604-bhp 1997 rating—but this was deceptive as they were less stressed. They were allowed to draw air through 35.2-mm/1.4-in twin air restrictors, rather than the usual FIA GT figure of 34.3

mm/1.35 in. Paul Rosche commented that an 8,000-rpm limit was imposed for fuel consumption reasons.

Rosche added that their Munich V12 assembly priorities had been to keep everything accessible for quick pit-stop service. They uprated the 165-amp alternator to support the increased demand for electricity in 24-hour events, with a margin for safety support should an electrical defect occur and start draining the battery.

Le Mans was the race in which McLaren-BMW was allowed to use the ITT Teves ABS it had developed at such enormous one-off expense. Other extra equipment included hydraulic power assistance for the eight-piston calipers and massive 15-in/380-mm front discs, 14-in/355-mm rears.

There was extra air cooling for the drivers, all in recognition of the fact that they were likely to be sitting for eight hours in four two-hour stints with cockpit temperatures that would otherwise exceed 90 degrees Fahrenheit. These "comfort" changes escalated the curb weight of the cars from their usual 950 kg /2,090 lbs to more like 1,000 kg/2,200 lbs.

Today, the 13.6-km/8.5-mile mile track has chicanes inserted into the 5.5-km/3.4-mile Hunaudieres main straight, but the McLaren GTRs still hit a solid 198.7 mph (320 km/h) during qualification.

Le Mans 1997 will probably be regarded as an historical disappointment for BMW directors, who wanted another LeMans victory badly enough to promise boosted future budgets. In fact, the 1997 second and third over-all—from six cars to make the cut—was an outstanding performance, but BMW's excellent fuel economy was not balanced by the Porsche-beating pace required. The final works Porsche suffered a terminal fire in the closing hours, leaving a Joest Porsche open sports car with no Stuttgart support to win for a second successive year.

McLaren-BMW suffered spectacular Le Mans fires as well: in final practice, one of the Gulf-backed GTC machines was burned beyond redemption. In the race, a sister Big Mac exploded shortly after the leading Porsche, but was not so badly damaged. In all three cases, the Porsche and BMW drivers escaped unhurt. That such top teams should suffer such terrifying high-speed blazes was a matter under intense scrutiny. The only known cause was a fractured gearbox oil line in the case of the pre-race Gulf McLaren incident.

Post-Le Mans 1997, BMW, with Schnitzer and McLaren, provided the major opposition to the ever-more successful Mercedes CLK squad. AMG-Mercedes drew ahead on points for its leading driver in September 1997.

At September 1997's Frankfurt Motor Show, BMW made a formal statement in Formula 1 with Williams Grand Prix Engineering, the car to be badged BMW Williams and pledged to debut in the year 2000. The word from factory insiders was that the V10 would run on the bench at Preussenstrasse for the first time in October 1997, but no commitment to in-car race testing was made before 1999.

During a hectic pre-show evening in which the new Rover Mini was unveiled three years (!) before its production date, BMW's Karl Heinz Kalbfell pledged that Williams and BMW would also field an open sports racer for Le Mans 1998. This BMW Williams would wear the kidney grille and could later adopt a hardtop to face up to Mercedes again in subsequent GT races.

That Williams move, with BMW Motorsport Ltd. scheduled to cozy up to the Williams base in Britain rather than McLaren, left links with McLaren officially severed at the close of 1997. These include FIA GT racing and touring car engineering. However, both Schnitzer and Bigazzi needed 1998 programs if their links with BMW were to be maintained, and it seemed likely that some measure of low-profile BMW Motorsport support would be forthcoming for 1998 FIA GT McLarens.

They build 'em tough at McLaren Cars. Here, touring-car tactics from the J. J. Lehto/Steve Soper entry, as they pressure the F1 over the curb beyond this Porsche's grasp in early 1997. The effective and spectacular pairing had scored three of the team's four wins at this stage.

Picture: BMW AG Presse, 1997

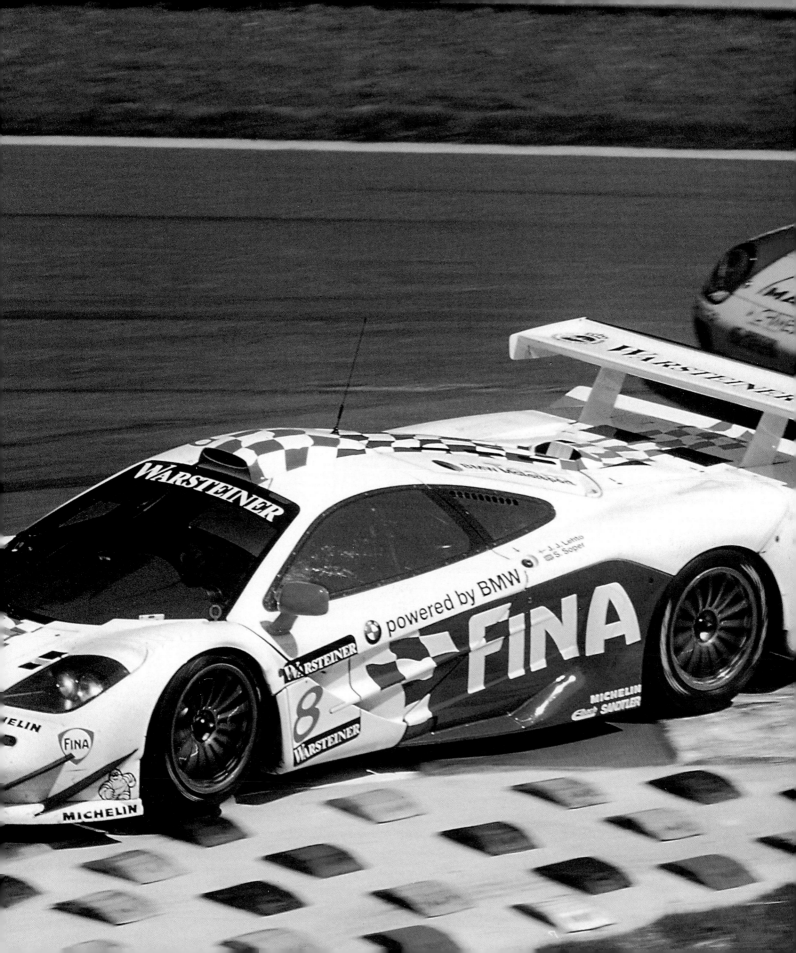

QUICK FACTS

Period

1992–97

Products

2-liter Supertourers, two- and four-door 318i/318iS/318is/320-homologated bodies (all 2-liters used S14-coded M3 motor variant exclusively until 1994, when Motorsport's M42-based S42 was developed)

Performance

1993 and 1997 span officially quoted at 270 and 305 bhp

Achievements

Against the best home and world opposition, the E36 2-liters won the national titles of Asia-Pacific (1994), Britain (1992/93), Germany (1994/95), Belgium (1994), Italy (1993/97), Japan (1995), and Australia (1994/95/97)

Chapter 29

SuperTourer!

The world-wide pursuit of glory for the 4-cylinder SuperTourer

Even as the factory prepared to battle out its last season with the obsolete four-cylinder M3 in the 1992 German Championship, some very special E36 bodies were undergoing pioneering race preparation at the headquarters of Winfried Matter GmbH in Graben Neudorf. Not only were they from newcomer E36, but conformed to the even fresher two-door coupe outline.

The E36 coupes were prepared on the orders of BMW Motorsport to provide a strong (25 percent stiffer than the E30 predecessor) foundation to a 2-liter competitor. Unlike common US practice, these cars—and the 1995–97 M3s in the US—stayed with their production steel shells. All received massive strength from chrome moly steel roll cage fabrication that is closely related to sophisticated builder's scaffolding.

They were destined for Britain (UK's British Touring Car Championship—the BTCC) and one season of glory with the professional Vic Lee Motorsport (VLM). Later, this outfit became Shellsport MTeam, after Lee was imprisoned on drug importation charges. Prodrive was the second of the UK MTeams.

Known in the UK as 318iS coupes, they maintained BMW's British Championship monopoly in the early 1990s, but Prodrive did

not enjoy its expected form with either the 1992 318iS BMWs or the 1994 Alfa Romeo campaigns. However, the company was back winning races with Honda Accords and World Championship rallies via Subaru in 1997.

All the British wins in 1992, and there were five, went to Tim Harvey and VLM preparation. Former production-sedan racer Vic Lee had the ear of the people who mattered inside Motorsport at Munich. Lee, who quipped in his racing days, "I may not be quick but I smell good," grabbed the tiny, but crucial, technical edge required in BTCC—a category that supports tightly-regulated racing in near-one-ton autos of less than 300 bhp.

The specification for a winning VLM E36 in 1992 embraced the 2-liter M3 motor of previous E30 UK deployment, but ran in dry-sump format for 1992 rather than 1991 UK-specification wet-pan technology. Bore-and-stroke dimensions were hidden by rival UK outfits, but Prodrive quoted me a BMW Motorsport figure of 93.4 mm versus an ultra short 72.6-mm stroke for 1,989 cc. VLM reported only 1,991 cc and BMW Motorsport moved on to 90.6 mm x 77.4 mm for 1,996 cc, when it released its first E36 customer cars (all four-doors) in 1993.

Such units were expected to give 270–275 bhp before the mandatory 8,500-rpm limiter. Torque was scarce at the 177-lb-ft /7,000-rpm factory figure to the 190 lb-ft reported at VLM and Prodrive by 7,000 to 7,500 rpm. Factory-engined BMWs often exhibited race-traffic ability that argued a broader power band and less sheer bhp than their rivals.

A trick 6-speed H-pattern gearbox from Hollinger in Australia and ABS race braking from Teves in Germany (rather than the road car's Bosch ABS) completed an international UK race specification. The most obvious difference in UK specifications was the use of Pirelli tires on 19-inch wheels at Prodrive, versus 18-inch rollers and more durable Yokohamas at VLM.

A former Prodrive employee told me frankly, "That was a nightmare season for us. We had a lap speed deficit you could measure in 1- to 1.5-second chunks and we were lucky if the Pirellis did five laps. Both Tim Sugden and Alain Menu (now with Williams at the wheel of

The E36 body brought BMW a far sleeker shape to race and was home to new six-cylinder (see last chapter) and four-cylinder power-plants from Motorsport. Here is a typical example of the 2-liter SuperTourer breed discussed in this section: a 1996 factory-backed 320i with more than 300 bhp, as seen in the German Championship.

Picture: Author, Monterey, 1996

The E36 coupe body had its moments of glory outside the M3 six-cylinder classes. Here at the Thruxton chicane, the 1992 British Touring Car Champion Tim Harvey shows us what kind of stress a top 2-liter had to resist to beat GM, Nissan, and the best of the rest.

Picture: John Colley, England, 1992

the winning Renault Laguna tourers) were fine drivers, but they had no chance that season."

It was not smooth sailing for VLM/Harvey. For a start, Sugden's teammate was the internationally-rated Steve Soper and the new BMWs were twitchy enough to induce a nervous breakdown in lesser drivers than Sugden and Soper. Then VLM learned to contain the multi-link rear suspension's behavior over the British bumps that caused BMW GB so much grief in 1994–96.

VLM got a handle on the flex that was occurring in the trailing arms at the rear and learned to minimize the violent behavior that the back end could show as cornering weight was abruptly transferred. The 1992 BMW 318iS was probably the most difficult-handling BMW raced in recent times.

Then VLM and Munich started to restrain its oafish waywardness so that the E36's sleek shape (0.30 Cd with no wings or chance of downforce), its rear-drive layout, wide power band, and god-like braking (14-inch fronts,

12.6-inch rears, clamped by a total of twenty carbon-fiber pads!) could assert themselves.

The turning point came at the Snetterton, a quick ex-USAAF airbase track in Norfolk. Harvey qualified the VLM machine third, challenging Toyota's previous dominance (TOMs was the first over 300 bhp from four-cylinders in the UK) to promise BMW would be back in winning mode.

It took a month, and a slightly revised minimum weight of 1,025 kg (down 25 kg from season-start) to produce a winning edge for the 318iS. Prodrive actually had the better result at Championship round 4 at Snetterton (Menu came in third).

By the double-header Donington's round 7, Harvey and VLM started a winning roll. In fact, Tim only failed to win three of the remaining eight events!

Finishing fourth in a dramatic final Silverstone was enough to decide a three-way championship fight and maintain BMW's succession of winners in the more prestigious

Not all E36 racers in Europe are 2-liter SuperTourers of 4-door specification. The Dutch national series ran to Group N (a restricted "showroom" formula) for many seasons and the 325i coupe was a regular front-runner.

Modifications were deliberately limited, so a standard 5-speed gearbox was retained rather than a SuperTourer's $32,000 6-speed sequential. The same Group N regulations governed the use of standard-issue alloy wheels on this professionally-presented machine from BMW Holland, but racing rather than road rubber was allowed.

Picture: BMW AG Presse, 1993

British Touring Car Championship for drivers. The Silverstone finale featured seven 2-liters in the same seven-second band with two laps to go, and all three championship challengers occupying four-five-six positions.

It could not last for long. Harvey saw a bruising way by Will Hoy's top Toyota, shoving it back to seventh on the grass. The final lap saw Soper's Bimmer T-bone GM's championship hope in John Cleland, this after its race had included the GM Cavalier navigating on two wheels, propped up against the Soper BMW it was passing!

Autosport's reporter, Nick Phillips, concluded of the E36's first and last 2-liter UK title in 318iS format, "When the dust settled, there were some very disgruntled people about and a nasty whiff of acrimony. It had been a mighty spectacular race, but a little too physical." The British talent for understatement is not forgotten.

1993: Four-door pioneers

For 1993, BMW pledged not to pursue any international "works activities" but to be "omnipresent through a wide range of customer activities." These centered on "an all-new racing car—the BMW 318i based on the current 3-series." BMW was as good as its word, and the 318i contested events from Britain to Australia, via the Asia-Pacific rim.

The 318i tag was still misleading. Just the shell of the four-door 1.8-liter remained, the two-door coupe variant—as raced in 1992 in Britain—having been banned from 2-liter racing, along with ABS.

Initially, teams were not allowed additional spoilers in 2-liter events, but this was blown apart in 1994. Then Alfa Romeo Corse squeezed through a unique tall rear wing and front splitter set and splattered the opposition

(particularly in 1994 in Britain). The FIA in Paris, France, let BMW have a recognized wing set from July 1, 1994. Then the car officially became a 318is, and it has raced since 1995 with yearly evolutions of that front and rear aerodynamic package, but homologated as 320i from 1996 onward.

Back in 1993, the 318i did not look so different from a street car. True, the driver sat 3.25 in/80 mm rearward, and it was over four inches lower at the roof line. Then, 8.0 x 18-inch wheels kissed the wheel arches, but today's 320s feature 8.3 x 19 BBS rollers within further sunken and stretched arches. Plus, constantly tested aerodynamics allow front downforce and at least cut rear-end lift or eliminate it completely (according to speed) at the back.

The first racing 318i for customers featured pneumatic air jacks, plus 40 m/130 ft of steel tubing to deliver roll-cage protection and torsional strength reckoned by BMW as an astonishing "seven times" that of the "standard production model."

For 1993, the 318i sedan retained an S14-coded 2-liter M3 motor of the previous season's 1,996 cc. BMW Motorsport revealed that a unique combustion chamber shape was required for 90.6 x 77.4-mm bore and stroke. This obtained in association with forged racing pistons (12.0:1 compression ratio), steel connecting rods, and a forged-steel crankshaft.

The 2-liter was now closer to 280 bhp, but also available with higher torque and lower bhp for tighter circuits and heavy race-traffic contests. Maximum engine rpm remained at 8,500 rpm, but a ride with Joachim Winkelhock during the pre-season revealed that he power-shifted on command from the change light set at 8,400 rpm. Winkelhock's starts during the season verged on sensational, until you recalled that a standing start imposed 65 percent of the vehicle weight over the driven rear wheels, whereas a front-drive car might only have 35 percent.

This weight distribution bias allowed a tremendous traction advantage off the line, enough to counter the 220-lb weight penalty, and resulted in Winkelhock winning a clutch of events from the front, demonstrating that he could get from 0–60 mph in closer to four seconds than the best of the rest.

The 1993 running gear retained the Hollinger 6-speed gearbox with an H-pattern shift, digital display, and data-collecting multi-mode instrumentation, plus the biggest brakes outside pro football. That meant an alliance of front and rear vented discs measuring 355 mm/304 mm of 32.4- and 25.0-mm vented thickness (14-inch fronts with 12-inch rears of 1.25-inch and 1.0-inch thickness, respectively) with the six- and four-piston calipers—a major racing asset made familiar in 1992 in Britain. ABS was banned from 2-liter racing from 1993 onward, so this sophistication from the 1992 British championship could not be repeated.

The suspension retained the MacPherson-strut front and multi-link rear end, but not a single part was from the production line—everything was fabricated for the high G strains of racing. BMW specified a limited-slip ZF differential with 75 percent locking action, but the 1992 British team's 318iS had on occasion used a solid spool differential and later seasons produced a lot of trick (electro-hydraulic) differential developments among the front drivers. This was a major reason why Alfa was so successful in 1994 and why the front-drive cars such as the 1997 Williams Renault handle so well, aside from having engines dropped so far back and down in the engine bay that it's a job to find them!

The E36 318i racer was an honorable successor to the E30 M3, selling to "more than 40" customers all over the world and lifting the hard-fought championships of Britain, Germany, and Italy in its 1993 debut season, runner-up in France.

Such achievements are what the customers expect from BMW competition sedans, but were hard to return in 1993 and almost impossible to duplicate today. The reason was not BMW company arrogance—it took drastic and courageous corporate action in the 1995/96 winter to counter increasingly-effective opposition—but the spread of lighter, better-handling, front-drive, 2-liter racing sedans.

Back in 1993, BMW faced seven other marques in the British series, all front drive. UK-based Fords (their ex-Probe Mazda aluminum V6s uprated by Cosworth Grand Prix techniques), GM Cavaliers, Nissans, Toyotas, et al., raced off 950-kg/2,090-lb minimum weights.

BMW's unique (in this category) rear-drive layout initially attracted a 100-kg/220-lb penalty and a total minimum race weight for the 318i of 1,050 kg/2,310 lbs, whereas its 318iS predecessor was given a UK mid-season dispensation to carry only 75 kg ballast. Over the seasons since, BMW's 2-liter race weight penalty and that of compatriots Audi have fluctuated, but the principle of punishment versus ever-more sophisticated front-drivers remains.

Back in 1993, Audi and its quattro 4x4 racing program were just beginning to make an impact on the national series (it was Audi who beat BMW into second in France that season) with their 80. When it came to fielding the A4 quattro, Audi became even worse news in 1995–96 for BMW than the front drive brigade: BMW then had to step up another technical gear.

Back in 1993, BMW used conventional methods and fine drivers to scoop those Italian and British titles for Roberto Ravaglia and Joachim Winkelhock. Keys to success were works-backed MTeams Schnitzer in the UK and the Italian championship-winning effort of CiBIEmme for Ravaglia, backed by Bigazzi's similarly solid performance behind Italian runner-up Johnny Cecotto (who is featured in chapter 27).

As a tail-piece to the 1993 season, the 318i fleet assembled to fight the first FIA 2-liter World Cup, which drew 43 drivers from 12 countries, including 14 pilots with Grand Prix experience. The venue was Italy's historic Milan parkland track of Monza, but the news was bad for BMW, their star drivers, and any of the 41 other cars that did not wear the Ford blue oval.

Just two Cosworth-engined Mondeo V6s (Contour in the US) were entered, but one carried off both 15-lap race results and the World Cup. The best BMW—and German manufacturer—result came from young Alex Burgstaller, who finished fifth. The German press was not amused.

The rest had to play second fiddle to Ford again in 1994's FIA shoot-out (New Zealander Paul Radisich was the winner on both occasions). It was the 1995 final edition of the FIA World Cup in France that finally saw German

Audis and BMWs wreak revenge for this upset, monopolizing the front rows of the grids and unchallenged by the front drivers.

1994: Wings and many new things

Although BMW Motorsport and its partners started the 1994 season with a machine that looked much like the 1993 318i, it had been reworked from the roll cage outward. It subsequently developed both new aerodynamics and a replacement motor to the M3 (running out of homologation recognition for 1995) during the 1994 season. Much of the rest of the running gear was replaced for 1994, too, including front and rear suspension layout and a sequential version of the BMW-Holinger-engineered 6-speed gearbox.

BMW Motorsport and Schnitzer tried running the 2-liter tourer at the 1994 Nürburgring 24-hours. It set the fastest time for Joachim Winkelhock, but was not mechanically-reliable enough to complete the course. It faced the usual action-packed adventures to avoid natural hazards (fog, thunderstorms), as well as a grid of cars so large that it was started in three separate packs!

Despite this works setback, other BMWs invariably prevail at the Nürburgring Marathon (back in the 1970s, Nürburgring's transplanted Marathon de la Route lasted 84 hours!) and the race has encouraged the more talented amateurs to make the six-cylinder M3 effective at a lower cost than the factory program.

Picture: Author, Germany, 1994

At start of 1994, BMW Motorsport had overhauled the 318i thoroughly. The relocated engineers of Motorsport came up with a yet-stiffer steel roll cage construction (by a staggering 40 percent, said official sources) and the left-hand-drive-only carbon/Kevlar Recaro seat was moved further rearward.

Motorsport could build a 318i at 2,200 lbs/1,000 kg or less, but the FIA rules at the beginning of the season put them at 2,310 lbs/1,050 kg versus 2,090 lbs/950 kg for the front drive majority. That was changed from July 1, when a 2,145-lb/975-kg minimum for front drive arrived. BMW was allowed to drop to 2,255 lbs/1,025 kg. In Britain, things were more complicated: Winkelhock started the year with another 44-lb/20-kg penalty as the 1993 Champion.

Internationally, the 1994 318's achievements were rewarding, despite an average 100-kg/220-lb weight penalty over front-drive. BMW scored a remarkable one-two-three-four result in the Spa 24-hours, securing the National Championships of Australia, Belgium, and South Africa. BMW was the FIA World Championship Manufacturer's team, taking runner-up spot in the FIA World Cup shoot-out for drivers, plus half the top six placings.

Nationally, BMW won the German 2-liter title (ONS/ADAC TourenWagen Cup) for Johnny Cecotto. Steve Soper won four races in the All-Japan series (plus one at home in the UK) to finish third overall. He would return and finish the job of defeating the local giants with Schnitzer in 1995.

BMW's traditional dominance of the biggest 2-liter series (Britain's BTCC) ended. Instead of basing the Schnitzer team in Britain again, BMW Motorsport had worldwide ambitions for Schnitzer, and this meant the all-new car did not hit the tracks with the test mileage advantage it had in 1993.

It was mid-season—actually, the British Grand Prix meeting—before Schnitzer-BMW looked its usual winning self, boosted by the new wing kit homologated for the four-door on July 1, 1994. Then the 3-series racer officially became a winged 318is and raced off a lower international weight versus a raised weight for front drive. Now BMW came to the grid at 2,255 lbs/1,025 kg versus 2,145 lbs/975 kg for front-drive.

In Germany, you could buy a 318is street replica that had the front and rear wing kit, plus the M42 16-valve motor that began its racing career in the 1994 German 2-liter Cup cars of Cecotto and Alex Burgstaller. Motorsport prepared the M42 units (coded S42) at 2 liters rather than the street 1.8 liters so familiar in 318-badged coupes, compacts and sedans, deploying 86.5 mm x 85 mm for 1,998 cc rather than the 1,796 cc and 84 x 81-mm street dimensions. Compression was set around 12.0:1 rather than a street car's 10.0:1.

Under the hood, the new S42 motor was immediately distinguished by its vertical stance, rather than the traditional BMW slant installation. From the start, it was a dry-sump unit and pre-season trials established a power output similar to the old M3 2-liters, reported to be 280 bhp at 8,500 rpm. The big benefit was to be torque and—after a lot of hard development work—a comparatively wide power band. Official 1994 torque reports centered on 180 lb-ft at 7,000 rpm.

The comparative failure in the 1994 BTCC Championship (BMW GB Ltd. finished fourth in the team category, Winkelhock and Soper were sixth and seventh-ranked drivers) was not a serious setback to the casual observer. Remember, BMW had won the 1991 through 1993 titles.

Yet the 1994 season forecast a pattern— BMW has not won that title again, and it abandoned the British series totally for 1997. During this period, the BTCC attracted Formula Car teams (Williams for Renault, TWR at Volvo) and the established order began to change. Despite massive efforts from traditional British event-winners BMW and Ford, neither were to be a major force in the 1995–97 seasons.

BMW and Jo Winkelhock finished 1994 as the most successful BTCC contestants in the four years that the series had been established. BMW had won most races: a total of 27, including five in 1994 (one to Soper between Japanese sorties, the rest to Winkelhock). Joachim Winkelhock had won the most races of any driver in that four-year period, racking up 10 victories in 1993–94. Things could only get worse....

1995: International success, bad news from Britain

Headline success for the racing E36 in 1995 centered on Steve Soper's first international title, the All Japan 2-liter series, plus a success-

Up and running in time for 1994/95 winter testing, the 1995 BTCC 2-liter (labled 318i that season for UK marketing reasons) did not respond to the ministrations of the (temporarily) Silverstone-domiciled Gunther Warthofer factory-backed team. An advanced aerodynamic package can be seen front and rear, but even the driving of Johnny Cecotto and David Brabham brought little more than a string of midfield results and racing accidents. It was the worst season record for a British-based BMW factory team.

Picture: BMW GB, 1995

ful home title run for Joachim Winkelhock in the German series.

Altogether, the company won five touring-car titles in 1995, including far-flung Australia, but the bumpy tracks of Britain and white-hot front-drive opposition (GM was champion, with John Cleland driving its Cavalier) were bad news for BMW in 1995. They left BMW's Gunther Warthofer/BMW Team Motorsport outfit languishing in sixth place on final points.

The biggest routine change was that the S42 (née M42) 2-liter was now the regular customer engine after its successful use in the 1994 German series. Running a regular 12.5:1 compression, the S42 was now rated at 285 bhp at 8,000 rpm with 184 lb-ft of torque on the usual 7,000-rpm peak.

Incidentally, if you try to race a 1995 factory-built Bimmer with later engine specification, you will find updates difficult. Motorsport did a lot of work between seasons on ancillaries like the dry sump (pressure pump and two extraction units in 1995) and it was not the simple transplant job you would expect.

The company now spoke of a roofline 110 mm/4.5 inches lower than a production 3-series and confessed that the roll-cage/body-strengthening moves had allowed a boost in torsional rigidity to a value ten times that of a production four-door E36.

For 1995, BMW felt it had gone as far as required on the body-strength route and concentrated on reducing chassis weight by 10 kg/22 lbs. The composite Keiper Recaro seat went rearward again—the driver basically sits on the floorspace normally used by rear seat passengers and their feet—but BMW did not go for the near-central driving position adopted by Peugeot and its followers.

The suspension was overhauled again, basically using lighter and stronger aluminum or magnesium parts. The racer began to pull its wheels well within the arches, the only outward sign of its marginally lower roofline over the

1993 car. Those oversize wheels could be either 18 or 19 inches in diameter in 1995.

The factory wheel was a BBS magnesium item, a cooperative effort with the Black Forest manufacturer (founded and partially owned by former BMW Motorsport founder-genius Martin Braungart) that has existed since 1970. However, customer cars also came on Speedline units from Italy in 1995.

You might also take it for granted that Bimmers raced on Bilstein gas dampers, but this was not necessarily so in 1995, and it is not so today. For 1995, the factory recommended Penske products, that is, Penske in Tamworth, England rather than Roger's Poole Dorset or US operations. Ironically, the troubled British 1995 race team reverted to Bilsteins. BMW still lists Penske as their partners in 1997 tourers. It also remains with Eibach at Finnentrop Germany on the massively stiff coil-spring specification and a wide choice of anti-roll bars, the front being cockpit-adjustable from the beginning of 318i's competition life.

By 1995, the disc brakes had grown again at the front, but were smaller for the rear. The vented units were specified at 342/283 mm (13.5/11.1 inches) and ran swing caliper designs of six-piston layout fronts, twin-piston rears. The official 1995 supplier was Brembo. BMW Motorsport has used a number of brake component suppliers: today, AP Racing in Britain is listed.

Winning the 2-liter series at home (re-christened the STW—Super Touring Wagen Cup—and challenging hard to be the best 2-liter racing in the world) was particularly sweet for BMW, because there was a season-long battle with a rival squad from Audi. The A4 quattro had to race at an even heavier weight than BMW (1,040 kg versus 1,025 kg) but the 4x4 element soaked up the wet races and the result was in doubt until the final at the Nürburgring new circuit.

Audi's Emanuele Pirro won, but the BMW warriors—Winkelhock, Kox, Soper—did what

The BMW Motorsport International development of the 2-liter 3-series was generally extremely effective through the 1990s on all but British terrain. Here are details of the Bimmers that, along with Audi, dominated premier positions at the FIA World Cup Finals of 1995. Note that Winkehock's rear brakes came from Brembo and that the car was used to promote the Z3's appearance in the James Bond film "Goldeneye," while the front end of another factory-backed contender has twin calipers from AP Racing on its monster cross-drilled discs. The tubular silver engine subframe/"cradle" boosted front-end strength (Right).

By summer 1995, the S42 motor was a well-established replacement for the old M3-derived 2-liters and developed just over 300 bhp: within a spit of the old Formula 2 M12/7s. Not bad for a rev-limited (8,500) unit running unleaded pump gas and a catalytic convertor!

Pictures: Author, Paul Ricard, France, 1995

was needed to give Jo Winkelhock a home title win. Since Soper had also won the Japanese title in a long-distance year for him and the Schnitzer boys, BMW was very happy with its year, especially since Yvan Muller took the 1995 French SuperTourisme Championship in the Oreca-run 320i.

The tremendously-effective trio of Kox, Winkelhock, and Soper had hauled home the Spa 24-hour spoils (BMW was also second in this edition, but Honda prevented a one-two-three). Steve Soper had also given Audi a good run (second and third) in the two World Cup races at Paul Ricard, France. Those awkward Brits and their front-drive formula car flotilla got a thrashing from Germany GmbH in the form of Audi (Frank Biela was overall FIA World Cup winner) and BMW. Ah yes, those bloody Brits. They were set to change the politics and practicalities of BMW in touring-car racing, forever....

The (Gunther) Warthofer team formed in 1992 and based itself at Nürburgring to run Johnny Cecotto's last-gasp M3. The winners of the 1994 German 2-liter title with the S42 motor development program, they set up a base at Silverstone for the 1995 British assault, but it was not enough to offset the increasing speed of the now all-winged front-drive brigade. The "wing-kits-for-all" FIA-dispensation meant extra stability for the front drivers, destroying much of BMW's traditional braking and tire-preserving race advantages.

In desperation, BMW Motorsport hired Australian race designer Ralph Bellamy to put in some parallel test-and-development input to the transplanted Warthofer team. It did not go well. Bellamy decided that the BMW wing kit was tailored to German speeds rather than the UK's need for downforce.

Warthofer felt it was not getting any practical assistance. British-based 1995 BMWs only really progressed in terms of power-to-weight ratio in that their 285 bhp was now harnessed to a 1,000-kg/2,200-lb minimum, whereas 1,025 kg was their international norm.

Warpaint! Here are the BMW Motorsport International colors seen on the E36 3,018-cc M3 GTR normally campaigned by Johnny Cecotto in the 1993 ADAC GT series, which Cecotto and BMW won, previewing later 1990s success for the M3 in the US.

Picture: Author, Monterey, 1996

In Germany, that aerodynamic package changed mid-season, a possibility not allowed in the UK. The results for ace of aces Johnny Cecotto and hard-trying David Brabham were so dire in the UK that the factory importer pleaded with Munich to withdraw the cars, a request refused. Image is all in the UK, so when the mass manufacturers do it to BMW, it hurts. Conversely, when BMW wins, that is just what is expected. It's a no-win situation that has always colored BMW GB's view of 2-liter racing.

By the close of 1995, BMW had slumped to its worst-ever UK race performances to finish sixth in the Manufacturer's 8-team league and place their drivers a dismal twelfth and thirteenth. Certainly, these 1995 statistics formed the worst results ever seen for Johnny Cecotto, who became totally disillusioned with their status of mid-field and worse. David Brabham battled mightily for every lap of every round, rewarded

with a revealing ninth place in the penultimate round of the 1995 UK series. Neither Warthofer BMW cracked the top ten in the closing event. It could not be allowed to continue.

BMW Motorsport Great Britain, Ltd.

The author chose December 1995's foggy ice and autobahn slush to drive a 323i coupe to BMW's annual press conference in Munich. It was perhaps the best-balanced package of smooth BMW attributes I have ever driven, but I was in for a big upset when I got to one of many BMW satellite offices in Munich.

I should have guessed there was something major coming up when I was asked to arrive a little early with the other five British journalists and possibly double that number of German

Assisted by McLaren and the importation of 1993/1995 British and German Champion Joachim Winkelhock to drive alongside Roberto Ravaglia, BMW began to crack the British series in 1996. The team took eight poles and five wins—the majority to Winkelhock, although Ravaglia (seen here) won the biggest UK touring car event of the year, supporting Grand Prix. Audi won all the UK titles that season as well as the national championships of virtually every major market in the world outside the US (which went to Honda in its inaugural year). BMW withdrew from the British series in 1997—the first time factory-backed cars had not been apparent in a decade.

Picture: BMW GB, 1996

media for a pre-awards briefing. While the huge marquee filled up with guests ready for an evening themed on brightly colored South American revelry, the media sat in dour confrontational lines within a silver-and-white conference room.

The atmosphere was already tense, before BMW management—headed by Karl Heinz Kalbfell and Paul Rosche—made the astonishing announcement: for 1996, BMW Motorsport would be setting up a satellite operation in Britain! All hardcore work outside the engine bay for the touring-car program was to be run in the UK, ostensibly through a

small office at BMW Bracknell. Later, a purpose-built British BMW Motorsport department and buildings were expected.

The German press were as dumbfounded as we British had been when BMW bought Rover. Germans obviously could not understand why one of their country's proudest names, one that is a major Bavarian attraction, would want to go to Britain.

From the welter of hostile questioning, it emerged that BMW Motorsport's commercial M-branded operations were not affected. Nor were Paul Rosche's engine-building staff, and no layoffs were expected. BMW wanted to

take advantage of Britain's extensive racing infrastructure (unsaid but true: labor rates are a lot lower) and extend the link with McLaren that had blossomed into GT racing and Le Mans-winning success.

The move distanced Motorsport from the grinding responsibility of increasingly hard-won 2-liter results. Motorsport and BMW AG wanted a higher international profile than 2-liter race sedans alone could bring. First came GT racing with McLaren, then Grand Prix with Williams.

BMW Motorsport's development of both the McLaren GTR and the 320i-branded 2-liter SuperTourer—outside the engine bay—had settled at two units on the McLaren Grand Prix race-car site at Woking in Surrey by 1997. The office in Bracknell had a couple of German personnel installed to process all the necessary purchase and materials ordering, smoothing the liaison with BMW Motorsport in Germany.

Although the McLaren-BMW link had tangible success—mostly in GT racing during 1995–97 rather than 2-liter racing during the 1996–97 season—the future of the British Motorsport operation was under review in the summer of 1997. Hidden from the public was the fact that BMW was about to climb into bed with McLaren's more-successful Grand Prix rivals, Williams, and that naturally had ramifications for McLaren and BMW. It seemed obvious that the winning McLaren-BMW GT racing program would continue into 1998, but it was equally obvious that a new car would be required, partially to meet the challenge of purpose-built racers from Porsche and Mercedes, but also because McLaren would not be making any more road versions of the F1/GTR series unless a major financial deal was completed.

Although nobody but nobody would publicly admit it, the fact that Mercedes and McLaren are aligned for Formula 1 racing cannot help at board level for BMW. What kept McLaren and BMW together was the personal, absolutely direct ("We don't even let others fax on our behalf," says Murray) working relationship between Paul Rosche and Gordon Murray.

The Motorsport boss—under the overall design leadership of Gordon Murray—was Jeff Hazell, and he recalled, "We examined the 1995 touring cars in November 1995. There was not much time to make a major input for the 1996 season, but we did construct two test 320s for both 1996 and 1997.

"We worked in partnership with Schnitzer to boost their 1996 assault on the BTCC, running a full test program whilst they got with the business of racing. Our changes were not just for Britain, but fed into BMW factory cars, wherever they appeared. Equally obviously, our input was greater in 1997 than 1996, and I would like to pay tribute to the huge test mileage done out of the limelight by Holland's Peter Kox for 1996 and France's Eric Helary in 1997."

Changing the 320s for 1996

What was done to the 1996 320s? Another extensive overhaul occurred at the Munich end. The Matter roll cage lost 7 percent of its overall weight (the cars raced at 2,200 lbs/1,000 kg that season) and looked totally different. They squatted much closer to the ground—particularly noticeable at the rear, where Motorsport noticeably eased out the wheelarch behind the doors. The 320i benefited from a new wing set that was biased toward slower British circuit use.

Underneath bulging steel skin, the motor had new muscles to push the power-to-weight ratio up to 304 bhp per ton, compared with the 1993 debut year at 262 bhp per ton, so the 320 had substantially quicker acceleration than the 318i of 1993. Official power output on unleaded pump gasoline was now just short of 150 bhp per liter in emission-controlled form: 298 bhp at 8,300 rpm with torque exceeding an official 190 lb-ft for the first time (192 lb-ft by 7,000 rpm).

Although there was no official confirmation, compression was surely increased during the 1996 season. The 1997 specification was up to 13.5:1, whereas the factory figure had been 12.5:1 in 1995. The S42 continued to cooperate with a catalytic converter and oxygen sensor.

For 1996, the 320i had dropped trackward again to lower the center of gravity. There was a replacement six-speed sequential gearbox from Holinger, and it too was dropped in the frame to provide a lowline stance in association with replacement front and rear axle suspension layouts. A sprint 50-liter (11 UK gallons) fuel tank was used in place of earlier, larger reservoirs.

Jeff Hazell—a keen weekend racer himself, who has a distinguished management record in both sports car racing and Grand Prix (Williams)—did not push the point, but BMW's 1996 record was vastly improved over 1995's dismal BTCC record. BMW employed 1993 British champion Joachim Winkelhock and their most successful title collector, Robert Ravaglia, and the cars proved winners...but not as often as they should have done.

Winkelhock took seven pole positions in a year dominated by Biela's BTCC Championship-winning Audi A4 quattro, but these converted into just four early season wins for "Smokin Jo." Ravaglia was not so happy in the rough-and-tumble of BTCC—in fact he gave it a bit too much rough in one well-publicized TV incident—but he won the most important race of the year, the British Grand Prix supporter at Silverstone. Ravaglia also took another pole position, so BMW accrued eight poles and five wins between the two drivers—a fine recovery from 1995's winless misery.

It was not, however, really enough for the effort that had been applied. Both drivers were involved in more incidents than expected, and the points-scoring consistency that

yields championships simply was not on the winning Audi pace.

In Germany, the 320s—fielded by Bigazzi for top BMW points-scorer Steve Soper—succeeded in winning against Audi, Honda and Peugeot three times. Soper, who preferred German racing to that in his native UK, looked to be a possible German champion. Then he was barged off by his teammate Alex Burgstaller, who was on his way to the pits at the time!

Soper took the runner-up spot in Germany, while Johnny Cecotto equaled that result in Italy. The dream-team combo of Winkelhock and Ravaglia came back from the UK with fifth and sixth to show from the Schnitzer-McLaren race-and-test-team alliance.

The US witnessed the birth of its own SuperTouring (NATCC) 2-liter contest in 1996, but only Chrysler took it seriously enough to field full-works cars for some thin grids, uplifted by some excellent racing. An ex-BTCC Honda took the inaugural US series, and there was no sign of BMW NA wanting more of the 2-liter action in 1997. However, with 1996 champion Randy Pobst in a BMW, there was hope for better results in 1997.

As the German press pointed out at the BMW Haus-top Motorsport conference for 1997, BMW's improved 320i had been absolutely blitzed by Audi worldwide. It was scant consolation that Ingolstadt had done it to every other manufacturer as they took home the biggest haul of national race titles the author can recall any manufacturer accruing in one season.

1997 and all that

The touring-car technical liaison with McLaren continued in 1997, but the BTCC was not a problem anymore—BMW withdrew for the first time in eight seasons. There seems little

By 1997, BMW had won the Spa 24-hours 20 times (21, if you included the class victory of 1938 in which a 328 was fifth overall). This formation finish from the 1996 edition of the Belgian night-and-day classic was a pretty typical example of how the E36 2-liter developed into a regular winner, although by 1997, BMW could get a 234-bhp (direct injection) turbo diesel version of the 320i to finish third overall!

Here, we see the 1996 winning Bigazzi BMW 320i (car number 2, closest to the camera) of Thierry Tassin and Jorg Muller, and Alex Burgstaller beside the delayed (alternator problem) number 1 Bigazzi-team Bastos 320i of Steve Soper, Peter Kox, and Marc Duez. BMWs filled five of the first six places, including a six-cylinder M3 assigned to Katy Raffanelli (daughter of the Bigazzi team boss, Gabrielle), Yolanda Surer, and Florence Duez.

Picture: BMW AG Historiches Archiv, reprinted 1997

prospect of a return in 1998, and BMW is set on a late 1990s course to emphasize higher status events such as GT racing until its return to Grand Prix.

McLaren's extensive use of wind-tunnel research yielded some aerodynamic benefits, and the 1997 320i featured a new front spoiler and back wing, with the emphasis on air supply to the radiator and brakes. The roll cage was further reinforced with safety rather than a competitive edge in mind. This was the responsibility of BMW at the Regensberg factory, which considerably improved the side-impact protection, an area which had cost non-BMW touring-car drivers their lives in Australia, Germany, and Belgium.

Other technical moves were Paul Rosche's engine-team responsibility. They had a hard look at the S42 motor—and the rest of the power train—to reduce friction. The motor sported twin injector nozzles per intake-manifold cylinder feed, the now traditional carbon fiber air collector, and a 13.2:1 compression

(on pump unleaded gasoline!). Details extended to low-friction crankshaft/bearing modifications (unspecified), reprogrammed BMW Motorsport engine management for the ECU, and fresh values for the inlet-and exhaust-valve timing.

Maximum power was now quoted as 305 bhp at 8,300 rpm and 195 lb-ft of torque at 7,000 rpm. These values were to full European Common Market new-car endurance procedures using 98 RON unleaded gas. Some rival teams thought up to 315 bhp was actually available for sprint racing.

The result was that the 1,000-kg/2,200-lb BMW came to the start line with a power-to-weight ratio of 311 bhp per ton. The ratio is the best on record for BMW's 2-liter tourers, but is exceeded by front-drive outfits such as Honda, as their equally powerful Neil Brown motors carry only 975 racing kg/2,145 lbs.

BMW's planned 1997 support of German, Australian, and Italian SuperTouring series was extremely successful. The German series was a

The wing kit has its annual change, the rear wheelarches blister to a more extensive bulge, and the power creeps toward 315 regular bhp. Joachim Winkelhock returns to his home Championship in Germany to seek another domestic title to sit alongside his 1995 victory in the booming series. Joined by Johnny Cecotto and benefiting from the McLaren "special relationship" with BMW Motorsport Ltd. (the UK arm of the company), the 1997-season 320i proved quick enough to score double victories over some racing weekends. But a factory Peugeot won the 1997 German series, despite a trick brake-balance system.

Picture: BMW AG Presse, 1997

struggle between Peugot's factory 406, Manfred Winkelhock and Johnny Cecotto's Bigazzi BMW 320s. BMW scored the initial home wins, but the factory Peugot 406 of Laurent Aiello went on winning right to the last round. It took home a title the French could be proud of in the backyard of BMW and Audi, the latter struggling to develop a front-drive car since 4x4 was banned for 1998.

In 1997, Australia, Belgium, and Italy BMW 320s were winning, the Italian series a runaway for BMW against an energetic Audi defense of its 1996 title. Former singer-seater ace Emanuel Naspetti had won five of six opening rounds in the CibiEmme/BMW Italia entry, and kept up that form for the season.

Paul Morris was a championship winner for BMW in Australia, where BMW also won the first 2-liter edition of the classic Bathurst "Great Race" to compliment its historic twentieth Spa 24-hour race victory. Belgium also gave BMW another sedan title for promising ex-motorcyclist Didier Radrigues.

BMW's worldwide haul of success in 1997 was completed with an FIA World Cup (given to the most successful manufacturer in

SuperTouring) and a dominant win for Steve Soper in the season-closing Macau Grand Prix. It was a fitting end to the bulk of BMW's interest in the 2-liter racing E36. The factory published pictures of their new 3-series for 1998, and distanced themselves from a 1998 domestic German title hunt, clearly assigning Schnitzer to that task.

Looking ahead, Audi's 4x4 transmission is scheduled to be banned from 1998 onward. How long before the international authorities ban BMW too, the only rear-drive layout in 2-liter?

There is also the fact that the new-for-1998 BMW 3-series has not been designed with 2-liter racing high on its priority list. It certainly will be a bigger, more refined car, but that is not expected to improve its race competitiveness.

As we leave the tale of BMW's core sporting business, almost 40 years in the circuit sedan racing business, it looks as though the company will keep the faith in the category it has dominated over the years, but on a much-reduced, sub-contract basis.

This fine study of the 3-series in popular privateer use at the Nürburgring looks as if the E36 was racing off into history. In Europe in 1997, late-season talk was all about how the new, enlarged 3-series for 1998 would be less suitable for racing. Senior BMW executives were also worried that rear-drive could follow 4x4 onto the internationally-banned list in 2-liter FIA regulations.

Picture: Chris Willows, Germany, 1994

1997 Team Schnitzer

It seems odd to outline Team Schnitzer in a mere panel box, because we have watched this organization develop from Josef Schnitzer's personal racing championships to a world force in BMW Motorsport team management. Yet there are some formal details that may be helpful.

Trading since 1963 from the German-Austrian border town of Freilassing, Schnitzer is owned today by the surviving Schnitzer brother, Herbert. The team manager is the legendary Karl "Charly" Lamm, half-brother to Herbert.

Schnitzer employs around 25 people, but also works in cooperation with other major teams, particularly McLaren and Munich members of BMW Motorsport in the 1997 FIA GT Championship, actually representing BMW Motorsport at Le Mans 1997.

Schnitzer's racing history starts with that 1966 German Championship for Josef Schnitzer (2000TI) and now covers major Championship titles in European Formula 2 (1975), European Touring Cars (1983/86/88); Germany (1978/89), Italy (1989/90), Japan (1995), Asia-Pacific (1994), and Britain (1993).

Schnitzer 24-hour racing success is a separate industry in itself, covering five separate Spa 24-hours (1985/86/88/95) and the 1989/91 Nürburgring marathons.

There is more, but you get the picture: Schnitzer is the best sedan racing team in the business.

1997 Team Bigazzi

Based in San Gimignano, Italy, Bigazzi had the reputation among BMW's drivers for being the most fun to work with...but they also bring back the results.

Owned by Gabrielle Rafanelli, BMW Team Bigazzi is the youngest of the regular BMW sub-contractors. Established in 1987, it employed 20 and was managed by Stefano di Ponti.

Bigazzi began in the toughest of European sedan competition, entering the World Touring Car Championship in 1987 and the European series of 1988. It was runner-up to the overall Italian title of 1989. Between 1989 and 1992, it scored ten outright German Championship wins for the M3 and established an excellent working relationship with Steve Soper.

From 1994–96, Bigazzi's reputation in long-distance racing accelerated, winning the Spa 24-hours twice for BMW and Nürburgring in 1995. Such a record brought them the 1996 contract to run a McLaren-BMW GT at Silverstone, Le Mans 24-hours, and two South American races. Bigazzi won the South American events and took the 1997 Brasilia 1,000-mile race for McLaren-BMW, but gave best to Schnitzer in the race to run the 1997 Le Mans and FIA GT assaults for BMW.

Bigazzi's 1997 contract was to represent the factory in the German 2-liter series with drivers Winkelhock and Cecotto, their 320s finishing one-two at Zolder in Belgium and finishing the season as second and third to the champion, Peugot.

In 1998, Rafanelli ran the BMW-Williams V12 prototype at Le Mans: the open sports racers were withdrawn at less than 1/4 distance, suffering repeated wheel-bearing failures.

1997 Team Isert

BMW Team Isert is based at Mainleus in Germany and was established in 1985. It's a family affair, owned by Heinz Isert and managed by Uwe Isert, with 17 employees.

Isert contested the German Championship with a 325i in 1986 and finished with a win and third overall in 1987's home series when it switched to an M3. Isert was a German Championship regular from 1988–92.

Isert's profile magnified in 1993. The move to the ADAC GT cup brought it second overall in the series, with the M3 GTR.

Since 1994, Isert has contested the 2-liter German Championship race, but ventured to Spa to score third overall in the 1995 edition with a 320i.

Isert's 1997 contract was to run a 320i for the promising Christian Menzel and Leopold "Poldi," Prince of Bavaria.

QUICK FACTS

Period

1993 to date

Products

3.2-liter M3, 3.0-liter M3, 2.0-liter Z3

Performance

380 bhp for GTS2 IMSA 3.2 M3; 325 bhp for M3 GTR 3.0-liter; 250 bhp for Z3 2.0-liter

Achievements

The M3 GTR 3-liter won the 1993 German ADAC GT Championship for Johnny Cecotto; Group N 3-liter M3 is a regular winner of Nürburgring 24-hours, and won 1995 German/Dutch/Hungarian production-car titles; the 3.2 M3 collected the 1996 IMSA GTS2-class Championship, the first IMSA title for a North American BMW since the 1981 Kenper Miller/David Cowart M1 blitz of 1981; Z3 by Oreca debuted at 2 liters in French ice-racing tournament, won division, placed driver third overall, and assisted BMW, placing second overall in Trophee Andros; in May 1997, the PTG M3s kept winning, with a one-two-three result at Lime Rock

People

Thomas Milner at PTG, Erik Wensberg at BMW NA, Inc., and Oreca with the Z3 ice-racing charm quota

Chapter 30

Star-Spangled Bimmers

Born in Germany as the M3 GTR, today's M3 is a serial winner in the US

It was inevitable that the new M3 would sizzle along the racetracks of the world, but we waited two long seasons to see the factory field such a machine. And then it was in a low-key domestic ADAC (Germany's biggest auto club) series.

BMW itself won with an M3, conservatively engineered at 325 bhp. It packaged better fuel economy and sustained pace than turbo Porsche and Ford opposition. But BMW Motorsport personnel dismissed that 1993 achievement as minimal—the result of a proper factory team with a talented driver (Johnny Cecotto) simply achieving what they had expected.

That 1993 ADAC title did not signify a major factory effort to promote the six-cylinder M3 in the tire tracks of its famous four-cylinder ancestor. BMW Motorsport just supported annual outings to the Nürburgring 24-hours with the M3 sixes, and supplied a 300-bhp customer car in Group N race stock trim.

So it was 1996 before we would see a benchmark BMW seize major championship honors. By then, the backdrop was America, specifically Winchester, Virginia, and the old site of Jaguar preparation specialists, Group 44. That IMSA result was a just reward for the 1995–96 seasonal persistence of PTG (Prototype Technology

Group) boss Tom Milner, who managed the M3s, from wet-sump, ex-Munich hybrids to IMSA-oriented category winners. Let's start with the factory E36 M3 of 1993.

BMW Motorsport decided to back the growing home-market interest in production sedan racing (Group N in FIA-speak) and a new ADAC GT Championship subbed "Festival of Great Makes." In both cases, BMW decided that the new six-cylinder M3 was the right tool for the job, and proved the point by securing the initial eight-race ADAC GT title. It took the combination of Johnny Cecotto and a fractionally-overbored M3 GTR deviant. The latter was the granddaddy of the 1995–97 IMSA GT2 warriors.

Granddad was officially called GT for the base road car, GTR on track. It looked the race part, to such effect that Germany's *auto motor und sport magazine* dubbed GT's appearance the "Schwarzenegger Look." As they demonstrated, this could be applied to a limited-production run of road-registered, all-white M3 GTRs. These were distinguished by wheelarch extensions and side sills that made the use of 18-inch-diameter BBS wheels (10-inch wide fronts, 11-inch rears) with 245/40 or 285/35 ZR rubber appear natural.

The M3 GT price was DM 250,000 in the winter of 1993, but you needed to pay more to have your street 286 bhp rebuilt as a 325-bhp GTR competition motor, which also boosted torque 6 percent. Although it was a mild 15-percent power boost, the motor had some expensive and fundamental changes to suit the power-to-weight formula.

The primary move was an 86.4-mm bore in place of the production 86-mm. Allied to the usual 3-liter six's stroke of 85.8 mm, this released 3,018 cc in place of the M3's production 2,990 cc. Compression escalated from 10.8:1 to 12.0:1, the motor drew breath from a competition air filter, and there were new Bosch Digital Motor electronics managing the show. The power band was moved from the M3's street-friendly 3,600-rpm torque peak to a 5,500 summit, 8,000 rpm as the upper limit and 7,000 the horsepower crescendo.

Technically, BMW did more outside the engine bay, backing up those Schwarzenegger looks with a sequential 6-speed gearbox for the works GTRs (three optional 5-speed and 6-speed boxes, plus three final-drive ratios were offered). Then it delivered Teves race ABS anti-lock braking, enormous disc brakes in steel (old Grand Prix sizes) and Uniball joints for suspension that retained production principles but was, like the 318i of the period, fabricated for the job.

The big brakes were required not so much for the performance of the car, but the arduous task of repeatedly stopping its 1,300-kg/2,860-lb allotted minimum race weight. The M3 GTR motor was little more powerful, because the ADAC regulations balanced power-to-weight ratios to bring a wide variety to the grid and predict how the revival of GT racing might be. Although BMW personnel did not seem terribly impressed with the series—"amateur" was the word I heard most after that winning season—it was terrifically successful in bringing together opposing motorsport philosophies.

The ADAC opening round at Avus-Berlin saw wall-to-wall Porsches of varying preparation standards and types (968 turbo, 911 Carrera 2, and RSRs) meet Honda's NSX, Wolf Racing Ford Escort Cosworths, a swift Abt Audi, and even a Callaway Corvette. All those brands featured in the final top ten, and Honda was just as seriously prepared as BMW. Honda grew out of the program into a class-winning Le Mans team of NSXs with UK-manufactured race monocoques.

Roundel serves over 40,000 BMW CCA members as of mid-1997 and they thought this bug burial ground on the winning PTG M3 was worthy of the front cover of the March 1997 magazine. So do I!

Picture: Klaus Schnitzer, US, 1997

The seasonal result? BMW drivers Cecotto and Kris Nissen, one-two! The season was not a walkover, for Honda and Armin Hahne did a consistent job in the normally-aspirated Honda NSX, and the turbo Porsches usually out-qualified or set faster race laps than the works M3s.

Yet the M3 could race faster for longer than the turbo opposition, as fuel-consumption limits had been set. This meant exceeding 5.9 US miles per gallon (7 UK mpg). That was hard for a flat-out turbo to manage, and the result was that many of the races saw the turbo Porsches and Fords reduced to an economy run to the final flag or out of fuel after a hard charge. Meanwhile the M3 and NSX (usually sneaking along in the M3's huge rear-wing

airstream!) were more fuel-efficient under duress. Score M3's first major title.

The M3 path to the USA

The M3 continued a slow development path in Europe. Most customers went for the Group N version, a very lightly-tuned (300 bhp) 3.0-liter, that could be little-modified in this category. Teams were allowed to strip the interior of trim and use slick racing tires, but the body had to remain showroom, and all areas of modification were either banned or

How the PTG Bimmer, one of a pair entered, looked at its Daytona 1995 debut, when it took a surprise class pole position. Note the lack of later-extended wheelarches and the fact that both had been rebuilt from that European/ Nürburgring hybrid Group A/N specification. They featured 9- and 10-inch rims, front and rear, for 18-inch Yokohamas. The 3-liter motors fed 6-speed Hollinger non-sequential gearboxes, but both threw connecting rods during the 35-degree night.

Picture: Courtesy Judy Stropus/PTG, USA, 1997

Stripes rule, OK? If you like your BMWs with pizzaz, then this is your eight-picture corner of a California heaven for Bimmerphiles.

Pictures: Author (8); BMW AG (M3 badge)

subject to very small production tolerances—just the sort of stuff that Rosche and his henchmen tended to avoid because there are so many gray regulation areas and no scope for radical engineering.

The 1993 ADAC Cup-winning program progressed the M3, but it was no more than a first step when compared to the tubular frame cars the Bimmer would be asked to beat in the US.

For the June 1994 Nürburgring 2- hours, BMW decided to field a brace of modified (340 PS) M3s for what they called the "BMW Dream Team Super Oldies" to conduct around the old 'Ring layout. Trailed as the "Green Hell," the majestic backdrop to the world's toughest 24-hours (because of the Eiffel mountain weather and blind crest circuit) would see many of BMW's legends back at the wheel. Even though most were 50 or more, the Super Oldies put in some stirring drives.

Multiple German champion (with Ford) Hans Heyer lapped the car he shared with still-current driver Leopold von Bayern well under Nürburgring's decisive 10-minute barrier. They averaged over 95 mph and fourth fastest overall—just eight seconds slower than the best of the works drivers (including Winkelhock and Heger) could manage in the pole-sitting 318i 2-liter serious entry. The other M3, whose crew included Hubert Hahne (then 58) and Jochen Neerpasch, was twelfth overall, some 25 seconds down on the quickest M3.

As for the imported American M3s of 1995, these 1994 M3s had a pretty strange specification. They covered bits of the Group N production racer and some more serious stuff, like the 340-horsepower/7,800-rpm 3-liter motors, which offered a slight torque bonus over 1993's ADAC-winning GTR specification (350 Nm at 4,750 rpm versus 340 Nm at 5,500 rpm).

The old-timers also had the full 2-liter race brakes, 75-percent preloaded limited-slip differential, and an excellent 1,200-kg minimum weight target. This meant that they had a much better power-to-weight ratio than the 1993 GTR Cup winner: some 283 bhp per ton versus 250 bhp per ton. Yet these 1994 M3s were clothed in two-door showroom M3 cues, right down to the color-coded white road wheels.

Neither of those two M3s gave BMW its traditional 24-hour finishing rate or the win that the company seems to preserve as its exclusive property in the German and Belgian epics. But quite a lot of the motor and associated technology arrived in the US for that 1995 debut.

When the 240-bhp American version of the M3 was released, competitive interest was almost as strong as the phenomenal (by European standards) M3 sales rates. For seasons, BMW North America's Erik Wensberg and the enormous BMW CCA club (over 40,000 members at press time) had been telling Munich that they needed another race program. It was a subject that made Munich flinch, remembering the aborted IMSA GTPs and forgetting the glorious deeds done in the

Another legendary lightweight coupe from BMW. The 1995 importation of 85 such M3s (up to 200 lbs. lighter than stock with many showroom features deleted, especially air conditioning and power assists) was unfortunately not accompanied by the 325-bhp motor offered in the European GT counterpart to the Lightweight series. Not even the usual European 286 bhp of the period was permitted, so the first M3s struggled in competitions such as the One Lap of America on a Federal 240 horsepower.

Picture: Klaus Schnitzer, US

name of Bavarian Motor Works by the CSLs and the McLaren-320t programs.

The sheer enthusiasm for BMW in the US takes Europeans back when they visit. Only Porsche parallels BMW's following in the US experience. Europeans often end up asking, "Why no official American race program?" Talking with German executives, the answer appears to be that there is no suitable category for the products to stand a winning chance.

Talking to bouncy BMW North America people, the answer seems to be lack of budget and commitment. Back in the winter of 1994/95, BMW NA supported Thomas H. Milner's Prototype Technology Group as it strove to sort out its first racing M3s. The cars arrived in time to contest February 1995's Daytona 24-hours, and expectations were high as there was an immediate pole position set.

The cars had wet-sump lubrication on their debut and Daytona's bankings terminated two units before the need for dry-sump layouts was

accepted. From the start, the PTG priority has been to get the weight out of the monocoque (unibody) construction in a category where tube-frame cars are the pace-setting norm.

Having put the M3 on a savage diet, PTG also had to keep at the handling, because it is easier to adjust a tubular chassis car to each track than it is for a machine that started life on the production line. It's the difference between creating a competition car that looks like a street machine and converting a street car into a competition car.

That diet returned a 2,300-lb/1,045-kg M3 on the lightest of four cars fielded at Daytona 1996, the remaining trio averaging out around 2,450 lbs/1,114 kg. On the stated 380 bhp from 3.2 liters (119 bhp per liter), this gave the lightweight 07 First Union/Valvoline the best power-to-weight ratio for a 3-series since the old McLaren turbo days: 390 bhp per ton.

As McLaren North America and John Nicholson discovered on either side of the

Human driving forces behind the major US race program for M3 have been Prototype Technology Group's Tom Milner (left) and BMW North America M-marketing manager Erik Wensberg (right).

Picture: Courtesy Judy Stropus/PTG, USA, 1997

For 1996, the wheelarches grew and the success rate mounted to the point where allies PTG, BMW North America, and an impressive array of sponsors secured a last gasp IMSA GTS2 national title: the first US major Championship since the 1980s reign of M1! Javier Quiros did the job when this lightweight model driven by Peter Halsmer suffered a broken oil line in the last seven minutes.

During 1996, adjustable FIA-sanctioned wings that boosted downforce considerably were adopted: the "lightweight's" 2,310 lbs. became usual for the 2-door racing coupes of 1997.

Picture: Courtesy Judy Stropus/PTG, US, 1997

Mechanical driving force has come from 3- and 3.2-liter versions of the fabled in-line six. At Daytona in 1995, they debuted with much the same 340 bhp as had appeared at Nürburgring 1994; but by 1997, a durable 380 bhp was exploited in the higher-temperature world of US endurance racing.

Picture: Courtesy Judy Stropus/PTG, US, 1997

Atlantic in the 320t program of the 1970s, European race and American conditions are so different that they can cause a lot of development heartache. BMW Motorsport in Munich had applied most of their data for four-door, 2-liter cars of different dimensions and weights to the PTG M3s, but the real killer was the availability of 100-plus octanes in the US, where 98-octane pump gas and catalytic converters featured in the most recent BMW 3-series experience. PTG redeveloped the engine around American conditions and reckoned to have added 60 reliable bhp to the original import total. The total of 380 horsepower was very accessible, running cleanly from pit-lane speeds and happy to run from 4,500 rpm upward.

When it came to carving up the body and designing a proper roll cage, Munich's 2-door coupe data went back to the 3-liter 1993 ADAC M3, or the 1992 British 2-liters. Overcoming these basic difficulties took time,

but BMW in Germany and the US were committed to seeing the M3 succeed. PTG got an unexpected insight into progressing the M3 when it had to rebuild New York customer Matt Cohen's M3 from scratch to contest the same IMSA GT S2 class.

On July 14, 1996 at Sears Point in northern California, PTG M3s scored their first IMSA GT S2 win. In fact, they finished one-two-three against the Porsches that provided BMW's principle opposition to winning its first IMSA title since 1981. There were three straight victories recorded before a quartet of PTG M3s lined up at Daytona as part of a World Sports Car Championship round, held in heavy Floridian rain. The driving teams behind Pete Halsmer included Bill Auberlen, Javier Quiros, Boris Said, and...and Dieter Quester!

Since veteran Pete Halsmer had scored a consecutive three wins on the way to Daytona, it was hoped that he would do the job again at

(Right) At the third attempt, BMW North America and PTG won their category at the Daytona 24-hours. The number 10 M3 was driven by the former Ferrari World Champion's son Derek Hill, IMSA title contender Bill Auberlen, and 1988 IMSA Lights Champion Tom Hessert, who is also a BMW dealer. Boris Said also did a stint in this car, which lost all but two forward gears in the closing stages.

Picture: Courtesy Judy Stropus/PTG, US, 1997

Night drama: beautifully caught by the Schnitzer lens, the number 6 BMW M3 at 1997 Daytona spent a lot of time in the pit lane, yet finished second in GTS3.

Picture: Klaus Schnitzer, US, 1997

The M3 lightweight inspired plenty of racing action from BMW loyalists in the US. This is one prepared by T. C. Kline, who provided Randy Pobst with his SCCA National Championship-winning M3. At those 1996 finals, M3s finished first, fourth, and fifth in their category. The SCCA changed the rules for 1997!

Picture: Author, US, 1996

Here, a dramatic pit stop was required for the Porsche-beating M3 at Daytona 1997 when the windscreen cracked up and required replacement. That done, the booming Bimmer departed on its way to ninth overall and the GTS3 win: a prophetic morale-booster for 1997's Championship chances.

Picture: Klaus Schnitzer, US, 1997.

Persistence pays. After seasons of heartbreak and intermittent promise, the BMW North America-backed E36s won through with numerous additional backers, including Valvoline, AC Schnitzer, and the ever-expanding (from 32,000 to beyond 40,000 members in 1997) BMW CCA (BMW Car Club of America).

BMW number 6 raced to the six-cylinder beat in the USA and won the IMSA GTS2 title. Here is the 1996 PTG machine, driven by Javier Quiros in the season they started to win in IMSA GT. For 1997, the rules were changed, weight was added, and the M3s moved up a class. They were still title winners in GTS3, the 2-door coupes joined by an M3-based 4-door that got wrecked its first time out, but was a winner within months.

Picture: BMW NA/Courtesy of Judy Stropus

Daytona, even if the odds played Porsche's 15 entries against BMW's four. For much of the race, it looked like Halsmer's number-four win was on the way, but seven minutes from the end, an oil line was severed and Halsmer's personal hopes were shattered.

BMW's honor was saved by lanky Javier Quiros, who surged by the remaining Porsche just five minutes from the finish to secure the 1996 IMSA GT S2 title for BMW.

The 1997 PTG M3s were still winning in one-two-three order within the revamped IMSA series at Lime Rock, and took first, third, and fourth places at Watkins Glen in June 1997. Just rewards for a lot of pioneering craftsmanship, including successfully racing the four-door M3.

BMW à la Oreca

In our enthusiasm for US racing, it is all too easy to miss out on some of the most fanatical BMW-based businesses. For sheer enjoyment of the marque in sporting use, I reckon you have to include the French Team Oreca. The story of how the Spartanburg Z3 made its international competition debut in ice racing (hard top firmly in place!) is truly astonishing.

First, a little history: Team Oreca was founded 23 years ago by former mathematics teacher and Renault racer Hugues de Chaunac. He founded Oreca in 1973 and heads the 48 employees today. Their primary base is by the Paul Ricard circuit in Southern France, but their promotions and racing activities are world-wide.

BMW North America and the resourcefulness of PTG brought us the world's first 4-door M3 racer in 1997. It was wrecked on its April 1997 debut (shown here alongside the US street M3 4-door) at Road Atlanta, but managed its first win in GTS3 within months. This meeting was also notable for finishing the sixth straight GTS2/GTS3 category-winning run of PTG and the M3.

Picture: Courtesy Judy Stropus/PTG, US, 1997

One of a trio of updated 1996 M3s that contested the 1997 Rolex 24-hours at Daytona, this machine served for a quartet of drivers: three newcomers to to the PTG team, plus the M3-experienced Boris Said. It finished second in its class, while a sister car cleaned up by two laps in GTS3 after a bruising race.

Picture: Courtesy Judy Stropus/PTG, US, 1997

Chamonix Ski resort in the French Alps hosts the annual Andros Trophy Ice-Racing Challenge: here, Yvan Müller fends off two GM-Opel Vectras in the very special Oreca Z3 4x4. Philippe Gache finished third overall in the demanding series, winning the 2-liter cup on the way.

Picture: Hugh Bishop, France, 1997

Oreca displays preparation skills as diverse as an 8-liter GT endurance racer and an annual winter foray into ice racing with the beastliest BMWs ever to bear the 3-series tag.

Most of the mechanics have done more than 10 years at Oreca. They work with an amiable efficiency that betrays experience from world-class rallying (Peugeot T16), Le Mans (Oreca won with Mazda in 1991), Rally Raids (Lada), through all forms of single-seater racing, including Grand Prix and F3000.

Drivers to carry the Oreca emblem include multiple world champion Alain Prost, current Benetton-Renault employee (just) Jean Alesi and—at that historic first Japanese Le Mans victory—Johnny Herbert, who was with Sauber-Ferrari (Petronas) in 1997 Grand Prix.

Loyal employee and practical engineer Arnaud Elizagaray reminded us of some less-obvious Oreca liaisons, and a number of unlikely BMW projects. These include an M1 mid-engined supercar of 3.5 liters for success-

ful stage use by Bernard Beguin, and the big M5 in France's version of production racing. It had to give best to the home team of turbo Renaults, but was a spectacle to behold in full flight, as fans of the David Donohue M5 outings in America would appreciate.

Oreca had three seasons representing BMW in 2-liter SuperTouring, a category that is not very popular in France, culminating in the 1995 national title for Yvan Müller in a 320i that also penetrated the top three in that year's FIA World Cup races.

So, to our amazing story: how do you take a Z3 ice racing? Well, when your main entry is the 1996 Trophy-winning 3.2 liter M3 Evolution-engined Compact (!), complete with 4-WS (Wheel Steer) and 4x4 drive, as was the case at Oreca, the challenge of building a 2-liter around a prediction of Z3's coupe outline probably does not seem so difficult.

Design work from Olivier Maroselli started in July 1996, and practical work overseen by

Mid-mounted and offset, the Z3 ice-racer from Oreca incorporates Vanos variable valve timing for the inlet camshaft of the 2-liter SuperTouring motor, providing much more accessible pulling power alongside its conservative 250 bhp and 8,000 rpm.

Picture: Hugh Bishop, 1997

Arnaud Elizagaray began the following month. The layout would be familiar in the US in that a tube frame is used, clothed in the lightest composite-construction panels possible.

For the Z3 pioneer, design basics were much the same as Oreca had employed on its extraordinary 3.2 Compact, running an offset front engine so far to the rear that it could be termed front mid-engined. Weight distribution is pretty even, front to rear, settling around 51 percent front and 49 percent back.

The four-cylinder Z3 motor offset helps run a simple 4x4 system and allows clearance for the front propshafts, which otherwise tend to plunge through the sump or other lubrication-sensitive hardware. The 1,998-cc (86.4 x 85.2 mm) engine is quite in the spirit of Z3, being based on the M42 unit that was found at 1.8 or 1.9 liters emerging from Spartanburg. Horsepower was augmented by something over 100 additional bhp, conservatively-tuned by Heini Mader in Switzerland to yield 250 bhp at 8,000 rpm.

More to the point, a wide power band is vital in ice-racing, so the unit should run cleanly from 2,500 rpm and gives maximum torque by 5,500, some 1,500 to 2,000 revs earlier than that at which an equivalent circuit-racer would cooperate fully. That was partially because Mader utilized the VANOS valve-timing control system on the inlet cam, and is investigating the possibility of running it on both inlet and exhaust cam timing, à la production M3.

Power freaks may like to know that Oreca's M3-Compact weighs 264 lb/120 kg more than the flyweight 1,826-lb/830-kg Z3, but delivers 340 bhp at 7,500 rpm and an even-beefier 280 lb-ft of torque by 4,500 revs. This means that Oreca's mutant Bimmers deliver 308.6 and 365.6 bhp per ton, so 4x4 and mechanically linked 4-wheel steering is needed to successfully tackle a variety of similarly hybrid opposition that included a VW-engined Daewoo and a mid-V6 motor Micra mini car!

Oreca has a long tradition of building race and rally BMWs, so this mid-motor Z3 combined both disciplines to produce a winning 4x4 tube-frame cousin to Spartanburg's finest. Driven by Philippe Gache—here demonstrating the sideways art to a suitably attentive passenger—the Oreca baby Bimmer proved to be a 2-liter winner and a podium finisher throughout the 1996/97 French ice-racing season.

Picture: Hugh Bishop, 1997

The Z3 has its M-badge sports and M-coupe cousins on stream at Spartanburg. How long before they join the 328 and ancestors in the BMW Motorsport Hall of Fame?

Picture: Author, US, 1996

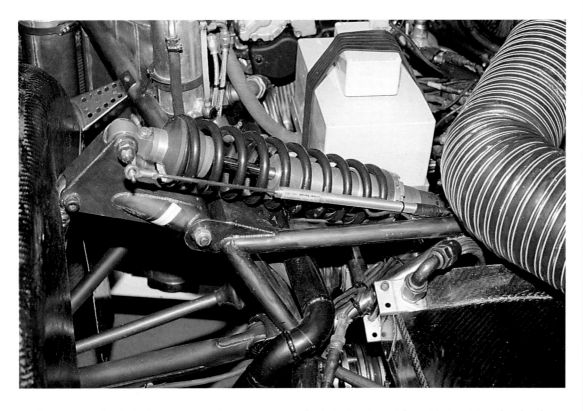

The inboard rear suspension of the Oreca Z3 racer displays its tubular frame and complexity of plumbing in so many technical features of this small sports car.

Picture: Hugh Bishop, 1997

The purpose-built 4x4 system employs an adapted Holinger 6-speed on the 2-liter Z3 and the heavy-duty X-trac 5-speed on the M3 Compact. Power transfer is by chain on the smaller-capacity Z3, and by gears (again from X-trac in Britain) for the bigger Bimmer. Steel propshafts are specified all around, with BMW Motorsport-sourced limited-slip differentials that have their ramp angles repeatedly tuned to the widely varying track surfaces. Data acquisition is by the British PI sensors (with bias to detect excess wheelspin and steering angles) that can be quickly downloaded since telemetry is banned, along with traction control and anti-lock braking.

Unlike the M-motored Compact, Oreca's Z3 has formula-car in-board rocker arm layouts and requires no anti-roll bars. Damping is by a mixture of Bilsteins and UK-built Quantum shock absorbers. Braking is not the circuit-racing priority on these low-grip surfaces and they get by with 10-inch/254-mm vented discs all around. Control wheels and tires are speci-fied: in 1997, spidery 135 x 16-inch wheels wore Michelins with 216 ice studs per tire.

Oreca drivers for the 1996–97 winter series included defending champion Yvan Müller, the 27-year-old who had won the preceding Trophee Andros in the M3 Compact as well as the 1995 SuperTouring title in a 320i. Philippe Gache and James Ruffier shared the Z3 and Gache came back third overall in the series, 2-liter category winner (a fiercely disputed honor), while Müller repeated his individual driver performance to snatch the Trophy.

In the counterpart points totals for manufacturers, BMW was runner-up to an extraordinary GM-Opel Tigra team. Gache commented, "It is hard to win with a 2-liter car at this altitude, especially if somebody spins or makes a mistake in front of you, but that's all part of the charm of racing!" It would be a boring world without such rugged individuals....

Appendix 1

1960–80 BMW competition-car specifications

Racing car development is a continuous process, making it practically impossible to give an exact technical specification, for it can only be right at the precise time it is given. I have attempted to classify the BMW sedans and single-seaters with the sources available, but there are often wide variations, particularly when it comes to power outputs and top speeds. These specifications do make interesting comparative reading, and for that reason alone, they are included.

	700 Sports CS	1800TI*	1800TI/SA**	2000TI	2002Ti/Tii†
Engine	Boxer, 2-cyl rear	il 4-cyl front	il 4-cyl front	il 4-cyl front	il 4-cyl front
Bore x stroke (mm)	78 x 73	84 x 80	84 x 80	89 x 80	89 x 80
Capacity (cc)	697	1,773	1,773	1,990	1,990
Bhp @ rpm	56 (Group 2), 75 (GT)	145/155 6,500 (Group 2)	158 to 165 max 6,500	170 7,500	180 (2 x Webers) to 210 (Kugelfischer fi) 7,500/7,800
Gearbox	4-speed, cr	4-speed, cr	Getrag 5-speed	Getrag 5-speed	Getrag 5-speed
Suspension	Production, ind. f & r, with Konis	Production, ind. f & r, with Konis, short springs	Modified production, ind. f & r, with Konis, short springs, f & r anti-roll bars	Modified production, ind. f & r, with Konis, short springs, f & r anti-roll bars	Heavily modified, lower & stiffer hard bushings, anti-roll bar f & r (choice)
Brakes	Drum f & r	Disc f, drum r	Disc f, drum r	Disc f, drum r	Disc f & r
Tires & wheels (in)	Dunlop, steel 4/4.5 x 12	Dunlop, steel 5 x 14	Dunlop, steel 5/6 x 14	Dunlop, steel 5/6 x 13	Dunlop, cast-alloy 7/10 x 13
Body & chassis	Production 2-door in steel	Production 4-door in steel	Production 4-door in steel	Production 4-door in steel	Modified production 2-door in steel with aluminum & fiberglass, extended wheelarches
Weight (kg)	630	1,040	1,020 or less	under 1,100	860/890
Top speed (mph)	95/105	115/125	circa 126	130	135/140
Competition Category	Group 1, 2 & GT, 1960–64	Group 1 & 2, 1964	Group 2, 1965–66	Group 2, 1966	Group 2/5, 1968–69

KEY: il=in-line; fi=fuel injection; v=valve; f=front; r=rear
*TI means Touring Internationale
**TI/SA means Touring Internationale Sonder Aüsfuhring (literally translates into Touring Internationale Special Equipment)
† The Tii was the fuel-injection designation for the Ti

	2002 turbo††	3.0 CSL◊	CSL turbo	320i	320i turbo◊◊
Engine	il 4-cyl, front	il 6-cyl, front	il 6-cyl, front	4-cyl	4-cyl
Bore & stroke (mm)	89 x 80	92 x 80/94 x 80/94 x 84	92x80	89.2 x 80	89/2 x 80
Capacity (cc)	1990	3191/3331/3498	3191	1999	1999
Bhp @ rpm	270/280 7,200	330 (early Group 2)/ 470 (late Group 5) 7,800/9,000	750+ 9000	300/305 9250	500/654√ 9000
Gearbox	Getrag 5-speed	ZF & Getrag 5-speed	Getrag 5-speed	Getrag 5-speed Type 245	Getrag 5-speed Type 265.3.5
Suspension	Heavily modified, lower and stiffer, Anti-roll bar f & r (choice)	Radically modified strut & trailing arm Bilsteins, wide, use of fabricated steel, aluminum & titanium. All adjust. for Group 5	Same as for Group 5 3.0 CS	Similar to 3.0 CSL, but all adjustable & steel-jointed, quick ride-height adjust.	Similar to 3.0 CSL, but all adjustable & steel-jointed, quick ride-height adjust.
Brakes	Disc f & r	Ate ventilated disc f & r, 4-piston front calipers	Ate ventilated disc f & r, 4-piston front calipers	Same as 3.0 CSL with balance bar	Same as 3.0 CSL with balance bar
Tires & wheels (in)	Dunlop, cast-alloy 8/10 x 13	Dunlop, BBS, 11.5 f & 13 r x 15/16 diam. (1973 Group 2); Goodyear, BBS, 12 f & 14 r BBS spun & cast-alloy, split-rim wheels)	Goodyear, BBS, 12 x 16 diam. f 14 x 19 diam. r (special rear tires)	Goodyear, BBS, 11 f & 12 .5 r x 16 diam.	Goodyear, BBS, 11 x 16 diam. f, 14 x 19 diam. r
Body & chassis	Modified production 2-door in steel with aluminum & fiberglass, ext. wheelarches with pop-riveted alloy panels.	Steel Karmann 2-door base, Lightweight, alloy hood, trunk doors, fiberglass wheelarch extensions, 8-part wing set	Group 5 CSL skeletal steel frame, fiberglass & alloy glass-panels ext., big water radiator	Skeletal steel production 2-door, base, fiberglass panels & side radiators, rear engine-oil cooler & dry-sump tank	320i specs plus detail aerodynamic changes— 120-liter fuel tank replaces 70/100
Weight (kg)	860	1,062 (Group 2 avg.) 1,030 (Group 5 avg.)	1,080	760	880
Top speed (mph [km/h])	155 (250)	167 (270) Group 2 175 (284) Group 5	178 (289), Silverstone; circa 190 (308), Le Mans	circa 160 (259)	circa 186 (300) at Nürburgring
Competition category	Group 5, 1969	Group 2, 1973/74 (factory) Group 5, 1976 (factory)	3 races only, 1976, Group 5 & LeMans, no finishes	Group 5 World & German Champ., 1977/78; IMSA, 1975/76 (factory); sold to many customers	Group 5, 1977/78/79

††The 2002 turbo was sometimes referred to as the 2002TIK (K for Kompressor), but it was not a designation used by the factory
◊CSL stands for Coupe Sport Lightweight ◊◊European specification
√320i turbo used a compression ratio of 7.5:1 instead of the conventionally aspirated engine's 11:1

	M1 ProCar	John Surtees Racing/BMW Lola T102 F2	Polifac-BMW Junior Team March 782 F2
Engine type	il 6-cyl mid	il 4-cyl rear (mid)	il 4-cyl rear (mid)
Bore & stroke (mm)	94 x 84	89 x 64.2	89.2 x 80
Capacity (cc)	3498	1598	1999
Bhp @ rpm	470 9,000	220 10,500	305/310 9,250/10,000 (late '78 dev.)
Gearbox	ZF 5-speed with oil cooler	Hewland 5-speed	Hewland FT200 5-speed with oil cooler
Suspension	Double wishbones f & r, magnesium uprights, alloy hubs, Bilsteins, adjustable anti-roll bars f & r, center-lock wheels	Triangulated f wishbones & parallel rod/transverse link r	Triangulated f wishbones & parallel rod/transverse link r
Brakes	Ate ventilated discs f & r, twin master cyl, balance bar	disc f & r, inboard at r	disc f & r, 2 team cars with ventilated r, others with solid discs, all vented disc front
Tires & wheels (in)	Goodyear, BBS, 11 f & 12.5 r x 16 diam.	Dunlop, Lola cast-alloy, 10 f & 12 r x 13 diam.	Goodyear, March cast-alloy, 10 f & 14 r x 13 diam.
Body & chassis	Tubular steel chassis, fiberglass bodyshell, 2-door, 2-seat	Aluminum monocoque with tubular engine bay, fiberglass panels, separate f aelerons, strut-mounted rear wing— electrically adjusted	Aluminum monocoque with tubular engine bay, full-width nose & twin-sideplate-supported r wing
Weight (kg)	1,020	409	500 (ballasted)
Top speed (mph [km/h])	192 (310)	circa 150 (243)	circa 165 (267)
Competition category	ProCar series, 1979 & eligible Group 4	European F2 Championship, 1968	European F2 Championship, 1978

1982–97 BMW competition-car specifications

Now we travel into the era of advanced aeorodynamics and heavily restricted formulae with yet more formidable BMW hardware, from the 528i to turbocharged Grand Prix fours and V12-energised GTs.

	1982 528i	1983 635CSi	1987 M3/2.3	1996 320i	1997 M3/3.2 USA
Engine	6-cyl	6-cyl	4-cyl	4-cyl	6-cyl
Valve gear	SOHC/12-v	SOHC/12-v	DOHC/16-v	DOHC/16-v	DOHC/24-v
Bore x stroke (mm)	86 x 80	92.6 x 86	94 x 84	93.4 x 72.6	86.3 x90
Capacity (cc)	2,788	3,473	2,332	1,999	3,200
Bhp @ rpm	245 6,500	285 6,800	300 8,000	305 8,400	380 8,200
Gearbox	5-speed H	5-speed H	5-speed H	6-speed S	5-speed H
Discs	Ate	Ate/AP	Ate/AP	Brembo/AP	Brembo
Tires & alloy wheels (in)	Pirelli/Dunlop/ Michelin, BBS 7 x 15 or x 16	Pirelli, BBS 11 x 16	Pirelli/Yokohama, BBS 9 x 17	Michelin, BBS 8.25 x 18	Yokohama, BBS cast-alloy 10.5 x 18 or 16 11.0 x 18
Body & chassis	Production 2/4-door in steel	Production 2-door in steel	Production 2-door in steel/plastics	Production 4-door in steel/carbons	Modified production 2-door in steel with extended wheelarches & wing kit
Weight (kg)	1,200	1,185	960	1,025	1,150
Top speed (mph)	140	155	160	155	170
Competition category	Group A	Group A	Group A	2-liter ST	IMSA/ProGTs-3

KEY: SOHC=single overhead camshaft; DOHC= double overhead camshaft; v=valves; H=H-pattern gear shift; S-=sequential shift; f=front; r=rear

	1997 McLaren F1 GT-R	1983 Brabham BT53-BMW
Engine	S70 V12	M12/13 Turbo 4-cyl
Bore & stroke (mm)	86 x 85.95	89.2 x 60
Capacity (cc)	5,990	1,499
Bhp @ rpm	604 7,500	Race: 640/Practice: 700 11,000
Gearbox	X-trac 6-speed S	Weissmann 6-speed H
Disc brakes front/rear (mm)	380/355	315 or less
Tires & wheels (in)	Michelin, OZ 10.85 x 18 13.0 x 18	Michelin, 11.5 x 13 16.5 x 13
Body & chassis	Composite carbon hull and panels	Aluminium tub with composite panel inserts
Weight (kg)	900	540
Power-to-weight ratio (race)	686 bhp/ton	1,207 bhp/ton
Top speed (mph)	205 (Le Mans)	195 (Silverstone)
0-60 mph (sec)	2.5	n/a
0-100 mph (sec)	n/a	5.0
Competition category	GT racing	Grand Prix

Appendix 2

BMW 3-series competition cars manufactured 1987–97

Until the closing months of 1995, these cars were all constructed directly under the wing of BMW Motorsport in Germany. For all but the last season of statistics, assume BMW kept 10 cars a year for their own use. For 1996–97 seasons, the SuperTourer was developed with McLaren as a pure works racer. That meant no new car sales to customers, but all 12 cars made were assigned new duties in 1997 and all were said to be sold, some to private owners, at the close of 1996.

Year	Cars Manufactured
1987	40
1988	40
1989	40
1990	25
1991	25
1992	25 (Ends M3)
1993	20 (as 318i with M3-motor)
1994	15 (318iS)
1995	15 (320i)*
1996	12 (BMW-McLaren)
Total	257

*Change during year to M42-based competition motors from M3 base

The following lists the various M-branded or pure motorsport products to come from Preussenstrasse (originally) Garching.

M1: 1978–81

Year	Production
1978	29
1979	115
1980	251
1981	55
Total	450*

*Of that 450 total, no less than 49 were constructed for racing, most in Procar.

M3 (E30): 1987–91, street cars	Production
Two-door sedans	17,184
Two-door cabriolets	786
Total First M3	17,970

M3 (E30): exports to the US	
1987	1,113
1988	1,675
1989	979
1990	764
1991	384
Total	4,915

M3 (E36): 1992–95*

The factory reported manufacture of 25,667 coupes, 1,570 of the 4-door sedans, and 1,981 cabriolets in the above period. The US model M3 was not released until 1994 but racked up 5,806 units in 1994–95, almost double the 2,953 achieved by all versions of the boxy original in four sales years.

*1995 was the last fully accounted period at press time. However, the factory production department summarized that 12,000 of all kinds of E36 M3s were made in 1996 to give the grand 1992–95 total of 41,218 in current M3 guise.

M5 (E28): 10/84 to 6/5/88

The Preussenstrasse Motorsport site hand-made 1,247 of these extremely desirable 24-valve Funfers before handing production over to Garching for the M5 (E34), including touring and four-doors, 5/9/88 to 12/10/95. The Garching site reports manufacture of 12,126 M5s in a total of six different models in the above period. Therefore, total production of all M5s was 13,373.

Appendix 3

BMW "Roll of Honor"

Here are the highlights of the BMW record in motorsports. Recalling so much success is near impossible, but this is the most complete catalogue of the company's major achievements that we can accommodate and that has been published to date.

Formula 2: European Championship Years

All used BMW M12/7 2-liter, except 1975, when a Schnitzer-developed BMW unit won the title.

1973: Jean Pierre Jarier	(March 732-BMW)
1974: Patrick Depailler	(March 742-BMW)
1975: Jacques Laffite	(Martini-Schnitzer BMW)
1978: Bruno Giacomelli	(March 782-BMW)
1979: Marc Surer	(March 792-BMW)
1982: Corrado Fabi	(March 882-BMW)

Grand Prix

1983: FIA World Champion Driver, Nelson Piquet (Brazil)

1983: FIA World Championship for Constructors; Brabham-BMW M12/13 were placed third overall, the BMW motor's best result to date.

GT endurance racing

All achievements using BMW Motorsport S70-based V12

1995: Winner Le Mans 24 hours. J.J. Lehto/Yannick Dalmas/Masanori Sekiya (6.1 McLaren F1 GTR). The world's most expensive rental car!

1995: BPR of Paris Global Cup. Champions Dr. Thomas Bscher/John Nielsen (6.1 McLaren F1 GTR). Run by Dave Price Racing for West.

1996: BPR of Paris Global Cup. Champion Ray Bellm (6.1 McLaren F1 GTR). Run by GTC Motorsports. Also McLaren-BMW, winner of Japanese GT Championship.

1997: FIA World Endurance GT Racing Championship. J.J. Lehto/Steve Soper (6.0 McLaren F1 GTR). Run by Schnitzer/BMW Motorsport/McLaren.

Touring car championships 1960–97

Recording sedan racing from the 1960s to the 1990s, BMW provides the benchmark against which others must measure up in all but NASCAR. The BMW company and privateer/works-assisted record in the European Championship is unlikely to ever be matched, since the European series was cancelled after the 1988 edition. Thus ended a continous championship with the accent on endurance—one that had opened in 1963 with a fine pan-European flavor as Peter Nocker of Germany won in a British Jaguar 3.8.

No rival matches BMW's sedan record of 16 European titles and one world championship title, 1966–88. You can add all the opposition up together and still not exceed the BMW winning record of outright victories in 20 editions of the 33 Spa Francorchamps 24-hour races held between 1964–1997.

Year	Driver	Mode	Title
1960	Hans Stuck Sr.	700 Sport Coupe	German Hillclimb Champion
1961	Walter Schneider	700 Sport	German Circuit Champion
1962	Heinrich Eppelein	700S	German Hillclimb Champion
1964	Hubert Hahne	1800TI	German Circuit Champion
1965	Pascal Ickx/Gerald v. Ophem	1800TI/SA	BMW's first Spa 24-hour win
1966	Josef Schnitzer	2000TI	German Circuit Champion
1966	Helmuth Bein	1602-2	German Rally Champion
1966	Hubert Hahne	2000TI	European Champion (Division 3)
1968	Dieter Quester	2002TI	European Champion (Division 3)
1969	Dieter Quester	2002Ti/turbo	European Champion (Division 3)
1970	Helmuth Bein/Christoph Mehmel	2002Ti	German Rally Champions
1973	Toine Hezemans	3.3/3.5 CSL	European Touring Car Champion
1975	Siggi Mueller/Alain Peltier	3.3 CSL	European Touring Car Champion
1976	Jean Xhenceval/Pierre Dieudonné	3.2 CSL	European Touring Car Champions
1977	Dieter Quester	3.2 CSL	European Touring Car Champion
1978	Umberto Grano	3.2 CSL	European Touring Car Champion
1978	Harald Ertl	1.4 turbo 320	German Circuit Champion
1979	Carlo Facetti/Manfred Finotto	3.2 CSL	European Champions
1980	Helmut Kelleners/Siggi Muller	2.0 320	European Champions
1981	Helmut Kelleners/Umberto Grano	3.5 635CSi	European Champions
1982	Helmut Kelleners/Umberto Grano	2.8 528i	European Champions
1983	Dieter Quester	3.5 635CSi	European Champion
1986	Roberto Ravaglia	3.5 635CSi	European Champion
1987	Winni Vogt	2.3 M3	European Champion
1987	Roberto Ravaglia	2.3 M3	World Touring Car Champion (driver)
1987	Eric v. Poele	2.3 M3	German Circuit Champion
1988	Roberto Ravaglia	2.3 M3	European Champion
1988	Frank Sytner	2.3 M3	British Champion
1988	Jean Pierre Malcher	2.3 M3	French Champion
1988	Patrick Snijers/Colebunders	2.3 M3	Belgian Rally Champions
1988	Francis Dosieres	2.3 M3	European Champion (Production class)
1989	Francois Chatriot/Michel Perin	2.3 M3	French Rally Champions
1989	Marc Duez/Alain Lopes	2.3 M3	Belgian Rally Champions
1989	Josep Bassas/A.Rodrigues	2.3 M3	Spanish Rally Champions
1989	John Bosch	2.3 M3	Dutch Rally Champion

1989	Silvan Lulik	Group N 2.3 M3	Yugoslavian Rally Champion
1989	Roberto Ravaglia	Schnitzer 2.3 M3	German Touring Car Champion
1989	Johnny Cecotto	Bigazzi 2.3	Italian Circuit Champion
1989	Jean-Pierre Malcher	Group A M3	French Circuit Champion
1989	Harri Toivonen	Group A 2.3 M3	Finnish Champion
1989	Peggen Andersson	Group A 2.3 M3	Swedish Circuit Champion
1990	Roberto Ravaglia	Schnitzer 2.5 Evo M3	German Touring Car Champion
1990	François Chatriot	Prodrive 2.3 M3	French Rally Champion
1990	J-P. Malcher	Group A 2.5 M3	French Touring Car Champion
1990	Jean-M. Martin	Group A 2.5 M3	Belgian Circuit Champion
1990	Cor Euser	Group N 2.3 M3	Dutch Circuit Champion
1990	Hansueli Ulrich	2.3 M3	Swiss Champion
1990	Heikki Salmenautio	2.3 M3	Finnish Circuit Champion
1990	Silvan Lulik	2.3 M3	Yugoslavian Rally Champion
1990	Xavier Riera	2.3 M3	Spanish Hillclimb Champion
1991	Will Hoy	Supertouring 2.0 M3	British Touring Car Champion
1991	Roberto Ravaglia	Schnitzer 2.5 M3	Italian Circuit Champion
1992	Tim Harvey	SuperTouring 2.0 318iS coupe	British Champion
1992	Dieter Quester	1.8 1800TI/SA	FIA Historic Champion
1993	Joachim Winkelhock	Schnitzer 2.0 318i	British Champion
1993	Roberto Ravaglia	2.0 318i	Italian Champion
1993	Johnny Cecotto	3.0 E36 M3 GTR 2dr	ADAC GT Cup of Germany
1994	Johnny Cecotto	2.0 318is 4dr	ADAC D1 German Champion
1995	Joachim Winkelhock	2.0 320i	ADAC D1 German Champion
1995	Steve Soper	2.0 320i	Japanese Touring Car Champion
1996	Various	3.2 M3 2dr	IMSA GTS-2 Category to BMW
1997	Emanuele Naspetti	2.0 320i	Italian Circuit Champion
1997	Didier de Radrigues	2.0 320i	Belgian Circuit Champion
1997	Various	3.2 M3	Pro SportsCar GTS-3 to BMW
1997	David & Geoff Brabham	2.0 320i	1st Bathurst 1000*

* First occasion this prestigious Australian event ran for SuperTourers and attracted a premium entry. Battle between BMW and Audi so intense that Audi protested a BMW 1–2 result and original BMW winners (Craig Baird/Paul Morris) disqualified, leaving Audi 2–3 positions.

In 1988, BMW M3 drivers also won the national titles of Asia-Pacific, Holland, Portugal, Sweden and finished as runners-up in the European Rally series. Prodrive (UK) entered rallying M3s at French and Belgian Championship levels until 1990. The 2.3- and 2.5-liter BMW M3s won every edition of the Spa 24-hours held between 1987 and 1992, bar 1988 and 1991. Except in rallying, the first (1987) Evolution E30 BMW M3 was usually used. The second Evolution M3 entered Group A racing during 1988; a third (2.5 liter) Evolution was readied for the 1990 season.

In 1994, the E36 Supertouring 318i 2-liter started to match the E30 M3 record and won national titles in Germany, Belgium, Australia and South Africa.

Appendix 4

BMW touring-car results, 1960–78

BMW 700 Sport Coupe

1960
Races

Grosser Preis der Tourenwagen (6-hr)	Nürburgring, D	Schneider/Levine,1st in class
ADAC races (500 km)	Nürburgring, D	Linge/Schwind, class win
German GP meeting	Nürburgring, D	Schneider, 1 litre GT win
12 Stunden von Hockenheim (12-hr)	Hockenheim, D	Stuck Sr./S.Gregor, class win

Rallies

Geneva Rallye	Switzerland	Verheye/Windler, class win
Oesterreich Alpenfahrt	Austria	A & K von Falkenhausen, 1st 601-700 cc Pilhatsch, 1st GT to 1300 cc
Rally of 1000 Lakes	Finland	Lyytikaines/Raunio, class win
Tour de France	France	1st Index of Performance: Prince von Metternich/Hohenlo
Deutschland Rallye	Germany	1st class, 7th overall: Block/Paul

Hillclimbs

Mont Ventoux	France	1st, std tourers: Robert Jenny
Gaisbergrennen	Salzburg, A	Hans Stuck, GT 1-litre class win Walter Schneider, 750 class win
Bergrekord	Freiburg, D	Hans Stuck, GT 700 cc, class win
Grosser Berpreis der Schweiz	Switzerland (CH)	Hans Stuck, GT 850 cc, class win

Title won: 1960 Deutsche Bergmeister, Hans Stuck Sr. (Hillclimb champion of Germany)

1961
Races

GP of Brussels	Brussels, B	A. von Falkenhausen, class win
Coppa Ascari (6-hr)	Monza, I	Stuck Sr./Greger, class win
Grosser Preis von Tourenwagen (6-hr)	Nürburgring, D	Schneider/Schwind, class win
British Empire Trophy Race, Silverstone	England, UK	1st in class, 3rd o/a; H. Linge
500 kms, Nürburgring	Germany, D	700 cc Class, Tourers: 1-2-3 GT Cars-700 cc: 2 & 3 in class
12 Stunden von Hockenheim (12-hr)	Hockenheim, D	Schneider/Schwind, class win

Rallies

Monte Carlo Rallye	Monaco, F	Class win & 5th o/a: Bloch/Paul 10th o/a: Metternich/Weicher
Mille Miglia	Brescia, I	1st in class, 700 cc: Bloch/Paul
Tulip Rallye	Holland	1st class &13 o/a: Bloch/Bertram
Acropolis Rallye	Athens, Greece	1st class & 8th o/a: Bloch/Herbert
Midnight Sun	Sweden	1st Group 2 700 cc: S. Lester/Gothe
Coupes des Alpes	F/I	1st Group1 850 cc: Courtois/Krause
Tour de France	F	1-2-3 Touring Category
Polish Rally	Poland	1st in class & 3rd o/a: S.Zasada/E.Zasada

Title won; 1961 Deutsche Rundstreckenmeister, Walter Schneider (German Race Circuit champion)

1962

Races

ADAC races (500 km)	Nürburgring, D	Fischhaber/Koch, class win
Coupe de Paris	Montlhèry, F	A.von Falkenhausen, class win
Nürburgring 6-hours	Nürburgring, D	700 cc class: 1-2-3
Nürburgring 12-hours	Nürburgring, D	700 cc class: 1& 2
German GP (support race)	Nürburgring, D	700 cc GT: W. Schneider
Berlin GP (support race)	Berlin, D	GT Race: 2nd, Schneider
Brands Hatch 6-hours	Kent, UK	Coupe des Dames: Timaro/Pearson

Rallies

Acropolis Rallye	Athens, Greece	1st in class, 7th o/a: Levi/Gottlieb
Midnight Sun	Sweden	1st in class 700 cc: Spjuth/Burgren
Coupes des Alpes	F/I	1-2-3 in touring classification
Polish Rally	Poland	Class win & 7th o/a: Dobrzanski/Murawski
Baden-Baden Rally	Germany	1-2-3 in 700 cc classification

Hillclimb

Mont Ventoux	France	1-2-3 in Modified 700 cc class plus 700 cc touring (Matheron)

1963

Races/hillclimbs (European Challenge, later Championship)

Mont Ventoux	France	1-7 in class! J. Grasser led Gp2
Nürburgring 6-hours	Nürburgring, D	Class 1-2-3, won at 67.8 mph
Motor 3-Hours	Mallory Park, UK	1st & 3rd, 850 cc class win 2nd overall: H. Hahne
Zolder races	Zolder, B	1st in class, 700 cc: J. Grasser
Zandvoort races	Zandvoort, N	1st in class & 3rd o/a: Hahne

Timmelsjoch Bergrennen	Austria	1st in class: Hahne
Budapest GP (support)	Budapest, Hungary	1st in class: Hahne

European Challenge result: Hubert Hahne, 3rd overall

Non-Championship international races

Sebring 2 hours	US	3rd o/a: J. Stevens
Montlehery Coupes Salon	Paris, France	1st, 700 cc: A von Falkenhausen

Rallies

Acropolis	Greece	1st, 700 cc: Zalmas/Kosmetator & 20th o/a
Midnight Sun	Sweden	1st, 700 cc Group 2: Arp/Arp
Route du Nord	France	1st, Coupes des Dames: Marthieuw/Martine
Wiesbaden	Germany	1st, 700 cc: Knoppel/Knoppel, 7th o/a
Sardinia	Sardinia, Med	1st overall: G. Pirons

This season effectively ends the 700's works career, as the 1800s were ready for factory use in 1964. However, works drivers Hahne/Schneider won their 1964 class at Mallory Park UK in a one-off appearance.

BMW 1800TI, 1800 Tisa, 2000TI

1964

Races/hillclimbs for European Touring Car Championship

Zolder GP (support)	Zolder, B	W. Schneider (1800TI), 4th o/a and class win
Mont Ventoux	France	3rd in class (1800TI) for Laroche
Grosser Preis von Tourenwagen (6-hr)	Nürburgring,	D Hahne/Fischhaber (1800TI), 7th o/a, class win
Karlskoga races	Sweden	Hahne (1800TI), 1st class, 6th o/a
St Ursanne, Hillclimb	France	Hahne (1800TI), 1st in class
Zandvoort Trophae	Zandvoort, NL	Hahne (1800TI), 1st o/a
Timmelsjoch	Austria	Josef Schnitzer (1800TI) 1st in class
Budapest GP	Budapest, H	Hahne (1800TI), 1st o/a

Non-championship internationals

12 Stundenrennen	Nürburgring, D	Hahne/Eppelein (1800TI), 1st o/a Glas 1204 was 3rd o/a
24 Heures de Francorchamps	Spa, B	Aaltonen/Hahne (1800TI) 2nd o/a, class win
German GP support race	Germany	Hahne (1800TI) 1st o/a & fastest lap

1964 Deutsche Rundstreckenmeister, Hubert Hahne (Race circuit champion of Germany)

Rallies 1964

Geneva	Switzerland	4th o/a: Walter/Lier (1800TI); 1st 2000 cc

Police Rallye Liege	Belgium	2nd o/a: Friedel/Schmitzberger (1800)

1965

Races

24 Heures de Francorchamps	Spa, B	P. Ickx/Langlois (1800 Tisa), 1st o/a
Internationale Flugplatzrennen	Innsbruck, A	Hahne (1800 Tisa), 2-liter class win
Sebring 3-hours	Sebring, USA	Glemser (1800 Tisa), 3rd o/a

1966

Races

Preis von Wein	Aspern, A	Quester (1800 Tisa), 3rd o/a, class win
Grosser Preis der Tourenwagen (6-hr)	Nürburgring, D	Glemser/Fischhaber; Otto/Zink 2nd and 3rd o/a (1800 Tisa), class winners
24 Heures de Francorchamps	Spa, B	J. Ickx/Hahne (2000TI), 1st o/a
Snetterton 500 km	Snetterton, UK	Hahne 2nd o/a, class win, Glemser 3rd (2000TI)

1966

European Touring Car Champion (drivers) Hahne, (marques) 2-liter class, BMW

1967

No works touring car for international events

BMW 2002Ti and turbo (TIK)

1968

European Touring Car Championship (ETC)

ETC-2, Vienna 4-Hours	Aspern, A	Quester (TI), 1st o/a @ 130.6 km/h
ETC-3, Snetterton 500 km	Snetterton, GB	Quester (TI), 4th o/a
ETC-4, Belgrade GP (4-hr)	Belgrade, YU	Quester (TI), 1st o/a @ 123.98 km/h
ETC-6, Grosser Preis von Tourenwagen	Nürburgring, D	Hahne/Hobbs 1st o/a @ 135.5 km/h, Ahrens/Quester 2nd o/a (TIs)
ETC-8, Brno GP (4-hr)	Brno, CZ	Hahne/Quester 2nd o/a, Basche/Hahne 4th o/a (TIs)
ETC-9, Zandvoort Trophae	Zandvoort, NL	Quester 3rd o/a, Hahne 4th, Basche 5th (TIs)
ETC-10, Madrid GP (3-hr)	Jarama, E	Quester 3rd o/a, Hahne 4th, Basche 5th (TIs)
ETC-11, Eigenthal Hillclimb	Eigenthal, CH	Basche (TI), 2nd o/a

1968 European Touring Car Champion Division 3 (drivers) Quester, (marques) 2-liter class, BMW

1969

European Touring Car Championship

ETC-3, Belgrade GP (3-hr)	Belgrade, YU	Quester (TIK), 1st o/a, Basche 2nd (TI)
ETC-4, Brno GP (4-hr)	Brno, CZ	Quester (TIK), 1st o/a, Basche 2nd (TI)
ETC-6, Motor 6-Hours	Brands Hatch, GB	Quester/Hahne (TIK), 1st o/a @ 135.76 km/h
ETC-9, Zanvoort Trophae	Zandvoort, NL	Basche 2nd o/a, Quester 4th (TIKs)
ETC-10, Madrid GP (3-hr)	Jarama, E	Quester (TIK), 1st o/a @ 11 5.15 km/h

1969 European Touring Car Champion Division 3 (drivers) Quester, (marques) 2-liter class, BMW

Many of the 1969 points which enabled BMW to take these titles came (directly or indirectly) from the efforts of Alpina. Subsequently, in 1970, they represented the company in touring-car racing, winning Division 2 (marques) with their 1600Ti.

At the close of the 1970 season, the BMW factory announced its overall withdrawal from motorsports. By this time, Alpina had developed the 2800CS into a race winner, its first international European Championship victory being recorded on April 12 at Salzburgring, Austria, by Spaniard Alex SolerRoig. Official factory cars were not seen again until 1973, when BMW Motorsport GmbH entered the ETC in Group 2. In the meantime, Alpina, Schnitzer, and Broadspeed had all carried out development work, albeit with some measure of factory support.

1973

BMW 3.2, 3.3, 3.5 CSL (Group 2), factory and Alpina or Schnitzer BMW-backed results

ETC-1, Monza 4-Hours	Monza, I	Works cars dnf, Alpina 3.0 CSL 1st o/a
ETC-2, Austria Trophae (4-hr)	Salzburgring, A	Works car dnf, Alpina 2nd, Schnitzer 3rd o/a
ETC-3, Mennen races (507 km)	Mantorp Park, S	No car entered, Alpina 2nd o/a
ETC-4, Grosser Preis von Tourenwagen (6-hr)	Nürburgring, D	Amon/Stuck Jr. 1st o/a @ 158.5 km/h, Hezemans/Quester 2nd (3.3s), Alpina 3rd
ETC-5, 24 Heures de Francorchamps	Spa, B	Hezemans/Quester (3-3) 1st o/a @ 192.62 km/h, other car dnf, Alpina withdrew
ETC-6, Zandvoort Trophae (4-hr)	Zandvoort, NL	Hezemans/Quester (3.5) 1st o/a @ 150.91 km/h, other car dnf, Alpina 2nd
ETC-7, Le Castellet Ricard (6-hr)	Paul Ricard, F	Hezemans/Quester 1st o/a @ 154.10 km/h, Alpina 2nd, Amon/Stuck 3rd (3.5s)
ETC-8, Tourist Trophy (4-hr)	Silverstone, GB	One works car dnf, other out of fuel (classified), Alpina 1st and 3rd

1973 European Touring Car Champion (drivers) Hezemans, (marques) overall

1973 BMW World Sports Car Championship (factory and Alpina)

1000 km	Spa, B	Stuck/Lauda/Muir (3.2), 7th o/a, class win; 8th o/a, class 2nd same drivers in 3.0. Both Alpina cars

ADAC 1000 km	Nürburgring, D	Hezemans/Quester 9th o/a and class 2nd; Amon/Stuck crashed by Stuck (3.3s)
24 Heures	Le Mans, F	Hezemans/Quester 11th o/a and class win; Amon/Stuck, crashed by Stuck 3.3s

1974 European Touring Car Championship

ETC-2, Austria Trophae (4-hr)	Salzburgring, A	Stuck/J. Ickx 1st o/a @ 188.35 km/h (3.5 24-v)

Peterson/Stuck and J. Ickx/Bell were entered in 4-valve Group 2 CSLs for the July 14 Nürburgring 6-hour race. Neither car finished in this, the factory's last official Group 2 racing appearance in Europe.

1976

BMW 3.5 CSL (Group 5) factory built for World Championship of Makes

Mugello 6-Hours	Mugello, I	None in first six
Vallelunga 6-Hours	Vallelunga, I	Grohs/Posey/de Fierlant 2nd o/a, Walkinshaw/Fitzpatrick 4th
BRDC (6-hr)	Silverstone, GB	Walkinshaw/Fitzpatrick 1st o/a @ 170.81 km/h; Grohs/de Fierlant 4th
ADAC 1000 km	Nürburgring, D	Quester/Krebs 1st o/a @ 161.66 km/h
Oesterreich 1000 km	Oesterreichring, A	Quester/Nilsson 1st o/a @ 184.10 km/h, Walkinshaw/Fitzpatrick 2nd
Watkins Glen 6-Hours	Watkins Glen, US	Gregg/Haywood 4th o/a, Peterson/Quester 5th
Dijon 6-Hours	Dijon, F	Quester/Krebs/Peterson 6th o/a

1976 World Championship of Makes: 2nd overall

1977

BMW 320i (2-liter) factory-built 3-series for World Championship of Makes

BRDC (6-hr)	Silverstone, GB	Peterson/Kelleners 4th o/a and class win
ADAC 1000 km	Nürburgring, D	Surer/Winkelhock 3rd o/a and class win
Mosport 6-Hours	Mosport Park, CDN	Villeneuve/Cheever 3rd o/a and class win
Hockenheim (two 3-hr heats)	Hockenheim, D	Surer/Cheever 3rd o/a and class win

1977 World Championship of Makes: 2nd overall and 2-liter class winners

1978

During 1978, BMW Motorsport GmbH parts and complete 320i racing cars were more freely available. They were widely used by privateers in the Group 5 World Championship—being virtually invincible in the 2-liter class—in which category BMW again came 2nd overall to Porsche's 1st, for the third year running. The 320i turbo appeared several times, but did not finish a race in international Group 5.

The 1978 German national Group 5 Racing Championship was won outright by the Schnitzer-prepared and works-supported 320i turbo of Harald Ertl. BMW-engined cars won 10 of the 11 2-liter class races in the German qualifying rounds.

1977/78 McLaren North America Inc. Race Results for BMW 320i/320i turbo.

The BMW 320i was supplied by BMW Motorsport GmbH and they gave support throughout the seasons. Englishman David Hobbs drove in the IMSA rounds, while he, Ronnie Peterson, Sam Posey, Tom Klausler, and Hans-Joachim Stuck drove in the Internationals. The car was turbocharged as from Road Atlanta in 1977, the second event.

1977

Event/circuit	Start pos.	Result
Daytona	19	dnf, engine
Atlanta	28	4th
Laguna Seca	1	24th
Mid America	5	dnf, ignition
Lime Rock	2	dnf, fire
Mid Ohio	2	1st
Brainerd	20	dnf, gearbox
Watkins Glen	2	dnf, accident
Sears Point	2	1st
Pocono	2	dnf, drive shaft
Mosport	2	9th
Mid Ohio	2	dnf, throttle
Atlanta	1	1st
Laguna Seca	1	1st
Daytona	4	dnf, accident

1978

Event/circuit	Start pos.	Result
Daytona	3	dnf, piston
Sebring	1	dnf, accident
Atlanta	2	dnf, accident
Laguna Seca	4	4th
Hallet	2	1st
Lime Rock	2	5th
Brainerd	2	dnf, wastegate
Daytona	3	29th
Watkins Glen	5	dnf, turbo
Sears Point	1	1st
Portland	2	dnf, turbo
Mid Ohio	3	2nd
Atlanta	4	dnf, gearbox

Appendix 5

Single-seater race results

I discovered that BMW competition records were virtually non-existent prior to the establishment of BMW Motorsport GmbH in 1972. I have limited results to those where BMW engines finished in the top three. It should be noted that the Dornier 269/270 series of cars were pure BMW projects (albeit using a UK designer), whereas the bulk of later success came using UK chassis from March. This makes the Dornier BMWs particularly significant as all-German projects, possibly the last we will ever see as motorsports have become so international.

I drew this material from my original book research of the 1970s and the Grand Prix work of Chris Willows. Chris logged these results as a private project in the late 1980s, between bouts of cataloguing a picture collection that would gladden the heart of any BMW enthusiast. The magazines *Motor Sport, Motoring News,* and *Autosport* filled the gaps.

BMW Grand Prix results

Note that works-supplied engines were also the only ones to achieve pole positions. BMW literature claimed 15 of these fastest practice times in 1997, but I could trace only 14. Of these, Piquet took 11, Fabi 2, and Patrese 1.

BMW Motorsport 1.5-liter turbocharged M12/13: Grand Prix results

Date	Venue	Driver	Car/winning speed
6/13/82	Montreal,Canada	Nelson Piquet	(Brabham BT50-BMW), 107.9 mph
3/13/83	Jacarepagua,Brazil	N.Piquet	(Brabham BT52-BMW), 108.9 mph
9/11/83	Monza,Italy	N.Piquet	(Brabham BT52B-BMW), 135.2 mph
9/25/83	Brands Hatch,UK	N.Piquet	(Brabham BT52B-BMW), 123.1 mph
10/15/83	Kylamai, S. Africa	Riccardo Patrese	(Brabham BT52B-BMW), 126.1 mph
1983	FIA World Champion	Driver Nelson Piquet, Brabham BT52-BMW M12/13; Riccardo Patrese finished 8th in the standings	
1983 FIA Championship for Constructors			Brabham-BMW was 3rd o/a
6/17/84	Montreal,Canada	Nelson Piquet	(Brabham BT53-BMW), 108.2 mph
6/24/84	Detroit,USA	N.Piquet	(Brabham BT53-BMW), 81.7 mph
7/7/85	Paul Ricard,France	N.Piquet	(Brabham BT54-BMW), 125.1 mph
10/12/86	Mexico City	Gerhard Berger	(Benetton B186-BMW),120.1 mph

NB: The 1983 FIA World rankings were never equalled by BMW-powered GP cars in subsequent years. See Chapters 21 and 22 for fuller details.

Formula 2: 1.6-liter formula, 1967–71

Date	Event	Circuit/country	Driver	Car/Result/Winning speed
1967				
4/23/67	Eifeirennen	Nürburgring, D	Surtees	Lola-BMW, 2nd o/a
8/6/67	German GP	Nürburgring, D	Hobbs	Lola-BMW, 3rd F2 sec
1968				
No top three placings in international F2 races				
1969				
4/13/69	J. Clark Trophy	Hockenheim, D	Hahne	Lola-BMW, 2nd o/a (2 heats)
4/27/69	Eifelrennen	Nürburgring, D	Siffert	Dornier-BMW, 2nd o/a
6/15/69	Rhein-Pokal	Hockenheim, D	Hahne	Dornier-BMW, 2nd o/a
1969 European F2 Championship for ungraded drivers: 2nd, Hahne				
1970				
6/14/70	Rhein-Pokal	Hockenheim, D	Hahne	BMW 269 1st o/a @ 186.2 km/h
6/28/70	Circuit of Rouen	Rouen, F	Siffert	BMW 270, 1st o/a, 190.9 km/h
8/23/70	Circuit of Enna	Enna-Pergusa, I	Siffert	BMW 270, 2nd; J. Ickx, BMW 270, 3rd
8/30/70	Festspielpreis	Salzburgring, A	J Ickx	BMW 270, 1st: Quester, BMW 269, 3rd Heat times added
9/13/70	J. Rindt Trophy	Hockenheim, D	Quester	BMW 270, 1st o/a, 186.17 km/h
10/25/70	Neubiberg Preis	Neubiberg Airfield, A	Quester	BMW 270, 1st o/a, 151.6 km/h
1970 European F2 Championship for ungraded drivers: 4th, Quester				
1971				
5/16/71	Madrid GP	Jarama, E	Quester	March, 712, 2nd
6/20/71	Lottery GP	Monza, I	Quester	March, 712, 1st @ 218.141 km/h
6/27/71	Circuit of Rouen	Rouen, F	Quester	March, 712, 2nd
9/12/71	Flugpfatzrennen Tulin	Langenlebarn, A	Quester	March, 712, 3rd
10/3/71	Wurtemburg Trophy	Hockenheim, D	Quester	March, 712, 2nd
10/10/71	Rome GP	Vallelunga, I	Quester	March, 712, 2nd
1971 European F2 Championship for ungraded drivers: 3rd, Quester				

1972

2-liter engine not eligible

1973

3/11/73	Radio Luxembourg Trophy	Mallory Park, GB	Jarier	March 732, 1st @180.64 km/h
4/8/73	J Clark Trophy	Hockenheim, D	Jarier	March 732, 1st @ 197.6 km/h
4/23/73	Esso Trophy	Thruxton, GB	Beuttler	March 732, 3rd
5/6/73	Circuit of Pau	Pau, F	Jarier	March 732, 2nd
6/10/73	GB GP	Nivelles, B	Jarier Brambilla	March 732, 1st @ 177.34 km/h; March 732, 3rd
6/17/73	J. Rindt Trophy	Hockenheim, D	Vandervell Coulon	March 732, 2nd; March 732, 3rd
6/24/73	GP des Essarts	Rouen, F	Jarier	March 732, 1st @ 177.07 km/h
6/29/73	Lottery GP	Monza, I	Williamson Coulon	March 732, 1st @ 200.59 km/h; March 732, 3rd
6/22/73	Circuit of Misano	Misano, I	Vandervell	March 732, 2nd; Coulon, March 732, 3rd
7/29/73	Mantorp Park	Mantorp, S	Jarier	March 732, 1st Heat, times added
8/12/73	Circuit of Karlskoga	Karlskoga, S	Jarier	March 732, 1st
8/27/73	Circuit of Enna	Enna Pergusa, I	Jarier Brambilla	March 732, 1st @ 200.90 km/h; March 732, 2nd
9/2/73	Festspielpreis	Salzburgring, A	Brambilla Coulon	March 732, 1st @ 212.76 km/h; March 732, 3rd
9/9/73	Norisring Trophy	Norisring, D	Pescarolo	Motul MI, 3rd
9/16/73	Circuit of Albi	Albi, F	Brambilla Jarier Beltoise	1st @ 187.99 km/h; 2nd; 3rd. All March 732
10/14/73	Circuit of Vallelunga	Vallelunga, I	Coulon Brambilla	March 732, 1st @ 157.78 km/h; March 732, 2nd
10/21/73	Circuit of Estoril	Estoril, P	Jarier Coulon	March 732, 1st @ 160.52 km/h; March 732, 2nd

1973 European F2 Championship for ungraded drivers: 1st, Jean Pierre Jarier

1974

3/24/74	Montjuich Park	Montjuich, E	Stuck Depailler Jabouille	March 742, 1st @ 156.75 km/h; March-BMW, 2nd; Elf-BMW, 3rd
4/7/74	J, Clark Trophy	Hockenheim, D	Stuck Leclere	March 742, 1st; Elf-BMW, 3rd. Heat times added
6.5.74	Circuit of Pau	Pau, F	Depailler Laffite Sutcliffe	March 742, 1st; 2nd; 3rd. March-BMW

6/2/74	Salzburg GP	Salzburgring, A	Laffite Purley	March-BMW, 1st @ 210.13 km/h; Chevron-BMW, 2nd
6/9/74	J. Rindt Trophy	Hockenheim, D	Jabouille Laffite Stuck	Elf-BMW, 1st @ 198.76 km/h; March-BMW, 2nd; March-BMW, 3rd
6/30/74	GP des Essarts	Rouen, F	Stuck Purley Leclere	March 742, 1st @ 155.63 km/h; Chevron-BMW, 2nd; Elf-BMW, 3rd
7/14/74	Mugello Int	Mugello, I	Depailler Paoli Pryce	March 742, 1st @ 169.60 km/h; March-BMW, 2nd; Chevron-BMW, 3rd
8/11/74	Circuit of Karlskoga	Karlskoga, S	Peterson Depailler Laffite	March 742, 1st @ 147.45 km/h; March-BMW, 2nd; March-BMW, 3rd
8/25/74	Circuit of Enna	Enna Pergusa, I	Stuck Purley Serblin	March 742, 1st @ 208.81 km/h; Chevron-BMW, 2nd; March-BMW, 3rd
9/22/74	Circuit of Nogaro	Nogaro, F	Tambay Schenken Leclere	Elf-BMW, 1st @ 149.12 km/h Surtees-BMW, 2nd; Elf-BMW, 3rd
9/29/74	Hockenheimpreis	Hockenheim, D	Depailler Stuck Jabouille	March 742, 1st; March-BMW, 2nd; Elf-BMW, 3rd. Heat times added
10/13/74	Vallelunga GP	Vallelunga, I	Depailler Stuck Laffite	March 742, 1st @ 162.29 km/h; March-BMW, 2nd; March-BMW, 3rd

1974 European F2 Championship for ungraded drivers, a 1-2-3 for BMW M-Power: 1st, Patrick Depailler; 2nd, Hans Joachim Stuck; 3rd, Jacques Laffite

1975

3/9/75	Estoril Int.	Estoril, P	Laffite Vonlanthen Leoni	Martini-BMW, 1st @ 137.22 km/h; March-BMW, 2nd; March-BMW, 3rd
3/31/75	BARC	Thruxton GB	Laffite Tambay Martini	Martini-BMW 1st @ 186,64 km/h; March-BMW, 2nd; March-BMW, 3rd
4/13/75	J. Clark Trophy	Hockenheim, D	Larrousse Stuck	Alpine-BMW, 1st @ 196.42 km/h; March-BMW, 2nd
4/27/75	Eifelrennen	Nürburgring, D	Laffite Tambay Ertl	Martini-BMW 1st @ 180.3 km/h; March-BMW, 2nd; Chevron-BMW, 3rd
5/4/75	Circuit Magny Cours	Magny Cours, F	Jabouille Serblin	Elf-BMW, 1st @ 165 5 km/h; March-BMW, 3rd
5/19/75	Circuit of Pau	Pau, F	Laffite Jabouille Depailler	Martini-BMW, 1st @ 131.14 km/h; Elf-BMW, 2nd; March-BMW, 3rd

6/8/75	Rhein Pokal	Hockenheim, D	Laffite Bourgoignie Flammini	Martini-BMW, 1st @ 198.3 km/h; March-BMW, 2nd; March-BMW, 3rd
6/15/75	Festspielpreis	Salzburgring, A	Jabouille Binder Serblin	Elf-BMW 1st @ 210.67 km/h; March-BMW, 2nd; March-BMW, 3rd
6/29/75	Rouen GP	Rouen, F	Leclere Tambay Bourgoignie	March, 752 1st @ 180.98 km/h; March-BMW, 2nd; March-BMW, 3rd
7/13/75	Mugello Int.	Mugello, I	Flammini Pesenti-Rossi "Gianfranco"	March 752, 1st @ 166.62 km/h; March-BMW, 2nd; March-BMW, 3rd
7/27/75	Circuit of Enna	Enna-Pergusa, I	Laffite Martini Larrousse Serblin	BMW, 1st @ 178.24 km/h; Alpine-BMW, 2nd; March-BMW, 3rd
8/24/75	Misano GP	Misano, I	Flammini Merzario	March 752, 1st; Osella-BMW, 2nd
8/31/75	BRDC	Silverstone, GB	Leclere Larrousse	March 752, 1st @ 199.19 km/h; Elf-BMW, 2nd
9/14/75	Circuit of Zolder	Zolder B	Leclere Tambay Flammini	March 752, 1st @ 168 65 km/h; March-BMW, 2nd; March-BMW 3rd
9/28/75	Circuit of Nogaro	Nogaro, F	Tambay Leclere Jabouille	March 752r 1st @ 150.71 km/h, March-BMW, 2nd; Elf-BMW, 3rd
10/12/75	Vallelunga GP	Vallelunga, I	Brambilla Laffite Flammini	March 752, 1st @ 1561 km/h Martini-BMW 2nd; March-BMW, 3rd

1975 European F2 Championship for ungraded drivers: 1st, Jacques Laffite, 2nd, equal Leclere and Tambay

1976

4/11/76	J Clark Trophy	Hockenheim, D	Stuck	March 762, 1st @ 199.25 km/h
4/19/76	BARC	Thruxton, GB	Flammini, March 762, 1st @ 187.15 km/h; Ribeiro	March-BMW, 2nd
5/2/76	Eifelrennen	Nürburgring, D	Kottulinsky	Ralt-BMW, 1st @ 177.91 km/h
5/9/76	Vallelunga GP	Vallelunga, I	Ribeiro	March 762, 3rd
5/23/76	Festspielpreis	Salzburgring, A	Flammini	March 762, 2nd
6/7/76	Circuit of Pau	Pau, F	Laffite	Chevron-BMW, 2nd
6/20/76	Rhein-Pokal	Hockenheim D	Stuck	March 762, 1st @ 200.19 km/h
6/27/76	Rouen GP	Rouen, F	Flammini Martini	March 762 1st @ 180.57 km/h; March 752r 3rd
7/25/76	Circuit of Enna	Enna-Pergusa, I	Ribeiro	March 762, 2nd
8/8/76	Estoril GP	Estoril P	Ribeiro	March 762, 3rd

8/22/76	Misano GP	Misano, I	Stuck Merzario Marazzi	March 762, 1st; Osella-BMW, 2nd; Chevron-BMW, 3rd

1977

3/6/77	Int. Trophy	Silverstone, GB	Neves	March 772P, 3rd
4/11/77	BARC	Thruxton, GB	Cheever Ribeiro	Ralt-BMW, 2nd; March-BMW, 3rd
4/17/77	J. Clark Trophy	Hockenheim D	Mass Patrese	March 772P, 1st @ 200.29 km/h; Chevron-BMW, 3rd
5/1/77	Eifelrennen	Nürburgring, D	Mass Cheever	March 772P, 1st @ 184.91 km/h; Ralt-BMW, 2nd
5/15/77	Rome GP	Vallelunga, I	Giacomelli Cheever	March 772P, 1st @ 162.17 km/h; Ralt-BMW, 3rd
5/30/77	Pau GP	Pau, F	Patrese	Chevron-BMW, 3rd
6/19/77	Mugello GP	Mugello, I	Giacomelli Patrese Colombo	March 772P, 1st @ 172.54 km/h; Chevron-BMW, 2nd; March-BMW, 3rd
6/26/77	Rouen GP	Rouen, F	Cheever Patrese	Ralt-BMW, 1st @ 184.21 km/h; Chevron-BMW, 2nd
7/10/77	Circuit of Nogaro	Nogaro, F	Patrese Hoffman	Chevron-BMW, 2nd; Ralt-BMW, 3rd
7/24/77	Mediterranean GP	Enna-Pergusa, I	Hoffman	Ralt-BMW, 3rd
8/7/77	Misano GP	Misano, I	Cheever Hoffman	Ralt-BMW, 2nd; Ralt-BMW, 3rd
10/2/77	Estoril GP	Estoril P	Cheever	Ralt-BMW, 3rd
10/30/77	BRSCC	Donington Park, GB	Giacomelli	March 772P, 1st @ 166.12 km/h

1977 European F2 Championship for ungraded drivers: 2nd, Eddie Cheever (US)

1978

Our last race-by-race analysis of BMW's immense success covers the 1978 European F2 Championship, in which the factory March and the BMW M12/7 motor was particularly successful.

Racing as the Polifac-BMW Junior Team, Bruno Giacomelli, Marc Surer, and Manfred Winkelhock produced such consistent results that Giacomelli won the twelve-round championship with eight victories—Surer finished as runner-up. The innovative Junior Team concluded the year with a 1–2–3 aggregate result at Hockenheim. The BMW 2-liter engine also won eleven international F2 events, scoring twelve second places and eleven third places.

3/27/78	Thruxton, GB	Giacomelli Surer Dougall,	March 782, 1st @ 190.28 km/h; March 782, 2nd; March 782, 3rd
4/9/78	Hockenheim, D	Giacomelli Surer Jarier	March 782r, 1st @ 202.71 km/h; March 782, 2nd; March 782, 3rd
4/30/78	Nürburgring, D	Ribeiro Cheever	March 782, 1st @ 185.23 km/h; March 782, 3rd

5/15/78	Pau, F	Giacomelli	March 782, 1st @ 129.71 km/h;
		Surer	March 782, 3rd
5/28/78	Mugello, I	Surer	March 782, 2nd;
		Giacomelli	March 782, 3rd
6/4/78	Vallelunga, I	Giacomelli	March 782, 2nd;
		Necchi	March 782-Osella, 3rd
6/18/78	Rouen, F	Giacomelli	March 782, 1st @ 185.65 km/h;
		Cheever	March 782, 2nd;
		Surer	March 782, 3rd
6/25/78	Donington, GB	Necchi	March 782 Osella, 2nd;
		Surer	March 782, 3rd
7/9/78	Nogaro, F	Giacomelli	March 782, 1st @ 153.6 km/h;
		Surer	March 782, 2nd
7/23/78	Enna-Pergusa, I	Giacomelli	March 782, 1st @ 189.99 km/h;
		Cheever	March 782, 2nd
8/6/78	Misano, I	Giacomelli	March 782, 1st @ 170.25 km/h;
		Surer	March 782, 2nd
9/24/78	Hockenheim, D	Giacomelli	March 782, 1st @ 202.4 km/h;
		Surer	March 782, 2nd;
		Winkelhock	March 782, 3rd

1978 European F2 Championship for ungraded drivers: 1st, Bruno Giacomelli

BMW drivers Marc Surer and Corrado Fabi also won the 1979 and 1982 European Formula 2 Championships.

Appendix 6

BMW competition-engine codes

The BMW factory system called for an M-prefix to each new engine engineering project of substance. So far as competition engines are concerned, this means we begin in 1966 with the Apfelbeck development of the four-cylinder engine, but that M10 code simply reflects the production in-line four-cylinder block around which it was created. More recently, an S-prefix has been adopted to distinguish Motorsport projects from the factory M-prefix norm for engines.

Ludwig Apfelbeck completed the extended development of the BMW motorcycle-based, opposed two-cylinder motor. Brief details of this are given within the chapter covering the BMW 700. Apfelbeck developed two versions of the overhead camshaft 700. The first was colloquially known as the Kellenhund ("chaindog"), having chain drive for the overhead camshafts on both cylinders. The second version had a complex system of shafts to take the drive from the central crankshaft location via separate driveshafts up to each overhead camshaft, thus, it was gear-and-shaft driven.

The smaller engines developed some 70–75 bhp from 697 cc, whereas the later OHC 800-cc motor described was capable of producing 85 bhp. The earliest four-cylinder sedan engines did not warrant a separate development program number, so the engine work was done under the car engineering project number of 0115 (for the 1500) or 0118 (for the 1800). Even later on, no separate number was given for sedan engine development, so details are confined to those given in the chapter concerned.

After I had completed the text to the book, a journey to Munich confirmed that it was Jack Brabham, three-time world motor racing champion, who coined the widely-used "high and heavy" description of the original Apfelbeck racing four-cylinder engine.

Code	M10	M10	M10	M12
Engine Type	il 4 cyl. Apfelbeck	il 4 cyl. Apfelbeck	il 4 cyl. Apfelbeck	il 4 cyl. diametral v
Capacity (cc)	1,991	1,991	1,598	1,598
Bore & stroke (mm)	89 x 80	89 x 80	89 x 64.2	89.2 x 80
Fuel feed	8 x Solex carbs 30% Nitro, 70% Methanol	Lucas fi	Lucas fi	Lucas fi
Power (bhp @ rpm)	330	260/270 8,500	210/225 9,800	220 10,500
Date & purpose	1966 Record breaking	1966 Record breaking; Race and hillclimb	1967 F2	1968 F2

Code	M12/1 and M12/4 (1969/70)	M12/2	M12/3
Engine type	il 4 cyl. diametral v	il 4 cyl. parallel v*	il 4 cyl. diametral v
Capacity (cc)	1,598	1,598	1,999
Bore & stroke (mm)	89.2 x 80	89.2 x 80	89.2 x 80
Fuel feed	Kugelfischer fi	Kugelfischer fi	Kugelfischer fi
Power (bhp@ rpm)	252 10,700	248 10,300	270 (approximately)
Date & purpose	1969 F2	1970/71 F2	1970, Quester (last all-BMW event) Neubiberg practice

Code	M12/5	M12/6	M12/7
Engine type	il 4 cyl parallel v	il 4 cyl parallel v	il 4 cyl parallel v
Capacity (cc)	1,999	1,999	1,999
Bore & stroke (mm)	89.2 x 80	89.2 x 80	89.2 x 80
Fuel feed	Kugelfischer fi	Kugelfischer fi	Kugelfischer fi
Power (bhp @ rpm)	240 (approx.)	275 8,500**	305/310 (1978/79) 10,000 (Max. 1979)
Date & purpose	1973/74 Experimental for rallying	1973 F2	1974/79 F2 Many sold

Code	M12/8	M12/9	M12/11
Engine type	il 4 cyl parallel v	il 4 cyl parallel v	il 4 cyl parallel v
Capacity (cc)	1,999		2,140
Bore & stroke (mm)	92 x 75	89.2 x 80	n/a
Fuel feed	Kugelfischer fi	Kugelfischer fi, Garrett AiResearch turbo	Kugelfischer fi, KKK turbo
Power (bhp @ rpm)		500/550 (to 1.3 bar)† 9,000 (9,500 max.)	n/a
Date & purpose	Prototype short stroke	IMSA & Group 5 World Championship	Experimental Never run

N.B. M12/10 coding was assigned to experimental 2-liter, unlisted statistically.

Code	M12/12	M38	M52	M52.1
Engine type	il 4 cyl. parallel v††	il 6 cyl. 12-v head	il 6 cyl. 12-v head	il 6 cyl. 12-v head
Capacity (cc)	1,400	2,987	3,191	3,191
Bore & stroke (mm)	89 x 57.5	89 x 80	92 x 80	92 x 80
Fuel feed	Kugelfischer fi 4 cyl KKK turbo	Kugelfischer fi normally aspirated	Kugelfischer fi normally aspirated	Kugelfischer fi normally aspirated
Power, (bhp @ rpm)	450 max rpm n/a	333 8,000	330/339 7,800	341/348 8,000
Date & purpose	1972 Prototype German Championship development Group 5	1972 Broadspeed Group 2 experimental CS, raced once	1973 Group 2	1973 Winter development and Group 2 race

Code	M52.2	M52.3	M49
Engine type	il 6 cyl. 12-v head	il 6 cyl. 12-v head	il 6 cyl. 12-v head
Capacity (cc)	3,331	3,498	3,191
Bore & stroke, (mm)	94 x 80	94 x 84	92 x 80
Fuel feed	Kugelfischer fi normally aspirated	Kugelfischer fi normally aspirated	Kugelfischer fi normally aspirated
Power, (bhp @ rpm)	352/366 8,200	365/370 8,000	405/420 rpm n/a
Date & purpose	1973 Group 2 race	1973 Group 2 race engine	Sept 1973 on Group 2 development

Code	M49/1	M49/2	M49/3	M49/4
Engine type	il 6 cyl. 24-v head	il 6 cyl. 24-v head	il 6 cyl. 24-v head	il 6 cyl. 24-v head
Capacity (cc)	3,331	3,498	3,498	3,200
Bore & stroke (mm)	94 x 80	94 x 84	94 x 84	Both 94 and 92 bore used. Raced as 92 x 80
Fuel feed	Kugelfischer	Kugelfischer	Kugelfischer	Kugelfischer, KKK turbo
Power (bhp @ rpm)	410/420 9,000	430/440 8,500	460/470 8,500/9,000	750-800[2] rpm n/a
Date & purpose	1973/74 Group 2 development	4/74 Group 2 race	1975/76 Overheating investigation[1]	1976 Group 5 race 1 x 3

Code	M49/5	M88	M90
Engine type	il 6 cyl. 24-v head	il 6 cyl. 24-v head[3]	il 6 cyl. 24-v head[4]
Capacity (cc)	3,423	3,423	3,423
Bore & stroke (mm)	93.4 x 84	93.4 x 84	93.4 x 84
Fuel feed	Kugelfischer	Kugelfischer fi butterfly system	Bosch electronic injection
Power (bhp @ rpm)	n/a n/a	277 6,500	218 5,200
Date & purpose	Test for M88	1977/78 Production for M1	1978 Production for 635CSi

KEY

il=in-line

fi=fuel injection

v=valve

Notes added by Paul Rosche to guide author:

* Engines built to 1,600-cc F2 regulations normally featured 10.5 or 10.6:1 compression ratios

** Maximum 9,200 rpm

† compression ratio according to country 7.0:1 to 7.5:1

†† 2-liter F2 engines had an optimum compression ratio of 11.2:1. The turbocharged compression ratio was 7.5:1 (or less for M12/9)

[1] Problem solved by vertical mounting, new water channelling and revised exhaust. Subsequently adopted by all works cars

[2] Bhp quotations vary for this engine. See text. A maximum of 1.3 atm was used

[3] Six-cylinder engines started at compression ratio 11.0:1 and optimized at 11.2:1, except for the turbo engines

[4] Compression ratio for M88 is 9.0:1; that for M90 635CSi production engine of 1979–82 was 9.3:1

Bibliographical Notes

This update meant I should cast my net much wider than I originally had for the first edition, and I would like to publicly acknowledge the work of some fellow authors.

If you want to know about the postwar fate of the BMW 328 and its extraordinary non-factory descendants, may I recommend the late Denis Jenkinson's *From Chain Drive to Turbocharger: The Story of AFN*, a 1984 book from PSL, with additional original references to BMW products in the 1930s and 1950s. It is an entertaining and educational title, which makes it even sadder that we will not read Jenkinson's pungent comments again. "Jenks" died while this book was being prepared, in December 1996, just before his 76th birthday.

The enormous BMW-backed book, *BMW 328: From Roadster to Legend* by Rainer Simons, is a must for anyone who wants to know anything about the 328, and is beautifully illustrated. Jenkinson's work features strongly here as well. I also received 328 help from some fierce American enthusiasts and Tim Hignett of L & C BMW Tunbridge Wells, Kent, UK.

I also referred to the following works:

Automobile Quarterly, Volume 36, Number 4 of July 1997 for further BMW Art Car information (another superbly researched article from Gordon Cruickshank) and a summary of BMW Mobile Tradition by Jonathan A. Stein. I should know about Mobile Tradition, having been around when most of the racing exhibits were performing, but I found Mr. Stein's overview a concise education.

BMW: Portrait einer grossen Marke by Hans Peter Rossellen. Heavyweight facts.

The BMW Story: A Company in its Time by Horst Monnich, and its German-language predecessor, *Vor der Schallmauer: BMW Eine Jahrhundertgesichte*, which has a lot more illustrations and is useful for purist references.

BMW from 1928: The Complete Story, by Werner Oswald and Jeremy Walton. Tackled for translation originally, I found this a handy source of quick facts. Unfortunately, BMW's later issues of production statistics means much of this information is obsolete.

BMW: A Celebration by Eric Dymock is one of the few BMW titles to treat all aspects of BMW in one book. Published in 1990 by Pavilion, it taught me how an elegant writer can make a tangled story comprehensible.

Brabham: The Grand Prix Cars by Alan Henry. Published by Osprey, this work by a former colleague at *Motoring News* is strong on racing recollections and reflects Henry's unmatched integrity in four decades of reporting on the Grand Prix scene.

Wie Kamm ich Blob vom Rennsport los, by Dieter Quester. The best of tall stories from BMW's longest-contracted competition driver. Equivalent to reading biographies of Gerry Marshall in Britain or Sam Posey in the US.

BMW: Vollgas in Weiss Blau by K. "Kalli" H. Hufstadt and Wolfgang Rausch is also good for gossip and strong on engine-building memories from a former insider.

M3: Szenen einer Karriere by former BMW Motorsport Press Officer Friedbert Holz, with stunning pictures from Walter Matthias Wilbert. The only weakness is that it does not cover the end of the original E30 M3's career and the text is in German only. The 1990 publisher was Edition Messner of Munster, the ISBN is 3–7022–16707–1990, and I think it's the best tribute the original M3 has received.

I also drew much 1975–1992 information from my own BMW 3-series books (there are two titles from separate publishers available in the US). You may find the *1992 Collectors Guide: BMW 3-series* from MRP in the UK (ISBN 0–947981–68–3) useful on the earlier "Threes," as it covers the E21 and E30 models in a neat factual package. I also authored Osprey's *Classic Marques: BMW Classics in 1994* (ISBN 1–85532–329X), for which I attended the 1992 BMW CCA Oktoberfest in Florida, so at least the pictures (and it is primarily a pictorial book) look pretty!

Motoring magazines are a vital source of facts in a work like this. I was employed by *Motoring News* and *Motor Sport* when the BMW bug bit, and their management was truly fanatical about German cars. I received maximum encouragement and every opportunity to drive some fabulous BMWs. A public thank you to W. J. Tee, the late proprietor of both titles (he also died while this book was being written). W. J. T.'s son Michael was the best boss I had before going out on my own.

Equally valuable references came from *Autosport* (UK, weekly), *Auto Hebdo* (France, weekly), *auto motor und sport* (Germany, fortnightly), *Classic & Sportscar* (UK, monthly), and from my fellow countrymen at *Classic Cars* in Britain.

Roundel, the monthly journal of the North American BMW Car Club of America, was vital not just for text but for the contributions of their Chief Photographer, Klaus Schnitzer. Another resource was *BMW CS Register*, an irregular but red-hot "fanzine" publication devoted to members of the BMW 2800/3.0 CS, CSi and CSL elements within BMW CCA. It offers excellent practical help and contact addresses.

McLaren's former driver David Hobbs and his late-1978 feelings came via *Autoweek* in the US, plus a hilarious Oktoberfest 20th Anniversary celebration in Florida in 1992.

I also referred to a video tape, *McLaren at Le Mans: Pursuit of Perfection*, released in 1996 by McLaren/Electronic Arts and produced by Tigermain Productions. This outstanding record of an historic achievement is the closest we can get to experiencing the BMW V12 unleashed at Le Mans. It gave me the fervor to attend Le Mans in 1996 and 1997, filling the gap since my first-time Le Mans attendance in 1971! Unfortunately, the BMW-powered "Big Macs" failed to deliver any more Le Mans wins.

Index

Author's Acknowledgements

This book would not exist without the personnel of BMW Motorsport and their overseas affiliates. Individuals are mentioned below, but this 1990s edition of the BMW sports record would not have appeared without the enthusiasm and encouragement of Americans.

Today, BMW has its Spartanburg, South Carolina, US factory on stream, but American enthusiasm for "Beemers" permeated my consciousness as far back as 1968. David E. Davis, then of Car & Driver, now founder and publisher of Automobile, wrote a paean of praise for the 2002's arrival on the US market. It was an inspired piece, drawing parallels of religious zeal in its fervor, but not particularly surprising. It was the US importer, Max Hoffman, who had initially suggested the larger engine in BMW's then-smallest sedan. I acknowledge that it was the champagne supplies of David E. Davis and Automobile's Jean Lindamood that made it possible to survey so much fresh paint and whitewalls at 1996 Pebble Beach Concours without wincing. In fact, I saw the best BMW 507s and Ferraris I have ever observed.

Now, we have an American publisher, Michael Bentley of Robert Bentley, Publishers, deploying Senior Editor John Kittredge, who made it all happen for this book in 1997/98.

Additionally, BMW Car Club of America's Roundel magazine is an inspiration to its 41,000 BMWCCA members. It was that membership's reactions to the prospect of this book, and courteous encouragement of Yale Rachlin (Editor) and correspondent Bob Roemer, which were decisive factors in disassembling and totally rebuilding this book. It is now twice the length some 18 years after the original British edition.

My individual thanks go to Richard Conway, Amy Lester, Arthur Porter, Clint and Pat de Witt, plus BMW North America's Erik C. Wensberg, for their sustained inspiration and support.

A 1992 trip to the BMW Car Club Oktoberfest reminded me forcibly that there was still a demand for this book, as folks kept telling me how wicked the second-hand prices were for a title that was out of print a decade previously.

The American initiative was repeated in 1996 when BMW was the honored marque at Monterey Historic Races (sponsored by Chrysler!). This time, BMW GB's Chris Willows had me transported with Alun Parry as the minder who shared most of that trip's outstanding joys and setbacks (he had to carry the cameras, because I was so much older and had the keys to our loaned Z3...).

To all at BMW Motorsport GmbH, a sincere thanks. I especially thank Dieter Stappert for reading it all in 1979, his organization, and his frankness; Jochen Neerpasch for his immense insights; Rainer Bratenstein for useful chassis information; and Rudi Gmeiner for his patience. Thanks also go to Martin Braungart for his humorous and precise interpretation of events while dealing with a hectic schedule that includes our infrequent meetings when he is on BBS directorial business these days.

My thanks also go to the BMW press departments in England and Germany for archive and photographic assistance. On a personal level, Chris Willows, Press Relations Manager at BMW GB, maintained the BMW faith in me throughout: not just the obvious access to cars and people, but to the point of lending me his own cars and providing much of the raw data that has transformed our early and Grand Prix racing results records for the Appendices.

I have dealt with the Hoepner family—father and daughter—in BMW's Munich press departments since the 1960s, and say thanks to Claudia Hoepner-Korinth for the welcome irreverence and laughter that stopped some of my earlier BMW research from becoming too solemn. "Claudi's" inspired freefall approach to the US in 1996 led to renewing a passing acquaintance with Nelson Piquet and to our first foreword to the second edition. It also provided an opportunity to watch Clint Eastwood's back disappear into the Carmel-sited Mission restaurant's private quarters when we mistook him for the parking lot supervisor in the twilight!

The following individuals provided vital information: Eva Maria Burkhardt, 1997 BMW Motorsport Press Officer; Karsten Engel, BMW Motorsport; Hughes de Fierlant, BMW Belgium; Dr. Fritz Indra, then of VW-Audi Engineering, Germany; Peter Hass, Euroracing, England; Eddie Keizan, South Africa; Teddy Mayer, then of McLaren Racing in America and England; Klaus Mahrlein, 1996–97 BMW Motorsport Manager; Gordon Murray, design director at McLaren International; John Nicholson, then of Nicholson McLaren Engines England; Charly Lamm, of Schnitzer, Germany; and Tom Walkinshaw, founder of TWR Racing, England.

Thanks for the race memories to Chris Amon, Jean-Claude Andruet, Dieter Basche, Johnny Cecotto, Chris Craft, Pierre Dieudonne, Hubert Hahne, Toine Hezemans, David Hobbs, Jacky Ickx, Eddie Joosens, Niki Lauda, and Australian gentleman and professional racer Brian Muir. Also to: Sam Posey, Dieter Quester (who contributed more than any other driver), and Brian Redman, the only Brit who will call you back from the US!

Many thanks also to Marc Surer for race administration and driver information, plus 19 years of dialogue with Steve Soper, international BMW Motorsport driver 1989–97. Also helpful were 1979 World Rally Champion Bjorn Waldegard of Sweden and Jean Xhenceval of Luigi BMW in Belgium.

Facility/information thanks to: British BMW and Alpina dealers Frank Sytner of Sytners Plc., Nottingham, and Tim Hignett of L&C Tunbridge, Kent.

Photographically, I must single out Klaus Schnitzer in the US, UK's Colin Taylor Productions, and the quality of work and consideration received from many German photographers, especially H.P. Seuffert. Bibliography magazine credits are alongside those for reference books, in the Appendices.

Jeremy Walton
March 1979/December 1997

About the Author

Born in Britain on July 4, 1946, Jeremy David Walton has authored more than 25 automotive marque histories and biographies, selling more than 245,000 copies. His work has been translated into French, German, and Italian; he has also translated BMW books into English.

An experienced motoring journalist and former racing driver (mostly in the sedan classes), Walton has worked as a staffer for *Motor Sport*, *Motoring News*, and *Cars & Car Conversions*.

Contact with BMW came through Walton's avid interest in piston-engined fighter planes and his employment at Ford Motorsport in Germany. The Blue Oval struggled to beat BMW when key ex-Ford employees established BMW Motorsport more than 25 years ago, and Walton witnessed that confrontation first-hand.

Personal enthusiasm for BMW was sealed for Walton when he had the privelege of racing a 3.0-liter CS in the 1972 Belgian 24-hours at Spa-Francorchamps. The virtually standard coupe, shared with Peter Hanson, finished seventh overall, won its class and covered 2,516 miles at an average of 104.9 mph with no mechanical maladies.

Walton currently resides in the UK with his wife Marilyn and his adopted BMW 635CSi.

Selected Automotive Books Available from Bentley Publishers

Enthusiast Books

Going Faster! Mastering the Art of Race Driving *The Skip Barber Racing School: Written by Carl Lopez with foreword by Danny Sullivan* ISBN 0-8376-0227-0

The Racing Driver *Denis Jenkinson* ISBN 0-8376-0201-7

Sports Car and Competition Driving *Paul Frère with foreword by Phil Hill* ISBN 0-8376-0202-5

The Technique of Motor Racing *Piero Taruffi with foreword by Juan Manuel Fangio* ISBN 0-8376-0228-9

Race Car Aerodynamics *Joseph Katz* ISBN 0-8376-0142-8

Think To Win *Don Alexander with foreword by Mark Martin* ISBN 0-8376-0070-7

The Design and Tuning of Competition Engines *Philip H. Smith, 6th edition revised by David N. Wenner* ISBN 0-8376-0140-1

Maximum Boost: Designing, Testing and Installing Turbocharger Systems *Corky Bell* ISBN 0-8376-0160-6

Glory Days: When Horsepower and Passion Ruled Detroit *Jim Wangers* ISBN 0-8376-0208-4

Small Wonder: The Amazing Story of the Volkswagen Beetle *Walter Henry Nelson* ISBN 0-8376-0147-9

Volkswagen Beetle: Portrait of a Legend *Edwin Baaske* ISBN 0-8376-0162-2

Harley Evolution V-Twin Owner's Bible™ *Moses Ludel* ISBN 0-8376-0146-0

Jeep Owner's Bible™ *Moses Ludel* ISBN 0-8376-0154-1

Ford F-Series Pickup Owner's Bible™ *Moses Ludel* ISBN 0-8376-0152-5

Chevrolet & GMC Light Truck Owner's Bible™ *Moses Ludel* ISBN 0-8376-0157-6

Toyota Truck & Land Cruiser Owner's Bible™ *Moses Ludel* ISBN 0-8376-0159-2

Alfa Romeo Owner's Bible™ *Pat Braden with foreword by Don Black* ISBN 0-8376-0707-9

The BMW Enthusiast's Companion *BMW Car Club of America* ISBN 0-8376-0321-8

New Directions in Suspension Design: Making the Fast Car Faster *Colin Campbell* ISBN 0-8376-0150-9

The Scientific Design of Exhaust and Intake Systems *Philip H. Smith and John C. Morrison* ISBN 0-8376-0309-9

BMW Service Manuals

BMW Z3 Roadster Service Manual: 1996–1998 4-cylinder and 6-cylinder engines *Robert Bentley* ISBN 0-8376-0327-7

BMW 5-Series Service Manual: 1989–1995 525i, 530i, 535i, 540i, including Touring *Robert Bentley* ISBN 0-8376-0319-6

BMW 5-Series Service Manual: 1982–1988 528e, 533i, 535i, 535is *Robert Bentley* ISBN 0-8376-0319-6

BMW 3-Series Service Manual: 1984–1990 318i, 325, 325e(es), 325i(is), and 325i Convertible *Robert Bentley* ISBN 0-8376-0319-6

Fuel Injection

Ford Fuel Injection and Electronic Engine Control: 1988–1993 *Charles O. Probst, SAE* ISBN 0-8376-0301-3

Ford Fuel Injection and Electronic Engine Control: 1980–1987 *Charles O. Probst, SAE* ISBN 0-8376-0302-1

Bosch Fuel Injection and Engine Management *Charles O. Probst, SAE* ISBN 0-8376-0300-5

Volkswagen Official Service Manuals

Jetta, Golf, GTI, Cabrio Service Manual: 1993–1997, including Jetta$_{III}$ and Golf$_{III}$ *Robert Bentley* ISBN 0-8376-0365-X

GTI, Golf, and Jetta Service Manual: 1985–1992 Gasoline, Diesel, and Turbo Diesel, including 16V *Robert Bentley* ISBN 0-8376-0342-0

Corrado Official Factory Repair Manual: 1990–1994 *Volkswagen United States* ISBN 0-8376-0387-0

Passat Official Factory Repair Manual: 1990–1993, including Wagon *Volkswagen United States* ISBN 0-8376-0378-1

Cabriolet and Scirocco Service Manual: 1985–1993, including 16V *Robert Bentley* ISBN 0-8376-0362-5

Volkswagen Fox Service Manual: 1987–1993, including GL, GL Sport and Wagon *Robert Bentley* ISBN 0-8376-0340-4

Vanagon Official Factory Repair Manual: 1980–1991 including Diesel Engine, Syncro, and Camper *Volkswagen United States* ISBN 0-8376-0336-6

Rabbit, Scirocco, Jetta Service Manual: 1980–1984 Gasoline Models, including Pickup Truck, Convertible, and GTI *Robert Bentley* ISBN 0-8376-0183-5

RB ROBERT BENTLEY, INC. | AUTOMOTIVE PUBLISHERS

Robert Bentley has published service manuals and automobile books since 1950. Please write Robert Bentley, Inc., Publishers, at 1734 Massachusetts Avenue, Cambridge, MA 02138, visit our web site at http://www.rb.com, or call 1-800-423-4595 for a free copy of our complete catalog, including titles and service manuals for Jaguar, Triumph, Austin-Healey, MG, and